NTOA 20

Majella Franzmann • The Odes of Solomon

# NOVUM TESTAMENTUM ET ORBIS ANTIQUUS (NTOA)

Im Auftrag des Biblischen Instituts
der Universität Freiburg Schweiz
herausgegeben von Max Küchler
in Zusammenarbeit mit Gerd Theissen

*About the author*

*Dr. Majella Franzmann*, b. 1952 in Charleville, Australia. Diploma of Teaching (1957). Secondary teaching, Brisbane (1976-1982). B.A. (1979). B.A. Hons. (1984) and PhD (1990), University of Queensland. DAAD scholarship for studies in Tübingen (1986/87). Currently Honorary Research Adviser and part-time lecturer in the Department of Studies in Religion at the University of Queensland. Since 1970, member of the Sisters of the Presentation of the Blessed Virgin Mary.

NOVUM TESTAMENTUM ET ORBIS ANTIQUUS    20

Majella Franzmann

# The Odes of Solomon

## An Analysis of the Poetical Structure and Form

UNIVERSITÄTSVERLAG FREIBURG SCHWEIZ
VANDENHOECK & RUPRECHT GÖTTINGEN
1991

Die Deutsche Bibliothek – CIP Einheitsaufnahme

**Franzmann, Majella:**
The Odes of Salomon: an analysis of the poetical structure and form /
Majella Franzmann. – Freiburg, Schweiz: Univ.-Verl.; Göttingen: Vanden-
hoeck und Ruprecht, 1991
  (Novum testamentum et orbis antiquus; 20)
  Einheitssacht. des kommentierten Werkes: Odae Salominis
  Zugl.: Saint Lucia, Queensland, Univ., Diss.
  ISBN 3-7278-0780-6 (Univ.-Verl.)
  ISBN 3-525-53921-5 (Vandenhoeck u. Ruprecht)
NE: The Odes of Salomon; EST des kommentierten Werkes; GT

Veröffentlicht mit Unterstützung des Hochschulrates
der Universität Freiburg Schweiz

© 1991 by Universitätsverlag Freiburg Schweiz
Paulusdruckerei Freiburg Schweiz
ISBN 3-7278-0780-6 (Universitätsverlag)
ISBN 3-525-53921-5 (Vandenhoeck und Ruprecht)

*For my parents*

# FOREWORD

The present work was submitted as a thesis for the degree of Doctor of Philosophy at the University of Queensland during 1990. I wish to thank the staff of the Department of Studies in Religion at the University of Queensland for their interest in my studies over many years. I am deeply grateful for the excellent teaching and encouragement of my doctoral supervisor, Assoc. Prof. Michael Lattke.

My appreciation goes also to the three examiners of the thesis for their helpful comments and meticulous reading - Prof. Dr. Sebastian Brock (Oxford), Prof. Dr. Dr. Peter Nagel (Halle), and Prof. Dr. Dr. Kurt Rudolph (Marburg).

My research in 1985 and 1987-89 was supported by an Australian Commonwealth Postgraduate Research Award, and twelve months research in 1986/7 at the University of Tübingen was made possible by a scholarship from the Deutsche Akademische Austauschdienst (DAAD).

Finally I wish to acknowledge the many friends who have shared with me the vicissitudes of the years of research and writing, and my congregation of the Sisters of the Presentation of the Blessed Virgin Mary who have encouraged and supported me in this project.

University of Queensland
December, 1990                                           M. Franzmann

# TABLE OF CONTENTS

# INTRODUCTION

As with other texts from the early centuries C.E. discovered in this century, the Odes of Solomon have suffered the effects of that overpowering scholarly temptation to "skim off" from a text what might shed light on other "more important" (read "canonical") works from the mainstream Hebrew or Christian traditions, with the result that often the newly discovered texts are treated as little more than footnoting material. When the excitement of the discovery wanes, or the text is exhausted of what it might offer regarding other texts, it comes time for it to be treated finally as a work in its own right and so begins that scholarship which is less exciting in the short-term but which offers a surer and more fundamental basis for interpretation; that is, the detailed analysis of the structure/form and of the system of images.

There has been concern to ask other questions within the scholarship on the Odes besides their relationship to other texts, but the eighty years of research have failed to resolve satisfactorily these perennial secondary questions of date, provenance, original language, and so on.

This study attempts to bring some balance to the previous scholarship on the Odes by providing the first analysis of the collection in its entirety from the aspect of the structure of its vocabulary and syntax, building towards grouping Odes according to these structures as well as by certain patterns of imagery/ motif.

The structure of vocabulary and syntax is the bare bones of the text. Allied with it and inseparable from it in the process of interpretation are the patterns of meaning and sound. The levels can never be entirely isolated from each other, yet the former structures must be accepted as the most appropriate framework upon which to build the analysis of the whole. To concentrate on the semantic level, as most of the previous study has done, without a firm basis provided by the analysis of vocabulary and syntax, is to run the risk of error in interpretation, ambiguity, and over-subjectivity.

The most extensive section of this study in Chapter II comprises the structural analysis of the individual (Syriac, Coptic, and Greek) Odes of the collection. It is what one might call the micro-analysis; that is, the analysis of the patterns of words/roots, cola, strophes, stanzas, and sub-odes, working from the most basic level to the larger relationships within an Ode and beyond to relationships between Odes. Within this analysis, there is much use made of lists of word-pairs, lists of frequently occurring phrases and associated words/ roots, and word-frequency tables, so as to bring as objective a perspective as possible to bear on the analysis.

Chapter III has two major sections. The first investigates the implications of the data collected in Chapter II for the interpretation of the text, and indicates how this might have been used to avoid error in earlier studies of the Odes. In the second section, micro-analysis leads to macro-analysis; that is, the investigation of how the Odes might be arranged into certain groups according to the shared patterns of syntax especially, and also of imagery.

The concluding chapter suggests that the direction for future research lies with the thoroughgoing analysis of the system of imagery in the Odes. Together with the structural analysis, this latter study will provide a strong basis for interpretation within the Odes and in the search for parallels in other literature.

# TECHNICAL PREFACE

## a. TRANSLATION METHOD

The translation is intended as a working text to be used in conjunction with the analysis in Chapters II and III. Thus it is as literal as possible without sacrificing intelligibility (cf. the translations [incomplete] of Barnstone and Freeman which are more literary but less helpful from a scholarly point of view). Where idiomatic expressions occur, this has been indicated generally in the notes to the translation. No reference is made, however, to the common constructions (e.g. ܟܡܪܝܐ ܪܘܚܗ [= lit. "his spirit of the Lord"]) for which a literal translation would be too laboured.

For the most part, word order has been preserved even to the detriment of good style, since it is more important for a working text to try to preserve the structure of the elements in the original language. Word order has not been maintained with the particles ܓܝܪ and ܕܝܢ, which never occur in the first position of the line in Syriac.

As far as possible, without distortion to the text (cf. Burchard 618; Nida and Taber 16), a consistent meaning has been kept, not only for single vocabulary items, but also for words related by a common root (thus ܚܝܠ ["strengthen"], ܚܝܠܐ/ܚܝܠ ["strength"], ܚܝܠܬܢ ["strong"]). For the reader with little knowledge of Syriac, such consistency can facilitate the recognition of passages where the same Syriac words/roots are used. Previous translations are sometimes unduly obscure where it would have been easy to be clear and helpful. Thus Charlesworth translates 4:4:

"Never wilt Thou be idle,
Nor wilt Thou be without fruits;" (1977, 22)

while for 11:23 he has:

"And there is nothing in it which is barren,
But everything is filled with fruit." (53)

To translate ܒܛܠ with both "idle" and "barren" obscures the relationship between these verses of Odes 4 and 11 for the reader unskilled in Syriac. Similarly in Ode 16, Charlesworth's translation of ܥܒܕܐ as "occupation" (1c) and "work" (6) and of ܦܘܠܚܢܐ as "service" (2a) and "labour" (6) conceals the connection between 1c-2a and 6 (70-1).

The attempt to be consistent is often simpler than it appears, since many times the choice between a number of variations is, in the end, arbitrary and depends more on the aesthetic judgment of the translator than on any strong indication from the text. Limiting oneself to the same translation for a word/ root where there is no danger of distortion can be something of a positive re-straining force. Admittedly, such a method can also limit the "poetry" of one's own translation but in this case (translating for textual analysis rather than for popular reading or liturgy) it seems an affordable restriction.

Arbitrary choice in translation is a danger, not only for single vocabulary items, but also for some syntactic constructions. For example, the imperfect may be translated in English by the future tense ("they will...") or by the ex-hortative ("let them..."). Difficulties arise where there is no indication, either in the Coptic and Greek Mss. or in the context of the Ode itself, as to which choice would be more suitable.

The translation of prepositions (esp. ܒ) is, in general, the most problemati-cal (cf. Burchard 618). Whether one translates ܒ as "in" or "by" may be, at times, of little consequence. At other times, the choice may determine the dif-ference between two different theological standpoints (e.g. 8:22b-d).

Where abstract words such as "truth" or "error" are clearly personified in the text, I have indicated this by the initial capital (Truth, Error) and used masculine and feminine referring pronouns rather than the neuter (e.g. 38:2-4). Where the presence of personification is debatable (e.g. 18:9-11), I have used neuter pronouns (*contra* Schökel, who suggests that one exaggerate rather than underestimate when it comes to difficulties in perceiving and determining personification in biblical poetry, 124).

The problem concerning the gender of various personifications cannot be solved until the question of the original language is resolved. If, for example, the Syriac is a translation of Greek, then what might appear to be a masculine character in the Syriac because of the gender of the noun (e.g. ܩܘܫܬܐ) may have been intended as a female personification in the original Greek (ἀλήθεια). One of the most important characters in the Odes is the Spirit, which is feminine in Syriac (ܪܘܚܐ) and neuter in Greek (πνεῦμα).

At least the English translation does not have to contend with further possible gender shifts as happens, for example, in Ode 36 where the feminine ܪܘܚܐ must be translated by the Germans as "der Geist" or by the French as "l'esprit" and the corresponding feminine pronouns in Syriac replaced by masculine pronouns in the translating language. This can seriously affect the very flavour of an Ode, as for example in 36:3a where the Spirit is associated with birthing imagery and the German and French translations must use the masculine.

Where differences occur between Mss. H and N (after 17:7b) and both variants are possible within the context, then N is preferred, since it is the older of the two manuscripts, and given the greater proportion of errors generally by the copyist of H.


### b. CONVENTIONS WITH THE SYRIAC

Within the English text, where the quotation of a number of phrases in Syriac is not completed in one line, the remainder in the next line follows from the last group of words separated by commas on the right of the previous line. In a list of Syriac words or in word-pairs separated by a hyphen, read the words from left to right.

When reference is made to the number of syllables in a line, this is always without taking account of the shewa or indistinct vowel (Robinson, T.H. 1962, 7).


### c. NUMBERING OF THE TEXT

The numbering of the verses of the Odes coincides with Harris and Mingana. The most accessible English edition at present is that of Charlesworth (1977) which unfortunately introduced yet another numbering system, only adding to the confusion begun with Harris and the first French and German editions. Line divisions in the edition follow, where possible, those indicated in the manuscripts (Charlesworth 1981). Other divisions made on the basis of structure are indicated in the translation notes.

Harris and Mingana vol. 2, Greßmann 1924, Bauer 1964, and Charlesworth 1985 give extensive reference to parallels to the Odes to be found in the Hebrew and Christian scriptures. In the present work, other primary texts are cited more to elucidate some difficulty with the text of the Odes rather than to suggest parallels. There is some reference to the Nag Hammadi material since, with the exception of <u>The Gospel of Truth</u> (Ménard 1962; 1972) and <u>The Gospel of Thomas</u> (Ménard 1975), the relationship of this material to the Odes has not been investigated to any great extent.

### d. ABBREVIATIONS FOR THE EDITION AND TRANSLATION IN CHAPTER II

[ ]      - completion of a gap in the text.

‹ ›      - editorial addition or correction.

( )      - addition in the English text where the Syriac, Coptic, Greek uses an
           abbreviated form; e.g. the omission of the verb "to be"
         - addition in the English text to make clear some ambiguity concerning
           reference (esp. with pronouns).
         - indication of a longer text in the Syriac, Coptic, Greek which would
           be better understood in abbreviated formed; e.g. (son of) man.

{ }      - editorial erasure.

...      - missing letters in the manuscript (number of dots = estimated number
           of letters).

---      - missing text in the manuscript of indefinite length.

### e. TECHNICAL TERMS FOR THE ANALYSIS IN CHAPTER II

In order to avoid confusion to the reader, an outline of some of the technical terms and their meanings is necessary[1]. My choice of terms is based primarily upon Watson 1986, albeit with modification. Other studies of terms/categories

---

[1] Terminology varies in meaning not only between biblical poetical studies and studies, for example, in English poetical literature, but also within biblical poetical studies themselves. A simple check through an English dictionary of literary terms shows, for example, that "colon" is used as a metrical term (Cuddon 128; the terms "bicolon" and so on do not occur in the dictionary) and that "strophe" can be used synonymously for "stanza" (662). Muilenberg suggests implicitly that "strophe" and "stanza" are synonymous, opting to use "stanza" with work on the Hebrew Scriptures because of the technical understanding of "strophe" for Greek verse (1969, 12).

are more detailed (e.g. Korpel and de Moor) but are often too complicated to be of practical use for the kind of analysis envisaged in Chapter II.

1. Basic categories of verse units

colon - a line of verse

monocolon - a single line which is not closely related to another colon (e.g. as an element of a bicolon) and may function as a strophe

bicolon, tricolon, quatrain - groups of two, three, and four cola

strophe - a unit (in Eng. lit. called a "verse paragraph") made up of one or more cola

stanza - a group of one or more strophes making a sub-section of an Ode

sub-ode[1] - a section of an Ode containing one or more stanzas which is a relatively independent (although not totally isolated) unit within the Ode

2. Categories of relationship between verse units

Types of parallelism and terms relating to parallelism:

alternate parallelism: parallelism over a number of lines, where alternate rather than adjacent lines are parallel; e.g. line 1 // line 3, line 2 // line 4 (cf. Willis)

chiasmus/reflexively congruent parallelism: A B // B' A' (cf. Watson 1986, 117).

insertion : a monocolon (AXB) or a bicolon (AXYB) inserted between two parallel lines (cf. Tsumura 1983; 1988).

internal parallelism: the second half of the colon is parallel to the first (cf. Watson 1989; cf. also aba-monocolon in Watson 1986, 150, 215).

---

[1] The use of the term "ode" is not to imply anything about the actual form of the section. It is used because in the tradition the work has been referred to as Odes.

pivot pattern: a parallel bicolon where the final word/s of line 1 are implied at the conclusion of line 2 (cf. Watson, 150, 214-5).

terrace pattern: the final part of a line is repeated at the beginning of the next line (cf. Watson 1986, 208-12).

Merismus: the totality of some thing/person or some system is expressed by reference to its parts, e.g. feet and head, body and soul, creeping thing and flying creature (cf. Watson 1986, 321-4).

Polysemy: where one word may have a number of meanings, e.g. זַ֭מָר = prune/ circumcise (cf. Watson 1986, 237-8).

# ABBREVIATIONS

## a. PUBLICATIONS

The abbreviations below follow Schwertner.

| | |
|---|---|
| AKG | Arbeiten zur Kirchengeschichte |
| AnBib | Analecta biblica |
| AnOr | Analecta orientalia |
| AThD | Analecta theologica Danica |
| BBET | Beiträge zur biblischen Exegese und Theologie |
| BGPhMA | Beiträge zur Geschichte der Philosophie und Theologie des Mittelalters |
| Bib | Biblica |
| BSOAS | Bulletin of the school of Oriental and African studies |
| BWAT | Beiträge zur Wissenschaft vom Alten Testament |
| BZAW | Beihefte zur Zeitschrift für die alttestamentliche Wissenschaft |
| CBQ | Catholic biblical quarterly |
| CCER | Cahiers du cercle Ernest-Renan |
| ChW | Christliche Welt |
| ClF | Classical folia |
| CSCO | Corpus scriptorum Christianorum orientalium |
| CSCO.S | - Scriptores Syri |
| CSEL | Corpus scriptorum ecclesiasticorum Latinorum |
| EeT | Église et théologie |
| EeV(M) | Esprit et vie. Maredsous |
| EPRO | Études préliminaires aux religions orientales dans l'empire romain |
| ET | Expository times |
| EtB | Études bibliques |
| Exp. | Expositor |
| FKDG | Forschungen zur Kirchen- und Dogmengeschichte |

| | |
|---|---|
| FRLANT | Forschungen zur Religion und Literatur des Alten und Neuen Testaments |
| FV | Foi et vie |
| GCS | Griechische christliche Schriftsteller der ersten drei Jahrhunderte |
| GTA | Göttinger theologische Arbeiten |
| HeTr | Helps for translators (series) |
| HO | Handbuch der Orientalistik |
| HR | History of religions |
| HSM | Harvard Semitic monographs |
| HUCA | Hebrew union college annual |
| Interp. | Interpretation |
| IWW | Internationale Wochenschrift für Wissenschaft, Kunst und Technik |
| JAC | Jahrbuch für Antike und Christentum |
| JBL | Journal of biblical literature |
| JSHRZ | Jüdische Schriften aus hellenistisch-römischer Zeit |
| JSOT | Journal for the Study of the Old Testament |
| JSOT Suppl. Ser. | - Supplement Series |
| JSP | Journal of social psychology |
| JThS | Journal of theological studies |
| KEK | Kritisch-exegetischer Kommentar über das Neue Testament |
| KHÅ | Kyrkohistorik årsskrift |
| KlT | Kleine Texte für (theologische und philologische) Vorlesungen und Übungen |
| LCL | Loeb classical library |
| LF | Liturgiegeschichtliche Forschungen |
| LOS | London oriental series |
| LZD | Literarisches Zentralblatt für Deutschland |
| MSSNTS | Monograph series. Society for New Testament studies |
| NedThT | Nederlands(ch)e theologisch tijdschrift |
| NHS | Nag Hammadi series |
| NKZ | Neue kirchliche Zeitschrift |
| NSGTK | Neue Studien zur Geschichte der Theologie und Kirche |
| NT | Novum Testamentum |
| NTG | Neue theologische Grundrisse |
| NTS | New testament studies |

| | |
|---|---|
| OBO | Orbis biblicus et orientalis |
| OLZ | Orientalische Literaturzeitung |
| OrChr | Oriens Christianus |
| OrChrA | Orientalia Christiana analecta |
| OrChrP | Orientalia Christiana periodica |
| OrSyr | Orient syrien |
| OstKSt | Ostkirchliche Studien |
| PLO | Porta linguarum orientalium |
| PRE | Paulys Real-Encyclopädie der classischen Altertumswissenschaft |
| RAC | Reallexikon für Antike und Christentum |
| RB | Revue biblique |
| RCHL | Revue critique d'histoire et de littérature |
| RdQ | Revue de Qumran |
| Refor. | Reformation |
| RGG | Religion in Geschichte und Gegenwart |
| RThPh | Revue de théologie et de philosophie |
| RThQR | Revue de théologie et de questions religieuses |
| RTP | Review of theology and philosophy |
| SBL | Society of biblical literature |
| SBL Semeia Suppl. | - Semeia supplement |
| SBLDS | - dissertation series |
| SBLSP | - seminar papers |
| SBLTT | - text and translation |
| SHR | Studies in the history of religions |
| SJTh | Scottish journal of theology |
| StANT | Studien zum Alten und Neuen Testament |
| StP.SM | Studi e testi di papirologia. Series maior |
| StUNT | Studien zur Umwelt des Neuen Testaments |
| SubBi | Subsidia biblica |
| Symb. | Symbolon |
| TaS | Texts and studies |
| Theop. | Theopaneia |
| ThGl | Theologie und Glaube |
| ThLZ | Theologische Literaturzeitung |
| ThSt(U) | Theologische studiën. Utrecht |
| TRE | Theologische Realenzyklopädie |

| | |
|---|---|
| TU | Texte und Untersuchungen zur Geschichte der altchristlichen Literatur |
| UTB | Uni-Taschenbücher |
| UUA | Uppsala universitets årsskrift |
| VT | Vetus Testamentum |
| WdF | Wege der Forschung |
| WUNT | Wissenschaftliche Untersuchungen zum Neuen Testament |
| ZKTh | Zeitschrift für katholische Theologie |
| ZNW | Zeitschrift für die neutestamentliche Wissenschaft (21, 1922ff:) und die Kunde der älteren Kirche |

## b. GENERAL AND TECHNICAL

| | |
|---|---|
| act. | active |
| adj. | adjective/adjectival |
| adv. | adverb/adverbial |
| cl./cls. | clause/s |
| comp./comps. | compiler/s |
| compl. | complement |
| conj. | conjunction |
| dat. | dative |
| dir. | direct |
| diss. | dissertation |
| ed./eds. | edition or editor/s |
| esp. | especially |
| gen. | genitive |
| imper. | imperative |
| imperf. | imperfect |
| indef. | indefinite |
| indir. | indirect |
| infin. | infinitive |
| lit. | literal |
| Ms./Mss. | manuscript/s |
| obj./objs. | object/s |
| part. | participle |
| pass. | passive |
| perf. | perfect |

| pl.         | plural                       |
|-------------|------------------------------|
| poss.       | possessive                   |
| prep.       | preposition/prepositional    |
| pres.       | present                      |
| pron.       | pronoun                      |
| ref.        | reference                    |
| rel.        | relative                     |
| rev.        | review/revised               |
| sing.       | singular                     |
| subj./subjs.| subject/s                    |
| trans.      | translator                   |
| vol./vols.  | volume/s                     |

# I. THE HISTORY OF RESEARCH AND THE PRESENT PROJECT

## a. THE HISTORY OF RESEARCH ON THE ODES

The Odes of Solomon were first published as a collection by J.R. Harris in 1909 (Ms. H, containing Odes 3 [the beginning of the Ode is missing] to 42). Prior to this publication, the Odes were known from five quotations of the text in the Coptic Gnostic work, Pistis Sophia (Odes 1:1-5; 5:1-11; 6:8-18; 22:1-12; 25:1-12; Schmidt 1978b, 114-115, 117, 132-133, 151-152, 157-158), and from Lactantius' quotation of 19:6-7 in Divinae Institutiones IV. 12,3 (Brandt and Laubmann 310). The Odes are listed together with the Psalms of Solomon in Pseudo-Athanasius' Synopsis Scripturae Sacrae 74 (PG 28: 432) and Nicephorus' Quae Scripturae Canonicae II, 6' (PG 100: 1057). A second Syriac manuscript (Ms. N containing 17:7b to 42) was discovered by F.C. Burkitt in 1912, and the Greek version of Ode 11 from Papyrus Bodmer XI was published by M. Testuz in 1959.

In the history of Odes research (cf. Lattke's annotated bibliography [1979-86, vol. 3]), several major phases may be discerned; the first from 1909 to 1915, the second gathering momentum in the late 1950's and early 1960's as the writings from Qumran and Papyrus Bodmer XI became available for study. The 1970's saw, finally, the publication of the Nag Hammadi writings and witnessed a new interest in the Odes encouraged principally by the work of Charlesworth and Lattke.

Over the eighty years of scholarship since 1909, a number of key questions have remained as the major focus of attention of the scholarly community (cf. the recent summary in Brock 1987). The area of poetical and form analysis will be dealt with in Section II below. Apart from that and the detailed philological work, editions and translations, the scholarship may be divided into some eight areas of investigation. Of these eight, the two which have consistently aroused the most interest are the community of origin/author and the relation of the Odes to other texts.

## 1. Date of composition

Scholarly opinion settled very early on dating the Odes in the second half of the second century. This has been disputed most recently by Drijvers (1981) who has pushed the dating of the Odes into the second half of the third century C.E. (cf., *contra* Drijvers, L. Abramowski 1984, 83-90, though Drijvers continues to hold his position [1987/88, 156]).

## 2. Place of origin

In early work, Egypt was considered as a possible place of origin[1], though the majority of scholars have opted for Syria. The choice between Antioch and Edessa as the city of origin was of interest briefly in the 1930's and 1940's but elicits little interest in later work.

## 3. Community of origin/author

Investigation of this question has tended to focus on imagery and motifs for which parallels could be found in the writings of other groups or individuals. The general discussion has centred on whether the Odes are Jewish, Gnostic or Christian, with more recent work focussing on the latter two. Opinion remains divided (cf. e.g. Rudolph 1980, 34, 238-40, for the Odes as Christian-Gnostic; Charlesworth 1969 for the Odes as not Gnostic). From the beginning too, there has been investigation of possible docetic tendencies in the Odes, with the discussion continuing more recently in the unpublished dissertation of McNeil (1978). Of more significance has been the investigation of a possible origin in, or certainly of links with, the Qumran and/or Johannine communities[2]. Suggestions for an author have been relatively few. Of these, Bardaiṣan has been the most frequent choice[3].

---

[1] Cf., e.g. Gunkel 1910, 327; Alès 769-70; Batiffol 33-4; Loisy 104; Dhorme 468; Greß-mann 1913, 203.

[2] For Qumran and the Odes, cf. e.g. Braun 226-31; Carmignac 1961; 1963; Charlesworth 1970; Ragot . For John and the Odes, cf. e.g. Bultmann; Braun 242-5; Charlesworth and Culpepper; Lattke 1975; Langbrandtner; Potterie; Barrett; Morrison. For Qumran, John and the Odes, cf. esp. Charlesworth 1972.

[3] Cf. Newbold; Bardenhewer 2: 321; Sprengling vii; Braun 238-42. Those who have argued against the theory include Haase (762), Rücker (172) and Altaner (97).

4. The relation of the Odes to other texts

This area of investigation is closely linked with the previous one. The search
for parallels to the Odes or, more frequently, the search for parallels in the
Odes to other literature, has covered a wide range of texts: canonical biblical
writings (esp. the Johannine literature, and more recently, the Wisdom of Solomon [Drijvers 1986; 1987]), early Syriac writings (esp. from Ignatius; cf.
Corwin; Paulsen), texts from Qumran, Nag Hammadi, the Montanists, the
Mandaeans, the Manichaeans, the Hermetica, and so on.

Harris studied the context of the Odes within the collection of the Odes and
Psalms of Solomon, and within Pistis Sophia (1909, 3-12, 16-35). A more detailed discussion of the interpretation of the Odes within Pistis Sophia has been
provided by Lattke (1979-86, 1: 207-25). As yet there has been no study of the
significance of Ode 11 within the collection of Papyrus Bodmer XI. Such study
is important to the discussion concerning the community of users of the Odes
and questions about "orthodoxy".

5. Original language of composition

The discussion of the relation of the Odes to other texts has been important for
the question of the original language. The debate remains unresolved as to a
Syriac or Greek original. In the latter part of the century most had opted for
Greek but there has been more recent defence of a Syriac original by Charlesworth (1977, 11-12), Drijvers (1980, 351) and L. Abramowski (1984, 80-3).

---

EXCURSUS: GREEK LOAN WORDS IN THE SYRIAC ODES

| ܐܐܪ | - | $\dot{\alpha}\dot{\eta}\rho$ | ܡܘܟܠܐ | - | $\mu o\chi\lambda\acute{o}\varsigma$ |
|------|---|------|------|---|------|
| ܟܣܢܝܐ | - | $\xi\acute{\epsilon}\nu o\varsigma$ | ܦܝܣ | - | $\pi\epsilon\tilde{\iota}\sigma\alpha\iota$ |
| ܓܝܪ | - | $\gamma\acute{\alpha}\rho$ | ܦܪܨܘܦܐ | - | $\pi\rho\acute{o}\sigma\omega\pi o\nu$ |
| ܓܢܣܐ | - | $\gamma\acute{\epsilon}\nu o\varsigma$ | ܩܝܢܕܘܢܘܣ | - | $\kappa\acute{\iota}\nu\delta\upsilon\nu o\varsigma$ |
| ܕܝܢ | - | $\delta\epsilon$ | ܩܝܬܪܐ | - | $\kappa\iota\theta\acute{\alpha}\rho\alpha$ |
| ܠܡܐܢܐ | - | $\lambda\iota\mu\acute{\eta}\nu$ | ܬܓܡܐ | - | $\tau\acute{\alpha}\gamma\mu\alpha$ |

---

6. Unity of authorship

Investigation of this question has been generally with reference to the theory of
Harnack (1910, esp. 74-124) who argued that the Odes are Jewish with Christian interpolation over against Harris' outline for the unity of Christian author-

ship (1909, 48-53)[1]. Scholars largely disagreed with Harnack and he himself later capitulated (1921, 7). Of all the areas of investigation, it is in this one that scholars seem to have lost interest, with only sporadic discussion since 1921.

Although Harnack may not have been correct with his theory of Christian interpolation of Jewish material, the question of the unity of the Odes has not been satisfactorily answered. The problem lies with the method of questioning. It is only after outlining his theory of interpolation, that Harnack promises to make, at some later time, "eine genaue Untersuchung der Strophik und der technischen Kunst des Dichters" (1910, 112). It will become clear in Chapter II below that, had Harnack done firstly what he promised for the future (and never fulfilled), he may have had a more solid basis for questioning the unity of the Odes.

7. The "I"/speaker(s) in the Odes

A major problem in this area of Odes research has been the continuing penchant of scholars for dividing some Odes into speeches of the Odist and speeches of Christ. The divisions made by Harris and Mingana in their 1920 edition, for example, turn up exactly reproduced in Charlesworth's 1977 edition (Odes 8, 10, 17, 22, 28, 31, 36, 41, 42). Although there may be some basis for division in the content of an Ode, all too often the method employed seems to have relied on the particular view which a scholar holds of what might be dogmatically suitable in the mouth of a particular character[2]. Although Aune follows Charlesworth 1977, he attempts at least to argue for the division from his discussion of the form of the Odes (1983, 297). Aune (1982; 1983, 296-9) and Franzmann (1987) are the most recent attempts to investigate the "I" of the Odes in a general way.

---

[1] This theory was based on Harris' grouping of Odes according to common themes. Elsewhere he gives a less rigorous basis for his opinion: "...the very elevation of the thought of the Odes is an index of a single personality: even if we cannot identify him, we are sure that the writer was a rare spirit, and rare spirits do not agree with multiple authorship." (1911a, 49)

[2] E.g. Bernard makes internal divisions in some Odes according to a number of speakers (the Church, God, Christ, the baptized; 39-40), excusing some doubt on his part as to where the divisions might occur because "the union of the believer with Christ, and his incorporation in the Church, are taken as certain, so that what the Church says might not unfitly be placed in the mouth of the believer, who is again a member of Christ..." (40).

8. The pseudonym "Solomon"

The early consensus was that the Odes are named for Solomon because of their connection with the <u>Psalms of Solomon</u> in the canonical lists. Other theories centre on Solomon's reputation as a poet (1 K 4:32) and possible parallels between the Odes and the Wisdom literature (esp. Canticles). Recent discussion focusses on the Wisdom of Solomon (Drijvers 1987), 1 Chr 22:9-10 and 2 Sam 12:25 (Franzmann 1985; 1987, 324-6).

Little has been done over the eighty or so years of research to question the methodology of scholars. The questions initially addressed to the Odes were simply accepted as *the* questions to ask. Most recently, L. Abramowski has argued for more honesty in the approach to the perennial questions of date, place of composition, and so on:

> "The anonymous or pseudonymous Syriac literature from the period before Aphraates and Ephraem is hedged round with so many uncertainties of date and place, of literal and historical connections that conclusions have to be drawn with the utmost care...to draw the map of this world one has to be conscious that the blank spaces would take up most of it." (1987, 219)

The Odes have been used repeatedly merely as footnotes to work on other texts, or have been treated in a piecemeal fashion, scholars culling a line or two from a number of Odes or a theme or two in the attempt to identify parallels in other texts. There were few who raised other methodological concerns. Of these, Bacon (194), G. Kittel (1914, 1: 6), R. Abramowski (213), Lattke (1979-86, 1: vii-viii), Drijvers (1980, 338), Blaszczak (3-4), and Franzmann (1986a, 365) plead (in a variety of contexts) for an approach which respects the collection as a literary text in its own right.The problem is ongoing (cf. Franzmann 1989) and Blaszczak's criticism is well-founded:

> "...all too often sweeping and ill-founded conclusions have been made, based on parallels of language and form that are either so strained or so common as to be of little real significance. In their efforts to establish the setting, external causes, influences, and general cultural and religious climate, scholars of the Odes have not infrequently neglected a careful study of the language, form and content of the texts of the Odes themselves." (3-4)

It is not only the way in which parallels have been sought between the Odes and other texts that has been at fault. Strict categories of Christian or Gnostic, orthodox or heterodox, seem now far too clear-cut for the very fluid and eclectic environment of the earliest centuries C.E. Drower indicates something of the prevailing spirit in the context of her discussion of Mandaean religious literature:

> "During the period 500 B.C. to A.D. 500, when syncretistic tendencies were active and many religious teachers bent on adapting old formulae and ancient rites to fresh conceptions, an operation hastened by conquest, free intercommunication, and occasional interchange of populations, one would expect to find amongst the widely diffused Aramaic-speaking peoples a common fund not only of religious ideas but of religious phrases. Hence it is difficult to determine priority when identical phrases are found in the religious literatures of the epoch, or to base precise conclusions upon such evidence alone." (21)[1]

It is becoming increasingly clear that categorising texts baldly as Christian or Gnostic is no longer satisfactory. One need only witness the difficulty with the attempt at an exact definition of what constitutes Gnosticism and its relationship to the development of the Christian tradition in the first centuries C.E.[2] Not only was there an extensive degree of syncretistic borrowing between groups in the early centuries C.E., but one is also aware that the drawing of boundaries between orthodox and heterodox practices and texts for "mainstream" Christianity was a long process in an anything but homogeneous church.

Then, too, the question about orthodoxy must be asked from a broader perspective. To question the orthodoxy of imagery or expression in the Syriac text is not enough. One must take all the texts which include Odes (Pistis Sophia, Divinae Institutiones, Papyrus Bodmer XI) and ask: What kind of texts/collections are these? Who used them? Were they groups considered to be orthodox? If there seems little basis one way or the other for judging the orthodoxy or heterodoxy of imagery/expression in the Odes (although we might find "tendencies" towards one or the other), then it seems the question must be left open and the possibility accepted that their expression is so ambiguous that a wide-

---

[1] Similarly, for the interaction of Greek language and culture in Palestine, cf. Hengel 1969, esp. "Kapitel II: Der Hellenismus in Palästina als kulturelle Macht und sein Einfluß auf die Juden", 108-95.

[2] Cf. e.g. Bianchi; Rudolph 1975; Widengren and Hellholm; Koschorke; Colpe 1981; Berger, K. 1984b; Wilson 1984.

ranging group felt able to use them, or at least some of them, as the text answered a need for religious expression.

### b. POETICAL ANALYSIS AND FORM-CRITICAL RESEARCH ON THE ODES OF SOLOMON

This area has evoked the least interest in studies of the Odes, although there has been some work on individual Odes or a few Odes, covering a variety of aspects: the similarity of the Odes to the canonical psalter, to Hebrew poetry in general, to the Hodajot of Qumran; strophe and line division; metre and rhythm; style (assonance, repetition, alliteration, parallelismus membrorum, ...); genre and setting.

The most important and helpful contribution so far in the area of poetical analysis has been Charlesworth's article on paronomasia (repetition, double entendre and double entente) (1970, 13-22) and assonance (22-3).

In the introduction to the most recent form-critical study on the Odes, Blaszczak gives a short history of research, outlining the work of the three scholars (Kroll [1921/22], R. Abramowski, and Schille) who had previously made the major contribution towards categorising the Odes according to genre (4-6), albeit in rather piecemeal fashion. Blaszczak himself offers a detailed analysis of four of the Odes (16, 31, 33, 36) and, although his concluding chapter gives some indication for classifying the remainder of the collection (75-99), Odes 4, 5, 6, 14, 26, 27, 30, 40, and 41 are not considered (cf. Lattke 1987).

Blaszczak's brief overview omits a discussion of the work of Gunkel who, although not producing any detailed analysis of individual Odes, wrote a number of times on the form of the Odes as a whole (1910, 293; 1913a, 165; 1913b, 12).

There has been great variation in opinion concerning the genre of the Odes. Although few scholars have produced detailed form-critical work, many have voiced an opinion about genre, whether for individual Odes, groups of Odes, or for the entire collection. The examples from the range of opinions given below will not include the work by Kroll, R. Abramowski, Schille or Blaszczak which will be discussed in Chapter III.

Suggestions for the collection as a whole include:

| | |
|---|---|
| Griechische Dichtungen | Zahn 764 |
| Semitische Poesie in griechischem Gewande | Greßmann 1911b, 5 |
| Psalmen | Wensinck 55 |
| Songs | Abbott 1912, vii |
| Hymns of the Catechumens/hymns of the newly baptised | Bernard |
| Griechische Gedichte in Nachahmung hebräischer poetischer Satzordnung | Gunkel 1913a, 165 |
| Hymnes antiochiennes | Dalmais 244 |
| Prophetic hymns | Aune 1982 |
| Hymnisch-enthusiastische Lobpreisungen der Erlösung | Baumeister 61 |
| Didactic poetry of a religious nature | Drijvers 1987, 128 |
| "Inspirierte"/"geistgewirkte" Liederdichtungen | Hengel 1987, 368 |

A number of scholars have categorised groups of Odes: Danklieder - 10, 22, 29 (Gunkel 1910, 183, 309, 311); Psalmen - 17, 36 (Gunkel 1910, 300, 307); Triumphlieder - 17, 22, 42 (Gunkel 1910, 303, 307, 309); apokalyptische Oden - 23, 24, 38, 39 (Harnack 1910, 115); Flood-hymns - 24 and 38 (Harris 1911b; 1911c); frälsareoden (Redeemer Odes) - 9, 10, 11, 15, 17, 22, 25, 28, 29, 31, 35, 36, 38 (Lindblom 9); Danklieder - 25, 29 (Gunkel 1933, 265, 292; Morawe 347); Danklieder - 22, 25 (Colpe 1982, 77).

The categorisation of single Odes includes:

| | |
|---|---|
| 1 - Doxologie | Colpe 1982, 77 |
| 5 - Vertrauenslied | Eißfeldt 828 n. 2 |
| 5 - Preisgelübde und Scheltrede | Colpe 1982, 77 |
| 6 - Lehrgedicht | .. |
| 9 - Verbindung von Selbstempfehlung und Predigtaufruf | Dibelius 284 |
| 11 - meditation | Carmignac 1961, 97 |
| 15 - Tauflied | Dölger 369-70 |
| 15 - Sonnenlied, Osterlied, Tauflied, Dankhymnus | Steidle 242 |
| 16 - Hymn | Eißfeldt 828 n. 2 |
| 24 - baptismal hymn | Burkitt 384 |
| 24 - Taufwunder | Dibelius 270-4 |
| 25 - Danklied | Eißfeldt 828 n. 2 |

| 26 - Hymnus | Greßmann 1911a, 635 |
| 28 - Dankpsalm | .. , 675 |
| 33 - Missionsrede | .. , 9 |
| 33 - Offenbarungsrede | Becker 16-8 |
| 38 - apocalyptic Ode | Harris 1931, 22 |

Analysis of sections of Odes include:

| Hallelujah - Schlußruf | Dölger 132 |
| - Gebetsruf | Severus 1206 |
| 5:10-15; 12:4b-f; 23:1-3; 26:5-7; 29:2-3(4) | |
| - Ode-within-the-Ode | Franzmann 1984, 397, 401-403 |
| 16:11-20 - Hymn | Gunkel 1933, 33 |
| 24:1-5 - Taufsage | Greßmann 1921, 27 |
| 24:1-8 - Taufbericht/ein Bericht über | |
| die Höllenfahrt | Reitzenstein 167 n. 2 |
| 26:4 - Erhöhungsdoxologie | Bertram 1966, 25 |
| 34:1-3 - Lehrgedicht | Amstutz 130 |
| 39:9ff - mythologische Möglichkeit | Dibelius 278 |
| 42:13ff - Hadespredigt | Bertram 1928, 1968 |
| 42:15c - Erbarmungsruf | Severus 1206 |
| 42:15c-18 - Ruf nach der endgültigen | |
| Erlösung | Dölger 135 |

Omissions are also noteworthy, most notably in the work of Bernard, who produced a detailed work on the Odes as baptismal hymns without one truly form-critical section.

A number of studies have attempted to integrate the analysis of form with analysis of some poetical features of the Odes. Grimme's (1911) translation of the Odes in acrostic Hebrew style depends in part on his work in strophe division and metre[1], and G. Kittel incorporated form-critical detail especially in the first part of his work ("Zur Stilistik der Oden Salomos" [1914, 12-44]).

---

[1] Critics of Grimme's work include Brockelmann (1912, 314), Dhorme (464-6) and, much later, Carmignac (1961, 102) and Lattke (1979-86, 3: 98-107).

EXCURSUS: "CATEGORISATION" OF THE COLLECTION ACCORDING TO PAPY-
RUS BODMER XI, PISTIS SOPHIA, MSS. N AND H, AND DIVINAE INSTITUTIONES

### Papyrus Bodmer XI, Pistis Sophia and Divinae Institutiones

The title, Odes of Solomon, for the collection appears to be known to the writ-
ers of the Greek Ode 11 in Papyrus Bodmer XI, Pistis Sophia, and Divinae
Institutiones. Ode 11 in Papyrus Bodmer XI has the superscript, $\Omega\Delta H$
$\Sigma O\Lambda OM\Omega NTO\Sigma$ (Testuz 46) and Lactantius introduces 19:6-7 with "Solomon
in ode undeuicesima" (Brandt and Laubmann 310). In Pistis Sophia, ⲱⲀH is
used in reference to the Odes in general (II,65,132; Schmidt 1978b, 264[1];
II,69,151; Schmidt 1978b, 302), and to Odes 1 ([Ode 19 according to the
Coptic] I,58,117; Schmidt 1978b, 234), 6:8-18 (II,66,136; Schmidt 1978b,
272), and 22:1-12 (II,71,157; Schmidt 1978b, 314). Each of the Odes cited is
referred to also as words which have been prophesied (ⲡⲢⲟⲫⲎⲧⲉ ⲩⲉ).

In Pistis Sophia, the Odes are clearly regarded as prophetic material, in the
double sense of prophecy and of interpretation. Apart from the references to
the Odes, the term ⲱⲀH (cf. the index, Schmidt 1978b, 793) occurs only once
in the citation of Ps 68:30 (I,33,55; Schmidt 1978b, 110; שיר [MT] ᾠδή [LXX]
ܐܬܒܫܘܚܬ [Pesh]).

In comparison with ⲱⲀH, ⳞⲨⲘⲚⲞⲥ and ⲯⲀⲗⲘⲞⲥ and their respective verb
forms are far more frequent in Pistis Sophia (cf. the index, Schmidt 1978b,
793). There seems little difference in style between the "hymns" which the
Odes are said to interpret and the Odes themselves[2]. It could be suggested that
the writer would have referred to the Odes as hymns had he/she not known of
the title for the collection.

### The Syriac manuscripts: N and H

Unlike N which has a number only preceding each Ode, H has ܐܬܝܪܡܙ and a
number. In H, the Psalms of Solomon follow immediately upon the Odes with
the first Psalm designated likewise with ܐܬܝܪܡܙ.

Within the Odes, a variety of terms is used for the action of composing or
singing: ܐܬܝܪܡܙ (14:7; 26:2,3,8; 36:2; 40:3); ܚܒܫ which occurs once in paral-

---

[1] MacDermot translates with "his ode", as if in reference to 6:8-18, but the text has
Ⲛⲉ Ⳟ ⲱⲀH ("his odes").

[2] Cf. the fourth section of Lattke 1979-86, vol. 1 ("Die gnostische Interpretation der Oden
Salomos in der Pistis Sophia"; 207-25) for a detailed study of the relationship of the Odes to
their context in the Pistis Sophia.

lel to ܟܐܬܘܪܬܐ (40:3); ܡܙܡܘܪܐ (16:1); ܬܫܒܘܚܬܐ (16:2,4; 26:1 [appears to be in parallel to ܟܐܬܘܪܬܐ in 26:2]; 40:2). ܡܙܡܘܪܐ is found in 7:17,22 where the Odist is not explicitly mentioned as singing/composing. ܬܫܒܘܚܬܐ occurs as a general term for praises sung to the Lord (13:2; 16:1; 41:4,16) and for the new song sung by the Lord in 31:3.

ܡܙܡܘܪܐ occurs in 26:12 and refers to the group to which the Odist belongs. ܚܝܠ (7:18) and perhaps ܡܙܘܪܝ (7:22) refer to the same group.

ܟܐܬܘܪܬܐ and ܬܫܒܘܚܬܐ are the most frequently used terms for the material produced/sung by the Odist. A number of equivalent Hebrew (MT) and Greek (LXX) terms can be found for these two terms as used in the Peshitta, for example:

ܟܐܬܘܪܬܐ

| | |
|---|---|
| זָמִיר | Ps 118:54; Amos 5:23 |
| שִׁיר | Amos 5:23; Is 23:15; Ez 33:32 |
| ψαλτός | Ps 118:54 |
| ψαλμός | Amos 5:23; Lam 3:14 |
| ᾠδή | Amos 5:23; Eph 5:19; Col 3:16 |
| ᾆσμα | Is 23:15 |

ܬܫܒܘܚܬܐ

| | |
|---|---|
| שִׁיר | Ex 15:1; Deut 31:19; Cant 1:1 |
| ᾠδή | Ex 15:1; Deut 31:19 |
| ᾆσμα | Cant 1:1 |
| ὕμνος | Eph 5:19; Col 3:16 |

Even such a small sample of equivalent terms supports the impression of the relative freedom enjoyed in the use of the Syriac terms ܟܬܝܒܬܐ and ܟܬܢܘܒܚܬܐ in the early centuries C.E. Thus the collection of the Odes itself makes no clear delineation concerning the categorisation of its material as hymns or songs or psalms.

### c. THE METHOD OF FORM CRITICISM IN GENERAL

Kroll, R. Abramowski and Schille completed their work on the Odes before the current dissatisfaction with form-critical method (particularly in the specific areas of genre categorisation and setting) had gained a hold in scholarly circles. Blaszczak may well be aware of the debate (6-8, 76-7) but nowhere refers to it explicitly.

The change in the approach to form-critical studies is evident in the report from the Old Testament Form-critical Project (Knierim, director) in the Institute for Antiquity and Christianity at Claremont:

"Increasingly it has become clear that the project, while attempting to preserve its identity as a form-critical endeavor, could not ignore the impact of insights derived from the disciplines of sociology, structural linguistics, style criticism, and rhetorical criticism, and from the studies of oral tradition and literature." (1981, 9)

In his Presidential Address to the Society of Biblical Literature in December 1968, Muilenburg notes in relation to form criticism that "signs are not wanting, both here (USA) and abroad, of discontent with the prevailing state of affairs, of a sense that the method has outrun its course." (1969, 4). Muilenburg suggests that the basic problem is the priority which form criticism gives to the typical with insufficient appreciation for what is unique about a text (5-7)[1]. Although the title of the address suggests that Muilenburg sees the solution in a move "beyond" form criticism, in effect he calls for the supplementing of form-critical work by what he terms rhetorical criticism (18), the practical

---

[1] In like manner Buss criticises Gunkel and form critics in general for the assertion of the purity of popular genres: "OT form critics have often not seen, as others have, that genres are abstractions ("ideal forms") and that virtually all human experiences involve a combination of categories applied simultaneously and that partly for this reason no more than statistical correlations between phenomena can be expected." (53). Cf. also Knierim 1973, 455.

working out of which appears to be closely synonymous with the analysis of poetical structure[1].

Knierim is right to point out that what Muilenburg proposes is not beyond form-critical method (1973, 458, n.91), as is clear from the work of Richter, especially under the aspect of criteria for form-analysis (79-103). Knierim suggests that the answer to some of the major problem-areas in form criticism (the relation of genre to setting and the relation of the genre of a text to its structure; the relation of the structure of a genre to its content, mood, function, intention, or concern) is to "conceptualize the methodology less ideologically than in the past...to set up a framework within which the specific form-critical tools can be applied flexibly" (459). He envisages the future direction for form criticism as incorporating the method of structural interpretation (459)[2], meaning by this the identification of the structural principles that underlie a text: rhetorical or stylistic devices, patterns of a particular literary type (decalogue, itinerary,...), the systematic viewpoint (process of thought, climax and anti-climax,...) and so on (460).

### d. THE PRESENT PROJECT

The present project provides preliminary steps towards a form-critical investigation of the collection of the Odes; preliminary, because certain control factors necessary for such an investigation in the fullest sense are missing and cannot be provided within the limits of this work. Ideally a study of form should go hand in hand with a thoroughgoing analysis of the imagery, such studies being complementary and in the nature of a mutual critique/control. Although the focus is towards form-critical study, the project is preliminary also with regard to other questions such as the original language of the Odes.

---

[1] Cf. the critique of Muilenburg's address by Melugin. Recently several scholars have described their work as an attempt to take up Muilenburg's challenge. Although Mosca carries out a careful analysis of the poetical structure of Ps 26 (217-29), his second section of form criticism focusses unfortunately on the semantic content of the psalm rather than on the form (229-36). Allen's analysis of Ps 69 is much more successful in its integration of the two aspects. Cf. also Meynet's rhetorical analysis of the prologue in the Gospel of John. For an overview of recent studies, cf. Black.

[2] The terminology has become problematical. Knierim obviously means by structural analysis something much broader than, for example, what constitutes the method for T. Collins' (1987) work on a structural approach to the psalter which focusses on semantic content, the units of meaning which can be identified within that, their relation to each other and the deeper structure revealed by that relationship. For a discussion of the difference in these two methods, cf. Girard, esp. "Analyse structurale et analyse structurelle", 12-15.

Taking its point of departure from the recent studies of form criticism in general, the analysis works "from the bottom up", Chapter II comprising the major section in which the text is analysed word by word, line by line, strophe by strophe, stanza by stanza...[1] The examination of each Ode is according to literary devices: inclusion, change in perspective by the shift in speaker/the one addressed or by the shift in verb forms (e.g. changes from imperative to inter-rogative), change in semantic focus, patterning of verb forms, patterning of words in pairs or phrases, repetitions of key words, use of particles, conjunc-tions and prepositions (esp. initially), forms of parallelismus membrorum (pivotal, staircase, chiasmus, ...), patterns of suffixes, patterning of sound (onomatopoeia, alliteration), patterning of line length ...

The limits of space have necessarily restricted the treatment of metre and rhythm, line length, alliteration and assonance. To cover all the aspects in de-tail for each Ode would have been impossible as is clear from the work of Blaszczak and similar text studies by B.P. Kittel on the Hodayot or T. Collins (1978) on the prophetic corpus of the Hebrew scriptures. It seemed imperative, however, to study the whole collection for the first time, even if in such a lim-ited way. After this initial work, individual Odes can be given a fuller treat-ment.

The texts under investigation are the texts in their final form as we have them and there is only minimal concern for identifying possible strata of un-derlying sources. With the question of the original language still open, one can do no more than be aware that a translation may effect profound changes in rhythm, word-play, rhyme and so on.

Chapter III builds upon the detailed analysis of Chapter II, taking the pat-terns of vocabulary and syntax and so on that have been identified and looking at the implications both for the interpretation of Odes and for possible group-ings of Odes. The latter section includes a brief discussion of imagery/motif and further suggestions for the groupings of Odes.

The main purpose of the project is to take seriously the new direction in form-critical study and to attempt to follow that in a preliminary way with the Odes. There are no final lists with specific genre and setting for each Ode or indeed for the collection, but the project does indicate the possibilities for this method and gives both basic data and a direction for further research.

---

[1] The methods outlined by Watson (1986, 15-20) and Meer and Moor (vii-ix) for a structural approach, esp. to the Hebrew Scriptures, provided a helpful starting point.

# II. STRUCTURAL ANALYSIS OF THE SYRIAC, GREEK, AND COPTIC ODES OF SOLOMON[1]

## (ODE 1)

1 ⲡⲁⲟⲉⲓⲥ ϩⲓⲁⲛ ⲧⲁⲁⲡⲉ ⲛⲑⲉ ⲛⲟⲩⲕⲗⲟⲙ
  ⲁⲩⲱ ⲛⲧⲛⲁⲣⲡⲉϥⲃⲟⲗ ⲁⲛ

2 ⲁⲩϣⲱⲛⲧ ⲛⲁⲓ ⲙⲡⲉⲕⲗⲟⲙ ⲛⲧⲁⲗⲏⲑⲓⲁ
  ⲁⲩⲱ ⲁϥⲧⲣⲉ ⲛⲉⲕⲕⲗⲁⲇⲟⲥ ϯⲟⲩⲱ ϩⲣⲁⲓ ⲛϩⲏⲧ

3 ϫⲉ ⲉϥⲉⲓⲛⲉ ⲁⲛ ⲛⲟⲩⲕⲗⲟⲙ ⲉϥϣⲟⲩⲱⲟⲩ ⲉⲙⲉϥϯⲟⲩⲱ

4 ⲁⲗⲗⲁ ⲕⲟⲛϩ ϩⲓⲁⲛ ⲧⲁⲁⲡⲉ
  ⲁⲩⲱ ⲁⲕϯⲟⲩⲱ ϩⲣⲁⲓ ϩⲓϫⲱⲓ

5 ⲛⲉⲕⲕⲁⲣⲡⲟⲥ ⲥⲉⲙⲉϩ ⲁⲩⲱ ⲥⲉϫⲏⲕ
  ⲉⲩⲙⲉϩ ⲉⲃⲟⲗ ϩⲙ ⲡⲉⲕⲟⲩϫⲁⲓ

---

1 The Lord (is) on my head like a wreath,
  and I will not flee from him.

2 The wreath of truth has been plaited for me,
  and it has caused your branches to sprout in me.

3 For it is not like a wreath which is dry, which does not sprout.

4 But you are alive on my head,
  and you have sprouted upon me.

5 Your fruits are full and ripe;
  they are full of your salvation.

---

1 Several scholars have more than one edition and translation. In the notes to the translations and the analysis, either the more recent (Harris 1911a; Bauer 1964) or more detailed (Charlesworth 1977) edition is used and reference made to the other/s only where they differ significantly. Page numbers are not given in the references where the editor provides notes to the translation on the same page as the edited text.

NOTES TO THE TRANSLATION

The Ode is numbered as 19 (ϨΝ ΤΕϤΜΕϨⲘⲚⲦⲮⲒⲦⲈ ⲚⲱⲀϨ; Charlesworth 1981, 16) by the author of <u>Pistis Sophia</u>, but is generally regarded by scholars as Ode 1, missing from both H and N. The difference in numbering is explained by the Coptic scribe's possessing a manuscript in which the 18 <u>Psalms of Solomon</u> were followed immediately by the Odes. In H, where the <u>Psalms of Solomon</u> follow the Odes, Psalm 1 is entitled Ode (or psalm) 43.

2a: Lit. "they have plaited for me the wreath of truth" (for the use of the pass., cf. Till § 326).

5b: ⲞⲨⲀⲀⲒ̈ means "health"/"safety" but also translates σωτηρία (Crum 512a). The Greek loan word ⲤⲰⲦⲎⲢ occurs in Copt 5:11.

ANALYSIS

Stanza 1 [1]

1a-b functions as an introductory confessional statement. The simile in 1a introduces the motif of the wreath which will be developed in more detail in stanza 2.

1a and 1b are parallel to a degree with chiasmus by the placement of the 1st sing. and ⲠⲀⲞⲈⲒⲤ/3rd sing. masc. 1a has ⲠⲀⲞⲈⲒⲤ as the subj. and the 1st sing. as the ultimate obj.; 1b has the 1st sing. as subj. and the 3rd sing. masc. (ⲠⲈϤ, ref. to the Lord) as obj.

1a and 5:12a are almost identical expressions. The motif of the wreath/ crown is associated with the idea of union with the Lord (expressed by negative terms in 1b) in 5:10-15; 20:7-9.

Stanza 2 [2-3, 4]

With stanza 2 there is a change from statements about the Lord in the 3rd sing. masc. to an address to the Lord in the 2nd sing. masc. The repetition of the verb (Ⲧ)ⲞⲨⲰ is a strongly unifying feature of the stanza.

2a-3 concerns the wreath of truth which is the subj. of each line (indirectly in 2a by the impersonal passive construction). 2a and 2b have a degree of parallelism by the use of the 3rd perf. I and the focus on the 1st sing. as the ultimate object of the action described. There is a terrace pattern by the placement of ⲠⲈⲔⲖⲞⲘ ⲚⲦⲀⲖⲎⲈⲒⲀ as obj. at the conclusion of 2a and the 3rd sing. masc. perf. I prefix ⲀⳠ- (ref. to ⲠⲈⲔⲖⲞⲘ ⲚⲦⲀⲖⲎⲈⲒⲀ) immediately following at the beginning of 2b.

3 functions as a concluding statement for the strophe, referring back to 2a by the repetition of ⲔⲖⲞⲘ and to 2b by the repetition of (ϯ)ⲞⲨⲰ and by the use of the 3rd sing. masc. subj. (ref. to the wreath of truth). The monocolon has a central position in the Ode, not only by its placement, but primarily by the contrast between its negative descriptions (dry, not sprouting) and those of 2b (branches sprouting) and 4a-b (alive and sprouting). The use of ⲈⲒⲚⲈ in 3 creates the simile. There is internal parallelism by the doubling of the *Umstandssatz* form (cf. Till § 328-34) with the 3rd sing. masc. (ref. to the wreath).

With 4a-b, there is a shift from statements about the wreath of truth in the 3rd sing. masc. to statements addressed to the Lord (= the wreath of truth) in the 2nd sing. masc. The bicolon is parallel on the pattern: conj. + 2nd sing. masc. verb (ref. to the Lord) + loosely equivalent phrases expressing place with the key prep. ⳌⲒⲀⲚ/ⳌⲒⲀⲰ ("on my head"/"upon me").

4a reiterates the statement of 1a by the repetition of ⳌⲒⲀⲚ ⲦⲀⲀⲠⲈ (ref. to the Lord as the wreath). The image of the Lord as a living and blossoming wreath on the head of the "I" is similar to the crowning of the "I" with a living crown in 17:1. There is parallelism between 4b and 2b, further emphasising the centrality of 3, by the use of (ϯ)ⲞⲨⲰ + ⳌⲢⲀⲒ (used to stress the prep. which follows).

## Stanza 3 [5]

With stanza 3, the focus shifts from the wreath to the fruits (consequence of the sprouting of the wreath?). The bicolon functions as a concluding confessional statement. There is a degree of parallelism by the repetition of the 3rd pl. pres. I (5a)/II (5b) form of ⲘⲞⲨⳌ (ref. to the fruits) and the focus on attributes of the Lord ("your fruits", "your salvation").

5a has internal parallelism by the doubling of the 3rd pl. perf. I form. The association of salvation with the wreath/crown (5b) occurs also in 5:11-12.

## ODE 3

1 ... ܡܠܒܫ ܐܢܐ
ܘܗܕܡܘܗܝ ܠܘܬܗ ܐܢܘܢ
ܘܒܗܘܢ ܬܠܐ ܐܢܐ

ܘܪܚܡ ܠܝ
3 ܠܐ ܓܝܪ ܝܕܥ ܗܘܝܬ ܠܡܪܚܡ ܠܡܪܝܐ
ܐܠܘ ܗܘ ܠܐ ܪܚܡ ܗܘܐ ܠܝ
4 ܡܢܘ ܡܫܟܚ ܠܡܦܪܫ ܪܚܡܬܐ
ܐܠܐ ܗܘ ܕܡܬܪܚܡ
5 ܪܚܡ ܐܢܐ ܠܪܚܝܡܐ
ܘܪܚܡܐ ܠܗ ܢܦܫܝ
ܘܐܝܟܐ ܕܢܝܚܗ
ܐܦ ܐܢܐ ܐܝܬܝ

6 ܘܠܐ ܐܗܘܐ ܢܘܟܪܝܐ
ܡܛܠ ܕܠܝܬ ܚܣܡܐ ܠܘܬ ܡܪܝܐ ܡܪܝܡܐ ܘܡܪܚܡܢܐ
7 ܐܬܡܙܓܬ
ܡܛܠ ܕܐܫܟܚ ܪܚܡܐ ܠܗܘ ܪܚܡܐ
ܡܛܠ ܕܐܪܚܡ ܠܗܘ ܒܪܐ
ܕܐܗܘܐ ܒܪܐ

8 ܗܘ ܓܝܪ ܕܡܬܢܩܦ ܠܗܘ ܕܠܐ ܡܐܬ
ܐܦ ܗܘ ܕܠܐ ܡܐܬܐ ܢܗܘܐ
9 ܘܗܘ ܕܨܒܐ ܒܚܝܐ
ܚܝܐ ܢܗܘܐ

10 ܗܢܘ ܪܘܚܗ ܕܡܪܝܐ ܕܠܐ ܕܓܠܘܬܐ
ܕܡܠܦܐ ܠܒܢܝ̈ܢܫܐ ܕܢܕܥܘܢ ܐܘܪ̈ܚܬܗ

11 ܐܬܚܟܡܘ ܘܕܥܘ ܘܐܬܬܥܝܪܘ

ܗܠܠܘܝܐ

1 --- I am putting on,
2 and his members are with him,
　and in them I hang.

　And he loves me.
3 For I should not have known to love the Lord,
　if he did not love me.
4 Who is able to distinguish love,
　but he who is beloved?
5 I love the Beloved,
　and my soul loves him.
　And where his rest (is),
　I am also.

6 And I shall not be a stranger,
　because there is no jealousy with the Lord Most High and merciful.
7 I have been united,
　because the lover has found the Beloved.
　Because I love the Son,
　I shall be the Son.

8 For he who cleaves to him who is immortal,
　he also will be immortal.
9 And he who delights in the life
　will be living.

10 This is the Spirit of the Lord who is without falsehood,
　who teaches men that they might know his ways.

11 Become wise and know and wake up.

　Alleluia.

NOTES TO THE TRANSLATION

1: Manuscript H commences with ܡܠܒܫ.

2b-c: This appears as one line in H. The division is made on the basis of the parallelism of 2c and 3b (cf. also Diettrich 1911).

5a-d: H reads as two lines. The further division of each line is based on the parallel structure (cf. also Diettrich 1911; Greßmann 1924).

7a-d: H has two lines. The division into four lines here is made on the basis of the parallel structure within 6-7 (cf. also Diettrich 1911; Greßmann 1924; Lattke 1979-86, vol. 1).

7a: Lit. "I have been mixed".

10a: The qualification ܕܠܐ ܡܬܚܒܠܐ may apply to either the Spirit or the Lord. Application to the Spirit is supported by the fact that the following ܕܡܠܬܗ refers to the Spirit.

ANALYSIS

The centrality of the motif of love is clear from the frequency with which the root רחם (x 10) and its synonym חבב (x 2; synonymity is indicated in the parallelism of 5a-b) occur.

Stanza 1 [(1)-2b]

The extent of the stanza cannot be known. There is parallelism between the conclusion of what must be counted tentatively as 1 and the conclusion of 2b by the use of the sing. masc. part. act. + ܐܢܐ. This may indicate that there is at least a bicolon to precede (1) which is alternately parallel with 2a-b. The key words/roots in (1)-2b do not occur elsewhere in this Ode.

Stanza 2 [2c-3, 4, 5]

Stanza 2 introduces the major theme of the love between the "I" and the Lord. 2c functions as the introductory confessional statement, forming an inclusio for the first strophe with 3b, both semantically and by the use of the sing. masc. verb ܣܘܚ/ܪܚܡ ܝ (subj. is the Lord) + ܠ.

3a-b is a reflection on the introductory statement. There is a change to the past tense with 3a. The bicolon is parallel to a degree by the use of ܪܚܡ ܝ + dir. obj. There is chiasmus by the placement of the 1st sing. and ܗܒܝܒ/3rd sing. masc. 3a has the 1st sing. subj. associated with ܪܚܡ ܝ and ܗܒܝܒ as dir. obj.; 3b has the 3rd sing. masc. (= ܗܒܝܒ) as subj. of ܪܚܡ ܝ and the 1st sing. as dir. obj.

The rhetorical question in 4a-b is a reiteration of the thought in 3a-b. 4a-b is parallel by the use of the part. act. form with the common 3rd sing. masc. subj. and the repetition of the key root ܪܚܡ ܝ.

The third strophe is linked with the first by the parallelism between 2c and 5a: ܢܩܒ + ܠ + dir. obj. There is chiasmus by the placement of the 1st sing. and ܢܫܘ ܝ/3rd sing. masc.: 2c has the 3rd sing. masc. as subj. (the Lord/Beloved is understood) and the 1st sing. as dir. obj.; 5a has the 1st sing. as subj. and ܢܫܘ ܝ (= the Lord) as dir. obj.

5a-b is parallel on the general pattern: part. act. of ܪܚܡ ܝ/ܣܘ + ܠ with synonymous dir. obj. (ܢܫܘ ܝ/substitute 3rd sing. masc. suffix). The parallelism is strengthened by the 1st sing. subj. in 5a and the indirect use of the 1st sing. 5c-d are connected semantically by the concepts of love and union (being with). The bicolon continues the juxtaposition of 3rd sing. masc. (ref. to the Lord) and the 1st sing. persons.


Stanza 3 [6, 7]

The limits of the stanza are delineated by the inclusio between 6a and 7d which are parallel on the general pattern: ܐ ܡ ܗ ܐ + noun obj. The parallelism is strengthened by the antithesis between "stranger" and "son". The stanza comprises three bicola which have a common pattern of principal clause + 1st sing. verb in one line and a clause introduced by ܝ ܡܛܠ in the other, expressing the reason for the action described in the principal cl. The bicolon in 7a-b has the central position in the stanza which emphasises the motif of the unity of the Lord/Beloved and the "I". That the "I" is not unique in being "the Son" is clear from 31:4.

6a and 6b are linked semantically by the association of the ideas of the "I" being close to the Lord (= not a stranger) and of the Lord who does not hold himself back (= has no jealousy). The Lord is described as being without jealousy in 7:3; 11:6; 15:6; 20:7; 23:4.

7a-b and 7c-d are more closely connected by the parallelism of 7b and 7c on the pattern: ܩ ܟܠ܊ + verb + ܠܗܢ (pleonastic ref. to the dir. obj. for emphasis) + noun obj. The parallelism is strengthened by the repetition of the root ܝܚܕ and by the synonymity of ܪܚܡܬܐ, ܚܘܒ.

7a and 7b are connected semantically by the concepts of union and love. 7b has internal parallelism by the doubling of the root ܝܚܕ. 7c-d is parallel on the general pattern: 1st sing. verb + dir. obj./compl. (ܚܘܒ).

Stanza 4 [8-9]

The stanza comprises two alternately parallel bicola. 8a and 9a are parallel with chiasmus on the pattern: A B C // A' C' B', where A = ܩ ܗܘ; B = 3rd sing. masc. part. act.; C = ultimate object of the action. The parallelism is enhanced by the semantic closeness of the concepts of immortality and life. 8b and 9b are parallel by the pattern of qualifying expression + ܠܗܡ. The parallelism is strengthened by the word-pair ܡܘܬܐ ܠܐ - ܚܝ.

8a-b is parallel with chiasmus on the general pattern: A B C // A' C' B', where A = ܩ ܗܘ; B = sing. masc. verb; C = obj./compl. using the expression ܡܘܬܐ/ܚܕ ܠܐ. 7a and 8a appear to be similar descriptions of union between a believer and the Lord. 9a and 9b are parallel on the general pattern: ܚܝ/ܚܝ + sing. masc. verb. There is a finality to 9b which is produced by the relatively short line, achieved by a decreasing length of line over the whole stanza (8a has 9 syllables, 8b has 7, 9a has 6, and 9b has 4).

Although the statements in 8-9 are couched in 3rd sing. masc. impersonal terms, they would surely apply to the "I". There is therefore a semantic connection between 6a, 7d, 8b, and 9b - one who is united/cleaving to the Beloved (= the one who is immortal) is no stranger, is the Son, is immortal and living.

Stanza 5 [10]

10a-b has no clear ref. to its context although one must be careful in making any judgement because of the missing initial material of the Ode. The bicolon contains parallel rel. expressions (ref. to the Spirit) and a focus on the Lord (his Spirit, his ways). There is a play on the consonants ܫ, ܗ, ܝ in ܫܒܝܠܘ, ܗܘܝܘ. The concept of spirits without guile (ⲃⲁⲗϨⲏⲧ) is found in On the Origin of the World 107, 14 (Facs. ed. 2: 119; Bethge and Wintermute 167).

Stanza 6 [11]

11 functions as a concluding exhortation to the community. There is internal parallelism by the triple pattern of 2nd pl. masc. imper. verbs (cf. the same concluding form in 34:6) The parallelism is strengthened by the word-pair ܣܥܘܪ - ܥ ܠܒ. There is a connection with 10a by the repetition of the root ܥ ܠܒ and by the semantic closeness of ܠܓܐ and ܣܥܪ.

## ODE 4

1 ܠܐ ܐܢܫ ܡܫܚܠܦ ܐܬܪܟ ܩܕܝܫܐ ܐܠܗܝ
ܘܠܐ ܕܢܫܚܠܦܝܘܗܝ ܘܢܣܝܡܝܘܗܝ ܒܐܬܪܐ ܐܚܪܢܐ
2 ܡܛܠ ܕܠܝܬ ܠܗܘܢ ܫܘܠܛܢܐ
ܘܩܕܫܟ ܓܝܪ ܐܬܪܥܝܬ
ܥܕ ܠܐ ܕܬܥܒܕ ܐܬܪ̈ܘܬܐ
3 ܘܩܕܝܫܐ ܠܐ ܢܫܬܚܠܦ
ܥܡ ܗܠܝܢ ܕܒ̈ܨܝܪܝܢ ܡܢܗ

ܝܗܒܬ ܠܒܟ ܡܪܝܐ ܠܡܗܝܡ̈ܢܝܟ
4 ܠܐ ܡܬܗܘܐ ܬܒܛܠ
ܘܠܐ ܬܗܘܐ ܕܠܐ ܦܐܪ̈ܐ

5 ܚܕܐ ܓܝܪ ܫܥܬܐ ܕܗܝܡܢܘܬܟ
ܡܝܬܪܐ ܡܢ ܟܠܗܘܢ ܝܘ̈ܡܬܐ ܘܫܢ̈ܝܐ

6 ܡܢܘ ܓܝܪ ܢܠܒܫ ܛܝܒܘܬܟ
ܘܢܬܛܠܡ
7 ܡܛܠ ܕܚܬܡܟ [ܝ]ܕܝܥ ܗܘ
ܘܝܕܥ ܠܗ ܒܪ̈ܝܬܟ
8 ܘܚܝܠ̈ܘܬ[ܟ ܐ]ܚܝܕܝܢ ܠܗ
ܘܓ̈ܒܐ ܡܠܐ̈ܟܐ ܓܒ̈ܝܐ ܠܒܝܫܝܢ ܠܗ

9 ܝܗܒܬ ܠܢ ܫܘܬܦܘܬܟ
ܠܐ ܗܘܐ ܕܣܢܝܩ ܐܢܬ ܡܢܢ
ܐܠܐ ܚܢ ܣܢܝܩܝܢ ܠܟ

10 ܪܣܣ ܥܠܝܢ ܪ̈ܣܣܝܟ
ܘܦܬܚ ܡܒ̈ܘܥܝܟ ܒܝܪ̈ܬܐ
ܕܡܪܕܝܢ ܠܢ ܚܠܒܐ ܘܕܒܫܐ

11 ܠܝܬ ܓܝܪ ܬܘܬܐ ܠܘܬܟ
ܕܬܬܘܐ ܟܠ ܡܕܡ ܕܐܫܬܘܕܝܬ
12 ܘܚܪܬܐ ܓܠܝܐ ܗܘܬ ܠܟ

ܘܡܕܡ ܓܝܪ ܕܝܗܒܬ ܒܡܓܢ ܝܗܒܬ 13
ܕܠܐ ܡܟܝܠ ܬܬܘܒ
ܘܬܣܒ ܐܢܝܢ
ܟܠܡܕܡ ܓܝܪ ܐܝܟ ܐܠܗܐ ܓܠܐ ܗܘܐ ܠܟ 14
ܘܡܬܩܢ ܗܘܐ ܡܢ ܒܪܫܝܬ ܩܕܡܝܟ

ܘܐܢܬ ܡܪܝܐ ܥܒܕܬ ܟܠ 15

ܗܠܠܘܝܐ

---

1 No one changes your holy place, my God;
nor does one change it, and set it in another place;
2 because there is no authority over it.
For your sanctuary you determined
before you made the places.
3 The eldest will not be changed
by those less than it.

You gave your heart, Lord, to your believers.
4 Never will you be idle,
nor will you be without fruits.

5 For one hour of your faith
is better than all days and years.

6 For who will put on your grace
and be rejected?
7 Because your seal is known;
and your creatures are known to it;
8 and your hosts possess it;
and the chosen archangels are clothed in it.

9 You gave us your fellowship;
not that you need us,
but we need you.

10  Sprinkle upon us your sprinklings,
and open your abundant springs
which let flow milk and honey to us.

11  For there is no regret with you,
that you might regret anything which you promised.
12  And the end was manifest to you.

13  For what you gave, you gave freely,
that no longer will you draw (them) in,
and take them away.

14  For everything was manifest to you as God,
and was fixed from the beginning before you.

15  And you, Lord, made all.

Alleluia.

## NOTES TO THE TRANSLATION

2c: ܬܠܕ is a dependent imperf. verb indicating action which occurs in the future relative to the action of the principal cl. (Nöldeke § 267). It is logically translated here in the past tense (cf. also 7:9; 8:7,15; 16:18; 28: 5).

5a: ܗܝܡܢܘܬܟ may also be translated "faithfulness" (cf. Diettrich 1911; Lattke 1979-86, vol. 1; Emerton). Flemming, Ungnad and Staerk, Bruston (1912b), Greßmann (1924), and Bauer (1964) interpret the sense as "faith in you".

9b: ܠܐ ܗܘܐ may have the meaning "not", "having nothing of the force of a verb" (Nöldeke § 299).

13c: The sense is "that no longer will you take them back". Diettrich (1911) is the first to suggest ܬܗܦܟ rather than ܬܗܦܟ.

ANALYSIS

Stanza 1 [1-2, 3a-b]

The stanza focusses on the holy place/sanctuary of the Lord which cannot be changed. The verb ܚܠܦ (x 3) and ܐܬܪܐ (x 3) occur only in this stanza. The inclusio for the stanza is formed between 1a-b and 3a-b, both by their semantic similarity and by the repetition of the root ܚܠܦ (1a, 3a).

1a and 1b are parallel with a general pattern of 3rd sing. masc. verb with ܐܬܪܟ ܩܕܝܫܐ or its equivalent pron. suffix as obj. The vocative expression, ܐܠܗܝ, forms the pivot of the parallel bicolon. The parallelism is strengthened by the repetition of ܚܠܦ and by ܐܬܪܐ + adj. at the conlusion of both lines. There is contrast intended, not only geographically, between the "holy place" and "another place". 1b has internal parallelism by the doubling of the pattern of 3rd sing. masc. imperf. verb with 3rd sing. masc. obj. suffix.

2a serves as a concluding statement to 1a-b. It is connected syntactically by the clause introduced by ܡܛܠ ܕ which expresses the reason for the negative actions described in 1a-b and by the 3rd sing. masc. suffix with ܥܠ which refers to ܐܬܪܟ ܩܕܝܫܐ.

2b-c continues the motif of the holy place, ܩܘܕܫܝܟ (2b) being the equivalent of ܐܬܪܟ ܩܕܝܫܐ (1a), and a contrast to ܐܬܪ̈ܘܬܐ (2c). The bicolon is connected with 1a-b by the repetition of the root ܩܕܫ and of ܐܬܪܐ (1a, 1b, 2b [pl.]). 2b and 2c are parallel with chiasmus on the pattern: A B // B' A', where A = noun obj.; B = 2nd sing. masc. verb.

The concluding confessional formula in 3a-b sums up the statements of 1-2c. There is antithesis by the use of the contrasting terms ܩܫܝܫܐ - ܒܬܪܝܢ, the latter referring back to ܐܬܪܐ ܐܚܪܢܐ in 1a and ܐܬܪ̈ܘܬܐ in 2c.

Stanzas 2, 5, and 8

The major divisions of the Ode are indicated by the parallel stanzas 2, 5, and 8 which function as a kind of response. The stanzas follow a general pattern of a first line containing ܝܗܒܬ (subj. is the Lord) followed by a parallel bicolon, the focus of which is the Lord (2nd sing. masc. verbs in 4a, 4b, 9b, 13b, 13c), with each line comprising a simple action introduced by a negative particle (understood for 13c). 3c and 9a are more closely parallel with chiasmus on the pattern: A B C // A' C' B', where A = ܝܗܒܬ (subj. is the Lord); B = noun (attribute of the Lord) with 2nd sing. masc. suffix; C = indir. obj. The parallelism is enhanced by the similarity of the concepts of giving one's heart and being in fellowship. 13a acts rather like a final summary about the giving of the Lord.

## Stanza 2 [3c-4]

The parallelism of 3c and 9a has been dealt with above. The connection between 3c and 4a-b is not clear. That the latter is a formula is indicated by 11:23.

4a and 4b are parallel by the use of the 2nd sing. masc. Peal imperf. The lines are semantically connected, the second description (being without fruits) being subsequent to/co-terminus with the first (being idle).

## Stanza 3 [5]

5a-b is a confessional formula, linked with 3c by the repetition of the root ܐܡܪ. The bicolon contains a series of terms connected with time in a logical progression: hour, day, year. The similarity with Ps 84:10 is clear.

## Stanza 4 [6, 7-8]

The stanza proper (7-8) focusses on the seal. With an inclusio between 6a and 8b by the repetition of the root ܝܗܒ, there appears to be a connection between grace and the seal.

6a-b comprises an introductory rhetorical question. The bicolon is parallel with antithesis by the use of the 3rd sing. masc. perf. forms of the word-pair ܝܗܒ - ܛܠܡ (cf. the same word-pair associated with grace in 33:12).

7-8 is connected syntactically with 6a-b by the cl. introduced by ܡܛܠ ܕ in 7a which expresses the reason why one will not be rejected. 7a-b is parallel with chiasmus on the pattern: A B // B' A', where A = noun subj. ("possession" of the Lord) with 2nd sing. masc. suffix; B = 3rd Peal part. pass. of ܛܥܐ.

8a-b is parallel on the pattern: pl. noun subj. + 3rd pl. Peal part. pass. (with act. meaning in 8a) + ܠܗ. The parallelism is strengthened by the semantic similarity of the hosts and the archangels. 7b follows the same pattern as 8a-b but with chiasmus, by the placement of the 3rd pl. Peal part. pass. + ܠܗ to precede the pl. noun subj. 7b-8b expresses merismus by the association of creatures and the hosts/archangels; that is, those who belong to the earthly and heavenly realms.

Stanza 5 [9]

The parallelism of 9a and 3c has been discussed above. The 1st person pl. appears for the first time in 9a, indicating a community aspect that is not evident in 1a (ܢܡܠܐ). 9a is connected semantically with 9b-c, by the associated concepts of giving and needing, fellowship with the Lord and the need for the Lord.

9b-c is parallel on the general pattern: negative expression + masc. Peal part. pass. + pron. (as suffix attached to the part. in 9c) + ܡܢ with pron. suffix. There is chiasmus by the use of 1st and 2nd person - in 9b, 2nd sing. masc. subj. and ܡܢ with 1st pl. suffix; in 9c, 1st pl. subj. and ܡܢ with 2nd sing. masc. suffix. Emphasis is given to 9c by the double use of the 1st pl. pron. which brings a certain finality to the line.

Stanza 6 [10]

With stanza 6 the style shifts from address to the Lord in statements to imperatives addressed to the Lord. 10a and 10b are parallel on the general pattern: 2nd sing. masc. Peal imper. (subj. is the Lord)... pl. noun obj. ("possession" of the Lord) with 2nd sing. masc. suffix. The parallelism is strengthened by the semantic connection between sprinklings and springs as sources of moisture. There is merismus by the use of these terms: what comes from above (sprinklings) and what comes from below (springs).

10a has internal parallelism by the doubling of the root ܝܣܐ. The association of ܦܝܐ and ܡܒܢܐ (with ref. to the Lord) in 10b is found in 30:1, ܡܒܢܐ with ܡܬܝ in 26:13.

10c is connected with 10a-b by the rel. cl. (ref. to ܡܒܢܣܝܢ). There is a degree of parallelism between 10a and 10c on the pattern: verb + ܠ/ܠܠ with 1st pl. suffix + noun obj./s. The parallel structure links the sprinklings with milk and honey (cf. the sprinkling of the Lord and milk/the dew of the Lord, 35:1, 5). ܢܝܐ and ܚܠܒ are also associated in 40:1.

Stanza 7 [11, 12]

There is a return to statements addressed to the Lord with stanza 7. 11a-b is parallel with a terrace pattern by the use of the root ܗܒ in assocation with the 2nd sing. masc. at the conclusion of 11a and immediately following at the beginning of 11b. There is alliteration and assonance at the conclusion of 11a (ܠܗܒܝ ܗܒܬܗ). There is a semantic connection with stanza 8 by the motif of the generosity of the Lord (gifts/promises without regret).

There appears to be little connection semantically between 11 and 12 and indeed stanza 8 appears to interrupt a logical flow from 12 to 14a, the latter being parallel on the pattern: subj... (14a adds ܐܠܗܐ ܐܝܟ) + sing. Peal part. pass. of ܓܠܐ + 3rd sing. Peal perf. of ܗܘܐ + ܠܗ (ref. to the Lord).

## Stanza 8 [13]

13a has internal parallelism by the doubling of the pattern: obj./adv. + ܢܝܗܒܬ. 13b-c is parallel by the use of the 2nd sing. masc. Peal imperf. (subj. is the Lord) + ܐܢܬ (understood in 13c). The parallelism is enhanced by the semantic similarity of ܬܗܦܘ and ܢܣܒ in this context. The inclusio for the stanza is formed between 13a and 13c by the polar word-pair ܢܝܗܒ - ܢܣܒ.

## Stanza 9 [14]

The parallelism of 12 and 14a has been discussed above. 14a and 14b form a parallel bicolon on the general pattern: sing. masc. part. pass. (subj. is ܟܠܡܕܡ [understood in 14b]) + ܗܘܐ ... prep. + 2nd sing. masc. suffix (ref. to the Lord). 14b forms a semantic inclusio with stanza 1 by the idea of things being fixed/unchangeable/determined by God from the beginning.

## Stanza 10 [15]

The concluding confessional statement in 15 reiterates the motif of the Lord as creator in 2c especially, by the repetition of the root ܥܒܕ. There is a degree of parallelism with 14a-b with chiasmus - 14a and 14b have (ܟܠܡܕܡ) ܟܠ as the subj. and the 2nd sing. masc. (ref. to the Lord) as the ultimate object of the action described; 15 has the 2nd sing. masc. (ref. to the Lord) as the subj. and ܟܠ as the obj. There is a semantic connection between 14b and 15 by the motif of creation with ref. to the Lord.

## ODE 5 [Syriac]

1 ܡܘܕܐ ܐܢܐ ܠܟ ܡܪܝܐ
ܡܛܠ ܕܪܚܡܬ ܐܢܐ ܠܟ
2 ܡܪܝܡܐ ܠܐ ܬܫܒܩܢܝ
ܡܛܠ ܕܣܒܪܝ ܐܢܬ ܗܘ
3 ܡܓܢ ܢܣܒܬ ܛܝܒܘܬܟ
ܐܢܐ ܡܢܗ̇

4 ܢܐܬܘܢ ܪ̈ܕܘܦܝ
[ܘ]ܠܐ ܢܚܙܘܢܝ
5 ܥܢܢܐ ܕܥܡܛܢܐ ܬܦܠ [ܥܠ] ܥܝ̈ܢܝܗܘܢ
ܘܐܐܪ ܕܥܪܦܠܐ ܢܚܫܟ ܐܢܘܢ
6 ܘܠܐ ܢܗܘܐ ܠܗܘܢ ܢܘܗܪܐ ܕܢܚܙܘܢ
ܕܠܐ ܢܐܚܕܘܢܝ
7 ܠܥܘ̈ܒܝܐ ܬܗܘܐ ܬܪܥܝܬܗܘܢ
ܘܡܕܡ ܕܐܬܚܟܡܘ ܢܗܦܘܟ ܥܠ ܪ̈ܫܝܗܘܢ

8 ܐܬܚܫܒܘ ܓܝܪ ܬܪܥܝܬܐ
ܘܠܐ ܗܘܬ ܠܗܘܢ
9 ܐܬܛܝܒܘ ܒܒܝܫܐܝܬ
ܘܐܫܬܟܚܘ ܟܕ ܡܚ̈ܝܠܝܢ

10 ܥܠ ܡܪܝܐ ܗܘ ܓܝܪ ܣܒܪܝ
ܘܠܐ ܐܕܚܠ
11 ܘܡܛܠ ܕܡܪܝܐ ܗܘ ܦܪܘܩܝ
ܠܐ ܐܕܚܠ
12 ܘܐܝܟ ܟܠܝܠܐ ܗܘ ܒܪܝܫܝ
ܘܠܐ ܐܬܬܙܝܥ
13 ܘܐܢ ܢܬܬܙܝܥ ܟܠܡܕܡ
ܐܢܐ ܩܐܡ ܐܢܐ
14 ܘܐܢ ܢܐܒܕ ܡܕܡ ܕܡܬܚܙܐ
ܐܢܐ ܠܐ ܐܡܘܬ
15 ܡܛܠ ܕܡܪܝܐ ܥܡܝ ܗܘ
ܘܐܢܐ ܥܡܗ

ܗܠܠܘܝܐ

1   I praise you, Lord
    because I love you
2   Most High do not leave me
    because you are my hope
3   freely I received your grace
    I shall live by it

4   my persecutors will come
    and let them not see me
5   let a cloud of gloom fall upon their eyes
    and let an air of thick mist darken them
6   and let them not have light to see
    that they might not seize me
7   let their mind become festers
    and let what they have devised cleverly return upon their heads

8   for they have taken counsel
    and it did not succeed for them
9   they made ready wickedly
    and they were found to be empty

10  for upon the Lord is my hope
    and I shall not fear
11  and because the Lord is my salvation
    I shall not fear
12  and like a crown is he on my head
    and I shall not be disturbed
13  and if everything should be disturbed
    I shall stand firm
14  and if that which is visible should perish
    I shall not die
15  because the Lord is with me
    and I with him

    alleluia

## ODE 5 [Coptic]

1 ϮⲚⲀⲞⲨⲞⲚⲌⲦ ⲚⲀⲔ ⲈⲂⲞⲗ ⲡⲀⲞⲈⲓⲥ
  ⲀⲈ ⲚⲦⲞⲔ ⲡⲈ ⲡⲀⲚⲞⲨⲦⲈ
2 ⲘⲠⲢⲔⲀⲀⲦ ⲡⲀⲞⲈⲓⲥ
  ⲀⲈ ⲚⲦⲞⲔ ⲡⲈ ⲦⲀⲌⲈⲗⲡⲓⲥ
3 ⲀⲔϮ ⲚⲀⲓ ⲘⲠⲈⲔⲌⲀⲡ ⲚⲀⲒⲚⲀϨ
  ⲀⲨⲱ ⲀⲒⲚⲞⲨⲌⲘ ⲈⲂⲞⲗ ⲌⲒⲦⲞⲞⲦⲔ̄

4 ⲘⲀⲢⲞⲨⲌⲈ Ⲛ̄ϬⲒ ⲚⲈⲦⲠⲎⲦ Ⲛ̄ⲤⲰⲒ
  ⲀⲨⲱ ⲘⲠⲢⲦⲢⲈⲨⲚⲀⲨ ⲈⲢⲞⲒ
5 ⲘⲀⲢⲈ ⲞⲨⲔⲗⲞⲞⲗⲈ Ⲛ̄ⲔⲢ̄Ⲙ̄ⲦⲤ̄ ⲌⲰⲂⲤ ⲈⲂⲞⲗ ⲈⲀ̄Ⲛ̄ ⲚⲈⲨⲂⲀⲗ
  ⲀⲨⲱ ⲞⲨⲚⲒϤ Ⲛ̄ⲀⲎⲢ ⲘⲀⲢⲈϤⲢ̄ⲔⲀⲔⲈ ⲈⲢⲞⲨ
6 ⲀⲨⲱ ⲘⲠⲢⲦⲢⲈⲨⲚⲀⲨ ⲈⲠⲈⲌⲞⲞⲨ
  ⲀⲈ Ⲛ̄ⲚⲈⲨⲀⲘⲀⲌⲦⲈ Ⲙ̄ⲘⲞⲒ
7 ⲘⲀⲢⲈϤⲢ̄ⲀⲦϬⲞⲘ Ⲛ̄ϬⲒ ⲠⲈⲨϢⲞⲀⲚⲈ
  ⲀⲨⲱ ⲚⲈⲚⲦⲀⲨϢⲞⲀⲚⲈ ⲈⲢⲞⲨ ⲘⲀⲢⲞⲨⲈⲒ ⲈⲌⲢⲀⲒ ⲈⲀⲰⲞⲨ

8 ⲀⲨⲘⲈⲔⲘⲞⲨⲔⲞⲨ ⲈⲨϢⲞⲀⲚⲈ
  ⲀⲨⲱ ⲘⲠϤϢⲰⲠⲈ ⲚⲀⲨ
  ⲀⲨⲱ ⲀⲨⲀⲢⲞ ⲈⲢⲞⲞⲨ ⲈⲨϬⲘ̄ϬⲞⲘ
9 ⲀⲨⲱ ⲚⲈⲚⲦⲀⲨⲤⲂ̄ⲦⲰⲦⲞⲨ ⲔⲀⲔⲰⲤ ⲀⲨⲌⲈ ⲈⲠⲈⲤⲎⲦ ⲈⲢⲞⲞⲨ

10 ⲈⲢⲈ ⲦⲀⲌⲈⲗⲡⲓⲥ Ⲍ̄Ⲙ̄ ⲡⲀⲞⲈⲓⲥ
  ⲀⲨⲱ Ⲛ̄ϮⲚⲀⲢ̄ϨⲞⲦⲈ ⲀⲚ

11 ⲀⲈ Ⲛ̄ⲦⲞⲔ ⲡⲈ ⲡⲀⲚⲞⲨⲦⲈ ⲡⲀⲤⲰⲦⲎⲢ

---

1 I will confess you, Lord,
  for you are my God.
2 Do not leave me, Lord,
  for you are my hope.
3 You gave me your judgment freely,
  and I have been saved by you.

4     May those pursuing me fall,
       and let them not see me.
5     May a cloud of darkness cover their eyes,
       and may an air of gloom darken them.
6     And let them not see the day,
       that they might not seize me.
7     May their counsel become powerless,
       and may what they have taken counsel about come upon them.

8     They have taken counsel,
       and it has not happened for them.
       And the powerful have been overwhelmed,
9     and what (things) they have prepared wickedly have fallen upon them.

10   On the Lord is my hope,
       and I will not fear.

11   For you are my God, my saviour.

NOTES TO THE TRANSLATION

4-7: The decision to interpret the imperf. verbs in the Syriac (4b, 5a, 5b, 6a, 7a, 7b) as jussive is based primarily on the use of the optative in the Coptic.

4a-b: The division into two lines (cf. also Bruston 1912b; Greßmann 1924; Carmignac 1986) is based on the structure of the Ode, which has one action per line throughout (with the exception of 7b), and on the parallelism of 4b and 6b.

8b: Lit. "and it was not to them".

8b,9b: The initial ܢ should be interpreted in the sense of "but" since the second cl. in each case presents a contrasting or negative outcome of the action in the first cl.

ANALYSIS [Syriac]

## Stanza 1 [1-3]

The confessional address of the "I" to the Lord/Most High in the 2nd sing. occurs only in this stanza. 1a functions as the opening doxology.

1a-b is parallel on the pattern: masc. sing. part. act. + ܐܘܪ + ܠܝ. The bicolon has a pivot pattern by the use of the vocative ܡܪܝ at the conclusion of 1a.

2a and 2b are connected by the clause introduced by ܕ ܡܛܠ in 2b which refers to ܬܫܒܘܚܬ ܠܐ in 2a. There is a degree of parallelism by the pattern of 1st and 2nd persons: 2nd sing. masc. as the subj. (ref. to the Most High), and the 1st sing. linked with the obj./compl. 1a and 2a are linked by the vocative address to the Lord/Most High.

3a and 3b are parallel on the general pattern of 1st sing. verb with a focus on grace as the obj. (3a) or agent (3b) of the action described. The concept of living by grace occurs also in 41:3.

## Stanza 2 [4, 5-6, 7]

The stanza focusses on the enemies of the "I" and the hindering of their action against the "I". The verbs are in the imperf. with the exception of ܐܬܚܙܒܢ in 7b which occurs in the cl. which functions as the subj. of the imperf. ܢܣܘܦܘܢ.

All the statements are negative in the sense that they refer to action against the persecutors of the "I". However, the syntactic pattern of positive and negative (main) verbs for 4-7 is: + - + + - - + + . There is an inclusio for the stanza by the use of the polar word-pair ܐܬܐ - ܣܘܦ.

4a-b functions as the introductory bicolon, presenting the group of persecutors in relation to the "I". The lines are parallel by the use of the 3rd pl. masc. Peal imperf. with a final emphasis upon the 1st sing.

The major section of the stanza, 5-7, is delineated by the inclusio between 5a and 7b, which are parallel on the pattern: subj. (noun in 5a, cl. in 7b) + sing. Peal imperf. verb + ܥܠ with pl. noun obj. (physical attribute of the persecutors) + 3rd pl. masc. suffix. This serves to place 6a-b in the central position of the stanza proper.

5-6 expands on 4b by providing detail of how the persecutors will not see the "I". 5a and 5b are parallel on the pattern: sing. noun subj. + qualifying expression (ܕ + noun) + 3rd sing. imperf. verb with the 3rd pl. masc. group as the ultimate object of the action described. The parallelism is strengthened by the semantic closeness of ܕܚܫܘܟܐ ܥܝܢܐ and ܕܥܪܦܠܐ ܐܐܪ.

6a and 6b are connected by the cl. in 6b which expresses the purpose of the action described in 6a. There is a degree of terrace parallelism by the doubling of the cls. expressing purpose, at the conclusion of 6a and immediately following in 6b, on the pattern: ܘ + 3rd pl. masc. Peal imperf. verb. Both 6a and 6b are linked with 4b - 6a, by the repetition of the root ܚܙܐ; 6b, by the parallel pattern: ܠܐ + 3rd pl. masc. Peal imperf. verb + 1st sing. suffix. The parallelism of 6b with 4b effectively closes off this section of the stanza dealing with the persecutors and their ability to see the "I".

7a-b introduces a new aspect of the action against the persecutors. The bicolon is parallel to a degree, with chiasmus: A B C // C' B' A', where A = indir. obj./phrase (with the 3rd pl. masc. group as the ultimate object of the action described); B = 3rd sing. Peal imperf. verb + subj. (noun in 7a, cl. in 7b). The parallelism is strengthened by the semantic closeness of the subjs. (the mind of the persecutors and what they have "wisely" devised). There is irony intended by the use of the root ܚܟܡ. The powerless counsel of the persecutors in 7a is in direct contrast to the counsel/mind of the Lord which is eternal life (cf. 9:4).


Stanza 3 [8-9]

The change of tense from imperf. to perf. indicates the division of stanzas although the motif of the persecutors continues in 8-9 and especially in relation to their action of conspiring (cf. the repetition of ܬܪܥܝܬܐ in 7a and 8a).

8a and 8b have a degree of parallelism with chiasmus by the placement of the 3rd pl. masc. and 3rd sing. fem. - in 8a, a 3rd pl. masc. subj. and sing. fem. noun obj.; in 8b, a 3rd sing. fem. subj. (ref. to the noun obj. in 8a) and 3rd pl. masc. indir. obj. 9a and 9b are parallel on the pattern: 3rd pl. masc. perf. verb + qualifying expression.


Stanza 4 [10-12, 13-14, 15]

With stanza 4, there is a return to the relationship of the "I" and the Lord. In contrast to stanza 1, the Lord is spoken of in the 3rd person rather than addressed in the 2nd person. The most obvious unifying feature of the stanza is the use of the 1st sing. subj. in the second line of each bicolon. The general pattern of the bicola is similar to the pattern in 39:5-6.

The first strophe, 10-12, comprises three alternately parallel bicola. 10a, 11a, and 12a focus upon the Lord, the final section of each line having the general pattern: copula (ܘܗ) ... noun (subj. in 10a, compl. in 11a) with 1st sing. suffix. 11a and 12a are further connected by the word-pair ܩܘܪܒܐ - ܒܥܠܕ.

10b, 11b, and 12b are more strictly parallel on the pattern: ܠܐ(ܢ) + 1st sing. imperf. verb (ܐܙܘܥ in 10a, 11a). The parallelism is strengthened by the word-pair ܪܘܙ - ܙܘܥ. 10a and 10b are semantically linked by the opposite concepts of hope and fear. 10a and 2b are connected by the repetition of ܣܒܪܝ, in relation to the Most High/Lord.

Strophes 1 and 2 are linked by the repetition of the root ܙܘܥ in a terrace pattern to conclude 12b and immediately following at the beginning of 13a. The two bicola of strophe 2 are alternately parallel.

13a and 14a are parallel on the pattern: ܘܐܢ + 3rd sing. masc. imperf. verb + subj. using ܡܘܬ (cl. in 14a). 13b and 14b are parallel with ܐܘܪ (emphatic function) + 1st sing. verb. The parallelism is strengthened by the word-pair ܡܘܬܐ - ܩܒܪܐ. The bicola are further linked by the word-pairs ܙܘܥ - ܡܘܬ (13a, 13b; cf. also 12b, 13b), ܡܘܬ - ܐܒܕ (13b, 14a). 14a and 14b have the similar concepts of perishing and dying.

The concluding confessional statement in 15a-b provides a balance with the opening confession in 1a-b. There is also a semantic connection with 2a by the similar concepts of the Most High not leaving the "I" (2a) and the Lord being with the "I" (15a).

The bicolon follows the basic pattern of strophes 1 and 2 by a focus on the Lord in 15a and the 1st sing. as the subj. of 15b. The lines are parallel on the pattern: subj. + ܥܡ with pron. suffix. There is chiasmus by the placement of the 3rd sing. and 1st sing. 15a has a 3rd sing. masc. subj. and ܥܡ with a 1st sing. suffix; 15b has a 1st sing. subj. and ܥܡ with a 3rd sing. masc. suffix. 15a and 11a are parallel with chiasmus on the pattern: A B C D // A' B' D' C', where A = ܝ ܒܝܕ; B = ܡܪܝܐ (subj.); C = ܗܘ (copula); D = element with 1st sing. suffix.

ANALYSIS [Coptic]

There are some differences in vocabulary and syntax between the versions, as well as an additional line (8c) in the Coptic. The latter version appears much more tightly structured than the Syriac.

Stanza 1 [1-3]

The stanza division is the same as for the Syriac. The major differences between the versions occur in 1b and 3a-b. 1a-b and 2a-b are more strongly

linked than in the Syriac, by the use of the parallel vocative ΠⲀⲞⲈⲓⲥ and by
the parallelism of 1b and 2b on the pattern: ⲀⲈ ⲚⲦⲞⲔ ⲠⲈ + 1st sing. poss.
pron. with noun compl. 1b and 2b appear to function as responsoria.

There are differences in vocabulary between the versions for 3a-b: in 3a,
grace (Syr) and judgment (Copt); in 3b, to live (Syr) and to save (Copt). In the
Coptic, both lines are in the past tense (Syriac has perf. in 3a and imperf. in
3b). There is a degree of parallelism with chiasmus by the placement of the 1st
and 2nd persons - in 3a, 2nd sing. masc. subj. of the perf. I verb + 1st sing. indir. obj.; in 3b, 1st sing. subj. of the perf. I verb + 2nd sing. masc. as the agent
of the action (ⲍⲓⲦⲞⲞⲦⲕ̄).

Stanza 2 [4-7]

There is variation in vocabulary between the Syriac and Coptic, but apart from
the use of ⲍⲈ in 4a, which gives the possibility of an inclusio with 9 for the entire section devoted to the persecutors (4-9), there is little real effect from
these differences.

As in the Syriac, the stanza consists of four parallel bicola. The link between
6a-b and 4b is stronger in the Coptic. Although the root ⲕⲱ occurs in 4b and
6a in the Syriac, the Coptic repeats the form of the verb exactly (3rd pl. masc.
negative optative of ⲚⲀⲨ). 4b and 6b are not as strongly connected syntactically in the Coptic, with a 3rd pl. masc. negative verb + 1st sing. obj.

As in the Syriac, 7a-b is parallel with chiasmus, the Coptic having a terrace
pattern by the use of ⲱⲞⲀⲚⲈ to conclude 7a and immediately following in 7b.

Stanza 3 [8-9]

The change from the general pattern of optative verbs to the perf. I verbs indicates the division of stanzas.

8c in the Coptic does not appear in the Syriac and 8c-9 in the Coptic is sub-
stantially different from 9a-b in the Syriac. 8c-9 has a degree of parallelism
with chiasmus on the pattern: A B // B' A', where A = 3rd pl. masc. perf. I
verb ...ⲈⲢⲞⲞⲨ; B = *Umstandsatz* (ref. to the obj.)/rel. cl. (functions as the
subj.).

The connections between stanzas 2 and 3 are very strong, much more so than
in the Syriac. 7a and 8c are linked both semantically (the concept of loss of
power) and by the repetition of ⲞⲞⲘ. 7b and 9 have a degree of parallelism on
the pattern: ⲀⲨⲱ + pl. particle with rel. pron. and 3rd pl. perf. I verb ... 3rd
pl. verb (subj. is the previous rel. cl.) + prep./s (expressing direction of the ac-

tion of the verb) + 3rd pl. pron. suffix (ref. to the subj. of the rel. cl.). 7b and 9 have semantically equivalent final phrases ("to come upon them"/"to fall down on them"). 7a, 7b, and 8a are connected by the repetition of ⲱⲟⲁⲛⲉ (the Syriac has ⲕⲁⲩⲓⲁ in 7a and 8a).

Stanza 4 [10]

10a-b in the Coptic is similar to the Syriac and the same connection exists between 10a and 2b by the repetition of ⲧⲁⲍⲉⲗⲡⲓⲥ in relation to the Lord. 11b-15 of the Syriac does not appear in the Coptic. For the confusion in <u>Pistis Sophia</u> at this point, cf. Lattke 1979-86, vol. 1, 216-20.

Stanza 5 [11]

With stanza 5, the Coptic returns to an address to the Lord in the 2nd sing. masc. as in stanza 1. 11a in the Syriac and 11 in the Coptic have the equivalent concept of the Lord/God as salvation/saviour, although the Syriac speaks of the Lord in the 3rd sing. masc.

11 functions as a concluding confessional statement. The balance with the opening confession in 1a-b is strong, not only with the use of the 2nd sing. masc. address to the Lord/God, but also especially by the exact repetition of 1b in the first half of 11. 11 and 3b are connected semantically by the equivalence of "I have been saved by you" and "you are...my saviour", although the verb is ⲛⲟⲩⲍⲙ in 3b while 11 uses ⲥⲱⲧⲏⲣ.

11 has internal parallelism by the doubling of the pattern of 1st sing. poss. pron. prefix + noun (equivalent expressions: God, saviour).

## ODE 6 [Syriac]

1 ܐܝܟ ܕܡܗܠܟܐ [. . .]ܐ ܒܟܢܪܐ
ܘܡܢܐ ܡܡܠܠܢ
2 ܗܟܢܐ ܡܡܠܠܐ ܒܗܕܡܝ ܪܘܚܗ ܕܡܪܝܐ
ܘܡܡܠܠ ܐܢܐ ܒܚܘܒܗ

3 ܡܚܒܠ ܗܘ ܓܝܪ ܡܕܡ ܢܘܟܪܝ
ܘܟܠܡܕܡ ܕܡܪܝܐ ܗܘ
4 ܗܟܢܐ ܓܝܪ ܗܘܐ ܡܢ ܒܪܫܝܬ ܘܥܕܡܐ ܠܐܚܪܬܐ
5 ܕܠܐ ܡܕܡ ܢܗܘܐ ܣܩܘܒܠܐ
ܘܠܐ ܡܕܡ ܢܩܘܡ ܠܘܩܒܠܗ

6 ܐܣܓܝ ܝܕܥܬܗ ܡܪܝܐ
ܘܛܢ ܕܢܬܝܕܥܢ ܗܠܝܢ
ܕܒܛܝܒܘܬܗ ܐܬܝܗܒ ܠܢ
7 ܘܬܫܒܘܚܬܗ ܝܗܒ ܠܢ ܠܫܡܗ
ܪ̈ܘܚܢ ܠܪܘܚܗ ܩܕܝܫܐ ܡܫܒܚܢ

8 ܢܦܩ ܓܝܪ ܬܦܩܐ
ܘܗܘܐ ܢܗܪܐ ܪܒܐ ܘܦܬܝܐ
ܓܪܦ ܓܝܪ ܟܠܡܕܡ ܘܬܒܪ
ܘܐܝܬܝ ܠܗܝܟܠܐ
9 ܘܠܐ ܐܫܟܚܘ ܟܠܝܘܗܝ ܟܠܝ̈ܢܐ ܕܒ̈ܢܝ ܐܢܫܐ
ܘܐܦܠܐ ܐܘܡܢܘ̈ܬܗܘܢ ܕܗܢܘܢ ܕܟܠܝܢ ܡܝ̈ܐ
10 ܐܬܐ ܓܝܪ ܥܠ ܐܦ̈ܝ ܟܠܗ̇ ܐܪܥܐ
ܘܡܠܐ ܟܠܡܕܡ

11 ܘܐܫܬܝܘ ܟܠܗܘܢ ܨܗ̈ܝܐ ܕܥܠ ܐܪܥܐ
ܘܨܗܝܐ ܐܫܬܪܝ ܘܕܥܟ
12 ܡܢ ܡܪܝܡܐ ܓܝܪ ܐܬܝܗܒ ܡܫܬܝܐ

ܛܘܒܝܗܘܢ ܗܟܝܠ ܠܡܫܡܫܢܘܗܝ ܕܗܘ ܡܫܩܝܬܐ 13
ܗܢܘܢ ܕܐܬܗܝܡܢܘ ܡ̈ܝܘܗܝ
ܐܢܝܚܘ ܣܦܘ̈ܬܐ ܝܒܝ̈ܫܬܐ 14
ܘܨܒܝܢܐ ܕܡܫܪܐ ܗܘܐ ܐܩܝܡܘܗ
ܘܢܦܫ̈ܬܐ ܕܩܪܝܒ ܗܘܝ ܠܡܦܩ 15
ܡܢ ܡܘܬܐ ܐܚܕܘ ܐܢܝܢ
ܘܗܕ̈ܡܐ ܕܢܦܠܘ ܗܘܘ 16
ܬܪܨܘ ܘܐܩܝܡܘ
ܝܗܒܘ ܚܝܠܐ ܠܡܐܬܝܬܗܘܢ 17
ܘܢܘܗܪܐ ܠܥܝ̈ܢܝܗܘܢ
ܡܛܠ ܕܟܠ ܐܢܫ ܐܫܬܘܕܥ ܐܢܘܢ ܒܡܪܝܐ 18
ܘܚܝܘ ܒܡ̈ܝܐ ܚܝܐ ܕܠܥܠܡ

ܗܠܠܘܝܐ

---

1 As [ ] moves in the harp,
and the strings speak;
2 so speaks in my members the Spirit of the Lord,
and I speak by his love.

3 For what is strange is destroyed,
and everything of the Lord is.
4 For so it was from the beginning and until the end,
5 that nothing might be an opponent,
and nothing might stand firm against him.

6 The Lord increased his knowledge,
and was jealous that these might be known,
which by his grace were given to us.
7 And his hymn he gave us to his name.
Our spirits glorify his Holy Spirit.

8    For a stream issued forth,
     and it became a river great and wide.
     For it flooded and shattered everything,
     and brought (everything) to the temple.

9    And the restraints of (the sons of) men were not able to restrain it;
     not even the skills of those who restrain water.

10   For it came upon the face of the whole earth,
     and filled everything.

11   And all the thirsty upon the earth drank,
     and thirst was alleviated and quenched.

12   For from the Most High the drink was given.

13   Blessed, therefore, are the ministers of that drink,
     they who are entrusted with his waters.

14   They refreshed dry lips,
     and the will which was paralysed they made to stand.

15   And souls which were near to expiring
     from death they seized.

16   And members which were fallen
     they set upright and made to stand.

17   They gave strength to their coming,
     and light to their eyes.

18   Because everyone recognised them in the Lord,
     and they lived by the living water of eternity.

     alleluia

---

## ODE 6 [Coptic]

8    ⲁⲥⲉⲓ ⲉⲃⲟⲗ ⲛ̄ϭⲓ ⲟⲩⲁⲡⲟϩⲣⲟⲓⲁ
     ⲁϭⲣ̄ⲟⲩⲛⲟϭ ⲛ̄ⲓⲉⲣⲟ ⲉϥⲟⲩⲟⲩⲱ̄ⲥ
     ⲁⲥⲥⲟⲕⲟⲩ ⲧⲏⲣⲟⲩ
     ⲁⲩⲱ ⲁⲥⲕⲟⲧⲥ̄ ⲉⲁ̄ⲙ ⲡⲉⲣⲡⲉ

9    ⲙ̄ⲡⲟⲩϣⲁⲙⲁϩⲧⲉ ⲙ̄ⲙⲟⲥ ϩ̄ⲛ ϩⲉⲛϣⲡ̄ⲁ̄ ⲙ̄ⲛ ϩⲉⲛⲙⲁ ⲉⲩⲕⲏⲧ
     ⲟⲩⲇⲉ ⲙ̄ⲡⲟⲩϣⲁⲙⲁϩⲧⲉ ⲙ̄ⲙⲟⲥ ⲛ̄ϭⲓ ⲛ̄ⲧⲉⲭⲛⲉ ⲛ̄ⲛⲉⲧⲁⲙⲁϩⲧⲉ ⲙ̄ⲙⲟⲟⲩ

10   ⲁⲩⲛ̄ⲧⲥ̄ ⲉⲁ̄ⲙ ⲡⲕⲁϩ ⲧⲏⲣϥ̄
     ⲁⲩⲱ ⲁⲥⲁⲙⲁϩⲧⲉ ⲙ̄ⲙⲟⲟⲩ ⲧⲏⲣⲟⲩ

11 ⲀⲨⳓⲱ Ⲛ̅ϬⲒ ⲚⲈⲦϢⲞⲞⲠ ϨⲒⲀⲘ̅ ⲠϢⲱ ⲈⲦϢⲞⲨϢⲞⲨ
   Ⲁ ⲠⲈⲨⲈⲒⲂⲈ ⲂⲰⲖ ⲈⲂⲞⲖ ⲀⲨⲱ ⲀϤⲱϢⲘ̅
12 Ⲛ̅ⲦⲈⲢⲞⲨϯ ⲚⲀⲨ Ⲙ̅ⲠⳠⲱ Ⲛ̅ⲦⲞⲞⲦϤ̅ Ⲙ̅ⲠⲈⲦⲀⲞⲤⲈ

13 ϨⲈⲚⲘⲀⲔⲀⲢⲒⲞⲤ ⲚⲈ Ⲛ̅ⲆⲒⲀⲔⲰⲚ Ⲙ̅ⲠⳠⲱ ⲈⲦⲘ̅ⲘⲀⲨ
   ⲚⲎ ⲈⲚⲦⲀⲨⲦⲀⲚϨⲞⲨⲦⲞⲨ ⲈⲠⲘⲞⲞⲨ Ⲙ̅ⲠⲀⲞⲈⲒⳞ
14 ⲀⲨⲔⲦⲞ Ⲛ̅ϨⲈⲚⲤⲠⲞⲦⲞⲨ ⲈⲀⲨϢⲞⲞⲨⲈ
   ⲀⲨⲀⲒ Ⲛ̅ⲞⲨⲞⲨⲢⲞⲦ Ⲛ̅ϨⲎⲦ Ⲛ̅ϬⲒ ⲚⲎ ⲈⲦⲂⲎⲖ ⲈⲂⲞⲖ
15 ⲀⲨⲀⲘⲀϨⲦⲈ Ⲛ̅ϨⲈⲚⲮⲨⲬⲎ ⲈⲨⲚⲞⲨϪⲈ Ⲙ̅ⲠⲦⲎⲨ ϪⲈ Ⲛ̅ⲚⲈⲨⲘⲞⲨ
16 ⲀⲨⲦⲀϨⲞ Ⲛ̅ϨⲈⲚⲘⲈⲖⲞⳞ ⲈⲢⲀⲦⲞⲨ ⲈⲀⲨϨⲈ
17 ⲀⲨϯϬⲞⲘ Ⲛ̅ⲦⲈⲨⲠⲀⲢϨⲎⳞⲒⲀ
   ⲀⲨⲱ ⲀⲨϯⲞⲨⲞⲒ̈Ⲛ Ⲛ̅ⲚⲈⲨⲂⲀⲖ
18 ϪⲈ Ⲛ̅ⲦⲞⲞⲨ ⲦⲎⲢⲞⲨ ⲀⲨⳞⲞⲨⲐⲚⲞⲨ ϨⲘ̅ ⲠⲀⲞⲈⲒⳞ
   ⲀⲨⲱ ⲀⲨⲚⲞⲨϨⲘ̅ ϨⲒⲦⲚ̅ ⲞⲨⲘⲞⲞⲨ Ⲛ̅ⲱⲚ̅Ϩ Ⲛ̅ϢⲀⲈⲚⲈϨ

---

8   A stream came forth;
    it became a river great and wide.
    It gathered everything,
    and it went around the temple.
9   It could not be restrained with secure places, (nor) with places built;
    nor could the skills of those who restrain water restrain it.
10  It was brought over the whole earth,
    and it restrained everything.

11  The dry ones on the sand drank;
    their thirst was satisfied and quenched,
12  when they were given the drink from the Most High.

13  Blessed are the ministers of that drink,
    who have been entrusted with the water of the Lord.
14  They turned dry lips;
    those perishing received joy of heart.
15  They restrained souls which were expiring, that they might not die.
16  They made to stand limbs which had fallen.
17  They gave power to their confidence,
    and they gave light to their eyes.
18  For all of them have known them in the Lord,
    and they were saved by water of eternal life.

NOTES TO THE TRANSLATION

1a: The manuscript is torn, with space for three or four letters before an ܐ which has been joined to a preceding letter (possibly ܘ or ܢ). Harris' (1909) conjecture of ܟܘܐ (followed by the majority of scholars) is therefore not possible. Barnes' suggestion of ܪܘܚܝ (1910a, 57) is followed by Charlesworth (1977), Lattke (1979-86, vol. 1), and Emerton.

3a: "For he destroys what is strange" is also possible. The interpretation of ܢܟܪܒ as pass. is based of the parallelism of 3a and 3b.

3b: Given the parallelism of 3a and 3b, the verb ܗܘܐ should be interpreted in the sense of existing/remaining in existence.

8c: The insertion of ܟܠܡܕܡ between two verbs for which it is subj./obj. may be found in 22:11; 23:19; 35:3.

8d: The majority of scholars interpret the ܠ preceding ܗܝܟܠܐ as *nota dativi*. For the *nota accusativi*, cf. Bruston 1912b; Harris and Mingana vol. 2; Greßmann 1924; Bauer 1964. For the "elimination" of the temple altogether, cf. Torrey's suggestion (qtd. in Bacon 199) that the Syriac is a translation of the Aramaic ואיתי להכלא, itself a corruption of the original ולא איתי להכלא ("and there was no holding it in check").

   Both *nota accusativi* and *nota dativi* are possible, although with the latter, one must assume an obj. for ܐܝܬܝ (ܟܠܡܕܡ is the obj. of the series of three verbs in 8c-d). Within the collection of the Odes, the Aphel of ܐܬܐ may take both dir. and indir. obj. with ܠ,

   8:2a      ܐܬܐ + dir.obj. + (ܠ) indir. obj.

   16:16b     ܐܬܐ + (ܠ) dir. obj. + subj.

   22:11c     ܐܬܐ + (ܠ) dir. obj. + (ܠ) indir. obj.

   The choice for the *nota dativi* here has its basis in the parallelism of 8d and 10a.

17a: The Syriac has ܢܘܒܐܬܗܝܟܡ ("their coming"). The Coptic ⲧⲉⲩⲛⲁⲣⲍ̄ⲏⲥⲓⲁ ("their confidence") may be a corruption of ⲧⲉⲩⲛⲁⲣⲟⲩⲥⲓⲁ.

ANALYSIS [Syriac]

The Ode comprises two distinct sub-odes (1-7, 8-18). The fact that the quotation in the <u>Pistis Sophia</u> comprises 8-18 gives added weight to such a division. A study of the vocabulary frequency table indicates that the repetition of key words/roots is confined, with the exception of ܐܒܠ, to one or the other sub-ode: ܢܘܢܐ, ܐܡܡ, and ܬܚܒܫ in sub-ode 1; ܐܡܪ and ܐܚܠܦ in sub-ode 2.

Stanza 1 [1-2] (= Stanza 1, Sub-ode 1)

The stanza comprises an introductory simile of the form, ...ܐܡܟ...ܟܝܐ. The verb ܐܡܡ occurs only in this stanza, in three of the four lines. The motif of inspired speech in relation to the "I" (the 1st sing. occurs only in this stanza) is appropriate as an introduction to the Ode (cf. Chapter III, Section b, 4.1).

The stanza comprises two alternately parallel bicola. 1a and 2a are parallel with chiasmus: A B C D // A' B' D' C', where A = ܟܝܐ/ܐܡܟ; B = fem. sing. Pael part. act.; C = subj.; D = ܒ with noun obj. The parallelism would be strengthened if the conjecture of ܢܘܢܐ for the missing subj. in 1a were correct. 1b and 2b are also parallel with chiasmus: A B // B' A' C, where A = masc. Pael part. act. of ܐܡܡ; B = subj.; C = phrase introduced by ܒ.

Within the bicola themselves there is parallelism. 1a and 1b have a general chiastic structure: A B C // B' A', where A = Pael part. act.; B = noun subj.; C = phrase introduced by ܒ. The placement of the root ܐܡܡ at the conclusion of 1b and immediately following to commence 2a provides a terrace pattern to link the bicola. 2a and 2b are parallel with chiasmus: A B C // A C' B', where A = sing. Pael part. act. of ܐܡܡ; B = ܒ + noun obj. with pron. suffix; C = subj.

1a and 2b form a kind of inclusio for the stanza by their parallelism on the pattern: sing. Pael part. act. + subj. + ܒ with noun obj.

Stanza 2 [3-5]

Stanza 2 moves from the description about the "I" and the Spirit of the Lord/ the Lord to a report about the Lord to whom everything belongs and against whom nothing can stand (cf. 4:1-3, 14-15). There is a possible inclusio for the stanza between 3a and 5b, both by their semantic similarity (nothing/what is strange cannot stand against the Lord from whom everything is), and by the word-pair ܦܘܡ - ܐܟܒܪ.

3a and 3b are parallel with chiasmus: A B // B' A', where A = 3rd sing. masc. verb/copula; B = subj. (ܟܠܡܕܡ/ܡܕܡ with qualifying expression). The lines are antithetical by the contrasting actions/states of being destroyed and existing and by the contrast of everything strange (cf. the translation notes for 20:6a) to everything of the Lord.

The monocolon in 4 is a confessional formula in the central position of the stanza. It interrupts the logical flow from 3a-b to 5a-b. There is internal parallelism by the phrases ܒܫܡܝܐ and ܠܥܠܡܐ ܕܐܬܐ in which the polar word-pair expresses merismus.

5a and 5b are parallel cls., expressing the purpose of 4, on the pattern: ܠܐ ܡܪܝܐ (subj.) + 3rd sing. masc. Peal imperf. verb + qualifying expression with the root ܩܒܠ (ref. to the subj.). The cls. are semantically equivalent (to be an opponent = to stand against someone). ܡܪܝܐ ܠܐ is in contrast to ܟܠܡܕܡ in 3b, 5a-b being a corrollary of 3a-b.

## Stanza 3 [6-7a, 7b]

Stanza 3 concludes the first sub-ode with the motifs of knowledge (ܝܕܥ in 6a, 6b), gifts to the community by the Lord (ܝܗܒ in 6c, 7a), and the praise of the name/holy Spirit of the Lord (ܫܒܚ in 7a, 7b). There is a focus on attributes of the Lord - his knowledge (6a), his grace (6c), his hymn and his name (7a), his holy Spirit (7b). The 1st pl. occurs only in this stanza.

6a and 6b are parallel to a degree by the 3rd sing. masc. perf. verbs (subj. is the Lord) and the repetition of the root ܝܕܥ. The rel. cl. in 6c refers to ܗܠܝܢ in 6b. The connection is strengthened by the word-pair ܝܕܥ - ܝܗܒ. 6a is very close to 12:3 (ܘܐܦܩ ܒܗ ܝܕܥܬܗ).

There is a certain degree of parallelism between 6c and 7a by the use of the root ܝܗܒ + ܠ. The lines are also connected by the word-pairs ܬܫܒܘܚܬܐ - ܡܘܗܒܬܗ (ref. to the Lord by the 3rd sing. masc. suffix), and ܫܒܚ - ܡܘܗܒܬܐ. 7a has internal parallelism by the word-pair ܬܫܒܘܚܬܐ - ܫܡܗ, each with a 3rd sing. masc. suffix (ref. to the Lord).

7b functions as the closing confessional formula for the stanza and for the first sub-ode. It is a description of a doxology rather than a doxology per se. It forms an inclusio for the first section with stanza 1 (esp. 2a) by taking up the motif of the Spirit of the Lord. There is a word-play by the double use of ܪܘܚܐ. The repetition of the root ܫܒܚ provides the link with 7a.

Stanza 4 [8a-b, 8c-10] (= Stanza 1, Sub-ode 2)

8a-b serves as the introduction to the stanza and to the entire second sub-ode by the description of the river which brings the water from the Lord (= the knowledge of the Lord from his spring, cf. 6 above, and 7:13-14,20-21;30:1-2,6; cf. also Sir 24:30-31 [the wisdom of the Lord]; Sir 39: 22 [the blessing of the Lord]). The bicolon has a degree of parallelism by the use of the initial 3rd sing. masc. Peal perf. verb (subj. is ܛܦܐ) and the semantically associated words ܛܦܐ - ܢܗܪܐ.

8c-d comprises a series of three 3rd sing. masc. perf. verbs, for which the subj. is ܢܗܪܐ (8b) and the obj. ܟܠܡܕܡ (8c). 8c has internal parallelism by the double pattern of the verbs between which the common obj. ܟܠܡܕܡ has been inserted.

8c-d is parallel to 10a-b with an inverted pattern: A B // B' A'. 8c and 10b are parallel by the use of the 3rd sing. masc. perf. verb/s (subj. is ܢܗܪܐ) + ܟܠܡܕܡ (obj.). The parallelism is strengthened by the semantic closeness of ܬܒܪ (8c) and ܡܠܐ (10b) in this context. 8d and 10a are parallel to a degree on the pattern: 3rd sing. masc. perf. of ܐܬܐ (subj. is ܢܗܪܐ) + ܠ/ܥܠ (indicating direction of the action) with noun obj.

10a and 10b are parallel by the use of an initial 3rd sing. masc. Peal perf. verb/verbal expression (subj. is ܢܗܪܐ) + obj. of the action (using ...ܟܠ). The parallelism is enhanced by the semantic closeness of ܥܠ ܐܬܐ and ܡܠܐ.

9a-b takes the central position of the second strophe between 8c-d and 10a-b. The bicolon is parallel to a degree (with ellipsis of ܐܫܟܚܘ ܟܠܐܘܗܝ in 9b) on the pattern: ܐܦܠܐ/ܠܐ ... pl. noun subj. + ܕ + gen. expression (ref. to the noun subj.). The lines are strongly linked by the repetition of the root ܟܠܐ. 9a has internal parallelism by the doubling of this root.

Stanza 5 [11-12]

The focus shifts to those who drink the water and its source in the Lord. 11a and 11b are parallel with a terrace pattern by the use of ܨܗܝ̈ܐ at the conclusion of 11a and ܨܗܝܐ to commence 11b. There is an echo of 10a in 11a by ܟܠܗܘܢ ܥܠ ܐܪܥܐ... 11b has internal parallelism by the doubling of the 3rd sing. masc. perf. verb (subj. is ܨܗܝܐ).

12 functions as the concluding summary statement for the stanza, linked with 11a-b by the repetition of the root ܫܬܐ.

Stanza 6 [13, 14-17, 18]

Stanza 6 focusses on the ministers of the drink and their healing actions on behalf of those in need (cf. the description of healing action associated with those
who have understanding/knowledge [ⲙⲚⲦⲡⲘⲚⲋ̄ⲎⲦ] in The Gospel of Truth 33,
1-9 (Facs. ed. 1: 37; MacRae 1984a, 44). The stanza flows easily from stanza 5
by the repetition of the root ܐܫܬ (11a,12a,13a) and by the link between the
Most High and the water (12,13b).

13a-b functions as the introductory beatitude, presenting the key group of
the ministers. The lines are parallel, comprising a double description of those
who are blessed. There is a further link by the semantic closeness of ܡܫܬܝ
and ܝܡܗ̈ܝ in this context. 13b forms an inclusio for the stanza with 18b by the
repetition of the key term ܡܝܐ.

The main unifying feature of 14-17 is the 3rd pl. masc. perf. verbs (ref. to
the ministers) in 14a, 14b, 15b, 16b (x 2), and 17a (understood in 17b). 14a-b
and 17a-b are loosely parallel, enclosing the alternately parallel bicola, 15a-b
and 16a-b. The general structure of 14-17 may be outlined as:

14   verb - obj.
     obj. + qualifying rel. cl. - verb
15   obj. + qualifying rel. cl.
     verb
16   obj. + qualifying rel. cl.
     verb (x 2)
17   verb - obj.
     obj.

14a and 14b are parallel with chiasmus on the pattern: A B // B' A', where A
= 3rd pl. masc. Aphel perf. verb; B = noun obj. (extended with a rel. cl. in
14b). The parallelism is strengthened by the word-pair ܢܦܫ - ܣܐܒ. 14b has internal parallelism by the polar word-pair ܣܐܒ - ܚܝܐ.

15a and 16a are parallel on the general pattern: ܐ + pl. noun subj. + ܘ + pl.
Peal part. + 3rd pl. perf. of ܗܘܐ. 14a has a similar initial pattern although
with subj. and verb in the sing. 15b and 16b are parallel by the use of the 3rd
pl. masc. perf. verb/s, the obj. of which is in the preceding line. The bicola are
also linked semantically by the generally negative descriptions in 15a and 16a,
followed by the positive reaction of the ministers in 15b and 16b.

15a and 15b are semantically associated by the related concepts of expiring and death. 16a and 16b are connected by the polar word-pair ܢܘܦܠ - ܩܡ.

17a-b follows the basic pattern of 14a-b by the use of a 3rd pl. masc. perf. verb (ܢܣܒ understood in 17b) + noun obj. The parallelism of 17a and 17b is stricter than 14a-b by the pattern of the noun obj. + ܠ with obj. + 3rd pl. masc. suffix. ܥܠܝܢ and ܢܘܗܪܐ are also associated in 5:5; 11:14.

18a-b functions as a concluding summary statement. The cl. introduced by ܕ ܡܪܟܠ in 18a appears to have little logical connection with the preceding lines. ܐܝܢܐ refers to the ones who have been healed, strengthened, and so on in 14-17. There is a further semantic link possible between 17b and 18a by the descriptions of the giving of light to the eyes (17b) followed by the ability to recognise (18a).

18b is connected to 18a by the 3rd pl. masc. perf. verb which refers logically to ܐܝܢܐ in 18a. There is a link between 18a and 6a by the motif of knowledge with some ref. to the Lord. 18b has internal parallelism by the doubling of the root ܚܝܐ, which, together with the use of ܠܥܠܡ, gives emphasis and an air of finality to the line. There is a similarity between the final phrase and 11:7 (ܗܢ ܗܝ ܚܝܐ ܕܠܐ ܡܘܬܐ).

## ANALYSIS [Coptic]

### Stanza 1 [8a-b, 8c-10] (= Stanza 1, Sub-ode 2 in the Syriac)

The most noticeable difference between the Coptic and Syriac versions of this stanza is in 8c-d where the syntax of the Coptic is unambiguous, in sharp contrast to the difficulty with the Syriac. The pattern of the stanza is the same as that of the Syriac, although the repetition of ⲁⲙⲁϩⲧⲉ in 9a-b (x 3) and 10b links these lines more closely than in the Syriac (where the root ܐܚܕ occurs only in 9a-b).

The parallelism of 9a-b is somewhat differently structured in the Coptic by the repetition of the initial ⲙⲡⲟⲩϣⲁⲙⲁϩⲧⲉ ⲙⲙⲟⲥ.

### Stanza 2 [11-12]

There is little difference between the versions in this stanza. The link between 10a and 11a is less pronounced since the Coptic does not repeat ⲡⲕⲁϩ (10a) but uses ⲡϣⲱ.

Stanza 3 [13, 14-17, 18]

The inclusio between 13 and 18 noted in the Syriac is also indicated in the Coptic (ΜΟΟⲨ in 13b, 18b) but is strengthened by the repetition of ΠⲀ ΟⲈ Ι Ϲ (13b, 18a).

The syntactic structure of the Coptic is somewhat different from the Syriac. The general pattern consists of an initial 3rd pl. perf. I verb + noun obj. 14a, 15 and 16 are more strictly parallel on the pattern: 3rd pl. perf. I verb + pl. noun obj. with the indef. article + rel. cl. with 3rd pl. verb (ref. to the pl. noun obj. of the initial verb). 14b is similar (with a sing. noun obj. with indef. art.) but the rel. cl. functions as the subj. of the initial verb.

17a-b is strictly parallel on the pattern: ⲀⲨ† (the Syriac does not repeat ܢܣܒ in 17b) + noun obj. + Ñ (signifying indir. obj.) + 3rd pl. poss. pron. prefix + noun.

As in the Syriac, 18a-b functions as a concluding statement with little apparent connection to the verses immediately preceding. The Coptic use of ΝΟⲨ ϨΜ̄ in 18b does not produce the same effect of emphasis and finality as the doubling of ܚܝ in the Syriac.

## ODE 7

1 ܐܝܟ ܪܘܓܙܗ ܕܚܡܬܐ ܥܠ ܥܘܠܬܐ
ܗܟܢܐ ܪܘܓܙܗ ܕܚܕܘܬܐ ܥܠ ܪܚܝܡܐ
ܘܡܢ ܦܐܪ̈ܘܗܝ ܡܥܠ ܕܠܐ ܟܠܝܐ
2 ܚܕܘܬܝ ܡܪܝܐ ܗܘ
ܘܪܘܓܙܝ ܠܘܬܗ
ܗܕܐ ܐܘܪܚܝ ܫܦܝܪܐ

3 ܡܥܕܪܢܐ ܓܝܪ ܐܝܬ ܠܝ ܠܡܪܝܐ
ܐܘܕܥܢܝ ܢܦܫܗ ܕܠܐ ܚܣܡܐ
ܒܦܫܝܛܘܬܗ ܪܒܘܬܗ ܓܝܪ ܒܡܣܟܢܘܬܗ ܐܙܥܪܬ

4 ܗܘܐ ܐܝܟܘܬܝ
ܡܛܠ ܕܐܣܒܘܗܝ
ܒܕܡܘܬܐ ܐܣܬܒܪ ܐܝܟܘܬܝ
ܡܛܠ ܕܐܠܒܫܘܗܝ
5 ܘܠܐ ܙܥܬ ܟܕ ܚܙܝܬܗ
ܡܛܠ ܕܗܘܐ ܚܢܢܝ
6 ܐܝܟ ܟܝܢܝ ܗܘܐ
ܡܛܠ ܕܐܠܦܘܗܝ
ܘܐܝܟ ܨܘܪܬܝ
ܡܛܠ ܕܠܐ ܐܗܦܟ ܡܢܗ

7 ܐܒܘܗ̇ ܕܝܕܥܬܐ
ܦܬܓܡܐ ܗܘ ܕܝܕܥܬܐ
8 ܗܘ ܕܒܪܐ ܚܟܡܬܐ
ܚܟܝܡ ܗܘ ܡܢ ܥܒ̈ܕܘܗܝ
9 ܘܗܘ ܕܒܪܢܝ ܥܕܠܐ ܐܗܘܐ
ܝܕܥ ܡܕܡ ܕܥܒܕ ܗܘܝܬ ܟܕ ܐܗܘܐ

10 ܡܛܠ ܗܢܐ ܚܢܢܝ ܒܚܢܢܗ ܣܓܝܐܐ
ܘܝܗܒ ܠܝ ܕܐܒܥܐ ܡܢܗ
ܘܐܣܒ ܡܢ ܕܒܚܬܗ
11 ܡܛܠ ܕܗܘܝܘ ܐܝܬܘܗܝ ܕܠܐ ܚܒܠܐ
ܫܘܡܠܝܐ ܕܥܠܡ̈ܐ ܘܐܒܘܗܘܢ

12 ܝܗܒ ܠܗ ܕܢܬܚܙܐ ܠܐܝܠܝܢ ܕܕܝܠܗ ܐܢܘܢ
ܡܛܠ ܕܢܫܬܘܕܥܘܢ ܠܗܘ ܕܥܒܕ ܐܢܘܢ
ܘܠܐ ܢܣܒܪܘܢ ܕܡܢ ܢܦܫܗܘܢ ܗܘܘ

13 ܠܝܕܥܬܐ ܓܝܪ ܐܘܪܚܗ ܣܡܗ̇
ܐܦܬܝܗ̇ ܘܐܘܪܟܗ̇ ܘܐܝܬܝܗ̇ ܥܠ ܟܠܗ ܫܘܡܠܝܐ
14 ܘܣܡ ܥܠܝܗ̇ ܥܩ̈ܒܬܐ ܕܢܘܗܪܗ
ܘܗܠܟܬ ܡܢ ܒܪܝܫܝܬ ܥܕܡܐ ܠܚܪܬܐ

15 ܡܢܗ ܓܝܪ ܦܠܚ ܗܘܐ
ܘܡܢܝܚ ܗܘܐ ܒܒܪܐ
16 ܘܡܛܠ ܦܘܪܩܢܗ ܢܐܚܘܕ ܟܠ ܡܕܡ

ܘܬܬܝܕܥ ܡܪܝܐ ܒܦܪ̈ܝܫܘܗܝ
17 ܠܡܫܒܚܘ ܠܐܝܠܝܢ ܕܐܝܬ ܠܗܘܢ ܡܙܡܘܪ̈ܐ ܕܡܐܬܝܬܗ ܕܡܪܝܐ
ܕܢܦܩܘܢ ܠܐܘܪܥܗ
ܘܢܙܡܪܘܢ ܠܗ ܒܚܕܘܬܐ
ܘܒܩܝܬܪܐ ܕܡܙ̈ܢܝܢ ܩܠ̈ܘܗܝ

18 ܢܐܙܠܘܢ ܩܕܡܘܗܝ ܚܙ̈ܝܐ
ܘܢܬܚܙܘܢ ܩܕܡܘܗܝ
19 ܘܢܫܒܚܘܢ ܠܡܪܝܐ ܒܚܘܒܗ
ܡܛܠ ܕܩܪܝܒ ܗܘ ܘܚܙܐ

20 ܘܬܬܥܩܪ ܣܢܐܬܐ ܡܢ ܐܪܥܐ
ܘܥܡ ܛܢܢܐ ܬܬܛܒܥ
21 ܐܬܚܒܠܬ ܠܗ̇ ܓܝܪ ܠܐ ܝܕܥܬܐ
ܡܛܠ ܕܐܬܬ ܠܗ̇ ܝܕܥܬܗ ܕܡܪܝܐ

22 ܢܙܡܪܘܢ ܐܝܠܝܢ ܕܡܙܡܪܝܢ ܛܝܒܘܬܗ ܕܡܪܝܐ ܡܪܝܡܐ
ܘܢܩܪܒܘܢ ܡܙܡܘܪ̈ܝܗܘܢ
23 ܘܐܝܟ ܝܘܡܐ ܢܗܘܐ ܠܒܗܘܢ
ܘܐܝܟ ܪܒܘܬ ܢܝܚܘܬܗ ܕܡܪܝܐ ܥܢ̈ܝܬܗܘܢ

ܘܠܐ ܢܗܘܐ ܡܕܡ ܕܢܦܫܐ
ܘܠܐ ܕܠܐ ܝܕܥܬܐ
ܘܠܐ ܕܚܪܫ
ܦܘܡܐ ܓܝܪ ܝܗܒ ܠܒܪܝܬܗ 24
ܠܡܦܬܚ ܩܠܐ ܕܦܘܡܐ ܠܘܬܗ
ܘܠܡܫܒܚܘܬܗ
ܐܘܕܘ ܚܠܝܘܬܗ 25
ܘܚܘܘ ܛܝܒܘܬܗ

ܗܠܠܘܝܐ

---

1 As the running of rage over wickedness,
so the running of joy over the Beloved,
and brings in from his fruits unhindered.
2 My joy is the Lord,
and my running towards him.
This is my beautiful way.

3 For I have a helper, the Lord.
He has made known to me himself without jealousy.
For by his extension, his gentleness reduced his greatness.

4 He became like me,
that I might receive him.
In likeness he was considered like me,
that I might put him on.
5 And I was not disturbed when I saw him,
because he had compassion on me.
6 Like my substance he became,
that I might learn him;
and like my form,
that I might not turn away from him.

7   The Father of knowledge
    is the Word of knowledge.
8   He who created wisdom
    is wiser than his works.
9   And he who created me before I was,
    knew what I would do when I was.

10  Because of this he had compassion on me in his great compassion,
    and granted to me that I might beseech from him,
    and might receive from his sacrifice.
11  Because he is incorrupted;
    the perfection of the aeons, and their Father.

12  He granted to him that he might be seen by those who are his,
    that they might recognise him who made them,
    and not consider that they were from themselves.

13  For towards knowledge he set his way;
    he spread it out widely, and lengthened it, and brought it to total
        perfection.
14  And he set upon it footprints of his light,
    and it went from the beginning until the end.

15  For by him he was served,
    and he was pleased in the Son.
16  And because of his salvation he will possess everything.

    And the Most High will be known by his saints;
17  to declare to those who have psalms of the Lord's coming,
    that they might go out to meet him,
    and might sing to him with joy,
    and with the many-toned harp.

18  Let the seers go before him,
    and let them be seen before him.
19  And let them glorify the Lord in his love,
    because he is near and sees.

20  And hatred will be lifted up from the earth,
     and with jealousy it will be drowned.
21  For ignorance was destroyed,
     because the knowledge of the Lord came.

22  Let the singers sing the grace of the Lord Most High,
     and let them offer their psalms.
23  And like the day let their heart be,
     and like the great beauty of the Lord their voices.

     And let there be nothing which breathes;
     neither which (is) ignorant,
     nor which (is) dumb.
24  For he gave a mouth to his creation;
     to open the voice of the mouth to him,
     and to glorify him.
25  Confess his might,
     and manifest his grace.

     Alleluia.

NOTES TO THE TRANSLATION

3a: The ܠ preceding ܡܪܢ indicates the obj. of ܠ ܐܝܬ in apposition with ܡܥܕܪܢܐ (cf. also Harris 1911a; Bernard; Brock 1975, 143; Charlesworth 1977). The concept of God/the Lord as a helper is found in 8:6; 21:2; 25:2 (cf. also <u>Didascalia Apostolorum</u> I, ܡܥܕܪܢܐ ܠܟ ܗܘܐ ܘܡܪܝܐ, "and the Lord will be to you a helper"; Vööbus 1: 14, line 1).

3b-c: H indicates a break before and after ܦܫܝܛܘܬ, which has been corrected in the margin to ܦܫܝܛܘܬܗ. Since the copyist's mistake occurs with the ending of ܦܫܝܛܘܬܗ, I am inclined to treat the punctuation after the word as the more unreliable of the two breaks indicated (cf. also, for this division, Bruston 1912b; Carmignac 1986). Every other case of ܠ ܚܕܐ in the Odes occurs at the conclusion of a line (11:6; 15:6; 17:12; 20:7; 23:4). If ܦܫܝܛܘܬܗ is relegated to 3c, ܠܝ would be in third position in the line which is unusual but also found in 21a.

3c: The root ܢܓܫ is used for the extension of the hands/the wood (cross?) in 27:1,3; 42:1-2 (cf. the note for Ode 42:2). If the same image is intended here, there may be a connection with the theology of Phil 2:5-8.

9a-b: In both lines ܟܢܗܟ is a dependent imperf. verb indicating action which occurs in the future relative to the action of the principal cl. (Nöldeke § 267) and must be translated here with the past tense (cf. also 4:2; 8:7,15; 16:18; 28:5).

10c: Nestle (587) conjectures that ܗܬܝܒܗ is a translation of οὐσία which was a copyist's error for θυσία (cf. Greßmann 1924, "Wesen").

12a: The ܗܠ is interpreted reflexively by Greßmann (1924); Bauer (1964); Carmignac (1986).

20a: The meaning of ܝܢܗܚ here should be interpreted negatively as opposed to other action of lifting up ( = exaltation) in the Odes.

23c: There is more intended here than people (*contra* Bauer 1964; Charlesworth 1977; the use of "soul" by others is ambiguous) as 24a makes clear.

ANALYSIS

There are three major sections to the Ode: 1-11, which concerns the relationship of the "I" and the Lord; 12-16a, which deals with the Most High and the Son, and the way of the Lord; and 16b-24, which comprises detail of various groups within the community, and finally of the whole creation, engaged in praise of the Most High. The sections share a number of motifs, the most significant being that of knowledge (the root ܢܕ occurs ten times).

Stanza 1 [1, 2]

Stanza 1 opens with a simile of the form ... ܗܘܒ...ܐܝܟ (cf. also Odes 6, 14, 15, 16, 28, 40). The two strophes are closely connected, both semantically (the joy over the beloved [1b] = the Lord as the joy of the "I" [2a]) and by the repetition of the key terms ܪܡܗ and ܚܕܘܬܐ.

1a and 1b are strictly parallel: ܐܝܟ/ܗܘܒ + ܢܝ݇ܡ + ܝ + noun + ܠܠ with noun obj. The bicolon is antithetical by the use of the opposites: rage and joy, wickedness and the beloved. 1c appears to be an addition, breaking what would be otherwise a logical flow to the second strophe. If not an addition, then 1c must be regarded as a conclusion to the action of 1b. ܟܚܘܬ is not otherwise associated with ܟܝܟ in the Odes (though cf. the connection of exultation and fruits in 8:1-2; 11:12) but there is mention of the fruits of the beloved/the Lord (4:4; 10:2; 12:2; 14:6; 16:2).

2a and 2b are parallel on the pattern: noun subj. with 1st sing. suffix + ref. to the Lord as the ultimate object of the joy/running + copula (understood in 2b). 2c provides a concluding statement which flows easily from the concept of running towards the Lord in 2b and also from the description of the running of joy in 1b. 2a and 15:1 contain the same formula: ܗܘ ܟܝܬ ,ܚܘܬ.

## Stanza 2 [3]

The stanza centres on the Lord as helper and his actions on behalf of the "I". It serves as a prelude to the greater detail in stanza 3 by introducing concepts of knowing the Lord and the Lord's reducing of his greatness (in order to become like the "I").

3a functions as an introductory statement for the stanza. 3b-c moves logically from the statement to give detail about the Lord's help. The bicolon is linked semantically rather than syntactically. 3b introduces the theme of knowledge. There is a connection with stanza 1 by the idea of the generosity of the Lord: his fruits are brought in unhindered (1c), he is without jealousy (3b).

## Stanza 3 [4, 5, 6]

The stanza is tightly structured with ܐ ܠܠܟܝ + cl. in the second line of each bicolon as the main unifying feature. The pattern of the strophes is A B A'.

4a-d and 6a-d are parallel strophes, both semantically and syntactically. 4a, 4c, 6a and 6c contain synonymous expressions concerning the Lord's taking on the likeness/substance/form of the "I". These expressions may be linked back to 3c, the reduction of the Lord's greatness being necessary to his becoming like the "I". Each of the lines contains a 3rd sing. perf verb (ref. to the Lord, understood in 6c) + an expression containing ܟܚܢܟܪ/ܘܝܟ (ref. to the "I"). 4a and 4c have the pattern: 3rd sing. perf. verb + ,ܚܢܟ. 6a and 6c are parallel with the pattern: ܘܝܟ + noun (attribute of the "I") + 1st sing. suffix + ܟܢܗ (understood in 6c). There is a degree of chiasmus between 4a, 4c and 6a, 6c by the placement of the verbs in relation to the expressions with the 1st sing. suffix.

4b, 4d, 6b and 6d follow the pattern: ܐ ܠܠܟܝ + 1st sing. Peal imperf. verb + 3rd sing. masc. pron. obj. (ܗܝܚ in 6d). Each line follows from the preceding line by expressing the (semantically similar) purpose of the action of the Lord described in that preceding line. 4b, 4d and 6d are linked further semantically by the contrasting concepts of receiving/putting on and turning away.

Although 5b follows the pattern of ܗ ܟܘܬܗ + cl., it is syntactically and semantically removed from the strict pattern of the first and third strophes. In this way it forms a central focus for the stanza, providing the detail of the outcome for the "I" (not being afraid, 5a) of the Lord's action in becoming like him (motivated by his compassion, 5b).

The second half of 5a and that of 5b are parallel to a degree on the pattern: conj. + perf. verb + pron. obj. suffix. There is chiasmus by the use of the persons - 1st sing. subj. with 3rd sing. masc. obj. in 5a; 3rd sing. masc. subj. with 1st sing. suffix in 5b. The pattern of persons for the subj. is the inversion of the pattern of subjs. in strophes 1 and 3 - 3rd sing. masc. subj. in 4a, 4c, 6a, (6c); 1st sing. subj. in 4b, 4d, 6b, 6d. 5a has internal parallelism by the double pattern of 1st sing. Peal perf. verbs.

Stanza 4 [7, 8-9]

The stanza focusses on the knowledge and wisdom of the Lord. 7 and 9b form the inclusio for the stanza by the repetition of the key root ܝܕܥ.

The confessional formula in 7a-b serves as the introduction to the stanza. The bicolon is parallel (with ellipsis of the copula ܗܘ in 7a) on the pattern: noun subj. + ܕܐܝܬܘܗܝ.

8a-b and 9a-b are alternately parallel. 8a and 9a have an initial pattern of ܐܝܟܢܐ ܗܘ + obj. 8b and 9b have the word-pair ܣܘܟܠ - ܝܕܥ in a masc. sing. form (ref. to the Lord) and repeat the root ܥܒܕ.

8a and 8b are parallel with a terrace pattern by the use of the root ܣܘܟܠ to conclude 8a and immediately following in 8b. There is a semantic connection between creation (8a) and works (= what has been created, 8b).

9a and 9b are parallel: initially, in a general pattern of 3rd sing. masc. verb with a 1st sing. obj./cl. of which the 1st sing. is the subj.; in the second half, on the pattern: conj. (ref. to time) + ܐܗܘܐ. As with 8a and 8b, there is a connection between the verbs ܟܝܢ and ܥܒܕ.

Stanza 5 [10, 11]

10a functions as an introductory statement concerning the compassion of the Lord, leading to detail about the actions of the Lord on behalf of the "I" (10b-c). 10a has a word-play on the root ܢܣ. There is a link with 5a by the use of this root with ref. to the Lord in association with action on behalf of the "I".

10b and 10c are parallel (with ellipsis of the principle cl. ܠ ܗܘܐ in 10c) on the pattern: ܘ (understood in 10c) + 1st sing. imperf. verb + ܗ + 3rd sing. masc. suffix/noun with 3rd sing. masc. suffix. There is a logic to the flow of the actions of beseeching and subsequently receiving.

The concluding confessional statement for the stanza in 11a-b is connected with 10a-c by the cl. introduced by ܘ ܡܛܠ in 11a which expresses the reason for the action in 10a-c. 11a-b contains parallel descriptions of the Lord with ellipsis of the shared clause ܐܝܬܘܗܝ ܕܗܘܐ ܡܛܠ in 11b. The parallelism is enhanced by the word-pair ܠ ܝܕܥ ܘ - ܚܟܡܬܐ. 11b has internal parallelism by the doubling of the pattern: noun (ref. to the Lord) + (synonymous) gen. expression (the 3rd pl. masc. suffix substitutes for ܠܟܘܢ).

With stanza 5, the use of the 1st sing. person ceases in the Ode.

## Stanza 6 [12a-c]

There is a shift in focus from the "I" and the Lord to the Most High and the Son and action done by the Son on behalf of those who belong to him (12b-c).

12a repeats the initial pattern of 10b: ܗܘܐ (ref. to the Lord) + ܠ with pron. suffix + ܘ + imperf. verb. 12a functions as an introductory statement to which the following cls. expressing purpose (12b, 12c) refer. There is a semantic connection between 12a and 12b by the equivalence of the concepts of belonging to the Lord and having been made by him (cf. 8:20).

12b and 12c have initial parallelism (with ellipsis of ܡܛܠ in 12c) on the pattern: ܘ + 3rd pl. masc. imperf. verb. The parallelism is strengthened by the word-pair ܢܕܥ - ܩܘܝ. There is also a semantic connection by the contrasting concepts of being made by the Lord and existing from themselves. 12c is linked with 12a by the word-pair ܚܝ - ܩܘܝ.

## Stanza 7 [13-14]

This stanza focusses on the motif of the way of the Lord, which was introduced in 2c. 13-14a comprises a series of 3rd sing. masc. perf. verbs with 3rd sing. fem. pron. objs. (with the exception of ܥܠܝܗ in 14a) referring to actions by the Lord concerning his way.

13a and 14a are more closely parallel by the repetition of the 3rd sing. masc. Peal perf. of ܣܡ. The parallelism has a terrace pattern by the placement of ܣܡܗ at the conclusion of 13a and of ܣܡ ܥܠܝܗ at the beginning of 14a.

13b is inserted into the parallel bicolon formed by 13a and 14a. It has internal parallelism by the triple pattern of 3rd sing. masc. perf. verb + 3rd sing. fem. pron. obj. The parallelism is strengthened by the word-pair ܟܬܒ - ܐܝܪ. There is a connection with 11b by the repetition of ܚܟܡܬܐ. There is also a link with 11:3-4 by a similar association of the way and knowledge (cf. 23:4).

14b concludes the stanza with a final summary statement concerning the way and its completion/fullness. The only other occurrence of the phrase, "from the beginning until the end", is with ref. to the way of the Lord in 11:4. There is a semantic link by the motif of fullness with 13b. 14a-b is strongly connected with 10:6 by the association of ܢܘܗܪܐ ܠܡܕܥܬܗ ... ܥܠ ܣܡ and ܗܠܝܢ. The combination of the motifs of the way of the Lord, walking, and footprints occurs also in 39:7-13. The association of footprints (ΪΧΝΟϹ) of the Father, the return to the Father, and the end as knowledge (ϹΑΥΝΕ), is found in The Gospel of Truth 37, 25-38, 4 (Facs. ed. 1: 41-2; MacRae 1984a, 46).

## Stanza 8 [15-16a]

Stanza 7 is concerned with the Father/Most High and the Son. 15a and 15b are parallel with chiasmus on the pattern: A B // B' A', where A = prep. + ܟܪܐ/ substitute 3rd sing. masc. suffix; B = sing. masc. part. + ܗܘܐ. The parallelism of ܡܪܗ and ܟܪܒܐ indicates that it is the Son to whom ref. is made in the former phrase. Ref. to the way of the Lord is precluded by the use of the 3rd sing. masc. suffix.

16a functions as a concluding confessional statement concerning the Son as saviour.

## Stanza 9 [16b-17]

The stanza exhibits a kind of semantic terrace effect by the pattern of the statements of purpose - 17a expresses the purpose of 16b, 17b-c expresses the double purpose of 17a.

16b opens the stanza and the entire second section of the Ode (16b-25), by introducing the key characters of the Most High and the saints (= the community). 17a is connected with 16b since it expresses the purpose of the action of knowing in 16b. The motif of the knowledge of the Lord/Most High provides the link between this section and the first section (cf. 3b, 7a-b, 12b).

17b-d must be regarded as a unit with the pattern: A B // A' B' C // C', where A = 3rd pl. masc. Peal imperf. verb; B = the 3rd sing. masc. (ref. to the Lord) as ultimate object of the action described in A; C = phrase with ܒ +

noun expressing the means of the action of singing. The root ܪܡܝ provides a link between 17a and 17c.

## Stanza 10 [18-19]

The limits of the stanza are indicated by the repetition of the root ܚܙܐ (18a, 18b, 19b) which underlies the key motif of the seers/seeing.

18a-19a has a degree of parallelism by the use of the initial 3rd pl. masc. imperf. verb with the 3rd sing. masc. (ref. to the Lord) as the ultimate object of the actions described. 18a and 18b are more strictly parallel (subj. ܚܙܐ understood in 18b) on the pattern: 3rd pl. masc. imperf. verb + ܠܩܘܒܠܗ. The parallelism is strengthened by the word-pair ܐܪܙ - ܚܙܐ. There is a terrace pattern to the two lines by the use of the root ܚܙܐ to conclude 18a and immediately following to begin 18b.

19b is connected with 19a by the cl. introduced by ܕ ܡܛܠ which gives the reason for the action of glorifying the Lord in 19a. It is a concluding confessional statement for the stanza, reiterating the key motif of seeing. There is an internal parallelism by the doubling of the sing. masc. part. form.

## Stanza 11 [20-21]

The stanza is concerned with the destruction of what is opposite to the knowledge of the Lord. The concluding focus on the knowledge of the Lord provides the link with the introduction to the section in 16b. There is antithesis between 20a-21a and 21b, both by the contrast between hatred/ignorance and knowledge and by the negative actions of being lifted up, drowned and destroyed over against coming. The combination of the actions of lifting up and of drowning expresses merismus .

20a and 20b are parallel with chiasmus on the pattern: A B C // C' A', where A = prep. with noun obj.; B = the subj. ܣܢܐܬܐ (understood in 20b); C = 3rd sing. fem. Ethpeel imperf. verb.

21a and 21b are parallel on the pattern: 3rd sing. fem. perf. verb + ܠܗ (pleonastic ref. to the subj. in each line; cf. Nöldeke § 224) + noun subj. (ܠܐ ܝܕܥܬܐ /ܝܕܥܬܐ).

## Stanza 12 [22-23b]

Stanza 11 returns to details concerning a group (singers) as in stanza 9 (seers). The repetition of the root ܪܡܝ provides a link with stanza 8. The use of initial

3rd pl. masc. imperf. verbs (22a-b) connects this stanza with both stanzas 8 and 9.

22a and 22b are parallel by the use of the initial 3rd pl. masc. Pael imperf. verbs (the subj. ܢܙܡܪܘܢ ܐܝܠ understood in 22b) + noun obj. The parallelism is strengthened by the repetition of the root ܙܡܪ and by the association of the concepts of singing and offering which is found also in 31:3-4. 22a has internal parallelism by the repetition of the root ܙܡܪ.

23a and 23b are parallel (with ellipsis of the verb in 23b) on the pattern: ܘܐܟܢ with obj... + noun subj. (attribute of the singers) with 3rd pl. masc. suffix. The parallelism of "heart" and "voices" is close to the association of "heart" and "lips" found also in 8:1; 16:2; 20:4; 21:8; 30:5; 37:2; 40:2).

## Stanza 13 [23c-e, 24]

Stanza 12 moves from the community groups to focus on the broader aspect of the whole creation ("anything which breathes", 23c).

The first strophe consists of three parallel negative statements on the pattern: ܘܠܐ + ܟܬܪܝ ܠܢܡܘܣ (understood in 23d and 23e) + ܗ + qualifying expression (ref. to ܟܬܪܝ). The descriptions of ignorance and of being dumb provide an antithesis to the key themes of the knowledge of the Lord and of the praise of the Lord in this section of the Ode.

24a-c takes up logically from the preceding strophe by asserting that the creation is fitted for praising (and is not therefore dumb). 24a functions as the introductory statement to which 24b-c refers by expressing the purpose for the Lord's giving in 24a. The latter is further linked with 24b by the repetition of ܦܘܡܐ.

24b and 24c are parallel by the use of the initial infin./extended infin. expression with the 3rd sing. masc. (ref. to the Most High) as the ultimate object of the action described. The parallelism is strengthened by the word-pair ܫܒܚ - ܦܬܚ ܠܘ ܦܘܡܗܐ.

## Stanza 14 [25]

25a-b functions as a final exhortation/invitation to the community, the first and only use of the 2nd pl. masc. in the Ode. The bicolon is parallel on the pattern: 2nd pl. masc. imper. verb + noun obj. (attribute of the Most High) with 3rd sing. masc. suffix. The parallelism is strengthened by the word-pair ܫܠܘܬܗ - ܛܝܒܘܬܗ.

## ODE 8

1 ܦܬܚܘ ܦܬܚܘ ܠܒܘܬܟܘܢ ܠܒܘܣܡܗ ܕܡܪܝܐ
ܘܢܣܓܐ ܚܘܒܟܘܢ ܡܢ ܠܒܐ ܘܥܕܡܐ ܠܣܦܘܬܐ
2 ܠܡܝܬܝܘ ܦܐܪܐ ܠܡܪܝܐ ܚܝܐ ܩܕܝܫܐ
ܘܠܡܡܠܠܘ ܒܥܝܪܘܬܐ ܒܢܘܗܪܗ

3 ܩܘܡܘ ܘܐܬܬܩܝܡܘ
ܗܢܘܢ ܕܡܟܝܢ ܐܬܬܪܝܡܘ
4 ܗܢܘܢ ܕܗܘܘ ܒܫܠܝܐ
ܡܠܠܘ ܕܐܬܦܬܚ ܦܘܡܟܘܢ
5 ܗܢܘܢ ܕܐܬܬܫܝܛܘ
ܡܟܝܠ ܐܬܬܪܝܡܘ ܕܐܬܬܪܝܡܬ ܙܕܝܩܘܬܟܘܢ

6 ܝܡܝܢܗ ܓܝܪ ܕܡܪܝܐ ܥܡܟܘܢ ܗܝ
ܘܗܘ ܗܘܐ ܠܟܘܢ ܡܥܕܪܢܐ
7 ܘܐܬܛܝܒ ܠܟܘܢ ܫܠܡܐ
ܡܢ ܩܕܡ ܕܢܗܘܐ ܩܪܒܟܘܢ

8 ܫܡܥܘ ܦܬܓܡܐ ܕܫܪܪܐ
ܘܣܒܘ ܝܕܥܬܗ ܕܡܪܝܡܐ
9 ܠܐ ܢܕܥ ܒܣܪܟܘܢ ܡܕܡ ܕܐܡܪ ܐܢܐ ܠܟܘܢ
ܐܦܠܐ ܠܒܘܫܟܘܢ ܡܕܡ ܕܡܚܘܐ ܐܢܐ ܠܟܘܢ
10 ܛܪܘ ܐܪܙܝ
ܗܢܘܢ ܕܡܬܛܪܝܢ ܒܗ
11 ܛܪܘ ܗܝܡܢܘܬܝ
ܗܢܘܢ ܕܡܬܛܪܝܢ ܒܗ̇
12 ܘܕܥܘ ܝܕܥܬܝ
ܗܢܘܢ ܕܒܫܪܪܐ ܝܕܥܝܢ ܠܝ
13 ܘܪܚܡܘܢܝ ܒܚܘܒܐ
ܐܝܠܝܢ ܕܪܚܡܝܢ

14 ܠܐ ܓܝܪ ܡܗܦܟ ܐܢܐ ܐܦܝ ܡܢ ܕܝܠܝ
ܡܛܠ ܕܝܕܥ ܐܢܐ ܠܗܘܢ
15 ܘܩܕܡ ܥܕ ܕܠܐ ܢܗܘܘܢ
ܐܣܬܟܠܬ ܐܢܘܢ
ܘܦܪ̈ܨܘܦܝܗܘܢ ܐܢܐ ܛܒܥܬ ܐܢܘܢ
16 ܐܢܐ ܐܬܩܢܬ ܗܕܡ̈ܝܗܘܢ
ܘܬܕ̈ܝܐ ܕܝܠܝ ܛܝܒܬ ܠܗܘܢ
ܕܢܫܬܘܢ ܚܠܒܐ ܩܕܝܫܐ ܕܝܠܝ ܕܢܐܚܘܢ ܒܗ
17 ܐܬܛܝܒܬ ܒܗܘܢ
ܘܠܐ ܒܗܬ ܐܢܐ ܒܗܘܢ

18 ܕܝܠܝ ܓܝܪ ܥܒܕܐ ܐܝܬܝܗܘܢ
ܘܚܝܠܐ ܕܡܚܫ̈ܒܬܝ
19 ܡܢܘ ܗܟܝܠ ܢܩܘܡ ܠܘܩܒܠ ܥܒܕܝ
ܐܘ ܡܢܘ ܕܠܐ ܡܫܬܡܥ ܠܗܘܢ
20 ܐܢܐ ܨܒܝܬ ܘܠܒܐ ܓܒܝܬ ܘܡܓܒܠܬ
ܘܕܝܠܝ ܐܝܬܝܗܘܢ

ܘܥܠ ܝܡܝܢܐ ܕܝܠܝ ܣܡܬ ܠܓܒ̈ܝܝ
21 ܘܐܙܠܐ ܩܘܕܡܝܗܘܢ ܙܕܝܩܘܬܝ
ܘܠܐ ܢܬܓܠܙܘܢ ܡܢ ܫܡܝ
ܡܛܠ ܕܥܡܗܘܢ ܗܘ

22 ܒܥܘ ܘܐܣܓܘ ܘܩܘܘ ܒܚܘܒܗ ܕܡܪܝܐ
ܘܚܒ̈ܝܒܐ ܒܚܒܝܒܐ
ܘܗܢܘܢ ܕܢܛܝܪܝܢ ܒܗܘ ܕܚܝܐ
ܘܦܪ̈ܘܩܐ ܒܗܘ ܕܐܬܦܪܩ
23 ܘܕܠܐ ܚܒܠܐ ܬܫܟܚܘܢ ܒܟܠܗܘܢ ܠܥܠܡ̈ܐ
ܠܫܡܗ ܕܐܒܘܟܘܢ

ܗܠܠܘܝܐ

---

1 Open, open your hearts to the Lord's exultation,
and let your love increase from the heart to the lips;
2 to bring fruits to the Lord, the holy life,
and to speak with wakefulness in his light.

3   Stand up and be established,
    you who once were brought low.
4   You who were in silence,
    speak since your mouth has been opened.
5   You who were despised,
    now be lifted up, since your righteousness has been lifted up.

6   For the right hand of the Lord is with you,
    and he is a helper for you.
7   And peace was prepared for you
    before your war was.

8   Hear the Word of truth,
    and receive the knowledge of the Most High.
9   Your flesh will not know what I am saying to you,
    nor your garment what I am manifesting to you.

10  Keep my mystery,
    you who are kept by it.
11  Keep my faith,
    you who are kept by it.
12  And know my knowledge,
    you who know me in truth.
13  Love me in love,
    you who love.

14  For I shall not turn my face away from mine,
    because I know them.
15  And before they yet were,
    I recognised them.
    And their faces I sealed;
16  I fixed their members.
    And my breasts I prepared for them,
    that they might drink my holy milk, and might live by it.
17  I was well pleased in them,
    and I am not ashamed by them.

18  For my work are they,
    and the strength of my thoughts.
19  Who then will stand against my work?
    Or who does not obey them?
20  I willed and formed mind and heart,
    and mine are they.

    And on my right hand I have set my chosen,
21  and my righteousness goes before them.
    And they will not be separated from my name,
    because it is with them.

22  Pray and increase and abide in the love of the Lord;
    and beloved ones in the Beloved,
    and you who are kept in him who lives,
    and saved ones in him who was saved.
23  And incorrupted will you be found in all the aeons,
    on account of the name of your Father.

    Alleluia.

NOTES TO THE TRANSLATION

3a: Lit. "stand up and be stood up".

4-5: The punctuation breaks in the Ms. after ܪ̈ܝܫܐ, ܦܩܘܕܝܗܘܢ, and ܐܬܬܩܝܡܘ
do not take account of the parallel structure of these two bicola.

7b: ܢܗܘܐ is a dependent imperf. verb indicating action which occurs in the future relative to the action of the principal cl. (Nöldeke § 267) and must be
translated here in the past tense (cf. also 4:2; 7:9; 8:15; 16:18; 28:5).

15a: As with ܢܗܘܐ in 7b, ܢܗܘܘܢ must be translated in the past tense. For the
understanding of ܩܕܡ ܕܠܐ ܕܐ as "before...yet", cf. Nöldeke § 267.

22a: Apart from Harris 1911a, Bernard, and Charlesworth 1977, the majority
of translations treat ܐܘܣܦ as an adv. modifying either ܒܥܘ (Flemming; Ungnad and Staerk; Diettrich 1911; Labourt and Batiffol; Greßmann 1924; Bauer

1964; Lattke 1979-86, vol. 1; Carmignac 1986), or ܩܢܘ (Harris and Mingana vol. 2; Emerton). The choice has been made to translate with the 2nd pl. masc. Aphel imper. on the basis of: a) the similarity of the association of the verb ܡܥܠ with ܢܘܒܪ in 1b to the association of ܡܥܠ with ܟܢܫܘܬܗ in 22a; b) other instances of a series of three verbs in the 2nd pl. masc. imper. joined by ܘ in 3:11 and 34:6b (cf. the three-verb series form in 7:13b; 31:10a; 33:5b; 34:6b; 38:17b,18a, and also 6:8c-d; 38:4a-b).

22c: The use of ܢܛܪ in the parallel structure of 22b-d is very subtle. That ܢܛܪ may connote "to preserve life" is clear in Ps 64:2, ܢܛܪ ܢܝ; תצר היי (MT); ἐξελοῦ τὴν ψυχήν μου (LXX).

ANALYSIS

Stanza 1 [1-2]

The stanza functions as an introductory exhortation to praise (cf. ܦܨܚܘ in 9:1; 13:1b).

1a and 1b are parallel on the general pattern: imper. verb/imperf. verb used as jussive + noun (obj. in 1a, subj. in 1b) with 2nd pl. masc. suffix + prep. phrase/s. The connection between the lines is strengthened by the repetition of ܠܒܐ.

2a and 2b are parallel by the initial infin. and a focus on the Lord as the ultimate object of the action described. The lines are linked semantically by the equivalence of bringing/producing fruits and speaking/praising (cf. 12:2; 14:7).

The associated elements of heart and lips, love, exultation, and speaking/praising, are found also to some degree in 16:2; 21:7-9; 40:2-4.

Stanza 2 [3-5]

The inclusio for the stanza is formed between 3a and 5b by the doubling pattern of the semantically similar roots ܩܥܩ and ܪܢܢ. The structure of the stanza may be outlined as: A B B' A' B" A", where A = a line introduced by a 2nd pl. masc. imper. verb (5b has ܡܛܠ before the imperative); B = ܘ ܡܢ ... 2nd pl. masc. perf. verb (cf. 31:6).

3a has internal parallelism both by the doubling of the imper. verb and by the doubling of the root ܩܥܩ. 4b and 5b are more strictly parallel on the pattern: 2nd pl. masc. imper. verb + ܘ + 3rd sing. Ethpeel perf. verb + noun subj. (attribute of the 2nd pl. group) with 2nd pl. masc. suffix. There is internal parallelism in both lines - in 4b, by the word-pair ܦܘܡܟ ܐܦܘ - ܠܒܟ; in 5b by the repetition of the root ܪܗܛ.

Each of the bicola is antithetical - 3a-b, by the polar word-pair ܩܘܡ - ܡܟ; 4a-b and 5a-b, by contrasting concepts of being silent and speaking (cf. 12:8), of being despised and lifted up. 3a-b and 5a-b are linked semantically by the similarity of both the negative and positive conditions described (standing up - being brought low, being despised - being lifted up).

The association of the imagery of praising (stanza 1) and of being lifted up (stanza 2) can be found in 21:6-9 (cf. also 36:1-2)

Stanza 3 [6-7]

With stanza 3 the style shifts from imperatives addressed to the community to statements about the community. Stanza 2 and stanza 3 are linked by the association of ܪܗܛ in 5b and ܪܚܡܘܗܝ in 6a (cf. 25:9). There may be a further connection between the stanzas if the war (7b) refers to the situation of being brought low in 3.

6a-b is parallel with chiasmus on the pattern: A B C // C' B' A', where A = noun subj./compl.; B = prep. + 2nd pl. masc. suffix; C = verb/copula. The parallelism is strengthened by the word-pair ܢܛܪܟ - ܢܛܪܗܘܢ. 7a follows a similar pattern to 6b: verb + ܠܟܘܢ + noun compl./subj. 7a and 7b are connected by the polar word-pair ܫܠܡܐ - ܩܪܒܐ.

Stanza 4 [8-9]

The stanza functions as an introduction to 10-21 which appears to constitute "the Word of truth" (8a)/"knowledge of the Most High" (8b). With 8a there is a return to the imperatives addressed to the community.

8a-b is strictly parallel on the pattern: 2nd pl. masc. imper. verb + noun obj. + ܘ + noun. The parallelism is strengthened by the word-pairs ܫܡܥܬ - ܩܒܠ and ܦܬܓܡܐ - ܝܕܥܬܐ.

9a-b is parallel on the pattern: ܐܝܟ/ܐܠ + ܝܕ (understood in 9b) + noun subj. (attribute of the community) with 2nd pl. masc. suffix + ܘ ܡܕܒ + masc. sing. part. act. + ܠܟܘܢ ܐܝܬ. 8b and 9a are connected by the repetition of the root ܝܕ.

Stanza 5 [10-12, 13]

Stanza 5 constitutes the first section of the Word of truth/knowledge of the Most High alluded to in 8a-b. The repetition of ܟܐܢܬ and the root ܝܕܥ (12a-b) provides the link with the introduction in stanza 4.

The bicola of stanza 5 follow the general structure of those in stanza 2, one line containing an initial 2nd pl. masc. imper. verb, the other commencing with ܗ ܐܝܟܢ. 10-11 are more strictly parallel, 10a and 11a having the pattern: ܗܝܠܕ + noun obj. (attribute of the "I") with 1st sing. suffix; 10b and 11b being equivalent except for the gender of the final suffixes which refer to the noun objs. in 10a and 11a. ܝܠܕ is repeated as the verb in both lines of each bicolon.

12a has the same pattern as 10a and 11a. 12b follows 10b and 11b to a degree with ܗ ܐܝܟܢ ... masc. pl. part. ܝܕܥ is repeated as the verb in 12a and 12b. There is also word-play in 12a by the repetition of that same root. There is further connection between 12a and 12b by the word-pair ܝܕܥܬܐ - ܟܐܢܬ.

13a-b does not follow the pattern of 10-12 as strictly but does have the 2nd pl. masc. imper. in the first line of the bicolon and, in the second line, ܐܬܠ ܗ (instead of ܗ ܐܝܟܢ) + masc. pl. part. As with 10-12, the verb of the first line is repeated in the second (ܪܚܡ). The pattern of doubling in 13a is similar to 12a except that the doubling is on the basis of the concept of love (by the synonymous roots ܪܚܡ and ܚܒ (cf. 22a-b), whereas 12a has a doubling of the same root. There is a connection between 10-11 and 13a-b by the word-pair ܚܒ - ܝܠܕ, between 12a and 13a by the word-pair ܝܕܥܬܐ - ܚܘܒ.

Stanzas 6-9

Stanzas 6-9 constitute the second section of the Word of truth/knowledge of the Most High alluded to in 8a-b. 14-21 comprises a report concerning the relationship of the "I" to his chosen ones. The inclusio for the section is formed between 14 and 21b-c - syntactically, by the structure of the initial negative verb...ܐܗܦܟ/ܐܬܠ ܗ in 14a and 21b, and ܗ ܡܢܗܘܢ + cl. with the 3rd pl. masc. as the ultimate object of the action; semantically, by the similarity of the concepts of the "I" not turning away from the chosen and of the chosen not being separated from the "I".

The designation of 14-21 as a section is supported by the use of -ܕܝܢ . This element occurs 25 times in the Odes. Of the thirteen cases of ܕܝܢ , six occur between 14-20.

Stanza 6 [14, 15-16, 17]

With stanza 6 there is a shift from the imperatives addressed to the community to a report concerning the "I" and his own. There is a connection with the introduction in stanza 4 by the repetition of the root ܝܕܥ in 14b.

14a-b and 17a-b form a semantic inclusio for the stanza by the similar concepts of the "I" not turning his face from his own and not being ashamed by them. The main focus of the action is in the present. The intervening lines, 15-16, comprise a report on past actions of the "I" towards his own - recognition before birth, establishment/creation, nursing.

14a and 14b have a degree of parallelism by the use of the masc. sing. part. act. + ܐܝܟ with a concluding focus on those who belong to the "I".

15a-b flows easily from 14b by the similarity of the concepts of knowing and recognising. 15b, 15c and 16a are parallel to a degree by the use of the 1st sing. perf. verb with a focus on the 3rd pl. masc. as obj. (indirectly by the 3rd pl. masc. suffix in 15c and 16a).

15c and 16a are more closely parallel with chiasmus on the general pattern: A B C // B' A", where A = pl. noun obj. (physical attribute of those belonging to the "I") with 3rd pl. masc. suffix; B = ܐܝܟ + 1st sing. perf. verb; C = ܐܢܘܢ (obj. in apposition with ܦܪܨܘܦܗܘܢ). The parallelism is strengthened by the synonymous verbs (cf. ܛܒܥ translated by ܬܩܢ in Prov 8:25). 15c has internal parallelism by the doubling of the obj. on either side of the 1st sing. perf. verb.

16b and 16c are initially parallel with chiasmus on the pattern: A B...// B' A'..., where A = noun obj. (physical attribute of the "I") with ܕܝܠܝ ; B = verb. The parallelism is strengthened by the word-pair ܚܕܐ - ܚܠܒܐ. There is a connection with 11:7 by the association of the roots ܚܙܐ - ܚܝ.

17a-b is parallel on the general pattern: 1st sing. perf. verb + ܒܗܘܢ. The lines are linked semantically by the similar concepts of being well-pleased and not being ashamed.

Stanza 7 [18-20b]

The stanza focusses on the creation of those who belong to the "I". The inclusio for the stanza is formed by 18a and 20b which are parallel on the pattern: compl. (ܕܝܠܝ as gen. expression in 18a, as the compl. per se in 20b) + ܐܬܒܪܝܘ.

18a-b is parallel with ܟܢܘܗܬܐ understood in 18b. There is chiasmus by the placement of the gen. expression with the 1st sing. suffix (ܝܠܝ , ܙܕܝܩܘܬܗ) and the noun compl. (ܥܒܕܐ, ܫܡܝ).

The double rhetorical question in 19a-b interrupts the report style, although the questions are connected with the statement in 18a by the use of ܝܕܝ in 19a. 19a and 19b are parallel by the use of ܡܢܘ + verb with a focus on those who belong to the "I" as the ultimate object of the action ("my work" = "them").

20a and 20b are linked semantically - those who are formed by the "I" are those who belong to the "I". The bicolon continues the motif of creation in 18a-b. 20a has internal parallelism by two doubling patterns: noun obj. + ܘ + noun obj.; 1st sing. Peal perf. verb + ܘ + 1st sing. Peal perf. verb.

## Stanza 8 [20c-21]

Stanza 8 completes the second section of the Word of the Most High by focussing on the establishment of the chosen on the right hand.

The connections between the lines of the stanza are more semantic than syntactic. There is a final emphasis in each line on attributes of the "I" ("my right hand" [20c], "my righteousness" [21a], "my name" [21b, understood as the subj. of the copula ܗܘ in 21c]) associated with action concerning the chosen. The combination of ܝܡܝܢܐ and ܣܡܬ in 20c is found in 18:7; 25:7.

21b and 21c have a degree of parallelism with chiasmus: A B // B' A', where A = verb/copula; B = prep. + obj. Chiasmus is also achieved by the placement of the 1st sing. and 3rd pl. persons. In 21b, the verb is 3rd pl. masc. and the obj. of the prep. is ܓܒܝܐ; in 21c, the copula has ܓܒܝܐ as the understood subj. and the 3rd pl. masc. as the obj. of the prep. The inclusio formed by 21b-c and 14a-b has been noted above.

## Stanza 9 [22-23]

With stanza 9 there is a shift from the report style to 2nd pl. imperatives addressed to the community. Since the Lord/the Father is spoken of in the 3rd person, it is clear that the Word of truth/knowledge of the Most High has come to an end with the preceding stanza.

22a has internal parallelism by the series of three 2nd pl. masc. imper. verbs. 22b-d comprises those who are the subject of the exhortation in 22a. There is a further connection between 22a and 22b by the association of the roots ܝܬܪ and ܣܓܐ.

22b-d is parallel to a degree by the use of the masc. pl. part. pass. + ܒ + obj. 22c and 22d are more strictly parallel on the pattern: masc. pl. part. pass. + ܘ ܟܡܗ + 3rd sing. masc. perf. verb. 22b and 22d have internal parallelism by the doubling of the root (ܥܒ in 22b, ܦܝܡ in 22d). There are further connections between the three lines by the word-pairs ܥܒ - ܠܒܝ (22b, 22c), ܠܒܝ - ܦܝܡ and ܣܟ - ܦܝܡ (22c, 22d).

22a-d is linked with stanza 5 by the repetition of the roots ܠܒܝ, ܝܣܝܪ, and ܥܒ.

23a-b moves from the exhortation in 22a. For the association of incorruption and the aeons, cf. 7:11. The final emphasis on ܫܡܗ links 23b and 21b-c (cf. Odes 16, 18, 20, 23, 39, 41, 42 for a concluding ref. to the name of the Lord/Most High; cf. also Ode 33).

## ODE 9

1 ܦܬܚܘ ܐܕ̈ܢܝܟܘܢ
ܘܐܡܠܠ ܠܟܘܢ
2 ܗܒ<ܘ> ܠܝ ܢܦܫܟܘܢ
ܕܐܦ ܐܢܐ ܐܬܠ ܠܟܘܢ ܢܦܫܝ

3 ܦܬܓܡܗ ܕܡܪܝܐ ܘܨܒ̈ܝܢܘܗܝ
ܡܚܫܒܬܐ ܩܕܝܫܬܐ ܕܐܬܚܫܒ ܥܠ ܡܫܝܚܗ
4 ܒܨܒܝܢܗ ܓܝܪ ܕܡܪܝܐ ܚ̈ܝܝܟܘܢ ܐܝܬܝܗܘܢ
ܘܬܪܥܝܬܗ ܚܝܐ ܕܠܥܠܡ
ܘܕܠܐ ܚܒܠܐ ܐܝܬܘܗܝ ܫܘܡܠܝܟܘܢ

5 ܥܬܪܘ ܒܐܠܗܐ ܐܒܐ
ܘܩܒܠܘ ܬܪܥܝܬܗ ܕܡܪܝܡܐ
ܐܬܚܝܠܘ ܘܐܬܦܪܩܘ ܒܛܝܒܘܬܗ

6 ܡܟܪܙ ܐܢܐ ܓܝܪ ܫܠܡܐ ܠܟܘܢ ܠܩܕ̈ܝܫܘܗܝ
ܕܟܠܗܘܢ ܐܝܠܝܢ ܕܩܢܝܢ ܠܐ ܢܦܠܘܢ ܒܩܪܒܐ
7 ܘܐܝܠܝܢ ܬܘܒ ܕܙܟܘܗܝ ܠܐ ܢܐܒܕܘܢ
ܘܕܗܘܢ ܕܩܢܘܢ ܠܐ ܢܒܗܬܘܢ

8 ܟܠܝܠܐ ܕܠܥܠܡ ܫܪܪܐ ܐܝܬܘܗܝ
ܛܘܒܝܗܘܢ ܠܐܝܠܝܢ ܕܣܡܝܢ ܠܗ ܒܪܫܝܗܘܢ
9 ܟܐܦܐ ܝܩܝܪܬ ܕܡܪܝܐ
ܘܩܪ̈ܒܐ ܓܝܪ ܡܛܠ ܟܠܝܠܐ ܗܘܘ
10 ܘܢܨܒܬܗ ܙܕܝܩܘܬܐ
ܘܠܟܘܢ ܝܗܒܬܗ
11 ܣܒܘ ܟܠܝܠܐ ܒܩܝܡܗ ܫܪܪܐ ܕܡܪܝܐ

ܘܟܠܗܘܢ ܐܝܠܝܢ ܕܙܟܘ ܢܬܟܬܒܘܢ ܒܟܬܒܗ
12 ܟܬܒܗܘܢ ܓܝܪ ܙ̇ܟܘܬܐ ܗܝ ܕܠܟܘܢ
ܘܚܙܐ ܠܟܘܢ ܡܩܕܡܗ̇
ܘܨܒܐ ܕܬܬܦܪܩܘܢ

ܗܠܠܘܝܐ

1   Open your ears,
    and I shall speak to you.
2   Give me yourself,
    that I also may give you myself.

3   The Word of the Lord and his desires (are)
    the holy thought which he thought about his Messiah.
4   For in the will of the Lord is your life,
    and his mind (is) eternal life,
    and incorrupted is your perfection.

5   Be rich in God the Father,
    and receive the mind of the Most High.
    Be strong and be saved by his grace.

6   For I declare peace to you, his holy ones,
    that all of those who hear might not fall in the war,
7   and those also who knew him might not perish,
    and that they who will take might not be ashamed.

8   An eternal crown is truth;
    blessed are those who set it on their head.
9   A stone of great price;
    for the wars were because of the crown.
10  And righteousness took it,
    and gave it to you.
11  Set on the crown in the true covenant of the Lord.

    And all of those who have been victorious will be written in his book,
12  for their book is the victory which is for you.
    And she sees you before her,
    and wills that you might be saved.

    Alleluia.

NOTES TO THE TRANSLATION

1b: The imper. ـحم in 2a must be taken as an error in view of the parallelism of 2a with 1a and the use of the 2nd pl. pron. suffix with ܟܢܘܢ.

7a: The failure of H to make a punctuation break after ܢܟܪܒܩܘ indicates the copyist was unaware of the syntactic pattern of 6b-7a.

11a: The line may also be translated "set the crown on the true standing one of the Lord" (cf. ܒ...ܩܡ, "to set on", in 8b). The standing "I" is a frequent image in the Odes (cf. e.g. 5:13; 15:2; 18:3; 26:12; 31:8,11; 36:2; 42:6). The Word also stands (12:6) as do the community (6:14,16; 8:3).

11b,12a: ܙܟܐ/ܙܟܘܬܐ may also be translated "to be justified"/"justification" (Smith, R.P. 1: 119-21). The imagery of war and crown seems to demand the meaning of "to be victorious"/"victory".

12b: The 3rd sing. fem. verb refers to ܙܟܘܬܐ ("Nike"; Greßmann 1924) in 12a.

ANALYSIS

The Ode has two basic sections: an exhortation and report/teaching to the community (1-7) and a report which concerns the crown (8-12). The motif of war (6-7, 9-12) and a focus on the community links the two sections.

Stanza 1 [1-2]

1a-b comprises a formula of introduction with imperatives addressed to the community (cf. introductory ܦܬܚܘ in 8:1a; 13:1b).
    1a-b and 2a-b are alternately parallel. 1a and 2a have a general pattern of 2nd pl. masc. imper. verb (cf. the translation notes for the emendation to ܗܒܡ in 2a) + noun (attribute of the 2nd pl. masc. group) with 2nd pl. masc. suffix. 1b and 2b have the pattern: 1st sing. imperf. verb + ܠܟܘܢ.
    1a and 1b are linked semantically, the action of 1a being required before that of 1b. There is a general parallel pattern by the initial verb with a dir./indir. obj. (ref. to the 2nd pl. masc. group). 2a and 2b are more strictly structured on the pattern: verb (ܗܒܡ/ܢܛܠ) + ܠ + suffix 1 + ܟܢܘܢ + suffix 2. The pattern is chiastic by the arrangement of persons: 2a has a 2nd pl. verb... 1st sing.

suffix 1... 2nd pl. suffix 2; 2b has a 1st sing. verb... 2nd pl. suffix 1... 1st sing. suffix 2.

## Stanza 2 [3-4]

The repetition of the root ܪܥܐ in 3a and 12c may indicate an inclusio for the Ode proper (3-12) which follows the introductory address to the community in stanza 1.

3a and 3b present the word/desires and thought of the Lord in apposition. Word and thought are associated in 16:8,19 although with ܡܠܬܐ rather than ܦܬܓܡܐ (cf. the excursus on "Word" following the analysis of Ode 12) and the link is further strengthened by the word-pair ܪܥܝ - ܡܚܫܒܬܐ. 3a has internal parallelism by the double pattern of noun (attribute of the Lord) + 3rd sing. masc. suffix, both nouns qualified by the centrally placed ܕܡܪܝܐ. 3b has a word-play on the root ܚܫܒ. There is some alliteration by the repetition of ܚ/ ܦ, ܫ.

3a-b and 4a-c are linked both semantically, by the concepts of desire/will (3a, 4a) and thought/mind (3b, 4b), and by the repetition of ܪܥܝ (3a [pl.], 4a).

4a and 4b are connected by the initial noun (attribute of the Lord) with 3rd sing. masc. suffix and by the repetition of ܚܝܐ as subj./compl. There is a degree of parallelism with chiasmus between 4a and 4c, on the pattern: qualifying expression ("in the will of the Lord"/"incorrupted") with ref. to the noun subj. (attribute of the group) + 2nd pl. masc. suffix. The chiasmus occurs in the conclusion of the lines by the placement of the verbs (ܐܝܬ + suffix) and noun subjs. 4b and 4c are semantically linked by the similarity of the concepts of eternal life (4b) and incorruption (4c).

## Stanza 3 [5]

With stanza 3 there is a return to a direct address to the community, each line commencing with a 2nd pl. masc. imper. verb (5c doubles the pattern) which refers to some attribute of God/the Most High as source or object of the action. 5b has central position between the more strictly parallel 5a and 5c on the pattern: 2nd pl. masc. imper. verb/s + ܒ + noun (ref. to God/the Most High). 5b and 5c are linked by the word-pair ܩܘܡ - ܡܠܟ. There is a connection with stanza 2 by the repetition of ܨܒܝܢܐ (4b, 5b; ref. to the Lord/Most High).

Stanza 4 [6-7]

The stanza focusses on the motifs of peace and war. 6a functions as the opening statement to which 6b-7b refer by giving the purpose for the declaration of peace. The motif of the "I" speaking to the community provides a kind of semantic inclusio for the first section of the Ode between stanzas 1 and 4.

6b-7b is parallel on the pattern: ܗܢܘܢ/ܐܝܠܝܢ + ܕ + 3rd pl. masc. verb + ܠܐ + 3rd pl. masc. imperf. verb. The parallelism is strengthened by the word-pair ܢܦܠ - ܐܒܕ. 6b is linked with 6a by the polar word-pair ܫܠܡܐ - ܩܪܒܐ.

Stanza 5 [8-11a]

With stanza 5, the primary focus becomes the crown, ܟܠܝܠܐ being repeated in the first (8a), central (9b), and final (11a) lines of the stanza. There is a link with the first section of the Ode (1-7) by the continuing motif of war. 8a-b and 11a form the inclusio for the stanza by the repetitions of ܟܠܝܠܐ, ܫܪܪܐ/ܫܪܝܪܐ and ܣܝܡ.

8a functions as the introductory statement for the stanza. 8a and 9a are parallel, ܟܐܦܐ ܝܩܝܪܬܐ ܕܡܪܝܐ being in apposition with ܟܠܝܠܐ ܕܠܥܠܡ. The beatitude in 8b has been inserted into the parallel bicolon formed by 8a and 9a. It flows easily from 8a by the ref. of ܠܗ to ܟܠܝܠܐ.

9b seems to follow logically from 9a, the idea being either that the stone/crown is precious because there were wars on its account, or that the wars were fought because the stone/crown is precious. The repetition of ܟܠܝܠܐ further links 9b with the bicolon formed by 8a and 9a.

10a and 10b are parallel, the two 3rd sing. fem. Peal perf. verbs with 3rd sing. masc. suffix (ref. to the crown) having the common subject ܙܕܝܩܘܬܐ. There is chiasmus by the placement of the verbs in relation to the noun subj. (10a) and the indir. pron. obj. (10b).

11a completes this section devoted specifically to the crown with an exhortation/invitation to the community. There is a degree of parallelism with 8b on the pattern: ܣܝܡ + obj. (ref. to the crown) + ܒ with obj. ܩܘܡ and ܫܪܝܪܐ are also found associated in 18:3 and 31:11.

Stanza 6 [11b-12c]

The motif of victory follows from the motif of war in stanza 5. 11b and 12a are closely connected by the repetition of the roots ܙܟܐ and ܟܬܒ. There is chiasmus between them by the reversal of the two roots in the repetition in 12a, and a terrace pattern by ܩܘܡܬܒ initially in 12a immediately following ܡܕܬܒ ܐܕܬܕܢ at the conclusion of 11b. The structure of 11b is very close to that of 6b: ܐ ܐܝܪ ܩܘܡܠܒ + 3rd pl. masc. verb + 3rd pl. masc. imperf. verb + ܒ + noun obj.

12b-c is linked with 11b-12a by the 3rd sing. fem. verb and 3rd sing. fem suffix which refer to ܟܬܢܕܝ in 12a. 12b and 12c are parallel by the initial 3rd sing. fem. Peal part. act. (subj. is "victory") and by the 2nd pl. masc. as ultimate object of the action described.

## ODE 10

1 ܬܪܨ ܦܘܡܝ ܡܪܝܐ ܒܡܠܬܗ
ܘܦܬܚ ܠܒܝ ܒܢܘܗܪܗ
2 ܘܐܥܡܪ ܒܝ ܚܝܘܗܝ ܕܠܐ ܡܘܬܐ
ܘܝܗܒ ܠܝ ܕܐܡܠܠ ܦܐܪܐ ܕܫܠܡܗ
3 ܠܡܦܢܝܘ ܢܦ̈ܫܬܐ ܕܐܝܠܝܢ ܕܨܒܝܢ ܠܡܐܬܐ ܠܘܬܗ
ܘܠܡܫܒܐ ܫܒܝܬܐ ܛܒܬܐ ܠܚܐܪܘܬܐ

4 ܐܬܚܝܠܬ ܘܐܬܥܫܢܬ ܘܫܒܝܬ ܠܥܠܡܐ
ܘܗܘܬ ܠܝ ܠܬܫܒܘܚܬܗ ܕܡܪܝܡܐ ܘܕܐܠܗܐ ܐܒܝ

5 ܘܐܬܟܢܫܘ ܐܟܚܕ ܥܡ̈ܡܐ ܕܡܒܕܪܝܢ ܗܘܘ
ܘܐܢܐ ܠܐ ܐܬܛܡܐܬ ܒܚܘ̈ܒܝ
ܡܛܠ ܕܐܘܕܝܘ ܠܝ ܒܡܪ̈ܘܡܐ
6 ܘܐܬܬܪܫܡܘ ܥܩ̈ܒܬܐ ܕܢܘܗܪܐ ܥܠ ܠܒܗܘܢ
ܘܗܠܟܘ ܒܚܝ̈ܝ ܘܐܬܦܪܩܘ
ܘܗܘܘ ܥܡܝ ܠܥܠܡܥܠܡܝܢ

ܗܠܠܘܝܐ

---

1 The Lord directed my mouth by his Word,
and opened my heart by his light,
2 and caused to dwell in me his immortal life,
and granted to me that I might speak the fruit of his peace;
3 to bring back the souls of those who desire to come to him,
and to capture a good captivity for freedom.

4 I grew strong and was strengthened and captured the world,
and it was mine for the glory of the Most High, and of God my Father.

5    And the peoples who had been scattered abroad were gathered together.
     And I myself was not defiled by my sins,
     because they confessed me in the heights.
6    And the footprints of light were set upon their heart,
     and they walked in my life and were saved.
     And they were my people for ever and ever.

Alleluia.

## NOTES TO THE TRANSLATION

4a: ܥܠܡܐ may also be translated "aeon" (Smith, R.P. 2: 2898-900). The decision concerning the use of the more technical term will depend on further investigation of the imagery of the Odes.

5b: Generally an emendation is made to ܚܘܒܝ ("my love"; exceptions are Bruston 1912b; Greßmann 1924; Bauer 1964; Lattke 1979-86, vol. 1; Emerton; Carmignac 1986) since it is judged inappropriate for the Messiah figure, who is presumed to be speaking, to refer to himself as a sinner (cf. e.g. the summary and argument in Charlesworth 1977, 48-9 n. 8).

6c: Labourt and Batiffol translate ܥܡܗ as "avec moi".

## ANALYSIS

Stanza 1 [1-2, 3]

Stanza 1 focusses on the Lord as the subject of action concerning the "I". The limits of the stanza are indicated by the semantic association of 1a and 2b which present the "I" as the one who speaks by the power of the Lord. 1b-2a forms the inclusio for the Ode with 6a-b by the repetition of ܠܒܐ, ܪܗܛܘ (1b, 6a), and ܚܝܝ (2a, 6b).

    The four lines of the first strophe (1a-2b) are linked by the initial 3rd sing. masc. perf. verb with the 1st sing. person as the object of the action (indirectly by the 1st sing. suffix in 1a-b) and by the concluding focus on some attribute of the Lord (word, light, life, peace).

    1a and 1b are parallel on the pattern: 3rd sing. masc. perf. verb (subj. the Lord) + noun ("physical" attribute of the "I") with 1st sing. suffix + ܒ + noun (attribute of the Lord) with 3rd sing. masc. suffix. The parallelism is strengthened by the word-pair ܟ̈ܬ̈ܠܗ - ܟܝܡܢܘ.

2a and 2b have a degree of parallelism by the initial pattern of 3rd sing. masc. perf. verb + prep./*nota dativi* with 1st sing. suffix and by the concluding focus on the noun (attribute of the Lord) + 3rd sing. masc. suffix.

With 3a there is a change of image to struggle, capturing and bringing back. 3a-b would be better placed with 4a because of the similarity of the motif of capture, especially since the root ܟܒܫ is repeated three times in 3b-4a. However, syntactically, the use of infinitives connects 3a-b with ܠܡܗ in 2b and, for this reason, 3a-b has been included as a second strophe for stanza 1.

3a and 3b are initially parallel on the pattern: infin. + noun obj. + qualifying expression. There is word-play in 3b on the root ܟܒܫ. The motifs of bringing back/return and capture/release of captives occur in 17:9-16; 22:4-10; 29:4-10; 42:10-20.

## Stanza 2 [4]

Stanza 2 is linked with stanza 1 by the repetition of the root ܟܒܫ (3b,4a). 4a-b comprises a report concerning action by/upon the "I" (capture and possession of the world). That this is a key action for the Ode is supported by the central position of the bicolon between stanzas 1 and 3, each of which consists of 6 lines.

4a and 4b are connected semantically, the possession of glory in 4b apparently resulting from the action in 4a. The latter has internal parallelism by the series of three 1st sing. perf. verbs. There is a degree of internal parallelism in 4b by the synonymity of the two concluding phrases ܟܢܝܬܗܝ and ܝܒܐ ܟܡܠܟܐ.

## Stanza 3 [5-6]

Stanza 3 is generally concerned with a description of the people who have been gathered together. The inclusio is formed by 5a and 6c with the repetition of ܟܢܠ.

5a functions as the introduction to the stanza, setting the focus for the detail which follows. It has internal parallelism by the 3rd pl. masc. verb forms from the polar word-pair ܟܠܝ - ܝܪܒ.

5b and 6a are connected by the cl. introduced by ܗ ܠܠܝܗܝ in 6a which refers to ܐܬܟܢܠܝܬܐܟ ܟܠ in 5b. 6a and 6b are linked semantically by the common motif of walking (ܟܬܣܩܠ in 6a and ܢܠܡ in 6b). The three verbs in 6a-b appear to form a series of logical actions: footprints are set down, the people walk (following the footprints; cf. 39:10-13) and are saved. 6b has internal parallelism by the double pattern of 3rd pl. masc. perf. verbs. The parallelism is strengthened by the word-pair ܗܠܟ - ܦܩܕ. ܟܢܫ may refer to both verbs.

6c functions as a concluding statement to the actions described for the gathered people in this stanza. It continues the general pattern of 3rd pl. masc. perf. verbs. The motifs of gathering/return, being saved, belonging, and, to some extent, walking (indirectly) are found also in 17:12-16; 33:5-13; 42:14-20.

## ODE 11 [Syriac]

1 ܐܬܓܙܪ ܠܒܝ
ܘܐܬܚܙܝ ܒܘܦܝܗ
ܘܢܒܬ ܒܗ ܛܝܒܘܬܐ
ܘܝܗܒ ܦܐܪܐ ܠܡܪܝܐ
2 ܡܪܝܡܐ ܓܝܪ ܓܙܪܢܝ ܒܪܘܚܗ ܩܕܝܫܐ
ܘܓܠܐ ܠܘܬܗ ܟܘ̈ܠܝܬܝ
ܘܡܠܢܝ ܡܢ ܚܘܒܗ
3 ܘܗܘܬ ܠܝ ܓܙܘܪܬܗ ܠܦܘܪܩܢܐ

ܘܪܗܛܬ {ܒܐܘܪܚܐ} ܒܫܠܡܗ ܒܐܘܪܚܐ ܕܫܪܪܐ
4 ܡܢ ܪܫܝܬܐ ܘܥܕܡܐ ܠܐܚܪܝܬܐ ܢܣܒܬ ܝܕܥܬܗ
5 ܘܐܫܬܪܪܬ ܥܠ ܫܘܥܐ ܕܫܪܪܐ
ܐܝܟܐ ܕܗܘ ܐܬܩܢܢܝ

6 ܘܡܝܐ ܡ̈ܡܠܠܐ ܩܪܒܘ ܠܣܦ̈ܘܬܝ
ܡܢ ܡܒܘܥܗ ܕܡܪܝܐ ܕܠܐ ܚܣܡ
7 ܘܐܫܬܝܬ ܘܪܘܝܬ
ܡܢ ܡܝܐ ܚܝܐ ܕܠܐ ܡܝܬܝܢ
8 ܘܪܘܝܘܬܝ ܠܐ ܗܘܬ ܕܠܐ ܝܕܥܬܐ

ܐܠܐ ܫܒܩܬ ܣܪ̈ܝܩܘܬܐ
9 ܘܐܬܦܢܝܬ ܠܘܬ ܡܪܝܐ ܐܠܗܝ
ܘܥܬܪܬ ܒܡܘܗܒܬܗ
10 ܘܫܒܩܬ ܠܫܛܝܘܬܐ ܫܕܝܐ ܥܠ ܐܪܥܐ
ܘܫܠܚܬܗ ܘܫܕܝܬܗ ܡܢܝ
11 ܘܡܪܝܐ ܚܕܬܢܝ ܒܠܒܘܫܗ
ܘܩܢܝ ܒܢܘܗܪܗ
12 ܘܡܢ ܠܥܠ ܐܢܝܚܢܝ ܕܠܐ ܚܒܠ

ܘܗܘܝܬ ܐܝܟ ܐܪܥܐ ܕܫܘܚܐ ܘܪܘܙܐ ܒܦܐܪ̈ܘܗܝ
13 ܘܡܪܝܐ ܐܝܟ ܫܡܫܐ ܥܠ ܐܦ̈ܘܗܝ ܕܐܪܥܐ
14 ܥܝ̈ܢܝ ܐܢܗܪ
ܘܦܪ̈ܨܘܦܝ ܩܒܠ ܛܠܐ
15 ܘܐܬܒܣܡܬ ܢܫܡܬܝ ܒܪܝܚܗ ܒܣܝܡܐ ܕܡܪܝܐ

16 ܘܐܘܒܠܢܝ ܠܦܪܕܝܣܗ
ܐܝܟܐ ܕܥܘܬܪܐ ܕܒܘܣܡܗ ܕܡܪܝܐ

17 ܘܣܓܕܬ ܠܡܪܝܐ ܡܛܠ ܬܫܒܘܚܬܗ
18 ܘܐܡܪܬ ܕܛܘܒܝܗܘܢ ܡܪܝܐ
ܠܐܝܠܝܢ ܕܢܨܝܒܝܢ ܒܐܪܥܟ
ܘܗܘܝܢ ܕܐܝܬ ܠܗܘܢ ܐܬܪܐ ܒܦܪܕܝܣܟ
19 ܘܪܒܝܢ ܒܡܪܒܝܬܐ ܕܐܝܠܢ̈ܝܟ
ܘܥܒܪܘ ܡܢ ܚܫܘܟܐ ܠܢܘܗܪܐ
20 ܗܐ ܟܠܗܘܢ ܦܠ̈ܚܝܟ ܫܦܝܪܝܢ
ܕܥܒܕܝܢ ܥܒ̈ܕܐ ܛܒ̈ܐ
21 ܘܗܦܟܝܢ ܡܢ ܒܝܫܘܬܐ ܠܒܣܝܡܘܬܐ ܕܝܠܟ
ܘܐܗܦܟܘ ܡܪܝܪܐ ܕܐܝܠܢ̈ܐ ܡܢܗܘܢ
ܟܕ ܕܐܬܢܨܒܘ ܒܐܪܥܟ ܕܝܠܟ
22 ܘܗܘܐ ܟܠܡܕܡ ܐܝܟ ܫܪܟܐ ܕܝܠܟ
ܘܕܘܟܪܢܐ ܕܠܥܠܡ ܕܥܒ̈ܕܝܟ ܡܗܝ̈ܡܢܐ
23 ܣܓܝ ܗܘ ܓܝܪ ܐܬܪܐ ܒܦܪܕܝܣܟ

ܘܠܝܬ ܒܗ ܡܕܡ ܕܒܛܝܠ
ܐܠܐ ܟܠܡܕܡ ܡܠܐ ܦܐܪܐ

24 ܫܘܒܚܐ ܠܟ ܐܠܗܐ ܒܘܣܡܐ ܕܦܪܕܝܣܐ ܕܠܥܠܡ

ܗܠܠܘܝܐ

---

1 My heart was circumcised,
and its flower appeared,
and grace budded in it,
and it bore fruits for the Lord.
2 For the Most High circumcised me by his Holy Spirit,
and exposed towards him my kidneys,
and filled me with his love.
3 And his circumcision was salvation for me.

And I ran {in the way} in his peace, in the way of truth;
4 from the beginning and until the end I received his knowledge.
5 And I was firmly set upon the rock of truth,
where he settled me.

6    And speaking water drew near to my lips
      from the spring of the Lord without jealousy.
7    And I drank and became intoxicated
      from the living immortal water.
8    And my intoxication was not without knowledge.

      But I abandoned vanities,
9    and turned back towards the Most High, my God,
      and was rich by his gift.
10   And I abandoned the folly cast upon the earth,
      and stripped it off and cast it from me.
11   And the Lord renewed me by his garment,
      and gained me by his light.
12   And from above he gave me rest without corruption.

      And I was like the earth which sprouts and exults by its fruits;
13   and the Lord like the sun upon the face of the earth.
14   My eyes he enlightened,
      and my face received dew,
15   and my breath delighted in the delightful fragrance of the Lord.

16   And he brought me to his paradise,
      where (are) the riches of the Lord's delight.

17   And I bowed down to the Lord because of his glory.
18   And I said, Blessed are they, Lord,
      those who are planted in your earth,
      and those who have a place in your paradise.
19   And they grow in the growth of your trees,
      and they have changed from darkness to light.
20   Behold, all your labourers (are) beautiful
      who work good works,
21   and turn away from wickedness to your kindness.
      And they turned the bitterness of the trees away from them
      when they were planted in your earth.
22   And everything was as your remnant,
      and an eternal remembrance of your faithful servants.
23   For great is the place in your paradise.

And there is nothing idle in it;
but everything is filled with fruits.

24  Glory to you, God, the eternal delight which (is) in paradise.

Alleluia.

---

## ODE 11 [Greek]

1  ΠΕΡΙΕΤΜΗΘΗ Η ΚΑΡΔΙΑ ΜΟΥ
ΚΑΙ ΕΦΑΝΗ ΤΟ ΑΝΘΟΣ ΑΥΤΗΣ
Η ΧΑΡΙΣ ΕΝ ΑΥΤΗ ΕΒΛΑΣΤΗΣΕΝ
[Κ]ΑΙ ΕΚΑΡΠΟΦΟΡΗΣΕΝ ΤΩ ΘΕΩ
2  Ο ΥΨΙΣΤΟΣ ΠΕΡΙΕΤΕΜΕΝ ΜΕ ΤΩ ΑΓΙΩ ΠΝΕΥΜΑΤΙ ΑΥΤΟΥ
ΚΑΙ ΕΓΥΜΝΩΣΕ ΠΡΟΣ ΑΥΤΟΝ ΤΟΥΣ ΝΕΦΡΟΥΣ ΜΟΥ
ΚΑΙ ΕΠΛΗΡΩΣΕΝ ΜΕ ΤΗΣ ΑΓΑΠΗΣ ΑΥΤΟΥ
3  ΕΓΕΝΕΤΟ ΜΟΙ ΕΙΣ ΣΩΤΗΡΙΑΝ Η ΠΕΡΙΤΟΜΗ ΑΥΤΟΥ

ΕΔΡΑΜΟΝ ΟΔΟΝ ΑΛΗΘΕΙΑΣ ΕΝ ΕΙΡΗΝΗ ΑΥΤΟ[Υ]
4  ΑΠ ΑΡΧΗΣ ΕΩΣ ΤΕΛΟΥΣ ΕΛΑΒΟΝ ΤΗΝ ΣΥΝΕΣΙΝ ΑΥΤΟΥ
5  ΕΣΤΗΡΙΧΘΗΝ ΑΠΟ [Σ]ΤΕΡΕΑΣ ΠΕΤΡΑΣ
ΟΠΟΥ ΜΕ ΣΥΓΚΕΚΑΘΙΚΕΝ

6  ΚΑΙ ΤΟ [Υ]ΔΩΡ ΤΟ ΛΑΛΟΥΝ ΗΓΓΙ[ΣΕ] ΠΡΟΣ ΤΑ ΧΕΙΛΗ ΜΟΥ
ΑΠΟ ΠΗΓΗΣ ΖΩΗΣ ΚΥΡΙΟΥ ΕΝ ΑΦΘΟΝΙΑ ΑΥΤΟΥ
7  ΕΠΙΟΝ ΚΑΙ ΕΜΕΘΥΣΘΗΝ ΥΔΩΡ ΤΟ ΑΘΑΝΑΤΟΝ
8  ΚΑΙ Η ΜΕΘΗ ΜΟΥ ΟΥΚ ΕΓΕΝΕΤΟ ΕΙΣ ΑΛΟΓΙΣΤΙΑΝ
ΑΛΛ ΕΞΕΤΡΑΠΗΝ ΤΩΝ ΜΑΤΑΙΩΝ   9  ΕΠΙ ΤΟΝ ΥΨΙΣΤΟΝ
ΘΕΟΝ ΜΟΥ
ΚΑΙ ΕΠΛΟΥΤΗΣΑ ΕΝ ΧΑΡΙΣΜΑΤΙ ΑΥΤΟΥ
10  ΑΦΗΚΑ ΤΗΝ ΑΦΡΟΣΥΝΗΝ ΧΑΜΑΙ ΚΕΙΜΕΝΗΝ
ΑΠΕΔΥΣΑΜΗΝ ΑΥΤΗΝ ΚΑΙ ΕΡΡΙΨΑ ΑΠ ΕΜΟΥ
11  Ο ΚΥΡΙΟΣ ΕΝΕΚΑΙΝΙΣΕΝ ΜΕ ΕΝ ΤΩ ΕΝΔΥΜΑΤΙ ΑΥΤΟΥ
ΚΑΙ ΑΝΕΚΤΗΣΑΤΟ ΜΕ ΤΩ ΦΩΤΙ ΑΥΤΟΥ
12  ΚΑΙ ΑΝΕΖΩΟΠΟΙΗΣΕΝ ΜΕ ΤΗ ΑΦΘΑΡΣΙΑ ΑΥΤΟΥ

ΕΓΕΝΟΜΗΝ ΩΣ Η ΓΗ ΘΑΛΛΟΥΣΑ ΚΑΙ ΓΕΛΩΣΑ ΤΟΙΣ ΚΑΡΠΟΙΣ
ΑΥΤΗΣ
13 [ΚΑ]Ι Ο ΚΥΡΙΟΣ ΜΟΙ ΕΓΕΝΕΤΟ ΩΣ Ο ΗΛΙΟΣ ΕΠΙ ΠΡΟΣΩΠΟΝ
ΤΗΣ ΓΗΣ
14 ΕΣΤΙΛΒΟΝ ΟΙ ΟΦΘΑΛΜΟΙ ΜΟΥ
ΚΑΙ ΕΔΡΟΣΙΣΘΗ ΤΟ ΠΡΟΣΩΠΟΝ ΜΟΥ
15 ΗΥΦΡΑΝΘΗ Η ΑΝΑΠΝΟΗ ΜΟΥ ΕΝ ΕΥΩΔΙΑ ΧΡΗΣΤΟΤΗΤΟΣ
ΚΥΡΙΟΥ

16 ΚΑΙ <Ε>ΠΗΓΑΓΕΝ ΜΕ ΕΙΣ ΠΑΡΑΔΕΙΣΟΝ ΑΥΤΟΥ
ΟΠΟΥ Ο ΠΛΟΥΤΟΣ ΤΗΣ [Τ]ΡΥΦΗΣ ΚΥΡΙΟΥ

ΕΘΕΑΣΑΜΗΝ ΔΕΝΔΡΑ ΩΡΑΙΑ ΚΑΙ ΚΑΡΠΟΦΟΡΑ
ΚΑΙ ΑΥΤΟΦΥΗΣ ΗΝ Ο ΣΤΕΦΑΝΟΣ ΑΥΤΩΝ
ΘΑΛΛΕΙ ΤΑ ΞΥΛΑ ΑΥΤΩΝ ΚΑΙ ΕΓΕΛΩΝ ΟΙ ΚΑΡΠΟΙ ΑΥΤΩΝ
ΑΠΟ ΑΘΑΝΑΤΟΥ ΓΗΣ ΑΙ ΡΙΖΑΙ ΑΥΤΩΝ
ΚΑΙ ΠΟΤΑΜΟΣ ΧΑΡΑΣ ΕΠΟΤΙΖΕΝ ΑΥΤΑΣ
ΚΑΙ ΚΥΚΛΩ ΤΗΣ ΓΗΣ ΖΩΗΣ ΑΙΩΝΙΑΣ ΑΥΤΩΝ

17 ΠΡΟΣΕΚΥΝΗΣΑ ΤΟΝ ΚΥΡΙΟΝ ΕΝΕΚΑ ΤΗΣ ΔΟΞΗΣ ΑΥΤΟΥ
18 Κ[ΑΙ] ΕΙΠΑ ΚΥΡΙΕ ΜΑΚΑΡΙΟΙ ΟΙ ΠΕΦΥΤΕΥΜ[Ε]ΝΟΙ ΕΠΙ ΤΗΣ
ΓΗΣ
ΟΙ ΕΧΟΝΤΕΣ ΤΟΠΟΝ ΕΝ ΤΩ ΠΑΡΑΔΕΙΣΩ ΣΟΥ
19 ΚΑΙ ΑΥΞΑΝΟΜΕΝΟΙ ΕΝ ΤΗ ΑΥΞΗΣΕΙ ΤΩΝ ΔΕΝΔΡΩΝ ΣΟΥ
ΜΕΤΑΒΛΗΘΕΝΤΕΣ ΑΠΟ ΣΚΟΤΟΥΣ ΕΙΣ ΤΟ ΦΩΣ
20 ΙΔΟΥ ΟΙ ΕΡΓΑΖΟΜΕΝΟΙ ΣΟΥ ΚΑΛΟΙ
ΜΕΤΑΒΟΛΑΣ ΠΟΙΟΥΣΙΝ ΑΓΑΘΑΣ
21 ΑΠΟ ΤΗΣ ΠΟΝΗΡΙΑΣ ΕΙΣ ΧΡΗΣΤΟΤΗΤΑ
ΜΕΤΑΛΛΑΣΣΕΤΑΙ ΤΟ ΠΙΚΡΟΝ ΤΩΝ ΦΥΤΩΝ ΕΝ ΤΗ ΓΗ ΣΟΥ
22 ΚΑΙ ΓΙΝΕΤΑΙ ΤΑ ΠΑΝΤΑ ΩΣ ΤΟ ΘΕΛΗΜΑ ΣΟΥ
ΕΥΛΟΓΗΜΕΝΟΙ ΟΙ <ΔΡΩΝΤΕΣ> ΤΩΝ ΥΔΑΤΩΝ ΣΟΥ
ΚΑΙ ΜΝΕΙΑΙ ΑΙΩΝΙΑΙ ΤΩΝ ΠΙΣΤΩΝ ΤΩΝ ΔΟΥΛΩΝ ΣΟΥ
23 ΠΟΛΥΣ Ο ΤΟΠΟΣ ΤΟΥ ΠΑΡΑΔΕΙΣΟΥ ΣΟΥ

ΚΑΙ ΑΡΓΕΙ ΟΥΔΕΝ
ΑΛΛΑ ΚΑΙ ΚΑΡΠΟΦΟΡΕΙ

24  ΔΟΞΑ ΣΟΙ ΤΩ ΘΕΩ ΠΑΡΑΔΕΙΣΩ ΣΟΥ ΤΡΥΦΗΣ ΑΙΩΝΙΑΣ

ΑΛΛΗΛΟΥΙΑ

---

1   My heart was circumcised,
    and its flower appeared.
    Grace budded in it,
    and it bore fruit for God.
2   The Most High circumcised me by his Holy Spirit,
    and exposed towards him my kidneys,
    and filled me with his love.
3   His circumcision was for me for salvation.

    I ran the way of truth, in his peace;
4   from the beginning until the end I received his understanding.
5   I was firmly set by solid rock,
    where he settled me down.

6   And the speaking water drew near towards my lips
    from the living spring of the Lord in his being without jealousy.
7   I drank, and was drunk - immortal water -
8   and my drunkenness was not into irrationality.

    But I turned aside from the vainities  9  to the Most High, my God,
    and was rich by his grace.
10  I let go the folly lying on the earth;
    I stripped it off and cast it from me.
11  The Lord renewed me by his garment,
    and regained me by his light,
12  and recalled me to life by his incorruption.

    I became like the earth, sprouting and laughing by its fruits;
13  and the Lord to me was like the sun upon the face of the earth.
14  My eyes shone,
    and my face was bedewed;
15  my breath was gladdened by the fragrance of the Lord's kindness.

16  And he brought me into his paradise,
    where (are) the riches of the Lord's luxury.

    I saw mature and fruitbearing trees.
    And their crown was natural;
    their timber sprouts,
    and their fruits were laughing.
    From immortal earth their roots,
    and a river of joy watered them,
    and round about the earth of their eternal life.

17  I bowed down before the Lord because of his glory.
18  And I said, Lord, blessed those planted upon the earth;
    those having a place in your paradise,
19  and growing in the growth of your trees,
    being changed from darkness into light.
20  Behold your beautiful labourers
    bring about good changes,
21  from wickedness to goodness.
    The bitterness of the plants in your earth is changed.
22  And everything was as your will -
    Praised be the servants of your waters -
    and eternal remembrances of your faithful servants.
23  The place of your paradise is great.

    And nothing is idle,
    but bears fruit.

24  Glory to you, God, to your paradise of eternal luxury.

    Alleluia.

NOTES TO THE TRANSLATION

1a: ܐܬܠܛܝ may also be translated as "was pruned" (Smith, R.P. 1: 699-700)
which would fit easily with the imagery of 1a-d. The play on words seems intended.

2b: ‚ܕܠܗܐ/ΤΟΥΣ ΝΕΦΡΟΥΣ ΜΟΥ = lit. "my kidneys", a ref. to the inner person, the place of emotion and affection.

3b: By comparison with the Greek text, it seems clear that the first ܪܝܘܪܐ in the Syriac text is a copyist's mistake.

5a: ܟܐܢܐ has connotations both of firmness/solidity and of truth (Smith, R.P. 2: 4303-4). The translation "rock of truth" is used on the basis of the parallelism with 3b. The translation does not indicate the word-play within 5a by the repetition of the root ܐܪ.

7: ΥΔΩΡ ΤΟ ΑΘΑΝΑΤΟΝ must be the dir. obj. of ΕΠΙΟΝ since there is no preceding word with which it could be in apposition.

9b: ܟܬܗܘܡܬܐ translates χαρίσματα in 1 Cor 1:7; cf. Smith, R.P. 1: 1567-8.

12a: Klijn (448) proposes emending ܗܢܝܢܐ to ܗܢܝܢ. Brock (1975, 143) suggests that if Syriac is the original, the Greek has not translated ܠܬܠ ܡܢ; if Greek is the original, then ܠܬܠ ܡܢ would correspond to ANA-. L. Abramowski (1984, 83) argues, on the other hand, that the Greek translator has rendered ܠܬܠ ܡܢ with ANA-. ἄνωθεν is the literal translation of ܠܬܠ ܡܢ and could mean "again" in later Greek; the rendering with ANA- shows that the Greek translator understood ܠܬܠ ܡܢ in this way.

15: ܒܣܝܡܐ has been rendered as "delightful" to indicate the word-play on the root ܒܣܡ. It has connotations also of sweetness and kindness (Smith, R.P. 1: 551), the latter being closer to the Greek for this line.

16c-i: These lines appear only in the Greek.

16f: Charlesworth (1977) proposes a Syriac Grundschrift (ܢܚܠ) to make sense of ΕΓΕΛΩΝ with ref. to fruits ("and their fruits were shining"); cf. similarly for shining/laughing trees, Apuleius Metamorphoses Bk XI, 7, 271:21, "germine foliorum renidentes"; Griffiths 78). He has failed to notice that 16e-f has the same word-pair, θάλλω - γελάω, as 12b, where the ref. is to the earth which sprouts and laughs. For the association of shining and exulting, cf. 40:4; 41:6-7.

20b: L. Abramowski (1984, 80-1) suggests the difference in the Syriac and Greek is explained by a change in the Syriac from ܟ̈ܝܒܠ to ܟ̈ܒܠ.

21b: *Contra* Lattke (1979-86, vol. 1) who has πηγῇ, Testuz's reading of TH ΓH (66) is correct (confirmed in a letter to the author by Dr. Hans Braun of the Bibliotheca Bodmeriana, 4.7.85).

22a: Philonenko argues for a Greek original on the basis that ܪܚܡܘ translates ΛΕΙΜΜΑ which has been corrupted to ΘΕΛΗΜΑ (264). L. Abramowski (1984, 81-2) suggests that ܪܚܡܘ should be emended to ܢܚܡܘ which may mean "gift" or "favour" (Smith, R.P. 2: 4154), the Greek translator having taken the meaning of "favour" and made it clearer by rendering it with ΘΕΛΗΜΑ.

22b (Greek): This line occurs only in the Greek. The Ms. has ΔΡΩΣΤΕΣ. The emendation of Lattke (1979-86, vol. 1), δρῶντες, has been followed here. Testuz suggests ΔΡΑΣΤΑΙ (66); Charlesworth (1977) has ΔΡΗΣΤΑΙ. The term has connotations also of those who serve in performing mystical rites (Liddel and Scott 449). My thanks to Dr. Lattke for pointing out the connection of chanting hymns with the mysteries (δρωμένοι) in Pausanias Description of Greece 9,30, 12 (4: 306).

ANALYSIS [Syriac]

Stanza 1 [1, 2, 3a]

The stanza comprises a double metaphor of spiritual pruning and circumcision (cf. Ferguson), the connection of the metaphors strengthened by the polysemy which occurs with the use of ܓܙܪ ("prune"/"circumcise"). ܓܙܪ is found only in stanza 1, in the first line of the two main strophes (1a, 2a) and in the concluding monocolon (3a). The repetition of the verb provides both the inclusio and the unifying element for the stanza.

1a-d comprises a series of actions in a logical sequence (circumcising/pruning, flowering, budding, fruit-bearing). Each line comprises a single action which refers to the heart of the "I" (ܠܒܝ in 1a; the masc. sing. suffixes in 1b and 1c; the subj. of the 3rd sing. masc. perf. verb in 1d).

1a and 1b are parallel on the pattern: 3rd sing. masc. Ethpeel perf. verb + noun subj. with pron. suffix. There is initial alliteration by the use of the Ethpeel form and the similarity of the first two consonants of the roots (ܓܠ ܚ).

The actions of budding and bearing fruit described for the heart of the "I" in 1c-d appear to indicate an image for the "I" (or his heart?) as a tree, thus providing a link with the latter section of the Ode and the description of those planted in paradise (18-23). The description of the "I" who produces fruits (ܦܐܪ̈ܐ ܥܒܕ) in/for the Lord is found also in 14:7.

2a-c is a parallel tricolon with a series of verbs in logical sequence (circumcision, exposure, filling), each of the three lines comprising a single action of the Most High. 2a and 2c are more strictly parallel on the pattern: 3rd sing. masc. Peal perf. verb (subj. the Most High) + 1st sing. dir. obj. + prep. with noun obj. (attribute of the Most High) + 3rd sing. masc. suffix. 2b follows the general pattern with a 3rd sing. masc. Peal perf. verb (subj. the Most High). The 1st sing. is indirectly the object of the verb by the use of the 1st sing. suffix with the noun obj. The latter section of the pattern of 2a and 2c is reversed in 2b by the inclusion of the prep. + 3rd sing. masc. suffix before the obj. which refers to the "I".

3a is a concluding confessional statement, referring to both strophes. The expression ܦܢܗ ܗܘܐ ܠ is found in 28:10; 35:2; 38:3.


Stanza 2 [3b-5]

The stanza focusses on the "I" with a description of two seemingly contrasting actions - running in the way of truth and being set firmly on the rock of truth. The motif of truth is the unifying element of the stanza (ܩܘܫܬܐ in 3b, 5a).

3b-5a follows a general pattern of 1st sing. perf. verbs. 3b and 4 are linked by the use of Peal perf. verbs and a focus on some aspect of the Most High (peace, knowledge) + 3rd masc. sing. suffix. 5a and 5b are connected by the cl. in 5b introduced by ܐܝܢܐ which refers to the rock of truth in 5a.

In contrast to the activity of the "I" in 3b, (running in the way of truth), the "I" in 5a-b is acted upon: the 1st sing. pass. verb in 5a and the 1st sing. pron. obj. in 5b. The actions of being firmly set and settled are semantically similar. There is internal parallelism in 5a by the repetition of the root ܫܪ.

4 is linked with 7:14 by the concept of the way towards knowledge combined with the expression ܡܢ ܒܪܝܫܝܬ ܠܝܕܥܬܐ.


Stanza 3 [6-8a]

The five lines of the stanza should be regarded as a unit. 6a-7b forms the major section, the limits indicated by the use of ܡܝ̈ܐ + qualifier in 6a and 7b. The action flows from 6a (waters drew near to the lips of the "I") to 7a (the "I" drinks and becomes intoxicated; cf. the contrasting image, 38:12-13; for intoxication as the result of ignorance, cf. The Teaching of Silvanus 94, 20-22 [Facs. ed. 7: 100; Wisse 1984b, 351]). 7a has internal parallelism by the double pattern of 1st sing. perf. verbs.

6b and 7b are parallel on the pattern: ܡ + noun obj. (with qualifying expression) + ܕܐ + part. The parallelism is strengthened by the semantic association of ܡܒܢܐ and ܡܪ. 7b has a degree of internal parallelism by the double qualification of ܡܪ with the word-pair ܚܝ - ܐ ܡܘܬ.

8a continues the pattern of 6b and 7b by the concluding descriptive expression introduced by ܕܐ. It functions as the concluding statement for the stanza, describing the outcome of the action (intoxication). Apart from this semantic connection, 7a and 8a are linked by the repetition of the root ܝܢܩ. The use of ܢܘܬܐ provides a link with 4.

## Stanza 4 [8b-9b, 10-12a]

8b-9b and 10-12a appear to be descriptions of the same movement of the "I" away from vanities/folly towards the Most High/Lord who subsequently acts upon the "I". The parallelism of the basic action described is strengthened especially in 8b and 10a: firstly, by the repetition of the root ܫܒܩ; secondly, by the initial parallelism of 1st sing. Peal perf. verb + noun dir. obj.

8b-9b comprises a logical series of three actions for the "I" (abandoning, turning back, being gifted; cf. 35:6). The lines are parallel to a degree with the key feature being an initial 1st sing. perf. verb. There is antithesis in 8b and 9a, both between the actions (abandoning and turning back towards) and between the characters/elements (vanities and the Most High). 9a and 9b are more closely parallel by the 1st sing. perf. verb + prep. + obj. (ref. to the Lord).

10a and 10b are initially parallel on the pattern: 1st sing. perf. verb/s + ܬܐܢܘܫ/equivalent pron. suffix. The parallelism is strengthened by the semantic similarity of ܫܒܩ and ܫܠܚ and by the repetition of the root ܠܒܫ. 10b has internal parallelism by the double pattern of 1st sing. Pael perf. verbs with fem. sing. suffix (ref. to folly). The verbs follow a logical order (stripping off then casting away).

11a-12a is linked with 10a-b by the polar word-pair ܫܠܚ - ܠܒܫ, by which the metaphor of dressing is continued into 11a. The tricolon comprises the detail of the action of the Lord towards the "I" and there is some parallelism between the lines by the 3rd sing. masc. perf. verbs with 1st sing. suffixes. 11a and 11b are more closely parallel on the pattern: 3rd sing. masc. perf. verb + 1st sing. suffix + ܒ with noun obj. (attribute of the Lord) + masc. sing. suffix.

There is some connection between this stanza and 15:6-8 by a similar semantic content (abandoning of vanities/error, turning back to the Lord, motifs of stripping off and putting on, gifts from the Lord) and by vocabulary - ܫܒܩ in 8b, 10a and 15:6; ܡܗܝܡܢܘܬܗ in 9b and 15:7; the roots ܠܒ - ܫܠܚ in 10b, 11a, and 15:8.

Stanza 5 [12b-13, 14-15]

The stanza commences with a double simile (12b-13). There is initial parallelism on a general pattern of subj. + ܐܝܟ + noun obj. with qualifying expression. The parallelism is strengthened by the word-pair ܐܝܪܐ - ܫܡܫܐ, and the repetition of ܐܝܪܐ. The strophe witnesses to the mixture of metaphors in this Ode. One would have expected perhaps ܐܝܠܢ rather than ܐܝܪܐ for the "I" in 12b, given the opening imagery in 1a-d.

14-15a comprises details of action upon some physical aspect of the "I". There are a number of syntactic connections possible between the three lines. 14a and 14b have a degree of parallelism initially on the pattern: noun subj./ obj. (physical attribute of the "I") with 1st sing. suffix + 3rd sing. masc. perf. verb. In each case the "I" is passive - in 14a, since the Lord is the subj. of the verb; in 14b, by the meaning of the verb. 14b and 15a are also parallel initially with chiasmus: A B // B' A', where A = noun subj. (physical attribute of the "I") with 1st sing. suffix; B = 3rd perf. verb. 15a has internal parallelism by the play on the root ܒܣܡ.

Stanzas 6-9

Stanzas 6-9 comprise a section devoted to the report of what the "I" sees and says to the Lord concerning the paradise to which he is taken. 16a-b and 24 form an inclusio for the entire section by the repetitions of the associated terms, ܒܦܪܕܝܣܐ and ܦܐܪܘܗܝ.

Stanza 6 [16]

Stanza 6 is linked with stanza 5 by the repetition of the root ܒܣܡ. It functions as an introduction to the entire section dealing with the Lord's paradise. 16b is connected with 16a by the cl. introduced by ܐܝܟ which refers to ܦܐܪܘܗܝ.

Stanza 7 [17, 18-23a]

17 functions as the introduction to the major section of 18-23a, setting the "I" in relation to the Lord whom he addresses. The action of worship finds an echo later in the Ode with the praise of God (repetition of the root ܫܒܚ) in 24. With 17, there is a shift from the passive role of the "I" in 11-16 to an active role. 17 and 18a are initially parallel with 1st sing. Peal perf. verbs.

With 18a there is a shift from reporting about the Lord in the 3rd person to an address to the Lord in the 2nd person. The major section of the stanza (18-23a) comprises a description of those planted in the Lord's paradise. The inclusio for the section is formed between 18b-c and 21c with 23a - in 18b and 21c, by the use of the root ܢܨܒ (ref. to the same 3rd pl. group) + ܒܟܐܪܥܐ/ܒܟܐܪܥܟ ܕܝܠܟ; in 18c and 23a, by the repetition of ܐܝܕܐ ܒܦܪܕܝܣܟ.

Within this major section, the beatitude in 18a-c serves to introduce the group who will be described in detail in 19-21b. 18b and 18c refer to the 3rd pl. masc. suffix in 18a. The two lines are parallel on the pattern: 3rd pl. masc. demonstrative pron. + ܕ + verbal expression (ref. to the 3rd pl. masc. group) ... ܒ + noun (ref. to a "place" of the Lord) with 2nd sing. masc. suffix. The parallelism is strengthened by the word-pair ܐܪܥܐ - ܦܪܕܝܣܐ.

19a-b and 21a-b are parallel bicola with an inverted pattern: A B B' A'. 19a and 21b are connected by the repetition of ܐܬܚܠܦ. 19b and 21a are parallel on the pattern: 3rd pl. masc. verb + ܡܢ + noun + ܠ + noun. The parallelism is strengthened by the semantic similarity of the verbs ("change", "turn away") and by the relationship of the two nouns in each line (in 19b in the polar word-pair ܚܫܘܟܐ - ܢܘܗܪܐ, in 21a by the semantic opposites ܡܪܝܪܘܬܐ - ܚܠܝܘܬܐ).

19a and 19b describe the action of those planted with initial 3rd pl. masc. verbs. 19a has a word-play by the doubling of the root ܚܝܐ. The latter is used of the action of grace in the heart of the "I" in 1c.

20a-b is an insertion into the parallel bicola, 19a-b and 21a-b. The bicolon presents two parallel positive descriptions (beautiful, working good works) concerning the labourers in the Lord's paradise. There is a word-play in 20b (cf. 19a) by the repetition of the root ܥܒܕ.

21a and 21b continue the detail in 19a-b concerning those planted. The bicolon is parallel by the use of the 3rd pl. masc. verbs with the root ܗܦܟ followed by ܡܢ. Both lines focus on turning from some negative element (wickedness, bitterness).

21c follows easily from 21a-b by the cl. introduced by ܕ which appears to refer to ܐܢܘܢ in 21b. 21c must be connected with 23a by the formation of the inclusio noted above with 18b-c. The same concluding parallel word-pair, ܪܚܝܩ - ܩܘܪܒܐ, is used for 21c and 23a as for 18b-c.

22a-b is an insertion into the bicolon formed by 21c and 23a. The lines are parallel, both ܪܚܝܩ and ܪܚܝܩܢ referring to the common subj. ܒܠܬܗ. The relationship of 22a-b to its context is not clear.

## Stanza 8 [23b-c]

23b-c is a formula used also in 4:4 with ref. to the Lord. The link between the bicolon and the previous stanza is effected by ܒܗ which refers to ܦܪܕܝܣܐ. 23b and 23c are parallel by the use of ܠܟ...ܒܢ ܬܗ (23b) and ܟܠܬܗ ܒܢ ܬܗ (23c), and by the antithetical concepts of idleness and being filled with/bearing fruits. There may be some connection between paradise (better still, the trees of paradise?) which is filled with fruits and the "I" who bears fruits for the Lord (1d) and is filled with his love (2c).

## Stanza 9 [24]

24 functions as the concluding doxology. It is connected with both 16 and 17 as noted above.

## ANALYSIS [Greek]

The major difference between the Greek and Syriac versions is the inclusion of 16c-i and 22b in the Greek for which there is no equivalent in the Syriac. There are other minor differences which in some cases affect the analysis of the poetical structure.

## Stanza 1 [1, 2, 3a]

There is no basic difference between the Greek and Syriac texts. The verb περιτέμνω fulfils the same function as ܓܙܪ

## Stanza 2 [3b-5]

The use of ΣΤΕΡΕΑΣ rather than ΑΛΗΘΕΙΑΣ in 5a means that the focus in the Syriac on the motif of truth does not occur in the Greek. The versatility of ܫܘܥܐ ܕܩܘܫܬܐ ("rock of truth"/"solid rock") cannot be duplicated in the Greek, although the word-play within 5a remains with the use of ΕΣΤΗΡΙΧΘΗΝ and ΣΤΕΡΕΑΣ.

Stanza 3 [6-8a]

The differences between the Mss. are relatively minor. ΖΩΗΣ is applied to the spring in 6b, whereas ܟܘ is associated with the water in 7b of the Syriac. The different placement of ΖΩΗΣ provides a connection between 6b (ΠΗΓΗ ΖΩΗΣ) and 7 (ΥΔΩΡ ΤΟ ΑΘΑΝΑΤΟΝ) which the Syriac does not have. 7 would require ΑΠΟ ΥΔΑΤΟΣ ΤΟΥ ΑΘΑΝΑΤΟΥ to maintain the parallelism of 6b and 7b in the Syriac.

Stanza 4 [8b/9a-9b, 10-12a]

The Greek text follows the basic pattern as in the Syriac. Where Syr. 9a contains a cl., the Greek has a simple phrase and syntactically seems to demand being placed together with 8b as one line (8b/9a). The parallelism of Syr 8b and 10a by the repetition of ܫܒܘܚ is not found in the Greek.

11-12a in the Greek is much more strictly parallel than in the Syriac with the pattern: 3rd sing. masc. aorist verb + ΜΕ + noun in the instrumental dat. (attribute of the Lord) + ΑΥΤΟΥ.

Stanza 5 [12b-13, 14-15]

There is little difference between the Syriac and Greek versions. The second strophe is more exactly parallel in the Greek on the pattern: 3rd person verb + noun subj. (physical attribute of the "I") + ΜΟΥ.

The Greek tends to support even more strongly the suggestion that the image for the Odist here would have been more aptly a tree rather than the earth, especially when the two verbs of 12b, (θάλλω, γελάω) are found in ref. to the trees of paradise in 16e-f.

Stanza 6 [16a-b]

As with the Syriac text, 16a-b forms an inclusio with 24 by the repetition of the associated words ΠΑΡΑΔΕΙΣΟΝ and ΤΡΥΦΗ, and 16a-b functions as the introduction to the entire section devoted to the Lord's paradise.

Stanza 7 [16c-f, 16g-i]

16c-i is not found in the Syriac text. The stanza comprises a description of the trees in the Lord's paradise. With 16c there is a subtle change in the action from the "I" as the object of action by the Lord (11a-16b) to the "I" as subject of the action.

The inclusio for the first strophe (16c-f) is indicated by ΚΑΡΠΟΦΟΡΑ (16c; cf. 23c) and ΚΑΡΠΟΙ (16f). 16c functions as the introductory statement which is followed by a detailed description of the trees. 16d-f is parallel on the pattern: verbal expression + noun subj. (attribute of the trees) + ΑΥΤΩΝ.

16g-i comprises a description of the external circumstances of the trees, focussing on the two complementary components of the immortal earth and the river of joy. The inclusio for the strophe is indicated by ΑΠΟ ΑΘΑΝΑΤΟΥ ΓΗΣ (16g) and ΤΗΣ ΓΗΣ ΖΩΗΣ ΑΙΩΝΙΑΣ ΑΥΤΩΝ in 16i.

There are connections between the second strophe and stanza 3 - ΑΠΟ ΠΗΓΗ ΖΩΗΣ (6b) and ΤΗΣ ΓΗΣ ΖΩΗΣ (16i); ΥΔΩΡ ΤΟ ΑΘΑΝΑΤΟΝ (7) and ΑΠΟ ΑΘΑΝΑΤΟΥ ΓΗΣ (16g).


Stanza 8 [17, 18-23a]

The structure of the Greek for 18a-23a is not as clear as in the Syriac. In the inclusio between 18a-b and 21b with 23a, 18a has ΟΙ ΠΕΦΥΤΕΥΜΕΝΟΙ ΕΠΙ ΤΗΣ ΓΗΣ and 21b has (ΤΟ ΠΙΚΡΟΝ) ΤΩΝ ΦΥΤΩΝ ΕΝ ΤΗ ΓΗ ΣΟΥ. The Syriac is more explicit in the ref. of the latter to those planted in the Lord's earth. 18b and 23a are closer to the Syriac - (ΕΧΟΝΤΕΣ) ΤΟΠΟΝ ΕΝ ΤΩ ΠΑΡΑΔΕΙΣΩ ΣΟΥ (18b), and Ο ΤΟΠΟΣ ΤΟΥ ΠΑΡΑΔΕΙΣΟΥ ΣΟΥ (23a).

The pattern of the beatitude in 18a-b continues into 19a-b with the 3rd pl. masc. nom. participles (ref. to those planted). 18-19a is more closely related on the pattern: 3rd pl. masc. nom. part. + ΕΠΙ/ΕΝ + article + noun. The parallelism strengthened by the association of earth, paradise and trees.

19b and 21a are parallel on the pattern: ΑΠΟ + noun + ΕΙΣ + noun, the nouns in each case forming an antithesis. The connection of 19a and 21b in the Syriac is not found in the Greek, since the latter uses ΔΕΝΔΡΩΝ (19a) and ΦΥΤΩΝ (21b).

21a is included with 18a-19b, with 20a-b as an insertion into the parallel bicolon formed by 19b and 21a, as in the Syriac. The link between 20a-b and its context is indicated by ΜΕΤΑΒΛΗΘΕΝΤΕΣ (19b) and ΜΕΤΑΒΟΛΑΣ (20b).

21b and 23a, which form the inclusio with 18a-b, are more closely connected in the Greek than the Syriac on the pattern: qualifying verbal/adj. expression + noun subj. + gen. article with noun ... ΣΟΥ (ref. to the Lord).

As in the Syriac, 22a and 22c (= 22b in the Syriac) function as an insertion into the bicolon formed by 21b and 23a. The structure is made more complex by the further insertion of the eulogy 22b (does not occur in the Syriac) into the bicolon formed by 22a and 22c.

A common feature in the section 21b-23a is the final focus in each line upon some attribute of the Lord (earth, will, waters, servants, paradise) + ΣΟΥ.

Stanza 9 [23b-c]

The same basic formula occurs as in the Syriac. There is a connection with 16c by the repetition of the verb καρποφορέω.

Stanza 10 [24]

24 functions as the concluding doxology as in the Syriac.

# ODE 12

1 ܡܠܢܝ ‹ܦܬܓܡܐ› ܕܫܪܪܐ
ܡܛܠ ܕܐܡܠܠ ܠܗ
2 ܘܐܝܟ ܪܕܝܐ ܕܡ̈ܝܐ
ܪܕܝܐ ܫܪܪܐ ܡܢ ܦܘܡܝ
ܘܣܦܘ̈ܬܝ ܚܘܝ ܦܐܖ̈ܘܗܝ
3 ܘܐܣܓܝ ܒܝ ܝܕܥܬܗ
ܡܛܠ ܕܦܘܡܗ ܕܡܪܝܐ ܦܬܓܡܐ ܗܘ ܫܪܝܪܐ
ܘܬܪܥܐ ܕܢܘܗܪܗ

4 ܘܝܗܒܗ ܡܪܝܡܐ ܠܥܠ̈ܡܘܗܝ
ܡܬܪ̈ܓܡܢܐ ܕܐܝܘܬܐ ܕܝܠܗ
ܘܡܬܢ̈ܝܢܐ ܕܬܫܒܘܚܬܗ
ܘܡܘܕ̈ܝܢܐ ܕܡܚܫܒܬܗ
ܘܡܟܣ̈ܝܢܐ ܕܬܪܥܝܬܗ
ܘܡܒܩ̈ܢܐ ܕܥܒ̈ܕܘܗܝ

5 ܩܠܝܠܘܬܗ ܓܝܪ ܕܦܬܓܡܐ ܠܐ ܬܘܚܐ ܐܝܬܝܗ̇
ܘܐܝܟ ܬܘܚܗ ܗܟܢܐ ܐܦ ܩܠܝܠܘܬܗ ܘܚܪ̈ܝܦܘܬܗ
ܘܠܐ ܣܟܐ ܐܝܬܝܗ̇ ܠܗܠܟܬܗ
6 ܘܠܐ ܡܬܬܘܒ ܢܦܠ
ܐܠܐ ܡܩܝܡ ܗܘ ܩܐܡ
ܘܠܐ <ܝܕܥ> ܡܚܝܬܗ ܐܦܠܐ ܐܘܪܚܗ
7 ܐܝܟ ܥܒܕܗ ܓܝܪ ܗܟܢܐ ܣܘܟܗ
ܢܘܗܪܐ ܓܝܪ ܘܕܢܚܗ̇ ܕܡܚܫܒܬܐ ܐܝܬܘܗܝ

8 ܘܥܠ̈ܡܐ ܒܗ ܡܡܠܠܘ ܚܕ ܠܚܕ
ܘܗܘܘ ܒܡܠܬܐ
ܗܢܘܢ ܕܫܬܝܩܝܢ ܗܘܘ
9 ܘܡܢܗ ܗܘܬ ܪ̇ܚܡܘܬܐ ܘܫܘܝܘܬܐ
ܘܡܠܠܘ ܚܕ ܠܘܬ ܚܕ ܡܕܡ ܕܐܝܬ ܗܘܐ ܠܗܘܢ
10 ܘܐܙܕܩܬܘ ܡܢ ܦܬܓܡܐ
ܘܝܕܥܘ ܠܗܘ ܕܥܒܕ ܐܢܘܢ
ܒܕ ܗܘܘ ܒܫܘܝܘܬܐ
11 ܡܛܠ ܕܡܠܠ ܠܗܘܢ ܦܘܡܗ ܕܡܪܝܡܐ
ܘܪܗܛܬ ܒܐܝܕܗ ܡܦܩܢܘܬܗ

ܗܘ ܐܝܟ ܒܪ ܦܘܚܠܐ ܓܠ ܡܫܒ̈ܚ 12
ܗܘ ܫܘܝ ܒܝܫܪ

ܘܠܡܘܗܒ ܐܝܬ ܗܘ ܡܢ ܐܠܗܐ ܗܘܐ ܐܫܬܘܕܝ ܠܟ ܗܒ̈ܝܢ 13
ܘܥܠ ܠܒ̈ܝ ܠܒܝܫܪ

ܗܠܠܘ

---

1 The Word of truth filled me,
in order that I might speak him.
2 And like the flow of waters,
flows truth from my mouth.
And my lips manifest his fruits,
3 and he increased in me his knowledge.
Because the mouth of the Lord is the true Word,
and the gate of his light.

4 And the Most High gave him to his aeons;
the interpreters of his beauty,
and the narrators of his glory,
and the confessors of his thought,
and the messengers of his mind,
and the purifiers of his works.

5 For the rapidity of the Word is without narration,
and as his narration, so also his rapidity and his swiftness.
And his path is limitless.
6 And he never falls,
but stands firm.
And not known (is) his descent nor his way.
7 For as his work, so his expectation;
for the light and dawning of thought is he.

8    And the aeons spoke to each other by him.
     And they were by the Word,
     those who were silent.
9    And from him were friendship and harmony,
     and they spoke to each other what was theirs.
10   And they were urged on by the Word.
     And they knew him who made them,
     because they were in harmony;
11   because the mouth of the Most High spoke to them,
     and his exposition ran by means of him.

12   For the tent of the Word is man,
     and his truth is love.

13   Blessed are they who by means of this have recognised everything,
     and have known the Lord by his truth.

     Alleluia.

NOTES TO THE TRANSLATION

1-12: In each case that a 3rd sing. masc. subj./pron. suffix has been used in relation to ܦܬܓܡܐ, it has been translated in the English by the masculine rather
than the neuter, since personification appears to be intended (cf. the excursus
on the Word following the analysis of Ode 12).

1a: Newbold (185) suggests the sing. ܦܬܓܡܐ as the subj. of ܡܠܝ. The pl.
ܦܬܓܡܐ appears to be a copyist's error. This is the only occurence of the pl.
form in this Ode which focusses so strongly on the Word of truth (cf. 8:8).
Other translations in general presume that ܡܢ is to be understood before
ܦܬܓܡܐ (e.g. "he filled me with words of truth"). However, one finds ܡܢ explicitly in such a construction in 11:2 (ܡܠܝܢܝ ܡܢ ܫܘܒܚܗ).

4f: For ܡܩܕܫ, Brockelmann gives "pudicum faciens" and "sanctificans (s. ob-
servans?)" (1966, 430), the latter specifically in relation to this verse. R.P.
Smith has "castigator" (2: 2378). The variety of meanings is found in the translations.

5a-b: The use of the 3rd sing. fem. suffixes with ref. to ⟨ܣܪ̈ܒܬܗ⟩ is an error by the copyist of the Ms.

Those who translate ⟨ܡܛܠܘܠܘ⟩ differently in 5a and 5b ("subtlety"/"swift-ness", Charlesworth 1977; "Schnelligkeit"/"fein", Greßmann 1924) do not appear to be aware of the structure of the bicolon.

5a: The majority of the translations render ⟨ܪܓܘܫ⟩ ⟨ܠܐ⟩ by an adj. ("inexpress-ible", "indescribable").

5b: ⟨ܬܢܦܝܘ⟩ also has connotations of sharpness/acuteness (Brockelmann 1966, 258; Smith, R.P. 1: 1381).

6c: Charlesworth's contention that H reads as ⟨ܠܝ⟩ with a point above the ⟨ܝ⟩ is erroneous (1977, 63 n. 10). The Ms. clearly has ⟨ܠܝ⟩ with the point above the ⟨ܝ⟩ signifying the masc. sing. Peal part. act.

The parallelism of 5c and 6c indicates that ⟨ܠܝ⟩ ⟨ܠܐ⟩ should be emended to ⟨ܠܐ⟩ ⟨ܠܝ⟩, as Harris and Mingana (vol. 2) suggest. If it is not a copyist's error, the reading in H could be explained by ἄγνωστος having been translated erroneously into the Syriac with an act. rather than a pass. meaning (Lewis and Short 12).

8b: The sense of this line is that the aeons came into being by the Word, a concept supported by 10b. Harris and Mingana (vol. 2) interpret ⟨ܒܡܠܬܗ⟩ ⟨ܗܘܐ⟩ as "to acquire speech" and declare it to be the only meaning that the Syriac sentence can have. The same expression used in relation to ⟨ܠܥܠ̈ܡܐ⟩ in 16:19 is given by them as "And the Worlds were made by His Word". Greßmann (1924), Charlesworth (1977), Emerton, and Carmignac (1986) follow Harris and Mingana in both cases.

9a: Although ⟨ܗܘܬ⟩ is a sing. verb, the English translation requires a pl. verb to follow the two fem. sing. nouns that form the subj.

ANALYSIS

Stanza 1 [1-3]

Stanza 1 functions as an introduction for the Ode, giving some detail concerning the inspiration of the "I" who speaks with truth and knowledge. The use of the 1st sing. person is limited to this stanza. Three of the key words/roots for this Ode are introduced - ܦܬܓܡܐ (x 5), ܫܪܪܐ (x 5), and ܝܕܥ (x 5). The inclusio for the stanza is formed by the association of ܦܬܓܡܐ and ܫܪܪܐ/ܫܪܝܪܐ in the first and final bicola (1a-b, 3b-c).

1a and 1b are parallel with chiasmus. 1a has a 3rd sing. masc. perf. verb (subj. ܦܬܓܡܐ) + 1st sing. pron. dir. obj.; 1b has a 1st sing. perf. verb + 3rd sing. masc. pron. dir. obj. (ref. to ܦܬܓܡܐ). There is alliteration with ܡ and ܠ in 1b.

2a-b is a simile with parallelism in a terrace pattern by the repetition of the part. form of ܪܕܐ and the noun to which the action refers at the conclusion of 2a and the beginning of 2b. The second bicolon is linked with the first by the repetition of ܫܪܪܐ.

2c-3a flows easily from the preceding bicolon by the logical progression of the action from mouth to lips (cf. the word-pair ܦܘܡܐ - ܣܦܘ̈ܬܐ). 2c and 3a are parallel to a degree by a similar focus on action performed by/upon the "I" with relation to some attribute of the Lord. The latter, with a 3rd sing. masc. suffix, has the final position in each line (ܦܐܪ̈ܘܗܝ, 2c; ܝܕܥܬܗ, 3a).

Although 3b comprises a cl. introduced by ܡܛܠ ܕ, there does not appear to be thereby a strong relation semantically between 3b-c and the preceding bicolon (but cf. the word-pair ܝܕܥܬܐ - ܫܪܝܪܐ...ܦܬܓܡܐ, 3a, 3b). 3b-c functions as a concluding confessional statement which refers to the true Word (the focus of the bicolon is actually the mouth of the Lord), thus providing a recapitulation of 1a. 3b and 3c are parallel with ellipsis, ܫܪܝܪܐ ܦܬܓܡܐ and ܬܪܥܐ ܕܢܘܗܪܗ each being a compl. of the subj. ܦܘܡܗ ܕܡܪܝܐ.

Stanza 2 [4]

The stanza is strictly structured, comprising for the most part a list of titles/offices with ref. to the aeons. 4a is an introductory monocolon, the initial nouns in 4b-f being in apposition with ܟ̈ܠܗܘܢ in 4a.

4b-f is parallel on the pattern: 3rd masc. pl. noun (ref. to the aeons) + ܕ + noun (attribute of the Most High/Word) with 3rd sing. masc. suffix (ܕܠܗ in 4b). The lines are connected by the word-pairs ܬܫܒܘܚܬܐ - ܐܘܕܝܬܐ (4b, 4c) and ܡ̈ܠܐ - ܡܫܡܫܢܘܬܐ (4d, 4f; cf. also 7a, 7b), and by the semantic closeness of ܡܫܡܫܢܘܬܗ (4d) and ܬܪܥܝܬܗ (4e). A certain degree of assonance occurs initially in each line since the nouns are constructed from part. forms.

Stanza 3 [5-7]

The stanza provides a detailed description of the Word. The structure of the strophes is chiastic: A B C B' A'.

5a-b (A) and 7a-b (A') are parallel with the pattern of 5a-b reversed in 7a-b. Thus 5a and 7b are parallel on the general pattern: noun subj./compl. + ܐ̣ܝܕ + ... ܐܝܬ with pron. suffix. Both lines focus on some attribute of the Word. 5b and 7a are parallel on the pattern: ܐܝܟ + noun (attribute of the Word) with 3rd masc. sing. suffix + ܘܗܒܝ + noun/s (attribute/s of the Word) with 3rd masc. sing. suffix. Each line has internal parallelism by the double pattern of ܘܗܒܝ/ܐܝܟ + noun + suffix.

5a and 5b are parallel with chiasmus by the placement of ܘܠܠܘܗܕ and ܬܘܢܪ. ܝܘ̣ܝ and ܘܠܠܝ (5b) are found associated in 39:4.

The combination of the elements of expectation and the light/dawning of thought in relation to the Word in 7a-b suggests some link with the Lord as the sun (cf. esp. in 15:1 where the aspect of expectation also occurs). There is a connection between 7a-b and 3b-c by the use of ܘܡܗܝܪ in association with the Word.

5c (B) and 6c (B') are parallel on the pattern: negative adj. expression ... subj. noun/s (ref. to the movement of the Word) with 3rd sing. masc. suffix. The parallelism is strengthened by the semantic closeness of ܡܗܠܘܬܗ and ܪܗܘܛܝܗ.

The bicolon 6a-b (C) is inserted into the parallel bicolon 5c and 6c, and functions as the central focus of the stanza. 6a and 6b are parallel on the general pattern of negative element + masc. sing. part. act. (ref. to the Word). The parallelism is strengthened by the polar word-pair ܢܦܠ - ܩܐܡ. The infin. absolute in 6b emphasises the contrasting action of standing over against falling (cf. Nöldeke § 295).

Stanza 4 [8-11]

The stanza presents a rather complex structure: A B C (with A' inserted) B' A". The three occurrences of the key root ܝܠܕ link 8a (A), 9b (A') and 11a (A") as the first, central and final lines of the stanza. 8a and 9b are more closely linked by the use of ܝܘ ܠܘܬܗ/ܠܘܬܝ ܝܘ with ܡܠܬܗ.

The bicola 8b-c (B) and 10b-c (B') are semantically parallel by the common motif of generation in relation to the aeons. 8b-c is similar both semantically and in form to 8:4. 8b and 10c are parallel on the pattern: ܗܘܐ + ܒ + noun. ܡܠܬܐ occurs only in 8b in this Ode in what appears to be a formula (cf.

16:19). Otherwise ܦܬܓܡܐ functions as the *terminus technicus*. 10c is linked with 9a by the repetition of ܚܘܫܒܐ.

9a and 10a (C) are parallel to a degree with chiasmus: A B // B' A', where A = ܡܢ + ܦܬܓܡܐ/equivalent pron. suffix; B = some attribute or action of the aeons which has its source in the Word.

11b seems to have no clear connection with its context except for the ܘ which links it with the preceding line.

Stanza 5 [12]

Stanza 5 introduces a new image for the Word as well as a shift in focus from the aeons to the human. 12a and 12b are parallel on the pattern: noun subj. (attribute of the Word) + gen. expression (ref. to the Word) + noun compl. + ܗܘ (copula). The stanza reiterates motifs of stanza 1 in the association of ܦܬܓܡܐ and ܝܕܥ, which also indicates the inclusio between 12a-b and 1a for the Ode proper (1-12).

Stanza 6 [13]

13a-b is the concluding beatitude. The bicolon is parallel, both cls. with the verb ܝܕܥ referring to those who are blessed. The parallelism may be intended to express merismus - recognising everything and knowing the Lord is the sum of knowledge possible for the blessed ones (cf. the concluding motif of recognition in 6:18). The repetition of ܝܕܥ provides the link with the Ode proper.

---

EXCURSUS: "WORD" IN THE ODES

Two Syriac terms may be translated by "word": ܦܬܓܡܐ (Smith, R.P. 2: 3335-6) and ܡܠܬܐ (2: 2110-2). Both terms may be used to translate λόγος and ῥῆμα.

Of the twelve occurences of ܡܠܬܐ in the Odes, seven are found within a phrase introduced by ܒ ("by his Word" [10:1; 16:19; 29:9,10; 39:9]; "by the Word" [12:8]; "by my Word" [15:9]). In general it can be said that ܡܠܬܐ is used in the sense of an agent, in parallel with other attributes of the Lord (his light [10:1], the thought of his heart [16:19], his power [29:9]). As well, 16:7-8 presents the Word of the Lord in parallel with his mercy and his thought. Activity associated with the agency of the Word includes inspiring speech (10:1), creation (12:8; 16:19), the destruction of Sheol (15:9), making war and destruction of an enemy (29:9,10), and bridging rivers (39:9).

ܦܬܓܡܐ is associated with truth ("Word of truth" [8:8]) and with knowledge ("Word of knowledge" [7:7]) and also occurs in parallel with knowledge (8:8), the desires and thought of the Lord (9:3) and his perfection (18:4-5). It is linked more generally with truth in 24:9-10 and 32:2, and with light in 32:1-2. It is spoken (24:9; 42:14), is heard (8:8), is with/in others (18:4; 32:2), and comes to give rest (= "the fruits of my labours", 37:3).

For the understanding of the use of both terms, Odes 12 and 41 are the most important sources. The former focusses on the Word (ܦܬܓܡܐ except for one occurrence of ܡܠܬܐ in the formula saying in 8b), giving an extensive description both of attribute and action. There is the association of the Word with truth (1-2), knowledge and light (3), and the relationship with the aeons (4). This is followed by a description of attributes of the word: indescribable rapidity, swiftness, having a limitless path and so on (5-6). The Word makes thought and speech possible, leading to friendship and harmony (7-10), dwells in humankind and brings love (12). There is surely a flavour here of the Sophia myth in Prov 8 and Wis 7 and 8.

Ode 41:11-16a comprises a listing of titles and actions associated with the Word (ܡܠܬܐ): he is with the community on their way; he is the saviour who gives life; he is the man who was humbled and lifted up by his own righteousness; he is the Son of the Most High; light comes from him; he is the one Messiah, known before the world was made.

Sanders concludes that there are two hypostatised Words in the Odes, ܡܠܬܐ which is feminine and ܦܬܓܡܐ which is masculine (115), the gender of the words giving a clue to how they should be understood:

> "The Melta is usually an instrument of God's action... and thus falls into the line of feminine hypostases in Judaism, headed by Wisdom, who are preexistent with God and who assist him at creation and in the further carrying out of his will... Petgama... seems indeed to be equated with Truth... The Melta is never a completely independent being; but when the swiftness of the Petgama is referred to (xii. 5), and when it is said that he 'came to me' (xxxvii. 3), one sees that the Petgama can be fully independent." (117)

While Sanders is correct in that ܡܠܬܐ is certainly used in the Odes with the sense of an instrument of God's action and ܦܬܓܡܐ is associated with truth, the argument concerning the understanding of the feminine and masculine hypostases cannot be sustained against the examination of Odes 12 and 41 above. In the former, ܦܬܓܡܐ is close to the line of Sophia which Sanders asserts for ܡܠܬܐ, and, in the latter, ܡܠܬܐ surely has full independence as the saviour-Son and is not a feminine hypostasis according to the imagery and titles used in parallel with it. Whether the hypostases are two complementary aspects of one character or two distinct characters is unclear (cf. also the masculine Truth and feminine Grace).

## ODE 13

1 ܗܐ ܡܚܙܝܬܢ ܡܪܝܐ ܗܘ
ܦܬܚܘ ܥܝܢܐ ܘܚܙܘ ܐܢܝܢ ܒܗ
2 ܘܝܠܦܘ ܐܝܢܐ ܐܝܬܝܗܘܢ ܐܦܝܟܘܢ
ܘܟܪܙܘ ܬܫܒܚܬܐ ܠܪܘܚܗ
3 ܘܫܘܘ ܨܝܕܬܐ ܡܢ ܐܦܝܟܘܢ
ܘܪܚܡܘ ܩܕܝܫܘܬܗ ܘܠܒܫܘܗ̇
4 ܘܬܗܘܘܢ ܕܠܐ ܡܘܡܐ ܒܟܠܙܒܢ ܠܘܬܗ

ܗܠܠܘܝܐ

---

1 Behold our mirror is the Lord.
Open the eyes and see them in him,
2 and learn how your faces are,
and declare hymns to his Spirit,
3 and wipe the huntress from your faces,
and love his holiness and put it on.
4 And you will be spotless always with him.

Alleluia.

### NOTES TO THE TRANSLATION

2a, 3a: With the exception of Labourt and Batiffol (and Flemming for 3a only), the translations render ܐܦܐ in the sing. Since it is possible to translate with either sing. or pl., the pl. has been chosen here on the basis of the 2nd pl. group which is addressed.

3a: ܨܝܕܬܐ means "huntress" (cf. Brockelmann 1966, 627). The points above and below the ܨ indicate the accompanying vowel as a pthāḥā (cf. Segal, J.B. 23, 28, 37-8) so that the translation "hunting"/"booty" is incorrect at least according to the Ms. (*contra* Charlesworth 1977, 64 n.3). For a summary of the various emendations proposed by scholars and my own argument for the emendation, ܙܢܝܘܬܐ ("harlotry"), cf. Franzmann 1986b. For the most recent conjecture of ܨܚܘܬܐ, cf. Lattke 1989.

ANALYSIS

The Ode is a unit with the pattern: A B C D C' B' A'.

1a (A) introduces the key metaphor of the Lord as mirror (cf. the Word as the spotless mirror in The Teaching of Silvanus 113, 4 [Facs. ed. 7: 119; Wisse 1984b, 359], and Wisdom as a spotless mirror in Wis 7:26). It is clearly divided from what follows by the change in focus from the speaker within a 1st pl. group ("our mirror") to the speaker addressing the group in the 2nd pl. There is a connection between 1a and 1b by the repetition of the root ܚܙ.

The major section of the Ode (1b-3b) is characterised by the use of at least one 2nd pl. imper. verb in each line. Except for 2b, the verbs follow a logical progression of action.

1b (B) and 3b (B') are parallel on the pattern: 2nd pl. imper. verb + noun obj. + ܘ + 2nd pl. imper. verb + pron. obj. (ref. to the preceding noun obj.). Each line has internal parallelism by the double pattern of verb + obj.

In contrast to the two verbs in each of 1b and 3b, 2a (C) and 3a (C') have one initial 2nd pl. imper. verb. The lines are connected by the repetition of the final ܐܦܝܟܘܢ. There is a logical progression in the actions of the group learning what their faces are like and wiping away what befouls them (cf. the notes to the translation). In his failure to recognise the structure of this Ode, Carmignac (1986) suggests that 3a would be better placed after 2a ("Il a pu facilement être déplacé par un saut visuel de 'votre visage' à 'votre visage'").

2b (D) functions as the key focus of the Ode by its position at the centre of the two reflexively congruent sections. Thus, what would normally have been expected as the final action of the series in 1b-3b, has been given prominence by its insertion within the parallel bicolon formed by 2a and 3a.

4 (A') functions as a concluding statement of assurance to the community, providing the balance to the introduction in 1a.

## ODE 14

1 ܐܝܟ ܥܝ̈ܢܘܗܝ ܕܒܪܐ ܥܠ ܐܒܘܗܝ
ܗܟܢܐ ܥܝ̈ܢܝ ܡܪܝܐ ܒܟܠܙܒܢ ܠܘܬܟ ܐܝܬܝܗܝܢ
2 ܡܛܠ ܕܠܘܬܟ ܐܝܬ ܬܕ̈ܝ ܘܦܘܢܩܝ

3 ܠܐ ܬܣܛܐ ܪ̈ܚܡܝܟ ܡܢܝ ܡܪܝܐ
ܘܠܐ ܬܣܒ ܡܢܝ ܒܣܝܡܘܬܟ
4 ܐܘܫܛ ܠܝ ܡܪܝ ܒܟܠܙܒܢ ܝܡܝܢܟ
ܘܡܕܒܪܢܐ ܗܘܝ ܠܝ ܥܕܡܐ ܠܚܪܬܐ ܥܠ ܨܒܝܢܟ
5 ܐܫܦܪ ܩܕܡܝܟ ܡܛܠ ܬܫܒܘܚܬܟ
ܘܡܛܠ ܫܡܟ ܐܬܦܪܩ ܡܢ ܒܝܫܐ

6 ܘܢܝܚܘܬܟ ܡܪܝܐ ܬܦܘܫ ܠܘܬܝ
ܘܦܐܪ̈ܘܗܝ ܕܚܘܒܟ
7 ܐܠܦܢܝ ܙܡܝܪ̈ܬܐ ܕܫܪ̈ܪܟ
ܕܐܥܒܕ ܡܢܟ ܦܐܪ̈ܐ
8 ܘܩܝܬܪܐ ܕܪܘܚܟ ܩܕܝܫܐ ܦܬܚ ܠܝ
ܕܒܟܠ ܩܠ̈ܝܢ ܐܫܒܚܝܟ ܡܪܝܐ

9 ܘܐܝܟ ܣܘܓܐܐ ܕܪ̈ܚܡܝܟ
ܗܟܢܐ ܬܬܠ ܠܝ

ܘܣܪܗܒ ܠܡܬܠ ܫܐܠ̈ܬܢ
10 ܘܐܝܬ ܗܘ ܡܫܟܚ ܠܟܠܗܝܢ ܣܢܝ̈ܩܘܬܢ

ܗܠܠܘܝܐ

---

1 As the eyes of a son upon his father,
so my eyes, Lord, are always towards you,
2 because towards you are my breasts and my luxury.

3   Do not turn aside your mercy from me, Lord,
    and do not take from me your sweetness.
4   Hold out to me, my Lord, always your right hand,
    and be a leader for me until the end according to your will.
5   Let me be beautiful before you because of your glory,
    and because of your name let me be saved from the Evil One.

6   And let your rest, Lord, abide near me,
    and the fruits of your love.
7   Teach me the odes of your truth,
    that I might bear fruits by you.
8   And the harp of your Holy Spirit open for me,
    that with all the tones I might glorify you, Lord.

9   And as the multitude of your mercy,
    so will you grant me.

    And hasten to grant our requests.
10  And you are able (for) all our necessities.

    Alleluia.

NOTES TO THE TRANSLATION

4b: H has a break after ⟨ᵃ⟩ and ⟨ᵇ⟩. The parallelism of ⟨ᶜ⟩ and ⟨ᵈ⟩
⟨ᵉ⟩ indicate that 4b should be read as one line.

5a-b: H has no break after ⟨ᶠ⟩ but after ⟨ᵍ⟩. The parallelism of 5a
and 5b demands a break after ⟨ᶠ⟩ and none after ⟨ᵍ⟩.

9a-b: H has no break, although the structure of the inclusio between 1a-b and
9a-b demands one (cf. also Bruston 1912b; Harris and Mingana vol. 2; Greßmann 1924; Carmignac 1986).

ANALYSIS

## Stanza 1 [1-2]

Stanza 1 comprises an introductory simile of the form, ... ܟܘܡ...ܝܟ. 1a and 1b
are parallel to a degree on the pattern: ܟܘܡ/ܝܟ + noun subj. (ܟܝܬ) with
pron. suffix + prep. with obj. The parallelism of "I" and "son", Lord and "father", serves to establish the relationship of the "I" and the Lord prior to the
main body of the address of the "I" to the Lord (3-9b).

The cl. introduced by ܕ ܠܛܠ in 2 refers to the reason for the action described in 1b. 1b and 2 are parallel with chiasmus: A B // B A', where A =
noun subj./s (attribute/s of the "I") with 1st sing. suffix; B = ܝܗܘܬ with 3rd
pl. verb/copula. The two lines have a terrace pattern by the placement of ܝܗܘܬ
at the conclusion of 1b and at the beginning of 2.

## Stanza 2 [3-5]

Each line of the stanza contains either an imper. verb (4a, 4b) or an imperf.
verb which is interpreted as imper. (3a, 3b) or cohortative (5a, 5b). There is a
general pattern of the Lord as the subject of the action, the "I" as the object of
the action (ܝܢܡ, ܠ), with some mention in each line of an attribute of the Lord
(mercy, sweetness, right hand, will, glory, name) which is connected with the
action desired by the "I".

3a and 3b are parallel with a pivot pattern by the placement of ܟܝܡ at the
conclusion of 3a. There is a chiastic structure: A B C // A' C B', where A =
2nd masc. sing. negative imperf. verb; B = noun obj. (attribute of the Lord)
with 2nd masc. sing. suffix; C = ܝܢܡ. The parallelism is strengthened by the
word-pair ܟܘܝ - ܟܗܘܝܡܘܒ. There is alliteration with ܡ in 3a (ܝܢܡ ܝܟܘܝ
ܟܝܡ).

4a follows the structure of 3b: 2nd masc. sing. verb + prep. with 1st sing.
suffix + noun (attribute of the Lord) with 2nd masc. sing. suffix. 4a and 4b
contain the semantically similar concepts of helping with the right hand (4a)
and leading (4b) which are found to some extent also in 22:7b. The lines are
parallel by the use of the 2nd masc. sing. imper. verbs + ܠ, by the time
phrases ܒܠܕܒ (4a) and ܟܗܝܠ ܟܡܢ (4b), and by the final nouns (attributes
of the Lord) with 2nd masc. sing. suffix.

5a and 5b are parallel with chiasmus: A B // B' A', where A = 1st sing. imperf. verb + prep. with obj.; B = ܠܛܡ + noun (attribute of the Lord) with

2nd masc. sing. suffix. The parallelism is enhanced by the word-pair ܟܕܘܢܙܝܬܗ - ܟܢܬ.

## Stanza 3 [6, 7-8]

Stanza 3 continues a similar pattern to stanza 2 with three parallel bicola. 6a, 7a and 8a contain either an imper. verb (7a, 8a) or an imperf. verb interpreted as a jussive (6a). The stanza is united semantically by a focus on the action of composing/singing odes. 26:3,10,12 indicate the connection between "rest" in 6a and the composing/singing of odes in 7-8 (cf. Franzmann 1985).

6a and 6b are parallel with ellipsis, ܝܬܢܠ ܟܢܬܗ ܟܝܙܐ understood for both the parallel noun subjs. (attributes of the Lord) with 2nd masc. sing. suffix. The parallelism is strengthened by the word-pair ܟܬܢܘܘ - ܟܝܟܐ. ܟܬܥ and ܟܝܟܐ are associated also in 16:2. The bicolon is given emphasis by its position in the centre of the main body of the address to the Lord (3-9b).

7a-b and 8a-b are alternately parallel. 7a and 8a are parallel with chiasmus: A B // B' A', where A = 2nd masc. sing. imper. verb + 1st sing. dir./indir. obj.; B = noun + ܝ + noun (attribute of the Lord) with 2nd masc. sing. suffix. 7b and 8b each comprise a cl. introduced by ܝ which provides the purpose of the action described in the preceding line. The general pattern of the parallelism is A B C // B' A'-C', where A = 1st sing. imperf. verb; B = ܒ with obj.; C = obj. of the verb.

There are a number of internal connections in the stanza apart from the parallelism and the vocabulary associated with the theme of composing/singing odes - the repetition of ܟܝܟܐ in 6b and 7b (cf. 11:1); the verbs ܝܬܗܒ and ܝܙܐ in 8a-b; and the word-pair ܟܝܝܬ - ܟܝܟܐ in 8a-b.

## Stanza 4 [9a-b]

The repetition of the initial ...ܟܬܗܡ...ܘܝܟ (cf. 15:7; 29:2-3; 36:5; 42:16) indicates that stanza 4 forms the inclusio with stanza 1 for the Ode proper (1-9b). The bicolon 9a-b concludes the preceding section of requests made to the Lord (3-8b) by making a general statement of belief in the Lord's generosity. The conclusion is more effective by the repetition of ܘܝܙܬܝ (3a, 9a).

## Stanza 5 [9c-10]

Stanza 5 is clearly an addition to the self-contained Ode in 1-9b. The focus shifts from the 1st sing. (1-9b) to a 1st pl. address to the Lord. The stanza appears to function as a communal response to the more personal "I" material of 1-9b. The connection with the Ode proper is made by the repetition of the verb ܢܚܬ (9b, 9c). The stanza itself flows easily from stanzas 2 and 3 by the use of the imper. addressed to the Lord. There is a semantic link between the concluding noun objs. (ܪܚܡܬܟ, ܢܝܚܬܟ) with 1st pl. suffixes.

## ODE 15

1 ܐܝܟ ܕܫܡܫܐ ܚܕܘܬܐ ܗܝ ܠܐܝܠܝܢ ܕܒܥܝܢ ܝܘܡܗ
ܗܟܢܐ ܚܕܘܬܝ ܡܪܝܐ ܗܘ
2 ܡܛܠ ܕܗܘܝܘ ܫܡܫܝ
ܘܙܠܝܩܘܗܝ ܐܩܝܡܘܢܝ
ܘܢܘܗܪܗ ܫܪܐ ܟܠ ܚܫܘܟܐ ܡܢ ܐܦܝ

3 ܩܢܝܬ ܒܗ ܥܝܢܐ
ܘܚܙܝܬ ܠܝܘܡܗ ܩܕܝܫܐ
4 ܗܘܝ ܠܝ ܐܕܢܐ
ܘܫܡܥܬ ܠܫܪܪܗ
5 ܗܘܬ ܠܝ ܡܚܫܒܬܐ ܕܝܕܥܬܐ
ܘܐܬܦܛܡܬ ܒܐܝܕܗ

6 ܐܘܪܚܐ ܕܛܥܝܘܬܐ ܫܒܩܬ
ܘܐܙܠܬ ܠܘܬܗ
ܘܩܒܠܬ ܦܘܪܩܢܐ ܡܢܗ ܕܠܐ ܚܣܡܐ
7 ܘܐܝܟ ܡܘܗܒܬܗ ܝܗܒ ܠܝ
ܘܐܝܟ ܪܒܘܬ ܫܘܦܪܗ ܥܒܕܢܝ
8 ܠܒܫܬ ܠܐ ܚܒܠܐ ܒܝܕ ܫܡܗ
ܘܫܠܚܬ ܚܒܠܐ ܒܛܝܒܘܬܗ
9 ܡܘܬܐ ܐܬܚܒܠ ܡܢ ܩܕܡ ܦܪܨܘܦܝ
ܘܫܝܘܠ ܐܬܒܛܠܬ ܒܡܠܬܝ

10 ܘܣܠܩ ܒܐܪܥܗ ܕܡܪܝܐ ܚܝܐ ܕܠܐ ܡܘܬܐ
ܘܐܬܝܕܥ ܠܡܗܝܡܢܘܗܝ
ܘܐܬܝܗܒ ܕܠܐ ܚܣܘܪܐ ܠܟܠܗܘܢ ܐܝܠܝܢ ܕܬܟܝܠܝܢ ܥܠܘܗܝ

ܗܠܠܘܝܐ

---

1 As the sun is joy to them who seek its day,
so my joy is the Lord,
2 because he is my sun.
And his rays have made me stand up,
and his light released all darkness from my face.

3　And I gained eyes by him,
　　and saw his holy day.
4　I had ears,
　　and I heard his truth.
5　I had the thought of knowledge,
　　and I was given pleasure by means of him.

6　The way of error I abandoned,
　　and went towards him,
　　and received salvation from him who (is) without jealousy.
7　And according to his gift, he gave to me;
　　and according to the greatness of his beauty, he made me.
8　I put on incorruption by means of his name,
　　and I stripped off corruption by his grace.
9　Death was destroyed before my face,
　　and Sheol has been brought to nothing by my word.

10　And it ascended in the Lord's land, immortal life.
　　And it was known to his faithful ones,
　　and it was given freely to all those who trust in him.

　Alleluia.

NOTES TO THE TRANSLATION

3-5: 3 and 4 are given as single lines in H. 5 is divided after ܟ̈ܬܥܕܐ. 3 and 4 must also be divided on the basis of the alternate parallel structure of 3-5.

4a: Lit. "ears were to me."

5a: Lit. "the thought of knowledge was to me."

10c: ܟ̈ܚܐ ܕܐ ܚܝ is not the subj. of ܣܠܩ. Although a sing. verb with ܚܝ is not unknown, (cf. Jn 1:4 ܟܐ ܚܝ ܗܘܐ; Nöldeke suggests that the construction rests "upon a dogmatic caprice..." [§321]), where ܟ̈ܚܐ ܕܐ ܚܝ functions as a subj. in the Odes (28:6; 40:6), it takes a pl. verb. Moreover, the pl. verbs in both 10b and 10c clearly refer back to ܟ̈ܚܐ ܕܐ ܚܝ as their subj. It is possible that ܟܕ̈ܡܝ ܟܠܐ ܚܘ has been misplaced and should be inserted after the initial ܘ of 10b.

ANALYSIS

Stanza 1 [1-2a, 2b-c]

Stanza 1 focusses on the image of the Lord as the sun (cf. 11:13), with a lesser motif of the Lord as the joy of the "I" (cf. 7:2).

1-2a comprises a simile of the form, ... ܟܐܡ... ܟܝܒܐ (cf. 16:1). The repetition of ܟܫܡܫ (1a, 2a) indicates the inclusio for the strophe. The structure of the tricolon is complex. The two key nouns of 1a (ܟܫܡܫ, ܟܕ̇ܘ) are repeated (with 1st sing. suffix) in reverse order as the key nouns in 1b (ܝܗܕܘ) and 2a (ܝܫܡܫ).

Omitting, for the moment, the second half of 1a from the discussion, the three lines are parallel with a triple chiastic structure. 1a and 1b are parallel on the pattern:  A B C D // A' C B' D', where A = ܟܐܡ/ܟܝܒܐ; B = noun subj.; C = ܟܕ̇ܘ (noun compl.); D = ܗܘ (copula). 1b-2a has the pattern: A B C // B'-C A', where A = noun compl. + 1st sing. suffix; B = noun/rel. pron. subj.; C = ܗܘ (copula). 1a and 2a have a loose chiasmus by the placement of ܟܫܡܫ.

The tricolon is constructed on a (circular) terrace pattern. The first half of 1a concludes with ܟܕ̇ܘ which is repeated at the beginning of 1b. 1b concludes with ܟܝܒ which is found at the beginning of 2a in the form of a substitute rel. pron. The concluding element in 2a, ܝܫܡܫ, is the repetition of the initial element in 1a.

The second half of 1a does not fit the tight structure outlined above and might be considered an addition. However, the second cls. in 1a and 10c form a syntactic inclusio for the Ode by their parallel pattern: ܝ ܥܠܝܟ + masc. pl. part. act. + obj. expression with 3rd masc. sing. suffix.

2b-c continues the motif of the Lord as sun from 1-2a. The bicolon is loosely parallel with a pattern of noun subj. (attribute of the Lord) with 3rd masc. sing. suffix + verb + 1st sing. as the ultimate object of the action. There is antithesis by the contrasting verbs ܢܗܡ - ܟܫܝ. 2c has internal parallelism by the polar word-pair ܟܝܡܡ - ܟܚܫܘܟ. 2c and 9a are linked by the descriptions of the destruction of darkness/Death, and by the phrases ܝܗܘ̈ܦܝ ܣܡ ܡܢ and ܡܢ ܐܦܘ.

Stanza 2 [3-5]

The three bicola are alternately parallel. 3a, 4a, and 5a describe some "possession" of the "I". 3a is semantically parallel to 4a and 5a, which are parallel on the pattern: perf. of ܟܐܡ + ܠ + noun subj. 3a and 4a are further linked by the word-pair ܟܝܢ - ܟܝܢܐ.

3b, 4b, and 5b report some action by/upon the "I" resulting from what is possessed by the "I" as described in the preceding line. The lines are parallel on the pattern: 1st sing. perf. verb + *nota accusativi*/prep. + noun (attribute of the Lord) with 3rd sing. masc. suffix. 3b and 4b are connected by the word-pair ܟܠ - ܫܒܠ.

Stanza 3 [6, 7, 8, 9]

Stanza 3 comprises a report about the "I" and how the Lord has acted on his behalf in the movement from error and corruption to salvation and incorruption. There is a link with the preceding stanza by the polar word-pair ܚܝܐ (4b) - ܚܒܠܘܬܐ (6a).

Beginning with 6b, there is an alternating pattern throughout the stanza. 6b-c and 8a-b have 1st sing. subjs. and the 3rd sing. masc. (ref. to the Lord) as the general object of the action described; 7a-b and 9a-b have 3rd sing. subjs. (only the subjs. of 7a-b ref. to the Lord) and the 1st sing. as ultimate object of the action.

6a provides the introduction to the ensuing action of the stanza. It follows the pattern of the first strophe by the use of the 1st sing. Peal perf. verb. 6b flows logically from 6a by the description of the movement away from error and towards the Lord. This is emphasised by the placement of the word-pair, ܫܒܩ - ܐܠܝ, so that ܐܠܝܗ follows immediately after ܫܒܩܗ (cf. 11:8b-9a). 6b and 6c are parallel on the general pattern: 1st sing. Peal perf. verb with prep. + 3rd sing. masc. suffix (ref. to the Lord).

7a flows easily from 6c by the description of the giving of the Lord (7a) which follows the statement that the Lord is without jealousy (6c). 7a and 7b are parallel on the pattern: ܐܝܟ + noun obj. (attribute of the Lord) with 3rd sing. masc. suffix + 3rd sing. masc. Peal perf. verb (subj. the Lord) + 1st sing. dir./indir. obj. The parallelism is strengthened by the word-pair ܝܗܒ - ܠܒܟ. The pattern introduced by ܐܝܟ occurs also in 14:9; 29:2-3; 36:5 (cf. also 42:16).

8a and 8b are parallel on the pattern: 1st sing. Peal perf. verb + *nota accusativi* with noun obj. + ܒ/ܒܝܕ + noun obj. (attribute of the Lord) with 3rd sing.

masc. suffix. The parallelism is enhanced by the use of the polar word-pairs, ܫܠܚ - ܠܒܫ and ܠܐ ܚܒܠܐ - ܚܒܠܐ, and by the word-pair ܫܡܐ - ܛܝܒܘܬܐ. There is some alliteration over the bicolon especially by the use of ܒ and ܠ .

9a is connected with the preceding strophe by the repetition of the root ܚܒܠ.

9a and 9b are parallel on the pattern: noun subj. + 3rd sing. Ethpaal perf. verb + prep./prep. construction with noun obj. (attribute of the "I") + 1st sing. suffix. The parallelism is strengthened by the word-pair ܡܘܬܐ - ܫܝܘܠ and by the synonymity of ܚܒܠ and ܒܛܠ.

Stanza 4 [10]

With stanza 4, the focus changes from the "I" and the Lord to a more impersonal report concerning the Lord and believers.

10a serves to introducte the bicolon in 10b-c. The subject of ܣܠܩ is the Lord as sun, indicating a return to the imagery of stanza 1, thus providing a semantic as well as syntactic inclusio (1a, 10c) for the Ode. The image of the sun ascending in the Lord's land is similar to the description of the Lord as the sun in 11:13. ܚܝܐ ܕܠܐ ܡܘܬܐ is in apposition with the 3rd masc. sing. subj. (cf. ܚܝܐ ܡܝܬܪ̈ܐ in apposition with ܦܐܪܐ in 8:2), so that one must equate sun, Lord, and eternal life.

10b and 10c are parallel on the pattern: 3rd pl. masc. Ethpeel perf. verb + equivalent obj. expressions, ܒܗܝܡܢܘܗܝ and ܟܠܗܘܢ ܐܝܠܝܢ ܕܬܟܠܝܢ ܥܠܘܗܝ. The parallelism is strengthened by the word-pairs ܢܣܒ - ܝܗܒ and ܐܡܢ - ܬܟܠ.

The relatively longer lines in 1a and 10c indicate perhaps that a singer would treat these in an antiphon mode, differentiating them by rhythm/melody from the remainder of the Ode to emphasise the introduction and conclusion.

## ODE 16

1 ܐܝܟܢܐ ܕܥܒܕܗ ܕܐܟܪܐ ܦܕܢܐ ܗܝ
ܘܥܒܕܗ ܕܡܕܒܪܢܝܬܐ ܓܪܪܗ ܕܐܠܦܐ
ܗܟܢܐ ܐܦ ܥܒܕܝ ܡܙܡܘܪܐ ܗܘ ܕܡܪܝܐ ܒܬܫܒ̈ܚܬܗ
2 ܐܘܡܢܘܬܝ ܘܦܘܠܚܢܝ ܒܬܫܒ̈ܚܬܗ ܐܝܢ
ܡܛܠ ܕܚܘܒܗ ܬܪܣܝ ܠܠܒܝ
ܘܒܡܐ ܠܣܦܘܬܝ ܢܒܥ ܗܘܐ ܦܐܪ̈ܘܗܝ
3 ܚܘܒܝ ܓܝܪ ܡܪܝܐ ܗܘ
ܡܛܠܗܢܐ ܐܙܡܪ ܠܗ
4 ܡܬܚܝܠ ܐܢܐ ܓܝܪ ܒܬܫܒ̈ܚܬܗ
ܘܗܝܡܢܘܬܐ ܐܝܬ ܠܝ ܒܗ

5 ܐܦܬܚ ܦܘܡܝ ܘܬܡܠܠ ܒܝ ܪܘܚܗ
ܬܫܒܘܚܬܗ ܕܡܪܝܐ ܘܐܝܩܪܗ
6 ܥܒܕܐ ܕܐܝ̈ܕܘܗܝ ܘܦܘܠܚܢܐ ܕܨ̈ܒܥܬܗ
7 ܠܣܘܓܐܐ ܕܪ̈ܚܡܘܗܝ ܘܠܚܝܠܐ ܕܡܠܬܗ

8 ܡܠܬܗ ܓܝܪ ܕܡܪܝܐ ܒܨܝܐ ܡܕܡ ܕܠܐ ܡܬܚܙܝܐ
ܘܓܠܐ ܡܚܫܒܬܗ
9 ܚܙܐ ܓܝܪ ܥܝܢܐ ܥܒ̈ܕܘܗܝ
ܘܐܕܢܐ ܫܡܥܐ ܠܡܚܫܒܬܗ

10 ܗܘ ܐܦܬܝ ܠܐܪܥܐ ܘܐܘܬܒ ܡܝ̈ܐ ܒܝܡܐ
11 ܡܬܚ ܫܡܝܐ ܘܐܬܩܢ ܒܟܘ̈ܟܒܐ
12 ܘܐܬܩܢ ܠܒܪܝܬܐ ܘܐܩܝܡܗ̇
ܘܐܬܬܢܝܚ ܗܘ ܡܢ ܥܒ̈ܕܘܗܝ

13 ܘܒܪ̈ܝܬܐ ܒܪ̈ܗܛܝܗܝܢ ܪܗܛ
ܘܥܒ̈ܕܝܗܝܢ ܥܒܕܝ
ܘܠܐ ܝܕܥܢ ܠܡܫܠܝ ܘܠܡܒܛܠܘ
14 ܘܚ̈ܝܠܘܬܐ ܡܫܬܥܒܕܢ ܠܡܠܬܗ

15 ܡܫܡܫܬܐ ܕܢܘܗܪܐ ܫܡܫܐ ܗܘ
ܘܡܫܡܫܬܐ ܕܚܫܘܟܐ ܠܠܝܐ ܗܘ
16 ܥܒܕ ܕܝܢ ܫܡܫܐ ܠܝܘܡܐ ܕܢܗܘܐ ܢܗܝܪ
ܐܝܬܝ ܕܝܢ ܠܚܫܘܟܐ ܠܠܝܐ ܥܠ ܐܦ̈ܝܗ̇ ܕܐܪܥܐ
17 ܘܚܘܠܦܗܘܢ ܕܚܕ ܡܢ ܚܕ ܫܘܦܪܗ ܕܐܠܗܐ ܡܡܠܠ

18 ܘܠܝܬ ܡܕܡ ܕܠܒܪ ܡܢ ܡܪܝܐ
ܡܛܠ ܕܗܘ ܐܬܩܢܗܝ ܗܘܐ ܡܢ ܩܕܡ ܕܟܠ ܢܗܘܐ
19 ܘܥܠܡ̈ܐ ܒܡܠܬܗ ܗܘܘ
ܘܒܡܚܫܒܬܐ ܕܠܒܗ

20 ܬܫܒܘܚܬܐ ܘܐܝܩܪܐ ܠܫܡܗ

ܗܠܠܘܝܐ

---

1 As the work of the ploughman is the plough-share,
and the work of the helmsman the steering of the ship;
so also my work is the psalm of the Lord in his praises.
2 My skill and my service are in his praises;
because his love nourished my heart,
and unto my lips it belched up his fruits.
3 For my love is the Lord;
because of this I will sing to him.
4 For I am strengthened in his praises,
and I have faith in him.

5 I will open my mouth and his Spirit will speak by me;
the glory of the Lord and his beauty,
6 the work of his hands and the service of his fingers,
7 the multitude of his mercy and the power of his Word.

8 For the Word of the Lord searches into that which is invisible,
and that which is manifested, his thought.
9 For the eye sees his works,
and the ear hears his thought.

10  He himself spread the land out widely and placed the waters in the sea;
11  he stretched out the heaven and fixed the stars;
12  and he fixed the creation and set it up.
      And he was at rest from his works.

13  And created things run their runnings,
      and work their works.
      And they do not know how to stand and to be idle.
14  And the hosts are in subjection to his Word.

15  The treasury of light is the sun,
      and the treasury of darkness is the night.
16  For the sun makes the day that it might be light;
      the night however brings darkness upon the face of the land.
17  And (by) their acceptance one from another they complete the beauty of
      God.

18  And there is nothing outside of the Lord,
      because he himself was before everything was.
19  And the aeons were by his Word,
      and by the thought of his heart.

20  Glory and honour to his name.

      Alleluia.

NOTES TO THE TRANSLATION

1b: Difficulty with the interpretation of ܘܝܪܗ was overcome by Harris and Mingana with evidence of a meaning of "steering" from Ephrem (2: 284). However, a problem remains in that 1a and 1c have ܣܟܘ (plough-share) and ܡܙܡܘܪܐ (psalm) in parallel to ܘܝܪܗ. Thus 1a and 1c deal with the material of the work rather than the action of the work as in 1b. For this reason, it may be well to reconsider the suggestion of Schulthess (254) and emend ܘܝܪܗ to ܘܝܪܗ ("mast"; Schulthess has ܘܝܪܗ; Diettrich (1911) has ܢܝܪܐ, "Signalstange [an einem Schiffsmast]"; Labourt and Batiffol have ܢܝܪܐ, and prefer Diettrich's interpretation).

1c: The break indicated in H after ‚ܠܒ cannot be correct according to the parallel structure of 1a-c.

2b-c: The liturgical indicator ܡ (= ܟܘܠܠܡ; cf. Lattke 1979-86, 1: 59) has been added after ‚ܠܠ, indicating that a break should be made at this point.

4b: Lit. "and faith there is to me in him."

6-7: There is one line indicated for both 6 and 7 in H. Although the majority of translators divide both lines into two, I have preferred to keep the structure of internally parallel lines from 5-7.

8b: For a summary of the discussion regarding the interpretation of this line and a new suggestion, cf. Charlesworth 1979. Given the parallelism of 8a-b and the repetition of the word-pair ܟܐܠܡ - (ܡܒܠܐ) ܟܐܒܟܘܡ in 19a-b, Brock's proposal ("For the Word of the Lord investigates that which is invisible, and His thought that which is revealed"; 1974, 624) remains the more credible (cf. also Blaszczak 34). As to the sense of the line, it would be wise to reconsider G. Kittel's suggestion that ܟܠ may have been inadvertently omitted by the copyist of H (1914, 77 n.1). Such an error has been made in 21:4. The emendation would further strengthen the parallelism of the lines:

"For the Word of the Lord searches into that which is invisible,
and that which is hidden, his thought."

13c: "and do not know how to stand idle"; cf. Matt 20:6, ܘܐܡܪ ܠܗܘܢ ܠܡܢ ܩܝܡܝܢ ܐܢܬܘܢ ܗܪܟܐ; Tί ὧδε ἑστήκατε ὅλην τὴν ἡμέραν ἀργοί.

16a: The parallelism in 15 and 16 points to the interpretation of ܟܫܡܫ as the subj. of ܥܒܕ (cf. also Bauer 1964; Lattke 1979-86, vol. 1; Blaszczak 28). Such a construction seems semantically unusual. There is an instance of the sun as subj. of a verb "to make" in The Teaching of Silvanus 98, 24-25: ⲚⲐⲎ ⲅⲀⲢ ⲘⲠⲢⲎ ⲈⲦⲞⲨⲞⲚⳒ ⲈⲂⲞⲖ ⲈⲦⲢⲞⲨⲞⲈⲓⲚ ⲈⲚⲂⲀⲖ ⲚⲦⲤⲀⲢⳅ (Facs. ed. 7: 104; "For in the manner of the sun which is revealed, which makes light [= shines] for the eyes of the flesh...").

The parallelism of 16a and 16b is weakened by the use of the 3rd masc. Peal perf. of ܥܒܕ in 16a (the point below the ܒ is clear in H) and the masc. sing.

Aphel part. act. of ܐܬܐ in 16b. A point above rather than below the ܒ would provide the part. form of ܥܒܕ.

17: Harris (1909) emended ܡܪܚܡ to ܡܪܚܡܠ (so also Flemming; Diettrich 1911; Harris 1911a; Labourt and Batiffol; Bernard; Harris and Mingana vol. 2; Greßmann 1924; Bauer 1964; Emerton; Blaszczak 28; Carmignac 1986). The emendation is supported by the association of ܪܚܡ and ܪܚܡܐ (ref. to the Lord) in 5a-b.

18b: ܢܗܘܐ is a dependent imperf. verb indicating action which occurs in the future relative to the action of the principal cl. (Nöldeke § 267) and must be translated here in the past tense (cf. also 4:2; 7:9; 8:7,15; 28:5).

19a: The sense is that the aeons came into being by his Word (cf. 12:8b; 41:10).

ANALYSIS

Stanza 1 [1-4]

Stanza 1 commences with an extended simile of the form, ... ܗܟܡܐ ... ܐܝܟ (cf. 15:1). The tricolon in 1 is parallel on the general pattern: ܗܡܐ/ ܐܝܟ (ܐܝܟ understood for 1b) + ܟܒܪ with pron. suffix + noun in gen. construction with ܟܒܪ (1a and 1b) + noun compl. (extended by gen. construction in 1b and 1c) + copula (1a and 1c). 1c is extended beyond the pattern by the concluding phrase ܒܬܫܒܚܬܗ.

Although not part of the preceding simile pattern, 2a reiterates the statement in 1c. The two lines are parallel by the synonymity of work (1c) with skill and service (2a), and by the repetition of ܒܬܫܒܚܬܗ. The syntactic pattern of both lines is similar with the synonymous nouns + 1st sing. suffixes as subjs. with a copula.

Although the semantic connection is not particularly strong, the bicolon in 2b-c is connected with 2a by the cl. in 2b introduced by ܕ ܡܛܠ. 2b and 2c are parallel with chiasmus: A B C // C' B' A', where A = noun (attribute of the Lord) with 3rd masc. sing. suffix; B = 3rd masc. sing. verb; C = *nota accusativi*/prep. + noun (attribute of the "I") with 1st sing. suffix. The parallelism is strengthened by the word-pairs ܢܘܚ - ܐܝܪ and ܠܒ - ܗܘܢܐ, and the association of ܢܘܚ and ܠܒ (cf. 8:1; 18:1), ܐܝܪ and ܗܘܢܐ (cf. 12:2).

3a-b continues the theme of love and praise in 2 by the repetition of ܚܘܒܐ (3a) and the use of ܐܘܕܝ. The cl. introduced by ܕܡܛܠܗ in 3b refers to the confessional statement in 3a. The bicolon has a degree of parallelism with the 1st sing. as subj. (indirectly by the noun with 1st sing. suffix in 3a) and the Lord as the compl./indir. obj.

4a follows easily from 3b by the association of the concepts of singing and praises. There is also a similarity between the short confessional statements in 3a and 4b. Both speak of some spiritual attribute of the "I" (love, faith) for which refer back to the Lord. With these connections, the two bicola have an inverted pattern of A B B A.

There is some parallelism between 4a and 4b by the concentration of the action on the "I" ("I am strengthened", "I have faith"), and by the description in parallel phrases (ܡܚܝܠܬܢܝ, ܒܗ) of the Lord as the source of the action.

## Stanza 2 [5-7]

Stanza 2 comprises the detail of the praising of the "I" which has been introduced generally in stanza 1 (1c, 2a, 2c, 3b, 4a). The two stanzas are strongly connected by the themes of praise and of work (1-2a, 6).

5a functions as the introduction to the praise of the Lord. The line has internal parallelism by the associated actions of opening the mouth and speaking (cf. 8:4; 31:3).

5b-7 constitutes the praise section proper. The three lines are parallel. 5b is simply constructed with internal parallelism: noun (attribute of the Lord) with 3rd masc. sing. suffix + ܕܒܝܪ (ref. to both nouns) + noun (attribute of the Lord) with 3rd sing. suffix. The concept of the Spirit speaking through the "I" is similar to that expressed in 6:2.

6 and 7 extend the pattern of 5b by the addition of gen. expressions with ܕ and are thereby more strictly parallel on the pattern: noun + ܕ + noun (attribute of the Lord) with 3rd masc. sing. suffix + ܘ + noun + ܕ + noun (attribute of the Lord) with 3rd masc. sing. suffix.

As with 5a, each line of 5b-7 has internal parallelism, strengthened by a number of word-pairs: ܬܫܒܘܚܬܗ - ܩܠܗ (5b); ܐܥܒܕ - ܦܘܠܚܢܝ, ܐܝܕ̈ - ܨܒܥ̈ (6).

## Stanza 3 [8-9]

Stanza 3 commences with the repetition of the concluding word of stanza 2, ܡܠܬܗ. There is a shift in focus from the Lord in 5b-7 to the Word of the

Lord in 8. The break in stanzas is further emphasised by the shift from the 1st person to a more impersonal reporting style.

8a-b is parallel, the rel. cl. ܘܕܓܠܐ in 8b being the antithesis of ܕܠܐ ܡܬܚܙܝܐ in 8a (both dependent upon ܡܕܪܟ [8a]; cf. the translation notes), and ܡܚܫܒܬܗ being the subj. of 8b (ܒܪܝܐ is understood) in parallel to ܡܠܬܗ in 8a.

9a-b is linked with 8a-b by the alternate repetition of ܚܙܐ (8a, 9a) and ܡܚܫܒܬܗ (8b, 9b). 9a and 9b are parallel with chiasmus: A B C // B' A' C', where A = 3rd fem. sing. Peal part. act. ; B = noun subj.; C = noun (attribute of the Lord) with 3rd masc. sing. suffix. The parallelism is strengthened by the three word-pairs: ܚܙܐ - ܫܡܥ, ܥܝܢܐ - ܐܕܢܐ, ܠܒܐ - ܡܚܫܒܬܐ.

Stanza 4 [10-12]

Stanza 4 provides the details of the creative work of the Lord.

10-12a constitutes a parallel tricolon, each line with internal parallelism by a double pattern of 3rd masc. sing. perf. verb (subj. is the Lord) + noun obj. (pron. obj. suffix in the second half of 12a). The pattern is extended by the phrase ܒܝܡܐ in 10. The internal parallelism of each line (cf. also 5-7) is enhanced by the word-pairs: ܐܪܥܐ - ܡ̈ܝܐ (10), ܫܡ̈ܝܐ - ܟܘܟ̈ܒܐ (11), ܬܩܢ - ܩܘܡ (12a). The parallelism of the tricolon is strengthened by the repetition of ܬܩܢ (11, 12a), by the word-pairs ܬܩܢ - ܩܘܡ (11, 12a) and ܐܪܥܐ - ܫܡ̈ܝܐ (10, 11), and by the semantic closeness of ܦܬܐ - ܡܬܚ (10, 11) and ܝܬܒ - ܬܩܢ (10, 11).

12b concludes the stanza. It is connected with 10-12a by the use of a 3rd masc. sing. perf. verb (subj. is the Lord). The relative shortness of the line compared to the three preceding lines and the use of one 3rd masc. sing. perf. verb rather than two as in 10-12a emphasises the finality of the statement. The use of ܠܟ̈ܠܗܘܢ recapitulates the action of the preceding tricolon.

Stanza 5 [13, 14?]

Stanza 5 continues logically from stanza 4, the focus shifting from the work of God to the work of the creation. The use of ܒܪ̈ܝܬܐ in 13a provides another link with the preceding stanza (12a).

13a and 13b are parallel on the pattern: ܒܪ̈ܝܬܐ (subj., understood in 13b) + pl. noun (activity of created things) with 3rd fem. pl. suffix + fem. pl. Peal part. act. In each of the lines, the noun denoting activity and the following part. are derived from the same root (ܪܗܛ in 13a, ܥܒܕ in 13b; cf. 11:20). There is alliteration by the repetition of the root in each line.

13c serves as a summary to the bicolon. Each of the infinitives (to stand, to be idle) is in contrast to the activities described for the created things (to run, 13a; to work, 13b). As a summary, it stands in contrast to the summary in 12b - the work of the Lord is followed by rest; the work of the created things never ceases.

The relationship of the hosts in 14 to the created things (13), the sun and night (15-17), or the aeons (19) is unclear. The monocolon stands between two structured sections, 13 and 15-17, and seems to have little relevance to either. Its closest syntactic relation is with 19 by the repetition of ܟܠܗ. If this indicates an inclusio with 19, then one must assume a semantic relationship between the hosts and the aeons and, further, a relationship between them and the sun and the night which are the focus of the section for which 14 and 19 would be the inclusio. This seems too much weight to place upon the repetition of ܟܠܗ, and such a conclusion would require the support of a thoroughgoing analysis of the imagery and characters of the Odes.

The decision to include 14 with stanza 4 is based on the word-pair ܟܕܝܒ - ܟܗܠܝܢ in 4:7-8, though in the latter case, the hosts appear to be equivalent to archangels and opposite to created things.


Stanza 6 [15-17]

The stanza focusses on four major elements: sun (ܫܡܫܐ 15a, 16a), night (ܠܠܝܐ 15b, 16b), light (ܢܗܝܪܐ/ܢܗܘܪ 15a, 16a), and darkness (ܚܫܘܟܐ 15b, 16b). The alternating pattern of repetition is similar to 8-9.

15a-b comprises two parallel descriptive statements on the pattern: ܡܢܗܕ + ܗ + noun + noun subj. + ܗܘ (copula). The parallelism is strengthened by the polar word-pair ܢܗܝܪܐ - ܚܫܘܟܐ, and by the contrast between ܫܡܫ and ܠܠ. That merismus rather than antithesis is intended is clear from the statement of 17.

The contrasting statements concerning the sun and darkness continue with 16a-b. The bicolon is parallel with chiasmus: A B C D // A' B D' C', where A = 3rd sing. verb; B = ܗ; C = noun subj.; D = noun obj. The syntactic parallelism which associates ܢܗܘ and ܚܫܘܟ does not exactly coincide with the more logical semantic parallelism between the concepts of the sun as the source of light and the night as the source of darkness in 15a-b.

17 functions as the summary for the stanza. The monocolon effectively mirrors the pattern of merismus by apparent antithesis in 15a-b and 16a-b. There is a subtle antithesis between ܩܘܡܠܩܒ (the root meaning of ܩܒܠ is "to be in

opposition"; Smith, R.P. 2: 3467-8) and ܡܣܩܒܠܐ. On the semantic level, it is clear that merismus is intended by the logic of the movement from opposition to completion.

## Stanza 7 [18, 19]

With stanza 7, the focus returns to the Lord as creator and the implications of that (cf., for priority by order in creation, 4:1-3,14-15; 28:17-18; 41:15).

The cl. introduced by ܕ ܡܛܠ in 18b serves as the basis for the statement in 18a. There is a degree of parallelism by the description of the Lord in relation to nothing (18a) and everything (18b). There is a semantic connection between the concepts of being outside and being before.

Although 19 appears to introduce a new element, there is a connection with 18 by the continuing focus on the Lord. The bicolon comprises a common subj. ܬܠܡܕܘ (19a) with parallel phrases: ܒ + noun/noun with gen. expression (creative attribute of the Lord) + 3rd sing. masc. suffix. There is a strong connection between 19a and 12:8b (cf. the translation notes for the latter).

## Stanza 8 [20]

The Ode concludes with a doxology (cf. 20:10). There is some connection with the preceding line by the concluding noun (attribute of the Lord) with 3rd masc. sing. suffix.

That this Ode is essentially about work (the work of the Odist, the work of God as creator, the work of created things) is apparent from the frequency of the repetition of the root ܥܒܕ and its derivatives (x 9).

## ODE 17

1 ܐܬܟܠܠܬ ܕܝܢ ܒܐܠܗܝ
ܘܡܠܝܠ ܚܝܐ ܗܘ
2 ܘܐܙܕܕܩܬ ܒܡܪܝ
ܦܘܪܩܢܝ ܕܝܢ ܕܠܐ ܚܒܠܐ ܗܘ

3 ܐܫܬܪܝܬ ܠܝ ܡܢ ܣܪ̈ܝܩܘܬܐ
ܘܠܐ ܐܝܬܝ ܡܚܝܒܐ
4 ܚܢ̈ܩܝ ܐܬܦܣܩܘ ܒܐܝ̈ܕܘܗܝ
ܐܦ̈ܐ ܘܕܡܘܬܐ ܕܦܪ̈ܨܘܦܐ ܚܕܬܐ ܢܣܒܬ

ܘܗܠܟܬ ܒܗ ܘܐܬܦܪܩܬ
5 ܘܡܚܫܒܬܐ ܕܫܪܪܐ ܕܒܪܬܢܝ
ܘܐܙܠܬ ܒܬܪܗ ܘܠܐ ܛܥܝܬ
6 ܘܟܠ ܕܚܙܘܢܝ ܐܬܕܡܪܘ
ܘܐܝܟ ܐܢܟܪܝܐ ܐܬܚܫܒܬ ܠܗܘܢ
7 ܘܗܘ ܕܝܕܥ ܗܘܐ <ܘܪܒܢܝ>
ܡܪܝܡܐ ܒܟܠܗ ܫܘܡܠܝܗ
ܘܫܒܚܢ ܒܒܣܝܡܘܬܗ
ܘܐܪܝܡ ܠܡܪܘܡܐ ܕܫܪܪܐ ܡܕܒܪ
8 ܘܡܢ ܬܡܢ ܝܗܒ ܠܝ ܐܘܪܚܐ ܕܫܒ̈ܝܠܘܗܝ

ܘܦܬܚܬ ܬܪ̈ܥܐ ܕܐܚܝܕܝܢ ܗܘܘ
9 ܘܬܒܪܬ ܡܘܟ̈ܠܐ ܕܦܪܙܠܐ
ܦܪܙܠܐ ܕܝܢ ܕܝܠܝ ܪܬܚ
ܘܐܬܦܫܪ ܩܕܡܝ
10 ܘܠܐ ܡܕܡ ܐܬܚܙܝ ܠܝ ܟܕ ܐܚܝܕ
ܡܛܠ ܕܦܬܚܐ ܕܟܠܡܕܡ ܐܢܐ ܐܝܬܝ ܗܘܝܬ
11 ܘܐܙܠ ܗܘܝܬ ܠܘܬ ܟܠܗܘܢ ܐܣܝ̈ܪܝ ܠܡܫܪܝܘ ܐܢܘܢ
ܕܠܐ ܐܫܒܘܩ ܠܐܢܫ ܟܕ ܐܣܝܪ ܘܐܣܪ

12 ܘܝܗܒܬ ܝܕܥܬܝ ܕܠܐ ܚܣܡ
ܘܒܥܘܬܝ ܒܚܘܒܐ ܕܝܠܝ
13 ܘܙܪܥܬ ܒܠܒܘܬܐ ܦܐܪܝ
ܘܫܚܠܦܬ ܐܢܘܢ ܒܝ
14 ܘܩܒܠܘ ܒܘܪܟܬܐ ܕܝܠܝ ܘܚܝܘ
ܘܐܬܟܢܫܘ ܠܘܬܝ ܘܐܬܦܪܩܘ
15 ܡܛܠ ܕܗܘܘ ܠܝ ܗܕܡܐ ܘܐܢܐ ܪܫܗܘܢ

16 ܬܫܒܘܚܬܐ ܠܟ ܪܫܢ ܡܪܢ ܡܫܝܚܐ

ܗܠܠܘܝܐ

---

1 Then I was crowned by my God,
and my crown is living.
2 And I was declared righteous by my Lord,
then my salvation is incorrupted.

3 I was released from vanities,
and I am not condemned.
4 My bonds were cut to pieces by her hands.
The face and shape of a new person I received.

And I walked in him and was saved,
5 and the thought of Truth led me,
and I followed it and did not err.
6 And all who saw me were amazed,
and like a stranger was I considered by them.
7 And he who knew and reared me,
the Most High in all his perfection.
And he glorified me by his sweetness,
and lifted up my understanding to the height of truth,
8 and thence he gave me the way of his steps.

And I opened the gates which were shut,
9    and dashed into pieces the bolts of iron.
Then my own iron grew hot,
and melted before me.
10   And nothing appeared shut to me,
because I was the opening of everything.
11   And I marched against all of my shut up ones to release them,
that I might not leave anyone bound and binding.

12   And I gave my knowledge without jealousy,
and my intercession by my own love.
13   And I sowed in hearts my fruits,
and changed them in me.
14   And they received my own blessing and lived,
and they were gathered together to me and were saved,
15   because they were my members and I their head.

16   Glory to you our head the Lord Messiah.

Alleluia.

## NOTES TO THE TRANSLATION

1a: ܟܠܠ may have connotations of being adorned with foliage (Smith, R.P. 1: 1731). This fits well with the image of the crown as a living wreath in 1:1-4; 11:16d; 20:7c (cf. Helderman 96-7).

1a-b: The division of the line, which is not indicated in H, is based on the parallelism between 1a-b and 2a-b. There is no division by Ungnad and Staerk or by Carmignac (1986).

3a-b: 3 stands as one line in H (cf. also Ungnad and Staerk; Diettrich 1911; Carmignac 1986). The division is made on the basis of the relative length of line and the structure of stanzas 1 and 2 in which each line contains one action by/effecting the "I".

4a: H has "her hands" but most translators, except for Flemming, Ungnad and Staerk, and Harris (1911) read "his hands".

5b: The 3rd sing. fem. suffix with ܝܗ̇ܒ refers to the thought of Truth. It is not the thought which is personified here but rather Truth (cf. also 38:4-5 where the "I" walks with Truth and does not err).

7a: H has ܝܗܒܪ. The emendation ܝܗܒܣ is preferred by Harris (1911a), Labourt and Batiffol, Bernard, Harris and Mingana (vol. 2), Bauer (1964), Lattke (1979-86, vol. 1; the assertion that the reading is "auch handschriftlich möglich" is very dubious), and Emerton. Diettrich's (1911) suggestion of mĕrab-bjânj ("mein Ernährer") requires a much more substantial emendation. Harris and Mingana note that ܟܐܗܒܪ might also be possible (cf. Charlesworth 1977). Greßmann (1924) and Carmignac (tentatively, 1986) interpret ܝܗܒܪ as "my master".

7b: Ms. N commences with ܒܠܚܡ.

7c: N has ܢܖܚܝܫ. The context of 7-8a demands the H reading.

9a: The reading from N, ܒܠܡܣܠܐ, makes less sense in the context.

10a: Lit. "and nothing appeared to me while being shut".

10b: The addition of ܠܝ after ܝܐܕܘܬ in N is superfluous.

11a: Harris and Mingana (vol. 2) and Carmignac (1986) prefer the N reading, ܐܝܣܝܐ.

11b: Lit. "that I might not leave a person while being bound and binding".
H has ܢܐܟܡܝ. N is smudged and very difficult to read. Charlesworth suggests N has ܐܟ ܝܐܟܡܝ (1977, 76-77 n. 16).

15a: H has mistakenly repeated ܝ̣ܒܖܟܠ ܝܗܡܡ ܠ.

ANALYSIS

Stanza 1 [1-2]

The two bicola are alternately parallel. 1a and 2a follow the pattern: 1st sing. Ethpaal perf. verb + ܒ + noun with 1st sing. suffix. The parallelism is strengthened by the synonymity of the word-pair ܐܝܕ̈ܝ - ܒܝܫ. Each line comprises an action done to the "I" by God/the Lord.

1b and 2b are parallel on the pattern: noun with 1st sing. suffix + adj. expression + ܗܘ (copula). The parallelism is enhanced by the word-pair ܛܠܠܐ - ܦܢܝܬܐ and by the semantic closeness of ܣܝܡ - ܒܥܠܕ̈ܒܒܐ. Each line is a statement connected semantically (esp. in 1a and 1b by the play on the root ܩܠ) with the action which precedes it.

Stanza 2 [3-4b]

With stanza 2, there is a shift from positive descriptions of action concerning the "I" (crowning and being declared righteous) to more negatively expressed detail (release from vanities/bonds, not being condemned).

There is a degree of parallelism between 3a and 3b by the impersonal verb + ܠ/1st sing. suffix. 3a and 4a are semantically parallel by the equivalent concepts of release and cutting bonds. 4b provides a positive conclusion to the more negative aspects of 3a-4a, the contrast emphasised by the use of ܢܣܒ in 4b over against ܫܪܝ ܡܢ in 3a.

Stanza 3 [4c-5, 6, 7-8a]

The inclusio for the stanza is formed between 4c-5a and 7d-8a with the repetition of ܫܪܪܐ (5a, 7d) and of the root ܗܠܟ.

4c and 5b are parallel on the pattern: ܘ + 1st sing. perf. verb + prep. with 3rd sing. pron. suffix + ܘ + 1st sing. perf. verb. The doubling of the verb form produces internal parallelism in each line. 5a appears to be linked with both 4c (walking in truth?) and 5a (following the thought of truth). Syntactically, it forms a central chiasmus with 4c and 5b by its reversal of the 1st sing. subj. and 3rd sing. obj. in the former lines, to 3rd sing. subj. and 1st sing. obj.

4c-5 is very strongly connected with 38:4-5, both semantically (walking with/following Truth and not erring) and by the vocabulary used (ܫܪܪܐ, ܐܝܟ, ܛܥܐ, ܗܠܟ).

The second strophe (6a-b) introduces another group of characters. The bicolon does not follow easily from the preceding tricolon, although there continues to be detail of action concerning the "I". There is a degree of chiasmus between the two lines by the reversal of the 3rd pl. perf. verb + 1st sing. obj. (6a) to 1st sing. perf. verb + 3rd pl. (indir.) obj. (6b), although semantically the "I" is the object of the action in 6b because of the pass. verb. It is possible to suggest semantic links with 4b and 7a from a study of the context of a similar statement in 41:8 (cf. also 28:8).

With the third strophe there is a shift in focus to the Most High as the subject of action upon the "I". 7a and 7d form the inclusio for the major section of the strophe (7a-d) by the repetition of the root ܣܠܩ. The unifying feature of 7a-8a is the 3rd masc. sing. perf. verb (ref. the Most High) with a 1st sing. obj./indir. obj. (indirectly in 7d by the noun obj. with 1st sing. suffix). 7b provides the subject for the section.

There is a loose concluding parallelism between 7b and 7c with ܒ + noun (attribute of the Most High) with 3rd sing. masc. suffix. The action of exaltation in 7d is given added emphasis by the repetition of the root ܪܡܪܡ. Although strongly linked syntactically and semantically with the third strophe, 8a functions also as a concluding monocolon to the entire stanza, returning to the initial motif of walking (4c-5c).

## Stanza 4 [8b-10, 11]

With stanza 4 the focus moves from the Most High to the "I" as the subject of the action.

8b and 10b form the inclusio for the first strophe by the repetition of the root ܦܬܚ. The strophe may be divided into three bicola (8c-9a, 9b-c, 10a-b), all of which are very closely linked semantically and by the repetition of some terms (ܦܬܚ, 8b, 10b; ܐܝܟ, 8b, 10a; ܦܪܙܠܐ, 9a, 9b).

8b-9a is parallel on the pattern: 1st sing. perf. verb + pl. noun obj. + descriptive expression related to the noun obj. 9b follows from 9a by the repetition of ܦܪܙܠܐ in a terrace pattern. 9b and 9c are parallel by the 3rd sing. masc. perf. verb with ref. to the common subj. ܦܪܙܠܐ (9b). On the semantic level, the action is not so much parallel as progressive (the iron grows hot, then melts).

10a-b is parallel with strong antithesis indicated by the polar word-pairs ܪܡܪܡ ܠܐ - ܡܬܬܪܝܡ, ܐܝܟ - ܦܬܚ, which are themselves interrelated: ܠܐ ܪܡܪܡ with ܐܝܟ, ܡܬܬܪܝܡܠܐ with ܦܬܚ. The (semantic) constant in both lines is the "I" who is the major focus of the action. The antithesis is given emphasis by the placement of the word-pair ܐܝܟ - ܦܬܚ in a terrace pattern, 10a concluding with ܐܝܟ and 10b commencing ܦܬܚ.

A new group of characters is introduced with 11a. The focus of the action changes slightly with this bicolon from the "I" and his release and opening of the gates to the ultimate object of his action - the ones who are shut up who are his. The shift in focus is also apparent in the use of ܥܒܕ which provides a link between 11a and 3a. In the latter, the "I" is released, in 11a it is the "I" who releases those who belong to him.

With the repetition of ܐܢܫ in 11a (cf. 8b, 10a) and the double play on ܚܒܫ in 11b (cf. similarly with ܫܒܩ in 38:9), the bicolon in 11a-b effectively concludes the key motif of imprisonment in stanza 4. The cl. introduced by ܕ in 11b expresses the purpose for the action in 11a. There is a degree of parallelism initially between the two lines by the 1st sing. verb + prep./*nota dativi* with 3rd person obj. (ref. to the same group of characters). There is antithesis both within 11a (ܐܢܫ - ܚܙܩ), and between 11a and 11b (ܚܙܩ - ܚܒܫ; cf. 22:4).

Besides the links between this stanza and Ode 42 (cf. stanza 6 below), Ps 107 and Is 45:2 (cf. Harris and Mingana vol. 2), there are similarities with <u>Trimorphic Protennoia</u> 41, 4-35 (Facs. ed. 13: 111; Turner, J.D. 465), <u>The Teaching of Silvanus</u> 110, 19-29 (Facs. ed. 7: 116; Wisse 1984b, 357-8), the Manichaean <u>Pss to Jesus</u> CCLXXI (Allberry 89, line 28) and <u>Pss of Heracleides</u> (Allberry 196, lines 15-16, 20-1).

## Stanza 5 [12-13, 14-15]

The stanza reports a series of actions by the "I" towards those he has released.

The 1st sing. perf. verbs and the frequent use of the 1st sing. suffix and the prep. ܒ provide the unifying features of the first strophe. 12a-b has a degree of parallelism on the pattern: ܣܝܡܬ (understood in 12b) + noun (attribute of the "I") with 1st sing. suffix. The parallelism is strengthened by the word-pair ܚܘܒܐ - ܢܝܚܘܬܐ.

13a-b is parallel with chiasmus: A B C // A' C' B', where A = 1st sing. perf. verb; B = ܒ with obj.; C = obj. of the verb. Semantically, there is no chiasmus since ܐܪܡܝܬ appears to refer to ܠܐܒܝܕܐ rather than ܦܪܩܬ. There is some parallelism also between 12a and 13a on the pattern: 1st sing. perf. verb with noun obj. + 1st sing. suffix.

There is a change to the 3rd masc. pl. subj. with the second strophe. The inclusio for the strophe is formed by the word-pair ܩܒܠ (14a) - ܦܘܩ (14b).

14a-b is parallel on the pattern: 3rd masc. pl. perf. verb + expression with 1st sing. suffix + ܗ + 3rd masc. pl. perf. verb. The parallelism is further strengthened by the word-pair ܢܣܒ - ܦܘܩ. Each line has internal parallelism by the double pattern of the verbs.

15 constitutes a summary line to the preceding bicolon, the cl. in 15 introduced by ܕ ܡܛܠ referring to the actions to the 3rd masc. pl. group in 14. The line has internal parallelism with chiasmus. The first half of the line has a

3rd masc. pl. subj. + the 1st sing. (ܠ) associated with the noun compl. The second half has a 1st sing. subj. + noun compl. + 3rd pl. suffix. The parallelism is enhanced by the merismus expressed by the complementary terms ܪܫܝ and ܪܘܚܐ.

Stanza 6 [16]

The 2nd person and 1st person pl. appear for the first time in this Ode in this stanza. 16 functions as the concluding doxology, the title ܪܫܝ following easily from ܢܩܘܫܝ in 15. ܪܫܝ is also associated with ܪܘܫܡ in 24:1, but the use of ܪܫܝ in the latter is literal rather than metaphorical.

There is a strong semantic link between this Ode and Ode 42 by the common thread of action: the "I" is firstly liberated from a situation of danger/persecution (17:3-4a,8b-10; 42:10-13); the "I" in turn liberates others who belong to him and bestows knowledge, fruits, faith and so on upon them (17:11-15; 42:14-20). There is also some connection by common vocabulary - ܪܬܝܕܐ/ ܪܬܝܕ...ܘܕܦ (17:8b; 42:17a); ܐܝܡܪ (17:11b; 42:16b); ܪܘ (17:14a; 42:14a); ܦܝܕ (17:14b; 42:18).

_____

EXCURSUS: THE "I" AS MESSIAH IN ODE 17 (cf. Chapter III, section 1.3)

The concluding doxology in 16 constitutes a response prompted by the description of the action of the "I" in the Ode but more specifically by the statement in 15. It is clear that the one addressed as "our head, the Lord Messiah" in 16 is the one who speaks in the 1st person in 15 of himself as the head of the members whom he has released, gathered and saved. It is the clearest indication in the Odes of an "I" who speaks who is not the Odist (for the early discussion, cf. Kittel, G. 1914, 78-88).

One assumes that the Odist would include himself with the group who speak the doxology. This raises the question as to whether he really perceives himself as included (in some mystically united way) in the "I" of the remainder of the Ode or whether he simply uses that stylistic device to express a direct dialogue between the Messiah and the community. This style can be observed even among modern hymn composers who sometimes use words from the Hebrew or Christian scriptures in which God or Jesus speaks in the first person, without thereby identifying themselves in some mystical way with the "I" who speaks.

If this is the case with the Odist then it should be possible, once the form-critical analysis and the analysis of imagery has been completed, to designate whole Odes or readily discernible parts of Odes to the Odist or to the Messiah or to the Most High and so on. Above all, if the analysis is thorough, the designation of Odes to certain characters will not be hampered by scholars' theological presuppositions; that is, by what may be considered appropriate material in the mouth of the Odist or other characters.

Franzmann 1990 offers, tentatively (since the analysis of form and imagery remains incomplete), some preliminary steps towards identifying criteria for designating Odes to one or other character.

## ODE 18

1 ܐܬܬܪܝܡ ܠܒܝ ܒܚܘܒܗ ܕܡܪܝܐ ܘܐܬܬܬܪ
ܕܐܫܒܚܝܘܗܝ ܒܗ ܒܫܡܝ
2 ܐܬܚܝܠܘ ܗܕܡܝ
ܐܝܟ ܕܠܐ ܢܦܠܘܢ ܡܢ ܚܝܠܗ
3 ܟܘܪܗܢܐ ܐܬܪܚܩܘ ܡܢ ܦܓܪܝ
ܘܩܡ ܠܡܪܝܐ ܒܨܒܝܢܗ
ܡܛܠ ܕܫܪܝܪܐ ܗܝ ܡܠܟܘܬܗ

4 ܡܪܝܐ ܕܠܡܐ ܡܛܠ ܐܝܠܝܢ ܕܚܣܝܪܝܢ
ܬܫܒܐ ܡܢܝ ܦܬܓܡܝܟ
5 ܐܦܠܐ ܡܛܠ ܥܒܕܝܗܘܢ
ܬܟܠܐ ܡܢܝ ܫܘܡܠܝܟ
6 ܠܐ ܢܙܟܐ ܢܘܗܪܐ ܡܢ ܚܫܘܟܐ
ܐܦܠܐ ܢܥܪܘܩ ܫܪܪܐ ܡܢ ܕܓܠܘܬܐ
7 ܠܙܟܘܬܐ ܬܗܘܐ ܦܘܪܩܢ ܢܨܚܢܟ
ܘܬܬܡܠܐ ܡܢ ܟܠ ܐܬܪ
ܘܬܬܢܛܪ ܡܢ ܠܟܠ ܕܒܒܝܫܬܐ ܐܚܝܕ
8 ܐܢܬ ܐܠܗܝ ܕܓܠܘܬܐ ܘܡܘܬܐ ܠܝܬ ܒܦܘܡܟ
ܐܠܐ ܐܝܬܘܗܝ ܫܘܡܠܝܐ ܨܒܝܢܟ

9 ܘܣܪܝܩܘܬܐ ܠܐ ܝܕܥ ܐܢܬ
ܡܛܠ ܕܐܦܠܐ ܝܕܥܐ ܠܟ
10 ܘܠܐ ܝܕܥ ܐܢܬ ܛܘܥܝܘܬܐ
ܡܛܠ ܕܐܦܠܐ ܗܝ ܝܕܥܐ ܠܟ

11 ܘܐܬܚܙܝܬ ܐܝܟ ܒܘܪܐ ܠܐ ܝܕܥܬܐ
ܘܐܝܟ ܣܪܝܩܘܬܗ ܕܝܡܐ
12 ܘܣܒܪܘ ܒܠܒܗ ܣܘܪܩܐ ܕܪܒܐ ܗܝ
ܘܐܬܘ ܐܦ ܗܢܘܢ ܐܝܟ ܕܡܘܬܗ ܘܐܣܬܪܩܘ

ܘܝܕܥܘ ܐܝܠܝܢ ܕܝܕܥܝܢ 13
ܘܐܬܚܫܒܘ ܘܠܐ ܐܬܛܢܦܘ ܒܡܚܫܒܬܗܘܢ
ܡܛܠ ܕܗܘܘ ܒܬܪܥܝܬܗ ܕܡܪܝܐ 14
ܘܓܚܟܘ ܟܠ ܐܝܠܝܢ ܕܡܗܠܟܝܢ ܒܛܠܘܡܘܬܐ
ܘܗܢܘܢ ܕܝܢ ܡܠܠܘ ܫܪܪܐ 15
ܡܢ ܢܦܚܐ ܕܢܦܚ ܒܗܘܢ ܡܪܝܐ

ܬܫܒܘܚܬܐ ܘܪܒܘܬ ܐܝܩܪܐ ܠܫܡܗ 16

ܗܠܠܘܝܐ

---

1 My heart was lifted up by the love of the Most High and was increased,
that I might glorify him by means of my name.
2 My members were strengthened,
that they might not fall from his power.
3 Infirmities departed afar from my body,
and it stood firm for the Lord by his will,
because solid is his kingdom.

4 Lord, because of those who are in need,
do not cast from me your Word;
5 nor, because of their works,
withhold from me your perfection.
6 Let not light be conquered by darkness,
nor let truth flee from falsehood.
7 To victory let your right hand set our salvation,
and let it receive from every place,
and let it keep whoever is shut up by evils.
8 You, my God, falsehood and death are not in your mouth,
but perfection is your will.

9 And nothingness you do not know,
because neither does it know you.
10 And you do not know error,
because neither does it know you.

11  And ignorance appeared like dust,
     and like the filth of the sea.
12  And the empty ones considered about it that it was great,
     and they came also like its likeness and were emptied out.

13  And they knew, those who know,
     and thought and were not polluted by their thoughts,
14  because they were by the mind of the Most High,
     and laughed at those who walk in error.
15  But they indeed spoke the truth
     by the breath which the Most High breathed in them.

16  Glory and greatness of beauty to his name.

Alleluia.

NOTES TO THE TRANSLATION

3b: N has ܩܡܪܗ but the context appears to demand the sing. reading from H, with ܦܠܚ̈ܝ as the (understood) subj. (*contra* Lattke [1979-86, vol. 1] who suggests ܡܗ ܝܗ̈ܒ as a possible subj.).

3c: ܫܪܝܪ may be translated as either "solid"/"firm" (Harris and Mingana vol. 2; Bauer 1964; Charlesworth 1977; Lattke 1979-86, vol. 1; Emerton; Carmignac 1986) or "true" (Flemming; Ungnad and Staerk; Diettrich 1911; Harris 1911a; Labourt and Batiffol; Bernard; Bruston 1912b; Greßmann 1924). "Solid" has been used on the basis both of the semantic context in 2-3 and of the association elsewhere in the Odes of the kingdom and rock (22:12).

4a-b: Lit. "Lord, that not, because of those who (are) needing, you might cast out from me your word". With the division into two lines, ܡܠܬܟ must be delayed in the English translation until the verb ܬܫܕܐ (H has ܬܫܕܐ) in the second line.
     Neither Ms. has an indication of a break after ܣܢܝܩܝܢ. However the parallelism of 5a-b (break indicated in H after ܠܒܗܘܢ̈) and 4a-b demands it. For the same reason of the parallelism, Diettrich (1911) chooses to disregard the break in 5 and reads 4-5 as a parallel bicolon.

7a: H has ܚܣܝܪܝ.

7c: Lit. "and let it keep from each which is ..."

9b, 10b, 12: The impersonal pron. has been used with ref. to "nothingness", "error", and "ignorance" since it is not clear that personification is intended.

10b: H has ܐܠܐ. N is preferred because of the parallelism of 9b and 10b.

12a: H has the sing. ܝܡܝܢܗ. The pl. verb ܢܣܒܘ requires the pl. reading of N.

14a: The line should be understood as meaning "because they came into being by the mind of the Most High". The interpretation is supported by the "creation" imagery in 15b (cf. Gen 2:7, ܢܘܦܚ ܐܟܬܘܫܬܐ, ܒܡܚܫܒܬܗ ܗܘܝܢ). There is a similar understanding for ܗܘܐ followed by ܒ in 12:8 and 16:19.

14b: H inserts ܗܘܐ after ܕܡܬܚܠ.

ANALYSIS

This Ode is a complex of two sub-odes; the first (1-8), a personal song incorporating confession and petition; the second (9-15), a teaching song about the Lord and believers over against nothingness, error, and ignorance. That a second sub-ode commences with 9a is evident from the vocabulary frequency table. The number of repetitions of ܝܕܥ and its derivatives in the second sub-ode (x 7) makes its absence from the first sub-ode most significant. Only ܚܝܐ is repeated in the two sections.

Stanza 1 [1-3] (= Stanza 1, Sub-ode 1)

1a-b and 2a-b are alternately parallel bicola. 1a and 2a have an initial pattern of 3rd perf. pass. verb + noun (physical attribute of the "I") with 1st sing. suffix. The parallelism is strengthened by the word-pair ܠܒܝ - ܗܕܡܝ. 1b and 2b comprise cls. expressing the reason for the action in 1a and 2a respectively. They follow the pattern: conj. + imperf. verb + prep. (ܒܝܕ functions as a prep.) + noun with pron. suffix.

1a has a degree of internal parallelism by the pass. verbs with a common subj. ܠܒܝ. ܢܛܪ occurs also in the first lines of Odes 21, 36 and 37 (cf. ܕܢܛܪܢܝ, 22:1). 1b is connected with 1a by the word-pair ܢܛܪ - ܢܕܥ.

2a and 3a are linked semantically by the parallel descriptions of the strengthening of the members and the departure of infirmities (cf. 25:9), and by the synonymity of ܗܘܝܬ and ܦܢܝ. 2b and 3b are connected by the word-pair ܢܦܠ - ܩܡ and the parallelism of the concluding phrases ܡܢ ܫܠܡ and ܒܩܘܝܡܗ (ref. to the Lord).

The past tense of 1-3b changes to present tense with 3c, which functions as a concluding confessional statement for the stanza. There is a clear word-play intended between ܫܪܝܪ and ܩܡ.


Stanza 2 [4-5, 6, 7-8]

The division between stanzas is indicated by the change from a report about the Most High in the 3rd person to an address to the Lord in the 2nd person. There is also a shift from action in the past tense (1-3b) to action in the pres./future.

The first strophe (4-5) comprises two alternately parallel bicola. 4a and 5a are more semantically than syntactically parallel, having the general pattern: negative expression + ܡܛܠ + description concerning a 3rd pl. group. There may be merismus intended with the latter, incorporating what the group does not have (their need) with what they have produced (their works). 4b and 5b are parallel on the pattern: 2nd sing. masc. imperf. verb + ܡܢ + noun obj. (attribute of the Lord) with 2nd masc. sing. suffix. There is end rhyme, assonance and an equivalent number of syllables (x 6) in 4b and 5b.

6a-b has central position in the stanza. The bicolon is set off from the rest of the stanza by the break it makes in the address to the Lord in the 2nd masc. sing. However, the interpretation of the negative imperf. verbs as negative jussives makes 6a-b an integral part of the stanza. The bicolon is parallel on the pattern: negative particle + 3rd masc. sing. imperf. verb + noun subj. + ܡܢ with noun obj. The two nouns in each line form polar word-pairs, ܚܝܘܗܝ - ܡܘܬܐ and ܫܪܝܪ - ܕܓܠܘܬܐ.

7a-c is linked with 6 by the repetition of the root ܝܕܥ. The 3rd fem. sing. imperf. verb in each line of the tricolon is interpreted as a jussive with the common subj. ܝܕܥܬܟ. ܐܠܗܘܬܐ has been given emphasis by its placement at the beginning of the strophe. 7b and 7c are initially parallel with a 3rd sing. fem. imperf. verb + ܡܢ with associated phrase/cl. 7a contains the only occurrence of the 1st pl. in this Ode.

With 8a, there is a change from the petitions of 4-7 to a concluding confessional statement concerning God. The bicolon is parallel with initial chiasmus: A B C // B A' C', where A = noun subj./s; B = ܝܕܥ/ܝܕܥ; C = ܒ + noun obj.

(attribute of God) with 2nd masc. sing. suffix. A study of the vocabulary frequency table indicates that 8 should be taken with stanza 2 rather than with stanza 3. ܟ̈ܘܠܗܝܢ occurs in 8a and 6b, ܟܣܡܚ in 8b and 5b. The repetition of ܚܘܒܐ (3b, 8b) provides a certain connection between the final lines of stanzas 1 and 2.

## Stanza 3 [9-10] (= Stanza 1, Sub-ode 2)

Although the second sub-ode commences with 9a there is some connection between the two sub-odes by the continuation of the address to the Lord in the 2nd person.

9-10 has alternately parallel lines. 9a and 10a are parallel with chiasmus on the pattern: A B // B A', where A = noun subj., and B = ܐܝܬ ܠܟ ܠܐ. 10b is an exact repetition of 9b, except for the addition of ܂ܗܘ for emphasis. The antithesis between the concepts of emptiness/nothingness and knowing is also found in 12 and 13a.

## Stanza 4 [11-12]

The division of the stanzas is indicated by the shift from pres. to past tense, and by the change from an address to God in the 2nd person to an impersonal report concerning ignorance and the empty ones. There is a connection with the preceding stanza by the repetition of the roots ܠܟ (11a) and ܣܪܩ (12a, 12b). The repetition of the latter in 9a indicates the inclusio for the two stanzas formed by 9a and 12a-b.

11a-b is parallel, the similes with ܐܝܟ referring to the common subj. ܠܐ ܟܕܝܠ in 11a. The parallelism is enhanced by the semantic similarity of the images (cf. 29:10). 12a-b is parallel with initial 3rd pl. perf. verbs and a wordplay on the root ܣܪܩ. There is a subtle irony in the antithesis of being great (12a) and being emptied out (12b).

## Stanza 5 [13-15]

Stanza 5 is the antithesis to stanza 3 - the ones who know over against the empty ones who are in the likeness of ignorance.

13a and 13b are parallel with initial 3rd pl. perf. verbs. Each line has internal parallelism by the doubling of the main root (ܝܕܥ in 13a; ܛܥܐ in 13b). There is a degree of parallelism in 14a-b by the initial 3rd pl. perf. verbs and the concluding antithetical phrases (mind of the Most High over against error) introduced by ܒ. The bicolon as a whole is antithetical, contrasting those who are created by the mind of the Most High with those who follow error.

15a follows easily from 14b by the antithesis of those who speak the truth over against those who walk in error (cf. the word-pair ܟܐܢܘܬܐ - ܛܥܝܐ). 15b has internal parallelism by the repetition of the root ܢܦܠ. 14 and 15 are further linked by the use of ܒܪܝܬܐ at the conclusion of 14a and 15b.


## Stanza 6 [16]

The concluding doxology in 16 forms the inclusio for the Ode with 1b by the repetition of ܬܫܒܘܚܬܐ and ܚܝܐ. The same vocabulary terms occur in the inclusio for Ps 144 (1-2, 21).

## ODE 19 [Syriac]

1 ܟܣܐ ܕܚܠܒܐ ܐܬܩܪܒ ܠܝ
ܘܐܫܬܝܬܗ ܒܚܠܝܘܬܐ ܕܒܣܝܡܘܬܗ ܕܡܪܝܐ
2 ܒܪܐ ܟܣܐ ܐܝܬܘܗܝ
ܘܗܘ ܕܐܬܚܠܒ ܐܒܐ
ܘܕܚܠܒܬܗ ܪܘܚܐ ܕܩܘܕܫܐ
3 ܡܛܠ ܕܬܕ̈ܘܗܝ ܐܬܡܠܝܘ
ܘܠܐ ܡܬܒܥܐ ܗܘܐ ܕܡܫܬܦܩܐܝܬ ܢܫܬܕܪ ܚܠܒܗ

4 ܦܬܚܬ ܠܥܘܒܗ ܪܘܚܐ ܕܩܘܕܫܐ
ܘܡܙܓܬ ܚܠܒܐ ܕܬܪܝܢ ܬܕ̈ܘܗܝ ܕܐܒܐ
5 ܘܝܗܒܬ ܚܘܠܛܢܐ ܠܥܠܡܐ ܟܕ ܠܐ ܝܕܥܝܢ
ܘܗܢܘܢ ܕܢܣܒܝܢ ܒܡܫܡܠܝܘܬܗ ܐܝܬܝܗܘܢ ܕܝܡܝܢܐ

6 ܓܦܬ ܪܚܡܗ ܕܒܬܘܠܬܐ
ܘܢܣܒܬ ܒܛܢܐ ܘܝܠܕܬ
7 ܘܗܘܬ ܐܡܐ ܒܬܘܠܬܐ ܒܪ̈ܚܡܐ ܣܓܝܐܐ
ܘܚܒܠܬ ܘܝܠܕܬ ܒܪܐ

ܘܠܐ ܟܐܒ ܠܗ̇
8 ܡܛܠ ܕܠܐ ܗܘܐ ܡܫܬܦܩܐܝܬ ܗܘܬ
9 ܘܠܐ ܒܥܬ ܚܝܬܐ
ܡܛܠ ܕܐܚܝܗ̇.....10.....ܐܝܟ ܓܒܪܐ

ܝܠܕܬ ܒܨܒܝܢܐ
ܘܝܠܕܬ ܒܬܚܘܝܬܐ
ܘܩܢܬ ܒܐܘܚܕܢܐ ܣܓܝܐܐ
11 ܘܐܚܒܬ ܒܦܘܪܩܢܐ
ܘܢܛܪܬ ܒܒܣܝܡܘܬܐ
ܘܚܘܝܬ ܒܪܒܘܬܐ

ܗܠܠܘܝܐ

1   A cup of milk was brought near to me,
    and I drank it in the sweetness of the Lord's gentleness.
2   The Son is the cup;
    and he who was milked, the Father;
    and she who milked him, the Spirit of holiness;
3   because his breasts were filled,
    and it was necessary that his milk might not be cast out without cause.

4   The Spirit of holiness opened her womb,
    and mixed the milk of the two breasts of the Father,
5   and gave the mixture to the world although they did not know.
    And they who receive are in the perfection of the right hand.

6   The womb of the Virgin caught,
    and she received conception and brought forth.
7   And the Virgin became a mother by great mercy,
    and she was in labour and brought forth a son.

    And it did not cause her pain,
8   because it was not without cause.
9   And she did not seek a midwife,
    because he gave her life     10     like a man.

    She brought forth with desire,
    and she brought forth with manifestation,
    and she gained with great force,
11  and she loved with salvation,
    and she kept with gentleness,
    and she manifested with greatness.

    Alleluia.

---

## ODE 19 [Latin]

6   infirmatus est uterus uirginis
    et accepit fetum et grauata est
7   et facta est in multa miseratione mater uirgo

6    The womb of the Virgin was weakened,
     and she received young and she was made pregnant.
7    And the Virgin became a mother in great compassion.

NOTES TO THE TRANSLATION

2c: H has ܡܬܒܠܘܢ. N preserves the parallel structure of 2b and 2c.

3b: Lit. "and it was not necessary that without cause his milk might be cast out."

4a: For the interpretation of ܥܘܒܗ as "womb" rather than "bosom", cf. Drijvers 1980, 341-5.

5a: The pl. ܝܗܒܝ is used in relation to ܥܠܡܐ. Either the latter must be regarded as a collective noun or it should be emended to the pl. (cf. Greßmann 1924). If the emendation is made, it appears that cosmological action is intended here and there are similarities with 12:4 ("And the Most High gave him to his aeons").

6a: There is difficulty with the meaning of ܦܪܣܬ both within the Syriac line and in its relation to Lactantius' "infirmatus est". Labourt and Batiffol interpret ܦܪܣܬ as "alas produxit" ("L'Esprit étendit ses ailes sur le sein de la Vierge") and propose that the original Greek ἐπέπτη was translated slavishly into Syriac without due care being taken that the prep. included in the Greek verb form be rendered by ܥܠ. The discrepancy between the Syriac and the version used by Lactantius is explained by a Latin translator's having misread the aorist of ἐπιπέτομαι as some form of πίπτω. The suggestion of Barnes that ܦܪܣܬ be emended to ܦܪܣ (1910b, 574) presents less difficulty.

Flemming's proposal of "umarmte" (from the Targum meaning for the Piel of נפק) is followed by Bruston 1912b and Emerton. In this case, the 3rd fem. sing. subj. refers to the Spirit of holiness (4a) and the obj. is ܒܬܘܠܬܐ ܕܡܪܝܐ.

6b: Lattke (1979-86, vol. 1) translates "grauata est" literally as "sie war beschwert". The semantic context seems to call for the metaphorical meaning "to make pregnant" (Lewis and Short 829).

9b/10a: ܐܝܟ ܓܒܪܐ has been placed at the conclusion of 9b on the basis of the structure of 10b-11c. Such an arrangement changes the whole discussion of the phrase ܐܝܟ ܓܒܪܐ from how the Virgin could be said to give birth like a man (cf. the summary and discussion in Lagrand 99-104 and Drijvers 1980, 348-9), to how he (the Father) gives her life like a man/husband.

Given the play on the root ܚܝܐ in 9a and 9b, it seems possible to follow the suggestion of Harris (1911a; Harris and Mingana vol. 2; cf. also Bernard, Carmignac 1986, and the discussion by Drijvers 1980, 346-7) that ܚܝܐ in 9b should be interpreted as the action of delivering a woman in childbirth. In this case 9b/10a would read "because he delivered her like a man." Since ܓܒܪܐ may mean "man" or "husband", it is possible to interpret 9a-9b/10a as meaning that the Virgin had no need of a midwife because the Father acted as midwife, as a woman's husband might (for Eve as the virgin/pregnant one who is also midwife, cf. On the Origin of the World 114, 9-11; Facs. ed. 2: 126; Bethge and Wintermute 171; cf. also The Thunder, Perfect Mind 13, 25-27; Facs. ed. 6: 17; MacRae 1984b, 272). Thus ܐܝܟ ܓܒܪܐ refers to the Father rather than to the Virgin. The use of the image of husband for the Father is strengthened by the earlier detail of the Ode. The milk of the breasts of the Father (his sperm? cf. Drijvers 1980, 341), which is mixed in the womb of the Spirit, becomes eventually the matter of conception by the Virgin.

10d: For the sake of consistency, ܩܢܐ is translated as "gained", although it has connotations here of "created" (cf. Deut 32:6), especially in its association with ܥܠ; cf. 41:9b.

ANALYSIS

Stanza 1 [1, 2, 3]

1a-b contains the only use of the 1st sing. in this Ode. The bicolon functions as a personal introduction to the rather more impersonal reporting/teaching sections of the Ode. It serves also to introduce the motif of "milk" in the first two stanzas. The action described in the bicolon may have connotations of a liturgical setting (Betz 17-8; cf. 11:6, ܐܢܐ ܫܬܝܬ ܡܢ ܡܝܐ ܚܝܐ ܕܠܐ ܡܝܘܬܝܢ).

There is a degree of chiasmus in 1a-b by the pattern of subj. and obj./indir. obj. 1a has ܟܣܐ ܕܚܠܒܐ as subj. and the 1st sing. as the indir. obj.; 1b has the 1st sing. as subj. and the 3rd sing. masc. suffix (ref. to ܟܣܐ ܕܚܠܒܐ) as obj. The lines are also connected by the word-pair ܫܬܐ - ܡܙܓ.

2a-c moves easily from 1a by the repetition of ܟܡܐ and the root ܝܠܕ. Each line of the tricolon comprises a description of a key character (Son, Father, Spirit of holiness) associated with the motif of "milk". The importance of the descriptions is emphasised by the central position which the strophe holds in the stanza between the initial and concluding bicola.

There is some chiasmus between 2a and 2b by the placement of the elements of the word-pair ܐܒܐ - ܒܪܐ and their respective descriptions ("cup", "he who was milked"). 2b and 2c are parallel on the pattern: ܕ (rel. particle) + ܝܠܕ (with suffix in 2c) + noun subj.

3a is connected to the preceding strophe by the cl. introduced by ܕ ܡܬܚܠܒ which refers to ܝܠܕܬܗ in 2c. 3a and 3b are linked semantically by the association of ܬܕܝܗ, and ܝܠܕܗ and the progression of the action from the breasts being full to the release of the milk. There is a degree of chiasmus by the placement of the noun subjs. with 3rd masc. sing. suffix (his breasts, his milk) in relation to the main verbs ("were filled", "might be cast out").

Stanza 2 [4-5]

Stanza 2 introduces a series of actions by the Spirit of holiness. There is a connection with the preceding stanza by the repetition of vocabulary in 4a-b - ܪܘܚܐ ܕܩܘܕܫܐ, ܝܠܕ, ܬܕܝܗ.

4a, 4b, and 5a are initially parallel on the pattern: 3rd sing. fem. perf. verb (subj. is the Spirit of holiness) + noun obj. The three verbs follow a logical sequence: opening the womb, mixing the milk, giving the mixture. 5b functions as a concluding confessional statement for the stanza. It is unclear whether the ones who receive (the mixture) are equivalent to the world in 5a or whether 5a and 5b are intended to be antithetical - the ignorant world over against those who receive the mixture. For the possible connection between 5 and the prologue of the Gospel of John, cf. Drijvers 1980, 342-4.

Stanza 3 [6-7b]

With stanza 3 the focus of the report shifts to the Virgin. Moreover, the central motif changes from the milk of the Father to the bearing of the Virgin, though there is a connection between the motifs (cf. the notes to the translation for 9b/10a). A study of the vocabulary frequency table indicates the change in motif. The root ܝܠܕ occurs only in stanzas 1 and 2 (x 5), the root ܢܣܒ only in stanzas 3, 4, and 5 (x 4), and these two roots are those most frequently repeated in the Ode. There is, however, some connection between stanza 3 and stanza

2 by the similarity of the series of three actions described for the Virgin in 6 (the womb of the virgin receives the mixture, she conceives and bears a son) to the three-verb series described for the Spirit of holiness in 4-5a.

6-7b comprises a quatrain with alternate parallelism, indicated principally by the alternate repetition of ܟܒ݁ܠܘܒ (6a, 7a) and ܕܠܬ (6b, 7b). There is also a degree of parallelism by the pattern of 3rd sing. fem. perf. verbs - one in 6a and 7a, two in 6b and 7b, the second of the two being in both cases ܕܠܬ. Semantically 6a-b and 7a-b are very closely connected, the description of the action in 7 elaborating on the final verb, ܕܠܬ, in 6b.

6b and 7b are parallel on the general pattern of two 3rd sing. fem. perf. verbs joined by ܘ. There is a degree of chiasmus between the lines by the use of a noun obj. with the first verb, ܕܒܡܘ, in 6b and with the second verb, ܕܠܬ, in 7b.

## Stanza 4 [7c-9b/10a]

The stanza provides detail concerned with the birth of the Son (7b). The two bicola have alternate parallelism, indicated by the initial patterning of elements: ܠܐܘ + verb in 7c and 9a, ܘ ܠܠܝܡ + cl. in 8 and 9b/10a. There is also semantic parallelism since 7c and 9a comprise a (negative) detail concerning the birth, 8 and 9b/10a following with a cl. introduced by ܘ ܠܠܝܡ giving the reason for the detail in 7c and 9a respectively. The parallelism is enhanced by the number of syllables per line - four in 7c and 9a, seven in 8 and 9b/10a.

9a and 9b/10a are strongly linked by the play on the root ܟܘ (cf. the translation notes). The repetition of ܕܒܩܘܣܐ in 3b and 8 may indicate a connection between the result of the milking of the Father and the bearing of a son by the Virgin (cf. Drijvers 1980, 346).

## Stanza 5 [10b-11c]

This strictly structured stanza which focusses on the action of the Virgin could be considered as a sub-ode, although it has a connection with stanza 3 by the repetition of the root ܠܬ and with stanza 1 by the repetition of ܟܒܢܡܘܒܡ.

The form of the stanza is very simple, each line comprising a 3rd sing. fem. perf. verb (subj. is the Virgin) + ܒ + noun. ܟܟܠܡ in 10d must be considered as an addition since not only does it disturb the otherwise strict parallelism of the lines but, without it, 10d would conform to what appears to be a deliberate pattern of five syllables per line for the stanza.

10b and 10c are more closely parallel by the repetition of the root ܢܠ. If the remaining four lines in the stanza are associated in two bicola, it is possible to detect (semantic) alternate parallelism. 10d and 11b speak of gaining/possessing (but cf. the notes to the translation for 10d) and keeping (inwardly directed action), 11a and 11c, of loving and manifesting (outwardly directed action). There is also parallelism between 11b and 11c by the use of the polar word-pair ܟܬܢܬܝܡܐܒ - ܟܬܢܒܝ.

## ODE 20

1 ܟܗܢܐ ܕܡܪܝܐ ܐܢܐ ܐܝܬܝ
ܘܠܗ ܗܘ ܡܟܗܢ ܐܢܐ
2 ܘܠܗ ܡܩܪܒ ܐܢܐ ܩܘܪܒܢܐ ܕܡܚܫܒܬܗ
3 ܠܐ ܗܘܬ ܓܝܪ ܐܝܟ ܥܠܡܐ
ܐܦܠܐ ܐܝܟ ܒܣܪܐ ܡܚܫܒܬܗ
ܐܦܠܐ ܐܝܟ ܗܢܘܢ ܕܦܠܚܝܢ ܒܣܪܢܐܝܬ
4 ܩܘܪܒܢܗ ܕܡܪܝܐ ܙܕܝܩܘܬܐ ܗܝ
ܘܕܟܝܘܬܐ ܕܠܒܐ ܘܕܣ̈ܦܘܬܐ
5 ܩܪܒ ܟܘ̈ܠܝܬܟ ܕܠܐ ܡܘܡܐ

ܘܪ̈ܚܡܝܟ ܠܐ ܢܐܠܨܘܢ ܪ̈ܚܡܐ
ܘܢܦܫܟ ܠܐ ܬܐܠܘܨ ܢܦܫܐ
6 ܠܐ ܬܩܢܐ ܢܘܟܪܝܐ ܒܕܡܐ ܕܢܦܫܟ
ܐܦܠܐ ܬܒܥܐ ܠܡܟܠ ܠܩܪܝܒܟ
ܐܦܠܐ ܬܫܠܘܚܝܘܗܝ ܠܟܣܝܘܬܐ ܕܦܓܪܗ

7 ܠܒܫ ܕܝܢ ܠܛܝܒܘܬܗ ܕܡܪܝܐ ܕܠܐ ܚܣܡܐ
ܘܬܐ ܠܦܪܕܝܣܗ
ܘܥܒܕ ܠܟ ܟܠܝܠܐ ܡܢ ܐܝܠܢܗ
8 ܘܣܝܡ ܥܠ ܪ̈ܝܫܟ
ܘܐܬܒܣܡ
ܘܐܣܬܡܟ ܥܠ ܢܝܚܘܬܗ

9 ܘܬܗܠܟ ܩܕܡܝܟ ܬܫܒܘܚܬܗ
ܘܬܩܒܠ ܡܢ ܒܣܝܡܘܬܗ ܘܡܢ ܛܝܒܘܬܗ
ܘܬܪܘܢ ܒܫܪܪܐ ܒܬܫܒܘܚܬܐ ܕܩܘܕܫܗ

10 ܬܫܒܘܚܬܐ ܘܐܝܩܪܐ ܠܫܡܗ

ܗܠܠܘܝܐ

1 A priest of the Lord am I,
and him indeed I serve as a priest,
2 and to him I offer the offering of his thought.
3 For it was not like the world,
nor like the flesh, his thought;
nor like them who serve according to the flesh.
4 The Lord's offering is righteousness,
and purity of heart and lips.
5 Offer your spotless kidneys.

And let not your bowels constrain bowels,
and let not your soul constrain a soul.
6 Do not gain a stranger by the blood of yourself,
nor seek to deceive your neighbour,
nor deprive him of the covering of his nakedness.

7 But put on the grace of the Lord without jealousy,
and come into his paradise.
And make for yourself a crown from his tree,
8 and set (it) upon your head.
And refresh yourself,
and lean upon his rest.

9 And his glory will go before you;
and you will receive from his gentleness and from his grace,
and you will be anointed in truth by the glory of his holiness.

10 Glory and honour to his name.

Alleluia.

NOTES TO THE TRANSLATION

5a: N has ܟ̈ܘܠܝܬ. The reading from H fits the context more aptly. The literal translation "kidneys" is to be understood as referring to the inner person, the place of emotion and affection.

5b: ܪ̈ܚܡܐ is clearly intended in parallel to ܢܦܫܐ, and should be translated literally as "bowels" (= flesh; cf. Lattke 1979-86, vol. 1) rather than metaphorically as "compassion" (Smith, R.P. 2: 3882-3).

6a: This line is one of the most difficult in the Odes. Harris (1909) emends ܒܕܡܐ (by the blood) to ܒܕܡܝܐ (by the price), (cf. also Flemming; Labourt and Batiffol; Ungnad and Staerk 21 n. 2). Diettrich (1911) divides ܒܕܡܐ into ܒܕ (denn [er]) and ܡܐ (dasselbe, was) to translate with: "denn er ist dasselbe, was du bist". Bruston's (1912b) reading of the verb as 3rd sing. fem. ("Qu'une étrangère ne s'enrichisse pas avec le sang de ton âme") takes no account of the parallel structure of 6a-c which demands a series of 2nd sing. masc. negative imperf. verbs. Charlesworth (1977) suggests interpreting ܕܡܐ as the part. act. of the verb "to be like" rather than the emphatic noun "blood". ܒ is translated as "because". Lattke (1979-86, vol. 1) emends the text to b‹d› dm' dnpšk ("da er dein eigenes Blut [ist]").

Köbert finds no difficulty with ܒܕܡܐ ܕܢܦܫܟ which occurs in Sir 33:31 (cf. also ܕܡܐ ܕܢܦ̈ܫܬܐ, Jer 2:34), but suggests treating ܢܘܟܪܝܐ as a vocative and emending ܡܢܐ to ܡܢܠ ("Beneide nicht, Fremdling, dein eigen Blut" [530]). This reading would require that ܢܘܟܪܝܐ be understood as a technical term in the Odes for a member of the community. ܐܟܣܢܝܐ is used for the "I" in relation to "all who saw me" in 17:6, but ܢܘܟܪܝܐ is used only in a negative sense for whatever is alien to the Lord (3:6; 6:3; cf. Franzmann 1990, n.14). Köbert's emendation takes no account of the (polar) parallelism of the stranger and the neighbour in 6a-b.

In the margin of his 1911 edition, Harris wrote: "? by a slight change: hate". The suggestion appears, with further emendation, in the critical notes in Harris and Mingana: ܠܐ ܬܣܢܐ ܢܘܟܪܝܐ ܕܒܕܘܡܝܐ ܕܢܦܫܟ ("Thou shalt not hate the stranger who is in thy own likeness"; 2: 313). The emendment ܬܣܢܐ certainly appears to fit the context of Sir 33:30-31,

> ܐܢ ܚܕ ܗܘ ܥܒܕܟ ܢܗܘܐ ܐܝܟܘܬܟ: ܡܛܠ ܕܐܝܟܘܬܟ ܗܢܐ ܢܦܩܬܟ. ܐܢ ܚܕ
> ܗܘ ܥܒܕܟ: ܐܝܟ ܐܚܘܟ ܚܫܘܒܝܗܝ. ܘܠܐ ܬܬܟܬܫ ܒܕܡܐ ܕܢܦܫܟ. ܡܛܠ
> ܕܐܢ ܬܦܪܘܥܝܗܝ...

"If one is your servant, he will be like you. Because like you (is) this your expense. If one is your servant, regard him as your brother. And do not contend in the blood of your soul. Because if you smite him..."

The verbs of contending and acquiring are somewhat similar in Coptic and it may be possible that ⲘⲡϤϢⲰⲡ has been read as ⲘⲡϤϢⲰⲬⲈ and the mistake passed into a Syriac translation.

9b: N has mistakenly copied ܡܐܢܒܠ.

9c: The verb ܡܢ occurs only in 40:3 apart from this line. Since 40:3 refers to the members of the "I" anointed by the Lord's Odes, it seems possible that here ܟܬܘܒܚܬܐ should be interpreted as "hymn" rather than "glory".

ANALYSIS

Stanza 1 [1-2, 3, 4-5a]

The first stanza focusses on the theme of offering to the Lord, with the root ܩܪܒ repeated in 2 (x 2), 4, and 5a.

1a-b functions as the introduction to the central motif by establishing the identity of the "I" as priest of the Lord. The bicolon has a degree of parallelism with the repetition of the root ܟܡܪ, the 1st sing. subj., and ref. to the Lord (by 3rd sing. masc. suffix in 1b) in association with the root ܟܡܪ. 1b and the first half of 2 are parallel on the pattern: ܡܠܐ + masc. sing. Pael part. act. + ܐܘܐ (copula). 2 has internal parallelism by the repetition of ܩܪܒ and by the inverted pattern: A B C B' A', where A = a focus on the Lord by the 3rd masc. sing. suffix; B = the root ܩܪܒ.

The final element of strophe 1, ܡܚܫܒܬܗ, becomes the subject of strophe 2 (3a-c), with the repetition of the term in the central line of the tricolon (3b). 3a-c is parallel on the pattern: (ܗܘܬ) ܠܐ/ܠܐܝܬ + ܠܝ with obj. (nouns in 3a-b; cl. in 3c). The parallelism is strengthened by the use of ܟܐܡܪܐ/ܕܟܐܡܪܐ (3b, 3c).

Strophe 3 (4-5a) presents the positive description of the offering to the Lord as opposed to the negative description given in strophe 2. 4a-b has the parallel compls. ܟܗܢܘܬܝ and ܟܕܢܘܬܐ (ref. to the common subj. ܠܝܒܐ ܡܩܪܒܝܢ in 4a). 4b has internal parallelism by the word-pair ܠܒܐ - ܟܕܘܝܗ, the elements of which depend, in a gen. contruction, on ܟܕܢܘܬܐ.

5a functions as the concluding exhortation/invitation of the first stanza. The occurrence of the 2nd sing. masc. imper. in this line, following the report style of 1-4b, would generally indicate a stanza division. Moreover, the imper. in 5a is followed by a series of negative imperf. verbs (5b-6c), which are interpreted as imperatives, and which either have the 2nd masc. sing. as subj. (6a-c) or associated with the noun subj. by the use of a suffix (5b-c).

However, the positive exhortation in 5a which fits easily within the theme of stanza 1 is in sharp contrast to the negative (ethical) commands in 5b-6c. More importantly, the use of ܩܪܒ in 5a means that the line effectively forms an inclusio for the strophe with 4a, and provides the conclusion for the motif of offering in the Ode (the root ܩܪܒ occurs in 6b but its use is not relevant to the motif of offering). Finally, 5a is linked with 4b by the semantic similarity of the concepts of purity and spotlessness and by the word-pair ܠܒ - ܩܕܝܫܘܬ.

## Stanza 2 [5b-c, 6]

This stanza comprises the total section of lines containing negative imperf. verbs either with a 2nd sing. masc. subj. or with a noun subj. + 2nd sing. masc. suffix.

5b-c is strictly parallel on the pattern: noun subj. + 2nd masc. sing. suffix + ܠܐ + 3rd imperf. of ܐܙܠ + noun obj. (repetition of the noun subjs. ܬܪܥܝܬ and ܢܦܫ produces internal parallelism in each line). The bicolon exhibits merismus by the use of the terms ܬܪܥܝܬܟ and ܢܦܫܟ. The command against restraint concerns the whole person, bowels (flesh) and soul.

6a-c repeats the form of the three initial negatives (...ܘܠܐ...ܘܠܐ...ܠܐ) found in 3a-c. The lines are parallel on the pattern: ܠܐ(ܐܘ) + 2nd sing. masc. imperf. verb. 6a and 6c are more closely parallel, the verb followed by obj. + prep. + noun obj. + ܘ + noun with pron. suffix. 6a and 6b are linked by the use of the polar word-pair ܢܘܟܪܝ - ܩܪܝܒ, which brings an element of merismus to the command (do not wrong anyone, neither the stranger nor your neighbour). ܩܪܝܒ functions as the common object of the action in 6b and 6c. The strophe is connected with 5b-c by the repetition of ܢܦܫ in 6a.

## Stanza 3 [7-8]

The stanza follows easily from stanza 2 by the semantic connection between the covering of nakedness in 6c and ܠܒܫ in 7a. The style shifts from the negative commands of stanza 2 to a series of positive invitations/exhortations. The logical semantic progression of the series of parallel initial 2nd masc. sing. positive imper. verbs brings an internal cohesion to the stanza.

Apart from the initial verb form, most of the lines are connected by an emphasis upon some attribute of the Lord (his grace, 7a; his paradise, 7b; his tree, 7c; his rest, 8c). There is a degree of parallelism between 8a and 8c on the pattern: 2nd masc. sing. imper. verb + ܠܟ + noun with pron. suffix. There are a number of associations of vocabulary found elsewhere in the Odes: ܛܝܒܘܬܐ with ܠܒܫ (4:6), the phrase ܛܝܒܘܬܗ ܕܡܪܝܐ ܕܠܐ ܚܣܡܐ (23:4), ܦܪܕܝܣܐ with ܐܝܠܢܐ (Ode 11, passim), ܟܠܝܠܐ with ܒܣܡ (9:8,11).

Stanza 4 [9]

Stanza 4 describes future actions which will result from the acceptance of the invitations in stanza 3. The division of stanzas is indicated syntactically by the change from the imper. to the indicative mood. The repetition of ܛܝܒܘܬܐ (7a, 9b) and the root ܒܣܡ (8b, 9b) links this stanza with stanza 3. There are no other significant links between stanzas in this Ode by the repetition of vocabulary. The repetition of ܬܫܒܘܚܬܐ in two of the three lines of this stanza provides an important internal unity.

9a functions as an introduction to 9b-c. There is a connection between the introduction and the bicolon by the use of the initial imperf. verbs and by the emphasis on the attributes of the Lord (his glory, 9a; his gentleness, his grace, 9b; his holiness, 9c). 9a is also connected with 9b by the word-pair ܬܫܒܘܚܬܐ - ܛܝܒܘܬܐ.

9b-c has a degree of parallelism by the use of the 2nd masc. sing. imperf. verbs with prep. phrases associated with some attribute of the Lord which is being given to/effecting some action upon the person addressed. The connection of the lines is further strengthened by the word-pair ܛܝܒܘܬܐ - ܒܣܝܡܘܬܐ. There is internal parallelism in 9b by the double pattern of ܒ + noun (attribute of the Lord) with 3rd masc. sing. suffix.

Stanza 5 [10]

10 functions as the concluding doxology for the Ode (cf. 16:20; 18:16). It is connected with the preceding stanza by the repetition of ܬܫܒܘܚܬܐ.

## ODE 21

1 ܐܝܕܝ ܐܪܝܡܬ ܠܡܪܘܡܐ
ܠܚܢܢܗ ܕܡܪܝܐ
2 ܡܛܠ ܕܐܣܘܪܝ ܫܪܐ ܡܢܝ
ܘܐܪܝܡܢܝ ܡܥܕܪܢܝ
ܠܚܢܢܗ ܘܠܦܘܪܩܢܗ

3 ܘܫܠܚܬ ܚܫܘܟܐ
ܘܠܒܫܬ ܢܘܗܪܐ
4 ܘܗܘܘ ܠܝ ܗܕܡܐ ܠܘܬ ܢܦܫܝ
ܟܕ ܠܐ ܐܝܬ ܒܗܘܢ ܟܐܒܐ
ܐܦܠܐ ܐܘܠܨܢܐ ܐܦܠܐ ܫܢ̈ܝܐ
5 ܘܝܬܝܪܐܝܬ ܡܥܕܪܢܝܬܐ ܗܘܬ ܠܝ
ܡܚܫܒܬܗ ܕܡܪܝܐ
ܘܫܘܬܦܘܬܗ ܕܠܐ ܚܒܠܐ

6 ܘܐܬܬܪܝܡܬ ܒܢܘܗܪܐ
ܘܥܒܪܬ ܩܕܡ ܐܦ̈ܘܗܝ
7 ܘܗܘܝܬ ܩܪܝܒ ܐܢܐ ܠܗ
ܟܕ ܡܫܒܚ ܐܢܐ
ܘܡܘܕܐ ܐܢܐ ܠܗ

8 ܐܒܥ ܠܒܝ
ܘܐܫܬܟܚ ܒܦܘܡܝ
ܘܕܢܚ ܥܠ ܣܦ̈ܘܬܝ
9 ܘܪܒ ܥܠ ܐܦ̈ܝ
ܕܘܨܗ ܕܡܪܝܐ ܘܫܘܒܚܗ

ܗܠܠܘܝܐ

---

1 My arms I lifted up to the height,
to the compassion of the Lord;
2 because my chains he cast from me.
And my helper lifted me up
to his compassion and to his salvation.

3   And I stripped off darkness,
    and put on light.
4   And members were mine with me,
    although there was no sickness in them,
    nor restraint nor sufferings.
5   And it was increasingly helpful to me;
    the thought of the Lord,
    and his incorrupted fellowship.

6   And I was lifted up by the light,
    and passed before his face.
7   And I was near him,
    while glorifying,
    and praising him.

8   My heart overflowed.
    And it was found in my mouth,
    and it dawned upon my lips.
9   And it became great upon my face;
    the Lord's leaping for joy and his glory.

Alleluia.

NOTES TO THE TRANSLATION

1a: All translators follow the more logical reading in H (ܕܖ̈ܕ, "my arms") rather than N (ܕܖܕ, "my arm").

4a: ܠ ܗܘܘ (were to me = were mine); ܢܦܫܝ ܠܘܬ (with my soul = with me).

4b: H omits ܠ. That the N reading is correct is clear from the following ܐܦܠܐ (x 2).

7b-c: No break is indicated in the Mss., although N is smudged and difficult to read. The division is made on the basis of the structure of 7a-c.

8a: The translations are fairly evenly divided between those which have ܠܒܝ as subj. of ܐܫܟܚ (Harris 1909, 1911a [with a correction in the margin to ܠܒܝ as obj.]; Flemming, Ungnad and Staerk, Diettrich 1911, Labourt and Batiffol, Bernard, and Bruston 1912b) and those which have it as the obj. (Harris and Mingana vol. 2, Bauer 1964, Charlesworth 1977, Lattke 1979-86, vol. 1, Emerton, Carmignac 1986). The choice for the former translation is made on the basis of Ps 45:1 (ܐܟܒܠ ܠܒܝ ܦܘܢܨܟ ܠܕܪ) and of the structure of 8a-c.

9b: Translators generally follow the reading from H, ܩܗܢܒܩܘܗܬܘ, rather than N, ܟܗܢܒܩܘܗܟ (cf. Lattke 1979-86, vol. 1), as the more logical of the variants.

ANALYSIS

Stanza 1 [1-2]

The inclusio for the stanza is formed by the parallel bicola, 1a-b and 2b-c, with the repetition of ܢܩܗ in the first line of the bicola (1a, 2b) followed by ܟܘܣ in the second line (1b, 2c).
1a-b is parallel, 1b comprising a second phrase introduced by ܠ in parallel to ܠܢܗܢܘܟ and dependent upon ܢܝ܀ ܐܝܪܒܘܗ. In the bicolon in 2b-c, the 1st sing. is the obj. of ܢܩܗ, whereas it is the subj. in 1a. ܟܘܣ is repeated in 2c, and extended to include another attribute of the Lord (ܦܢܘܠܗ).
2a has the central position between the parallel bicola. It effectively provides the reason for the subsequent action in both parallel bicola. There is some parallelism between 1a and 2a (pl. noun obj. with 1st sing. suffix + perf. verb), and between 2a and 2b (3rd sing. masc. perf. verb + 1st sing. obj. suffix/ܢܝ܂). The unity of the stanza is emphasised by the pattern of the number of syllables - 8, 5, 7, 5, 7.

Stanza 2 [3, 4, 5]

The stanza focusses on action concerning the "I" subsequent to his release from chains (2a).
3a-b is exactly parallel on the pattern: ܩ + 1st sing. Peal perf. verb + noun obj. There is antithesis by the use of the polar word-pairs ܢܠܣ - ܢܣܠ and ܟܝܡܩ - ܟܩܣܝ. The connection of the two lines is enhanced by the assonance between the parallel elements.
4a functions as the introductory statement for the tricolon 4a-c. The double pattern of the semantically similar phrases ܢܣܘ ܠܗܢ and ܠ with ܩܩܗ serves to emphasise the description of the "I" who acquires members, perhaps in com-

parison with the Lord who also has members (cf. 3:2; 17:15-16). There is some (antithetical) parallelism between 4a and 4b by the use of ܟܐܡ/ܐܝܟ ܐܠ + *nota dativi*/prep. + pron. suffix + noun subj./compl.

4b-c comprises a series of three parallel descriptions of the members. ܐܝܟ ܟܡܣ is understood in the second and third descriptions (4c). 4c has an internal parallelism by the double pattern of ܐܦܠ + noun. It is possible that it should be further divided into two parallel lines. Elsewhere in the Odes, ܐܦܠ appears in two consecutive parallel lines (20:3,6) or in constructions with alternate parallel lines (18:5-6,9-10; 34:1-2). If 4c remains as one line then it would represent the only double occurrence of ܐܦܠ within a single line. The triple (negative) parallel structure of this strophe is similar to 7:24.

5a introduces a basic statement for which the compound subj. is found in 5b-c. The two elements of the subj. are parallel on the pattern: noun (attribute of the Lord) with 3rd masc. sing. suffix + descriptive element.

Stanza 3 [6-7]

6a reiterates the initial descriptions of stanzas 1 and 2, emphasised by the repetition of ܗܢܘ (1a) and ܟܐܡܘ (3b). The connection of 1a, 3b, and 6a is strengthened by the use of the 1st sing. perf. verb.

6a-b has a degree of parallelism on the pattern: 1st sing. perf. verb + prep. with noun obj. The parallelism is enhanced by the equal number of syllables (x 5) to each line. The tricolon in 7 is parallel on the pattern: 3rd sing. masc. part. + ܐܝܟ + ܠܡ (understood for 7b). 7b and 7c are more closely linked since they comprise two cls. introduced by ܒ (understood in 7c), describing actions simultaneous with the action in 7a.

The stanza has semantic links with 36:2-3 with some common vocabulary, ܗܢܘ, ܟܐܡܘ/ܟܝܡܢ, ܫܒܚ, ܟܐܦܘܡ (ref. to the Lord), and the image of the "I" who continues to praise the Lord in the region above.

Stanza 4 [8-9]

Stanza 4 follows easily from 7b-c, giving a more detailed description of the action of praise by the "I". A number of divisions seem possible. Firstly, 8a-9a may comprise a sequence of four 3rd sing. masc. perf. verbs for which the subj. is ܠܟ (8a). In this case 9b would be an addition or would function as a kind of incomplete concluding confessional statement. Secondly, 8a may be the introductory statement of the stanza with the verbs in 8b-9a dependent upon the compound subj. in 9b. Thirdly, 8a-c may comprise the first section, with the common subj. ܠܝ followed by the bicolon in 9a-b.

The exact parallelism of 8b and 9a indicates that they should not be divided into separate sections of the stanza, thus leaving the choice for either the first or second possibility outlined above. Of these, the second is preferable for two reasons: first, 9b need not be treated as an addition; second, there are similar descriptions of the action of praising in other Odes (cf. esp. 40:2-4a, but also 8:1; 11:1).

Thus 8a serves as the introduction for the stanza, linked syntactically with the lines that follow by the use of the 3rd sing. masc. perf. verb + noun (physical attribute of the "I") with 1st sing. suffix; and semantically, since 9b describes what it was that overflowed in the heart of the "I".

8b-9a is parallel on the pattern: 3rd sing. masc. perf. verb + prep. + noun (physical attribute of the "I") with 1st sing. suffix. 8c and 9a are more closely parallel by the repetition of the prep. ܥܠ. The physical aspects of the Odist mentioned in the four lines are variously connected in word-pairs: ܠܒܐ - ܣܘܬܐ, ܠܒܐ - ܐܕܢ, and ܦܘܡ - ܣܦܘܬܐ. The series of actions described follows a logical sequence from heart to mouth to lips.

9b comprises the compound subj. for the verbs in 8b-9a. It has internal parallelism by the double pattern of the noun (attribute of the Lord) with 3rd masc. sing. suffix. ܕܡܪܝܐ refers to both nouns. The use of a compound (pl.) subj. with a sing. verb occurs also in 5, where the noun subjs. in 5b-c refer to the sing. verb in 5a.

The use of the 1st sing., either as subject or object (sometimes indirectly by the use of 1st sing. suffix with nouns or preps.) of the action in each bicolon makes this an intensely personal Ode of the "I".

## ODE 22 [Syriac]

1 ܗܘ ܕܡܚܬ ܠܝ ܡܢ ܡܪܘܡܐ
ܘܡܣܩ ܠܝ ܡܢ ܬܚܬܝ̈ܬܐ
2 ܘܗܘ ܕܡܟܢܫ ܡܨܥ̈ܝܬܐ ܘܪܡܐ ܠܗܝܢ ܠܝ
3 ܗܘ ܕܒܕܪ ܠܒܥܠܕܒ̈ܒܝ ܘܠܒܥܠܕܝ̈ܢܝ
4 ܗܘ ܕܝܗܒ ܠܝ ܫܘܠܛܢܐ ܕܐܣܘܪܐ ܐܝܟ ܕܐܫܪܐ ܐܢܘܢ
5 ܗܘ ܕܡܚܐ ܒܐܝ̈ܕܝ ܠܬܢܝܢܐ ܕܫܒܥܐ ܪ̈ܫܘܗܝ
ܘܐܘܩܡܬܢܝ ܥܠ ܥܩܪܗ ܕܐܘܒܕ ܙܪܥܗ

6 ܐܢܬ ܗܘܝܬ ܬܡܢ ܘܥܕܪܬܢܝ
ܘܒܟܠ ܐܬܪ ܫܡܟ ܚܕܪ ܗܘܐ ܠܝ
7 ܚܒܠܬ ܝܡܝܢܟ ܠܡܪܪܬܗ ܕܒܝܫܬܐ
ܘܐܫܘܬ ܐܝܟ ܐܘܪܚܐ ܠܐܝܠܝܢ ܕܡܗܝܡܢܝܢ ܒܟ

8 ܘܓܒܝܬ ܐܢܘܢ ܡܢ ܩܒ̈ܪܐ
ܘܦܪܫܬ ܐܢܘܢ ܡܢ ܡܝ̈ܬܐ
9 ܢܣܒܬ ܓܪ̈ܡܐ ܡܝ̈ܬܐ
ܘܪܟܒܬ ܠܗܘܢ ܦܓܪ̈ܐ
10 ܘܠܐ ܡܬܬܙܝܥܝܢ ܗܘܘ
ܘܝܗܒܬ ܡܥܒܕܢܘܬܐ ܠܚܝ̈ܐ

11 ܕܠܐ ܚܒܠܐ ܗܘܬ ܐܘܪܚܟ
ܘܦܪܨܘܦܟ
ܐܝܬܝܬ ܠܥܠܡܟ ܠܚܒܠܐ
ܕܢܬܫܪܐ ܒܟܠܡܕܡ ܘܢܬܚܕܬ
12 ܘܬܗܘܐ ܫܬܐܣܬܐ ܠܟܠܡܕܡ ܟܐܦܟ
ܘܥܠܝܗ ܒܢܝܬ ܡܠܟܘܬܟ
ܘܗܘܬ ܒܝܬ ܡܥܡܪܐ ܕܩܕ̈ܝܫܐ

ܗܠܠܘܝܐ

1   He who makes me descend from the height,
    and makes me ascend from parts below.
2   And he who gathers together the middle parts and lays them to me.
3   He who scattered abroad my enemies and my adversaries.
4   He who gave me the authority of chains that I might release them.
5   He who threw down by my hands the seven-headed dragon.
    And you set me over his root that I might destroy his seed.

6   You were there and you helped me,
    and in every place your name surrounded me.
7   Your right hand corrupted the bitterness of evil,
    and your hand levelled the way for those who have faith in you.

8   And you chose them from the graves,
    and separated them from the dead.
9   And you took dead bones,
    and spread bodies over them.
10  And they were motionless,
    and you gave energy for life.

11  Incorrupted was your way,
    and your face.
    You brought your world to corruption;
    that everything might be dissolved and renewed,
12  and that your stone might be the foundation for everything.
    And upon it you built your kingdom,
    and it was the habitation of the holy ones.

Alleluia.

## ODE 22 [Coptic]

1  ΠΕΝΤΑϤⲚⲦ ΕΠΕϹΗⲦ ΕΒΟⲗ ⲌⲚ ⲘⲘΑ ΕⲦⲀΟϹΕ <Ε>ⲦϹΑⲦΠΕ
   ΑⲨⲰ ΑϤⲚⲦ Ε2ΡΑⲓ ⲌⲚ ⲘⲘΑ ΕⲦⲘⲠ6ΟΝ ⲘΠΕϹΗⲦ
2  ΠΕΝⲦΑϤϤΙ ⲘⲘΟⲨ ⲚⲚΕⲦⲌⲚ ⲦⲘΗⲦΕ
   ΑⲨⲰ ΑϤⲦϹΑΒΟΟⲨ ΕΡΟΟⲨ
3  ΠΕΝⲦΑϤⲀⲰΡΕ ΕΒΟⲗ ⲚΝΑⲀⲀⲀΕ ⲘⲚ ΝΑΑΝⲦΙⲆΙΚΟϹ
4  ΠΕΝⲦΑϤϯ ΝΑⲓ ⲚΟⲨΕ3ΟⲨϹΙΑ Ε2ΡΑⲓ ΕⲀⲚ 2ΕΝⲘⲢⲢΕ ΕΒΟⲗΟⲨ ΕΒΟⲗ
5  ΠΕΝⲦΑϤΠΑⲦΑϹϹΕ ⲘϤΟϤ ΕⲦΟ ⲚϹΑⲱϤΕ ⲚΑΠΕ ⲌⲚ ΝΑ6ΙⲀ
   ΑϤⲦΑ2Οⲓ ΕΡΑⲦ 2ΙⲀⲚ ⲦΕϤΝΟⲨΝΕ
   ⲀΕΚΑϹ ΕⲓΕϤⲰⲦΕ ΕΒΟⲗ ⲘΠΕϤϹΠΕΡΜΑ

6  ΑⲨⲰ ⲚⲦΟΚ ΝΕΚⲚⲘΜΑⲓ ΠΕ ΕΚϯ ⲚⲦΟΟⲦ
   2ΡΑⲓ ⲌⲘ ΜΑ ΝΙΜ ΑϤΚⲰⲦΕ ΕΡΟⲓ ⲚϬΙ ΠΕΚΡΑΝ
7  Α ⲦΕΚΟⲨΝΑⲘ ⲦΑΚΕⲦΜΑⲦΟⲨ ⲘΠΡΕϤⲀΕΠΕΘΟΟⲨ
   Α ⲦΕΚϬΙⲀ ΚΕ2ⲦΕ2ΙΗ ⲚΝΕΚΠΙϹⲦΟϹ

8  ΑΚϹΟⲦΟⲨ ΕΒΟⲗ ⲌⲚ ⲚⲦΑϤΟϹ
   ΑⲨⲰ ΑΚΠΟΟΝΟⲨ ΕΒΟⲗ ⲌⲚ ⲦΜΗⲦΕ ⲚⲚΚⲰⲰϹ
9  ΑΚⲀΙ Ⲛ2ΕΝΚΑϹ ΕⲨΜΟΟⲨⲦ
   ΑΚϯ 2ΙⲰΟⲨ ⲚΟⲨϹⲰΜΑ
10 ΑⲨⲰ ΝΕⲦΕ ⲚϹΕΚΙΜ ΑΝ
   ΑΚϯ ΝΑⲨ ⲚΟⲨΕΝΕΡΓΙΑ ⲚⲰⲚ2

11 Α ⲦΕΚⲀΙΗ ⲱⲰΠΕ ⲚΟⲨⲘⲚⲦΑⲦⲦΑΚΟ
   ΑⲨⲰ ⲘⲚ ΠΕΚ2Ο
   ΑΚⲚΠΕΚΑΙⲰΝ ΕⲀⲘ ΠⲦΑΚΟ
   ⲀΕΚΑϹ ΕⲨΕΒⲰⲗ ΕΒΟⲗ ⲦΗΡΟⲨ ΑⲨⲰ ⲚϹΕⲢⲂⲢΡΕ
12 ΑⲨⲰ ⲚⲦΕ ΠΕΚΟⲨΟⲓΝ ⲢϹⲚⲦΕ ΝΑⲨ ⲦΗΡΟⲨ
   ΑΚΚΕⲦⲦΕΚⲘⲚⲦⲢⲘΜΑΟ 2ΙⲰΟⲨ
   ΑⲨⲰ ΑⲨⲢΟⲨΜΑⲚⲱⲰΠΕ ΕϤΟⲨΑΑΒ

1    He who brought me down from the places which are high above,
     and brought me up from the places which are in the deep below.
2    He who has taken thence those in the middle,
     and taught them about them.
3    He who brought to naught my enemies and my adversaries.
4    He who gave me authority over chains to release them.
5    He who smote the serpent with seven heads by my hands.
     He set me over his root,
     that I might wipe out his seed.

6    And you were with me helping me;
     in every place your name surrounded me.
7    Your right hand destroyed the poison of the one speaking evil;
     your hand levelled the road for your faithful.

8    You turned them out of the graves,
     and moved them from the middle of the corpses.
9    You took dead bones,
     and laid a body upon them.
10   And to those not moving,
     you gave energy of life.

11   Your way became incorruptible,
     and your face.
     You brought your aeon to corruption;
     that everything might be dissolved and might become new,
12   and that your light might become foundation for everything.
     You built your wealth upon them,
     and they became a holy dwelling place.

NOTES TO THE TRANSLATION

3: H has ܢܝܢ ܠܟܚܘܢ.

5b: H has ܠܥܘܢܘܗܝ. The sing. reading in N has been preferred (cf. also Lattke 1979-86, vol. 1) since it occurs also in the Coptic.

6b: H has mistaken the ܒ for ܟ in writing ܒܟܝ.

7a: H has ⟨ꝋ⟩. The choice for the N reading (cf. also Lattke 1979-86, vol. 1) has been made on the basis of its closeness to the Coptic.

8a, 8b, 9a, 9b, 10b: The Coptic gives the verbs in the 2nd masc. sing. In the margin of his personal copy of his 1911 edition, Harris changed the translation of the verbs from 2nd masc. sing. to 3rd fem. sing. (subj. ⟨ꝋ⟩). The changes found their way into Harris and Mingana vol. 2 and subsequently into Charlesworth 1977 and Emerton. Charlesworth indicates for 8a (91, n. 11) that the unpointed Syriac text could be interpreted either as 2nd masc. sing. or as 3rd fem. sing. This is only true if the verb is Pael rather than Peal. One must question how Charlesworth has arrived at the Pael for 8a rather than the Peal which he has used for the remaining verbs of 8b, 9a, 9b and 10b. The choice of the Pael would appear to have been made for the convenience of supplying the possibility of a 3rd fem sing. subj.

10b: H has ⟨ꝋ⟩. The Coptic agrees with the N reading.

11a-c: H and N indicate a break after ⟨ꝋ⟩ and ⟨ꝋ⟩. The Coptic has a break after ⲚⲞⲨⲘⲚ̄ⲦⲀⲦⲀⲔⲞ, ⲠⲈⲔⳅⲞ, and ⲠⲦⲀⲔⲞ. Flemming rightly calls Harris (1909) to task for reading the masc. ⟨ꝋ⟩ as subj. of the fem. ⟨ꝋ⟩ (53 n. †). Diettrich prefers to emend the verb to ⟨ꝋ⟩ (1911, 83 n. 8). ⟨ꝋ⟩ may be either 2nd masc. sing. or 3rd fem. sing. The Coptic equivalent (ⲀⲔⲚ̄) is 2nd masc. sing. It seems preferable to follow the punctuation of the Coptic, regarding the Syriac as having lost the break after ⟨ꝋ⟩ early in the transmission of the text.

12b: Carmignac (1986) makes ref. to a personal letter received (6.1.64) from A. Guillaumont in which the latter suggests that ⲦⲈⲔⲘ̄Ⲛ̄ⲦⲢ̄Ⲙ̄Ⲙⲁⲟ ("your wealth") should be emended to ⲦⲈⲔⲘ̄Ⲛ̄ⲦⲢ̄ⲢⲞ ("your kingdom").

12c: H has ⟨ꝋ⟩.

ANALYSIS [Syriac]

Stanza 1 [1-5 (5b?)]

Stanza 1 is differentiated from the remainder of the Ode by the pattern of the initial ⟨ꝋ⟩ and by the 3rd masc. sing. as subj. There is a difficulty with 5b which has a 2nd masc. sing. verb and therefore should be placed in stanza 2. Although the change in subj. is an extremely important consideration, there are also strong reasons for suggesting that 5b may be included with 5a. Firstly, there is a semantic connection by the two masc. sing. pron. suffixes which refer to ܪܟܘܚ in 5a; secondly, the bicolon at 5 provides a symmetrical balance with the bicolon in 1; thirdly, 5b provides a second aspect to the action in 5a (cf. 31:13 for the salvation of the seed of the patriarchs as opposed to the destruction of the seed of the dragon here). With regard to the third point, each line/bicolon beginning with ܗܘ ܘ has a second aspect to it, be it a parallel action (1b, 2, 5b), a second obj. for the verb (3), or an associated cl. (4). Although it also contains an associated cl., the main action of 5b is the setting of the "I" at the root of the dragon.

The difficulty does not occur in the Coptic which has a 3rd masc. sing. verb in 5b. Since the semantic argument for including 5b with 5a is strong, it would seem preferable to follow the Coptic and consider the 2nd masc. sing. verb in the Syriac as corrupted text.

The introductory bicolon in 1 is parallel on the pattern: ܗܘ ܘ (understood in 1b) + masc. sing. Aphel part. act. + ܠ + ܡܢ with noun obj. It provides a dramatic opening by its antithesis (ܡܪܝܬܐ - ܡܪܡܘܡ, ܐܒܢܐܢܪ - ܐܚܕܘܬܐ).

2-4 constitutes the central part of the stanza. Apart from the initial ܗܘ ܘ, there is little else that links the lines of the tricolon. 2 and 4 are closest with a general pattern of ܗܘ ܘ + 3rd masc. sing. verb + pl. noun obj. + associated cl. in which the 3rd pl. pron. obj. refers to the pl. noun obj. of the first cl. The associated cl. in 2 and the first cl. in 4 are similar, both semantically (the Lord gives something to the "I" who thereby has authority) and by the pattern of masc. sing. verb + ܠ. 3 has internal parallelism by the use of the double (synonymous) objs. ܒܚܠܬܕܪ and ܒܚܠܢܙ.

## Stanza 2 [6-7]

With this stanza the subj. changes from the 3rd masc. sing. to (generally) the 2nd masc. sing. (sometimes indirectly by the use of a noun with 2nd masc. sing. suffix).

6a and 6b are linked semantically and syntactically, each of the series of three perf. verbs with 2nd masc. sing. subj. (indirectly by ܝܝܡܒ in 6b) describing a presence and care for the "I" who is the obj. 7a-b contains some initial parallelism on the pattern: 3rd fem. sing. perf. verb + noun subj. with 2nd masc. sing. suffix + noun obj. The parallelism is strengthened by the word-pair ܚܝܠܐ - ܐܝܟ.

There is some connection between 6 and 7 by the association of ܚܝܠܐ and ܝܠܕ, the latter in the noun form found associated with ܚܝܠܐ in 8:6 and 25:2.


Stanza 3 [8-10]

The stanza centres on the image of resurrection/resuscitation of the dead. Each line, with the exception of 10a, describes one simple action with an initial 2nd masc. sing. perf. verb.

8a-b is strictly parallel: ܘ + 3rd fem. sing. Peal perf. verb + ܐܝܕ + ܝܡ with a pl. noun obj. The repetition of ܡܝܬܐ provides the link between 8b and 9a. 9a-b has a degree of parallelism by the use of the 2nd masc. sing. Peal perf. verb and the ref. of the indir. obj. in 9b to ܝܗܒܬ ܠܗܘܢ in 9a. 10a and 10b are semantically connected, the action in 10b being the result of the state described in 10a. There is a loose kind of antithesis between the descriptions of being motionless and the giving of energy.


Stanza 4 [11a-c, 11d-12]

The focus remains on the 2nd masc. sing. character but there is a shift from the description of the resurrection/resuscitation of the dead to a report of the dissolution of the world and the foundation of the kingdom as habitation of the holy.

The inclusio for the first strophe is formed by the repetition of ܚܝܠ in 11a and 11c. 11a-b is parallel, with (ܟܗܡ) ܗܘܐ ܚܝܠ ܠܐ understood for ܦܨܝܗܝ. 11a-b is in antithesis to 11c, "your way" and "your face" being incorrupted over against the corruption of "your world".

11d-12a comprises two cls. introduced by ܘ (understood in 12a) which express the purpose of the action in 11c. 11d has internal parallelism by the double pattern of verbs for which ܟܠܡܕܡ is the subj. 11d and 12a are connected by the repetition of ܟܠܡܕܡ and the antithesis between the concepts of the dissolution of everything and the foundation of everything.

In a kind of terrace pattern, each of the lines of the bicolon 12b-c is dependent upon the final word of the preceding line. Thus 12b refers to ܐܪܥܐ in 12a, and 12c refers to ܡܠܟܘܬܗ in 12b.

ANALYSIS [Coptic]

Of the four Coptic Odes with a corresponding Syriac version, Ode 22 has fewest variations between the versions.

Stanza 1 [1-2, 3-5a, 5b-c]

As in the Syriac, 1a-b is tightly structured, the repetition of the verb ЄІНЄ and the noun Ма (as well as ЄСНТ, though it has less significance) serving to reinforce the parallelism. By its nature, the Syriac is far more concise than the Coptic.

2 (a-b in the Coptic) is quite different in the two versions, albeit equally obscure in both. The common element is the focus on the "middle" (ܪܨܘܢܐ, МНТЄ). The difference lies in the verbs ܟܢܫ (gather) - ϥΙ (take) and ܣܡ (lay) - ТСаВО (teach), which are perf. I in the Coptic and participles in the Syriac, and in the 1st sing. as indir. obj. of ܣܡ in the Syriac where the Coptic employs the 3rd pl.

3-5a is virtually the same in the Coptic as in the Syriac, with minor differences in vocabulary and syntax.

A major difference in the versions occurs in 5b-c (5b in the Syriac). The Coptic continues with the 3rd sing. masc. verb where the Syriac changes to a 2nd sing. masc. verb.

Stanza 2 [6-7]

Apart from minor syntactic differences, 6a-b is the same in both versions. 7a-b is parallel in both Coptic and Syriac versions. In 7b the Syriac uses a rel. cl., ܗܝܡܢܘܬܗ ܐܠܗܐ, while the Coptic has the more succinct ЙЙЄКΠІСТОС.

Stanza 3 [8-10]

There are only minor differences between the Syriac and Coptic in this stanza. In 8a, there is a slight variation in meaning with СШТ ЄВОΛ (turn out) in the Coptic and ܓܒܐ (choose) in the Syriac. 9b and 10b are more clearly parallel in the Coptic on the pattern: аКϯ + prep. with 3rd pl. suffix/3rd pl. indir. obj. + Й (indicating the obj.) + indef. art. + noun obj.

Stanza 4 [11-12]

11 is virtually the same in both versions. 12 contains the most important differences with theological implications between the two versions. Firstly, in 12a, the Coptic has ΠЄΚΟΥΟΪΝ (your light) where the Syriac has ܟܐܦܟ (your stone). If the difference is not deliberate but a scribal error, the Coptic should read ΠЄΚШΝЄ (your stone). However, in the interpretation which follows in <u>Pistis Sophia</u> (Schmidt 1978b, 322-3), light is the central focus even from the preceding verse.

The second variation occurs in 12b where the Coptic has TЄΚΜΝΤΡΜΜαΟ (your wealth) and the Syriac has ܡܠܟܘܬܟ (your kingdom). It is possible that the difference is due to a scribal error, TЄΚΜΝΤΡΜΜαΟ having been read for TЄΚΜΝΤΡΡΟ (cf. translation notes).

In 12b-c the 3rd pl. in the Coptic refers to ΝαΥ ΤΗΡΟΥ in 12a. This, together with the two differences outlined above, causes a profound variation in the concepts presented by the two versions. In the Syriac, the stone is the foundation of everything, the kingdom is built on the stone, and the kingdom is the habitation of the holy. In the Coptic, the light is the foundation of everything, the wealth is built, not upon the light, but upon everything, and everything becomes a holy dwelling.

## ODE 23

1 ܚܕܘܬܐ ܕܩܕܝ̈ܫܐ ܗܝ
ܘܡܢܘ ܢܠܒܫܝܗ̇
ܐܠܐ ܐܢ ܗܢܘܢ ܒܠܚܘܕ
2 ܛܝܒܘܬܐ ܕܓܒܝ̈ܐ ܗܝ
ܘܡܢܘ ܢܩܒܠܝܗ̇
ܐܠܐ ܐܢ ܗܢܘܢ ܕܬܟܝܠܝܢ ܒܗ̇ ܡܢ ܒܪܝܫܝܬ
3 ܚܘܒܐ ܕܓܒܝ̈ܐ ܗܝ
ܘܡܢܘ ܢܠܒܫܝܘܗܝ
ܐܠܐ ܐܢ ܗܢܘܢ ܕܩܢܝܘܗܝ ܡܢ ܒܪܝܫܝܬ

4 ܗܠܟܘ ܒܝܕܥܬܗ ܕܡܪܝܐ
ܘܬܕܥܘܢ ܛܝܒܘܬܗ ܕܡܪܝܐ ܕܠܐ ܚܣܡܐ
ܘܠܪ̈ܘܙܗ ܘܠܫܘܠܡܐ ܕܝܕܥܬܗ

5 ܘܡܚܫܒܬܗ ܗܘܬ ܐܝܟ ܐܓܪܬܐ
ܘܨܒܝܢܗ ܢܚܬ ܡܢ ܡܪܘܡܐ
6 ܘܐܫܬܕܪܬ ܐܝܟ ܓܐܪܐ ܡܢ ܩܫܬܐ
ܕܐܫܬܕܪܬ ܒܩܛܝܪܐ

7 ܘܪ̈ܗܛ ܥܠ ܐܓܪܬܐ ܐܝ̈ܕܝܐ ܣܓܝ̈ܐܬܐ
ܠܡܚܛܦ ܘܠܡܣܒ ܘܠܡܩܪܝܗ̇
8 ܘܥܪܩܬ ܡܢ ܨܒ̈ܥܬܗܘܢ

ܘܕܚܠܘ ܡܢܗ̇
ܘܡܢ ܚܬܡܐ ܕܥܠܝܗ̇
9 ܡܛܠ ܕܠܐ ܫܠܝܛ ܗܘܐ ܠܗܘܢ ܠܡܫܪܐ ܚܬܡܗ̇
ܚܝܠܐ ܓܝܪ ܕܐܝܬ ܗܘܐ ܥܠ ܚܬܡܐ
ܡܝܬܪ ܗܘܐ ܡܢܗܘܢ

10 ܐܙܠܘ ܕܝܢ ܒܬܪܗ̇ ܕܐܓܪܬܐ ܗܢܘܢ ܕܚܙܐܘܗ̇
ܕܢܕܥܘܢ ܐܝܟܐ ܫܪܝܐ
ܘܡܢܘ ܩܪܐ ܠܗ̇
ܘܡܢܘ ܫܡܥ ܠܗ̇

11 ܓܝܓܠܐ ܕܝܢ ܡܩܒܠܬܗ̇
ܘܐܬܐ ܗܘܬ ܥܠܝܗ̇
12 ܘܐܬܐ ܐܝܬ ܗܘܐ ܒܡܗ̇
ܕܡܠܟܘܬܐ ܘܕܡܕܒܪܢܘܬܐ
13 ܘܟܠܡܕܡ ܕܡܙܝܥ ܗܘܐ ܠܓܝܓܠܐ
ܚܨܕܐ ܗܘܬ ܠܗ
ܘܡܦܣܩܐ ܗܘܬ ܠܗ
14 ܘܣܘܓܐܐ ܚܒܠܬ ܕܣܘܩܒ̈ܠܐ ܗܘܘ
ܘܓܙܪܬ ܢܗܪ̈ܘܬܐ 15 ܘܥܒܪܬ
ܥܩܪܬ ܥܒ̈ܐ ܣܓܝ̈ܐܐ
ܘܥܒܕܬ ܐܘܪܚܐ ܦܬܝܬܐ
16 ܢܚܬ ܪܝܫܐ ܠܘܬ ܪ̈ܓܠܐ
ܡܛܠ ܕܥܕܡܐ ܠܪ̈ܓܠܐ ܪܗܛܬ ܓܝܓܠܐ
ܘܟܠܡܕܡ ܕܐܬܐ ܗܘܐ ܥܠܝܗ̇

17 ܐܓܪܬܐ ܗܘܬ ܕܦܘܩܕܢܐ
ܘܡܛܠ ܕܐܬܟܢܫܘ ܐܟܚܕܐ ܟܠܗܘܢ ܐܬܪ̈ܘܬܐ
18 ܘܐܬܚܙܝ ܒܪܫܗ̇ ܪܝܫܐ ܕܐܬܓܠܝ
ܘܒܪܐ ܕܫܪܪܐ ܡܢ ܐܒܐ ܡܪܝܡܐ
19 ܘܝܪܬ ܟܠܡܕܡ ܘܢܣܒ

ܘܐܬܒܛܠܬ ܕܝܢ ܡܚܫܒܬܐ ܕܣܓܝ̈ܐܐ
20 ܐܡܪܚܘ ܕܝܢ ܟܠܗܘܢ ܡܣܛܝ̈ܢܐ ܘܥܪܩܘ
ܘܪܕܦܘ ܐܝܠܝܢ ܕܪ̈ܕܦܝܢ ܘܐܬܒܛܠܘ

21 ܘܗܘܬ ܕܝܢ ܐܓܪܬܐ ܦܘܩܕܢܐ ܪܒܬܐ
ܕܟܬܝܒܐ ܒܨܒܥܗ ܕܐܠܗܐ ܡܫܡܠܝܐܝܬ
22 ܘܫܡܐ ܕܐܒܐ ܥܠܝܗ̇
ܘܕܒܪܐ ܘܕܪܘܚܐ ܩܕܝܫܐ
ܠܡܡܠܟܘ ܠܥܠܡ ܥܠܡܝܢ

ܗܠܠܘܝܐ

1    Joy is of the holy ones;
     and who will put it on,
     but they alone?
2    Grace is of the chosen ones;
     and who will receive it,
     but they who have trusted in it from the beginning?
3    Love is of the chosen ones;
     and who will put it on,
     but they who gained it from the beginning?

4    Walk in the knowledge of the Lord,
     and you will know the grace of the Lord without jealousy,
     both for his exultation and for the perfection of his knowledge.

5    And his thought was like a letter,
     and his will descended from the height.
6    And it was sent out like an arrow from a bow,
     which is shot with force.

7    And many hands ran at the letter,
     to snatch and take and read it.
8    And it fled from their fingers.

     And they were afraid of it,
     and of the seal which was upon it,
9    because it was not lawful for them to open its seal.
     For the power which was upon the seal
     was better than they.

10   Then those who saw it went after the letter,
     that they might know where it would be opened;
     and who would read it,
     and who would hear it.

11  But a wheel received it,
    and it (letter) came upon it.
12  And a sign was with it (letter),
    of the kingdom and of rule.
13  And everything which was disturbing to the wheel,
    it mowed it down,
    and cut it to pieces.
14  And it gathered in a multitude who were opponents,
    and it covered rivers with earth    15    and passed over.
    It uprooted many thickets,
    and made a wide way.
16  The head descended to the feet,
    because unto the feet ran the wheel,
    and whatever came upon it.

17  The letter was of commandment,
    and because all places were gathered together.
18  And the head which manifested itself was seen at its (letter) head,
    and the Son of truth from the Father Most High.
19  And he took possession of everything and took.

    And then the thought of many was brought to nothing.
20  Then all the apostates were hasty and fled,
    and those persecuting were extinguished and blotted out.

21  But the letter became a great tablet
    written entirely by the finger of God.
22  And the name of the Father was upon it,
    and of the Son and of the Holy Spirit,
    to reign for ever and ever.

    Alleluia.

NOTES TO THE TRANSLATION

1b: N is in error with ܘܡܫܒܠܝ.

4a: H has ܕܡܒܝܢ ܟܠ.

4b: H omits 4b except for ܚܘܡܘ ܐ݈ܢ (cf. the notes for 3:6b).

4c, 5b: H has no initial ܢ in each of these lines.

7a: N has ܠܗܘܝܐ.

10a: H is in error with ܐܚܗ݈ܬܝܐ.

10d: N has ܢܒܪܗ. The parallelism of 10c and 10d demands the H reading.

13a: The ܐܝܠ in N following ܟܐܡ appears to be an afterthought.

14a: H has ܐܠܒܚܘܡܐܢ.

14b/15a: The obj. of ܚܒܝܬ is obviously ܐܚܢܝܡܝ. Two verbs with a shared obj. inserted between them occurs also in 19a and 20b. For the division of the line as I have it, cf. Ungnad and Staerk; Diettrich 1911; Bruston 1912b. Harnack (1910) implies the division: "und es überdeckte Ströme und überschritt sie,..."

15a: N has ܐܚܝܒܚܝ. The H reading fits the context better.

16b: H has ܐܠܝܓܝ.

17a: N has ܐܘܩܦܗܢ. Both H and N are awkward constructions, but N would require a sing. masc. verb with ܐܘܩܦ to make the translation syntactically correct, "and it was a letter and a commandment."

17b: H has no initial ܢ.

19b: N has ܚܠܠܒܗܢ. The pass. as in H seems to be required in this context.

20b: H is in error with ܢܠܒܚܚܐܢ.

22b: H has ܐܫܗܩܐܢ (cf. also 19:2,4).

ANALYSIS

The Ode comprises two basic sections: the first (1-4) being a description of the attributes of the chosen/holy ones and an exhortation to the community; the second (5-22) being a detailed report of the action of a letter and wheel. The two sections are semantically quite distinct from each other (although they share some vocabulary) and must be regarded as sub-odes (*contra* G. Kittel 1914, 20-21).

Stanza 1 [1-3] (= Stanza 1, Sub-ode 1)

This is a tightly structured stanza comprising three alternately parallel tricola. Each tricolon consists of a confessional statement + associated rhetorical question. The particular form of the rhetorical question (... ܐ ܐ ... ܢ) occurs in 3:4.

The pattern of each tricolon may be outlined as:

line 1: sing. noun 1 subj. + ܘ + pl. noun 2 + copula

line 2: ܢ + 3rd sing. masc. imperf. verb + pron. suffix (ref. to noun 1)

line 3: ܗ ܐ ܐ + ref. to ܗ.

In addition, the parallelism is strengthened by the word-pair ܐ -
ܐ (1a, 2a), and by the repetition of vocabulary - ܠ in 1b, 3b; ܟ in 2a, 3a; ܝ in 2c, 3c.
In 1c the ref. to ܗ is by the adv. ܠ; in 2c and 3c it is by a cl. on the pattern: ܘ + verb/part. + pron. obj. (ref. to noun 1) + ܝ ܢ.
There is a relatively even number of syllables in the parallel lines: 1a and 2a (x 6), 3a (x 5); 1b, 2b, and 3b (x 4); 2c (x 12) and 3c (x 11).

Stanza 2 [4]

There is a shift in style with this stanza from the description of the holy/chosen ones to an exhortation to a 2nd pl. group. The tricolon focusses on "knowing" (ܝܕܥ occurs in each line): the knowledge of the Lord and the community's knowledge of his grace. The inclusio for the stanza is formed by the repetition of ܡܕܥ in 4a and 4c.

4a and 4b are parallel. If one brackets out the final ܕܠܐ ܚܣܡܐ of 4b (but cf. 20:7), the pattern is: 2nd pl. verb + noun + 3rd sing. masc. suffix + ܕܡܪܝܐ. The parallelism is enhanced by the word-pair ܝܕܥܬܐ - ܛܝܒܘܬܐ and the equivalent number of syllables (x 7) for each line. 4c has internal parallelism by the double pattern of ܘ + *nota dativi* + indir. obj. expression + 3rd sing. masc. suffix (ref. to the Lord).

There is a link between the first two stanzas by the repetition of the key word ܛܝܒܘܬܐ.

Stanza 3 [5-6] (= Stanza 1, Sub-ode 2)

With stanza 3 the second sub-ode begins with ref. to the key motif of the letter. The stanza consists of two bicola, the first line of each containing a simile with ܐܝܟ.

5a-b is parallel on the pattern: noun subj. + 3rd sing. masc. suffix (ref. to the Lord) + 3rd sing. perf. verb + ܐܝܟ/ܒ with a noun obj. A further link is provided by the word-pair ܡܚܫܒܬܐ - ܨܒܝܢܐ. 6a combines the pattern of the final phrase of 5a (ܐܝܟ + noun) and 5b (ܒ + noun) into ܐܝܟ + noun + ܒ + noun. 6a and 6b are linked by the rel. cl. in 6b which refers to ܓܐܪܐ in 6a, and by the word-play with the semantically similar ܫܕܪ and ܫܕܐ.

Stanza 4 [7-8a]

Stanza 4 describes the beginning of action involving the letter over against a group who want to take it and read it.

The central focus of the tricolon is the violent intention expressed by the series of three Peal infinitives in 7b. 7a and 8a are closely connected semantically, the action in 8a following easily from 7a. The lines have a degree of parallelism on the pattern: perf. verb + prep. + noun obj. The parallelism is strengthened by the semantic association of ܪܗܛ - ܚܛܦ. 7a and 8a also exhibit chiasmus: 7a has a 3rd pl. verb (subj. is ܐܝ̈ܕܐ) + prep. with ܐܓܪܬܐ as obj.; 8a has a 3rd sing. verb (subj. is ܐܓܪܬܐ understood) + prep. with ܨܒ̈ܥܬܗܘܢ (ref. to ܐܝ̈ܕܐ) as obj.

Stanza 5 [8b-9]

This stanza appears to interrupt the flow of the report from stanza 4 to stanza 6, by providing a commentary on the attitude towards the letter of those against it and a statement about the power of its seal. Although there is connection with the sub-ode in which it occurs (5-22), the stanza may well be treated as a further sub-section because of its exclusive use of the key word ܚܬܡܐ. Moreover, the key term of sub-ode 2, ܐܓܪܬܐ does not occur in this stanza.

8b-c is parallel on the pattern: ܕܚܠܘ (understood in 8c) + ܡܢ with obj. (ܚܬܡܐ/substitute pron. suffix). 9b-c also has a degree of parallelism on the pattern: ܚܝܠܐ as subj. (understood in 9c) + verbal expression + prep. with obj. There is a kind of semantic terrace pattern from 8c to 9b: the seal is upon the letter (8c) and the power is upon the seal (9b). The lines are further linked by the repetition of ܚܬܡܐ.

The connection of 8c and 9b emphasises the central position of 9a, which is strengthened by the use of ܚܬܡܐ in this line (the central repetition of this word in the stanza). 9a provides the connection between 8b-c and 9b-c. It points back to 8b-c, giving the reason for the fear of those against the letter, and leads into 9b-c which in turn provides the reason why these people are unable to open the seal.

Stanza 6 [10]

The stanza consists of two bicola. 10a and 10b are connected by the cl. in 10b which refers to ܐܙܠܘ in 10a. The latter has internal parallelism by the double pattern of 3rd pl. masc. perf. verb ... 3rd fem. pron. obj./suffix (ref. to the letter). The internal connection is strengthened by the word-pair ܐܙܠ - ܚܙܐ.

The second cl. of 10b, ܐܢܫܐ ܐܚܪܢܐ, as well as the cls. in 10c and 10d, function as objs. of ܚܛܦܘܗ̇. 10c-d is strictly parallel on the pattern: ܘܪܕܦܘ + sing. masc. Peal part. act. + ܠܗ̇ (ref. to the letter).

Stanza 7 [11-12, 13, 14-15, 16]

The limits of the stanza are clearly delineated by the exclusive use of the key word ܓܝܓܠܐ and by the inclusio formed between 11a-b and 16b-c by the occurrence of ܓܝܓܠܐ in 11a and 16b and by ܐܬܝܐ ܗܘܬ/ܐܬܐ ܗܘܐ ܠܟܠܗ̇ in 11b and 16c. There is a link with stanza 6 by the 3rd fem. sing. suffix in 11a and 12a which refers to ܐܓܪܬܐ in 10a. The stanza has strong semantic links with 39:7-9 (the sign from the Lord, the disturbing/dangerous action of passing over rivers) with some common vocabulary - ܐܬܐ, ܥܒܪ, ܢܗܪ̈ܘܬܐ, ܐܘܪܚܐ.

11-12 concerns the wheel and the letter. 11a and 11b are somewhat chiastic in structure: the subj. of 11a (the wheel) is (indirectly) the object of the action in 11b, while the obj. in 11a (the letter) is the subj. of 11b. 11a-12b follows a simple pattern of perf. verb + object of the action. The parallelism is more pronounced in 11b and 12a where the verbal expression is followed by a prep. + pron. suffix. There is also a degree of parallelism between 11a and 12a by the similarity of the concepts of receiving and being with, and the repetition of the fem. sing. pron. suffix (ref. to the letter). 12b has internal parallelism by the double pattern of ܝ + noun, both nouns being closely associated semantically.

With the second strophe, the report of the destructive actions of the wheel commences. 13a is connected with 13b-c by its apposition with the pron. obj. suffix in both lines of the bicolon. 13b-c is parallel on the pattern: fem. sing. part. act. (subj. is ܟܠܗܝܢ understood) + ܡܠ ܗܘܐ.

14a-15c continues the report of the destruction by the wheel. The main feature of the strophe is the series of 3rd fem. sing. perf. verbs + obj., made more complex in 14b/15a by the use of two verbs with their common obj. (ܟܬܝܒܬܐ) inserted between them (cf. 19a).

There is some initial chiasmus in the bicolon in 14a-14b/15a by the placement of the noun objs. and verbs (ܒܝܕܗ in 14b/15a). 15b-c is more closely parallel on the pattern: 3rd fem. sing. Peal perf. verb + noun obj. + adj. There is word-play with the verbs in 14b/15a-15c (ܒܝܕܗ, ܒܝܕܗ, ܒܝܕܗ).

16a-b is parallel with chiasmus: A B // B' A', where  A = 3rd sing. Peal perf. verb + noun subj.; B = prep. + ܟܠܗ. There is a terrace pattern by the placement of the prep. and ܟܠܗ at the conclusion of 16a and at the beginning of 16b. 16c functions as the second part of the subj. of ܐܝܠܝܢ with ܟܠܗܝܢ ܐܝܠܝܢ at the conclusion of 16c refers to ܟܠܗ which concludes 16b.


Stanza 8 [17-19a]

The focus of the stanza is the authority of the letter and of the Son of truth associated with it.

17a functions as the introductory statement concerning the letter. It is reminiscent of the statement concerning the sign in 12 - the sign with the letter is of the kingdom and of rule, the letter itself is one of commandment. The ref. of 17b is not entirely clear. Semantically it seems close to the concept of the possession of everything by the Son of truth (19a).

18a is the central focus of the stanza. The main feature of the monocolon is the word-play with ܪܫܝ, the first occurrence referring back to ܟܬܝܒܬܐ in 17a, the second referring forward to ܣܝܡܬܐ ܕܟܠ in 18b. There is a loose of chiastic parallelism within 18a on the general pattern: verb + ܪܫܝ + ܪܫܝ + verb. The parallelism of the 3rd masc. sing. Ethpeel perf. verbs is enhanced by the word-pair ܟܘ - ܠܠ. The chiasmus also applies to the pattern of vowels: rbhā-ṣā + ḥbhāṣā, ḥbhāṣā + zqāphā // ḥḥbhāṣā + zqāphā /rbhāṣā + ḥbhāṣā.

18b is in apposition with the second occurrence of ܪܢ in 18a, and is also the understood subject of the action in 19a. The latter comprises two 3rd sing. masc. perf. verbs with their common obj. inserted between them (cf. also 14b/15a). The internal parallelism of the line is strengthened by the use of the word-pair ܕܝܘ - ܣܡܟ.

## Stanza 9 [19b-20]

With stanza 9, the focus changes to the negative reaction of the apostates/persecutors to the letter. 19b serves as a summary introduction to the stanza. There is a connecting link with the previous stanza by the antithesis of the thought brought to nothing over against the Son's possesion of eveything.

20a-b is parallel on the pattern: 3rd pl. masc. perf. verb + subj. expression + ܢ + 3rd masc. pl. perf. verb. There is similarity with 14b/15a and 19a, except that the common subj. is inserted rather than a common obj. The internal parallelism of each line is enhanced by the semantic association between the two verbs, ܘܝܣܗ - ܣܝܠ and ܠܟܢܗ - ܠܠ.

## Stanza 10 [21-22b, 22c]

21a describes the fate of the letter (cf. the similar form in 6:8).

The rel. cl. in 21b refers to ܟܕܡܩܝ in 21a. The description of the letter in 22a has been extended to a trinitarian formula in 22b, the two parallel gen. phrases (ܢ + ܝ + noun) dependent upon ܟܢܙ in 22a. 22c extends the trinitarian formula. As a concluding confession it is similar to Ex 15:18, ܡܠܪܘ ܟܝܗ ܝܗܠܠ ܪܠܠܠ. Association between a trinitarian formula and a motif of everlasting kingly rule occurs in a variant reading to Matt 6:13,

...πονηροῦ, ὅτι σοῦ ἐστιν ἡ βασιλεία καὶ ἡ δύναμις καὶ ἡ δόξα, τοῦ πατρὸς καὶ τοῦ υἱοῦ καὶ τοῦ ἁγίου πνεύματος εἰς τοὺς αἰῶνας. ἀμήν. (Aland 18-9)

## ODE 24

1 ܝܘܢܐ ܦܪܚܬ ܥܠ ܪܫܗ ܕܡܪܢ ܡܫܝܚܐ
ܡܛܠ ܕܪܝܫܐ ܗܘܐ ܠܗ
2 ܘܙܡܪܬ ܥܠܘܗܝ
ܘܐܫܬܡܥ ܩܠܗ

3 ܘܕܚܠܘ ܥܡܘܪܐ
ܘܐܬܬܙܝܥܘ ܬܘ̈ܬܒܐ
4 ܦܪܚܬܐ ܫܒܩܬ ܟܢ̈ܦܝܗ
ܘܪܚܫܐ ܟܠܗ ܡܝܬ ܒܚܘܠܗ

5 ܘܬܗ̈ܘܡܐ ܐܬܦܬܚܘ ܘܐܬܟܣܝܘ
ܘܗܘܘ ܒܥܝܢ ܠܡܪܝܐ ܐܝܟ ܗܢܝܢ ܕܝܠܕܢ
6 ܘܠܐ ܐܬܝܗܒ ܠܗܘܢ ܠܡܐܟܘܠܬܐ
ܡܛܠ ܕܠܐ ܗܘܐ ܕܝܠܗܘܢ ܗܘܐ

7 ܘܛܒܥܘ ܕܝܢ ܬܗ̈ܘܡܐ ܒܛܒܘܥܗ ܕܡܪܝܐ
ܘܐܒܕܘ ܒܗܝ ܡܚܫܒܬܐ
ܕܐܝܬܝܗܘܢ ܗܘܘ ܡܢ ܠܩܕܡ
8 ܚܒܠܘ ܓܝܪ ܡܢ ܒܪܫܝܬ
ܘܫܘܠܡܐ ܕܚܒܠܗܘܢ ܐܝܬܘܗܝ ܗܘܐ ܚܝܐ

9 ܘܐܒܕ ܡܢܗܘܢ ܟܠ ܕܚܣܝܪ ܗܘܐ
ܡܛܠ ܕܠܝܬ ܗܘܐ ܠܗܘܢ
ܠܡܬܠ ܦܬܓܡܐ ܐܝܟ ܕܢܚܘܢ

10 ܘܡܪܝܐ ܡܚ̈ܫܒܬܐ ܐܘܒܕ
ܕܟܠܗܘܢ ܐܝܠܝܢ ܕܠܝܬ ܠܘܬܗܘܢ ܫܪܪܐ
11 ܚܣܪܘ ܓܝܪ ܡܢ ܚܟܡܬܐ
ܗܢܘܢ ܕܡܬܪܝܡܝܢ ܗܘܘ ܒܠܒܗܘܢ
12 ܘܐܣܬܠܩܘ
ܡܛܠ ܕܠܝܬ ܗܘܐ ܠܘܬܗܘܢ ܫܪܪܐ

ܡܪܢ ܕܡܫܝܚܐ ܪܝܫܗ ܥܠ     13
ܐܦܪܚܬ܂ ܝܘܢܐ ܗܘܬ
ܘܡܢ ܐܫܬܡܥ ܩܠܗ     14
ܠܥܠ ܙܡܪܬ ܗܘܬ

ܗܠܠܘܝܐ

---

1    The dove flew above the head of our Lord Messiah,
     because the head was hers.
2    And she sang above him,
     and her voice was heard.

3    And the inhabitants were afraid,
     and the sojourners were disturbed.
4    The flying creature abandoned its wings,
     and each creeping thing died in its hole.

5    And the deep abysses were opened and covered,
     and they sought the Lord like those who are bringing forth.
6    And he was not given to them for food,
     because he was not theirs.

7    But the deep abysses sank in the submersion of the Lord,
     and they perished in the thought,
     who were from the first.
8    For they corrupted from the beginning,
     and the completion of their corruption was life.

9    And each one who was in need perished from them,
     because they could not give the Word,
     that they might abide.

10   And the Lord destroyed the thoughts
     of all those with whom the truth was not.
11   For they were in need of wisdom,
     they who were haughty in their heart.
12   And they were rejected,
     because the truth was not with them.

13   Because the Lord manifested his way,
     and spread out widely his grace.
14   And they who recognised it
     know his holiness.


Alleluia.

NOTES TO THE TRANSLATION

1a: H does not have ܡܫܝܚܐ ܕܡܪܝܐ. The reading from N makes better sense of
1b, although the reading from H would give a stricter parallelism between 1a
and 2a.

1b: Since ...ܠ ܗܘܐ denotes possession (Smith, R.P. 1: 984; Brockelmann 1966,
173), 1b indicates that the dove possesses the head (of the Lord Messiah).
Smith gives as example Jn 4:18, which has an identical syntactic structure to
1b, ܫܡܫܐ ܠܟ ܐܝܬ ܒܥܠܝܢ ܗܘܐ ܠܗ.

4a: ܦܪܚܬܐ has been rendered by "the flying creature" rather than "bird" to
make clear the parallelism with ܪܚܫܐ. Such a translation avoids the ambiguity
by which it might be supposed that ܦܪܚܬܐ is referring to the dove in 1a. The
parallelism is the basis for the choice of the H reading over N (ܦܪܚܝ).

     Those translators who interpret 4a with a positive image (e.g "the birds took
to flight", Harris and Mingana vol. 2; "the bird began to fly", Charlesworth
1977) have not understood that the parallelism between 4a and 4b demands that
the action in 4a be interpreted negatively - the flying creature has abandoned
its wings (= can no longer fly/has fallen from flight) and the creeping thing has
died in its hole.

4b: H has ܪܚܫܐ...ܡܘܬܗ. The variants in N (the later addition of the ܘ to ܡܘܬ
is to be disregarded) are preferred because of the continuing use of sing. suffixes in this line.

6a: H omits the necessary ܠ before ܡܒܗܠܬܐ.

9a: H has incorrectly inserted a ܘ before ܒܠ.

9b: H has omitted ܠܗܘܢ after ܗܘܐ.

9b-c: Lattke makes a division into two lines here, but after ܠܗܘܢ (1979-86, vol. 2).

ANALYSIS

Stanza 1 [1-2]

Stanza 1 focusses on the action of the dove. The two bicola of the first strophe have a degree of alternate parallelism. 1a and 2a have a pattern of 3rd sing. fem. perf. verb (subj. is ܝܘܢܐ) + ܥܠ + ܪܫܝܗܝ ܕܗܘ ܡܫܝܚܐ/substitute 3rd masc. sing. suffix. 1b and 2b refer in some measure to the action in 1a and 2a respectively. There is direct ref. in 1b by the repetition of ܪܫܐ and indirect ref. in 2b by the use of ܩܠ. ܡܫܝܚܐ and ܪܫܐ are also associated in 17:16.

Stanza 2 [3-4]

With stanza 2 the focus shifts from the activity of the dove to the effects of that activity upon people and living things. The word-pairs ܠܒܢܝܢܫܐ - ܚܝܘܬܐ and ܦܪܚܬܐ - ܪܫܐ express merismus, indicating the totality of the disturbed reaction of all that live (human and animal) to the voice of the dove.

3a and 3b are parallel on the pattern: 3rd. pl. masc. perf. verb + noun pl. subj. The parallelism is strengthened by the word-pair ܢܚܘ - ܩܥܘ. 4a and 4b are not so strictly parallel, following the general pattern: noun sing. subj. ... 3rd. sing. Peal perf. verb ... noun + pron. suffix (ref. to the noun subj.).

Stanzas 3-6

With stanza 3, the focus shifts from the dove and the results of her actions to the deep abysses over against the Lord. The complete shift in focus together with the fact that stanzas 1-2 and stanzas 3-6 (and 7) are self-contained with regard to the repetitions of vocabulary (except for the occurrence of the ubiquitous ܡܪܝܐ) may indicate that the Ode is a complex of at least two sub-odes. The self-containment of the stanzas is the more remarkable by the number of connections between stanzas 3-6 by the repetition of vocabulary: ܬܗܘܡܐ (5a, 7a); ܐܝܟ with ܕܡܬܬܪܥܝܢ/ܕܡܬܪܥܝܢ (7b, 10a); ܐܝܟ (7b, 9a, 10a); ܚܕܝܘ (9a, 11a). Such a number of connections makes a clear division of stanzas very difficult.

Stanza 3 [5-6]

The personification of the deep abysses is indicated by the use of the simile which speaks of giving birth (5b) and by the ref. to eating (6a).

5a-b comprises three major actions for the deep abysses: being opened, closed, and seeking the Lord. 5a has internal parallelism by the double pattern of 3rd pl. masc. pass. verbs (ref. to ܬܗܘܡܐ). 5b comprises a simile introduced by ܐܝܟ, in which the actions of seeking and bringing forth are compared.

With 6, the focus changes from the 3rd pl. masc. (deep abysses) to the 3rd sing. masc. (the Lord). The bicolon has a degree of parallelism on the pattern: ܠܐ + 3rd sing. masc. verb + ܠ/ܠܗ + ܗܘܐ. The lines are semantically similar, concerned with the lack of the Lord experienced by the deep abysses ("he was not given to them... he was not theirs").

Stanza 4 [7-8]

Stanza 4 introduces a new aspect of the action with the deep abysses, emphasised by the use of ܕ. The abysses are the subj. of each line except for 8b where they are indirectly the subject of the action.

7a and 7b are parallel on the general pattern: 3rd pl. masc. perf. verb + ܒ + obj. 7c comprises a rel. cl. referring to the 3rd pl. masc. subj. of 7b (ܬܗܘܡܐ understood). The force of the destruction in 7a is given emphasis by the double play on the root ܚܒܠ.

Although 7c belongs with 7a-b, it is strongly connected with the following bicolon by its parallelism with 8a on the pattern: 3rd masc. pl. perf. verb + the synonymous phrases ܡܢ ܩܕܡܝܗܘܢ, ܡܢ ܒܪܝܫܝܬ. 8a and 8b are linked by the double word-play on the root ܚܝܐ and by the merismus expressed by the polar word-pair ܒܪܝܫܝܬ - ܥܠܡܐ.

Stanza 5 [9]

9b is linked with 9a by the use of the cl. introduced by ܕ ܡܛܠ which refers to ܐܒܐ. The cl. in 9c refers back to ܠܡܪܗܛܐ in 9b. There is a marked syntactic similarity between 9b and 12b (cf. also 10a) by the repetition of the pattern: ܗܘܐ ܠܝܬ ܡܛܠ + ܠܗܕܐ + ܗܘܐ + compl. (infin. + obj. [9b], ܒܪܝܬ [12a]).

Stanza 6 [10-12]

The inclusio for the stanza is formed by the repetition of ܠܘܬܗܘܢ (ܗܘܐ) ܠܝܬ
ܫܪܪ in 10b and 12b. 10a and 12a are connected by the word-pair ܐܒܕ - ܡܠܐ.
The two bicola describe the destruction of those who do not have the truth with
them. Given the link between 10b and 12b, the destruction of thoughts in 10a is
equivalent to the rejection in 12a. The central bicolon in 11 refers semantically
to both the surrounding bicola by giving further reasons for the destruction of
this group.

10b is connected with 10a as a gen. expression dependent upon ܡܚܫܒܬܗܘܢ.
11b comprises a rel. cl. with ref. to the 3rd masc. pl. subj. of 11a. 12b is connected with 12a by the cl. introduced by ܕ ܡܛܠ which refers to ܐܠܗܐ.

The synonymous descriptions in 11a and 11b (lack of wisdom, haughtiness
of heart) are also ironically antithetical: being needy/lacking over against being
haughty (lit. "lifted up"). The association of wisdom and heart occurs in 28:19.
The themes of humbling, exaltation, and rejection are found also, albeit positively, in 41:11-12.

Stanza 7 [13-14]

The opening of ܕ ܡܛܠ for 13a is unusual since the line (and the stanza in
general) does not fit especially well in the context. 13a-b is parallel on the pattern: A B C // B' C', where A = ܡܛܠ ܕܡܪܝܐ (understood in 13b), B = 3rd
masc. sing. perf. verb, and C = noun obj. with 3rd masc. sing. suffix (ref. to
the Lord). The bicolon is similar to 7:13, both semantically and by the use of
vocabulary (ܐܪܝܡ with ref. to the Lord; the Aphel of ܦܬܚ).

14a-b is parallel by the use of the 3rd masc. pl. verb + obj. There is a terrace pattern by the repetition of the root ܝܕܥ. The parallelism is further enhanced by the word-pair ܛܝܒܘܬܗ - ܝܕܥܬܗ. Ode 6 also concludes with the
motif of recognition.

The generally negative flavour of the Ode results, in part, from the number of
statements about those not having (6b, 9b, 10b, 12b), those lacking (9a, 11a),
and those not given (6a).

## ODE 25 [Syriac]

1 ܐܬܦܠܛܬ ܡܢ ܐܣܘܪܝ
ܘܠܘܬܟ ܥܪܩܬ ܐܠܗܝ
2 ܡܛܠ ܕܗܘܝܬ ܝܡܝܢܐ ܕܦܘܪܩܢܐ
ܘܡܥܕܪܢܐ ܕܝܠܝ

3 ܟܠܝܬ ܠܐܝܠܝܢ ܕܩܡܝܢ ܠܘܩܒܠܝ
ܘܬܘܒ ܠܐ ܐܬܚܙܝܘ
4 ܡܛܠ ܕܦܪܨܘܦܟ ܥܡܝ ܗܘܐ
ܗܘ ܕܦܪܩ ܗܘܐ ܠܝ ܒܛܝܒܘܬܟ

5 ܐܬܬܫܝܛܬ ܕܝܢ ܘܐܣܬܠܩܬ ܒܥܝܢ̈ܝ ܣܓ̈ܝܐܐ
ܘܗܘܝܬ ܒܥܝܢ̈ܝܗܘܢ ܐܝܟ ܐܒܪܐ
6 ܘܗܘܐ ܠܝ ܟܢܫܐ ܡܢ ܠܘܬܟ
ܘܡܥܕܪܢܐ

7 ܫܪܓܐ ܣܡܬ ܠܝ ܡܢ ܝܡܝܢܝ ܘܡܢ ܣܡܠܝ
ܕܠܐ ܢܗܘܐ ܒܝ ܡܕܡ ܕܠܐ ܢܘܗܪܐ

8 ܘܐܬܟܣܝܬ ܒܟܣܝܬܐ ܕܪܘܚܟ
ܘܐܪܝܡܬ ܡܢܝ ܠܒܘ̈ܫܝ ܕܡܫܟܐ
9 ܡܛܠ ܕܝܡܝܢܟ ܐܪܝܡܬܢܝ
ܘܐܥܒܪܬ ܟܘܪܗܢܐ ܡܢܝ

10 ܘܗܘܝܬ ܚܝܠܬܢܐ ܒܫܪܪܟ
ܘܩܕܝܫܐ ܒܙܕܝܩܘܬܟ
11 ܘܕܚܠܘ ܡܢܝ ܟܠܗܘܢ ܕܠܘܩܒܠܝ
ܘܗܘܝܬ ܕܡܪܝܐ ܒܫܡܗ ܕܡܪܝܐ
12 ܘܐܙܕܕܩܬ ܒܒܣܝܡܘܬܗ

ܘܢܝܚܗ ܠܥܠܡܥܠܡܝܢ ܗܘ

ܗܠܠܘܝܐ

1   I escaped from my chains,
    and towards you I fled my God;
2   because you were the right hand of salvation,
    and my helper.

3   You withheld those rising against me,
    and again they were not seen;
4   because your face was with me,
    which saved me by your grace.

5   But I was despised and rejected in the eyes of many,
    and I was in their eyes like lead.
6   And I had power from (being) with you,
    and help.

7   A lamp you set for me on my right hand and on my left,
    that there might not be in me anything without light.

8   And I was covered with the covering of your Spirit,
    and I removed from me my garments of skin;
9   because your right hand lifted me up,
    and you caused infirmity to pass from me.

10  And I was strong by your truth,
    and holy by your righteousness.
11  And all of those against me were afraid of me.
    And I was the Lord's by the name of the Lord,
12  and I was declared righteous by his gentleness.

    And his rest is for ever and ever.

    Alleluia.

## ODE 25 [Coptic]

1 ⲁⲓⲛⲟⲩ⳧ⲙ ⲉⲃⲟⲗ ⳥ⲛ ⳩ⲙⲣⲣⲉ
  ⲁⲓⲡⲱⲧ ⲉⲣⲁⲧⲕ̄ ⲡⲁⲟⲉⲓⲥ

2 ⳨ⲉ ⲁⲕϣⲱⲡⲉ ⲛⲁⲓ̈ ⲛ̄ⲟⲩⲛⲁⲙ ⲉⲕⲛⲟⲩ⳧ⲙ ⳩ⲙⲟⲓ̈
  ⲁⲩⲱ {ⲉⲕⲛⲟⲩ⳧ⲙ ⳩ⲙⲟⲓ̈ ⲁⲩⲱ} ⲉⲕϯ ⲛ̄ⲧⲟⲟⲧ

3 ⲁⲕⲕⲱⲗⲩ ⲛ̄ⲛⲉⲧϯⲟⲩⲃⲏⲓ̈
  ⲁⲩⲱ ⳩ⲡⲟⲩⲟⲩⲱⲛ⳧ ⲉⲃⲟⲗ

4 ⳨ⲉ ⲛⲉⲣⲉ ⲡⲉⲕⳭⲟ ϣⲟⲟⲡ ⲛ̄ⲙⲁⲓ̈ ⲡⲉ
  ⲉ⳷ⲛⲟⲩ⳧ⲙ ⳩ⲙⲟⲓ̈ ⳥ⲛ ⲧⲉⲕⲭⲁⲣⲓⲥ

5 ⲁⲓ̈ⳇⲓⲥⲱϣ ⳩ⲡⲉⲙⲧⲟ ⲉⲃⲟⲗ ⲛ̄ⲟⲩⲙⲏⲏϣⲉ
  ⲁⲩⲱ ⲁⲩⲛⲟⳍⲧ ⲉⲃⲟⲗ
  ⲁⲓ̈ⲣ̄ⲑⲉ ⲛ̄ⲟⲩⲧⲁ⳧ⲧ ⳩ⲡⲉⲩⲙⲧⲟ ⲉⲃⲟⲗ

6 ⲁⲥϣⲱⲡⲉ ⲛⲁⲓ̈ ⲛ̄ϭⲓ ⲟⲩϭⲟⲙ ⲉⲃⲟⲗ ⳥ⲓⲧⲟⲟⲧⲕ̄
  ⲁⲥϯ ⲛ̄ⲧⲟⲟⲧ

7 ⳨ⲉ ⲁⲕⲕⲱ ⲛ̄⳥ⲉⲛ⳥ⲏⲃⲥ̄ ⲛ̄ⲥⲁ ⲟⲩⲛⲁⲙ ⳩ⲙⲟⲓ̈ ⲁⲩⲱ ⲛ̄ⲥⲁ ⳥ⲃⲟⲩⲣ ⳩ⲙⲟⲓ̈
  ⳨ⲉⲕⲁⲥ ⲛ̄ⲛⲉ ⲗⲁⲁⲩ ⲛ̄ⲥⲁ ⳩ⲙⲟⲓ̈ ϣⲱⲡⲉ ⲉ⳷ⲟ ⲛ̄ⲁⲧⲟⲩⲟⲉⲓⲛ

8 ⲁⲕⲥⲕⲉⲡⲁⲍⲉ ⳩ⲙⲟⲓ̈ ⳥ⲁ ⲑⲁⲓ̈ⲃⲉⲥ ⳩ⲡⲉⲕⲛⲁ
  ⲁⲩⲱ ⲁⲓ̈ⲣ̄ⲡⲉⲧⲡⲉ ⲛ̄ⲛⲉϣⲧⲏⲛ ⲛ̄ϣⲁⲁⲣ

9 ⲧⲉⲕⲟⲩⲛⲁⲙ ⲧⲉ ⲛ̄ⲧⲁⲥ⳨ⲓⲥⲉ ⳩ⲙⲟⲓ̈
  ⲁⲩⲱ ⲁⲕ⳷ⲓⲡϣⲱⲛⲉ ⲛ̄ⲥⲁⲃⲟⲗ ⳩ⲙⲟⲓ̈

10 ⲁⲓ̈ϣⲱⲡⲉ ⲉⲓ̈ϭⲙ̄ϭⲟⲙ ⳥ⲛ ⲧⲉⲕ⳩̄ⲛ̄ⲧⲙⲉ
  ⲉⲓ̈ⲧⲃ̄ⲃⲏⲩ ⳥ⲛ ⲧⲉⲕⲇⲓⲕⲁⲓⲟⲥⲩⲛⲏ

11 ⲁⲩⲟⲩⲉ ⲉⲃⲟⲗ ⳩ⲙⲟⲓ̈ ⲛ̄ϭⲓ ⲛⲉⲧϯⲟⲩⲃⲏⲓ̈

12 ⲁⲩⲱ ⲁⲓ̈ⲧⲙⲁⲓ̈ⲟ ⳥ⲛ ⲧⲉⲕ⳩̄ⲛ̄ⲧⲭⲣⲏⲥⲧⲟⲥ

  ⳨ⲉ ⲡⲉⲕ⳩̄ⲧⲟⲛ ϣⲟⲟⲡ ϣⲁⲉⲛⲉ⳥ ⲛ̄ⲧⲉ ⲡⲓⲉⲛⲉ⳥

---

1 I was saved from chains,
   and fled to you, Lord;

2 for you became for me a right hand saving me,
   and {saving me and} helping me.

3   You hindered those who rise against me,
    and they have not appeared;
4   for your face was with me,
    saving me by your grace.

5   I was scorned before a multitude,
    and was cast forth.
    I became like lead before them.

6   A power from you became for me,
    helping me;
7   for you put lamps on my right side and on my left,
    that no side of me might become without light.

8   You sheltered me with the shadow of your mercy,
    and I surmounted garments of skin.
9   Your right hand it is that exalted me,
    and you took away the sickness from me.

10  I became powerful by your truth,
    and pure by your righteousness.
11  Those who rise against me became far from me.
12  And I have been justified by your goodness.

    For your rest is forever and ever.

NOTES TO THE TRANSLATION

2b: The Coptic scribe is mistaken in repeating ⲉⲕⲛⲟⲩⳅⲙ ⲙⲙⲟⲓ̈ after ⲁⲩⲱ.

3b: The reading from H, ܡܢܘܟ, makes less sense than N in the context.

7b: H has ܠܐ. N and the Coptic agree.

8a: The Coptic scribe appears to have misread ⲡⲉⲕⲛⲁ for ⲡⲉⲕ̄ⲛ̄ⲁ̄.

8b: ܐܝܪܬܗ may be 1st sing. (Harris and Mingana vol. 2; Bauer 1964; Charlesworth 1977; Emerton), 2nd sing. masc. (Harris 1911a; Diettrich 1911; Labourt and Batiffol; Bernard; Bruston 1912b; Lattke 1979-86, vol. 2; Carmignac 1986), or 3rd sing. fem. (Flemming; Ungnad and Staerk). The choice for 1st sing. has been made on the basis of the Coptic which also uses 1st sing., and because of the parallelism with 8a.

H has ܡܕܪܟ.

9b: ܐܟܒܪܬ may be 1st sing., 2nd sing. masc. (Lattke 1979-86, vol. 2), or 3rd sing. fem. (Harris 1911a; Flemming; Ungnad and Staerk; Diettrich 1911; Labourt and Batiffol; Bernard; Bruston 1912b; Harris and Mingana vol. 2; Bauer 1964; Charlesworth 1977; Emerton; Carmignac 1986). The choice for the 2nd masc. sing. is made because the Coptic has it also. The parallelism of 9a and 9b would favour using the 3rd sing. fem., although "your right hand" and "you" are also semantically closely equivalent. The same difficulty occurs in 18:7a-b.

10a: H has ܒܚܝܝܟ. N and the Coptic agree. The N reading is also supported by the parallelism of 10a and 10b.

12a-b: Lattke (1979-86, vol. 1) translates ܒܒܣܝܡܘܬܗ with "in deiner Milde (Güte)" instead of "in seiner Milde (Güte)", and ΠΕΚΜ̄ΤΟΝ with "seine Ruhe" instead of "deine Ruhe".

ANALYSIS [Syriac]

Stanza 1 [1-2]

1a-b is parallel with chiasmus on the pattern: A B // B' A' C, where A = 1st sing. perf. verb; B = prep. with obj. (expressing movement); C = vocative expression. The bicolon presents two antitheses; firstly, between the prep. phrases (ܡܢ - ܠܘܬ), and secondly, between the final nouns with 1st sing. suffix (my chains, my God).

2a-b is connected with 1a-b by the cl. introduced by ܡܛܠ ܕ which refers to ܢܝܪܘܗܝ (1b) and perhaps also ܐܣܘܪ̈ܝ. 2a and 2b are parallel, with ܡܛܠ ܕܗܘܐ understood in 2b. The compls., ܝܕ ܕܝܡܝܢܗ (2a) and ܡܪܝܐ ܕܝܠܝ (2b), are semantically synonymous. The parallelism between the gen. element of each compl. is enhanced by using ܕܝܠܝ instead of the pron. suffix (ܕܡܪܝܐ).

The stanza is connected semantically with 21:1-2 with some common vocabulary - ܐܝܕܝ̈, ܦܘܩܢ̈ܐ, ܐܪܝܡ ܚܬܝ̈ܪܐ (ܚܬܝܪ in 21:2), the latter two terms with ref. to the Lord.

## Stanza 2 [3-4]

Stanza 2 repeats the basic four-line pattern of stanza 1: two bicola with the second bicolon introduced by ܡܛܠ܊ 3 presents a new group of characters, the adversaries of the "I". The cl. introduced by ܡܛܠ܊ in 4a refers to the action of God in 3. As with 2a-b the cl. comprises details of some attribute of God with ref. to its helpfulness to the "I". There is a further link between 2a and 4b by the repetition of the root ܦܪܩ.

4b is linked with 4a by the rel. cl. introduced by ܗܘ referring to ܦܪܩܘܗܝ. There is some degree of parallelism between the two lines on the pattern: A B C // C' B' A', where A = noun + 2nd masc. sing. suffix (ref. God); B = prep. + 1st sing. suffix; C = verb.

## Stanza 3 [5-6]

Stanza 3 continues the general theme of the previous stanzas. The "I" is under oppression ("chains" [1a], "those rising against me" [3a], "despised and rejected...in their eyes like lead" [5a, 5b]) but can withstand his enemies by the help of God. The 1st sing. subj. is used throughout the stanza.

5a and 5b are semantically equivalent. There is some parallelism by the repetition of ܐܬܚܫܒܬ/ܐܣܬܠܝܬ ܩܕܡ ܥܝ̈ܢܝܗܘܢ. 6a-b is parallel, 6b providing the second noun compl. for ܗܘܐ ܠܝ. 6a-b is similar both semantically and syntactically to 2a-b, the similarity emphasised by the repetition of the root ܥܒܪ for the second noun compl. in 2b and 6b.

With the repetition of ܥܒܪ and the syntactic structure of 2 and 6 which links stanzas 1 and 3, there is a loose pattern of A B A' for the first three stanzas. Stanza 3 effectively completes the first section of the Ode in which the "I" describes his escape from enemies with the help of God.

## Stanza 4 [7]

The single bicolon in 7 breaks the flow of the pattern of the previous four-line stanzas. By its position, 7 is a central focus of the Ode, describing a watershed action by God which moves the "I" out of the situation of oppression. Thus 7 provides the bridge between the first descriptions of oppression and the second section of the Ode (8-12) which details the lifting up, healing, strengthening, sanctifying and so on of the "I".

The focus of the action in both lines is the "I" (ﺏ, ﺝ). There is a loose kind of inclusio by the close semantic association of ﺭﺥﻳﺭ and ﺭﻳﻣﻧ. 7b is similar in form to 11:23b and 34:3b.

## Stanza 5 [8-9]

The stanza returns to the four-line pattern (two bicola with the second bicolon introduced by ﺭ ﺏﺏﻳﺭ) of stanzas 1 and 2. As in stanza 1, the subj. of the first bicolon is the 1st sing., while that of the second bicolon is the 2nd masc. sing. (indirectly in 9a).

8a-b is parallel on the pattern: 1st sing. perf. verb ... noun 1 (object of the action of the verb and associated with the clothing motif) + ﺭ + noun 2. There is antithesis between the verbs ﺭﻣﺯ and ﻳﻧﺭ, and the nouns 2, ﺭﻧﻧﺭ and ﺭﺯﻳﻧ. Nouns 1, ﺭﻳﻣﺯﺝ and ﺭﺯﺯﺏ, are semantically equivalent. 8a has a double play on the root ﺭﻣﺯ.

The second bicolon is connected with the first by the cl. introduced by ﺏﺏﻳﺭ ﺭ which refers to the action in 8a-b, and by the repetition of the root ﻳﻧﺭ. There is a degree of parallelism in 9a-b by the use of the Aphel perf. verbs which have the 1st sing. as dir./indir. obj., and by the semantic equivalence of the subjs. ("your right hand", "you"). The parallelism is strengthened by the word-pair ﻳﻧﺭ - ﺯﺏﺝ.

## Stanza 6 [10-12a]

It is not entirely clear if the one addressed as "you" (= God) in 10 (and up to this point in the Ode) is equivalent to the one spoken of as "he" (= the Lord) in 11b-12. If this is the case then one would have expected to make a division in the stanza between these verses because the change in personal pron. would underline a change in style from a direct address to God to a report about God.

However, 10 and 11c-12a are strongly linked. The lines are parallel on the pattern: 1st sing. perf. verb (ﺏﻳﻧﺯ understood in 10b) + adj. expression (attribute of the Odist, contained within the verb in 12a) + ﺯ (signifying agency in each case) + noun (attribute of the Lord/God) with masc. sing. suffix. There is a further connection by the repetition of the root ﺯﻳﺭ in 10b and 12a.

11a has the central position of the stanza. The surrounding bicola give the reasons for the fear of the adversaries in 11a. It has internal parallelism with each half section having two elements, the first using the 3rd pl. masc. and the second consisting of a prep. with 1st sing. suffix. There is a connection with 3a by the repetition of ܠܩܘܒܠܝ.

## Stanza 7 [12b]

12b continues the pattern of noun (attribute of the Lord) with 3rd sing. masc. suffix found at the conclusion of 12a (and 11b). The line functions as a concluding confessional statement for the Ode.

This is a thoroughly personal Ode with the focus squarely on the "I". Every verse makes ref. to the "I", either by an action which the "I" performs or an action which is performed to him/on his behalf.

ANALYSIS [Coptic]

## Stanza 1 [1-2]

As with the Syriac, the bicolon in 1 is parallel. The Coptic has ΝΟΥϨΜ in 1a and 2a, which further strengthens the connection between the two bicola.
    In 2a, the ܪܩܝܦܗ of the Syriac is a fully fledged cl. in the Coptic, ΕΚΝΟΥϨΜ ΜΜΟΪ, parallel to the cl. which follows in 2b on the pattern: 2nd sing. masc. pres. II verb + obj.
    The Coptic mirrors the structure of the four-line stanza in the Syriac: two bicola with the second bicolon introduced by ΔЄ.

## Stanza 2 [3-4]

The versions are very similar, the Coptic following the four-line pattern of stanza 1.

## Stanza 3 [5]

The Coptic has two lines (5a-b) where the Syriac has one (5a). Within the tricolon, 5b is the central focus between 5a and 5c which are parallel on the pattern: 1st sing. perf. I verb...ΜΠΕΜΤΟ ЄΒΟΛ ΝΟΥΜΗΗϢЄ/ΜΠΕΥΜΤΟ ЄΒΟΛ.

## Stanza 4 [6-7]

The division of stanzas here differs from the Syriac. The Coptic of 6 has a 3rd sing. fem. subj. (ΟΥϬΟΜ) rather than the 1st sing. of the Syriac which continues from 5. It is possible that 6-7 follows the four-line pattern of stanzas 1 and 2, although ⲀⲈ which introduces 7a may not be intended to be interpreted as strongly as ⲁ ⲗⲗⲁ.

The connection between 6b and 2b found in the Syriac is stronger in the Coptic since the repetition involves ï in the pres. II (2nd masc. sing. in 2b, 3rd fem. sing. in 6b) with ⲚⲦⲞⲞⲦ in each case. 6b and 2b are linked semantically by the equivalence of the right hand and power. 6a (initially) and 2a are parallel on the pattern: perf. I of ϢⲰⲠⲈ (2nd masc. sing. in 2a, 3rd fem. sing. in 6a) + ⲚⲀï + noun (compl./subj.)

The use of ⲦⲞⲞⲦ links 6a and 6b. 7a and 7b are connected by the repetition of ⲤⲀ. There is a slight variation between the Syriac and Coptic in 7b which has no major effect on the overall meaning.

## Stanza 5 [8-9]

The Coptic does not follow the four-line pattern of stanzas 1 and 2 as does the Syriac. However both versions are similar by the strong semantic links within this stanza - the antithetical concepts of sheltering and surmounting in 8a-b; the parallelism of being above or exalted in 8b and 9a, and of surmounting and taking away in 8b and 9b.

## Stanza 6 [10-12a]

There are a number of significant differences between the Syriac and Coptic in this stanza. 11b in the Syriac does not occur in the Coptic, and the Coptic uses the 2nd sing. masc. prefix in 12a where the Syriac has the 3rd sing. masc. suffix. Because of the latter difference, 10 and 12a in the Coptic are more strictly parallel than 10 and 11b-12a in the Syriac and there is no question regarding the division of the stanza. The pattern of the parallel lines is: 1st sing. perf. I verb (ⲀïϢⲰⲠⲈ understood in 10b) + 1st sing. pres II verb used as an adj. expression (attribute of the "I", contained within the verb in 12a) + ⳈⲚ (signifying agency in each case) + 2nd sing. masc. prefix + noun (attribute of the Lord).

As in the Syriac, the monocolon in 11 interrupts the pattern of parallel lines and has a connection with 3a (ⲚⲈⲦϯⲞⲨⲂⲎï). If the monocolon is an addition, then the stanzas of the Ode (excluding the concluding confessional statement) would follow a double pattern of two four-line stanzas + one three-line stanza. The three-line stanzas (stanzas 3 and 6) are linked by their exclusive use of a 1st sing. subj. throughout.

Stanza 7 [12b]

The concluding confessional statement in 12b continues the pattern of 2nd masc. sing. prefix + noun (attribute of the Lord) found at the conclusion of 12a. It comprises direct address to the Lord rather than being an indirect statement as in the Syriac.

## ODE 26

1 ܐܪܒܝܬ ܬܫܒܘܚܬܐ ܠܡܪܝܐ
ܡܛܠ ܕܕܝܠܗ ܐܢܐ
2 ܘܐܡܠܠ ܙܡܝܪ̈ܬܐ ܩܕܝܫܬܐ ܕܝܠܗ
ܡܛܠ ܕܠܒܝ ܠܘܬܗ ܗܘ
3 ܩܝܬܪܗ ܓܝܪ ܒܐܝ̈ܕܝ
ܘܠܐ ܢܫܠܝܢ ܙܡܝܪ̈ܬܐ ܕܢܝܚܗ
4 ܐܩܥܐ ܠܘܬܗ ܡܢ ܟܠܗ ܠܒܝ
ܐܫܒܚ ܘܐܪܝܡܝܘܗܝ ܡܢ ܟܠܗܘܢ ܗܕ̈ܡܝ

5 ܡܢ ܡܕܢܚܐ ܓܝܪ ܘܥܕܡܐ ܠܡܥܪܒܐ
ܬܫܒܘܚܬܐ ܕܝܠܗ ܗܝ
6 ܘܡܢ ܬܝܡܢܐ ܘܥܕܡܐ ܠܓܪܒܝܐ
ܕܝܠܗ ܗܝ ܬܘܕܝܬܐ
7 ܘܡܢ ܪܫܐ ܕܪ̈ܘܡܐ ܘܥܕܡܐ ܠܣܘܦܗܘܢ
ܫܘܡܠܝܗ ܕܝܠܗ ܗܘ

8 ܡܢܘ ܕܟܬܒ ܙܡܝܪ̈ܬܗ ܕܡܪܝܐ
ܐܘ ܡܢܘ ܕܩܪܐ ܠܗܝܢ
9 ܐܘ ܡܢܘ ܕܕܪܐ ܢܦܫܗ ܠܚܝ̈ܐ
ܕܬܬܦܪܩ ܢܦܫܗ
10 ܐܘ ܡܢܘ ܕܡܬܬܢܝܚ ܥܠ ܡܪܝܡܐ
ܕܢܡܠܠ ܡܢ ܦܘܡܗ
11 ܡܢܘ ܡܫܟܚ ܕܢܦܫܩ ܬܕܡܪ̈ܬܗ ܕܡܪܝܐ
ܡܛܠ ܓܝܪ ܕܗܘ ܕܡܦܫܩ ܢܫܬܪܐ
ܘܢܗܘܐ ܗܘ ܕܡܬܦܫܩ

12 ܣܦܩ ܓܝܪ ܠܡܕܥ ܘܠܡܬܬܢܚܘ
ܕܡܙ̈ܡܪܐ ܓܝܪ ܩܝܡܝܢ ܒܫܝܢܘܬܐ
13 ܐܝܟ ܢܗܪܐ ܕܐܝܬ ܠܗ ܡܒܘܥܐ ܥܬܝܪܐ
ܘܪܕܐ ܠܡܥܕܪܢܐ ܕܐܝܠܝܢ ܕܒܥܝܢ ܠܗ

ܗܠܠܘܝܐ

1    I poured forth a hymn to the Lord,
      because I am his.

2    And I will speak his holy ode,
      because my heart is with him.

3    For his harp is in my hands,
      and the odes of his rest will not be still.

4    I shall implore him with all my heart;
      I will glorify and exalt him with all my members.

5    For from the east and unto the west
      the hymn is his;

6    and from the south and unto the north
      his is the confession;

7    and from the summit of the heights and unto their extremity
      the perfection is his.

8    Who is it who writes the odes of the Lord?
      Or who is it who reads them?

9    Or who is it who leads his soul to life,
      that he himself might be saved?

10   Or who is it who rests upon the Most High,
      that he might speak from his mouth?

11   Who is able to interpret the wonders of the Lord?
      Because he who interprets will be dissolved,
      and what is interpreted will abide.

12   For it suffices to know and to be at rest;
      for the singers stand up in rest;

13   like a river which has an abundant spring,
      and flows to the help of those who seek it.

Alleluia.

NOTES TO THE TRANSLATION

1a: I have translated ܐܬܒܘܚܫܬ as "hymn" (cf. Diettrich 1911; Labourt and Batiffol; Lattke 1979-86, vol. 2) because of the parallelism between 1a and 2a.

5-7: Both Mss. have a single line only for each of 5, 6, and 7. The division into two lines has been made because of the otherwise overly long lines when compared to the rest of the Ode. The parallelism is also clearer when each verse is set out as two lines.

5b: I have kept to the translation of ܬܫܒܘܚܬܐ as "hymn" for consistency (cf. 1a), and because of the parallelism between 5a and 6a. However, ܬܫܒܘܚܬܐ occurs elsewhere in the Odes in word-pairs with both ܐܘܕܝܬܐ (6b) and ܬܫܒܚܬܐ (7b).

9b: H has ܝܘܕܝܬܗ.

11b: H has omitted the ܘ before ܗܘ.

ANALYSIS

Stanza 1 [1-4]

1a and 13a form the inclusio for the Ode by the repetition of the root ܢܒܥ. The repetition indicates that the image of 13 is implicit in 1a (cf. also e.g. 40:2). The inclusio for the stanza is formed by the repetition of the root ܫܒܚ in 1a and 4b.

    1-2 comprises two alternately parallel bicola. 1a and 2a have the pattern: 1st sing. verb + noun obj. + prep./poss. particle + ܡܪܝܐ/substitute pron. suffix. The lines are also connected semantically by the equivalence of pouring out a hymn and reciting an ode. 1b and 2b are two parallel associated cls. introduced by ܘ ܡܛܠ. There is chiasmus by the placement of the expressions associated with 1st sing. and 3rd sing. masc. persons: ܠܘܬܗ - ܠܒܗ, ܐܢܐ - ܠܗ. The concepts of being with the Lord and one's heart being with him are synonymous. There is a semantic similarity between 1-2 and 21:7-8 (the heart of the "I" in the action of praising the Lord).

    The lines of the bicolon in 3 are connected semantically especially by the association of ܩܝܬܗ and ܟܢܪܗ ܕܚܝܠܗ. 3a flows easily from 2b with a chiastic structure by the placement of the 1st sing. and 3rd masc. sing. persons: ܠܗ - ܐܝܟ, ܠܩܝܬܗ - ܩܝܬܗ. 2 and 3 are further connected by the repetition of ܟܢܪܐ in the pl. in 3b.

4a-b is parallel on the pattern: 1st sing. imperf. verb/s + masc. sing. pron. obj. + ...ܠܒ ܕ + pron. suffix (ref. to subsequent noun) + noun + 1st sing. suffix. The parallelism is strengthened by the word-pair ܠܒ - ܗܝܢ.

It is possible that another structure may be operating in the stanza. When one focusses on the repetition of ܫܒܚ in 1a and 4b and of ܟܐܝܘܬܝ in 2a and 3b, then 2b-3a becomes the centre of the stanza. The chiasmus between 2b and 3a has been noted. The lines are also parallel on the general pattern: noun + pron. suffix + prep. with obj. Working out from 2b-3a, 2a and 3b have a degree of parallelism by ܟܐܝܘܬܝ/ܟܐܝܘܬܝ + descriptive expression with 3rd masc. sing. suffix (ref. to the Lord), although ܟܐܝܘܬܝ in 2a is the obj. and ܟܐܝܘܬܝ in 3b is the subj.

## Stanza 2 [5-7]

With this stanza, the style of the Ode shifts from a description of the action of the "I" to a confessional section. The three bicola are alternately parallel. 5 and 6 are more strongly connected semantically with merismus expressed by the two pairs of opposite compass points (5a, 6a), and by the close association of "hymn" (5b) and "confession" (6b) over against "perfection" in 7b. 7 follows logically from 5-6 since it expresses what might be termed "vertical merismus" (the summit of the mountains to their base) to complement the "horizontal merismus" of 5-6.

5a, 6a, and 7a follow the pattern: ܕ + noun 1 (combination of two nouns in 7a) + ܠ ܟܢܬܐܐ + noun 2. In each case noun 1 and noun 2 are semantic opposites. 5b, 6b, and 7b are parallel with chiasmus by the placement of the noun and the gen. expression with copula. 5b and 7b have the pattern: noun + ܡܠܗ + copula. 6b has ܡܠܗ + copula + noun.

## Stanza 3 [8, 9-10, 11]

The limits of the stanza are indicated by the occurrence of the initial ܐܝܟܢ. What may have been originally a simple series of rhetorical questions has been expanded and several subdivisions must be made.

8a-b is parallel on the pattern: ܢ ܐܝܟ + masc. sing. Peal part. act. + noun obj./substitute pron. suffix. The parallelism is enhanced by the word-pair ܒܗܒ - ܟܝܐ. There is a connection with stanza 1 by the repetition of ܟܐܝܘܬܝ in 8a.

9-10 keeps the pattern of the rhetorical question with ܢ ܐܝܟ but adds a second line containing an associated cl. expressing purpose. The two bicola are therefore alternately parallel - 9a and 10a on the pattern: ܢ ܐܝܟ ܐܟ + masc.

sing. part. act. ... prep. with noun obj.; 9b and 10b on the pattern: ܘ + 3rd masc. sing. imperf. verb ... noun (attribute of the "I") with 3rd masc. sing. suffix. 9a and 9b are connected by the repetition of ܢܦܫܗ and by the association of ܫܝܢ and ܦܐܝܘ.

The tricolon in 11 must be included in the stanza because of the intial ܡܢܘ but it also stands as a self-contained strophe by the repeated use of the key root ܬܚܘܡ. 11a differs from 8a, 8b, 9a and 10a by the omission of the rel. ܘ after ܡܢܘ and by the use of a complex of two cls. in place of the simple part. act. 11a sets the question. 11b-c is associated with 11a by the initial ܘ ܡܛܠ in 11b, and semantically provides the reasons why the answer to 11a must be "no one". 11b-c are parallel with chiasmus by the placement of ܘ ܗܘ + 3rd masc. sing. part. (root ܬܚܘܡ) and the 3rd masc. sing. imperf. verb. There is antithesis by the use of the word-pair ܫܝܐ - ܩܡ.

## Stanza 4 [12-13]

The final stanza reiterates some motifs of the first and third stanzas - rest and the odes/singers (3b, 10), the action of pouring forth associated with the "I" (1a, 13).

12a and 12b are connected by the repetition of the root ܢܘܚ, 12b taking up one of the necessary attributes outlined in 12a and applying it to the singers.

The simile in 13 may apply to the singers in 12b although the connection is not entirely clear, especially since the simile uses "a river" rather than "rivers" as would have been expected after "singers". It would be easier, therefore, to see the connection of the simile with the impersonal expression of 12a (Dietrich 1911, 94 has 12b as an addition). If the simile is connected with 12b, then it appears that the singers experience the rest of the Lord when they stand (the attitude adopted for prayer but also meaning a great deal more than a liturgical posture; cf. 36:2; Grundmann passim) and it is this experience of rest which enables them to flow to the help of others (cf. the rest given upon the spring of the Lord in 30:2b).

13 is similar to 4:10b-c by the use of ܒܝܬ ܡܩܒܠ (pl. in 4:10b and with the 2nd masc. sing. suffix) and ܢܗܪ.

ODE 27

,ܐ̈ܢܠ ܕܫܒܩ ,ܐܝܟ ܕܠܝܫܛ  1
,ܡ ܡܕܟ ,ܐܝܟܗ ܪܘܕܝܗܗ ܠܠܝܛ  2
ܓܐܕܗ ܪܡܘܚ ,ܕܢܠܝܫܛܗ  3

ܪܢܠܠܡ

---

1    I extended my hands and hallowed my Lord;
2    because the stretching out of my hands is his sign,
3    and my extension the wood which (is) upright.

Alleluia.

NOTES TO THE TRANSLATION

1: A number of translators have difficulty with the concept of hallowing the Lord and suggest an understood obj. for ܕܫ ܗܡ, referring to "my hands", so that it is the hands of the "I" which are hallowed to/for the Lord (cf. Ungnad and Staerk; Diettrich 1911; Harris and Mingana vol. 2; Carmignac 1986; Labourt and Batiffol indicate this possibility in a footnote).

2-3: cf. The Untitled Text, Chapter 2, "And the stretching out of his hands is the manifestation of the cross (ⲤⲦⲁⲨⲢⲟⲤ)"; Schmidt 1978a, 227, lines 14-15. Cf. the note for Ode 42:2.

2: N has ,ܡܕܕܟ, but has ܡܕܟ in 42:1b.

ANALYSIS

This is the shortest of the Odes, combining in three lines a description of physical (liturgical?) action with a commentary on its theological significance.

1 functions as the introduction, giving the basic physical description of the action of the "I". The monocolon has internal parallelism by the double pattern of 1st sing. perf. verb + noun obj. with 1st sing. suffix. 1 is linked to both 2 and 3 by the repetition of the key words ,ܐܝܟ and ܠܝܫܛ.

2-3 is a parallel bicolon where subjs. (ܡܬܚܐ ܕܐܝܕܝ and ܦܫܝܛܘܬܝ) and compls. (ܐܬܘܬܗ and ܩܝܣܐ ܕܬܪܝܨ) are semantically equivalent . There is chiasmus by the placement of the single (ܐܬܘܬܗ and ܦܫܝܛܘܬܝ) and double (ܡܬܚܐ ܕܐܝܕܝ and ܩܝܣܐ ܕܬܪܝܨ) construction of elements.

---

EXCURSUS: COMPARISON OF 27:1-3; 35:7; 37:1; 42:1-2

27:1-3

1 ܦܫܛܬ ܐܝܕܝ ܘܩܕܫܬ ܠܡܪܝ
2 ܡܛܠ ܕܡܬܚܐ ܕܐܝܕܝ ܐܬܘܬܗ ܗܝ
3 ܘܦܫܝܛܘܬܝ ܩܝܣܐ ܕܬܪܝܨ

35:7

7 ܘܦܫܛܬ ܐܝܕܝ ܒܡܣܠܩܗ ܕܢܦܫܝ
ܘܐܬܬܪܨܬ ܠܘܬ ܡܪܝܡܐ
ܘܐܬܦܪܩܬ ܠܘܬܗ

37:1

1 ܦܫܛܬ ܐܝܕܝ ܠܘܬ ܡܪܝ
ܘܠܘܬ ܡܪܝܡܐ ܐܪܝܡܬ ܩܠܝ

42:1-2

1 ܦܫܛܬ ܐܝܕܝ ܘܐܬܩܪܒܬ ܠܘܬ ܡܪܝ
ܡܛܠ ܕܡܬܚܐ ܕܐܝܕܝ ܐܬܘܬܗ ܗܝ
2 ܘܦܫܝܛܘܬܝ ܩܝܣܐ ܦܫܝܛܐ
ܕܐܬܬܠܝ ܥܠ ܐܘܪܚܗ ܕܬܪܝܨܐ

The basic form has two elements: the first, ܦܫܛܬ ܐܝܕܝ; the second comprising a 1st sing. perf. verb + ܠ/ܠܘܬ + ܡܪܝ as found in 27:1 and 42:1. 35:7 inserts a descriptive expression ܒܡܣܠܩܗ ܕܢܦܫܝ before the second element (adapted: ܡܪܝܡܐ replaces ܡܪܝ) in 7b, which is followed by a parallel expression, ܘܐܬܦܪܩܬ ܠܘܬܗ, in 7c. 37:1 has separated the first element from the second (adapted and in reverse order: ܠܘܬ ܡܪܝܡܐ ܐܪܝܡܬ ܩܠܝ) by the construction of the parallel bicolon with chiasmus.

27:1-3 and 42:1-2 have a more extended form, which includes the reflection upon the meaning of the action of the "I". Both have the same third element ‍‍‍ܝܗ ܗܬ݂ܐ ,ܘܪ݂ܐܐ ܟܕܬܗܢ ܡ̈ܠܝܟܘ and a parallel fourth element ܟܣ݂ܘܣ ,ܬ݂ܢܠ݂ܝܫܦܘ ‍ܝܗܬ݂ܐ/ܟܝܫܦ which repeats the root ܠ݂ܝܫܦ (x 2 in 42:2a) from the first element. The final descriptive cl. in 42:2b refers to its preceding fourth element and is linked with 27:3 and 35:7b by the use of the root ‍ܝܗܬ݂.

## ODE 28

1 ܐܝܟ ܓܦܐ ܕܝܘܢܐ ܥܠ ܦܪܘܓܝܗܘܢ
ܘܦܘܡܗܘܢ ܕܦܪܘܓܝܗܘܢ ܠܘܬ ܦܘܡܗܘܢ
ܗܟܢܐ ܐܦ ܓܦܘܗܝ ܕܪܘܚܐ ܥܠ ܠܒܝ
2 ܡܬܒܣܡ ܠܒܝ ܘܕܐܨ
ܐܝܟ ܥܘܠܐ ܕܕܐܨ ܒܟܪܣܐ ܕܐܡܗ

3 ܗܝܡܢܬ ܡܛܠ ܗܢܐ
ܐܦ ܐܬܬܢܝܚܬ
ܡܛܠ ܕܡܗܝܡܢ ܗܘ
ܗܘ ܕܗܝܡܢܬ ܒܗ

4 ܡܒܪܟܘ ܒܪܟܢܝ
ܘܪܫܝ ܠܘܬܗ ܗܘ
ܘܚܪܒܐ ܠܐ ܬܦܠܓܢܝ ܡܢܗ
ܐܦܠܐ ܣܦܣܪܐ
5 ܡܛܠ ܕܐܬܛܝܒܬ ܡܢ ܩܕܡ ܕܢܐܬܐ ܐܒܕܢܐ
ܘܐܬܬܣܝܡܬ ܒܟܢܦܘܗܝ ܕܠܐ ܚܒܠܐ

6 ܘܓܦܘܢܝ ܚܝ̈ܐ ܕܠܐ ܡܘܬܐ ܘܢܫܩܘܢܝ
7 ܘܡܢܗܘܢ ܐܝܬܝܗ ܪܘܚܐ ܕܒܝ
ܘܠܐ ܡܫܟܚܐ ܠܡܡܬ
ܡܛܠ ܕܚܝܐ ܗܝ

8 ܐܬܕܡܪܘ ܐܝܠܝܢ ܕܚܙܝܢ ܗܘܘ ܠܝ
ܡܛܠ ܕܐܬܪܕܦܬ
9 ܘܣܒܪܘ ܕܐܬܒܠܥܬ ܠܝ
ܡܛܠ ܕܐܬܚܙܝܬ ܠܗܘܢ ܐܝܟ ܚܕ ܡܢ ܐܒܝ̈ܕܐ

10 ܘܛܠܘܡܝܐ ܕܝܢ ܕܝܠܝ
ܦܘܪܩܢܐ ܗܘܐ ܠܝ

11 ܘܣܘܠܓܗܘܢ ܕܝܢ ܗܘܝܬ
ܡܛܠ ܕܛܢܢܐ ܠܝܬ ܗܘܐ ܒܝ
12 ܡܛܠ ܕܠܟܠܢܫ ܥܒܕ ܗܘܝܬ ܛܒܬܐ
ܐܣܬܢܝܬ

13 ܘܫܪܘܢ ܐܝܟ ܡܠܟ̈ܐ ܦܩܪܐ
ܗܢܘܢ ܕܠܐ ܢܟܬܐ ܐܝܠܝܢ ܟܠ ܡܪ̈ܝܗܘܢ
14 ܡܛܠ ܕܡܣܟܠܐ ܗܝ ܬܪܥܝܬܗܘܢ
ܘܡܫܚܠܦ ܪ̈ܥܝܢܗܘܢ

15 ܐܢܐ ܕܝܢ ܡ̈ܝܐ ܐܚܝܕ ܗܘܝܬ ܒܝܡܝܢܝ
ܘܠܡܪ̈ܝܪܘܬܗܘܢ ܣܝܒܪܬ ܒܚܠܝܘܬܝ

16 ܘܠܐ ܐܒܕܬ
ܡܛܠ ܕܠܐ ܗܘܝܬ ܐܚܘܗܘܢ
ܐܦܠܐ ܓܝܪ ܝܠܝܕܘܬܝ ܐܝܟܘܬܗܘܢ
17 ܘܒܥܘ ܡܘܬܝ ܘܠܐ ܐܫܟܚܘ
ܡܛܠ ܕܩܕܝܡ ܗܘܝܬ ܡܢ ܕܘܟܪܢܗܘܢ
ܘܣܪܝܩܐܝܬ ܢܦܣܝܢ ܗܘܘ ܥܠܝ
18 ܘܐܝܠܝܢ ܕܡܢ ܒܬܪܝ ܗܘܘ
ܣܟ̈ܝ ܕܒܥܐ ܕܗܘܘ ܕܡܢ ܦܘܡܗܘܢ ܒܗ ܠܡܘܒܕܘ

19 ܡܛܠ ܕܠܐ ܡܬܡܨܝܐ ܬܪܥܝܬܗ ܕܡܪ̈ܝܡܐ
ܘܠܒܗ ܡܬܪ ܗܘ ܡܢ ܟܠ ܚܟܡܐ

ܗܠܠܘܝܐ

---

1 Like the wings of doves over their nestlings,
and the mouths of their nestlings toward their mouths;
so also the wings of the Spirit over my heart.
2 My heart is delighted and leaps for joy,
like a foetus which leaps for joy in the womb of his mother.

3 I had faith because of this,
also I was at rest;
because he is faithful,
he in whom I had faith.

4    He has surely blessed me,
     and my head is near him.
     And the dagger will not divide me from him,
     nor the sword;
5    because I made ready before destruction came,
     and I was set incorrupted in his wings.

6    And immortal life embraced me and kissed me,
7    and from it is the Spirit which (is) in me.
     And she cannot die,
     because she is life.

8    They marvelled those who saw me,
     because I was persecuted.
9    And they were convinced that I was swallowed up,
     because I appeared to them like one of the lost.

10   But my oppression
     was salvation to me.

11   But their refuse was I,
     because there was no jealousy in me.
12   Because to everyone I did good,
     I was hated.

13   And they surrounded me like mad dogs,
     they who in ignorance attack their lords;
14   because corrupt is their mind,
     and perverted their intellect.

15   But I was holding water in my right hand,
     and their bitterness I bore by my sweetness.

16 And I did not perish,
   because I was not their brother,
   for neither (was) my birth like theirs.
17 And they sought my death and did not attain it,
   because I was older than their memory.
   And in vain they cast lots against me.
18 And those who were after me,
   without cause they sought to destroy the memory of him who was before
   them.

19 Because the mind of the Most High is not to be anticipated,
   and his heart is better than all wisdom.

Alleluia.

NOTES TO THE TRANSLATION

1b: H has ܪܣܩܦܩ. Context requires the pl.

2a: N appears to have ܝܪܩܩ.

3a: H omits ܐܦ. Context demands a conj. of some kind.

5a: ܪܣܣܝ is a dependent imperf. verb indicating action which occurs in the future relative to the action of the principal cl. (Nöldeke § 267) and must be
translated here in the past tense (cf. also 4:2; 7:9; 8:7,15; 16:18).
   H has ܕܝܪܬܬܝ. N is preferred because of the parallelism of 5a and 5b.

5b: Although the placement of ܪܠܣܘ ܪܠܝ suggests a reference to ܝܡܩܨܩ, the
adj. is sing. It appears that the only possible referent is the 1st sing. subj.

6: H has ܝܩܩܦܝܩ. N is preferred because of the parallelism of ܝܩܩܦܠ and
ܝܩܩܫܝ.

7a: H has omitted the ܝ before ܩ.

7b: I have interpreted ܪܘܨܫܩ as the fem. sing. part. act. in the absolute state.
Thus the line refers to the Spirit which cannot die. It is also possible that the

line refers to the "I", in which case ܟܘܿܣܚܘ would be read as the masc. sing. part. act. in the emphatic state and the line translated impersonally, "and it is impossible to die".

7c: H has ܟܘܢ. The reading from N is preferred because of the link between 6 and 7c.

11a: H has ܩܘܝܪܐܘܘܘ.

12a: N's reading of ܣܝܟ ܣܠܠܐܝ is confused.

13b: H has ܟܠܒܝ.

15b: N has ܕܝܠ. H is preferred because of the semantic similarity with 31:12.

16a-b: Only Lattke (1979-86, vol. 1) follows N by reading two lines here. The choice for N has been made on the basis of the parallelism between 16b and 16c.

16c: N has ܂ܐܘܠ ܘܠܘܐܣܟ. H is preferred because of the parallelism of 16b and 16c and for the final alliteration and rhyme of ܩܘܘܟ and ܩܘܐܘܟ.

17b: Charlesworth (1977) is mistaken in reading ܩܘܝܟܘܘ in N. Both Mss. have ܩܘܝܒܘܘ.

17c: H's reading of ܟܘܐ has been corrected in the margin.

18a: N has ܐܕܒ. H is preferred because of the structure of the antithetical cls.

ANALYSIS

Two sub-odes are easily distinguished here. The joy and confidence of the first (1-7) contrasts sharply with the details of persecution in the second (8-19). The two are not entirely unconnected as there is ref. to dagger, sword and destruction in the first sub-ode (4c-5a), and 1c, 2a, and 19b form an inclusio for the Ode by the repetition of ܟܠ.

Stanza 1 [1, 2] (= Stanza 1, Sub-ode 1)

Both strophes of the stanza comprise a simile that focusses on the heart of the Odist. As well, both are related semantically by the motif of a parent caring for/bearing young.

1a and 1c are strictly parallel on the pattern: ܐܝܟ/ܗܟܢܐ + ܟܢ̈ܦܐ + ܕ + noun + ܥܠ + noun + pron. suffix. 1b provides the second expression associated with ܐܝܟ and is parallel with 1a in a terrace pattern by the repetition of ܦܪ̈ܘܓܝܗܘܢ. The parallelism may be outlined generally as: noun 1 (attribute of noun 2) + ܕ + noun 2 + prep. + noun 3 with 3rd masc. pl. suffix. There is chiasmus of a semantic nature between 1a and 1b by the placement of ܦܪ̈ܘܓܝܗܘܢ (noun 3 in 1a, noun 2 in 1b) and ܦܘ̈ܡܝܗܘܢ/ܝܘ̈ܢܐ (noun 2 in 1a, noun 3 in 1b). 1b has internal parallelism by the use of ܦܘ̈ܡܐ as the initial and concluding element. If 1b is taken into account as an integral part of the tricolon, one would have expected a fourth line such as ܘܦܘܡܝ ܠܘܬ ܦܘܡܗ to provide a balance for the strophe.

The simile with ܐܝܟ in strophe 2 is the inversion of the pattern (comparison with ܐܝܟ followed by the experience of the "I") in strophe 1. 2a-b has a terrace pattern by the repetition of ܕܝ. 2a has internal parallelism by the double pattern of the two semantically similar verbs (is delighted, leaps for joy) between which the subj. ܠܒܝ is inserted.

Stanza 2 [3]

3a and 3d form the inclusio for the stanza by the repetition of ܗܝܡܢܬ. Although the four lines are closely connected by the use of the root ܐܡܢ (occurring only in this stanza), they may be divided into two parallel bicola. 3a-b has a pivot pattern with parallel 1st sing. perf. verbs, ܡܛܠ ܗܢܐ in 3a referring to both verbs. 3c-d is parallel by the repetition of ܐܡܢ and the equivalence of the 3rd masc. sing. subj. (3c) and obj. (3d).

Stanza 3 [4-5]

4a-b is parallel with chiasmus: 4a with a 3rd masc. sing. subj. and 1st sing. obj.; 4b with a noun subj. with 1st sing. suffix and 3rd masc. sing. object of the action. 4a contains the only occurrence of the infin. absolute in the Odes. There is a semantic connection between 4b (the "I" is near him) and 4c (the "I" will not be divided from him).

4c-d is parallel on the pivot pattern, ܠܐ ܬܬܦܠܓ ܡܢܗ being understood in 4d, ܚܪܒܐ and ܣܦܣܪܐ being the parallel noun subjs. 5a-b contains two parallel cls., with ܡܛܠ ܕ understood in 5b. The parallelism is supported by the initial 1st sing. Ethpeel perf. verbs and by the antithesis of ܐܒܕܢܐ - ܠܐ ܚܒܠܐ.

Stanza 4 [6-7]

The stanza is tightly constructed on the association of the two key antithetical terms ܚܝܐ and ܡܘܬܐ (cf. 10:2; 11:7; 15:10; 31:7; 38:3; 40:6), which are introduced together in 6 (ܚܝܐ ܕܠܐ ܡܘܬܐ) and repeated in reverse order in 7b (ܡܝܬ) and 7c (ܚܝܐ) in relation to ܪܘܚܐ in 7a. There is a connection between stanza 4 and the introductory simile by the repetition of ܪܘܚܐ (1c, 7a) and the associated motif of new life (the foetus in 2b and the implied "conception" [?] of the Spirit [7a] from the actions of embracing and kissing [6]).

6 has internal parallelism by the double pattern of verbs + pron. suffixes between which the common subj. is inserted (cf. 2a). The parallelism is strengthened by use of the word-pair ܓܦܦ - ܢܫܩ and by the rhyming of these elements. 7a is linked to 6 by ܡܢܗܘܢ which refers to ܚܝܐ, and by the continuation of the 1st sing. as object of the action. 7b-c contains two semantically equivalent statements with ref. to ܪܘܚܐ using the polar word-pair ܡܝܬ - ܚܝܐ.

Stanza 5 [8-9] (= Stanza 1, Sub-ode 2)

8a introduces a 3rd pl. group of enemies in this section concerned with the details of the persecution of the "I".

The two bicola of the stanza are alternately parallel. 8a and 9a have an initial 3rd masc. pl. perf. verb followed by a second cl., the obj. of which is the 1st sing. 8b and 9b comprise cls. introduced by ܡܛܠ ܕ with a 1st sing. Ethpeel perf. verb. 8b and 9b are semantically equivalent by the concepts of being persecuted and being one of the lost. 8a is strikingly similar to 41:8a, both in vocabulary and construction:

8a ܐܬܕܡܪܘ ܐܝܠܝܢ ܕܚܙܘ ܗܘܘ ܠܝ

41:8a ܢܬܕܡܪܘܢ ܟܠܗܘܢ ܐܝܠܝܢ ܕܚܙܝܢ ܠܝ

Stanza 6 [10]

10a-b is a positive commentary/confessional statement in the midst of the descriptions of persecution. The bicolon is antithetical by the opposition of ܛܠܘܡܐ - ܦܘܪܩܢܐ and both lines have a concluding emphasis on the 1st sing.

(cf. 8a, 9a). The parallelism is further enhanced by the equivalent number of syllables (x 5) in each line.

Stanza 7 [11-12]

The four-line stanza follows an inverted pattern: A B B A, where A = principal cl. (11a, 12b); B = an associated cl. introduced by ܩ ܡܛܠ (11b, 12a). 11a and 12b have 1st sing. perf. verbs and are semantically equivalent (being their refuse, being hated). 11b and 12a are also connected semantically (having no jealousy, doing good to all).

Stanza 8 [13-14]

The focus shifts in stanza 8 from the "I" to the persecuting group. 13a-b contains a simile over the two lines, 13b referring to ܠܒܐ in 13a. The conditions of madness and ignorance are also associated to some extent in 38:13-14. 14a-b comprises two cls. referring to 13a-b (ܩ ܡܛܠ understood in 14b). The bicolon is parallel on the pattern: 3rd sing. part. act. + noun (from the root ܢܩܐ) + 3rd masc. pl. pron. suffix. The copula is understood in 14b.

Stanza 9 [15]

With stanza 9 there is a return to a 1st sing. subj. The parallel bicolon follows the pattern: noun obj. + 1st sing. perf. verb + ܒ + noun + 1st sing. pron. suffix. 15b has internal parallelism by the antithesis of ܒܬܪܥܝܬܐ - ܒܢܦܫܐ.

Stanza 10 [16, 17-18]

The strophic divisions within the stanza are not entirely clear because of a number of connections between the lines, both semantically and syntactically, and by the repetition of vocabulary. 16a and 18b form the inclusio for the stanza proper by the repetition of the root ܐܒܪ.

16 continues with the 1st sing. subj. (noun subj. + 1st sing. suffix in 16c). The three lines are connected, 16c referring to 16b, which in turn refers to 16a. 16a and 16b have a degree of parallelism with 1st sing. perf. verbs. 16b and 16c conclude with a focus on the 3rd masc. pl. (noun/prep. + 3rd masc. pl. suffix) with a degree of alliteration and rhyme in the final element of each line (ܐܢܘܢ - ܐܒܗܬܗܘܢ). There is also a semantic link by the concepts of kinship and birth.

There is some connection between 16 and 17-18, since 17a reiterates the statement of 16a concerning the "I" who holds out under threat of death. 17a and 18b form the inclusio for the second strophe by the repetition of ܪܚ݁ܒ .

17a has internal parallelism by the double pattern of verbs between which the common obj. is inserted (cf. 23:20, though with a common subj.). The cl. in 17b refers to 17a. It is not clear if 17c belongs to 17a-b or 18. The pattern of 1st sing. and 3rd pl. masc. persons in 17a-c suggests that these lines constitute a unit with a loose chiastic structure throughout:

17a     3rd pl. masc. (subj.) - 1st sing. (obj. suffix) - 3rd pl. masc. (subj.)

17b     1st sing. (subj.) - 3rd pl. masc. (obj. [of prep.] suffix)

17c     3rd pl. masc. (subj.) - 1st sing. (obj. [of prep.])

18 is closely connected to 17 by the repetition (in reverse order) of the key terms ܪܚ݁ܒ and ܪܚܝܢܘ̈ܗܝ. 18a-b is parallel by the antithesis of ܐ݂ܠܝ ܚܢ݁ ܒܬ݂ܝ, and ܗܡ ܚܢ݁ ܡܐ ܒܡܘܬܗܢ̈ . The syntactic structure is complex, the verb to which the cl. in 18a belongs occurring at the end of 18b.

## Stanza 11 [19]

Although the bicolon in 19 commences with a cl. introduced by ܡ݁ܛܠ ܕ, the link to 18 appears minimal since the narrative ends abruptly with 18, and 19 introduces an entirely new character, the Most High. 19 is a concluding confessional statement with a loose chiastic pattern by the placement of the key words ܬܗܪܘܣܗ and ܠܒܗ and their respective qualifiers.

Throughout the Ode, there is a frequent use of cls. introduced by ܡ݁ܛܠ ܕ, especially in a variety of four-line units. Stanza 2, strophe 2 in stanza 3, and stanza 8 follow the pattern:

line 1     principal cl.
line 2     associated cl.
line 3     ܡ݁ܛܠ ܕ + cl.
line 4     associated cl.

Stanza 4 contains the cl. with ܡ݁ܛܠ ܕ in the fourth line rather than the penultimate, with principal cls. in lines 1, 2, and 3. Stanza 5 has two bicola on the pat-

tern: principal cl. + cl. introduced by ܐ ܡܛܠ. Stanza 7 has a variation on
stanza 5 with inversion: principal cls. in 11a and 12b and cls. introduced by
ܐ ܡܛܠ in 11b and 12a.

## ODE 29

1 ܡܪܝܐ ܗܘ ܣܒܪܝ
ܠܐ ܐܒܗܬ ܒܗ

2 ܐܝܟ ܬܫܒܘܚܬܗ ܓܝܪ ܥܒܕܢܝ
ܘܐܝܟ ܛܝܒܘܬܗ ܗܟܢܐ ܐܦ ܝܗܒ ܠܝ
3 ܘܐܝܟ ܪ̈ܚܡܘܗܝ ܐܪܝܡܢܝ
ܘܐܝܟ ܪܒܘܬ ܫܘܦܪܗ ܪܡܪܡܢܝ

4 ܘܐܣܩܢܝ ܡܢ ܥܘܡܩ̈ܝ ܫܝܘܠ
ܘܡܢ ܦܘܡܗ ܕܡܘܬܐ ܢܓܕܢܝ
5 ܘܡܚܒܬ ܠܒܥܠܕܒܒ̈ܝ
ܘܙܕܩܢܝ ܒܛܝܒܘܬܗ
6 ܗܝܡܢܬ ܓܝܪ ܒܡܫܝܚܗ ܕܡܪܝܐ

ܘܐܬܚܙܝ ܠܝ ܕܗܘܝܘ ܡܪܝܐ
7 ܘܚܘܝ ܠܝ ܐܬܗ
ܘܕܒܪܢܝ ܒܢܘܗܪܗ
8 ܘܝܗܒ ܠܝ ܫܒܛܐ ܕܚܝܠܬܢܘܬܗ
ܕܐܫܥܒܕ ܡܚܫܒ̈ܬܐ ܕܥܡ̈ܡܐ
ܘܠܥܫܝܢܐ ܕܓܒܪ̈ܐ ܠܡܡܟܟܘ
9 ܠܡܥܒܕ ܩܪܒܐ ܒܡܠܬܗ
ܘܙܟܘܬܐ ܠܡܣܚܦ ܒܚܝܠܗ

10 ܘܐܡܝܪ ܠܒܥܠܕܒܒܝ ܡܪܝܐ ܒܡܠܬܗ
ܘܗܘܐ ܐܝܟ ܥܘܪܐ ܕܫܩܠܐ ܠܗ ܪܘܚܐ

11 ܘܝܗܒܬ ܬܫܒܘܚܬܐ ܠܡܪܝܡܐ
ܡܛܠ ܕܐܘܪܒܗ
ܠܥܒܕܗ ܘܠܒܪ ܐܡܬܗ

ܗܠܠܘܝܐ

1    The Lord is my hope;
     I shall not be ashamed in him.

2    For according to his glory he made me;
     and according to his grace so also he gave me;
3    and according to his mercy he lifted me up;
     and according to the greatness of his beauty he exalted me.

4    And he made me ascend from the depths of Sheol,
     and from the mouth of Death he drew me out .
5    And I brought low my enemies,
     and he declared me righteous by his grace.
6    For I had faith in the Messiah of the Lord.

     And he appeared to me who is indeed the Lord,
7    and he manifested to me his sign,
     and led me by his light,
8    and gave to me the rod of his power;
     that I might bring into subjection the thoughts of the gentiles,
     and to bring low the power of the mighty;
9    to make war by his Word,
     and take victory by his power.

10   And the Lord cast down my enemy by his Word,
     and he was like the chaff which the wind carries up.

11   And I gave glory to the Most High,
     because he made him great ,
     his servant and the son of his maidservant.

     Alleluia.

NOTES TO THE TRANSLATION

2b: H has ܡܕܒܠܝ.

6b: The Lord, rather than the impersonal "it", is the subj. of ܐܬܚܝ, as indicated by the structure of 6b-8a. For the rendering of ܕܗܘܝܘ, cf. Smith, R.P. 1: 980.

7a: H has ܠܗ. The reading from N is preferred because of the parallelism of 7a and 7b.

10a: H has ܠܒܥܠܕܒ̈ܒܝ. Although the pl. occurs in 5a, the sing. subj. in 10b requires a sing. referent in 10a.

ANALYSIS

Stanza 1 [1]

1 introduces the Ode. Athough there is no connection by form (cf. 5:11) or by vocabulary with the remainder of the Ode, in its theological content it serves to summarise the Odist's attitude to the Lord based on the activity of the Lord on his behalf which is decribed there.

Stanza 2 [2-3]

2a and 3b form the inclusio for the stanza by the word-pair ܬܫܒܘܚܬܐ - ܐܝܩܪܬܐ. All four lines of the stanza follow the general pattern: ܐܝܟ + noun (attribute of the Lord) with 3rd sing. masc. suffix ... 3rd sing. masc. perf. verb + 1st sing. pron. obj. (cf. 15:7; 36:5). The structure of 2b is more complex by the addition of ܗܟܢܐ ܐܦ (cf. 14:9; 36:5). The repetition of the same vocabulary or of synonyms in the other examples of this particular form is quite remarkable: ܡܣܒܪܢܘܬܐ ܕܪ̈ܚܡܝܟ (14:9) and ܕܪ̈ܚܡܘܗܝ (29:3); ܗܟܢܐ ܬܬܠ ܠܝ (14:9) and ܝܗܒ ܠܝ (15:7); ܪܒܘܬ ܐܝܩܘܬܗ (15:7; 29:3) and ܪܒܘܬܗ (36:5); ܝܗܒ ܠܝ... ܟܒܪܝ (15:7; 29:2 [reverse order]) and ܟܒܪܬܝ (36:5).

There are further connections by the word-pair ܬܫܒܘܚܬܐ - ܬܘܒܠܬܐ in 2 and the repetition of ܪܘܡ in 3. 2b breaks the pattern of assonance and rhyme with which the other three lines conclude: ܟܒܪܝ, ܐܪܝܡܢܝ, ܪܘܪܒܢܝ.

Stanza 3 [4, 5-6a]

Stanza 3 continues initially with the focus on a 3rd sing. masc. subj. and 1st sing. obj. The bicolon in 4 exhibits chiasmus: A B // B' A', where A = 3rd sing. masc. perf. verb + 1st sing. pron. suffix; B = ܒ + noun 1 + 3rd sing.

suffix (ref. to noun 2) + ܘ + noun 2. The parallelism is enhanced by the word-pair ܟܐܒܐ - ܠܥܠ. There is a certain appropriate heaviness to the alliteration with ܡ in 4b. The bicolon has a semantic (ascent from the regions below/Sheol) and syntactic similarity with 22:1.

There is a degree of parallelism in 5a-b on the pattern: 1st/3rd masc. sing. perf. verb (with suffix in 5b) + *nota dativi*/prep. + noun obj. with 1st/3rd masc. sing. pron. suffix. 6a comprises a concluding confessional statement/indirect doxology in a similar way to 11.

Stanza 4 [6b-8a, 8b-9]

Although with 8b the subj. changes from the 3rd masc. sing. to the 1st sing., the use of the dependent cl. in 8b which refers to 8a indicates that the two strophes (6b-8a and 8b-9) must belong in the one stanza.

ܒܪܝ in 6b is the subj. of the 3rd sing. masc. verbs in the first strophe. The four lines are initially parallel on the general pattern: 3rd masc. sing. verb + ܠ (1st sing. dir. obj. in 7b). 7-8a extend the pattern with a concluding noun (attribute of the Lord) with 3rd masc. sing. suffix. 7b makes effective use of the repetition of ܒ, ܝ, and ܢ.

By semantic content (the reasons for the giving of the rod of power) and by syntax (cls. and infinitives referring to ܒܗ in 8a), the four lines of the second strophe are dependent on the statement in 8a, and this is reiterated by the final ܡܠܟܘܬܗ in 9b. 8c-9 provides a section of infinitives which function in a similar syntactic way to the cl. in 8b which could be translated more generally as "to bring into subjection".

8b-c is chiastic by the placement of the verbs and the obj. phrases. The latter must be considered as semantically equivalent. 9a-b is parallel with chiasmus: A B C // B' A' C', where A = infin.; B = noun obj.; C = ܒ + noun (attribute of the Lord) with 3rd masc. sing. suffix.

An investigation of the verb forms and their objs. in 8b-9 reveals an alternating chiastic pattern for the strophe:

8b   verb + obj.
8c   obj. + verb
9a   verb + obj.
9b   obj. + verb

Stanza 5 [10]

With 10a there is a shift in subj. to the 3rd sing. masc. The bicolon serves to summarise the action described in the Ode from 5 onwards. There is a connection with the preceding stanza by the repetition of ܒܛܝܠܘܬܗ (9a, 10a). 10b is semantically similar to 18:11 by the negative image of dust/chaff.

Stanza 6 [11]

11 functions as an indirect doxology. 11a and 11b are linked by the cl. in 11b which refers to 11a. 11c has internal parallelism by the double pattern of noun objs. (in apposition with the pron. obj. suffix of the verb in 11b) which form the word-pair ܥܠܒܐ - ܒܝܐ ܕܐܝܡܬܐ.

ODE 30

ܟܠܘ ܠܟܘܢ ܡܝܐ ܡܢ ܡܒܘܥܐ ܚܝܐ ܕܡܪܝܐ    1
ܡܛܠ ܕܐܬܦܬܚ ܠܟܘܢ

ܘܬܘ ܟܠܟܘܢ ܨܗܝܐ ܘܣܒܘ ܫܩܝܐ    2
ܘܐܬܬܢܝܚܘ ܥܠ ܡܒܘܥܗ ܕܡܪܝܐ

ܡܛܠ ܕܫܦܝܪ ܗܘ ܘܢܨܝܚ ܘܡܢܝܚ ܠܢܦܫܐ    3

ܡܢ ܕܒܣܐ ܓܝܪ ܣܓܝ ܚܠܝܢ ܡܝܗ̈ܝ    4
ܘܟܟܪܝܬܐ ܕܕܒܘܪܝܬܐ ܠܐ ܡܬܦܚܡܐ ܠܗ

ܡܛܠ ܕܡܢ ܣܦܘܬܗ ܕܡܪܝܐ ܢܦܩ    5
ܘܡܢ ܠܒܗ ܕܡܪܝܐ ܫܡܗ

ܘܐܬܐ ܕܠܐ ܣܘܦ ܘܠܐ ܡܬܚܙܐ    6
ܘܥܕܡܐ ܕܐܬܝܗܒ ܒܡܨܥܬܐ ܠܐ ܝܕܥܘܗܝ

ܛܘܒܝܗܘܢ ܐܝܠܝܢ ܕܐܫܬܝܘ ܡܢܗ    7
ܘܐܬܬܢܝܚܘ ܒܗ

ܗܠܠܘܝܐ

---

1   Fill for yourselves water from the living spring of the Lord,
    because it was opened for you.
2   And come all of you thirsty and take a drink,
    and rest upon the spring of the Lord,
3   because it is beautiful and fresh and gives rest to the soul.

4   For much sweeter than honey its water,
    and the honeycomb of bees is incomparable to it;
5   because from the lips of the Lord it issued forth,
    and from the heart of the Lord its name.
6   And it came infinite and invisible,
    and until it was given in the middle they did not know it.

7   Blessed are those who have drunk from it,
    and have been at rest by it.

    Alleluia.

NOTES TO THE TRANSLATION

5b: Bruston argues for ܫܡܗ as a perf. verb (1912c, 441-2; cf. also Charlesworth 1977). Certainly one expects a verb because of the parallelism between 5a and 5b. To the emendations suggested in Harris and Mingana vol. 2 (ܫܦܥܗ "its overflow") and Bruston 1912b (ܫܡܪܗ "elle s'écoule") might be added ܫܪܐ ("it flowed").

7a-b: Both Mss. have one line (cf. Ungnad and Staerk; Diettrich 1911; Bruston 1912b; Lattke 1979-86, vol. 1). The division is made on the basis of the structure of the bicolon.

ANALYSIS

Stanza 1 [1-3]

Stanza 1 comprises the invitation/exhortation section of the Ode, focussing on a 2nd pl. group. It has a pattern of imper./s (1a, 2) + cl. introduced by ܡܛܠ ܕ expressing reason for the imper. However there seems to be a deliberate inclusio for 1-2 by the repetition of ܡܒܘܥܐ ܕܡܪܝܐ in 1a and 2b, in which case 3 would function as a summary monocolon for the stanza.

There is some parallelism in 1 by the initial pattern of verb + ܠܟܘܢ. 1a and 2b are more closely connected by the imper. verb ... prep. + ܡܒܘܥܐ ܕܡܪܝܐ. There is alliteration in 1a by the repetition of ܡ.

2a-b comprises a series of three imperatives, forming a logical progression of actions. 3 follows with a series of three descriptions of the qualities of the spring of the Lord. It is connected with 2b by the repetition of the root ܢܘܚ.

2a is similar to 6:11a, both syntactically (verb + ܠܒ with pron. suffix + ܡܝܐ) and by the use of ܫܬܐ. 2b is linked with 26:10 and 36:1 by the pattern of the root ܢܘܚ + ܥܠ + ܡܒܘܥܗ ܕܡܪܝܐ or ܡܪܘܡܐ or ܪܘܚܗ ܕܡܪܝܐ. The entire stanza is connected with 11:6-7, both semantically and by common vocabulary (ܡܝܐ ܚܝܐ, ܫܬܐ, ܡܒܘܥܗ ܕܡܪܝܐ).

2-3 and 7 provide the external boundaries of stanza 2 by the repetition of the associated roots ܫܬܐ, ܢܘܚ.

Stanza 2 [4, 5-6]

With this stanza there is a change in style to a report about the spring of the Lord. The comparison of the water and honey in 4 is the central focus of the

Ode, preceded by the exhortation section and followed by the report of the origin of the spring.

4 has a loose parallelism by the initial semantic connection between ܟ‌ܣܢ and ܟ‌ܘ‌ܒܩ, by the comparative descriptions (much sweeter, incomparable), and by the 3rd sing. masc. suffixes (ref. to the spring).

5a-b is parallel on the pattern: ܩ‌ܢ + noun ("physical" attribute of the Lord) with 3rd sing. masc. suffix + ܟ‌ܝܣ‌ܢ + verb/noun (ref. to the spring). The parallelism is enhanced by the word-pair ܟ‌ܐ‌ܩ‌ܣ‌ܡ - ܟ‌ܠ. One would have expected a 3rd masc. sing. perf. verb at the conclusion of 5b (cf. the notes to the translation) to fit with the strict parallelism of the remainder of the bicolon. However one does not always find consistency in the Odes, and it is possible with this line that ܟ‌ܝܣ‌ܢ ܡ‌ܒܠ ܩ‌ܢ‌ܩ must be considered as a second cl. dependent upon ܢ‌ܦܩ. If so, ܡ‌ܣ‌ܝ‌ܬ would still seem out of place at the end of 5b, although there are other instances in the Odes where words or phrases are not clearly contextualised (e.g. 8:2; 9:3).

6 introduces three descriptions of the spring as infinite, invisible, and unknown. The roots ܢ‌ܦܩ - ܟ‌ܐܬܟ (5a, 6a) are also associated in 6:8 and 7:17. The 3rd pl. masc. subj. introduced in the conclusion of 6b has no clear ref. point in the Ode.

Stanza 3 [7]

This stanza and 12:13 provide the only examples of a concluding beatitude in the Odes. The two cls. of 7a-b (ref. to ܐ‌ܝ‌ܠ‌ܟ) follow the pattern: 3rd masc. pl. perf. verb + prep. with 3rd masc. sing. suffix (ref. to ܟ‌ܐ‌ܒ‌ܣ‌ܡ). Given the link between 7 and 2-3, one would have expected ܝ‌ܡ‌ܢ‌ܠ‌ܠ in 7b rather than ܡ‌ܒ (although ܢ‌ܩ‌ܢ is found with ܒ in 35:6).

Since this Ode focusses on the single motif of the spring, one might have expected more repetition of key words/roots. The highest number of repetitions is for the root ܢ‌ܩ‌ܢ (x 3) which is of great importance in considering the effect of the spring of the Lord (cf. 26:12-13).

## ODE 31

1 ܐܬܦܫܪܘ ܡܢ ܩܕܡ ܡܪܝܐ ܬܗܘ̈ܡܐ
ܘܐܬܚܒܠ ܚܫܘܟܐ ܡܢ ܚܙܘܗ
2 ܛܥܬ ܛܥܝܘܬܐ ܘܐܒܕܬ ܡܢܗ
ܘܫܝܛܘܬܐ ܫܒܝܠܗ̇ ܠܐ ܗܘܬ
ܘܛܒܥܬ ܡܢ ܫܪܪܗ ܕܡܪܝܐ

3 ܦܬܚ ܦܘܡܗ
ܘܡܠܠ ܛܝܒܘܬܐ ܘܚܕܘܬܐ
ܘܡܠܠ ܬܫܒܘܚܬܐ ܚܕܬܐ ܠܫܡܗ
4 ܘܐܪܝܡ ܩܠܗ ܠܘܬ ܡܪܝܡܐ
ܘܩܪܒ ܠܗ ܒܢܝܐ ܗܢܘܢ ܕܒܐܝ̈ܕܘܗܝ ܗܘܘ
5 ܘܐܙܕܕܩ ܦܪ̈ܨܘܦܗ
ܡܛܠ ܕܗܟܢܐ ܝܗܒ ܠܗ ܐܒܘܗܝ ܩܕܝܫܐ

6 ܦܘܩܘ ܗܢܘܢ ܕܐܬܐܠܨܘ
ܘܣܒܘ ܚܕܘܬܐ
7 ܘܐܬܘ ܢܦܫܟܘܢ ܒܛܝܒܘܬܐ
ܘܣܒܘ ܠܟܘܢ ܚܝܐ ܕܠܐ ܡܝܘܬܐ

8 ܘܚܝܒܘܢܝ
ܟܕ ܩܡܬ
ܠܗܘ ܕܠܐ ܐܝܬܝ ܗܘܝܬ ܚܝܒܐ
9 ܘܦܠܓܘ ܒܙܬܝ
ܟܕ ܡܕܡ ܠܐ ܡܬܚܝܒ ܠܗܘܢ

10 ܐܠܐ ܕܝܢ ܣܝܒܪܬ ܘܫܬܩܬ ܘܫܠܝܬ
ܐܝܟ ܕܠܐ ܐܬܬܙܝܥ ܡܢܗܘܢ
11 ܐܠܐ ܩܡܬ ܕܠܐ ܙܘܥܐ ܐܝܟ ܟܐܦܐ ܫܪܝܪܬܐ
ܗܝ ܕܡܬܢܓܕܐ ܡܢ {ܟܐ̈ܦܐ} ܓܠ̈ܠܐ ܘܡܣܝܒܪܐ

12 ܘܣܒܠܬ ܡܪܝܪܘܬܗܘܢ ܡܛܠ ܡܟܝܟܘܬܐ
ܡܛܠ ܕܐܦܪܘܩ ܠܥܡܝ ܘܐܪܬܝܘܗܝ
13 ܘܕܠܐ ܐܒܛܠ ܠܡܘܠܟܢܐ ܕܠܘܬ ܪ̈ܝܫ ܐܒܗ̈ܬܐ
ܗܢܘܢ ܕܐܫܬܘܕܝܬ ܠܦܘܪܩܢܐ ܕܙܪܥܗܘܢ

ܗܠܠܘܝܐ

---

1 Deep abysses melted before the Lord,
and darkness was destroyed by his appearance.
2 Error erred and perished by him;
and contempt received no path,
and she sank by the truth of the Lord.

3 His mouth he opened,
and he spoke grace and joy;
and he spoke a new hymn to his name,
4 and lifted up his voice to the Most High.
And he offered him sons, those who were by means of him,
5 and his face was declared righteous,
because thus his holy Father gave to him.

6 Go forth, you who have been constrained,
and receive joy.
7 And take possession of your souls by means of grace,
and take unto you immortal life.

8 And they condemned me,
while I stood firm;
me, who had not been condemned.
9 And they divided my spoil,
while nothing was owing to them.

10 But I myself endured and kept silence and was still,
that I might not be disturbed by them.
11 But I stood undisturbed like solid rock,
which is beaten by {rocks} waves and endures.

12  And I suffered their bitterness because of lowliness,
    in order that I might save my people and instruct it,
13  and might not render void the promises which (were) to the patriarchs,
    which I promised for the salvation of their seed.


Alleluia.


NOTES TO THE TRANSLATION


2b: The difficulty of this line is attested by the variety of translations. Lattke (1979-86, vol. 1) alone reads ܐܠܗܘܬܐ ܠܐ as the subj. The same syntactic structure in relation to the verb may be found in 29:11b, verb + pron. obj. suffix + noun obj. ܐܠܗܘܬܐ ܠܐ is translation Syriac from the Greek ἀνοδία (Liddell and Scott 145a; Lampe 146b). Philo uses ἀνοδία in a similar way to 2b in De Agricultura 101 (Colson and Whitaker 160-161) where licentiousness (ἀκολασία) finds no path. ἀνοδία occurs together with πλάνη (as in 31:2a, ܐܠܗܘܬܐ) in Stromata VI, X, 82,2 (Stählin and Früchtel 472).
    H has ܡܗܘܬܗ. N makes more sense in the context.


4b: N is very smudged but does not appear to have a final ܝ for a reading of ܝܡܘܪܟܗܝ as in H. The latter is preferred because of the poor state of the N Ms.


9a: N has ܠܠܥܘ. The context demands the pl. as in H.


11b: N has ܐܠܠܟ ܟܘܟܐ. The copyist has mistakenly read ܟܘܟܐ from the preceding line.


ANALYSIS


Stanza 1 [1-2] (= Stanza 1, Sub-ode 1)


1a-b is parallel on the pattern: A B C // A' C' B', where A = the verb; B = a phrase introduced by ܡܢ; C = noun subj. There is alliteration in 1a by the repetition of ܡܢ.

    2a functions as the central focus of the stanza, its position further enhanced by the doubling of the root ܥܠ. 2a and 2c are strongly linked: firstly, by the word-pairs ܐܠܗܘܬܐ - ܟܐܢܬ, ܐܪܒ - ܠܩܠ; secondly, by the parallelism (in the second half of each line) of 3rd fem. sing. Peal perf. verb + ܒܗ with obj. (ref. to the Lord).

2a-b has an initial chiastic pattern by the placement of verb and noun subj. 2b and 2c are linked by the common subj. ܫܒܝܚܘܬܗ. Given the strong links between 2a and 2c, and the fact that the prep. ܒܗ, a particular feature of this stanza, does not occur in 2b, it seems that 2b is an addition.

The stanza is connected with 24:7-10, both semantically and by the use of vocabulary (ܬܗܘܡܐ, ܢܚܠ, ܐܟܬ, ܥܒܕ, ܫܝܢ).

## Stanza 2 [3-4a, 4b-5]

3-4a are strongly connected by the vocabulary associated with the action of praise (ܡܪ, ܦܬܚ, ܦܘܡܗ, ܬܫܒܘܚܬܐ [ܫܒܚ], ܝܗܒ, ܩܠ) which occurs in a variety of combinations in the Odes (cf. e.g. 7:24; 8:4; 16:5).

There are a number of connections between the four lines. ܡܪ is repeated in 3b and 3c. 3a and 4a are linked by the word-pair ܦܘܡܗ ܦܬܚ - ܩܠ ܝܗܒ. 3c and 4a are parallel to some degree on the pattern: 3rd masc. sing. perf. verb + noun obj. + ܠܗܠ/ܠ + obj. (ref. to the Most High). The use of ܫܘܒܚܬܐ and ܚܝܘܬܐ in 3b provides a link with 6a-7b.

There is parallelism initially for 4b and 5b by the pattern of 3rd masc. sing. perf. verb + ܠܗ + noun (obj./subj.), in which the word-pair ܐܟܬ - ܡܝܐ occurs. 5a and 5b are connected by the cl. in 5b which refers to 5a.

The association of the motifs of destruction in stanza 1 and the lifting up of the Lord's voice in stanza 2 are similar to the description of the destruction accompanying the singing of the dove in Ode 24.

## Stanza 3 [6-7]

The style changes from a report to a series of 2nd pl. imper. verbs. It appears at first that this stanza might be either the introduction to, or the entire new hymn of the Lord (3c). However, the hymn is described as addressed "to his name" (cf. also 6:7) while in this stanza the afflicted are exhorted and the remaining stanzas contain a report of the sufferings and triumph of the "I" (cf. Kittel, G. 1914, 26).

The four lines of the stanza are linked by the initial 2nd masc. pl. imper. verbs. They may be divided into two bicola. 7a-b follows a pattern of A B C // A' C' B', where A = 2nd masc. pl. imper. verb; B = noun obj.; C = prep./*nota dativi* with obj.

Stanzas 4-6 (= Stanzas 1-3, Sub-ode 2)

With the exception of ܟܐܝܪܝܟ, the repetition of vocabulary is particular to each of the three stanzas. These repetitions are indicative of the major themes of the sub-ode - in stanza 4, condemnation of the "I" (ܚܝܒ); in stanza 5, endurance of the "I" (ܣܡܟ, ܢܣܒ ܠܐ); and in stanza 6, the "I" who promises salvation and is saviour (ܦܪܩ, ܚܝ).

Stanza 4 [8-9]

With stanza 4 the focus of the Ode shifts to the persecution of the "I" and the style changes to a report by a 1st sing. subj. 8a and 9b form the inclusio for the stanza by the repetition of ܚܝܒ. 8c takes the central position of the stanza, presenting the innocence of the "I". The statement is enclosed by the alternately parallel bicola 8a-b and 9 which describe the action taken by the enemies of the "I".

8a and 9a are parallel on the pattern: 3rd masc. pl. perf. verb + obj. (ref. to 1st sing.). 8b and 9b are parallel by the pattern of the cls. introduced by ܒ. There is antithesis within 8a-b and 9a-b, although this is not quite as obvious with 8a-b. It is necessary to be aware that ܩܡܝܢ (8b) in the Odes connotes far more than the simple physical description of standing (cf. Grundmann). 8a, 8c and 9b are connected by the repetition of ܚܝܒ.

Stanza 5 [10-11]

10a and 11b form the inclusio for the stanza by the repetition of the Paiel of ܣܡܟ. The repetition of ܣܡܟ and ܢܣܒ provides a mirror pattern (A B B A) for the four lines.

10a and 10b are connected by the cl. in 10b which refers to 10a. The latter has internal parallelism by the series of three 1st sing. perf. verbs.

11a emphasises the statement in 10b, not only by the repetition of ܢܣܒ, but also by the image of immovability and stillness ("solid rock") in the simile. 11a and 11b are connected by the cl. in 11b which refers to ܟܐܦ in 11a.

Stanza 6 [12-13]

The four lines of the stanza are variously connected - 12b and 13a have cls. referring to 12a; the cl. in 13b refers to ܚܐܝܘܬ in 13a; ܦܪܩ is repeated in 12b and 13b; ܚܝ occurs in 13a and 13b.

There is antithesis in 12a between the bitterness of the enemy and the lowliness of the "I". 12b has internal parallelism by the double pattern of 1st sing. imperf. verbs + obj. (ref. to ܟܘܠ). 13a continues from ܡܠܠܬ in 12b. 13b concludes the stanza strongly by the repetition of the key roots ܚܝ, ܦܪܩ.

There is some similarity between stanzas 5 and 6. The initial lines (10a, 12a) contain a description of the action of the "I"; the second lines (10b, 12b) have a cl. referring to the purpose of the action in the preceding line (the third line also in stanza 6 [13a]); the fourth lines (11b, 13b) comprise a rel. cl. (ref. to the key noun in the third line).

## ODE 32

1 ܠܛܘܒܢܐ ܚܕܘܬܐ ܡܢ ܠܒܗܘܢ
ܘܢܘܗܪܐ ܡܢ ܗܘ ܕܥܡܪ ܒܗܘܢ
2 ܘܡܠܬܐ ܡܢ ܫܪܪܐ
ܗܘ ܕܗܘܐ ܡܢ ܢܦܫܗ
3 ܡܛܠ ܕܐܬܥܫܢ ܒܚܝܠܗ ܩܕܝܫܐ ܕܪܘܡܐ
ܘܗܘܐ ܕܠܐ ܙܘܥܐ ܗܘ ܠܥܠܡ ܥܠܡܝܢ

ܗܠܠܘܝܐ

---

1 For the blessed ones joy (is) from their heart,
and light from him who dwells in them,
2 and the Word from the Truth,
who was from himself;
3 because he has been strengthened by the holy power of the Most High,
and he is undisturbed for ever and ever.

Alleluia.

### NOTES TO THE TRANSLATION

2a-b: Neither Ms. reads two lines here. The division has been made because of the structure of the bicolon.

2b: Lattke (1979-86, vol. 1) omits the ܡܢ as in N. The structure supports the reading of ܡܢ , as does the similar phrase in 7:12c, ܡܢ ܢܦܫܗܘܢ ܗܘܘ.

3b: H has ܠܥܠܡܝܢ.

### ANALYSIS

The six lines of the Ode comprise one stanza of two strophes (1-2, 3).
ܠܛܘܒܢܐ in 1a, to which ܚܕܘܬܐ, ܢܘܗܪܐ, and ܡܠܬܐ refer, functions as the introduction and focus for the first strophe. The structure of the strophe centres on the use of the prep. ܡܢ. In general the pattern may be outlined as: noun

1 (attribute of the blessed ones) + ܡܢ + noun 2/cl. (source of noun 1). 1a-b are further linked by the final phrases with 3rd masc. pl. suffixes.

The pattern of the strophe is made more complex by 2b, where the initial noun is replaced by the rel. pron. ref. to ܟܐܢܘܬ (2a). Thus 2a-b has a kind of terrace pattern:

2a      noun 1 (attribute) + ܡܢ + noun 2 (source of noun 1)

b      rel. pron. (= noun 2) + (verb) + ܡܢ + noun 3 (source of noun 2)

1b and 2a are linked by the word-pair ܟܝܢܐ - ܦܬܓܡܐ. 1a and 2b have the closely associated words ܠܒܐ and ܦܘܡ.

3a is connected with the preceding strophe by the cl. which seems to refer logically to 2b, although there are a number of instances in the Odes when such cls. appear to have no real relevance to the preceding verses (cf. e.g. 4:7; 6:18; 12:3,11; 16:2...). If it is the case of the latter here, then one cannot be sure that it is Truth to which ref. is made rather than one of the blessed ones.

3a-b is parallel by the initial 3rd masc. sing. verb and by the semantic similarity of the expressions ܠܥܠ and ܠܐ ܐܝܬܘܗܝ ܣܘܦܐ. ܠܥܠܡ ܠܥܠܡܝܢ at the conclusion of 3b suggests that either 3b or 3a-b may function as an indirect doxology (if ref. is to the Truth).

## ODE 33

1 ܐܠܐ ܕ ... ...

2

3

4

5

6

7

8

9

10

11

12

13     ܟܕ ܗܠܟܬ ܟܠ

ܠ ܚܠܦܝܗ ܠܗܘܢ ܐܡܪ ܐܬܝܬܝ, ܘܟܢܫܬ

ܘܐܬܕܟܪ ܐܢܘܢ ܠܠ ܫܡܥ

ܗܠܠܘܝܐ

---

1   Then again Grace ran,
     and abandoned Corruption,
     and descended into him,
     that she might render him void.

2   And he caste out destruction before him,
     and corrupted all his handiwork.

3   And he stood upon the top of the height,
     and let loose his voice,
     from the uttermost parts of the land
     unto its uttermost parts.

4   And he drew to him all those who hearkened unto him,
     and he did not appear like the Evil One.

5   But the Perfect Virgin stood,
     preaching and crying out and saying,

6   Sons of men, turn back,
     and their daughters, come;

7   and abandon the ways of this Corruption,
     and draw near to me.

8   And I will enter into you,
     and I will bring you forth from destruction,
     and I will make you wise in the ways of truth.

9   Do not be corrupted,
     nor perish.

10  Listen to me,
     and be saved.
     For the grace of God am I speaking in you.

11  And by means of me you will be saved,
     and will be blessed.

Your judge am I.

12  And they who have put me on will not be rejected,
    but will gain incorruption in the new world.

13  My chosen, walk in me.
    And my ways I shall make known to them who seek me,
    and I will lead them to trust in my name.

Alleluia.

NOTES TO THE TRANSLATION

1b: The three occurrences of ܚܒܠܐ in this Ode (1b, 7a, 12b) have a point above the ܒ in both Mss. Since ܠܐ ܚܒܠܐ can only be read as "incorruption" (12b), on the Ms. evidence alone, ܚܒܠܐ in 1b and 7a should be translated as "Corruption" rather than "Corruptor" as in Diettrich 1911, Harris and Mingana vol. 2, and Charlesworth 1977 (cf. the pointing in Smith, R.P. 1: 1178-9). The translation of "Corruption" does not negate the interpretation of a change with 2a to a masc. personification at enmity with the fem. personification, Grace.

    G. Kittel (1914, 123) argues that the character in 2-4 should not be interpreted as different from Grace/the Perfect Virgin, contending that Diettrich is incorrect in reading 4b as a negative statement ("und nicht erschien er [ward er erkannt] als der Böse"; Diettrich 1911, 114). The argument hinges on what Kittel regards as the strong connection between 4b and 5a by the use of ܐܦ in 5a. Certainly the lines are connected, but by antithesis rather than by the synonymity of the characters. The antithetical use of ܐܦ is attested by 4:9; 11:23.

5b: H has ܩܘܡ.

6b: H has ܬܘܝ. N has ܬܐܝ.

12a: H has ܕܠܒܫܘܗܝ.

12b: The treatment of ܚܝܬܐ ܒܥܠܡܐ or ܚܒܠܐ ܠܐ ܚܝܬܐ ܒܥܠܡܐ as the obj. of ܢܣܒܘܢ (Flemming; Ungnad and Staerk; Harris 1911a; Diettrich 1911; Labourt and Batiffol; Bernard; Bruston 1912b; Carmignac 1986) is precluded by the prep. ܒ.

13a: That the verb is 2nd pl. imper. rather than 3rd masc. pl. perf. (as in Harris and Mingana vol. 2; Charlesworth 1977; Carmignac 1986) is clear from the punctuation in N, especially when one compares the punctuation for 6, where the same point (samka; cf. Segal, J.B. 72-3) occurs just below the line after ܒ̈ܢܝܢܫܐ and ܒ̈ܢܬܗܘܢ to indicate a pause between the vocative expression and the imper. verb.

ANALYSIS

One of the most interesting aspects of this Ode is the repetition of roots with regard to action involving the major characters: for Corruption and Grace/the Perfect Virgin, ܐܒܕ (2a, 8b) and ܩܡ (3a, 5a); for Grace/the Perfect Virgin and the 2nd masc. pl. group who are the subject of her exhortations, ܥܒܕ... ܐܘܪ̈ܚܬܗ ܕܚܒܠܐ/ܚܒܠܐ (1b, 7a) and ܐܒܕ (8b, 9b); for Corruption and his group, and the 2nd masc. pl. group addressed by the Perfect Virgin, ܚܒܠ (2b, 9a) and ܥܒܪ (4a, 10a).

Stanza 1 [1]

The major unifying feature of the four-line stanza is the 3rd fem. sing. perf. verb (ref. to the subj. ܛܝܒܘܬܐ) at the beginning of each line. 1b, 1c and 1d are linked by the common obj. ܚܒܠܐ (substitute 3rd masc. sing. suffix in 1c and 1d). Other connections are provided by the cl. in 1d which refers to ܢܚܬܬ in 1c, and the word-pair ܢܚܬ - ܪܗܛ in 1a and 1c.

Stanza 2 [2, 3, 4]

The stanza focusses on the actions of a 3rd masc. sing. subj. (the personified "Corruption"), each line having the general pattern of 3rd masc. sing. perf. verb + obj. A connection with stanza 1 is made by the word-pair ܐܒܕ - ܚܒܠ (2a-b) and by the repetition of the root ܚܒܠ (2b).

There is parallelism in 2a-b by the word-pair ܐܒܕ - ܚܒܠ; by the pattern of 3rd masc. sing. perf. verb + obj.; and by the use of the 3rd masc. sing. suffixes (ref. to Corruption).

3a-b is semantically similar to 5 by the repetition of ܩܡ (3a, 5a) and by the expressions ܥܒܕ ܩܠܗ (3b) and ܩܪܝ, ܐܡܪ (5b). 3c-d is parallel by the use of the phrases ܡܢ ܣܘܦ̈ܝܗ and ܥܕܡܐ ܠܣܘܦ̈ܝܗ (the pivot is provided by ܕܐܪܥܐ in 3c). The two parallel phrases express merismus (= the whole land).

4a-b has a pattern of initial 3rd sing. masc. perf. verbs (ref. to Corruption). 4a provides another link with the Perfect Virgin by the use of ܐܠܝ (= ܗܝܒ, 7b) and ܫܚܠܦ (10a).

Stanzas 3-4

Strophes 2 and 3 of stanza 3 and the two strophes of stanza 4 follow an alternating pattern, A B A' B', where A = a strophe of four lines with 2nd pl. imper./imperf. verbs; B = a strophe of three lines with, generally, a 1st sing. subj. and 2nd masc. pl. obj. In 11a-b the subj. of the pass. verbs is the 2nd masc. pl., but the 1st sing. is the agent of the action (ܟܐܝܕ,).

Stanza 3 [5, 6-7, 8]

5 functions as the introduction for the monologue of the Perfect Virgin (6-13). The use of ܐܠܐ in 5a implies immediately an antithesis between the action of the Perfect Virgin and the action of Corruption as described in the preceding stanza (cf. the notes to the translation). 5b contains a series of three participles, with alliteration (esp. ܝ, but also ܒ/ܡ) and assonance.

The bicolon in 6 is parallel on the pattern: noun/s subj. + 2nd pl. imper. verb. The parallelism is strengthened by the word-pairs ܒܪܐ - ܒܪܬܐ and ܐܒ - ܐܬܐ. 7a-b has a degree of parallelism by the use of the initial 2nd pl. imper. verbs. The antithesis of the ways of Corruption over against the Perfect Virgin is already clear in the word-pair ܫܚܒ - ܗܝܒ. The use of ܫܚܒ in association with ܚܝܠܐ in 7a provides a link with 1a.

Strophe 3 follows from strophe 2, describing the action which will result when the 2nd pl. group have carried out the commands issued by the Perfect Virgin. The strophes are further connected by the antithesis of ܐܘܪܚܬܗ ܕܫܒܠܐ - ܐܘܪܚܬܐ ܕܫܪܝܪܐ in 7a and 8c.

The tricolon in 8 follows the general pattern of 1st sing. imperf. verb (+ 2nd masc. pl. obj. [b and c]) + prep. with pron./noun obj. The three verbs of the strophe follow a logical semantic order, building to the climax in 8c. The gradual increase in length of line from 8a-c enhances the impact of the final statement in 8c.

Stanza 4 [9-10b, 10c-11b]

The negative imperf. verbs in 9 are interpreted as negative imperatives. They provide a parallel structure (four lines with 2nd pl. imper. verbs) with strophe two in stanza 3. The four-line strophe is divided into two parallel bicola. 9a-b follows the pattern of negative particle + 2nd pl. verb. The parallelism is strengthened by the word-pair ܠܟܘ - ܐܒܐ (cf. 2). 10a-b is parallel with 2nd pl. verbs.

The second strophe contains the reasons for which the 2nd pl. group should carry out the commands of 9-10b. There is a connection with strophe 1 by the repetition of the root ܦܪܩ (10a, 11a). 10c and 11b form the inclusio for the strophe by the repetition of the root ܝܠܦ (initially in 10c and at the conclusion of 11b).

10c functions in two directions, providing a reason for the following out of the commands in 9-10a, and introducing the bicolon in 11a-b. The latter is parallel by the use of the 2nd masc. pl. imperf. verbs (ܐܪܬܐ is understood in 11b). The roots ܦܪܩ and ܝܠܦ are also associated in 9:5; 25:4; 34:6 (although in each case it is the noun ܝܘܠܦܢܐ which is used rather than ܝܠܦ).

Stanzas 5-6

Stanzas 5 and 6 follow an alternating pattern: A B A' B', where A = an introductory monocolon using 1st sing. and 2nd masc. pl. persons; B = a bicolon using 1st sing. and 3rd masc. pl. persons. The use of the persons follows an alternating pattern: 11c has a 1st sing. subj., 13a has a 2nd masc. pl. subj.; 12a-b has a 3rd masc. pl. subj., 13b-c has the 1st sing. (for the main verb).

The relatively short lines of the two monocola in comparison to the bicola, emphasises the succinct nature of their introductory statements over against the detail which follows in the bicola.

Stanza 5 [11c, 12]

The motif of the Perfect Virgin as judge in 11c leads into the bicolon, since the root ܥܠܒ in 12a has connotations of injustice through false accusation (cf. Smith, R.P. 1: 1476-7). 12a-b is parallel by the use of the synonymous 3rd masc. pl. imperf. verbal expressions ܘܠ ܐܕܥܠܠܗܢ and ܘܢܦܩܘܢ.....ܘܠ ܐܢܚܘܢ ܐܒܕ and ܘܠ ܐܟܘ are also associated in 15:8.

Stanza 6 [13a, 13b-c]

Each line of the stanza concludes with a 1st sing. suffix. 13a has internal parallelism by the use of the 1st sing. suffixes (ܝ...ܝ). The association of ܡܠܟ and ܐܘܪܝܬܝ in 13a-b occurs also in 3:10 and 12:6. The bicolon is further linked by the word-pair ܡܠܟ - ܝܕܥ.

13b-c has the pattern A B C // B' C' A', where A = noun (attribute of the Perfect Virgin) with 1st sing. suffix; B = 1st sing. imperf. verb; C = 3rd masc. pl. pron./pron. with dependent cl. [dir./indir. obj. of the 1st sing. imperf. verb]).

## ODE 34

1 ܠܝܬ ܐܘܪܚܐ ܩܫܝܬܐ
ܐܝܟܐ ܕܠܒܐ ܦܫܝܛܐ
ܐܦܠܐ ܡܚܘܬܐ
ܒܡܚܫܒܬܐ ܬܪܝܨܬܐ
2 ܐܦܠܐ ܠܠܠܐ
ܒܥܘܡܩܗ ܕܡܚܫܒܬܐ ܢܗܝܪܬܐ
3 ܐܝܟܐ ܕܚܕܝܪ ܡܢ ܟܠ ܐܬܪ ܫܦܝܪܐ
ܠܝܬ ܒܗ ܡܕܡ ܕܦܠܝܓ

4 ܕܡܘܬܗ ܕܗܘ ܕܠܬܚܬ
ܗܘܝܘ ܗܘ ܕܠܥܠ
5 ܟܠܡܕܡ ܓܝܪ ܠܥܠ ܗܘ
ܘܠܬܚܬ ܠܝܬ ܡܕܡ
ܐܠܐ ܡܣܬܒܪ ܠܐܝܠܝܢ ܕܝܕܥܬܐ ܠܝܬ ܒܗܘܢ

6 ܛܝܒܘܬܐ ܐܬܓܠܝܬ ܠܦܘܪܩܢܟܘܢ
ܗܝܡܢܘ ܘܚܝܘ ܘܐܬܦܪܩܘ

ܗܠܠܘܝܐ

---

1 There is no rough way,
where (there is) a simple heart;
nor an obstacle
in upright thoughts;
2 nor a whirlwind
in the depth of light thought.
3 Where the beautiful one surrounds from every place,
there is in him nothing which (is) divided.

4 The likeness of what (is) below
is what (is) above;
5 for everything is above,
and below there is nothing;
but it is considered so by those in whom there is no knowledge.

6    Grace has been manifested for your salvation.
     Have faith and live and be saved.


     Alleluia.

NOTES TO THE TRANSLATION

1-3: In dividing the lines of the strophe, I have followed the punctuation of N. If H were preferred, the bicola I have designated as 1c-d and 2a-b would be read as single lines. Division according to N gives more continuity to the relative length of line.

1a-b: Both H and N have two lines. Only Bruston (1912b), Lattke (1979-86, vol. 1) and Carmignac (1986) seem to have realised the structure of the strophe and divided accordingly. Although Ungnad and Staerk have kept 1a-b as one line, they have at least done the same for 3a-b. Those who have made one line of 1a-b and kept two lines for 3a-b have clearly misunderstood the structure of the strophe (Diettrich 1911; Harris and Mingana vol. 2; Bauer 1964; Charlesworth 1977; Emerton).

3a: Although pass. in form, ܒܪܝ may also be translated by the act. (Nöldeke § 280).
     ܡܢ ܟܠ ܐܬܪ is equivalent to πάντοθεν ("from every side", 3 Macc 4:2; Smith, R.P. 1: 426).

4b: N has omitted ܗܘ after ܗܘܐܠ.

ANALYSIS

Repetitions of words/roots in this Ode are limited to the stanzas in which they first appear.

Stanza 1 [1-3]

The structure of the stanza is clearly indicated by the pattern of the initial elements of each line:

1a    ܕܠܐ + noun (compl.) + adj.

b    ܕ ܐܝܟܐ + noun (compl.) + adj.

c    ܐܝܟܐ + noun (compl.)

d    ܒ + noun + adj.

2a    ܐܝܟܐ + noun (compl.)

b    ܒ + noun + ܕ (gen. construction) + noun + adj.

3a    ܕ ܐܝܟܐ + part. + phrase + adj. (functions as noun subj.)

b    ܕܠܐ + phr. + noun (compl.) + adj. expression

1c-2 has the central position in the stanza between the bicolon in 1a-b and its mirror image (by the reverse order of the initial elements) in 3. The two bicola in 1c-2 are alternately parallel, 1c and 2a being strictly parallel, 1d and 2b somewhat less so by the added phrase ܕ ܡܚܫܒܬܐ in 2b. However 1d and 2b are strongly connected by the repetition of ܚܘܫܒܬܐ (pl. in 1d, sing. in 2b).

1a-b is a parallel bicolon with the verb understood in 1b. The parallelism is enhanced by the end rhyme, ܕܚܝܠܐ - ܦܫܝܛܐ. 3a-b has a degree of parallelism by the pattern: verb + phrase + subj./compl. Both bicola follow the same general pattern of a principal cl. introduced by ܕܠܐ and a cl. introduced by ܐܝܟܐ ܕ. There is a similarity in form between 3b and 11:23b and 25:7b, and in expression between 3a and 22:6b.

1a, 1c, 2a, and 3b follow the general pattern of negative + noun compl. All four compls. (a rough way, an obstacle, a whirlwind, something divided) belong to the same negative category, just as the elements in 1b, 1d and 2a (simple heart, upright thoughts, the depth of light thought) belong to the same positive category. G. Kittel (1914, 126) recognised the connections, although he took them further to include 4, through his misunderstanding of the structure of the stanza.

There is some connection between 1b, 1d, 2b, and 3a by a preoccupation with place, by the cls. introduced by ܐܝܟܐ ܕ and the phrases introduced by ܒ. 1b is more strictly connected with 1d and 2b since the absence of the verb in 1b means that ܐܝܟܐ ܕ functions rather like the prep. ܒ, and thereafter the general pattern (noun + adj.) is the same for the three lines. With the addition of the phrases in 3 to those already discussed, the emphasis upon place in this stanza provides an interesting backdrop for the whole discussion about above and below which follows in stanza 2.

The word-pairs ܠܒܐ - ܡܚܫ̈ܒܬܐ and ܦܫܝܛܐ - ܬܪ̈ܝܨܬܐ provide the connection between 1b and 1d, 2b. Merismus is expressed by ܒܪܝܟ ܡܢ ܟܠ ܐܬܪ (3a) and ܒܗ (3b), and by ܬܪ̈ܝܨܬܐ (1d) and ܠܩܘܒܠܐ (2b). There may also be an intention of antithesis between ܦܫܝܛܐ (1b) and ܦܠܝܓ (3b).

Stanza 2 [4-5b, (5c)]

The focus of the stanza is found in the polar word-pair ܠܥܠ - ܠܬܚܬ, by the use of which there is an inverse pattern (A B B A) created in the four lines.

Although the stanza functions as a closely-knit unit, it may be divided into two parallel bicola. 4a-b follows the pattern: noun subj./ܗܘܝܘ + ܕ ܗܘ + ܠܥܠ/ ܠܬܚܬ. There is chiasmus in 5a-b by the placement of the word-pairs ܠܥܠ - ܠܬܚܬ and ܠܡܕܒܪܟ - ܠܐ ܡܕܒܪܟ (ܠܬܚܬ). The chiasmus increases the dramatic effect of the bicolon since both word-pairs comprise antithetical elements.

G. Kittel (1914, 125-6) argues against the structure outlined here on semantic grounds, the problem being ܕܡܘܬܐ in 4a which suggests to him that to link 4a and 4b would be to imply that the region above and the region below are alike. He seems unaware of the negative interpretation possible for the root ܕܡܐ within the Odes (cf. e.g. 38:11a where the Deceiver and Error imitate/are in the likeness of the Beloved and his bride). Moreover, the negative interpretation of ܕܡܐ in 4a is supported by the antithesis of ܠܥܠ - ܠܬܚܬ in 5a-b. Finally, the isolation of 4-5b from 1-3 is absolutely clear by the highly structured pattern of 1-3.

5c is a rather clumsy addition to this stanza. Syntactically and semantically it refers to 5b but it cannot be fitted into the strict structure of the four-line unit.

Stanza 3 [6]

Stanza 3 makes a decisive break with the first two stanzas, both by introducing new subject matter concerning salvation and by the change from the report style to a direct address to a 2nd masc. pl. group.

There is a degree of parallelism in the bicolon by the repetition of the root ܦܪܩ at the conclusion of both lines. In the series of three verbs in 6b, two of the verbs form the word-pair, ܚܝܐ - ܦܪܩ. Odes 3 and 7 also conclude with 2nd pl. masc. imperatives, those in Ode 3 having the same form as 6b.

# ODE 35

1 ܪܣܤܗ ܕܡܪܝܐ ܒܢܝܚܘܬܐ ܡܛܠܠ ܥܠܝ
ܘܥܢܢܐ ܕܫܠܡܐ ܐܩܝܡ ܠܥܠ ܡܢ ܪܝܫܝ
2 ܕܢܛܪܬܢܝ ܒܟܠܙܒܢ
ܘܦܘܪܩܢܐ ܗܘܬ ܠܝ

3 ܐܬܬܙܝܥܘ ܟܠܡܕܡ ܘܐܬܪܗܒܘ
ܘܢܦܩ ܡܢܗܘܢ ܬܢܢܐ ܘܕܝܢܐ

4 ܘܐܢܐ ܫܠܐ ܗܘܝܬ ܒܬܓܡܗ ܕܡܪܝܐ
ܘܝܬܝܪ ܡܢ ܛܠܠܐ ܗܘܐ ܠܝ
ܘܝܬܝܪ ܡܢ ܫܬܐܣܬܐ
5 ܘܐܝܟ ܛܠܝܐ ܡܢ ܐܡܗ ܡܬܛܥܢ ܗܘܝܬ
ܘܝܗܒ ܠܝ ܚܠܒܐ
ܛܠܗ ܕܡܪܝܐ
6 ܘܐܬܪܒܝܬ ܒܡܘܗܒܬܗ
ܘܐܬܢܝܚܬ ܒܫܘܡܠܝܗ

7 ܘܦܫܛܬ ܐܝܕܝ ܒܣܘܠܩܗ ܕܢܦܫܝ
ܘܐܬܬܪܝܨܬ ܠܘܬ ܡܪܝܡܐ
ܘܐܬܦܪܩܬ ܠܘܬܗ

ܗܠܠܘܝܐ

---

1 The sprinkling of the Lord with rest overshadows me,
and a cloud of peace he set over my head,
2 which kept me always,
and was salvation for me.

3 And all were disturbed and disquieted,
and smoke and judgment issued forth from them.

4    And I indeed was quiet in the company of the Lord.
     And more than shade was he to me,
     and more than a foundation.
5    And like a child by its mother I was carried.
     And he gave me milk,
     the dew of the Lord.
6    And I grew up by his gift,
     and was at rest in his perfection.

7    And I extended my hands in the ascent of myself;
     and I stood erect towards the Most High,
     and was saved towards him.

     Alleluia.

NOTES TO THE TRANSLATION

1a: H has ܟܬܝܒܐ.

2a: Harris and Mingana vol. 2, Charlesworth 1977 ("that it might guard...");
and Lattke 1979-86, vol. 1 ("damit sie...bewahren sollte"), are incorrect, since
such translation requires the imperf. rather than the perf. verb as it stands in
the text. ܕ has been interpreted here as the rel. pron., although it is somewhat
removed from its antecedent ܚܝܠܐ (but cf. Nöldeke § 342). It is also possible to
render 2a as, "since he kept me always..." (Nöldeke § 366 B).

2b: H has mistakenly copied ܒ instead of ܩ before ܦܪܘܩܝ.

3a: H has ܐܬܬܠܝ. The internal parallelism of the line demands that both verbs
be pl.

4b: N has ܗܘܐ ܠܝ ܛܠܠܐ, confusing the order of the elements in the sentence.

5b-c: A pause after ܚܠܒܐ is indicated in N.

ANALYSIS

Stanza 1 [1-2]

1a-b is parallel on the pattern: subj./obj. (noun + ܕ + noun) + 3rd masc. sing.
Aphel perf. verb + ܠܥ/ܡܢ ܠܥ + obj. with 1st sing. suffix. The antithesis of
1b appears in 5:5.

2a-b is parallel with chiasmus: A B C// B' A C, where A = ܗܘܐ; B = part./
noun compl.; C = ܠ. The chiasmus is not based on syntax except that the
expression ܗܘܐ ܦܪܝܣܐ (also found in 11:3; 28:10; [38:3]) functions as a verb.
The chiasmus would be more exact by emending ܡܪܚܝ to ܡܪܚܝܘ. The parallelism is strengthened by the word-pair ܠܝܢ - ܦܪܣ.

1 and 3 are similar to 24:1a,3, both semantically and by the vocabulary used
(ܠܥ...ܪܝܚܐ; ܐܬܬܢܝܚܬ).

Stanza 2 [3]

There is a shift in focus from the "I" and the Lord to a 3rd masc. pl. group.
Semantically, the stanza stands in antithesis to stanzas 1 and 3.

3a has internal parallelism by the double pattern of synonymous 3rd masc.
pl. Ethpeel perf. verbs between which the common subj. is inserted (cf. also
22:11; 23:19 [ܠܒܘܬܗܘܢ as obj.]). 3b, which is connected semantically with 3a by
ܡܢܗܘܢ, also has a double element by the compound subj. formed by two sing.
nouns. There is an alliterative effect in 3b by the repetition of ܢ.

Stanza 3 [4-5, 6]

The first strophe has a double three-line pattern of monocolon (1st sing. subj.)
+ bicolon (3rd sing. masc. subj.).

The monocola, 4a and 5a, are parallel to a degree. Semantically, both present the serenity of the "I" over against the general disturbance of all others.
There is chiasmus by the placement of the verbal expressions ("I was quiet", "I
was carried") and the descriptive expressions ("in the company of the Lord",
"like a child by its mother").

4b-c is parallel with a pivot pattern: A B C // A B', where A = ܘܐܝܬ; B =
ܡܢ + noun obj.; C = ܠ ܗܘܐ (pivot). The noun objs. express merismus -
"shade" above and "foundation" below. Each A B section contains 6 syllables.

5b-c is parallel, 5c being in apposition with ܟܠܒ in 5b. The bicolon is similar to 4b-c by the use of the 3rd masc. sing. verbs (ref. to the Lord) + ܠ in each first line, which is then understood for the second line.

5b-c moves easily from the simile in 5a, using implicitly in 5b the mother imagery for the Lord (ܟܠܒ is associated with the motif of motherhood in 8:16; 19 [passim]; 40:1). The metaphor of the milk of the Lord is complex since it uses another metaphor, dew of the Lord, as its referent. Thus 5b-c constitutes a kind of double level metaphor. The phrase ܢܛܠܐ ܠܝܡ in 5c provides a subtle link to ܐܢܛܠ ܘܡܪܚܡ in 1a (cf. 4:10), especially since the key elements form the word-pair ܠܝܡ - ܪܚܡ.

6a-b continues the motif of motherhood, not only by ref. to the gift of the milk in 5b (ܒܒܣܡܘܬܗ) but also by the use of ܪܒܐ with its connotation of rearing. The bicolon is parallel on the pattern: 1st sing. perf. verb + ܒ + noun (attribute of the Lord) with 3rd masc. sing. suffix. 6a and 11:9 have a similar pattern of 1st sing. perf. verb (expressing increase) + ܒܒܣܡܘܬܗ (ref. to the Lord).

6b and 4a form the inclusio for the stanza, having a loose parallel structure of 1st sing. perf. verb + ܒ + noun with 3rd sing. masc. suffix (ref. to the Lord). 6b also forms an inclusio for the first three stanzas with 1a by the repetition of the root ܢܘܚ.

Stanza 4 [7] (cf. the excursus following the analysis of Ode 27)

This stanza with its strong liturgical overtones seems a little out of place at the conclusion of the Ode, since other variations function as either the introduction to an Ode (37:1; 42:1-2) or comprise an entire Ode (27:1-3) which may have been used in some introductory way to liturgical action.

7a introduces the setting for 7b-c which is closely parallel on the pattern: ܘ + 1st sing. Ethpeel perf. verb + ܠܗ + ܕܝܫܘܥ/substitute 3rd masc. sing. suffix.

# ODE 36

ܐܬܬܢܝܚܬ ܥܠ ܪܘܚܗ ܕܡܪܝܐ 1
ܘܐܪܝܡܬܢܝ ܠܪܘܡܐ
ܘܐܩܝܡܬܢܝ ܥܠ ܪ̈ܓܠܝ 2
ܒܪܘܡܗ ܕܡܪܝܐ
ܩܕܡ ܡܫܡܠܝܘܬܗ ܘܬܫܒܘܚܬܗ

ܟܕ ܡܫܒܚ ܐܢܐ ܒܬܘܩܢܐ ܕܙܡܝܪ̈ܬܗ
ܝܠܕܬܢܝ ܡܢ ܩܕܡ ܐܦ̈ܘܗܝ ܕܡܪܝܐ 3
ܘܟܕ ܒܪ ܐܢܫܐ ܐܝܬܝ
ܐܫܬܡܗܬ ܢܘܗܪܐ
ܒܪܗ ܕܐܠܗܐ
ܟܕ ܡܫܒܚ ܐܢܐ ܒܡܫܒ̈ܚܢܐ 4
ܘܪܒ ܐܢܐ ܒܪ̈ܘܪܒܢܐ

ܐܝܟ ܪܒܘܬܗ ܓܝܪ ܕܡܪܝܡܐ 5
ܗܢܐ ܥܒܕܢܝ
ܘܐܝܟ ܚܘܕܬܗ
ܚܕܬܢܝ

ܘܡܫܚܢܝ ܡܢ ܡܫܡܠܝܘܬܗ 6
ܘܗܘܝܬ ܚܕ ܡܢ ܩܪ̈ܝܒܘܗܝ
ܘܐܬܦܬܚ ܦܘܡܝ 7
ܐܝܟ ܥܢܢܐ ܕܛܠܐ
ܘܢܒܥ ܠܒܝ
ܐܝܟ ܡܒܘܥܐ ܕܙܕܝܩܘܬܐ
ܘܗܘܐ ܩܘܪܒܝ ܒܫܠܡܐ 8
ܘܐܫܬܪܪܬ ܒܪܘܚܐ ܕܡܕܒܪܢܘܬܐ

ܗܠܠܘܝܐ

---

1 I was at rest upon the Spirit of the Lord.
And she lifted me up to the height,
2 and made me stand on my feet
in the height of the Lord,
before his perfection and his glory.

While I gave glory by the composition of his odes,
3  she bore me forth before the face of the Lord.
And while I was a (son of) man,
I was called light,
the Son of God.
4  While I gave glory among those giving glory,
and the greatest (was) I of the great.

5  For according to the greatness of the Most High,
so she made me;
and according to his renewal,
he renewed me.

6  And he annointed me from his fullness,
and I was one of those near him.
7  And my mouth was opened
like a cloud of dew,
and my heart belched up
like a belching of righteousness.
8  And my nearness was in peace,
and I was solidly set by the Spirit of rule.

Alleluia.

NOTES TO THE TRANSLATION

1b: H has ܠܬܪܝܬܗ.

2d, 4a: A lit. translation should render ܡܫܒܚ ܐܢܐ in the present. The context indicates that the sense of the expression is a continuous action in the past.

3b: The lit. translation of ܒܪ ܐܢܫܐ ("a son of man") should be understood as meaning simply "a man". Charlesworth (1977) alone continues to translate with "the Son of Man", though Brock (1974, 624) cast doubt on the legitimacy of such a translation in his review of Charlesworth's first (1973) edition. For the difference, cf. Mk 2:27-28,

ܘܫܒܚܬܐ ܕܟܠܠ ܒܪܢܫܐ ܐܬܒܪܝܬ: ܘܠܐ ܗܘܐ ܒܪܢܫܐ ܕܟܠܠ ܫܒܚܬܐ. ܒܪܗ ܗܘ
ܗܟܠ ܘܐܦ ܕܫܒܚܬܐ ܒܪܗ ܕܐܠܗܐ.

4a: H has ܒܡܫܒ̈ܚܐ.

4b: As with 4a, the context demands the past tense for the copula which would normally be translated in the present tense.

7a: H has ܕܠܐܠܐ.

7d: H has ܐܝܟ at the beginning of the line. Bauer (1964), Lattke (1979-86, vol. 1) and Blaszczak (9) prefer the reading from N. H has been preferred here because of the parallelism within 7a-d.

ANALYSIS

Stanza 1 [1-2c]

1a serves as as an introduction to the ensuing action as well as forming the inclusio for the Ode with 8b by the parallel pattern of 1st sing. perf. pass. verbs + prep. + ܪܘܚܐ + ܕ + noun (ref. to ܪܘܚܐ). There is some connection between 1a and 2a by the use of the phrase introduced by ܥܠ.

1b-2a is parallel on the pattern: 3rd fem. sing. Aphel perf. verb + 1st sing. suffix + phrase (denoting place). 1b has internal parallelism by the doubling of the root ܪܘܡ.

2b-c follows from ܐܩܝܡܬܢ in 2a, and comprises a series of phrases denoting place. 2c has internal parallelism by the use of the word-pair ܬܫܒܘܚܬܐ - ܫܘܒܚܐ.

Stanza 2 [2d-3a, 3b-d, 4]

There is a link between stanzas 1 and 2 by the terrace pattern of the repetition of the root ܫܒܚ in 2c-d. 2d-3a and 4a-b form the inclusio for the stanza, 4a being an exact repetition of 2c with the exception of the obj. of ܒ.

The connection of 2d-3a and 4a-b emphasises the central position of 3b-d. 3b and 3c are chiastic by the placement of the 1st sing. perf. verbs and the descriptive expressions referring to the "I" (a [son of] man, light). 3c and 3d are parallel, 3d being in apposition to ܢܘܗܪܐ in 3c. 3d is linked to 3b by the apparent antithesis of ܒܪܢܫܐ - ܒܪܗ ܕܐܠܗܐ. The parallelism of the latter expressions is weakened by the determination in the second element ("<u>the</u> Son of God") where the first has none ("a son of man").

4a-b is parallel on the pattern: part./adj. + ܐܢܫ + ܒ + pl. part. (functions as a noun)/pl. noun. The parallelism is enhanced by the pattern of repetition of the key root in each line: ܫܒܚ (4a) and ܪܒܐ (4b). The repetition gives strong alliteration in both lines: ܫ, ܒ and ܚ in 4a, ܪ and ܒ in 4b.

## Stanza 3 [5]

There is some connection between stanzas 2 and 3 by the repetition of the root ܪܒܐ (x 2 in 4b, x 1 in 5a).

5a-d is alternately parallel. 5a and 5c follow the general pattern: ܐܝܟ + noun (attribute of the Lord) with 3rd masc. sing. suffix. 5b and 5d have a 3rd sing. perf. verb + 1st sing. suffix (cf. 15:7; 29:2-3). There is a dramatic effect in the steady decrease in relative length of line over the four lines. The terrace pattern of the repetition of the root ܚܝܠ in 5c-d also provides alliteration.

The 3rd fem. sing. verb in 5b makes the parallelism of 5b and 5d less exact syntactically. Though both Mss. have the verb in this form, it may well be an error since this pattern with ܐܝܟ in all other cases has the Lord as the subj. of the verb. On the other hand, the concept of "making" is apt for the Spirit who bears the "I", according to 3a.

## Stanza 4 [6, 7, 8]

In a similar pattern to stanza 2, the bicola in 6 and 8 form the boundary (by the repetition of the root ܝܗܒ) for the more strictly structured central strophe.

6a-b is parallel to a degree by the pattern of the phrase introduced by ܡܢ + noun/adj. (functions as a noun) + 3rd masc. sing. suffix. The focus in both cases is the "I", as obj. in 6a and subj. in 6b.

7a-d has the central position in the stanza, with the four lines alternately parallel. 7a and 7c follow the pattern: 3rd masc. sing. perf. verb + noun subj. with 1st sing. suffix. The parallelism is strengthened by the use of the word-pair ܩܕܡܘ - ܠܒܝ. 7b and 7d are parallel on the pattern: ܐܝܟ (in H only for 7d) + noun + ܘ + noun. There is a strong link between 7c and d by the repetition of the root ܥܠܬ. ܠܒ is found associated with ܥܠܬ in 40:2.

8a and 8b are only loosely connected by a focus on the "I" - 1st sing. suffix with the noun subj. in 8a; 1st sing. subj. in 8b.

A number of roots are repeated throughout the Ode: ܫܒܚ (x 4), ܪܒܐ (x 3), ܪܘܡ (x 3), especially within a single line or within adjacent lines. The Ode has strong links with 21:1-2,6-8 both semantically (the exaltation of the "I" to the height and the continued praise of the Lord) and the use of vocabulary: ܪܘܡ, ܕܝܡܝܢܐ, ܢܝܚܐ, ܐܩܝܡܗ ܩܡ, ܫܒܚ, ܠܐ and ܦܐܪܐ (associated with praise), ܗܘܬ ܐܝܟ ܩܝܒ ܠܗ and ܗܘܬ ܘܝ ܟܝ ܩܝܒܘܗܝ, (ref. to the Lord).

## ODE 37

ܦܪܣܬ ܐܝܕܝ̈ ܠܘܬ ܡܪܝܐ      1
ܘܠܘܬ ܡܪܝܡܐ ܐܪܝܡܬ ܩܠܝ
ܘܡܠܠܬ ܒܣܦܘ̈ܬܗ ܕܠܒܝ      2
ܘܫܡܥܢܝ
ܟܕ ܢܦܠ ܠܘܬ ܩܠܝ
ܦܢܬܓܡܗ ܐܬܐ ܠܘܬܝ      3
ܘܝܗܒ ܠܝ ܦܐܪ̈ܐ ܕܥܡܠܝ
ܘܝܗܒ ܠܝ ܢܝܚܐ ܒܛܝܒܘܬܗ ܕܡܪܝܐ      4

ܗܠܠܘܝܐ

---

1    I extended my hands towards the Lord,
     and towards the Most High I lifted up my voice.
2    And I spoke by the lips of my heart,
     and he heard me,
     when my voice fell towards him.
3    His Word came towards me,
     so that he gave me the fruits of my labours,
4    and gave me rest by the grace of the Lord.

Alleluia.

NOTES TO THE TRANSLATION

1a: H has ܡܪܝ. Although there is precedence for the reading, established by
27:1 and 42:1, the N reading is preferred because of the parallelism of 1a and
1b, and the inclusio of 1a with 4.

ANALYSIS

The strong interrelation of the verses, and the inclusio between 1a and 4 by the
repetition of ܡܪܝܐ, indicate that this Ode should be treated as a single stanza.

1a-b is parallel with chiasmus: A B // B' A', where A = 1st sing. perf. verb
+ noun obj. (physical attribute of the Odist) with 1st sing. suffix; B = ܡܪܝܡܐ/
ܠܘܬ ܡܪܝܐ (cf. the excursus following the analysis of Ode 27). The placement

of the latter phrases forms a terrace pattern. There is a subtlety to the repetition of the root ܪܥܡ in 1a.

2a-b follows easily from 1, both semantically, by the word-pair ܪܥܡ - ܩܠܐ (1b, 2a), and syntactically, by the pattern of 1st sing. perf. verb + noun (physical attribute of the "I") with 1st sing. suffix (1, 2a). The two lines of the bicolon are connected by the word-pair ܩܠܐ - ܡܠܬܗ.

The action of the Lord in 2b brings to a conclusion the previous actions of the "I". Although there seems a finality to the rather bald statement of 2b, the loose parallelism between 2c and 1b by the repetition of ܩܠ, by the phrases introduced by ܠܘܬ (ref. to the Lord), and by the contrasting verbs ܪܥܡ and ܥܢܐ, precludes making a definite stanza division after 2b.

2c-3a follows the pattern: A B C// B' A' C', where A = 3rd masc. sing. Peal perf. verb; B = noun subj. + pron. suffix (1st sing. in 2c; 3rd sing. in 3a); C = ܠܘܬ + pron. suffix (3rd sing. in 2c; 1st sing. in 3a). Apart from the initial chiasmus, there is also a more subtle chiasmus with the inversion of the order of the pron. suffixes ("my voice... towards him"; "his word...towards me").

The bicolon in 3b-4, which refers to 3a, has the general pattern: ܝܗܒ ܠܝ + noun obj. The parallelism is strengthened by the word-pair ܚܝܠ - ܦܐܪܐ.

## ODE 38

1 ܣܠܩܬ ܠܢܘܗܪܐ ܕܫܪܪܐ
ܐܝܟ ܕܠܡܪܟܒܬܐ
ܘܕܒܪܢܝ ܫܪܪܐ ܘܐܝܬܝܢܝ
2 ܘܐܥܒܪܢܝ ܦ̈ܩܥܬܐ ܘܫ̈ܩܝܦܐ
ܘܡܢ ܫܩܝܦܐ ܘܓ̈ܠܠܐ ܦܨܢܝ
3 ܘܗܘܐ ܠܝ ܠܠܡܐܢܐ ܕܦܘܪܩܢܐ
ܘܣܡܢܝ ܥܠ ܪ̈ܓܠܐ ܕܚܝܐ ܕܠܐ ܡܘܬܐ
4 ܘܐܙܠ ܥܡܝ ܘܐܢܝܚ ܠܝ
ܘܠܐ ܫܒܩܢܝ ܕܐܛܥܐ
ܡܛܠ ܕܫܪܪܐ ܐܝܬܘܗܝ ܗܘܐ ܘܗܘܝܐ

5 ܘܠܐ ܗܘܐ ܠܝ ܩܘܕܘܢܘܣ
ܕܥܡܗ ܡܗܠܟ ܗܘܝܬ
ܘܠܐ ܛܥܝܬ ܒܡܕܡ
ܡܛܠ ܕܐܫܬܡܥܬ ܠܗ

6 ܥܪܘܩܐ ܗܘܬ ܓܝܪ ܡܢܗ ܛܥܝܘܬܐ
ܘܠܐ ܐܪܥܐ ܗܘܬ ܠܗ
7 ܫܪܪܐ ܕܝܢ ܐܙܠ ܗܘܐ ܒܐܘܪܚܐ ܬܪܝܨܬܐ
ܘܟܠܡܕܡ ܕܠܐ ܝܕܥ ܗܘܝܬ ܠܗ
ܡܚܘܐ ܗܘܐ ܠܝ
8 ܠܟܠܗܘܢ ܣܡ̈ܡܢܐ ܕܛܥܝܘܬܐ
ܘܠܚ̈ܘܬܐ ܗܠܝܢ ܕܡܣܒܪܢ ܕܚܠܝܘܬܐ ܗܝ ܕܡܘܬܐ
9 ܘܠܡܚܒܠܢܘܗ ܕܚܒܠܐ
ܚܙܐ ܗܘܝܬ ܟܕ ܡܬܛܟܣܐ ܗܘܬ ܟܠܬܐ ܕܡܚܒܠܐ
ܘܚܬܢܐ ܕܡܚܒܠ ܘܡܬܚܒܠ

10 ܘܫܐܠܬ ܠܫܪܪܐ
ܕܡܢ ܐܢܘܢ ܗܠܝܢ
ܘܐܡܪ ܠܝ
ܗܢܘ ܡܛܥܝܢܐ ܘܛܥܝܘܬܐ
11 ܘܡܬܕܡܝܢ ܒܚܒܝܒܐ ܘܒܟܠܬܗ
ܘܡܛܥܝܢ ܠܥܠܡܐ
ܘܡܚܒܠܝܢ ܠܗ

12 ܘܩܪܝܢ ܠܣܟܠ̈ܐ ܠܡܫܬܘܬܐ
ܘܝܗܒܝܢ ܠܗܘܢ ܕܢܫܬܘܢ ܚܡܪܐ ܕܪܘܝܘܬܗܘܢ
13 ܘܡܬܒܝܢ ܚܟܡ̈ܬܗܘܢ ܘܡܕܥ̈ܝܗܘܢ
ܘܥܒܕܝܢ ܠܗܘܢ ܕܠܐ ܪܥܝܢܐ
14 ܘܗܝܕܝܢ ܫܒܩܝܢ ܠܗܘܢ

ܘܗܢܘܢ ܕܝܢ ܗܘܝܢ ܡܬܒܪܝܢ
ܟܕ ܦܩܪܝܢ ܘܡܚܒܠܝܢ
ܟܕ ܠܝܬ ܒܗܘܢ ܠܒܐ
ܐܦܠܐ ܒܥܝܢ ܠܗ

15 ܘܐܬܚܟܡܬ ܐܢܐ
ܕܠܐ ܢܦܠܬ ܒܐܝ̈ܕܝ ܡܛܥܝܢܐ
ܘܚܕܝܬ ܠܢܦܫܝ
ܡܛܠ ܕܐܙܠ ܗܘܐ ܥܡܝ ܫܪܪܐ
16 ܘܐܫܬܪܪܬ ܕܝܢ ܘܚܝܬ ܘܐܬܦܪܩܬ
ܘܐܬܬܣܝܡܘ ܫܬܐܣ̈ܝ ܥܠ ܐܝܕܗ ܕܡܪܝܐ
ܡܛܠ ܕܗܘ ܢܨܒܢܝ

17 ܗܘ ܓܝܪ ܣܡ ܥܩܪܐ
ܘܐܫܩܝܗ ܘܐܬܩܢܗ ܘܒܪܟܗ
ܘܦܐܪ̈ܘܗܝ ܠܥܠܡܝܢ ܗܘܝܢ

18 ܐܥܡܩ ܘܣܠܩ ܘܐܦܬܝ
ܘܡܠܐ ܘܐܬܪܘܪܒ

19 ܘܐܫܬܒܚ ܡܪܝܐ ܒܠܚܘܕܘܗܝ
ܒܢܨܒܬܗ ܘܒܦܘܠܚܢܗ
20 ܒܢܨܦܘܬܗ
ܘܒܒܘܪܟܬܐ ܕܣܦܘ̈ܬܗ
ܒܢܨܒܬܐ ܝܐܝܬܐ ܕܝܡܝܢܗ
21 ܘܒܫܒܘܚܬܐ ܕܢܨܒܬܗ
ܘܒܡܕܥܐ ܕܬܪܥܝܬܗ

ܗܠܠܘܝܐ

1   I went up into the light of Truth,
as into a chariot.
And Truth drove me and brought me.

2   And he caused me to pass over chasms and fissures,
and from precipices and waves he saved me.

3   And he was for me a harbour of salvation,
and he set me upon the arms of immortal life.

4   And he went with me and gave me rest,
and did not abandon me that I might err,
because he was and is the Truth.

5   And there was no danger for me,
since I walked with him.
And I did not err in anything,
because I hearkened unto him.

6   For Error fled from him,
and did not meet him.

7   But Truth went by the upright way.
And everything which I did not know,
he manifested to me:

8   all the poisons of Error,
and those scourges which are supposed that sweetness is of Death,

9   and the corrupting of Corruption.
I saw while the corrupting bride was adorned,
and the corrupting and corrupted bridegroom.

10  And I asked the Truth,
Who are these?
And he said to me,
They are the Deceiver and Error,

11  and they imitate the Beloved and his bride.
And they make the world to err,
and corrupt it.

12  And they call many to the wedding feast,
    and give them that they might drink the wine of their intoxication.
13  And they vomit up their wisdoms and their minds,
    and they make them senseless,
14  and then they abandon them.

    But they go round in circles,
    while mad and corrupting,
    while there is no heart in them,
    for neither do they seek it.

15  And I indeed learnt wisdom ,
    so that I did not fall into the hands of the Deceiver.
    And I was glad (to) myself,
    because Truth went with me.
16  But I was solidly set and lived and was saved;
    and my foundations were set upon the hand of the Lord,
    because he planted me.

17  For he set the root,
    and watered it and fixed it and blessed it.
    And his fruits are forever.

18  It penetrated deeply and grew tall and spread out widely,
    and was full and was made great.

19  And the Lord alone was glorified,
    by his planting and by his cultivation,
20  by his care;
    and by the blessing of his lips,
    by the beautiful planting of his right hand,
21  and by the existence of his planting,
    and by the understanding of his mind.

    Alleluia.

NOTES TO THE TRANSLATION

2a: N has ܟܘܪܡܐ ܟܘܝܡ. The parallelism of 2a and 2b favours the H reading.

3a: N has ܘܪܟܠܠ. H is preferred because of the general structure in the Odes of ܠ ܟܗܘ without a *nota accusativi*; cf. e.g. 38:5a.

3b: N has ܟܝܪܝ. Charlesworth (1977), Lattke (1979-86, vol. 1), and Carmignac (1986) opt for this reading. Harris crossed out "arms" in his 1911 edition and wrote in "step", but Harris and Mingana vol. 2 has "arms". Either reading will make sense in the context. Although "step" suits the general theme of the movement of Truth and the "I", "arms" fits well with the more passive image of a haven in 3a. The final choice for the H reading has been made on the basis of the similarity in concept with 28:5d.

4c: H has ܗܘ.

5a: N appears to have ܘܗܘܚܘܗ.

6a: H is confused with ܡܠ where N has ܗܗܘ.

8b: H has ܝܪܡܘܝ. Context favours the pass. as in N.

9a-b: Both Mss. indicate a break after ܟܠܚܘܝ. I have followed this punctuation (cf. Charlesworth 1977; Emerton), because of the structure of 8-9a.

9b: H omits ܗܗܘ and has ܟܠܚܘܗܪܝ.

13b: N has ܝܡܠ. Context demands the masc.

14c: H has mistakenly written ܝ for ܝ.

15b: N has ܟܘܫܠܝܪ. H is preferred because of the link to 10d.

16b: H has ܝܪܘܡܗܗܟܐ.

17c: H has ܝܪܠܠ.

18a: H has ܘܩܛܠܗ ܟܡܐܢ ܠܒܝܬܗ. N seems more apt in the context of growth.

ANALYSIS

The finer points of the division of this Ode are difficult, although the larger division into two sub-odes is quite clear, especially by the repetition of vocabulary. In sub-ode 1 (1-16), the most frequent terms are: ܫܪܪܐ (x 6)/ܫܪ (x 1), ܗܝܡܢܘܬܐ (x 3)/ܗܝܡܢ (x 5), ܚܝܐ (x 6). These do not appear in sub-ode 2 (17-21) and in fact only three (ܣܠܩ, ܝܗܒ, ܪܚܡ) of the fourteen roots repeated in sub-ode 1 are repeated (once) in sub-ode 2. ܢܨܒ is the most frequent (x 3) and central term in sub-ode 2, and appears in sub-ode 1 in what can only be regarded as a deliberate bridging verse (16c) into sub-ode 2. Semantically the two sub-odes deal with two separate actions - the heavenly journey and instruction of the "I"; the planting of the "I" by the Lord.

Stanza 1 [1a-b, 1c-4] (= Stanza 1, Sub-ode 1)

1a-b sets the scene for sub-ode 1 by introducing the major character, Truth. The bicolon is parallel by the use of ܠ + noun and the shared verb ܣܠܩܬ. The parallelism indicates the connection of the light of Truth and the chariot. Strictly speaking the simile refers to the action of going up rather than to the equivalence of the light of Truth and the chariot.

1c-4 continues the metaphor from 1a-b, with a change of subj. to 3rd sing. masc. Each line of the second strophe has a 3rd masc. sing. subj. with 1st sing. dir./indir. obj.

1c functions as the introduction to the second strophe. It has internal parallelism by the double pattern of 3rd masc. sing. perf. verbs with 1st sing. suffix between which the common subj. is inserted. There is assonance and alliteration in the initial verbs + suffix of 1c and 2a, ܘܕܒܪܢܝ...ܘܐܚܕܢܝ.

2a-b is parallel with chiasmus: A B // B' A', where A = 3rd masc. sing. perf. verb + 1st sing. suffix; B = pl. noun + ܘ + pl. noun (objs. of a prep. contained in/associated with the verb: "[over] chasms and fissures"; "from precipes and waves").

3a-b is parallel by the general pattern of 3rd sing. masc. verb + 1st sing. indir./dir. obj. + ܠ (sign of the dir. obj.)/ܥܠ + noun + ܕ + qualifying expression. The parallelism is strengthened by the word-pair ܚܝܐ ܕܠܐ ܡܘܬܐ - ܦܪܩܘܗܝ.

3a is linked to 2b by the repetition of the root ܩܘܡ at the conclusion of each line (cf. 34:6). Syntactically, 3a is close to 5a on the pattern: ܐܢܐ/ܐܢܐ ܐܠ + ܠ + noun compl. (cf. 11:3; 28:10; 35:2).

4a-b contains a series of three 3rd masc. sing. perf. verbs. 4a has internal parallelism by the double pattern of ܗ + 3rd sing. masc. verb + prep. with 1st sing. suffix. Although 4b follows the general pattern of 3rd sing. masc. verb and 1st sing. object of the action, the structure is extended by the cl. with a 1st sing. subj.

The concluding formula in 4c is linked to the preceding verses by the cl. introduced by ܕ ܡܛܠ and by the antithetical association between ܚܝܐ and ܐܒܕ (4b; cf. the word-pair ܚܝܐ - ܐܒܕܢܐ in 6a, 7a).

## Stanza 2 [5]

The division in stanzas is indicated by the change generally to a 1st sing. subj. The two bicola have a loose alternate parallelism with the negative expressions of 5a and 5c, and with the chiasmus in 5b and 5d by the placement of the 1st sing. verbs and ܡܛܠ/ܡܠ. There is a link between 5b and 5c by the association of ܗܘܝ and ܐܒܕ (cf. 17:4b-5; 18:14).

There is a marked similarity, both semantically and by the vocabulary (ܚܝܐ, ܐܝܟ, ܐܒܕ) between 4-5 and 17:5.

## Stanza 3 [6-7, 8-9a, 9b-c]

6 introduces a new detail of the narrative, prepared for by the previous appearances of the root ܐܒܕ. The division of stanzas is indicated also by the change in subj. from 1st sing. to 3rd sing. fem. 6a-b is parallel to a degree by the pattern: fem. sing. Peal part. act. + ܗܘܐ + prep. with masc. sing. suffix. There is alliteration and assonance in the participles.

7a provides the contrast to 6, emphasised by the antithetical word-pair ܚܝܐ - ܐܒܕܢܐ) and by the use of ܕ. The association of ܚܝܐ and ܐܝܟ occurs also explicitly in 15f and implicitly in 4a.

7b-c is parallel on the pattern: part. + ܐܢܐ + ܠ with pron. suffix. There is chiasmus by the 1st sing. subj. and 3rd masc. sing. suffix in 7b, and the 3rd masc. sing. subj. and 1st sing. suffix in 7c.

The unifying feature of 8-9a is the initial ܠ which is the sign in each case of the dir. obj. of ܐܢܐ ܐܚܕܬ in 7c, the tricolon as a whole being in apposition with 7b. The three-part pattern of the tricolon (pl. noun + ܕ + noun) is extended in 8b by the inclusion of a qualifying cl. (ref. to scourges). The final noun of each of the lines is a key negative element in the Odes (Error, Death, Corruption).

9b-c introduces the imagery of bride and bridegroom which will continue into the next stanza and be extended to the wedding feast imagery of the stanza thereafter. The bicolon is parallel, with ellipsis of the verb in 9c. ܕܚܠܬܐ ܕܡܚܝܢܗ parallels ܠܡܚܝܢܗ ܚܬܘ, the latter being extended by the use of the part. pass. (cf. 17:11). The root ܚܝܐ is repeated five times within 9.

## Stanza 4 [10-11]

The break in stanzas is indicated by the shift to the report of direct speech between the "I" and Truth, in which the subj. for the most part is the 3rd pl. masc. The question and answer of 10 provide the introduction for the following verses. 10a and 10c are parallel on the pattern: verb (associated roots ܠ ܪܚܡ - ܐܡܪ) + ܠ with obj. There is chiasmus by the placement of the 1st sing. subj. and 3rd sing. masc. obj. in 10a and 3rd sing. masc. subj. and 1st sing. obj. in 10c. The question in 10b, in the central position by its insertion into the bicolon, supplies the impetus for the report which follows.

10d-11a is parallel on the pattern: verbal expression + double compl./obj. The two elements of the compl./obj. are a pair of associated characters, ܕܚܢܘܬܐ ܘܪܚܡܬܐ being the polar opposites of ܡܘܬܐ ܘܚܣܝܪܐ. 11b-c is parallel on the pattern: 3rd pl. part. + ܠ + noun/suffix (substitute for the noun). The parallelism is strengthened by the word-pair ܪܚܡ - ܚܝܐ. 11b-c is linked to 10d-11a by the repetition of the root ܪܚܡ.

## Stanza 5 [12-14a]

The Deceiver and Error continue as the general subject of the action, this stanza depicting their corrupting actions within the extended metaphor of the wedding feast. Semantically, the stanza is in direct contrast with stanzas 1 and 2 which contain descriptions of the actions of Truth on behalf of the "I". In each case, the final action reported of these contrasting characters uses the root ܣܒܪ (4b, 14a).

The major unifying element of the stanza is the initial 3rd pl. part. act. in each line (second position in 14a). The obj. of the part. in each case (ܐܢܘܢ in 12b, 13b and 14a; two noun objs. with 3rd masc. pl. suffix in 13a) is connected by ref. to ܡܪܝܐ in 12a. The simplicity of the pattern for the five lines is broken by the clausal extension in 12b.

13a is the central focus of the stanza, the subj. changing with this line to the many invited to the wedding feast, whereas the subj. of 12 and 13b-14a is the Deceiver and Error. The structure moves out from 13a in two groups of parallel lines: 12b with 13b (3rd pl. part. act. + ܠܗܘܢ + ܕ...) and 12a with 14a (3rd pl. part. act. + obj. [ܣܓܝܐܐ in 12a, pron. substitute in 14a]). 12b and 13b are further connected semantically by the theme of drinking and its effects (cf. 11:7-8).

## Stanza 6 [14b-e]

The division of stanzas is indicated syntactically by the termination of the pattern of part. + obj. with 14a, and semantically by the change of focus from the Deceiver and Error to the group of those who have been corrupted (the new 3rd masc. pl. subj.).

14b-c contains a variation (by the division into two cls. introduced by ܟܕ) of the familiar three-part verb pattern. The use of participles in the pattern is infrequent (cf. 33:5b). 14d-e is parallel to a degree by the use of negative expressions and the equivalence of the final ܠܐ, ܠܗ.

## Stanza 7 [15, 16]

The final stanza of the first sub-ode is a personal confession by the "I". The subj. shifts to the 1st sing.

15b and 15d comprise cls. associated with their respective preceding lines. 15a-c has an initial 1st sing. perf. verb. 15d is linked with 4a by the similar expressions, ܐܝܬ ܗܘܐ ܠܥܠ and ܐܝܬ ܠܥܠ, for which Truth is the subj., and serves to recapitulate the theme of the first stanzas of the Ode.

The connection between the two strophes is effected by the terrace pattern of the repetition of the root ܢܨܒ at the conclusion of 15d and the beginning of 16a. 16 serves as the bridge into the second sub-ode. The series of three 1st sing. perf. verbs in 16a effectively concludes the first sub-ode in a similar fashion to 34:6b. Although it appears to be linked by the planting motif to 17, 16b-c must be included with 16a because of the use of the 1st sing. person.

16b is closely linked to 15b by the contrasting final phrases ܟܐܒ, ܪܚܡܝܢܬܐ and ܥܠ ܐܝܕܗ ܕܡܪܝܐ, and to 3b by the use of ܣܡ...ܠܠ and by the similarity (if not equivalence) of the expressions, "the arms of immortal life" and "the hand of the Lord".

Stanza 8 [17] (= Stanza 1, Sub-ode 2)

The change to the image of the plantation and the change in vocabulary as noted above indicates very clearly that a second discrete section of material has been added to the larger first section. The division of the stanzas is supported by the change in the ref. to the one planted from the 1st sing. in 16c to the 3rd sing. in the sub-ode.

17a-b comprises a description of four actions of the planting. 17b contains a series of three 3rd sing. masc. perf. verbs with 3rd sing. masc. suffix. 17c provides a concluding confessional statement (cf. 1:5).

Stanza 9 [18]

The division of stanzas is indicated by the change in focus from the action of the Lord to the action by the plant/root. The 3rd sing. masc. obj. of stanza 8 becomes the subj. in this stanza. 18a and 18b are parallel and have internal parallelism by the series of five 3rd masc. sing. verbs which describe, in logical order, the growth pattern of the root (cf. Franzmann 1989).

Stanza 10 [19-20a, 20b-21]

Stanza 10 functions as a kind of litany, an extended indirect doxology to conclude the Ode. The division of the lines is difficult given the placement of ܐ and the clear parallel pattern beginning with ܡܬܩܒܠܢ ܟܐܒܝܢܒܒܐ (20a). A break after ܡܬܩܢܪܒܐ, apparent in N, has been preferred here, although it seems unusual that 20a should comprise this phrase without an initial ܐ.

19-20a consists of an introductory line followed by a bicolon comprising a three-part pattern of ܒ + noun (attribute/"possession" of the Lord) with 3rd masc. sing. suffix.

Except for the adj. ܟܐܝܪ in 20c, the second strophe follows a stricter pattern: ܒ + noun + ܝ + noun (attribute/"possession" of the Lord) with 3rd sing. masc. suffix. The quatrain may be further divided into two bicola for semantic reasons: in 20b-c, the two nouns with suffix at the end of each line refer to "physical" aspects of the Lord; those in 21a-b refer more to an "abstract" aspect of the Lord (21b) or something associated with him (21a).

## ODE 39

1 ܢܗܪ̈ܘܬܐ ܥܫܝ̈ܢܐ ܚܝܠܗ ܕܡܪܝܐ
ܕܠܐܝܠܝܢ ܕܡܒܣܪܝܢ ܠܗ ܡܗܦܟܝܢ ܠܒܪ ܪܝܫܗܘܢ
2 ܘܡܥܪܩܠܝܢ ܗܠܟ̈ܬܗܘܢ
ܘܡܣܪܚܝܢ ܡܥܒܪ̈ܬܗܘܢ
3 ܘܚܛܦܝܢ ܦܓܪ̈ܝܗܘܢ
ܘܡܚܒܠܝܢ ܢܦ̈ܫܬܗܘܢ
4 ܚܪܝܦܝܢ ܐܝܟ ܒܪ ܡܢ ܒܪ̈ܩܐ
ܘܩܠܝܠܝܢ

5 ܘܗܠܝܢ ܕܥܒܪܝܢ ܠܗܘܢ ܒܗܝܡܢܘܬܐ
ܠܐ ܡܬܬܙܝܥܝܢ
6 ܘܗܠܝܢ ܕܡܗܠܟܝܢ ܒܗܘܢ ܕܠܐ ܡܘܡܐ
ܠܐ ܡܬܕܠܚܝܢ
7 ܡܛܠ ܕܐܬܐ ܒܗܘܢ ܡܪܝܐ ܗܘ
ܘܐܬܐ ܗܘܐ ܐܘܪܚܐ
ܕܗܠܝܢ ܕܥܒܪܝܢ ܒܫܡܗ ܕܡܪܝܐ

8 ܠܒܫܘ ܗܟܝܠ ܫܡܗ ܕܡܪܝܡܐ
ܘܕܥܘܗܝ
ܘܬܥܒܪܘܢ ܕܠܐ ܦܘܣܘܣ
ܟܕ ܢܗܘܘܢ ܢܗܪ̈ܘܬܐ ܡܫܬܡܥܝܢ ܠܟܘܢ

9 ܥܒܪ ܐܝܟ ܡܪܝܐ ܒܡܠܬܗ
ܘܗܠܟ ܘܥܒܪ ܐܝܟ ܡܢ ܪܓܠ

10 ܘܥܩܒ̈ܬܗ ܩܝܡܝܢ ܥܠ ܡ̈ܝܐ
ܘܠܐ ܐܬܚܒܠ
ܐܠܐ ܐܝܬܝܗܝܢ ܐܝܟ ܩܝܣܐ ܕܡܬܩܢ ܒܫܪܪܐ
11 ܘܡܚܐ ܘܡܚܐ ܡܬܬܪܝܡܝܢ ܗܘܘ ܓ̈ܠܠܐ
ܘܥܩܒ̈ܬܗ ܕܝܢ ܕܡܪܢ ܡܫܝܚܐ ܩܝܡܝܢ ܐܝܟ
12 ܘܠܐ ܡܬܛܠܩܝܢ ܐܦܠܐ ܡܬܚܒܠܝܢ

ܡܝܕܐ ܪܝܬܐ ܐܠܐ ܐܘܝܢܐ ܕܬܚܒܘܬܗܟܐ   13
ܡܬܩܘܒܡܝ ܟܕܠܡܠ ܐܝܠܝ ܢܘܡܠܐ
ܡܫܪܠ ܪܪܦܘܐ

ܟܠܠܡ

---

1   Mighty rivers, the power of the Lord,
    that bring those who despise him head downwards.
2   And they entangle their steps,
    and destroy their fords,
3   and snatch their bodies,
    and corrupt their souls.
4   For swifter are they than lightning,
    and (more) rapid.

5   And they who pass over them in faith
    will not be disturbed;
6   and they who walk in them spotlessly
    will not be agitated;
7   because the sign in them is the Lord,
    and the sign is the way
    of them who pass over in the name of the Lord.

8   So put on the name of the Most High,
    and know him.
    And you will cross over without danger,
    while the rivers will obey you.

9   The Lord bridged over them by his word,
    and walked and crossed over them on foot.

10   And his footprints remained upon the waters,
    and were not destroyed;
    but they were like wood that is fixed in truth.
11   And on this side and on that the waves were lifted up;
    but the footprints of our Lord Messiah remain,
12   and were not blotted out nor destroyed.

13   And the way was set for those crossing over after him,
       and for those following the path of his faith,
       and doing reverence to his name.

Alleluia.

NOTES TO THE TRANSLATION

4a: H has ܟܘܒ.

7b-c: The division into two lines is supported only by Carmignac (1986),
       "parce que le Seigneur est un signe sur eux
       et (que ce) signe devient une route
       pour ceux qui traversent au nom du Seigneur"

8c: As with 38:5a, N has ܣܢܝܫܡ.

10b: H has ܐܬܘܒܠ.

10c: Most translate ܩܝܣܐ with "wood", or with a phrase such as "piece of
wood", "beam of wood". Bruston (1912b) uses "poutre" and Carmignac (1986)
"pieu". Harris (1911a) alone translates with "tree".
       ܒܩܘܫܬܐ is interpreted in the sense of "truly" by Harris 1911a; Bernard; Bauer
1964; Lattke 1979-86, vol. 1. The noun is used by Flemming; Ungnad and
Staerk; Diettrich 1911; Charlesworth 1977. The sense of "firmness" or "solidi-
ty" is found in Labourt and Batiffol; Harris and Mingana vol. 2; Emerton;
Carmignac 1986. I have preferred to translate literally ("in truth") but with the
sense of "truly".

ANALYSIS

Stanza 1 [1, 2-3, 4]

1a introduces the metaphor of the rivers. 1b is linked to 1a by the descriptive
cl. introduced by ܘ referring to ܐܬܘܗܢ. The second half of 1b introduces the
general pattern for 2-3, and on this basis it would be possible to make a break
after ܢܘܗܠܥ so as to include the second half of 1b with 2-3. It is only the associated ܘ at the beginning of 1b which precludes such a division.

The parallel quatrain 2-3 follows the pattern: ܢ + part. + pl. noun + 3rd masc. pl. suffix. The word-pair ܡܠܝ - ܠܒܪ occurs also in 5-6, 9b, 13a-b. There is a certain rhythm to the lines which are of similar length (2a-b and 3b have 6 syllables, 3a has 5 syllables), and a pattern of end-rhyme by virtue of the participial ending and the 3rd masc. pl. suffix (cf. Schökel 23-4).

4a-b is parallel with a pivot pattern: A B C // A', where A = adj. (attribute of the rivers); B = ܐܘܢ (understood in 4b); C = ܒܪܗ ܡܝ (pivot). The parallelism is strengthened by the word-pair ܚܝܠܐ - ܩܠܝܠܐ.

Stanza 2 [5-6, 7]

The inclusio for the stanza is formed by 5a and 7c which are parallel on the pattern: ...ܡܢܘ ܘܕܠܒܪ܀ + ܒ + noun. The parallelism is enhanced by the word-pair ܡܩܘܡܬܗ - ܫܒܚ.

The two bicola, 5a-b and 6a-b, are alternately parallel. 5a and 6a follow the pattern: ܢ ܡܢܘ + 3rd pl. part. + prep. + 3rd masc. pl. suffix + adv. expression. The parallelism is strengthened by the word-pair ܡܠܝ - ܠܒܪ. 5b and 6b are parallel on the pattern: ܠܐ + 3rd pl. masc. imperf. pass. verb. The lines are further connected by the synonymous verbs ܙܐܥ - ܕܚܠ. There is a similarity between the semantic content (the absence of fear/agitation when under the protection of the Lord) and structure of 5-6 and 5:10-14.

Both Mss. have two lines for 7. The second line has been deliberately divided here into 7b-c so as to indicate clearly the parallelism of 5a and 7c. The break is difficult however since the initial ܢ of 7c is strongly associated as a gen. expression with ܐܝܕܗ in 7b. 7a and 7b are parallel on the general pattern: A B C D // A' B D' C', where A = conj.; B = ܐܬܐ; C = compl.; D = copula/verb.

Stanza 3 [8]

The division in stanzas is indicated by the shift to the 2nd pl. imper. in 8. Stanza 3 is closely connected with stanza 2, ܕܢܗܪܝ ܫܒܚܗ in 8a and the root ܠܒܪ in 8c both providing a link to 7c.

8a-b is parallel on the pattern: 2nd pl. imper. verb + obj. (ܫܒܚ/substitute pron.). 8c and 8d are semantically linked by the equivalence of the lack of danger and the obedient rivers. This is in contrast to the description of destructive rivers in 1-4 and effectively serves to conclude this particular section of the Ode.

Stanza 4 [9]

With stanza 4 there is a return to a report style. Although the focus remains on the rivers, the metaphor changes subtly here from rivers as the power of the Lord (and the contrast between those who may cross safely and those for whom the rivers are dangerous) to the Lord's action of bridging the rivers.

9a-b is parallel on the pattern: 3rd sing. masc. perf. verb (x 2 in 9b) + ܐܢܘܢ + prep. with noun obj. 9b has internal parallelism by the double pattern of 3rd sing. masc. perf. verbs which form the word-pair ܗܠܟ - ܥܒܪ. The three verbs in 9a-b follow a logical progression of action.

Stanza 5 [10-12]

The limits of the stanza are indicated by the parallelism between 10a-b and 11b-12.

10a-b contains parallel 3rd pl. fem. verbs with a common subj. ܥܩ̈ܒܬܐ. The parallelism is strengthened by the word-pair ܩܘܡ - ܠܐ ܚܒܠ. 10c is linked to the bicolon by ܐܝܬܝܗܝܢ, which refers back to ܥܩ̈ܒܬܐ as its understood subj., and by the word-pair ܚܒܠ - ܬܩܢ.

11a fits more easily with 11b than with the preceding lines. There is a clear antithesis intended between the roots ܪܘܡ - ܩܘܡ, and chiasmus by the placement of the subj. and verb in each line. 11b-12a is strongly parallel to 10a-b: 10a and 11b with ܥܩ̈ܒܬܗ...ܩܝܡܢ (subj.); 10b and 12a with ܐܦܠܐ/ܠܐ + 3rd pl. fem. negative Ethpaal perf./part. of ܚܒܠ. The parallelism is only slightly disrupted by the addition of ܠܐ ܡܬܛܠܫܢ, which creates internal parallelism in 12 by its synonymity with ܐܦܠܐ ܡܬܚܒܠܢ. Both parallel bicola contain the word-pair ܩܘܡ - ܠܐ ܚܒܠ.

Stanza 6 [13]

That this tricolon serves as a kind of summary of important themes in the Ode is apparent in the vocabulary - ܐܘܪܚܐ, ܥܒܪ, ܗܠܟܬܐ, ܗܝܡܢܘܬܐ, ܫܡܐ. 13a may be further divided after ܐܘܪܚܐ. Such a division would make clearer the parallelism of the three final cls. with 3rd pl. participles act. + obj. In each case the Lord is the referent of the 3rd masc. sing. suffix. The structure is similar to 1b-3, especially in its use of the pres. participles.

## ODE 40

1  ܐܝܟ ܕܢܛܦ ܕܒܫܐ ܡܢ ܟܟܪܝܬܐ ܕܕܒܘܪ̈ܝܬܐ
ܘܢܪܕܐ ܚܠܒܐ ܡܢ ܐܢܬܬܐ ܪܚܡܬ ܒܢ̈ܝܗ
ܗܟܢܐ ܐܦ ܣܒܪܝ ܥܠܝܟ, ܡܪܝ ܗܘ ܐܠܗ,

2  ܐܝܟ ܕܡܒܥܐ ܡܒܘܥܐ ܡ̈ܝܗ,
ܗܟܢܐ ܡܒܥ ܠܒܝ ܠܬܫܒܘܚܬܗ ܕܡܪܝܐ
ܘܣ̈ܦܘܬܝ, ܡܒܥ̈ܢ ܠܗ ܬܫܒܘܚܬܐ

3  ܘܚܠܝ ܠܫܢܝ ܒܥܢ̈ܝܢܘܗܝ,
ܘܗܕܡ̈ܝ ܡܫܝܚܝܢ ܒܙܡܝܪ̈ܬܗ
4  ܘܢܨܚ ܐܦ̈ܝ ܒܚܕܘܬܗ
ܘܕܐܨ ܪܘܚܝ ܒܚܘܒܗ
ܘܡܒܗܐ ܢܦܫܝ ܒܗ

5  ܘܚܝܠ ܒܗ ܕܚܠܬܐ
ܘܦܘܩܢܐ ܒܗ ܢܝܚܬܐ
6  ܘܩܢܝܘ ܒܗ ܚܝ̈ܐ ܐܝܠܝܢ ܕܐܬܩܢܘ
ܘܡܒܣܡܝ̈ܗܘܢ ܕܠܐ ܫܠܘ,

ܗܠܠܘܝܐ

---

1  Like honey dripping from the honeycomb of bees,
   and milk flowing from the woman who loves her sons,
   so also is my hope upon you, my God.

2  Like a spring belching up its waters,
   so my heart belches up the Lord's hymn,
   and my lips bring forth a hymn to him.

3  And my tongue is sweet by his antiphons,
   and my members are anointed by his odes,
4  and my face greatly rejoices in his exultation,
   and my spirit exults in his love,
   and my soul shines in him.

5    And fear will trust in him,
     and salvation will be solidly set in him.
6    And his gain is immortal life,
     and the incorrupted receive it.


Alleluia.

NOTES TO THE TRANSLATION

2a: Charlesworth (1977) is mistaken in reading N as ⲕⲟⲟ̄ⲭ̇. The point indicating the ⲓ rather than ⲓ̇ is under the lower tail of the ⲭ as the Ms. shows for
ⲕⲑⲛⲭ̄ⲓ in 18:6,8. That the point above is intended for the ⲭ rather than indicating a ⲓ̇ is clear from ⲕⲟⲟⲭ in the next line of the Ms.

2b: N appears to have ⲙⲑⲩⲃⲝ̈ⲑ. Lattke (1979-86, vol. 1) alone uses this reading in the text. The choice for the sing. as in H is based on the parallelism of
2b with 2c where the sing. appears.

3: H omits ⲓ̈ⲏ̇ⲓⲙ...ⲕⲭⲩ. It appears from the Ms. that ⲋ before ⲙⲑⲓ̇ⲃⲟ̄ⲓ has
been erased.

4a: N has ⲋⲕ. H is preferred because of the pattern of noun + 1st sing. suffix
in 3-4.

5a: ⲕⲭⲩⲓ has been interpreted as the noun (Harris 1911a; Flemming; Ungnad
and Staerk; Diettrich 1911; Labourt and Batiffol; Bruston 1912b; Bauer 1964;
Carmignac 1986) or the part. (Harris and Mingana vol. 2; Lattke 1979-86, vol.
2; Charlesworth 1977; Emerton). The pointing of the Mss. differs. N has a
point below the word and H a point above. On the basis of J.B. Segal's summary that "the point above the line marks a full pronunciation or a comparatively
dominant form, the point below the line some 'weakening' or modification or a
less dominant form" (11), N would appear to have the noun and H the part.
The reading from N has been preferred because of the parallelism between
ⲕⲭⲩⲓ (5a) and ⲕⲟⲟⲓ̇ⲛⲋ (5b).

ANALYSIS

## Stanza 1 [1]

This stanza contains the first of two metaphor sections using ܐܝܟ ܕ... ܗܟܢܐ... In this case the first element of the two-part form is doubled, ܐܝܟ ܕ being understood in 1b. 1a-b is parallel on the pattern: ܐܝܟ ܕ (understood in 1b) + 3rd masc. sing. part. act. + noun subj. + ܡܢ + noun (source of the action) + descriptive expression qualifying the preceding noun. The parallelism is strengthened by the word-pair ܕܕܒܪܐ - ܚܠܒܐ and the semantic similarity of the verbs ܢܛܦ and ܪܕܐ. ܟܘܪܝܬܐ with ܕܟܘܪ̈ܝܬܐ also occurs in 30:4 and the association of ܚܠܒܐ - ܐܢܬܬܐ - ܒܢ̈ܐ is similar to 35:5.

1c is unusual. Following 1a-b, one expects either that one of the main verbs (ܢܛܦ, ܪܕܐ) will be repeated or a verb expressing similar or synonymous action will be used, 1c thus providing a conclusion in which the "I" (or perhaps God) is presented as a source in a similar fashion to the woman or the honeycomb.

## Stanza 2 [2]

The division of the stanzas is indicated by the change from the address to the Lord/God in the 2nd person to a report which refers to the Lord in the 3rd person. The tricolon presents another variation of ܐܝܟ ܕ... ܗܟܢܐ... Here the second element of the two-part form is doubled, ܗܟܢܐ being understood in 2c.

2a-b is parallel on the pattern: ܐܝܟ/ܗܟܢܐ ܕ + ܓܥܐ + noun subj. + noun obj. 2b-c is also parallel with chiasmus initially by the placement of the part. and the noun subj. with 1st sing. suffix. The parallelism of 2b-c is strengthened by the word-pair ܠܒܐ - ܣܦܘ̈ܬܐ and the repetition of ܬܫܒܘܚܬܐ. There is a variation of the terrace pattern in the repetition of ܓܥܐ (2a, b) and ܬܫܒܘܚܬܐ (2b, c).

Besides the use of ܐܝܟ ܕ... ܗܟܢܐ..., there is a similarity between the first two stanzas in the action (dripping, flowing, belching, bringing forth) of fluids (honey, milk, water).

## Stanza 3 [3-4]

The stanza continues easily from 2b-c by the focus on the two characters of the "I" and the Lord and by the word-pair ܣܦܘ̈ܬܐ - ܠܫܢܐ (2c, 3a). However, a division is indicated by the rather strict pattern of 3-4. Each line contains three

major elements - noun subj. (attribute of the "I") with 1st sing. suffix; part.; ܒ
+ noun (not in 4c; attribute of the Lord) with 3rd masc. sing. suffix. 3a and 4c,
which form the boundary of the stanza, open with noun subj. + 1st sing. suffix
followed by the part. 3b-4b has a part. initially, followed by noun subj. with
1st sing. suffix.

The nouns used in ref. to the "I" are both physical (3-4a) and abstract (4b-c)
as are those referring to the Lord. The latter are arranged in word-pairs, ܟܘܬܐ
- ܪܚܡܬܗ (3), ܪܚܡ - ܚܘܒܐ (4a-b). Apart from these, there are other connections by vocabulary in 4 - the closely associated roots ܝܗܒ and ܢܗܪ (4a-b), the
repetition of the root ܢܗܪ (4a-b), the word-pair ܢܗܪ - ܢܛܪ (4b-c).

Although a similar pattern has been noted for 3a and 4c and 3b-4b, the stanza should be divided into two parallel bicola, 3a-b (with initial chaismus) and
4a-b. By its parallelism with 3a, 4c provides the second element of the inclusio
for the stanza. Although it is not strictly parallel with 4a-b, nevertheless it follows easily from the bicolon and provides a finality to the stanza by its brevity
in relation to 3a-4b.

There is an alliterative effect in the two phrases, ܪܚܡܝ ܡܪܚܒ (4a-b) and
ܡܟܝܒܗ ܝܗܒ (4b).


Stanza 4 [5, 6]

The division of stanzas is clear with the shift in focus from the "I", although
the ܒܗ of 4c is carried over into the parallel bicolon in 5. If ܪܚܝܐ is accepted
as the noun rather than the part., then the bicolon is exactly parallel on the pattern: ܗ + noun subj. + ܒܗ + 3rd sing. masc. imperf. pass. verb.

There is a degree of parallelism in 6a-b by the semantic equivalence of the
concluding ܪܚܡܘ ܠܐ - ܪܚܠܝ ܠܐ. The link between the strophes is provided by
the word-pair ܪܘܝܗܒ - ܪܚܡܘ ܠܐܕ ܚܝ.

## ODE 41

1 ܢܫܒܚܘܢ ܠܡܪܝܐ ܟܠܗܘܢ ܝ̈ܠܘܕܘܗܝ
ܘܢܩܒܠܘܢ ܫܪܪܐ ܕܗܝܡܢܘܬܗ
2 ܘܢܬܝܕܥܘܢ ܠܘܬܗ ܒܢ̈ܘܗܝ

ܡܛܠ ܗܢܐ ܢܙܡܪ ܒܚܘܒܗ
3 ܚܝܝܢ ܒܡܪܝܐ ܒܛܝܒܘܬܗ
ܘܚܝܐ ܡܩܒܠܝܢ ܒܡܫܝܚܗ
4 ܘܝܘܡܐ ܓܝܪ ܪܒܐ ܐܢܗܪ ܠܢ
ܘܬܡܝܗ ܗܘ ܕܝܗܒ ܠܢ ܡܢ ܬܫܒ̈ܘܚܬܗ

5 ܢܗܘܐ ܗܟܝܠ ܟܠܢ ܐܟܚܕܐ ܒܫܡܗ ܕܡܪܝܐ
ܘܢܝܩܪܝܘܗܝ ܒܛܝܒܘܬܗ
6 ܘܢܢܗܪܢ ܐܦ̈ܝܢ ܒܢܘܗܪܗ
ܘܢܬܗܓܝܢ ܠܒ̈ܘܬܢ ܒܚܘܒܗ ܒܠܠܝܐ ܘܒܐܝܡܡܐ
7 ܢܕܘܨ ܡܢ ܕܚܢܗ ܕܡܪܝܐ

8 ܬܬܕܡܪܘܢ ܟܠܗܘܢ ܐܝܠܝܢ ܕܚܙܝܢ ܠܝ
ܡܛܠ ܕܡܢ ܓܢܣܐ ܐܚܪܢܐ ܐܢܐ
9 ܐܒܐ ܓܝܪ ܕܫܪܪܐ ܐܬܕܟܪܢܝ
ܗܘ ܕܩܢܝ ܡܢ ܒܪܫܝܬ
10 ܥܘܬܪܗ ܓܝܪ ܝܠܕܢܝ
ܘܡܚܫܒܬܐ ܕܠܒܗ

11 ܘܡܠܬܗ ܥܡܢ ܒܟܠܗ ܐܘܪܚܢ
ܦܪܘܩܐ ܕܡܚܐ
ܘܠܐ ܡܣܠܐ ܢܦ̈ܫܬܢ
12 ܓܒܪܐ ܕܐܬܡܟܟ
ܘܐܬܬܪܝܡ ܒܙܕܝܩܘܬܐ ܕܝܠܗ
13 ܒܪܗ ܕܡܪܝܡܐ ܐܬܚܙܝ
ܒܫܘܡܠܝܐ ܕܐܒܘܗܝ
14 ܘܢܘܗܪܐ ܕܢܚ ܡܢ ܡܠܬܐ
ܗܝ ܕܡܢ ܩܕܝܡ ܒܗ ܗܘܬ
15 ܡܫܝܚܐ ܒܫܪܪܐ ܚܕ ܗܘ
ܘܐܬܝܕܥ ܡܢ ܩܕܡ ܬܪ̈ܡܝܬܗ ܕܥܠܡܐ
16 ܕܡܚܐ ܢܦ̈ܫܬܐ ܠܥܠܡ ܒܫܪܪܐ ܕܫܡܗ

ܗܘܝܢ ܕܒܚܘܒܗ ܗܘܐ ܠܒܪܐ ܡ̇ܢ ܐܠܗ ܐܠܟ ܕܡܝܢܘ̇ ܠܗ

ܗܠܠܘܝܐ

---

1   Let all his babes glorify the Lord,
    and let them receive the truth of his faith,
2   and let his sons be known to him.

    Because of this, let us sing by his love.
3   We live in the Lord by his grace,
    and life we receive by his Messiah.
4   For a great day enlightened us,
    and amazing is he who gave us from his praises.

5   So let all of us agree together upon the name of the Lord,
    and let us honour him in his goodness,
6   and let our faces shine in his light,
    and let our hearts meditate on his love by night and by day.
7   Let us exult from the exultation of the Lord.

8   They will marvel, all those who see me,
    because from another race am I.
9   For the Father of truth remembered me,
    he who gained me from the beginning.
10   For his wealth brought me forth,
    and the thought of his heart.

11   And his Word (is) with us in all our way;
     the saviour who gives life,
     and does not reject our souls;
12   the man who humbled himself,
     and was lifted up by his own righteousness.
13   The Son of the Most High was seen
     in the perfection of his Father.
14   And light sprang forth from the Word,
     the one who was before in him.
15   The Messiah in truth is one.
     And he was known before the foundation of the world,
16   that he might give life to souls forever by the truth of his name.


A new hymn for the Lord from those who love him.


Alleluia.

NOTES TO THE TRANSLATION

1a-2a: There is disagreement between the Mss. concerning the person of the verbs. H has all the verbs in the 3rd pl. while N has 1a (ܢܣܬܟܠ) and 1b (ܢܣܒ) in the 1st pl. and 2a in the 3rd pl. The choice for H is made on the basis of the structure.

3a: N has ܚܝܘ (cf. Lattke 1979-86, vol. 1). Charlesworth bases his choice for H on a number of similarities with other Odes (1977, 141 n.6). One should also be aware that, although the verb ܚܝܐ may only occur in 38:15 apart from the N reading for this Ode, ܚܝܘܬܐ and ܠܚܝܘܬܐ are to be found as a word-pair in 23:1-2 and 31:6-7. The choice for H in this translation has been made on the basis of the close similarity between this verse and 5:3.

4b: N omits ܠ.

6a: For ܐܘܪ rendered in the sing., cf. Flemming; Ungnad and Staerk; Labourt and Batiffol; Diettrich 1911; Bauer 1964; Lattke 1979-86, vol. 2. The parallelism of ܐܘܪ and ܠܒܘܬܐ indicates that the pl. is the better choice.

9b: Cf. 19:10d.

10a: Diettrich (1911) transliterated ܡܐܬܪܐ into his translation and Lattke (1979-86, vol.2) translated with "Reichtum" but gave "UTHRA" in parenthesis. It is possible that the term should be so understood technically (cf. Drower and Macuch 347), especially if one compares this verse, where ܡܐܬܪܐ is parallel to ܡܒܠܗ ܟܕܒܝܠܘܬ and the imagery is that of birth, to 16:19, where ܡܠܬܗ is parallel to ܡܒܠܗ ܟܕܒܝܠܘܬ and the imagery is that of creation. With such a technical interpretation, the 'uthra of the Father of truth and his Word are one and the same.

15b: Although ܡܬܪܥܝܬ is pl., the phrase ܟܢܠܗܐ ܡܬܪܥܝܬ is used to translate the Greek καταβολὴ κόσμου or κτίσις κόσμου (Smith, R.P. 2: 3928).

ANALYSIS

Stanza 1 [1-2a]

1a and 2a are parallel on the pattern: imperf. verb + ܠ/ܬܢܠ + ܟܝܒܪ/substitute suffix + pl. noun subj. (children of the Lord) with 3rd masc. sing. suffix. The parallelism is strengthened by the word-pair ܟܐܢܠ - ܟܝܒ. The H reading of the 3rd pl. imperf. in 1a is supported by the parallelism of 1a and 2a and by ܝܡܐܢܐܠ ܢܩܡܠܒ as the subj. of 1a. It seems reasonable to continue the pattern of an initial 3rd pl. imperf. verb for 1b, which is inserted into the bicolon of 1a,2a.

Stanza 2 [2b, 3-4]

The change from the 3rd pl. subj. to 1st pl. in 2b indicates the division in stanzas. 2b is connected with 3 by the concluding pattern of ܒ + noun (attribute of the Lord) with 3rd masc. sing. suffix. However, it is closer syntactically to 5b-6b, by the initial 1st pl. imperf. verb as well as the concluding pattern of ܒ + noun (attribute of the Lord) with 3rd masc. sing. suffix and it may well be misplaced from an original position in stanza 3.

There is a degree of parallelism in 3 by the initial repetition of the root ܟܚ (according to H) and the concluding pattern of ܒ + noun (attribute of the Lord) with 3rd masc. sing. suffix as for 2b. The initial chiasmus of the bicolon is not exact, the pattern being indicated by the placement of the part. + 1st pl. suffix in relation to the phrase introduced by ܒ in 3a and the noun obj. of the verb in 3b.

4a-b seems to have little relation to the verses preceding and following it. There is parallelism by the use of the 3rd sing. masc. perf. verb + ܠܢ. It may be that the 3rd sing. masc. subjs. (the great day, the amazing one) are to be interpreted synonymously (cf. 7:23; 15:1-2).

Stanza 3 [5-7]

The major unifying feature of the stanza is the series of five initial imperf. verbs which focus on a 1st pl. group (5a-b and 7 with 1st pl. subj., 6a-b with pl. noun subj. + 1st pl. suffix). 5a and 7 form a parallel bicolon with an inserted tricolon, 5b-6.

5a and 7 are parallel on the pattern: 1st pl. imperf. verb ... prep. + sing. noun (attribute of the Lord) with 3rd sing. masc. suffix + ܕܡܪܝܐ. The tricolon, 5b-6, has a degree of parallelism on the pattern: 1st pl. imperf. verb ... ܒ + noun (attribute of the Lord) with 3rd sing. masc. suffix. 6a-b is more strictly parallel on the pattern: 1st pl. imperf. verb + noun (attribute of the "we") + 1st pl. suffix + ܒ + noun (attribute of the Lord) with 3rd sing. masc. suffix. The parallelism is enhanced by the word-pair ܐܦ̈ܐ - ܠܒܐ. The concluding phrase of 6b, ܒܠܠܝܐ ܘܒܐܝܡܡܐ, appears to be an addition influenced by Ps 1:2, ܘܒܢܡܘܣܗ ܢܬܗܓܐ ܐܝܡܡܐ ܘܠܠܝܐ.

The repetition of the root ܕܘܨ in 7 provides a strong conclusion to the stanza. A similar pattern with ܢܗܪ occurs in 6a.

There is alliteration with ܟ in 5a (ܗܟܝܠ ܟܠܢ ܐܟܚܕܐ), and with ܕ and ܨ in 7 (ܢܕܘܨ ܟܕ ܕܝܨܗ). 5b-6b has end rhyme: ܒܚܘܒܗ, ܒܢܘܗܪܗ, ܒܛܝܒܘܬܗ.

6-7 has a strikingly similar vocabulary to 40:4 (ܢܗܪ, ܐܦ̈ܐ, ܕܘܨ, ܕܝܨܐ), although the combination of the words is different.

Stanza 4 [8, 9-10]

The change from the 1st pl. to the 1st sing. speaker marks the division of the stanzas. Stanza 4 focusses on the kinship of the "I" with the Father because of his creation/birth (ܩܢܐ [cf. Deut 32:6], ܝܠܕ) from the Father. The motif provides a link back to the Lord's babes and sons in stanza 1.

Semantic emphasis upon the "I" in 8 is strengthened by the final position of ܠܝ in 8a and ܐܢܐ in 8b. 8a is strikingly similar to 28:8 (cf. the analysis of Ode 28 above). The repeated final sound in 8b (ܐܚܪܢܐ ܐܢܐ) brings a flavour of finality to the conclusion of the bicolon.

The structure of 9-10 is complex. 9a and 10a form a parallel bicolon on the pattern: noun subj. (ref. to the Father - explicitly in 9a, by pron. suffix in 10a)

+ ܬ݂ܒ + 3rd sing. masc. perf. verb + 1st sing. suffix. 9b is a modifying insertion into the bicolon which leads into 10a by the motif of creation/birth. The complexity arises in that 10a forms another parallel bicolon with 10b in a pivot pattern: A B // A', where A = noun subj. (attribute of the Lord; extended by the gen. expression in 10b) with 3rd sing. masc. suffix; B = ܥܠܘܗܝ (pivot).

Apart from the connection noted for 8a and 28:8, there are a links between this stanza and 4:3; 11:11; 23:3.

## Stanza 5 [11a, 11b-12, 13-14, 15-16a]

With 11 there is a change from the 1st sing. to a 1st pl. speaker. 11a functions as the introduction to the new section, which focusses on the central character of the Word. The inclusio for the stanza proper (11b-16a) is formed by the association of ܚܝ and ܬܫܒܘܚܬܐ in 11b-c and 16a.

The subjs. of 11b, 12a and 13a (ܦܪܘܩܐ, ܡܠܐܟܐ, ܕܡܪܝܐ ܕܒܗ) are in apposition with the subj. of 11a (ܡܠܬܗ). The bicola, 11b-c and 12a-b, are alternately parallel - 11b and 12a on the pattern: noun subj. (ref. to the Word) + ܗ + 3rd masc. sing. verb; 11c and 12b with ܗ + 3rd masc. sing. verb... 11b-c is parallel on the pattern: A B // B' C, where A = noun subj. of B and B'; B = 3rd sing. masc. part. act. ; C = noun obj. (understood for 11b). The parallelism is strengthened by the antithesis of ܚܝ and ܡܠܐ. 12a-b follows the same pattern as 11b-c: A B // B' C, where A = noun subj. of B and B'; B = 3rd sing. masc. pass. verb; C = phrase expressing manner. The parallelism is enhanced by the use of the antithetical word-pair ܪܚܩ - ܩܪܒ.

Although 13a is connected semantically to 11-12, there is a shift in style beginning with this verse. 11b-12 is in the form of a list: ...ܘ ܦܪܘܩܐ, ...ܘ ܡܠܐܟܐ. 13-14 takes up a more straightforward narrative style, although there is a reversion to the former pattern in 14b with ...ܘ ܗܘ referring to ܡܠܬܐ in 14a. The use of ܡܠܬܐ in 11a and 14a followed by the word/s in apposition on the pattern of noun + rel. pron., indicates the inclusio for the first three strophes of the stanza.

The confessional statement in 15a in the pres. tense makes an abrupt break in the narration in the past tense which continues thereafter in 15b. 14b and 15b are connected, both semantically and by the repetition of ܩܕܡ ܡܢ/ܡܢ ܩܕܡ.

The division into strophes is difficult here. The inclusio between 11a and 14a has already been discussed and it is also possible that there is an inclusio for the fourth strophe by the repetition of ܩܪܝܢ in 15a and 16a. Yet the connection between 14b and 15b, and more generally between 13-14 and 15b-16a by the narrative style in the past tense, suggests that 13-16a comprises the third strophe.

Stanza 6 [16b]

16b functions as a description, either of the total Ode or of some final section of it. It includes a confessional element by the declaration of love for the Lord. There is a connection with the opening line of the Ode by the repetition of the root ܚܒܒ.

## ODE 42

1 ܦܫܛܬ ܐܝܕܝ ܘܐܬܩܪܒܬ ܠܘܬ ܡܪܝ
ܡܛܠ ܕܡܬܚܬܐ ܕܐܝܕܝ ܐܬܗ ܗܝ
2 ܘܦܫܝܛܘܬܝ ܩܝܣܐ ܦܫܝܛܐ
ܕܐܬܬܠܝ ܥܠ ܐܘܪܚܗ ܕܬܪܝܨܐ

3 ܘܗܘܝܬ ܕܠܐ ܚܫܚܘ ܠܗܘܢ ܕܐܚܕܝܢ ܠܝ
ܡܛܠ ܕܐܬܛܫܝܬ ܠܗܘܢ ܕܠܐ ܐܚܕܘܢܝ ܗܘܘ ܠܝ
4 ܘܐܗܘܐ ܠܘܬ ܗܢܘܢ ܕܪܚܡܝܢ ܠܝ

5 ܡܝܬܘ ܟܠܗܘܢ ܪ̈ܕܘܦܝ
ܘܒܥܘܢܝ ܗܢܘܢ ܕܣܒܪܘ ܒܝ
ܡܛܠ ܕܚܝ ܐܢܐ
6 ܘܩܡܬ ܠܝ
ܘܐܝܬܝ ܒܡܢܗܘܢ
ܘܐܡܠܠ ܒܦܘܡ̈ܗܘܢ
7 ܐܣܠܘ ܓܝܪ ܠܐܝܠܝܢ ܕܪ̈ܕܦܝܢ ܠܗܘܢ

ܘܐܪܡܝܬ ܥܠܝܗܘܢ ܢܝܪܗ ܕܚܘܒܝ
8 ܐܝܟ ܕܪܥܗ ܕܚܬܢܐ ܥܠ ܟܠܬܐ
ܗܟܢܐ ܢܝܪܝ ܥܠ ܐܝܠܝܢ ܕܝܕܥܝܢ ܠܝ
9 ܘܐܝܟ ܓܢܘܢܐ ܕܡܬܦܫܛ ܒܒܝܬ ܚܬܢܐ
ܗܟܢܐ ܚܘܒܝ ܥܠ ܐܝܠܝܢ ܕܡܗܝܡܢܝܢ ܒܝ

10 ܠܐ ܐܣܬܠܝܬ ܐܝܟ ܐܣܬܒܪܬ
ܘܠܐ ܐܒܕܬ ܐܝܟ ܪܢܘ ܒܝ

11 ܫܝܘܠ ܚܙܬܢܝ ܘܐܬܬܘܝܬ
ܘܡܘܬܐ ܐܦܩܢܝ ܘܠܣܓܝܐܐ ܥܡܝ

12 ܚܠܐ ܘܡܪ̈ܪܐ ܗܘܝܬ ܠܗ
ܘܢܚܬܬ ܥܡܗ ܟܡܐ ܕܐܝܬ ܗܘܐ ܒܗ ܠܥܘܡܩܐ
13 ܘܪ̈ܓܠܐ ܘܪܫܐ ܐܪܦܝ
ܡܛܠ ܕܠܐ ܐܫܟܚ ܠܡܣܝܒܪܘ ܦܪ̈ܨܘܦܝ

ܘܥܒܕܬ ܟܢܘܫܬܐ ܕܚܝ̈ܐ ܒܡܝ̈ܬܝܗܘܢ 14
ܘܡܠܠܬ ܠܗܘܢ ܒܣܦܘ̈ܬܐ ܚܝ̈ܬܐ
ܡܛܠ ܕܠܐ ܢܗܘܐ ܒܛܠ ܦܬܓܡܝ
ܘܪܗܛܘ ܠܘܬܝ ܗܢܘܢ ܕܡܝܬܘ 15
ܘܩܥܘ ܘܐܡܪܘ
ܚܘܣ ܒܪܗ ܕܐܠܗܐ
ܘܥܒܕ ܥܡܢ ܐܝܟ ܒܚܢܢܘܬܟ 16
ܘܐܦܩܢ ܡܢ ܐܣܘܪ̈ܐ ܕܚܫܘܟܐ
ܘܦܬܚ ܠܢ ܬܪܥܐ ܕܒܗ ܢܦܘܩ ܠܘܬܟ 17
ܚܙܝܢ ܓܝܪ ܕܠܐ ܡܬܩܪܒ ܠܟ ܡܘܬܢ
ܢܬܦܪܩ ܐܦ ܚܢܢ ܥܡܟ 18
ܡܛܠ ܕܐܢܬ ܗܘ ܦܪܘܩܢ

ܐܢܐ ܕܝܢ ܫܡܥܬ ܩܠܗܘܢ 19
ܘܣܡܬ ܒܠܒܝ ܗܝܡܢܘܬܗܘܢ
ܘܣܡܬ ܥܠ ܪܫܗܘܢ ܫܡܝ 20
ܡܛܠ ܕܒܢ̈ܝ ܚܐܪ̈ܐ ܐܢܘܢ
ܘܕܝܠܝ ܐܢܘܢ

ܗܠܠܘܝܐ

---

1 I extended my hands and drew near towards my Lord;
because the stretching out of my hands is his sign,
2 and my extension (is) the extended wood,
that was hung up upon the way of the upright one.

3 And I was useless to them who knew me;
because I will hide myself from them who did not lay hold of me,
4 and I will be near them who love me.

5 All my persecutors died,
and they who hoped in me sought me;
because I am living,
6 and I stood myself up.
And I am with them,
and I will speak by their mouths,
7 for they have rejected those who persecute them.

And I laid upon them the yoke of my love.

8  As the bridegroom's arm upon the bride,
   so is my yoke upon those who know me.

9  And as the bridal bed spread out in the house of the bridal couple,
   so (is) my love upon those who have faith in me.

10 I was not rejected although I was considered so,
   and I did not perish although they thought so about me.

11 Sheol saw me and was shattered,
   and Death vomitted me up and many with me.

12 Vinegar and bitterness was I to it,
   and I descended with it as far as its depth.

13 And the feet and the head it let loose,
   because it was not able to endure my face.

14 And I made a congregation of living among its dead,
   and I spoke to them by living lips,
   because my word will not fail.

15 And they who had died ran towards me,
   and cried out and said,
   Have compassion on us, Son of God,

16 and do with us according to your gentleness,
   and bring us forth from the chains of darkness,

17 and open the gate for us by which we might issue forth towards you.
   For we see that our death does not come near you.

18 Let us also be saved with you,
   because you are our saviour.

19 Then I myself heard their voice,
   and set in my heart their faith,

20 and set upon their head my name;
   because they are free,
   and they are mine.

   Alleluia.

NOTES TO THE TRANSLATION

2a: "Wood" may well be a metaphor for "cross" (Charlesworth 1977) or for "tree" (Harris 1911a). It seems preferable to leave the lit. translation since either would be a plausible interpretation. Most of the translations indicate the repetition of the root ܩܝܣܐ, with the exception of Charlesworth 1977 ("common cross") and Lattke 1979-86, vol. 2 ("richtige Holz").

3a: The Mss. are problematical. H omits ...ܠܗܘܢ ܕܢܒܥܐ. As McNeil points out, neither H nor N makes sense (1980, 194), but to follow H as he suggests does not do justice to the text. Some translations emend the text from N for 3a with a negative (Charlesworth 1977, Freeman, Barnstone). It would appear that the problem with N is that the negative which belongs in 3a has been erroneously transferred to 3b. That the verb ܢܣܒ should be interpreted positively in this Ode is clear from 8. The translation of ܐܚܕ by "possess" (Charlesworth 1977) is ambiguous, an obvious attempt to mollify the difficulty with the text. The negative meaning of the verb in this context is similar to its usage in Jn 7:44 and 10:39. Bauer's reference to Jn 1:5 for the meaning of "nichtergreifen" as opposed to "liebevolle Aneignung" is much weaker (1964, 623 n.5).

4: *Contra* Charlesworth (1977) who reads H as ܪܚܡܘܢܝ, it appears that the copyist has managed to squeeze in the ܘ.

12a: H has ܘܒܪܝܟ.

13b: H has ܐܫܟܚ. The context demands the sing.

14b: H has ܠܡܘܬܐ.

19b: ܣܒܪ ܒܠܒܐ = to think of, consider (Smith, J.P. 1903, 233b).

19b-20a: H has omitted ܗܘܐܬ ܒܠܕ ܣܒܪܘ ܘܣܒܪܬܗܘܢ. Lattke (1979-86, vol. 2) mistakenly reads H as ܣܒܪܬܗ rather than ܣܒܪܬܐ.

ANALYSIS

Stanza 1 [1-2] (cf. the excursus following the analysis of Ode 27)

The stanza functions as a liturgical introduction. That it is distinct from the material which follows is clear from the vocabulary frequency table. The key words/roots ܐܝܝ and ܦܫܛ occur only in this stanza.

There are a number of close links between each of the four lines. ܐܝܝ is repeated in 1a and 1b and ܦܫܛ and ܡܬܚ are synonymous. ܦܫܛ is repeated in 1a and 2a. 1b and 2a are parallel on the pattern: subj. with 1st sing. suffix + compl. The parallelism is strengthened by the semantic equivalence of ܡܬܚ, ܐܝܝ and ܦܫܛ. 2a and 2b are connected by the word-pair ܦܫܛ - ܝܬ, as well as by the ref. of the cl. in 2b to ܩܘܡ in 2a.

1a and 2a have internal parallelism - 1a by the doubling of the pattern of 1st sing. perf. verb + noun + 1st sing. suffix; 2a by the repetition of the root ܦܫܛ.

1a and 1b are of similar length (9 and 10 syllables), as are 2a and 2b (7 and 8 syllables). 2a and 2b have an end rhyme (ܦܫܛ ܩܘܡ, ܝܬ).

Stanza 2 [3-4]

Even without the emendation of N (the negative in 3b transferred to 3a), there is a strict parallelism for the three lines of the stanza on the pattern: 1st sing. verb + ܠ/ܗܢ + ܗ ܗܢܘ + 3rd pl. part. act. + ܠ. If the emendation is accepted, then 3a-b is semantically parallel (those who do not know the "I" = those who lay hold of him). 3a-b provides the antithesis to 4.

Apart from the difficulty with the Mss., there is a semantically disturbing change in tense from the past in 3a to the future followed by past in 3b and the future followed by pres. (part.) in 4.

Stanza 3 [5-7a]

The inclusio for the stanza is indicated by the repetition of the root ܪܕܦ in 5a and 7a. Semantically, 5a introduces a new action, although it may be a result of what is previously described in 3.

5a-b is parallel on the pattern: 3rd pl. perf. verb + 3rd pl. subj. + descriptive element (ref. to the 3rd pl. subj.). There is antithesis between those who persecute and those who trust.

With 5c there is a change in subj. from 3rd pl. to 1st sing. 5c and 6a are parallel on the pattern: conj. + sing. verb (subj. is 1st sing.) + copula/dir. obj. (focus on the 1st sing.). The verbs ܟܡܕ and ܚܘ combine to form a delayed antithesis to ܒܪܬ in 5a.

6b-c is parallel on the general pattern: 1st sing. verb + prep. + 3rd pl. suffix/noun with 3rd pl. suffix.

The subj. returns to the 3rd pl. with 7a, so that the 1st sing. subj. section of 5c-6c is enclosed by the two sections (5a-b, 7a) with a 3rd pl. subj. 5b and 7a have a degree of parallelism: 3rd pl. perf. verb + 3rd pl. subj./obj. + ܘ + 3rd pl. verb (ref. to preceding subj./obj.) + prep. + pron. suffix.


Stanza 4 [7b, 8-9]

Although 7b may be linked semantically with 7a, it functions as the introduction to the two similes in 8-9. Each of the two nouns which form the obj. in 7b (ܚܒܘܥ, ܚܝܘ) is repeated, in the same order, as a major element in the second (ܚܒܡ) line of the similes, ܚܝܘ in 8b and ܚܒܘܥ in 9b.

8-9 is alternately parallel. 8a and 9a follow the pattern: ܐܝܟ + noun subj. + ܘ with noun qualifying the subj. + prep. and phrase (ܒܪܬܐ becomes ܒܪܬ by haplological ellipsis of the syllable; Brockelmann 1951, 42). The parallelism is emphasised by the imagery connected with marriage in both lines.

8b and 9b are more strictly parallel: ܚܒܡ + noun subj. + 1st sing. suffix + ܘ ܐܠܝ ܠܥ + 3rd pl. part. act. + prep. with 1st sing. suffix. The parallelism is strengthened by the word-pair ܥܠ - ܐܪܝ and by the associated words ܚܝܘ, ܚܒܘܥ.

ܠܥ occurs frequently in the stanza (7b, 8a, 8b, 9b).


Stanza 5 [10]

Both stanzas 5 and 6 function as summary introductions to the detail in stanza 7. The division has been made between them because of the change in the main subj. from 1st sing. to 3rd sing., the clear change in the syntactic pattern, and the semantic change from the rather abstract to the more detailed and concrete (in terms of the personification).

10a and 10b are parallel on the pattern: ܠܐ + 1st sing. perf. verb + ܐܦ + verbal expression. With regard to the latter, the use of the 1st sing. Ethpeel in 10a and the 1st sing. suffix with ܠܥ in 10b effectively establishes the "I" as the object of the equivalent actions of considering and thinking. The parallelism of the bicolon is strengthened by the word-pair ܚܠܐ - ܐܪܒ. For one who is persecuted and appears to die but does not in reality, cf. The Second Treatise of the Great Seth 55, 9-56, 19 (Facs. ed. 7: 61-2; Wisse 1984a, 332).

## Stanza 6 [11]

11a and 11b are parallel initially on the pattern: noun subj. + 3rd sing. perf. verb + 1st sing. pron. suffix ... Each line has internal parallelism by the double pattern of two fem. sing. perf. verbs in 11a and two objs. in 11b. The word-pair, ܟܬܒܝܢ - ܠܘܼܚ, strengthens the parallelism of the lines.

## Stanza 7 [12-13]

This stanza flows easily from stanza 6 since the image of the "I" as vinegar/ bitterness descending into the depths of Sheol/Death provides the background for the description in 11b of Death's vomiting up the "I".

12a and 12b are linked by the terrace effect of the pattern of 1st sing. perf. verb + prep. + masc. sing. suffix (ref. to ܟܬܒܝܢ), which occurs at the end of 12a and is repeated immediately at the beginning of 12b. The general pattern of verb + prep. + 3rd sing. suffix continues into the second cl. of 12b.

The four lines of the stanza may be divided into two bicola according to the 1st sing. subj. in 12a-b and the 3rd sing. masc. subj. in 13a-b. 13a and 13b are also linked by the cl. in 13b which refers to 13a.

12a and 13a have a similar pattern of double noun compl./obj. + verb. The relative brevity of the lines (7 and 6 syllables respectively) in comparison to 12b (10 syllables) and 13b (11 syllables) enhances the connection. The use of the word-pair ܠܓܝ - ܪܓܠܝ in 13a (denoting the physical extremities of the body) expresses merismus. It is the whole person which is released, whether one interprets that literally as the "I" who speaks or metaphorically as the "I" and the congregation of the living (= the head and members; cf. 17:15).

There is an alliterative effect by the repetition of ܚ in 13a.

## Stanza 8 [14]

Although the stanza is bound semantically to some extent with the preceding one by the events taking place with ref. to Sheol/Death, 14a introduces a new aspect of the action and a new group of characters (prepared for by the "many" in 11b), so that the focus on the confrontation between Sheol/Death and the "I" in stanza 7 changes to a focus on the "I" and the group of "its dead" in this stanza.

There is some connection with stanza 7 by the pattern in 13b and 14c of a concluding cl. introduced by ܟܕ ܡܠܠ + verbal expression + concluding noun (obj. in 13b, subj. in 14c) with 1st sing. suffix.

14a and 14b are parallel on the general pattern: 1st sing. perf. verb + obj./ indir. obj. (ref. to the congregation) + ܒ with noun obj. The connection is strengthened by the use of the antithetical word-pair ܡܘܬܐ - ܚܝܐ in the phrases introduced by ܒ. The same word-pair creates antithesis within 14a.

The cl. in 14c refers to 14b. 14c is a concluding confessional statement for the stanza.

There is repetition of ܠ and ܕ/ܠܝ in 14b ( ܡܠܝܬ ܠܗܘܢ ) and 14c ( ܡܠܠ ܡܠܠܬ ... ܟܕܝ).

## Stanza 9 [15a-b, 15c-18]

With 15a-b the subj. changes from the 1st sing. to the 3rd pl. There is a connection with 14a by the equivalence of ܡܘܬܐ and ܚܝܐ ܢܘܚ. The bicolon comprises a series of three 3rd pl. perf. verbs, and acts as the introduction to the direct speech which constitutes the major part of the stanza.

The unifying feature of the second strophe (15c-18) is the series of petitions in 15c-17a on the pattern: 2nd sing. imper. verb + 1st pl. suffix/prep. with 1st pl. suffix.

Each of the lines in 15c-17a contains one cl., with the exception of 17a which contains two. Charlesworth (1977) divided 17a after ܐܝܕ but there is no basis for this in N or H. Moreover there are other factors to be considered. As one line, the length of 17a follows well from 16b (10 syllables each). More importantly, there is an inclusio formed by ܦܬܚ in 16b and ܦܬܚ ܠܢ in 17a. Chiasmus is produced by the 2nd sing. masc. verb with 1st pl. obj. in 16b and the 1st pl. verb with 2nd sing. masc. obj. in 17a. 16b and 17a are also linked semantically by the equivalence of ܚܒܠܝܢ ܘܐܣܘܪܐ and ܐܝܕ as the forces which bind those who are speaking.

17b is semantically ambiguous and its syntactic function thereby unclear. If one interprets that the "I" is not affected adversely by the death state of the "we", then 17b functions as a summary for 15c-17a; that is, 17b presents the reason for the possibility of making the petitions to the "I". If 17b is taken more literally as meaning that the death state of the "we" prevents them from approaching the "I", then 17b functions more as a summary for 16b-17a; that is, it presents the reason for the opening and bringing forth actions of the "I".

18a contains the final petition for the stanza, the 1st pl. subj. in contrast to the 2nd sing. masc. subj. of 15c-17a. 18a and 18b are parallel with chiasmus by the placement of the personal prons. (1st pl. verb + prep. with 2nd sing. masc. suffix in 18a; 2nd sing. masc. verb + noun compl. with 1st pl. suffix in 18b) and by the repetition of ܦܪܩ at the beginning of 18a and at the conclusion of 18b.

There are a number of combinations of vocabulary in this stanza found elsewhere in Odes with a similar thematic content: ܐܣܝܘܬܐ with ܚܝ̈ܢܘ (21:2, 3); ܦܪܩ with ܐܝܕܐ (17:8).

Stanza 10 [19-20]

The direct speech reported by the "I" comes to an end with 18b. The division of stanzas is further indicated by the use of ܝܢ and the initial emphatic pronoun ܐܢܐ which stresses the change to the 1st sing. subj. from the previous focus on 1st pl. and 2nd sing. masc. prons.

19a follows logically from the detail of 15b. 19a and 19b have a degree of parallelism on the pattern: 1st sing. perf. verb ... noun obj. with 3rd pl. masc. suffix.

19b and 20a are parallel on the pattern: ܘܣܡܬ + prep. with noun obj. + pron. suffix (1st sing. in 19b, 3rd pl. masc. in 20a) + noun obj. of the verb + pron. suffix (3rd pl. masc. in 19b, 1st sing. in 20a). There is chiasmus by the placement of the pron. suffixes. The parallelism is strengthened by the repetition of ܣܡܬ and by the word-pair ܡܚܘܒܝܗܘܢ - ܚܘܒܝ.

20b and 20c are equivalent confessional statements, which repeat the structure of cls. introduced by ܕ ܡܛܠ to conclude a stanza (cf. 13b, 14c, 18b). The bicolon is parallel on the pattern: ܡܛܠ ܕ (understood for 20c) + descriptive expression + 3rd pl. masc. verb/copula.

One of the important themes of the Ode is the struggle against and victory over Death, emphasised by the frequently recurring root ܡܘܬ (x 5).

III. PATTERNS OF VOCABULARY, SYNTAX, AND IMAGERY:
IMPLICATIONS FOR INTERPRETATION AND FOR THE GROUPING OF
ODES

The chapter comprises two major sections. The first uses the analysis in the previous chapter to indicate how the identification of patterns of vocabulary and syntax is basic to the interpretation of the text. Section b suggests some preliminary steps towards the grouping of Odes according to patterns of vocabulary, syntax, small forms and imagery.

a. PATTERNS OF VOCABULARY AND SYNTAX AND THE INTERPRETATION OF THE TEXT

The patterns of vocabulary and syntax represent the most basic level of relationship in the text between words, lines, strophes, and stanzas, and between Odes. Although the related levels of semantics and sound are also indispensable to the whole process of interpretation, the analysis of the former level is fundamental in that process. Attempting to interpret the text on the semantic level without prior analysis to identify patterns of vocabulary and syntax or, worse, allowing a concern with semantics to cut across that more fundamental level, may well result in a poorer if not incorrect interpretation. This is well-illustrated by G. Kittel's analysis of 34:1-5b, where serious distortion of the clearly identifiable structure of 1-3 and 4-5b is caused by the attempt to accommodate an (ill-informed) interpretation of the use of ܪܚܡܬܐ (1914, 125-6).

Kittel's difficulty is resolved by a proper knowledge of the concept of imitation/likeness in the Odes. Yet, even if this were not the case, it is preferable to allow apparent ambiguity to remain rather than distort the basic foundation of a clearly identifiable pattern built on syntactic and vocabulary relationships.

1. Single terms - vocabulary frequency (cf. Appendix A)

Roots/words which occur with the greatest frequency in an Ode may indicate a central image/motif. This is well illustrated by the repetition of ܝܫܪ (x 10) and the synonymous root ܚܒ (x 2) in Ode 3 (motif of love); and the use of ܥܒܕ (x 9) in Ode 16 (motif of work).

The discrete limitation of multiple repetitions of key words/roots to a certain section of an Ode can indicate the division of stanzas (ܚܠܦ [x 3] and ܐܬܪܐ [x 2] in 4:1-3b [stanza 1]; ܓܙܪ [x 3] in 11:1-3a [stanza 1]); the division of groups of stanzas (ܚܠܒ [x 5] in stanzas 1 and 2 of Ode 19; ܝܠܕ [x 4] in stanzas 3, 4, and 5 of Ode 19); and the division of sub-odes (ܝܕܥ [x 7] in 18:9-15 [sub-ode 2]).

-ܕܝܠ occurs 25 times in the Odes. Isolated use of the element is not noteworthy, but the frequency of use in 8:14-20 (x 6) and 26:1-7 (x 6) is significant for the analysis of style and the question of sources.

## 2. Association of vocabulary items

### 2.1 Initial elements of lines

The identification of a pattern to the initial elements of lines indicates the division of these lines from the remainder of the Ode and the limits of their relatedness. Perhaps the best example of this for the collection is Ode 34, stanza 1. Only a minority of scholars seem to have recognised the structure of the stanza to some limited degree (Ungnad and Staerk; Bruston 1912b; Lattke 1979-86, vol. 1; Carmignac 1986).

### 2.2 Word-pairs/associated words in phrases (cf. Appendices B and C)

Where parallel word-pairs occur frequently, apart from the expected synonyms (e.g. ܚܒܠ - ܐܒܕ, 24:7b,8a,9a; 31:1-2; 33:2,9) or antonyms (e.g. ܢܦܠ - ܩܘܡ, 6:16; 12:6; 18:2b,3b), the recognition of the relationship between the elements can be important to the understanding of the theology of the collection (e.g. ܚܝܐ - ܦܪܘܩ, 8:22c-d; 17:15; 26:9 [with ܚ̈ܝܐ]; 34:6; 38:16) or for the analysis of the imagery (e.g. ܠܒܐ - ܣܦܘ̈ܬܐ, 16:2; 21:8; 30:5; 40:2).

Similarly, identification of a recurring association of roots/words (including non-parallel word-pairs; cf. Schökel 62), apart from the usual connections (e.g. ܚܝܐ and ܡ̈ܝܐ, 5:4,5; 13:1; 15:3; 16:9), can be invaluable for the study of imagery, theology, or style (e.g. ܚ̈ܝܐ and ܡܘܬܐ ܠܐ, 10:2; 11:7; 15:10; 28:6; 31:7; 38:3; 40:6; ܦܬܓܡܐ and ܫܪܪܐ, 8:8; 12:1,3,12; 24:9,10; 32:2; ܗܘܐ ܠ ܦܘܪܩܢܐ, 11:3; 28:10; 35:2; 38:3 [ܡܐܢܐ ܕܦܘܪܩܢܐ]).

Placement of a word-pair can be significant. The antithesis in 17:10 is strengthened by the close proximity of the polar word-pair ܐܣܪ (concludes 10a) - ܦܬܚ (follows immediately in 10b after the initial conjunction).

That the recognition of a word-pair can be crucial to text work is well illustrated in 11:16f. Charlesworth objects to ΕΓΕΛΩΝ on the grounds that fruits do not laugh (1977, 57 n. 33) and suggests that the Syriac *Grundschrift* ܢܟܘܚ has been incorrectly translated into Greek. He has failed to recognise the word-pair θάλλω - γελάω in 11:16e-f which occurs also in 11:12b (ref. to the "I" as the earth, "sprouting and laughing by its fruits").

3. Patterns of syntax

In the interpretation of the text, the implications of patterns of grammatical construction (syntactic parallelism) take precedence over what might appear to be general semantic connections.

Charlesworth (1977, 99 n. 4) asserts that ܦܪܚܬܐ in 24:4a is a reference back to the dove of 1a. However, the syntactic structure of 3-4, together with the word-pairs which build merismus (ܠܬܚܬܐ - ܠܥܠܐ; ܦܪܚܬܐ - ܪܚܫܐ), indicate that ܦܪܚܬܐ is to be interpreted, not as "the bird" (i.e. specific ref. to the previously mentioned dove), but in the general sense of "flying creature", in parallel with "creeping thing" (cf. Gen 1:20, 21...).

The recognition of the syntactic pattern in 19:10b-11c demands the "relocation" of ܐܝܟ ܓܒܪܐ at the conclusion of 9b, thus changing the whole focus of the discussion of the meaning of this phrase.

The identification of syntactic patterns between lines which are not adjacent provides a more-informed basis for interpretation. Thus the shared grammatical pattern of 3:6a and 7d underlines the antithesis between being a stranger and being a son; the parallelism of 36:2d and 4a brings into question a division of the Ode which allocates 3-8 to speech by the Christ (Harris and Mingana vol. 2; Aune 1983, 297; Charlesworth 1977); the syntactic relationship of 39:10a-b and 11b-12 indicates the inclusio for the stanza; the parallelism of 6:8d and 10a supports the interpretation of ܠܗܝܟܠܐ as a dative expression ("to the temple").

Patterns may also be found across Odes. Similar associations of vocabulary items occur, for example, in 11:6-7 and 30:1-3; 11:8b-12a and 15:6-8; 17:4c-5 and 38:4-5; 21:1-2 and 25:1-2; 28:8a and 41:8a; 40:4 and 41:6-7). Grammatical constructions with the same vocabulary items, when frequent, are easily identified as formula sayings (e.g. 27:1-3; 35:7; 37:1; 42:1-2). Others have not been so obvious to scholars. Thus 12:8b and 16:19, which share the same grammatical pattern and basic vocabulary, require a similar interpretation (*contra* Harris and Mingana vol. 2; Greßmann 1924; Charlesworth 1977; Emerton; Carmignac 1986).

4. Patterns of personal pronouns, tense/mood

The use and change of personal pronouns and changes in tense/mood will be discussed in some detail in Section b. The recognition of these patterns can often be helpful for interpretation in combination with some other pattern.

The change from the 1st sing. pronouns to 1st pl. in 14:9c-10, together with the inclusio between stanza 1 (1-2) and stanza 4 (9a-b) by the repetition of the ... ܟܘܡ... ܝܪܟ form, supports the interpretation of 9c-10 as an addition.

In Ode 41, the pattern of past tense is broken abruptly by the present tense in 15a. Its formula-like statement sets it apart as an interjection - either as a response or as a later addition.

The division of stanzas 1 (1-3) and 2 (4-8) in Ode 18 is indicated by a change from past indicative (section of description) to imperative (petitions) and from the description of the Lord in the 3rd person to an address to the Lord in the 2nd person.

b. GROUPING ODES ACCORDING TO PATTERNS OF VOCABULARY, SYNTAX, SMALL FORMS, AND IMAGERY

In the history of research, the form-categorisation of an Ode or section of an Ode has been based, for the most part, on the imagery/motifs (baptismal hymn, redeemer Ode, victory song, ...) or the use of personal pronouns (Individual Ode, Gemeindelied, ...).

Multiple categorisations of a single Ode by the same scholar are rare. Exceptions are found in the work of R. Abramowski (cf. e.g. Ode 12 as Lehrdichtung [50]; 12:1-3 as Individualode [52] and 12:4ff as Gemeindelied [51]) and Blaszczak (cf. e.g. Ode 11 as an Individual Confession Ode, sub-group Ascent Ode [77] and Hellenistic mission speech [83-5]).

Although Blaszczak (77-99) and Schille (47-8, 79-85, 90-1, 100-1, 114-5, 128-33) proclaim their intention to investigate both formal aspects and motifs in the grouping of Odes, in practice the emphasis is squarely on the latter, the motif or thematic complexes marking, in general, the fundamental differentiation between the various categories. As Blaszczak himself suggests, such a reliance on imagery or theological motif as a basis for grouping Odes cannot produce as clear or precise a result as a reliance on form-critical categories (76-7).

The discussion in this section will focus on a number of different features by which an Ode might be related to other Odes. For this reason, there will be no final list in which Odes are allotted to one specific group. The first three sub-sections proceed from the analysis in Chapter II: the use and change of personal pronouns; the smaller forms (petition, exhortation/invitation...); and the small structured sections. The final sub-section makes some preliminary suggestions for the grouping of Odes according to imagery/motif.

The question of the setting of the Odes will not be a major concern of the discussion, but a few points may be made in conjunction with the work on categories. The setting in which an Ode is to be used may serve to emphasise one of the groups to which it may be allocated over another. Within a community setting, an Ode may be chosen for singing/reciting because of a particular theme which has been established for the setting. Within a broader action of the community, an Ode may be chosen according to the part of the action in which it is to occur (petition, reflection, gathering, conclusion, and so on). Thus the dominant category for an Ode may be a fairly fluid thing. On the other hand, if a community uses an Ode exclusively in one setting, perhaps because of its particular complex of images, then the grouping of that Ode according to its imagery may always take precedence for the community over some other equally valid grouping by form.

Odes might also be selected according to who is to sing/recite - the community, a group, a solo singer, or combinations of these. Thus, in Ode 17, one person might sing 1-15, the community responding with 16; in Ode 33, a singer or the community might take the first section (1-5), setting the scene of the drama, while another singer might take the section for the Perfect Virgin (6-13). In discussing the "antiphonal or responsory character of the Odes", Aune demonstrates a similar possibility for Ode 41, with the change of speaker from 1st pl. in 1-7 to 1st sing. in 8-10 and back to 1st pl. in 11 (1982, 443).

As well as the sections identified by a specific change of speaker, the community might well be involved in singing responses like the doxologies (the more frequent would be easily remembered - "glory and honour to his name" [16:20; 20:10] or "glory and greatness of beauty to his name" [18:16]) or a series of responses such as 10b, 11b, 12b, 13b, 14b, and 15b in Ode 5.

1. Use and change of personal pronouns for speaker/s, "audience", and subject matter

## 1.1 The speaker

### 1.1.1 The dominant speaker as "I" (21 of the 41 Odes, 51.2% of the collection)

In Odes 1, 5, 10, 11, 15, 17, 21, 25, 27, 28, 29, 35, 36, and 37, virtually the entire Ode (over 90%)[1] comprises speech by the "I" to a variety of "audiences" about relationship with the Most High/Messiah and/or about events where the "I" has acted or has been the object of action.

The major portion (over 50%, but under 90%) of the following Odes comprises speech by the "I" as outlined in the preceding paragraph: 3 (72%), 8 (57.7%), 9 (59.3%), 14 (89.5%), 38 (57.6%), 40 (73.3%), 42 (84.1% [not including the reported speech]).

### 1.1.2 "We" as the dominant speaker (1 of the 41 Odes, 2.4% of the collection)

Ode 41 comprises speech by the "we" for 50% of its material.

### 1.1.3 No identified speaker (6 out of 41 Odes, 14.6% of the collection)

There is no identified speaker for Odes 23, 24, 30, 32, 34, 39.

### 1.1.4 Assumed speakers

Although there may be no speaker specified for much of an Ode, there may be some reference in part to an "I" or "we". The "I" is assumed as speaker in Odes 7, 12, 16, 18, 19, 20, 22, 26, 31; the "we" for Odes 4 and 13. The speaker is both "I" and "we" in Ode 6.

### 1.1.5 Speakers in reported speech

Reported speech occurs in four of the Odes. The "I" of the preceding material is the speaker in 11:18-24 and 38:10b; the Perfect Virgin, in 33:6-13; Truth, in 38:10d-14; and the dead, in 42:15c-18.

---

[1] The percentages are calculated on the number of lines in which the feature occurs in comparison to the total number of lines in the Ode, according to my edition.

1.2 The audience

Percentages are of little assistance here. The community is still the "audience", whether it is addressed explicitly for the major portion of the Ode, as in Ode 9 (85.2%), or only in a final exhortation, as in Ode 3 (4%).

1.2.1 The audience of the "I"

The Messiah/Most High: Odes 1, 5, 14, 18, 22, 25, 40.

The community: Odes 3, 7, 8, 9, 17 (from the final doxology), 20, 31.

1.2.2 The audience of the "we"

The Lord: Odes 4, 17 (only verse 16).

The community: Odes 13, 41.

1.2.3 The audience of the impersonal Odes

The community: Odes 23, 30, 34, 39.

1.2.4 Unspecified audience

Of the "I": Odes 10, 11, 12, 15, 16, 19, 21, 26, 27, 28, 29, 35, 36, 37,   38, 42.

Of the "I"/"we": Ode 6.

Of the impersonal Odes: Odes 24, 32, 33.

1.3 The "I" Odes

The identification of the "I" in the Odes is a continuing problem. The basic question has been, "Is the 'I' the Odist or the Messiah figure or some sort of mystical union of the two?" This is, even at first glance, a little simplistic since there are other characters to be considered - Grace, Truth, the Perfect Virgin - and the relationship of these characters to the Messiah figure has yet to be satisfactorily clarified. The most popular approach to the problem has been to suggest that, because the Odist is so closely united to the Messiah figure, when he speaks, it is as if the two characters merge mystically somehow (cf. e.g. Greßmann 1913, 212-3).

In his attempt to assign Odes to either the Odist or to the Saviour figure, Langbrandtner asserts the difficulty of making a distinction between the two:

> "Ganz so deutlich... ist der Unterschied zwischen dem Glaubenden, dem adoptierten Sohn, und Christus nicht. Im Gegenteil, die Oden stellen beide auf eine Stufe und bemühen sich zugleich, die Trennungslinien zu verwischen, damit beide Gestalten in eins fließen. Daher ist es nicht immer leicht, manchmal unmöglich, den Sprecher der Oden mit dem einen oder dem anderen zu identifizieren." (165)

When the concept of the mystical union of Odist and Messiah figure is taken to extremes, it tends to override the more objective conclusions one may make about an Ode. Blaszczak, for example, suggests that in Ode 17 "the Odist sets his own individual experience against the background of the <u>Descensus</u>" (96; Langbrandtner, too, assigns this Ode to the Odist [164]). However, Ode 17 is the clearest example of speech by the Messiah figure as the "I". The Odist, who must be logically included in the "our" of 17:16, cannot be the "I" who has been speaking in the Ode proper, the one addressed as "our head the Lord Messiah".

The union of Odist/community and the Messiah figure/Most High is certainly attested in the Odes but this motif should not be given emphasis to the exclusion of all other considerations when considering the style of the Odes. An Ode which uses "I" for the Messiah figure/Most High need not necessarily indicate that the Odist is thereby to be identified with the "I", producing a kind of conglomerate speaker of the Messiah figure/Most High and himself. The use of such a style might be a quite deliberate attempt by the Odist to express a direct dialogue between the Messiah figure/Most High and the community which might be more psychologically effective than some other style in inducing certain reactions in the community.

Ode 17 is the clearest indication of the "I" as the Messiah figure. By a variety of clues, other Odes suggest that certain "I" sections do not belong to the Odist. In 8:10-21, for example, the imagery associated with the "I" appears to refer to the Most High (most notably in 16). Such a point of view is supported by the introduction in 8:8, "hear the Word of truth, and receive the knowledge of the Most High". Thus the "I" within an Ode may have more than one referent.

The analysis of the structure of the individual Odes in Chapter II can assist in identifying the limits of sections accorded to a particular referent. Together with the consideration of the structure, the process of allocating the "I" to various referents will depend upon a thorough understanding of the system of interrelated imagery which operates in the Odes. Above all, the establishment of criteria for the process of identification must not be hampered by preconceptions of what might be theologically appropriate material for a particular referent[1].

### 1.3.1 The "I" Odes as Individual Odes

The predominance of the "I" as speaker in an Ode does not thereby indicate that the Ode should be classified necessarily as an Individual Ode. Firstly, there are "I" Odes in which there is a reference, perhaps only in one line, to the Odist as a community member by the use of "our" or "us" (14:9c-10; 18:7). This raises the question as to whether what the "I" sings might be regarded as exclusively individual material or if, rather, the experience or action could just as easily be applied by the community to themselves.

Secondly, although the "I" might be the dominant/assumed speaker, the community may in fact be the real focus of attention, as in Ode 20. The "I" is assumed as speaker from the introduction (1-2, 12.5%) but the community is specifically addressed in 5-9 (62.5%), 50% of the Ode comprising imperatives addressed to the community. Similarly, there are "I" Odes in which the "I" material serves as no more than an introduction to description which focusses on some third party (cf. Ode 19).

An investigation of the predominant tenses in the "I" material can be helpful in the identification of the proper focus in the "I" Odes. Some Odes describe action in the past which seems to be more specific to an individual (cf. the past tense as "alienating" of the subject, Goodman 195) than the material of a more general kind (petitions about protection and so on) with a present or future aspect which might validly be sung by the community out of their own experience. It is a difference really between what is mediated to the community and what might be immediate to the community.

Of the Odes with a dominant/assumed "I" speaker, Odes 1, 3, 5, 9, 14, 16, 20, 26, and 40 are in the present tense; Odes 7, 8, 12, 18, and 27 have a mixture of present and past; Odes 10, 11, 15, 17, 19, 21, 22, 25, 28, 29, 31, 35,

---

[1] Such an attitude has already appeared in work on the text; cf. the translation notes for 10:5b.

36, 37, 38, and 42 are in the past tense. On the basis of the content of the Odes using present tense, only Ode 20 might be strictly an Individual Ode, depending on whether the function of priest is the prerogative of the Odist or whether all the members of the community might so designate themselves. Within the mixed-tense Odes, Ode 8 must be categorised overall as Individual since the "I" of 10-21 refers to the Most High. All Odes in the past tense are to be categorised as Individual (though it might be argued that Ode 37 describes what might be a general experience of any member of the community).

## 1.4 Summary of the grouping according to personal pronouns

"I" Odes A (Individual Odes): the "I" is the central character; action in the past tense - 10, 11, 15, 17, 21, 22, 25, 28, 29, 35, 36, 37, 38, 42.

"I" Odes B: the "I" is the central character; action has a present or future aspect - 1, 5, 16, 26, 27, 40.

"I" Odes C: the "I" is the central character but the community is addressed/included to some degree - 3, 7, 14, 18, 31.

Community Odes A: the emphasis is on the community either as subject or audience - 13, 20, 41.

Community Odes B: the community is referred to but not in an explicitly predominant way - 4.

Mixed Odes: the emphasis is (relatively) equally on the "I" and the community - 8, 9.

Impersonal Odes A: the attention is exclusively upon a third party - 24, 32, 33.

Impersonal Odes B: the emphasis is on a third party but there is reference to speaker, audience or community: 6, 7, 12, 19, 23, 30, 34, 39.

## 1.4.1 The sub-odes

Although the analysis of the use and change of pronouns has concentrated on each Ode as an entity in its final form, those Odes which may be divided into sub-odes should also be considered in their parts since the sub-ode in each case is a discrete section within an Ode.

6:1-7 (sub-ode 1), Mixed Ode
6:8-18 (sub-ode 2), Impersonal Ode A

18:1-8 (sub-ode 1), "I" Ode C
18:9-15 (sub-ode 2), Impersonal Ode B

23:1-4 (sub-ode 1), Impersonal Ode B
23:5-22 (sub-ode 2), Impersonal Ode A

28:1-7 (sub-ode 1), "I" Ode A/"I" Ode B (mixture of present and past tenses)
28:8-19 (sub-ode 2), "I" Ode A

31:1-7 (sub-ode 1), Impersonal Ode B
31:8-13 (sub-ode 2), "I" Ode A

38:1-16 (sub-ode 1), "I" Ode A
38:17-21 (sub-ode 2), Impersonal Ode A

The allocation of the Mixed Odes to "I" or Community remains inconclusive and thus open to debate. Kroll, for example, designates Ode 8 as an "Ich-Stil" Ode rather than as a Mixed Ode (75 n. 2).

The Odes grouped as "I" Odes C and Impersonal Odes B are also open to question. Although there may be a strong focus upon the "I" in the "I" Odes C and upon some third party in the Impersonal Odes B, there is reference also to a speaker, or audience, or community, and it would be possible to categorise such Odes according to the secondary reference rather than according to the focus.

R. Abramowski identifies Odes 12, 30, and 39 (cf. my Impersonal Odes B) as Gemeindelieder (51-2; cf. Ode 30 as an "Ihr"-Psalm in Harnack 1910, 115). Odes 30 and 39 exhibit a degree of involvement of the community but Ode 12 makes more significant reference to the "I" (1-3a) than the community (13). Thus Blaszczak's categorisation of Ode 12 as a Theological Reflection Ode within the Individual Confession Odes seems more appropriate (88). The similar treatment of Ode 19 (cf. my Impersonal Odes B) is also feasible since the sub-group is identified principally by a reflection section in which "the speaker disappears, and no audience is addressed or referred to" (88).

Odes 14 and 18 (cf. my "I" Odes C) are nominated as Gemeindelieder by R. Abramowski (51). This is possible since there is reference to the community. However, the similar designation of Ode 16 (cf. my "I" Odes B) is inappropriate since there is no explicit reference to the community (but cf. 16:1-7 as an Individualode [52]). On the other hand, R. Abramowski's categorisation of Ode 20 (cf. my Community Odes A) as an Individualode (52) is ill-advised since the speaker is concerned with his own experience only in the introduction (1-2), while the major section of the Ode (5-9) is specifically addressed to the community.

## 2. The smaller forms

### 2.1 Summons to action

The syntactical forms associated with a summons to action, whether directed to the Messiah figure/Most High or the community, are the imperative, jussive and cohortative. The identification of Odes for which these forms are a significant feature must remain rather tentative, given the difficulty with the imperfect tense in Syriac which may be rendered with either the future or the jussive/cohortative. The difficulty can be allayed to a degree where a Coptic version of the particular Ode is available for comparison. Thus the use of the optative in the Coptic of 5:4b, 5a, 5b, 6a, 7a, 7b supports the interpretation of the imperfect in the Syriac as the jussive.

### 2.1.1 Summons to action (petition) addressed to the Messiah figure/Most High

Ode 14 contains petitions within 78.5%[1] of the Ode. R. Abramowski designates it as "reines Bittgebet" (52). Petition is also a feature in Odes 5 (33.3% in the Syriac, 47.6% in the Coptic) and 18 (27.3%). Also noteworthy is the reported speech in 42:15c-18 which is composed entirely of petitions. Severus (1206) and Dölger (135) refer to this passage as "Erbarmungsruf" and "Ruf nach der endgültigen Erlösung" respectively.

### 2.1.2 Summons to action (exhortation/invitation/command) addressed to the community

Exhortation, invitation and command are combined since it is impossible to judge in which way an imperative to the community is intended by the form alone.

---

[1] The percentages are calculated on petition "sections"; that is, the petition itself together with any clause expressing either the reason for or the expected result of the petition.

The summons to action is a significant feature in Odes 8 (46.2%), 13 (71.4%), 20 (50%), and the reported speech of the Perfect Virgin in 33:6-13 (60% of the speech, 35.3% of the total Ode). Although the percentages are not high in Odes 7 (20.3%), 9 (29.6%), 30 (38.5%), and 41 (34.4%), the form is prominent in those sections in which the community is directly addressed, the remainder of these Odes comprising, for the most part, decription of a third party. Imperatives addressed to the community serve as the opening to Odes 9 and 30 and the reported speech in 33:6-13 (cf. also the opening jussives in Ode 41 which refer to the community), and the conclusion for Odes 3, 7, 23:1-4 (sub-ode 1), and 34.

Of the Odes which Blaszczak categorises as Invitation Songs (98-9) or Odes of Instruction and Exhortation (99), only Odes 31 (Invitation Song) and 39 (Ode of Instruction and Exhortation) are not included in the discussion above. Ode 31 contains imperatives addressed to the community only in 6-7 (16.7%). Moreover in the detailed analysis of the Ode, Blaszczak states that 6-7 does not sit well in its present position in the Ode ("The address gives the impression of having been tacked on..." [57]). This seems all the more reason not to categorise the Ode on the basis of these two verses. The remainder of the Ode comprises description of events in the past (about the Lord and the Most High [1-5], and about the "I" [8-13]). In classifying Ode 39 as an Ode of Instruction and Exhortation, Blaszczak has relied for the latter half of the category on verse 8 only. It would seem to be more appropriate to designate the Ode simply as an Ode of Instruction.

The majority of the Odes discussed above (including 31 and 39) are contained within Schille's "Wecklieder" (94-101). Only Odes 12 and 32 appear to be misplaced in the section, "II. Der Weckruf im Offenbarungslied" (98-101), and then only from the point of view of the term "Weckruf". With regard to Ode 32, even Schille is not wholly convinced: "Sie verzichtet ganz auf Rufe. Daher ist ihre Einordnung in unsere Gattung nicht völlig gesichert" (100). The closest that one could come to a "Ruf" in Ode 12 would be in the concluding beatitude (*Makarismus*), although even here the beatitude is not directly addressed to the community.

2.2 Information/explanation/description

The basic syntactic unit of the Odes is the simple statement, often combined with a clause/clauses expressing reason for/result of what is described in the statement. Thus much of the collection comprises information by way of description or explanation whether it be for the purpose of teaching, exhorting, vindicating, remembering, raising feelings of gratitude, and so on. The categorisation of such material up till now has been based primarily upon the motivation for the giving of information (Propagandarede, Missionsrede, and so on).

Odes 23:5-22 (sub-ode 2), 24, 32, 33, and 38:17-21 (sub-ode 2) comprise information about a third party, as do large sections of Odes 6 (8-10, 14-18), 7 (11-16a), 9 (8-10, 11b-12), 12 (4-12), 16 (8-19), 18:9-15 (sub-ode 2) (11-15), 19 (2-11), 23:1-4 (sub-ode 1) (1-3), 30 (3-6), 31:1-7 (sub-ode 1) (1-5), 34 (1-5), 39 (1-7, 9-13).

Odes 10, 11, 15, 17, 21, 27, 28, 29, 31:8-13 (sub-ode 2), 35, 36, 37, 38:1-16 (sub-ode 1) and 42 comprise information given by the "I" about himself (much of it confessional material) to the community. Such information is also found in considerable sections of Odes 3 (1-3, 5-10), 7 (1-10), 8 (14-18, 20-21), 16 (1-7), 22 (Syr 1-5a, Copt 1-5), 40 (2-6).

## 2.2.1 Sub-group: Story

The sub-group is identified by material in the past tense in which events are arranged in a progressive time-related sequence. Thus the category does not include descriptions in the past tense of events which do not appear to be so arranged as, for example, in 6:14-18. Odes 11, 17, 23:5-22 (sub-ode 2), 28:8-19 (sub-ode 2), 31:8-13 (sub-ode 2), 33, 35, 36, 37, and 38:1-16 (sub-ode 1) comprise stories, as do the following sections of Odes: 6:8-10; 10:4-6; 19:4-7b; 24:1-13; 29:4-11; 31:1-5; 39:9-13; 42:10-20.

## 2.2.2 The rhetorical question

The rhetorical question does not function as a "true" question to elicit information (Schökel 150; cf. also Watson 1986, 338). In the Odes the rhetorical question is used to capture the attention of the community more forcefully so as to emphasise information already given or about to be given. Thus the statement by the "I" in 3:3, that he could not have loved the Lord unless he had been first loved himself by the Lord, is given extra emphasis by the rhetorical question which follows: "Who is able to distinguish love but he who is beloved."

Each of the rhetorical questions in the Odes (3:4; 4:6; 8:19a, 19b; 23:1b-c, 2b-c, 3b-c; 26:8a, 8b, 9, 10, 11) is introduced by ܡܢܘ ("who") and demands firstly the answer "no one" and secondly, in most cases, a further qualification, "no one except for...". The form is considerably employed in 23:1-4 (sub-ode

1) (series of three questions and associated clauses, 50% of the sub-ode) and in Ode 26 (series of five questions and associated clauses, 33.3% of the Ode).

Kroll's Ich-Stil/Offenbarungsreden[1] (8:15ff; 10:4ff; 11; 15; 17; 21; 28; 31:3-6, 6-11; 35; 36; 38; 42 [75 n. 2]), the Lehrdichtungen of R. Abramowski (16:8ff; 19:6ff; 20 [instruction about the true offering]; 23; 24; 31; 32; 34; 37; 40 [50-2]), and Blaszczak's Odes of Instruction and Exhortation (23:1-4; 34; 39 [99]), Didactic Story Odes (23:5-22; 24 [99]), and brief instruction lacking imperatives (33 [99]), can all be included within this broad grouping of the Odes which give information/explain/describe.

## 2.3 Similes/metaphors

The simple simile/metaphor[2] is employed in Odes 1, 5, 6, 7, 9, 11, 12, 13, 14, 15, 16, 17, 18, 19, 20, 23, 24, 25, 26, 28, 29, 31, 33, 35, 36, 38, 39, 40, 42 (70.7% of the collection), either as a single, double (e.g. 7:23; 11:22; 18:11; 36:7) or triple form (20:3).

### 2.3.1 Similes formed with ... ܐܝܟ ...ܗܟܢܐ

Lattke has indicated the frequency of the simile with ... ܐܝܟ ...ܗܟܢܐ (1982, 101-2: "Die Stilfigur des Vergleichs ['wie...so'] in den Oden"). The simplest type of the form over two lines occurs in 7:1; 12:5, 7; 14:1; 40:2; 42:8, 9 with the variation, ... ܐܝܟܢܐ ...ܗܟܢܐ, in 15:1. The form is extended over three lines, .... ܗܟܢܐ...(ܐܝܟ)... ܗܟܢܐ...ܐܝܟ in 28:1; 40:1 (cf. the variation with ܐܝܟܘ in 16:1), and over four lines, ...(ܗܟܢܐ)... ܗܟܢܐ...(ܐܝܟ)... ܐܝܟ in 6:1-2.

### 2.3.2 Simile/metaphor as introduction

The simile/metaphor is an important opening stylistic device for the Odes, occurring in Odes 1, 6, 7, 13, 14, 15, 16, 28, 38, 39, 40 (26.8% of the collection), and in 23:5-22 (sub-ode 2) (cf. also the opening allegory in Ode 19). Only Ode 26 concludes with a simile.

In Odes 1 (the Lord as wreath), 13 (the Lord as mirror), 23:5-22 (sub-ode 2) (the thought of the Lord as a letter), and 39 (the power of the Lord as

---

[1] "Der Myste beschreibt in manchen Gedichten seine Erlösung, seine Erlebnisse im Jenseits" (Kroll 1921/22, 75).

[2] By using the term "simple", I am limiting the discussion to the following forms or slight variations on them:
simile - X is like Y (e.g. "the Lord is like a wreath")
metaphor - X is Y (e.g. "the Lord is a mirror")

mighty rivers), the opening simile/metaphor is sustained throughout the Ode/ sub-ode.

The introductory simile in Odes 6, 15, and 28 functions as one element of an inclusio for a major section of the Ode, with the second element indicated by the reiteration of the initial image/motif (6:1-2 and 7; 15:1-2 and 10; 28:1-2 and 6-7; cf. to a lesser extent, 7:1-2 and 13-14).

## 2.4 Doxology

Deichgräber identifies two basic elements necessary for a doxology: firstly, the one who receives praise is in the dative or occasionally in the genitive; secondly, there is a predicate of praise, as a rule δόξα (1983, 258; cf. the addition of the *Ewigkeitsformel* in 1967, 25 ).

In the broadest sense, each Ode concludes with a doxology because of the final ϲ (= ܐܠܠ ܡ). There is some doubt as to whether the Hallelujah (and the intra-Ode Hallelujah in Ms. H) stems from the original composition (cf. esp. Lattke 1979-86, 1:36, 57, 59). It does not occur in the Coptic versions of Odes 5, 6, 22, and 25 (Ode 1 does not have a Syriac version for comparison) although it occurs at the end of the Greek version of Ode 11.

Leaving the final Hallelujah aside from the discussion, Odes 11, 16, 17, 18, and 20 conclude with a doxology[1] while Ode 5 opens with one. Apart from these, the small structured section in 26:5-7 comprises doxology.

The recognition of doxology in an Ode leads to the question of whether the Ode is thereby a hymn, if one accepts the broad definition of a hymn as "Preislied auf einen Gott, Helden oder erhabenen Gegenstand" (Träger, Chr. 225). The doxology itself is certainly a "short-hand" hymn but if the Ode itself is to be so classified, it must be clear that the doxology is integral to the content of the Ode. Thus Odes 5 and 17 cannot be classified as hymns; Ode 5 being more concerned with petition than with praise[2], the doxology of Ode 17 being the response of the community and quite distinct from the Ode proper which comprises speech by the Messiah.

Odes 16 (cf. Eißfeldt 828 n. 2; 16:11-20 in Gunkel 1933, 33) and 18 and, to a lesser degree, Odes 11 (cf. Schille 77) and 20, may be regarded as containing sufficient material in praise of the Lord in order to justify their designation as

---

[1] Lattke (1991, B.III.b) includes 29:11 in the list, but the verse comprises a description of the giving of glory rather than praise per se.

[2] Cf. Kroll's differentiation between prayer (Gebet) and hymn (Hymnus): "Auch zum Gebete gehört Lobpreis und Dank, aber es dominiert doch eben die Bitte, das andere lenkt nur darauf hin" (1921/22, 11).

hymns. 26:5-7 must be considered as a hymn inserted into the Ode proper (Greßmann [1911a, 635] and R. Abramowski [52] designate the entire Ode as a hymn). Of the hymns identified here only Ode 11 finds a place in Schille's categories of Initiations-Hymnen (11; 15; 17:5ff; 28; 29; 38; 42; [76-9]) or Epiphanie-Hymnen (7; 19; 23; 24; [114-6, 119]).

The classification of Odes as hymns involves more than the identification of the doxology form since praise may be given to God or others in other ways. Further investigation will necessitate a thorough analysis of the general motif of praise together with its associated imagery (cf. Lattke's [1991, B.III.b] discussion of the terms used for praising in the Odes, and the excursus in Chapter I.b above). Although the motif of praise permeates the collection, the Odes more often describe the action of praise rather than give praise. It seems significant in this regard that the Most High/Messiah figure is not directly addressed in Odes 3, 6, 7, 8, 12, 16, 21, 24, 27, 28, 29, 30, 31, 32, 33, 34, 35, 36, 37, 38, 39, and 41; that is, in 53.7% of the Odes.

The identification of hymns will also need to take account of the beatitude form in Odes 6, 9, 11, 12, and 30 in which there is praise of persons such as the ministers of the drink or those planted and so on. Also of importance are the small structured sections where form and praise content are often combined so effectively (cf. e.g. 12:4b-f [praise of the aeons], 16:5b-7 [praise of the Lord as creator], 19:10b-11 [praise of the virgin], 23:1-3 [praise of the holy/chosen ones], 29:2-4 [praise of the Lord]).

## 2.5 Patterns of small forms

As outlined above, many Odes share similar small forms. However, there seems to be no significant pattern to the arrangement of the small forms across a number of Odes. What patterning there is, has its basis more in content than in form. Thus, for example, Odes 1, 7, 16, 28, 38, 40 open with a simile which leads into description extending the image/motif of the simile and then moves to confession about the Lord. Apart from the simile, there is nothing about this pattern that has to do with the small forms per se.

## 3. The small structured sections

In Franzmann 1984 (397, 401-3), six highly structured sections were identified in the collection (5:10-15; 12:4b-f; 19:10b-11; 23:1-3; 26:5-7; 29:2-3[4]) and categorised as "Ode-within-the-Ode". The category seems less appropriate now since, in the present work, the term "sub-ode" has been used for large sections of independent material. However, the idea of the category remains the same - these are small sections with a highly structured style which sets them apart from the rest of the Ode in which they occur.

The first reaction to such material is to assume that it is borrowed material that has not been effectively integrated into the Odes. Such a reaction is supported by what seems to be a reluctance on the part of the Odist to take advantage of opportunities for highly structured material (cf. e.g. 8:22b-d). This suggests rather strongly that, where highly structured material does occur in the Odes, it is not the original work of the Odist.

However, a study of the unique occurrences of roots within the collection of the Odes (cf. Appendix E), which would be expected to support the identification of material from other sources, gives no indication that these particular sections of highly structured material are not the work of the Odist. Indeed, on the contrary, most of the sections above do not contain any occurrences of a unique root.

One is also aware that the Odes have a quality of "Buntscheckigkeit", as Greßmann so aptly put it (1911b, 18). They are "untidy" structurally with numerous levels ranging between what appears to be sections with little regard for any formal structure (apart from the ubiquitous parallelism) to the strictly structured material identified above. The analysis of the individual Odes in Chapter II indicates that at least 7:4, 6; 8:10-11(12); 16:5b-7; 34:1-3, 4-5b; 39:2-3, 5-6 should be added to the six sections identified earlier. There are other sections of Odes (e.g. 3:6-7, 8-9; 12:5-7; 22:1-5; 26:8-10; 38:19b-21; 40:3-4) which are less highly structured but nevertheless are clearly identified within the material in which they are set.

## 3.1 Sub-group: series of parallel lines with equivalent syntactic structure

Some of the highly structured sections consist of a series of parallel lines with the same syntactic structure: 12:4b-f; 16:5b-7; 19:10b-11 (Deichgräber [1983, 260] gives this as a parallel in form to 1 Tim 3:16); 39:2-3. 38:19b-21 and 40:3-4 are close to this form but the structure appears to have undergone some deterioration.

## 4. Imagery/motif

As has been noted already, much of the categorisation of the Odes up to the present has been based upon the interpretation of imagery/motif. The work has been hampered to a great degree through the lack of a comprehensive analysis of the connections between images within the total system of images upon which the Odes are constructed[1]. Thus to establish a category such as Redeemer Odes, one would need to discuss a number of motifs (struggle and victory, ascent and descent, death and Sheol, salvation, exaltation, gathering of a people...) in conjunction with the basic material to be found associated with the titles Messiah and Saviour (cf. this method to some extent in Blaszczak's identification of Ascent Odes [77-81], or the Saviour Speeches [97-8]). The work on the motifs must also take account of the analysis of the structure of individual Odes in order to identify, for example, the limits of sections for the "I" who is the Messiah figure.

The importance of an image/motif cannot be judged by the frequency of its use although frequency might also indicate importance. Thus the image of the letter (= the thought of the Lord) occurs only in Ode 23 but a significant proportion of that Ode is devoted to the story concerning it (5-22 [sub-ode 2]). The image of bride and bridegroom/beloved in reference to the Lord and the "I"/believers occurs explicitly only in 38:11 and 42:8-9, yet the image serves to differentiate between this group and the enemy (the Deceiver and Error) and must be recognised as significant.

The following sub-sections give some indication of how imagery might be used in the grouping of Odes.

### 4.1 General grouping of the collection - the Odes as inspired speech

The description of or invitation to speech inspired by the Lord/Spirit is a frequent motif of the Odes with reference both to the "I" and the community (e.g. 6:1-2, 7a; 8:1-2, 4; 10:1-2; 11:6(?); 12:1-2, 4, 8; 14:7; 16:2, 5; 18:1, 15; 26:2, 10-11; 28:1(?); 36:7; 41:4b; 42:6c). The identification of a number of associated images/motifs serves to broaden the basis for the discussion of the phenomenon of inspired speech: the harp and the Spirit (6:1; 14:8; 26:3), the Word (10:1; 12:1, 3, 12; 32:2; 37:3a), the composition of Odes (14:7; 16:1-2; 26:1-3, 8, 10-11; 36:2d; 40:2-3), heart and mouth and lips (10:1; 11:6; 12:2; 16:2, 5; 21:8-9; 26:2, 10; 37:1b-2a; 40:2b-3a), fruits (10:2; 12:2c; 14:7; 16:2c; 37:3b), the spring/water (11:6; 12:2a-b; 26:13; 40:2), the knowledge of the Lord (7:21, 23c-24; 11:7-8a; 12:3; 26:12a), standing (8:3; 26:12b; 36:2), and rest (14:6a; 26:3b, 10, 12b; 36:1; 37:4). Even taking into account these relatively

---

[1] Lattke 1982 is an early pilot study on the imagery. To date, the most extensive study of the imagery has been Morrison's dissertation on the literary and theological relationship between the Odes and the Johannine literature.

few associated images/motifs, the number of Odes cited represents 43.9% of the collection.

The discussion has been limited to images/motifs which can be found directly related to the descriptions of inspired speech. Aune's (1982) study of this phenomenon in the Odes which led to his categorising of them as Prophetic Hymns includes some of the images/motifs above (harp, water, rest, fruit) but also considers visions and auditions (439-43) and Christ as the speaker (443-5). Both the brief outline above and Aune's work indicate that inspired speech is a basic dynamic of the Odes.

4.2 Grouping by a motif - change in status/difference

Change in status and difference are two major related motifs of the Odes, whether referring to the "I", the community or the Messiah figure. Images/motifs which might be considered within these broad motifs include the gaining of new physical attributes (face, eyes, members), ascent into the region above and instalment before the Lord, stripping off and putting on, birth, sonship, strangeness, imitation and so on.

The investigation of each of these requires a further identification of related images/motifs. Thus, even in a limited discussion of the motif of sonship as applied to the "I" who is not the Messiah figure (3:7c-d; 14:1; 31:4b; 36:3; 41:2a), related images/motifs would include birth (36:3), creation (7:9; 8:18, 20a; 36:5a-b), rearing (35:6a), motherhood of God (8:16; 35:5), parenthood of God (41:1a), strangeness (3:6), likeness (7:4,6), and union (3:3-5, 7a-b; 5:15; 8:14, 20b-21; 11:2c; 14:2; 25:11b; 26:1-2; 28:4b-6; 40:4; 41:3; 42:6b, 7b-9, 20c).

The broad motifs of change in status and difference suggest that many Odes might be used appropriately in a setting in which initiation or change in status occurred (or perhaps was remembered and celebrated) for members of a community or for those wishing to become members.

Other broad motifs might relate Odes not so much to a ritual setting but rather to a specific situation of the community. Thus Odes which include a motif of struggle/persecution and subsequent victory/salvation (with associated images/motifs of war, death and Sheol, lifting up, stripping off/putting on, corruption and incorruption, rescue, healing, the Lord as keeper/helper, the right hand of the Lord,...) might be appropriately grouped as Odes to be sung in times of crisis for the encouragement of the community as much as to be sung in victory celebrations.

## 4.3 Grouping by an activity - drinking

Certain descriptions of action in the Odes may be allusions to ritual activity. There is mention of drinking, for example, which results in the quenching of thirst (6:11, 14a; 30:2), healing (6:15), strengthening (6:14b, 16-17a), the giving of light (6:17b), and knowledge (11:7-8), union with the Son/Father (19:1), rest (30:2-3, 7; 35:6), and life/growth (35:6). The drink comes from the Lord, whether from his breasts (19:1-3; 35:5), his spring which gives milk and honey (4:10) and water (11:6 ["speaking water"]; 30:1, 5), his sprinkling (4:10), his dew (11:14b; 35:5 [=his milk]), or his stream/river (6:8-10, 12). Such imagery may indicate a ritual action of drinking associated perhaps with healing, or with the acquisition of the knowledge of the Lord, and so on.

Other ritual action may lie behind the description of putting on a wreath/ crown (1; 5:12; 9:8-11; 17:1; 20:7-8) - e.g. celebration of victory or initiation/ change in status; extending the hands (27; 35:7; 37:1; 42:1-2) - e.g. opening/ closing ritual action and/or imitiation of the Christian crucifixion/exaltation symbol (cf. The Gospel of Philip 63:21-23, which explains that Jesus is known in Syriac as Pharisatha [ⲫⲁⲣⲓⲥⲁⲑⲁ], "the one who is spread out", for he came "crucifying the world" [ⲉϥⲥⲧⲁⲩⲣⲟⲩ ⲙ̄ⲡⲕⲟⲥⲙⲟⲥ]; Facs. ed. 2: 75; Isenberg, W.W. 138); stripping off and/or putting on (3:1; 4:6; 7:4; 11:10-11; 13:3; 15:8; 20:7; 21:3; 23:1-3; 25:8; 33:12; 39:8) - e.g. rite of initiation/change in status or rite of protection.

Section b of this chapter presents only preliminary steps in the grouping of Odes within the collection. Further work remains to be done on individual Odes. As Knierim (1973, 462-3) suggests, there will always be a complex set of questions to be asked: how do all the facets of this Ode (poetical structure, small forms, images/motifs, suggestions of liturgical setting) interact? What is the priority of the interaction? Which one/s of them will be dominant in the search for a category? What is most typical about this Ode?

# IV. CONCLUSION: TOWARDS THE STUDY OF THE IMAGERY

The close analysis of the text in its entirety for the first time in Chapter II provides a solid basis for future interpretation as shown, even to a small degree, in Chapter III. With this project completed, a study of the system of imagery in the Odes becomes the highest priority for the continuing research on the text. The more secondary questions of provenance, date, community of origin and so on are important but it is imperative that scholars recognise that the study of form and imagery provides the fundamental base from which work on the secondary questions might be done with more integrity than has been the case over the previous years of research. No doubt knowing the provenance and dating of the text and so on would be extremely helpful for interpretation, but over eighty years of research have thus far provided no certain answers to these questions, and so often researchers can be lured into a circular or limited methodological path if they begin from assumptions about these secondary questions.

Research on the imagery must begin by assembling the entire system of images so that subsequent work on single images might be informed by the context of that image in relation to the whole system. On the simplest level, the reason is that often the single image itself is not of great importance. Thus the helmsman and the ship, the ploughman and the plough (Ode 16), are important only in so far as they serve to illustrate workers and their tools, building towards the description of the Odist and the work of composing Odes.

More importantly, single images can so easily be manipulated to fit a chosen context if they are studied without attention to their context in the total system of images of their own text. This might be illustrated with the image of the Saviour figure who opens the doors and breaks the bars of Sheol/Death. One of the Manichaean Pss of Heracleides appears to be very close in its wording and image to 17:8b-9a,

"And I opened the gates which were shut,
and dashed into pieces the bolts of iron." (17:8b-9a)

"He opened the gates that were shut by his resurrection;
the gates and bolts of the men of Hades he broke."
(Allberry 196, lines 15-16, translation mine)

One might easily conclude that the Odes and the Manichaean psalms have some close connection, that one text has influenced the other, or that both texts are working from a common source. Yet, as has been noted in Chapter II, this same image and basic vocabulary can be found in a number of very different contexts (e.g. Ps 107; Is 45:2; Manichaean Pss to Jesus CCLXXI; Trimorphic Protennoia XIII, 41, 4-35; The Teaching of Silvanus VII, 110, 19-29). In order to say which of these texts (or others) might be closest to the Odes, one would have to investigate the image in its context within the total system of images in all the texts and subsequently compare the patterns of related imagery. The world of images is a living system of relationships - the single image in isolation from that world is meaningless.

Spurgeon's work on Shakespeare indicates the advantage of assembling images in a systematic fashion for the analysis of literature:

"They (the images) are not selected to point or to illustrate any preconceived idea or thesis, but they are studied, either as a whole, or in groups, with a perfectly open mind, to see what information they yield, and the result comes often as a complete surprise to the investigator. It seems scarcely necessary to say that the images form, when thus collected, a world in themselves..." (x)

As a first step in the analysis, images could be grouped in much the same way as Spurgeon has done for Shakespeare (cf. esp. the charts, 410-11, 418-9; cf. also Arnold-Döben's grouping of Manichaean imagery):

Nature

- growing things and products/elements of nature: tree, fruit, blossom, bud, wreath, water, honeycomb/honey, milk, dew, light, wind, dust, chaff, sea-spume, smoke, shade, wave, darkness...

- weather: lightning, rain, mist, whirlwind...

- physical formations: plantation, mountain, forest, harbour, ocean, river, spring, rock, sun, star, abyss, path, precipice...

- animals: dove, dog, flying creature, creeping thing...

Domestic and daily life

- relationships/roles: bride and groom, father/mother and child, father and son, lord and servant, enemy, midwife, stranger, gardener/planter, labourer, ploughman, helmsman, judge...

- small implements/products: bow and arrow, seal, book, wheel, lamp, yoke, garment, mirror, harp, chain, gate, bolt, dagger/sword, crown, bed, wine...

- large constructions: temple, chariot, bridge, ship, plough, house...

- activities/events: war, parenting, wedding feast, birth, work, sickness, gardening, planting, drinking, drunkenness, dressing...

- arts: writing, reading, singing, composing...

Cultic life

- roles: servant of the water, seer, singer, priest...

- constructions/places: temple, high place.

- activities: healing, drinking, dressing, putting on a wreath, singing, composing...

"Mythical" life and environment

- environment: regions above and below, Death/Sheol, paradise...

- characters: Most High, Messiah figure, Spirit, Grace, Truth, the Virgin, the Perfect Virgin, Error, the Deceiver, aeons, archangels, hosts, the seven-headed dragon/serpent...

- activities: ascending, descending, singing praise and composing, journeying, questioning, warring...

At this level, the data can be used in comparing the Odes with other authors/ writings, since, as Spurgeon asserts from her comparison of Shakespeare with Marlowe and Bacon,

"...quite apart from style and method of forming the images... each writer has a certain range of images which are characteristic of him, and... he has a marked and constant tendency to use a much larger number of one or two kinds" (13).

Murray's summary (Table III, 354-63) of some twenty images in the Odes and a variety of writings/authors (including the Acts of Judas Thomas, the Manichaean Psalms, the Macarian Homilies, the Acts of John, the Doctrine of Addai, the writings of Aphrahat, Ephrem, and Cyril), indicates what might be done on a small scale although, once again, the whole system of imagery should be collected first before comparisons are made. Other authors/writings for comparison would include the Gospel of John, Qumran, Bardaiṣan, and Ignatius of Antioch.

Inevitably, one is drawn to consider what images do not occur in the Odes. There is, for example, a great deal of agricultural and sea imagery but no desert imagery (except perhaps implied in "the dry ones on the sand" in Copt 5:11). There is no imagery associated with commerce and nothing specifically urban (the setting of the bridegroom's house and the temple is not specified). Ritual activity can only be guessed at from the descriptions of singers and seers and of activity such as drinking water/milk (cf. Chapter III, 4.3). There is little concern for a hierarchy of roles, except for the general distinction between God and the believer (lord and servant; but cf. also the prevailing imagery of union between the same), while the community is constantly encouraged to experience the same "authorising" inspiration as the "I".

Attempting to draw implications from perceived omissions in the imagery (e.g. that Egypt is less likely to have been the country of origin because of the lack of imagery about deserts) is less helpful since the physical world of the author is bound to be broader than what is described in the text. Speculation on the literal level of the imagery has not been terribly successful in the past as can be shown, for example, from the early debate between Loisy (104) and Alès (769) concerning the interpretation of Ode 6 with regard to Egypt and the flooding of the Nile. There is, quite simply, not enough specific physical evidence in the text to make any concrete suggestions about the provenance of it.

The analysis of the images is very complex since they may inform on a number of levels, depending on the questions asked of them and in what way they are grouped. When one moves from the more literal investigation of the images, it is possible to ask more subtle questions. One may ask, for example, in what way patterns of images mirror the patterns of the social experience of the originating community (cf. e.g. this approach to the Gospel of John in Meeks 1972). Such an investigation focusses on the form of the images rather than their literal content.

One is aware, for example, of the motif of real and threatened violence which runs through the Odes, indicating some situation of confrontation for the community. This social situation appears to be mirrored in the text by a predominance of images in a polar/antithetical relationship: e.g. flesh/world vs righteousness/purity, skin vs spirit, above vs below, knowledge vs ignorance, the Beloved and his bride vs the Deceiver and Error, following vs erring, corruption vs incorruption, idleness vs fruitfulness, truth vs error, falling/perishing vs standing firm, son vs stranger, death vs life, light vs darkness, apostates/persecutors vs the elect, open vs shut...

Investigating the patterns of polar images suggests a further step to images of mediation, especially those which mediate between the regions above and below: e.g. ascending/descending instruments (letter, chariot, voice, river of the Lord, way of truth...), and ascending/descending characters (Saviour figure, Word, Grace, Truth, Spirit, the Odist). One might also study the role of the Odist as mediator of the entire human-mythological structure and the legitimation of this role which the system of images works towards (cf. the legitimating function of symbolic universes in Berger and Luckmann, esp. 110-46).

In a similar way, but from a different perspective, one might examine the imagery of ordering (the footprints of the Most High/Messiah figure upon the river, creation, planting, setting up fallen limbs,...), and disordering (the voice of the dove, the overflowing river, the wheel, the breaking of bonds and doors, drunkenness which results in loss of knowledge...); imagery of liminality (strangeness, experience of ecstasy...; for the concept of liminality, cf. Turner, V. 1969, 94-130; 1974, 13-7; 1985, 158-61, 294-96) and so on.

Even more specifically, the body-imagery of the Odes may be studied for what it might indicate regarding the self-understanding of the originating group[1]. Such a step proceeds from the theory that "symbols based on the human body are used to express different social experiences" (Douglas 1982, vii)[2]. In his discussion of Gnosis, Rudolph asserts a two-fold congruence that may just as easily be applied to the Odes - between anthropological and cosmological images on the one hand and between anthropological imagery and natural and social human experience on the other:

"Das Menschenbild einer Religion oder Weltanschauung ist keine bloß abstrakte Konstruktion, auch wenn es über den notwendigen Weg der Reflexion in seinen unterschiedlichen Zügen und Ausformungen auf den ersten Blick so scheinen mag, dahinter steckt die sehr konkrete Auseinandersetzung des Menschen mit seiner natürlichen und gesellschaftlichen Umwelt." (1979, 19)

Douglas uses the analysis of body-imagery to draw the characteristics of what she refers to as a religion of ecstasy over against a religion of control (1969, esp. 74). A productive discussion might be engaged between the body-imagery of the Odes and the description of a religion of ecstasy, especially with regard to the spirit/matter dichotomy, the lack of emphasis upon specific ritual differentiation of roles or upon the control of consciousness and spontaneous expression (with the corresponding exaltation of the intoxicating knowledge of the Lord), and the informality between the Lord and the "I"/believers which encourages familiarity and intimacy. Lack of control appears in the Odes in more subtle ways also, as in the vagueness that exists with regard

---

[1] For an investigation of anthropological imagery for the understanding of Gnosis, cf. Nagel 1979b, esp. the articles by Rudolph, Colpe, Nagel, and Ullmann.

[2] For a review of Douglas' work, cf. S.R. Isenberg and Owen. The theory has been applied by Douglas herself to the Arian controversy (1969), and although criticised for misunderstanding the nature of that controversy (cf. e.g. Richard 141), nevertheless her basic theory is proving increasingly helpful to scholars (cf. e.g. Gager on the development of the Christian concepts of incarnation, resurrection, and asceticism; A.F. Segal [1981] on mediating figures in Gnosticism; Malina on the Gospel of John; S.R. Isenberg [1975] on Qumran).

to the differentiation of male and female, for example, in the androgynous image of the Father with breasts in Ode 19.[1]

The imagery of alienation found in the Odes (esp. the alienation of the "I"/believers from those around them who appear to be kin) serves to reinforce the idea of the originating community as engaged in a religion of ecstasy, withdrawn from or moving against the established order (Douglas 1969, 72), at the fringes rather than in the mainstream of a particular tradition, according to the theory developed by Gager with regard to the Christian tradition:

> "Specifically, I would anticipate that we should find, at the centre of the movement, a shift from symbols of alienation to symbols of integration and that we should discover a return to earlier symbols of alienation wherever we come upon expressions of protest or reform at the fringes of the movement." (348)

This level of analysis of the imagery which can be used to situate the community firmly within or on the edges of a tradition might prove more successful than the endless discussion concerning the orthodoxy or heterodoxy of the Odes. The apparent lack of interest in clearly-defined dogmatic statements can indicate that there is nothing against their orthodoxy or, just as easily, that there is nothing to support their orthodoxy.

Finally, a cautionary note. The image is always "more than", full of potential, with infinite possibilities for interpretation. In the final analysis, there can be no definitive answer to what a single image or the system of images itself means. There are merely clues and guesses, some better than others, depending upon the care taken in formulating and asking the questions. It is the positive (and frustrating) aspect of Gödel's theorem that no system contains within itself the solution of that system (70; cf. also Wittgenstein 71 [6.41: "The sense of the world must lie outside the world..."]). The images of the Odes do not contain, in their assembled system, the solution to their own puzzle.

---

[1] For the image of the androgyn in general, cf. Meeks 1973/74. Although Meeks makes reference to Odes 41:8 (167) and 25:8 (188), it seems unusual that he does not deal with this most striking example of the androgynous Father.

# APPENDIX A: WORD FREQUENCY TABLES

The repetition of elements within individual odes is categorised according to whether the element occurs throughout the Ode or within one discrete stanza (cf. Watson 1986, 291). Ideally each element should occupy one column for itself. This has not been done for the second ("in part") section in the interests of keeping all the data in view as much as possible, and since some Odes have a large number of repeated elements. For the few Odes which have many repeated elements in the first ("throughout") section, the number of columns has occasionally been abbreviated where possible to give all the relevant data across two facing pages.

The superscript number following an element indicates the number of repetitions of that element within the single line.

ODE 1

| | throughout | | in part |
|---|---|---|---|
| 1a | ⲁⲡⲉ | ⲕⲗⲟⲙ | |
| b | | | |
| 2a | | ⲕⲗⲟⲙ | |
| b | | | ⲟⲩⲱ |
| 3 | | ⲕⲗⲟⲙ | ⲟⲩⲱ |
| 4a | ⲁⲡⲉ | | |
| b | | | ⲟⲩⲱ |
| 5a | | | ⲙⲟⲩⳅ |
| b | | | ⲙⲟⲩⳅ |

ODE 3

| | throughout | | | | in part | |
|---|---|---|---|---|---|---|
| 1 | | | | | | |
| 2a | | | | | | |
| b | | | | | | |
| c | | | | | ܚܒ | |
| 3a | ܟܠ | ܪܚܡ | ܡܪܝܐ | | | |
| b | | ܪܚܡ | | | | |
| 4a | | ܪܚܡܬܐ | | | | |
| b | | ܪܚܡ | | ܗܘ ܕ | | |
| 5a | | ܪܚܡ | | | ܚܒ | |
| b | | ܪܚܡ | | | | |
| c | | | | | | |
| d | | | | | | |
| 6a | | | | | | |
| b | | ܪܚܡ | ܡܪܝܐ | | ܡܛܠ ܕ | |
| 7a | | | | | | |
| b | | ܪܚܡ 2 | | | ܡܛܠ ܕ | |
| c | | ܪܚܡ | | | ܡܛܠ ܕ | ܒܪܐ |
| d | | | | | | ܒܪܐ |
| 8a | | | | ܗܘ ܕ | ܠܐ ܡܐܬ | |
| b | | | | | ܠܐ ܡܝܘܬܐ | |
| 9a | | | | ܗܘ ܕ | | ܚܝܐ |
| b | | | | | | ܚܝܐ |
| 10a | | | ܡܪܝܐ | | | |
| b | ܟܠ | | | | | |
| 11 | ܟܠ | | | | | |

## ODE 4

| | throughout | | | in part | |
|---|---|---|---|---|---|
| 1a | | | | ܣܘܠܦ | ܐܪܬܐ |
| b | | | | ܣܘܠܦ | ܐܪܬܐ |
| 2a | | | | | |
| b | ܟܬܒ | | | | |
| c | | | | | ܐܪܬܐ |
| 3a | | | | ܣܘܠܦ | |
| b | | | | | |
| c | | ܢܣܒ | | | |
| 4a | | | | | |
| b | | | | | |
| 5a | | | | | |
| b | | | | | |
| 6a | | | | ܠܒܫ | |
| b | | | | | |
| 7a | | | | | ܥܠ |
| b | | | | | ܥܠ |
| 8a | | | | | |
| b | | | | ܠܒܫ | |

| | | | | | |
|---|---|---|---|---|---|
| 9a | | ܠ ܗܝ | | | |
| b | | | | ܘܣܘܝ | |
| c | | | | ܘܣܘܝ | |
| 10a | | | | ܗܣܘ ܝ, ܟܣܘܣܟ | |
| b | | | | | |
| c | | | | | |
| 11a | | | | ܟܬܢܬ | |
| b | | | | ܟܢܬ | |
| 12 | | | ܐܠ | | |
| 13a | | ܠ ܗܝ $^2$ | | | |
| b | | | | | |
| c | | | | | |
| 14a | | | ܐܠ | | |
| b | | | | | |
| 15 | ܒܠ | | | | |

ODE 5 [Syriac]

| | throughout | | | in part | | | | |
|---|---|---|---|---|---|---|---|---|
| 1a | | | | | | | | |
| b | | | | | | | | |
| 2a | | | | | | | | |
| b | ܩܘܕܐ | | | | | | | |
| 3a | | | | | | | | |
| b | | | | | | | | |
| 4a | | | | | | | | |
| b | | | | ܚܘ | | | | |
| 5a | | | | | | | | |
| b | | | | | | | | |
| 6a | | | | ܚܘ | | | | |
| b | | | | | | | | |
| 7a | | | ܬܘܠܕܬ | | | | | |
| b | | ܪܚܝ | | | | | | |
| 8a | | | ܬܘܠܕܬ | | | | | |
| b | | | | | | | | |
| 9a | | | | | | | | |
| b | | | | | | | | |
| 10a | ܩܘܕܐ | | | | | | | |
| b | | | | ܠܐ + verb | ܕܚܝܠ | | | |
| 11a | | | | | | | | |
| b | | | | ܠܐ + verb | ܕܚܝܠ | | | |
| 12a | | ܪܚܝ | | | | | | |
| b | | | | ܠܐ + verb | | ܗܘܠ | | |
| 13a | | | | | | ܗܘܠ | | |
| b | | | | | | | ܐܪܐ | |
| 14a | | | | | | | | |
| b | | | | | | | ܐܪܐ | |
| 15a | | | | | | | | ܩܒܠ |
| b | | | | | | | ܐܪܐ | ܩܒܠ |

ODE 5 [Coptic]

| | throughout | | | | | in part |
|---|---|---|---|---|---|---|
| 1a | | | | | | |
| b | NOYTE | | | | | |
| 2a | | | | | | |
| b | | ϨЄΛΠΙϹ | | | | |
| 3a | | | | | | |
| b | | | | | | |
| 4a | | | ϨЄ | | | |
| b | | | | | | NⲀY |
| 5a | | | | | | |
| b | | | | | | |
| 6a | | | | | | NⲀY |
| b | | | | | | |
| 7a | | | | ϬOM | ϢOⲀNЄ | |
| b | | | | | ϢOⲀNЄ | |
| 8a | | | | | ϢOⲀNЄ | |
| b | | | | | | |
| c | | | | ϬOM | | |
| 9a | | | | | | |
| b | | | ϨЄ | | | |
| 10a | | ϨЄΛΠΙϹ | | | | |
| b | | | | | | |
| 11 | NOYTE | | | | | |

ODE 6 [Syriac]

| | throughout | | | | | | | |
|---|---|---|---|---|---|---|---|---|
| 1a | | | | | | | | |
| b | | | | | | | | |
| 2a | ܪܘܚܐ | ܡܗܝܡܢܐ | | | | | | |
| b | | | | | | | | |
| 3a | | | | | | | | |
| b | | | | | | | | |
| 4a | | | | | | | | |
| b | | | | | | | | |
| 5a | | | | | | | | |
| b | | ܩܘܡ | | | | | | |
| 6a | | | ܢܥܠܬܐ | | | | | |
| b | | | ܥܠ | | | | | |
| c | | | | ܢܚܒ | | | | |
| 7a | | | | | | | | |
| b | ܪܘܚܐ 2 | | | | | | | |
| 8a | | | | | | | | |
| b | | | | | | | | |
| c | | | | | | | | |
| d | | | | | | | | |
| 9a | | | | | | | | |
| b | | | | | | ܡܝܐ | | |
| 10a | | | | | | | ܐܪܥܐ | |
| b | | | | | | | | |
| 11a | | | | | | | ܐܪܥܐ | ܫܬܐ |
| b | | | | | | | | |
| 12 | | | | | ܢܚܒ | | | ܡܫܬܐ |

| in part | |
|---|---|
| ܡܛܠ | |
| ܡܛܠ | |
| ܡܛܠ | |
| | |
| | |
| | |
| | |
| ܡܛܠ ܕ ܡܛܠ | ܡܛܠ |
| ܡܛܠ ܕ ܡܛܠ | ܡܛܠ |
| | |
| | |
| | |
| ܬܫܡܫܬܐ | |
| ܫܡܫ | |
| | |
| | |
| | |
| ܐܬܐ | |
| | ܥܠ, ܥܠܘ |
| | ܥܠ |
| ܐܬܐ | |
| | |
| ܥܡܐ | |
| ܥܡܐ | |
| | |

| 13a | | | | | | | | ܡܚܘܬܐ | |
| b | | | | | | ܗܪܟ | | | |
| 14a | | | | | | | | | |
| b | | | ܦܩܕ | | | | | | |
| 15a | | | | | | | | | |
| b | | | | | | | | | |
| 16a | | ܡܗܪܘܬܐ | | | | | | | |
| b | | | ܦܩܕ | | | | | | |
| 17a | | | | | ܢܗܒ | | | | |
| b | | | | | | | | | |
| 18a | | | ܒܥ | | | | | ⋅ | |
| b | | | | | ܗܪܟ | | | ܚܝܐ, ܚܝܘ | |

ODE 6 [Coptic]

| | | throughout | | | | |
|------|------|------|------|------|------|------|
| 8a | | | | | | |
| b | | | | | | |
| c | | | | | | |
| d | ⲕⲱⲧⲉ | | | | | |
| 9a | | ⲁⲙⲁϩⲧⲉ | | | | |
| b | | ⲁⲙⲁϩⲧⲉ 2 | ⲙⲟⲟⲩ | | | |
| 10a | | | | | | |
| b | | ⲁⲙⲁϩⲧⲉ | | | | |
| 11a | | | | ⲥⲱ | ϣⲟⲟⲩⲉ | |
| b | | | | | | ⲃⲱⲗ (ⲉⲃⲟⲗ) |
| 12 | | | | ⲥⲱ | | |
| 13a | | | | ⲥⲱ | | |
| b | | | ⲙⲟⲟⲩ | | | |
| 14a | ⲕⲧⲟ | | | | ϣⲟⲟⲩⲉ | |
| b | | | | | | ⲃⲱⲗ (ⲉⲃⲟⲗ) |
| 15 | | ⲁⲙⲁϩⲧⲉ | | | | |
| 16 | | | | | | |
| 17a | | | | | | |
| b | | | | | | |
| 18a | | | | | | |
| b | | | ⲙⲟⲟⲩ | | | |

ODE 7

| | throughout | | | | | | | |
|---|---|---|---|---|---|---|---|---|
| 1a | ܟܬܘܒܚܐ | | | | | | | |
| b | | | | | | | | |
| c | | | | | | | | |
| 2a | ܟܬܘܒܚܐ | | | | | | | |
| b | | | | | | | | |
| c | | ܐܢܪܘܟ | | | | | | |
| 3a | | | | | | | | |
| b | | | ܠܝ | ܟܦܪ | | | | |
| c | | | | | ܪܒܘܬܐ | | | |
| 4a | | | | | | | | |
| b | | | | | | ܕ ܠܠܬܡ | | |
| c | | | | | | | ܣܒܚ | |
| d | | | | | | ܕ ܠܠܬܡ | | |
| 5a | | | | | | | | ܗܠ |
| b | | | | | | ܕ ܠܠܬܡ | | |
| 6a | | | | | | | | |
| b | | | | | | ܕ ܠܠܬܡ | | |
| c | | | | | | | | |
| d | | | | | | ܕ ܠܠܬܡ | | |
| 7a | | | ܟܬܠܝ | | | | | |
| b | | | ܟܬܠܝ | | | | | |
| 8a | | | | | | | | |
| b | | | | | | | | |
| 9a | | | | | | | | |
| b | | | ܠܝ | | | | | |
| 10a | | | | | | | | |
| b | | | | | | | | |
| c | | | | | | | | |
| 11a | | | | | | ܕ ܠܠܬܡ | | |
| b | | | | | | | | |

| | | | | | | | in part | |
|---|---|---|---|---|---|---|---|---|
| | | | | | | | ܐܘܝ | |
| | | | | | | | ܐܘܝ | |
| | | | | | | | | |
| | | | | | | | | |
| | | | | | | | ܐܘܝ | |
| | | | | | | | | |
| | | | | | | | | |
| | | | | | | | | |
| | | | | | | | | |
| | | | | | | | ܐܢܫܬܐ | |
| | | | | | | | | |
| | | | | | | | ܐܢܫܬܐ | |
| | | | | | | | | |
| ܐܦ | | | | | | | | |
| | | | | | | | | |
| | | | | | | | | |
| | | | | | | | | |
| | | | | | | | | |
| | | | | | | | | |
| | ܐܪܥ | | | | | | | |
| | | | | | | | | |
| | | | | | | | ܒܝܪ | ܫܒܒܘܬܐ |
| | | ܒܝܬ | | | | | | ܩܪܒܬܐ |
| | | | | | | | ܒܝܪ | |
| | | ܒܒܬ | | | | | | |
| ܐܦ, ܐܢܫ | | | ܦܐܐܪ | | | | | |
| | | | | ܢܡܒ | | | | |
| | | | | | ܫܠܒ | | | |
| | ܐܪܥ | | | | | ܫܡܠܒܐ | | |

| | | | | | | | | | | |
|---|---|---|---|---|---|---|---|---|---|---|
| 12a | | | | | | | | ܚܝܐ | | |
| b | | | ܓܠ | | | ܕܠܛܓܗ ܝ | | | ܠܕܒ | |
| c | | | | ܩܥܗ | | | ܗܒܩ | | | |
| 13a | | ܐܒܝܕܐ | ܓܬܥܝ | | | | | | | |
| b | | | | | | | | | | |
| 14a | | | | | | | | | | |
| b | | | | | | | | | | |
| 15a | | | | | | | | | | |
| b | | | | | | | | | | |
| 16a | | | | | | | | | | |
| b | | | ܓܠ | | | | | | | |
| 17a | | | | | | | ܗܒܩ | | | |
| b | | | | | | | | | | |
| c | ܓܗܢܕ | | | | | | | | | |
| d | | | | | | | | | | ܦܠܐܐ |
| 18a | | | | | | | | ܚܝ̈ܐ | | |
| b | | | | | | | | ܚܝܐ | | |
| 19a | | | | | | | | | | |
| b | | | | | | | | ܚܝܐ | | |
| 20a | | | | | | | | | | |
| b | | | | | | | | | | |
| 21a | | | ܠܐ ܓܬܥ | | | | | | | |
| b | | | ܓܬܥ | | | | | | | |
| 22a | | | | | | | | | | |
| b | | | | | | | | | | |
| 23a | | | | | | | | | | |
| b | | | | | ܐܝܗܢܕ | | | | | |
| c | | | | ܩܥܗ | | | | | | |
| d | | | ܠܐ ܓܬܥ | | | | | | | |
| e | | | | | | | | | | |
| 24a | | | | | | | | | | |
| b | | | | | | | | | | |
| c | | | | | | | | | | |
| 25a | | | | | | | | | | |
| b | | | | | | | | | | |

| | | | | | | | |
|---|---|---|---|---|---|---|---|
| ܝܗܒ | | | | | | | |
| | | | | | | | |
| | | | | | | | |
| | | | | | | | ܝܣܦ |
| | ܝܚܝܕܝܐ | ܐܬܐ | | | | | |
| | | | | | | | ܝܣܦ |
| | | | | | | | |
| | | | | | | | |
| | | | | | | | |
| | | | | | | | |
| | | | | | | | |
| | | ܡܕܝܢܬܐ | ܐܘܪܚܬܐ | | | | |
| | | | | | | | |
| | | | ܕܝܢ, | | | | |
| | | | | | | | |
| | | | | | | | ܝܪܒ |
| | | | | | | | ܝܪܒ |
| | | | | ܫܒܚ | | | |
| | | | | | ܕܒ | | |
| | | | | | | | |
| | | | | | | | |
| | ܝܠܠ | | | | | | |
| | | ܐܬܐ | | | | | |
| | | | ܕܝܢ, 2 | | | ܠܒܘܬܐ | |
| | | | ܐܘܪܚܬܐ | | ܕܒ | | |
| | | | | | | | |
| | | | | | | | |
| | | | | | | | |
| | | | | | | | |
| ܝܗܒ | | | | | | | ܦܣܩ |
| | | | | | | | ܦܣܩ |
| | | | | ܫܒܚ | | | |
| | | | | | | ܠܒܘܬܐ | |
| | | | | | | | |

## ODE 8

| | throughout | | | | | | |
|---|---|---|---|---|---|---|---|
| 1a | ܩܘܝ [2] | ܠܚܬ̈ܐ | | | | | |
| b | | ܠܐ | ܦܐ | | | | |
| 2a | | | | | | | |
| b | | | | ܠܒ̇ | | | |
| 3a | | | | | ܘܗ ܪ [2] | | |
| b | | | | | | ܗܡܢ ܕ | |
| 4a | | | | | | ܗܡܢ ܕ | |
| b | ܩܘܝ | | | ܠܒ̇ | | | |
| 5a | | | | | | ܗܡܢ ܕ | |
| b | | | | | | | ܕܢܩܘܗ̈ܐ |
| 6a | | | | | | | |
| b | | | | | | | |
| 7a | | | | | | | |
| b | | | | | | | |
| 8a | | | | | | | |
| b | | | | | | | ܝܠܬܐ |
| 9a | | | | | | | ܝܠ |
| b | | | | | | | |
| 10a | | | | | | | |
| b | | | | | | ܗܡܢ ܕ | |
| 11a | | | | | | | |
| b | | | | | | ܗܡܢ ܕ | |
| 12a | | | | | | | ܝܠ, ܝܠܬܐ |
| b | | | | | | ܗܡܢ ܕ | ܝܠ |
| 13a | | | | | | | |
| b | | | | | | | |

| | | | | | | | in part |
|---|---|---|---|---|---|---|---|
| | | | | | | | |
| | | | | | | | |
| | | | | | | | |
| | | | | | | | |
| | | | | | | | |
| | | | | | | | |
| | | | | | | | |
| | | | | | | | |
| | | | | | | | |
| | | | | | | | זֹחֵק 2 |
| | | | | | | | |
| | | | | | | | |
| | | | | | | | |
| | | | | | | | |
| | | | | | | | ܙܘܙܐ |
| | | | | | | | |
| | | | | | | | |
| ܙܘܝ | | | | | | | |
| ܙܘܝ | | | | | | | |
| ܙܘܝ | | | | | | | |
| ܙܘܝ | | | | | | | |
| | | | | | | | ܙܘܙܐ |
| | | | | | | | |
| | זֹעֵק | ܫܘܐ | | | | | |
| | זֹעֵק | | | | | | |

| | | | | | | | | |
|---|---|---|---|---|---|---|---|---|
| 14a | | | | | | | | |
| b | | | | | | | | ܠܝ |
| 15a | | | | | | | | |
| b | | | | | | | | |
| c | | | | | | | | |
| 16a | | | | | | | | |
| b | | | | | | | | |
| c | | | | | | | | |
| 17a | | | | | | | | |
| b | | | | | | | | |
| 18a | | | | | | | | |
| b | | | | | | | | |
| 19a | | | | ܩܡܩ | | | | |
| b | | | | | | | | |
| 20a | | ܠܬ | | | | | | |
| b | | | | | | | | |
| c | | | | | | | | |
| 21a | | | | | | | ܟܢܣܘܬܐ | |
| b | | | | | | | | |
| c | | | | | | | | |
| 22a | | | ܦܪ | | | | | |
| b | | | | | | | | |
| c | | | | | | | | |
| d | | | | | | | | |
| 23a | | | | | | | | |
| b | | | | | | | | |

| | | | | | | | |
|---|---|---|---|---|---|---|---|
| | | | ܕܠܝ | | | | |
| | | | | | | | |
| | | | | | | | |
| | | | | | | | |
| | | | | | | | |
| | | | | | | | |
| | | | | | | | |
| | | | ܕܠܝ | | | | |
| | | | ܕܠܝ | ܫܐ | | | |
| | | | | | ܕܝ | | |
| | | | | | | | |
| | | | ܕܠܝ | | | | |
| | | | | | | | |
| | | | | | | | ܓܒܐ |
| | | | | | | | ܓܒܐ |
| | | | | | ܕܝ | | |
| | | | ܕܠܝ | | | | |
| | | | ܕܠܝ | | | | |
| | | | | | | | |
| ܕܘܠܝ | | | | | | ܫܡܐ | |
| | | | | | | | |
| | ܪܟܘܒܐ | | | | | | |
| | | ܝܠ 2 | | | | | |
| | | | | ܫܐ | | | |
| | | | | | | | ܦܘܡ 2 |
| | | | | | | | |
| | | | | | | ܫܡܐ | |

# 336  APPENDIX A

ODE 9

|  | throughout | | | | | | in part | | |
|---|---|---|---|---|---|---|---|---|---|
| 1a | | | | | | | | | |
| b | | | | | | | | | |
| 2a | ܝܗܘ ܒ | | | | | | ܦܘܪܐ | | |
| b | ܠܒܝ | | | | | | ܦܘܪܐ | | |
| 3a | | ܐܬܚܪ | | | | | | | |
| b | | | | | | | ܟܬܒܘܬܐ, ܣܒܪ | | |
| 4a | | ܐܬܚܪ | | | | | | ܚܢܝ | |
| b | | | ܬܝܕܘܬܐ | | | | | ܚܢܝ | |
| c | | | | | | | | | |
| 5a | | | | | | | | | |
| b | | | ܬܝܕܘܬܐ | | | | | | |
| c | | | | ܦܘܦ | | | | | |
| 6a | | | | | | | | | |
| b | | | | | ܦܘܪܐ | | | | |
| 7a | | | | | | | | | |
| b | | | | | | ܗܣܒ | | | |
| 8a | | | | | | | ܒܠܠ | ܫܪܪܝ | |
| b | | | | | | | | | ܩܘܡ |
| 9a | | | | | | | | | |
| b | | | | | ܦܘܪܐ | | ܒܠܠ | | |
| 10a | | | | | | ܗܣܒ | | | |
| b | ܝܗܘ ܒ | | | | | | | | |
| 11a | | | | | | | ܒܠܠ | ܫܪܪܝ | |
| b | | | | | | | ܩܕܒ, ܩܕܐ | ܐܪ | |
| 12a | | | | | | | ܩܕܐ | ܩܘܡܐ | |
| b | | | | | | | | | |
| c | | ܐܚܪ | | ܦܘܦ | | | | | |

ODE 10

| | throughout | | | | in part |
|---|---|---|---|---|---|
| 1a | | | | | |
| b | ܠܐ | ܐܝܬܘ | | | |
| 2a | | | ܚܝ | | |
| b | | | | | |
| 3a | | | | | |
| b | | | | ܥܒܪ, ܥܒܘܪ | |
| 4a | | | | ܥܒܪ | |
| b | | | | | |
| 5a | | | | | ܠܬܚܬ |
| b | | | | | |
| c | | | | | |
| 6a | ܠܐ | ܐܝܬܘ | | | |
| b | | | ܚܝ | | |
| c | | | | | ܠܥܠ |

ODE 11 [Syriac]

| | | | throughout | | | |
|---|---|---|---|---|---|---|
| 1a | | | | | | |
| b | ܠ | | | | | |
| c | | | | | | |
| d | | ܠܕ | ܦܐܪ̈ | | | |
| 2a | | | | | | |
| b | | | | | | |
| c | | | ܗܠ | | | |
| 3a | | | | | | |
| b | | | | | | |
| 4 | | | | ܙܠܬܐ | | |
| 5a | | | | | | |
| b | | | | | | |
| 6a | | | | | | |
| b | | | | | | |
| 7a | | | | | | |
| b | | | | | | |
| 8a | | | | ܠܐ ܙܠܬܐ | | |
| b | | | | | | |
| 9a | | | | | ܠܕܙ | |
| b | | | | | | |
| 10a | | | | | | ܐܠܕ |
| b | | | | | | |
| 11a | | | | | | |
| b | | | | | | |
| 12a | | | | | | |
| b | | ܦܐܪ̈ | | | | ܐܠܕ |
| 13 | | | | | | ܐܠܕ |
| 14a | | | | | | |
| b | | | | | | |
| 15 | | | | | | |
| 16a | | | | | | |
| b | | | | | ܠܗܘܠ | |

| | | | in part | | |
|---|---|---|---|---|---|
| | | | ܠܓܪ | | |
| | | | | | |
| | | | | | |
| | | | | | |
| | | | ܠܓܪ | | |
| | | | | | |
| | | | | | |
| | | | ܠܓܪܬܐ | | |
| | | | ܐܓܪܘܢ ² | ܫܓܪ | |
| | | | | | |
| | | | | ܫܓܪ, ܫܪ | |
| | | | | | |
| | | | ܡܕ | | |
| | | | | | |
| | | | | ܝܡܐ | |
| | | | ܡܕ | | |
| | | | | ܝܡܡܬܐ | |
| | | | ܫܡܒ | | |
| | | | | | |
| | | | | | |
| | | | ܫܡܒ | ܫܡ | |
| | | | | ܫܡ | |
| | | | | | |
| ܢܡܝܐ | | | | | |
| | | | | | |
| | | | | | |
| | | | | | |
| ܢܡܝ | | | | | |
| | | | | | |
| | ܒܡܪ, ܒܡܪܬܐ | | | | |
| | | ܦܪܝܡܐ | | | |
| | ܒܡܪܐ | | | | |

| | | | | | | | |
|---|---|---|---|---|---|---|---|
| 17 | | | | | | | |
| 18a | | | | | | | |
| b | | | | | ܐܝܟ | | |
| c | | | | | | | |
| 19a | ܥܠ, ܡܛܠܬܗ | | | | | | |
| b | | | | | | ܘܡܢ | |
| 20a | | ܠܘܬ, ܠܘܬܐ | | | | | |
| b | | | | | | | |
| 21a | | | | | | | ܘܣܥܪܬܗ |
| b | | | | | | | |
| c | | | | | ܐܝܟ | | |
| 22a | | | | | | | |
| b | | ܠܘܬ | | | | | |
| 23a | | | | | | | |
| b | | | | | | | |
| c | | | ܩܪܝܐ | ܡܠ | | | |
| 24 | | | | | | | ܒܡܫܟ |

| | ܬܫܒܘܚܬܐ | | | | | |
|---|---|---|---|---|---|---|
| | | | | | | |
| | | | ܢܛܪ | | | |
| ܦܪܝܫܘܬܐ | | | | ܐܬܪܐ | | |
| | | | | | ܐܠܟܐ | |
| | | | | | | |
| | | | | | | |
| | | | | | | |
| | | | | | | ܡܦܩ |
| | | | | | ܐܠܟܐ | ܡܦܩ |
| | | | ܢܛܪ | | | |
| | | | | | | |
| | | ܪܡܠܠ | | | | |
| ܦܪܝܫܘܬܐ | | | | ܐܬܪܐ | | |
| | | | | | | |
| | | | | | | |
| ܦܪܝܫܘܬܐ | ܫܒܚܘ | ܪܡܠܠ | | | | |

ODE 11 [Greek]

| | throughout | | | | | | | |
|------|------------|------|------|------|------|------|------|------|
| 1a | | | | | | | | |
| b | | | | | | | | |
| c | | | | | | | | |
| d | καρποφορέω | | | | | | | |
| 2a | | | | | | | | |
| b | | | | | | | | |
| c | | | | | | | | |
| 3a | | | | | | | | |
| b | | | | | | | | |
| 4 | | | | | | | | |
| 5a | | | | | | | | |
| b | | | | | | | | |
| 6a | | | | | | | | |
| b | | ζωός | | | | | | |
| 7 | | | ἀθάνατος | | | | | |
| 8a | | | | | | | | |
| b/9a | | | | | | | | |
| b | | | | πλουτέω | | | | |
| 10a | | | | | | | | |
| b | | | | | | | | |
| 11a | | | | | | | | |
| b | | | | | φῶς | | | |
| 12a | | | | | | | | |
| b | (καρποί) | | | | | θάλλω | γελάω | |
| 13 | | | | | | | | γῆ |
| 14a | | | | | | | | |
| b | | | | | | | | |
| 15 | | | | | | | | |
| 16a | | | | | | | | |
| b | | | | πλοῦτος | | | | |

| | | | in part | |
|---|---|---|---|---|
| | | | περιτέμνω | |
| | | | | |
| | | | | |
| | | | | |
| | | | περιτέμνω | |
| | | | | |
| | | | | |
| | | | περιτέμνω | |
| | | | | |
| | | | | |
| | | | | |
| | | | | |
| | | | ὔδωρ | |
| | | | | |
| | | | ὔδωρ | μεθύω |
| | | | | μέθη |
| | | | | |
| | | | | |
| | | | | |
| | | | | |
| | | | | |
| | | | | |
| | | | | |
| | | | | |
| | | | πρόσωπον | |
| | | | | |
| | | | πρόσωπον | |
| χρηστότης | | | | |
| | παράδεισος | | | |
| | | τρυφή | | |

| | | | | | | | |
|------|-----------|-------|----------|-----|--------|----|-----------|
| c | καρποφορέω | | | | | | |
| d | | | | | | | |
| e | (καρποί) | | | θάλλω | | | |
| f | | | ἀθάνατος | | γελάω | | |
| g | | | | | | γῆ | |
| h | | | | | | | |
| i | | ζωός | | | | γῆ | |
| 17 | | | | | | | |
| 18a | | | | | | γῆ | |
| b | | | | | | | |
| 19a | | | | | | | |
| b | | | | φῶς | | | |
| 20a | | | | | | | |
| b | | | | | | | |
| 21a | | | | | | | χρηστότης |
| b | | | | | | γῆ | |
| 22a | | | | | | | |
| b | | | | | | | |
| c | | | | | | | |
| 23a | | | | | | | |
| b | | | | | | | |
| c | καρποφορέω | | | | | | |
| 24 | | | | | | | |

| | | δένδρον | | | | |
|---|---|---|---|---|---|---|
| | | | | | | |
| | | | | | | |
| | | | | | | |
| | | | | | | |
| | | | | | | |
| | | αἰώνιος | | | | |
| | | | δόξα | | | |
| | | | | | | |
| παράδεισος | | | | | τόπος | |
| | | δένδρον | | | | αὐξάνω, αὔξη |
| | | | | | | |
| | | | | | | |
| | | | | | | |
| | | | | | | |
| | | | | | | |
| | | | | | | |
| | | | | | | |
| | | | | | | |
| παράδεισος | | | | | τόπος | |
| | | | | | | |
| | | | | | | |
| παράδεισος | τρυφή | | αἰώνιος | | | |

## ODE 12

| | | | throughout | | | | | |
|---|---|---|---|---|---|---|---|---|
| 1a | ܦܘܠܚܢܐ | ܢܗܝܪ̈ | | | | | | |
| b | | | ܠܒ | | | | | |
| 2a | | | | | | | | |
| b | | ܢܗܝܪ̈ | ܦܘܡܐ | | | | | |
| c | | | | | | | | |
| 3a | | | | | | | | ܥܕܠܬ |
| b | ܦܘܠܚܢܐ | ܢܗܝܪ̈ | ܦܘܡܐ | | | | | |
| c | | | | ܟܝܢܐ | | | | |
| 4a | | | | | ܥܠ | | | |
| b | | | | | | | | |
| c | | | | | | | | |
| d | | | | | | ܫܬܝܩܘܬܐ | | |
| e | | | | | | | | |
| f | | | | | | | ܥܠܬ | |
| 5a | ܦܘܠܚܢܐ | | | | | | | |
| b | | | | | | | | |
| c | | | | | | | | |
| 6a | | | | | | | | |
| b | | | | | | | | ܠܥ |
| c | | | | | | | | |
| 7a | | | | | | | ܥܠܬ | |
| b | | | | | ܟܝܢܐ | ܫܬܝܩܘܬܐ | | |
| 8a | | | ܠܒ | | ܥܠ | | | |
| b | | | | | | | | |
| c | | | | | | | | |
| 9a | | | | | | | | |
| b | | | ܠܒ | | | | | |
| 10a | ܦܘܠܚܢܐ | | | | | | | |
| b | | | | | | | ܥܠ | ܠܥ |
| c | | | | | | | | |
| 11a | | | ܠܒ | ܦܘܡܐ | | | | |
| b | | | | | | | | |

| in part | | |
|---|---|---|
| | | |
| | | |
| ܐܪܝ | | |
| ܐܪܝ | | |
| | | |
| | | |
| | | |
| | | |
| | | |
| | | |
| | | |
| | | |
| | | |
| | | |
| | | |
| ܩܠܬܚܕ | ܬܚܘܪ | |
| ܩܠܬܚܕ | ܬܚܘܪ | |
| | | |
| | | |
| | | ܩܡܣܝ [2] |
| | | |
| | | |
| | | |
| ܚ ܠܚܝ | | |
| | | |
| | | |
| | ܫܥܢܬܩ | |
| ܚ ܠܚܕܬ ܚ | . | |
| | | |
| | | |
| | ܫܥܢܬܩ | |
| | | |
| | | |

| 12a | ܦܘܬܟܐ | | | | | | | |
|-----|-------|---|---|---|---|---|---|---|
| b | | ܫܝܪܐ | | | | | | |
| 13a | | | | | | | | ܙܠ |
| b | | ܫܝܪܐ | | | | | | ܙܠ |

## ODE 13

| | throughout | |
|-----|------------|---|
| 1a | ܡܫܝܚܘܬܐ | |
| b | ܚܝ | |
| 2a | | ܐܦܐ |
| b | | |
| 3a | | ܐܦܐ |
| b | | |
| 4 | | |

## ODE 14

| | throughout | | | | in part |
|-----|------|-------|------|---|---------|
| 1a | ܐܟ... | | | | ܢܚܬ |
| b | ...ܗܘܐ | ܟܠܒܩ | | | ܢܚܬ |
| 2 | | | | | |
| 3a | | | ܪܚܡܐ | | |
| b | | | | | |
| 4a | | ܟܠܒܩ | | | |
| b | | | | | |
| 5a | | | ܕܫܩܒܘܬܐ | | |
| b | | | | | |
| 6a | | | | | |
| b | | | | | ܦܐܪܐ |
| 7a | | | | | |
| b | | | | | ܦܐܪܐ |
| 8a | | | | | |
| b | | | ܫܚܝ | | |

| | | | | | |
|---|---|---|---|---|---|
| 9a | ...ܐܝܟ | | ܝ̇ܢܐ | | |
| b | ܗܘܐ... | | | | ܬܠ |
| c | | | | | ܬܠ |
| 10 | | | | | |

## ODE 15

| | throughout | | | in part | |
|---|---|---|---|---|---|
| 1a | ܢܘܗܪ | | | ܫܡܫܐ | ܚܫܘܟܐ |
| b | | | | | ܚܫܘܟܐ |
| 2a | | | | ܫܡܫܐ | |
| b | | | | | |
| c | | | | | |
| 3a | | | | | |
| b | ܢܘܗܪ | | | | |
| 4a | | | | | |
| b | | | | | |
| 5a | | ܚܕܘܬܐ | | | |
| b | | | | | |
| 6a | | | | | |
| b | | | | | |
| c | | | | | |
| 7a | | | ܢܣܒ, ܡܗܝܡܢܘܬܐ | | |
| b | | | | | |
| 8a | | | | ܚܝܠܐ | |
| b | | | | ܚܝܠܐ | |
| 9a | | | | ܢܛܪ | |
| b | | | | | |
| 10a | | | | | |
| b | | ܢܛܪ | | | |
| c | | | ܢܣܒ | | |

## ODE 16

| | throughout | | | | | | |
|---|---|---|---|---|---|---|---|
| 1a | ܐܠܬܐ | | | | | | |
| b | ܐܠܬܐ | | | | | | |
| c | ܐܠܬܐ | ܬܫܒܘܚܬܐ | | | | | |
| 2a | | ܬܫܒܘܚܬܐ | ܩܠܝܐ | | | | |
| b | | | | ܠܬܐ | | | |
| c | | | | | | | |
| 3a | | | | | | | |
| b | | | | | | | |
| 4a | | ܬܫܒܘܚܬܐ | | | | | |
| b | | | | | | | |
| 5a | | | | | | | |
| b | | ܬܫܒܘܚܬܐ | | | ܐܘܪܬܐ | | |
| 6 | ܐܠܬܐ | | ܩܠܝܐ | | | | |
| 7 | | | | | | ܟܠܬܐ | |
| 8a | | | | | | ܟܠܬܐ | |
| b | | | | | | | ܬܒܘܪܟܬܐ |
| 9a | ܐܠܬܐ | | | | | | |
| b | | | | | | | ܬܒܘܪܟܬܐ |
| 10 | | | | | | | |
| 11 | | | | | | | |
| 12a | | | | | | | |
| b | ܐܠܬܐ | | | | | | |
| 13a | | | | | | | |
| b | ܐܠܬܐ, ܠܬܐ | | | | | | |
| c | | | | | | | |
| 14 | ܠܬܐ | | | | | ܟܠܬܐ | |

| | | in part |
|---|---|---|
| | | |
| | | |
| | | |
| | | ܘܬܐ |
| | | |
| | | |
| | | ܘܬܐ |
| | | |
| | | |
| | | |
| | | |
| | | |
| | | |
| | | |
| | | |
| | | ܗܝ |
| | | |
| | | ܗܝ |
| | | |
| ܐܪܥܐ | | |
| | | ܬܗ |
| | ܒܪܬܐ | ܬܗ |
| | | |
| | ܒܪܬܐ | ܟܡܐ, ܟܡܐ |
| | | |
| | | |
| | | |

| | | | | | | | |
|---|---|---|---|---|---|---|---|
| 15a | | | | | | | |
| b | | | | | | | |
| 16a | | | | | | | |
| b | | | | | | | |
| 17 | | | | | ܐܢܬܬܐ | | |
| 18a | | | | | | | |
| b | | | | | | | |
| 19a | | | | | | ܒܠܬܐ | |
| b | | | | ܠܐ | | | ܚܡܫܬܐ |
| 20 | | ܬܐܡܪܘܬܐ | | | | | |

ODE 17

| | throughout | | | | | | |
|---|---|---|---|---|---|---|---|
| 1a | | | | | | | |
| b | ܐܝ | | | | | | |
| 2a | | | | | | | |
| b | ܦܪܘܩܐ | | | | | | |
| 3a | | | ܚܪܝ | | | | |
| b | | | | | | | |
| 4a | | | | | | | |
| b | | | | | | | |
| c | | ܦܘܦ | | | | | |
| 5a | | | | | | | |
| b | | | ܐܪܝ | | | | |
| 6a | | | | ܐܝ | | | |
| b | | | | | | | |
| 7a | | | | | ܢܠ | | |
| b | | | | | | | |
| c | | | | | | | |
| d | | | | | ܢܠ | | |
| 8a | | | | | | ܠܡܗ | |

| | | ܡܫܡܫܬܐ | ܢܗܝܪܐ | ܫܒܚܬܐ | | |
|---|---|---|---|---|---|---|
| | | ܡܫܡܫܬܐ | | | ܫܠܚܘܢ | ܠܠܐ |
| | | | ܢܗܝ | ܫܒܚܬܐ | | |
| ܐܝܢܐ | | | | | ܫܠܚܘܢ | |
| | | | | | | |
| | | | | | | |
| | | | | | | |
| | | | | | | |
| | | | | | | |
| | | | | | | |

| in part | | | |
|---|---|---|---|
| ܒܠ | | | |
| ܒܠܠܐ | | | |
| | | | |
| | | | |
| | | | |
| | | | |
| | | | |
| | | | |
| ܗܠܝ | | | |
| | ܫܝܪܐ | | |
| | | | |
| | | | |
| | | | |
| | | | |
| | | | |
| | | | |
| | ܫܝܪܐ | ܝܗܪ, ܣܘܪܬܐ | |
| ܗܠܬܐ | | | |

| | | | | | | | |
|---|---|---|---|---|---|---|---|
| b | | | | | | | |
| 9a | | | | | | | |
| b | | | | | | | |
| c | | | | | | | |
| 10a | | | | ܐܬܐ | | | |
| b | | | | | | | |
| 11a | | | ܐܝܠ | | | | |
| b | | | | | | | |
| 12a | | | | | ܘܬܠܐ | ܢܡ ܠ | |
| b | | | | | | | |
| 13a | | | | | | | |
| b | | | | | | | |
| 14a | ܐܬ | | | | | | |
| b | | ܦܘܒ | | | | | |
| 15 | | | | | | | ܗܪܐ |
| 16 | | | | | | | ܗܪܐ |

## ODE 18

| | throughout | | | | | | |
|---|---|---|---|---|---|---|---|
| 1a | | | | | | | |
| b | ܚܒܝ | ܚܒܪܐ | | | | | |
| 2a | | | | | | | |
| b | | | | | | | |
| 3a | | | | | | | |
| b | | | ܗܒܪܐ | | | | |
| c | | | | ܚܪܝܬ | | | |

| ܦܘܫ | ܐܚܝ | | |
|---|---|---|---|
| | | ܦܘܪܬܐ | |
| | | ܦܘܪܬܐ | |
| | | | |
| | ܐܚܝ | | |
| ܦܘܫ | | | |
| | ܐܚܝ | | |
| | | | ܐܡܪ [2] |
| | | | |
| | | | |
| | | | |
| | | | |
| | | | |
| | | | |
| | | | |
| | | | |

| in part | | |
|---|---|---|
| | | |
| | | |
| | | |
| | | |
| | | |
| | | |
| | | |

| | | | | | | | | |
|---|---|---|---|---|---|---|---|---|
| 4a | | | | | | | | |
| b | | | | | | | | |
| 5a | | | | | | | | |
| b | | | | | | | | |
| 6a | | | | | | | | |
| b | | | | ܟܝܢܫ | | | | |
| 7a | | | | | | | | |
| b | | | | | | | | |
| c | | | | | | | | |
| 8a | | | | | | | | |
| b | | | ܟܝܢܕ | | | | | |
| 9a | | | | | ܟܬܩܘܝܣܐ | ܠܝ | | |
| b | | | | | | ܠܝ | | |
| 10a | | | | | | ܠܝ | ܟܬܠܝ | |
| b | | | | | | ܠܝ | | |
| 11a | | | | | | ܟܬܠܝ | | |
| b | | | | | | | | |
| 12a | | | | | ܟܘܝܣ | | | ܟܪ |
| b | | | | | ܘܝܣ | | | |
| 13a | | | | | | ܠܝ $^{2}$ | | |
| b | | | | | | | | |
| 14a | | | | | | | | |
| b | | | | | | | ܟܬܠܝ | |
| 15a | | | | ܟܝܢܫ | | | | |
| b | | | | | | | | |
| 16 | ܟܬܢܫܬ | ܟܪܫ | | | | | | ܟܬܢܝ |

| | | |
|---|---|---|
| | | |
| | | |
| | | |
| ܐܚܡܠܬܐ | | |
| | ܐܝ | |
| | | ܐܠܚܬܐ |
| | ܐܡܚܬܐ | |
| | | |
| | | |
| | | ܐܠܚܬܐ |
| ܐܚܡܠܬܐ | | |
| | | |
| | | |
| | | |
| | | |
| | | |
| | | |
| | | |
| | | |
| | | |
| ܐܡܫܚܬܐ, ܫܚܒ | | |
| | | |
| | | |
| | | |
| | ܢܦܝ, ܢܦܐ | |
| | | |

## ODE 19

| | | throughout | | | | | | |
|---|---|---|---|---|---|---|---|---|
| 1a | ܚܠܒܐ | | | | | | | |
| b | | ܟܣܘܬܗ | | | | | | |
| 2a | | | ܒܪܐ | | | | | |
| b | ܚܠܒܐ | | | ܐܒܐ | | | | |
| c | ܚܠܒܐ | | | | ܪܘܚܐ ܕܩܘܕܫܐ | | | |
| 3a | | | | | | ܬܕܝܗ | | |
| b | ܚܠܒܐ | | | | | | ܒܠܐ | ܣܦܩܘ ܬ |
| 4a | | | | | ܪܘܚܐ ܕܩܘܕܫܐ | | | . |
| b | ܚܠܒܐ | | | ܐܒܐ | | ܬܕܝܗ | | |
| 5a | | | | | | | | |
| b | | | | | | | | |
| 6a | | | | | | | | |
| b | | | | | | | | |
| 7a | | | | | | | | |
| b | | | | | | | | |
| c | | | | | | | | |
| 8 | | | ܒܪܐ | | | | | ܣܦܩܘ ܬ |
| 9a | | | | | | | ܒܠܐ | |
| b/10a | | | | | | | | |
| b | | | | | | | | |
| c | | | | | | | | |
| d | | | | | | | | |
| 11a | | | | | | | | |
| b | | ܟܣܘܬܗ | | | | | | |
| c | | | | | | | | |

| | | in part |
|---|---|---|
| | | ܟܡܣ |
| | | |
| | | ܟܡܣ |
| | | |
| | | |
| | | |
| | | |
| | | |
| | | |
| | | |
| ܝܡܣ | | |
| | | ܟܬܠܢܬܒ |
| ܝܡܣ | ܠܝ | |
| | | ܟܬܠܢܬܒ |
| | ܠܝ | |
| | | |
| | | |
| | | ܟܬܚ |
| | | ܟܚ |
| | ܠܝ | |
| | ܠܝ | ܟܬܚܚܬ |
| | | |
| | | |
| | | |
| | | ܚܚܝ |

ODE 20

| | throughout | | | | |
|---|---|---|---|---|---|
| 1a | | | | | |
| b | | | | | |
| 2 | ܩܘܪܒܐ, ܗܘ܏ | | | | |
| 3a | | ܠܐ... | | | |
| b | | ..ܐܘܠܐ | | | |
| c | | ..ܐܘܠܐ | | | |
| 4a | ܩܘܪܒܐ | | | | |
| b | | | | | |
| 5a | ܗܘܩ | | | | |
| b | | | | | |
| c | | | | | |
| 6a | | ܠܐ... | | | |
| b | ܩܘܗ | ..ܐܘܠܐ | | | |
| c | | ..ܐܘܠܐ | | | |
| 7a | | | ܠܒܥܬܗܐ | | |
| b | | | | | |
| c | | | | | |
| 8a | | | | | |
| b | | | ܩܕܡܒ | | |
| c | | | | | |
| 9a | | | | | ܗܟܒܫܘܬܗ |
| b | | | ܠܒܥܬܗܐ | ܗܣܒܩܗܐ | |
| c | | | | | ܗܟܒܫܘܬܗ |
| 10 | | | | | ܗܟܒܫܘܬܗ |

| in part | | |
|---|---|---|
| ܟܡܐ | | |
| ܟܡ | | |
| | ܟܬܘܫܬܐ | |
| | | |
| | ܟܬܘܫܬܐ | ܟܡܣ |
| | | ܟܡܣܘܬ |
| | | |
| | | |
| | | |
| ܟܢܘܫܝܐ [2] | | |
| | ܟܢܥ [2] | |
| | ܟܢܥ | |
| | | |
| | | |
| | | |
| | | |
| | | |
| | | |
| | | |
| | | |
| | | |
| | | |
| | | |
| | | |
| | | |

ODE 21 (cf. page 368)

ODE 22 [Syriac]

| | throughout | | | | | in part | |
|---|---|---|---|---|---|---|---|
| 1a | | | | | | ܗ ܗܘ | |
| b | | | | | | | |
| 2 | | | | | | ܗ ܗܘ | |
| 3 | | | | | | ܗ ܗܘ | ܟܠܬܟܐ, ܟܠܬܐ |
| 4 | ܢܗܒ | ܫܪܐ | | | | ܗ ܗܘ | |
| 5a | | | ܐܢܬ | | | ܗ ܗܘ | |
| b | | | | | | | |
| 6a | | | | | | | |
| b | | | | | | | |
| 7a | | | | ܚܠܒ | | | |
| b | | | ܐܢܬ | | ܐܘܪܚܐ | | |
| 8a | | | | | | | |
| b | | | | | | ܒܝܬܐ | |
| 9a | | | | | | ܒܝܬܐ | |
| b | | | | | | | |
| 10a | | | | | | | |
| b | ܢܗܒ | | | | | | |
| 11a | | | | ܚܝܠܬ | ܐܘܪܚܐ | | |
| b | | | | | | | |
| c | | | | ܚܝܠܬ | | | |
| d | | ܫܪܐ | | | | ܠܟܬܒܝ | |
| 12a | | | | | | ܠܟܬܒܝ | |
| b | | | | | | | |
| c | | | | | | | |

ODE 22 [Coptic]

| | throughout | | | | | | | | in part |
|---|---|---|---|---|---|---|---|---|---|
| 1a | EINE | MA | | | | | | | ECHT |
| b | EINE | MA | | | | | | | ECHT |
| 2a | | | MHTE | | | | | | |
| b | | | | | | | | | |
| 3 | | | | | | | | | |
| 4 | | | | † | BWλ (EBOλ) | | | | |
| 5a | | | | | | 6IA | | | |
| b | | | | | | | | | |
| c | | | | | | | | | |
| 6a | | | | † | | | | | |
| b | | MA | | | | | | | |
| 7a | | | | | | | TAKO | | |
| b | | | | | | 6IA | | ϩIH | |
| 8a | | | | | | | | | |
| b | | | MHTE | | | | | | |
| 9a | | | | | | | | | |
| b | | | | † | | | | | |
| 10a | | | | | | | | | |
| b | | | | † | | | | | |
| 11a | | | | | | | TAKO | ϩIH | |
| b | | | | | | | | | |
| c | EINE | | | | | | TAKO | | |
| d | | | | | BWλ (EBOλ) | | | | EIPE |
| 12a | | | | | | | | | EIPE |
| b | | | | | | | | | |
| c | | MA | | | | | | | EIPE |

## ODE 23

| | throughout | | | | | | | |
|---|---|---|---|---|---|---|---|---|
| 1a | ܡܪܝܐ | | | | | | | |
| b | | ܟܠ | | | | | | |
| c | | | | | | | | |
| 2a | | | | | | | | |
| b | | ܟܠ | ܚܘܒܐ | | | | | |
| c | | | | ܪܥܝܢܝ | | | | |
| 3a | | | | | | | | |
| b | | ܟܠ | | | | | | |
| c | | | | ܪܥܝܢܝ | | | | |
| 4a | | | | | ܝܕܥܬܐ | | | |
| b | | | | | ܥܠ | | | |
| c | | | | | ܝܕܥܬܐ | ܨܒܝܢܐ | | |
| 5a | | | | | | | ܡܚܫܒܬܐ | ܐܝܕܐ |
| b | | | | | | | | |
| 6a | | | | | | | | |
| b | | | | | | | | |
| 7a | | | | | | | | ܐܝܕܐ |
| b | | ܚܘܒܐ | | | | | | |
| 8a | | | | | | | | |
| b | | | | | | | | |
| c | | | | | | | | |
| 9a | | | | | | | | |
| b | | | | | | | | |
| c | | | | | | | | ܐܝܕܐ |
| 10a | | | | | | | | |
| b | | | | | ܥܠ | | | |
| c | | ܟܠ | | | | | | |
| d | | ܟܠ | | | | | | |

| | | | | | | | | | in part | |
|---|---|---|---|---|---|---|---|---|---|---|
| | | | | | | | | | ܠܒܫ | |
| | | | | | | | | | | ܠܐܝ |
| | | | | | | | | | | ܠܐܝ |
| | | | | | | | | | ܠܒܫ | |
| | | | | | | | | | ܡܪܐ | |
| | | | | | | | | | ܡܪܐ | |
| ܚܝܬ | ܡܪܘܬܐ | | | | | | | | | |
| | | ܪܡܝ | ܡܠܐܬܐ | | | | | | | |
| | | | ܩܪܐ | | | | | | | |
| | | | | ܢܒܕ | ܓܠܘܬܐ | | | | | |
| | | | | | | | | | ܚܕܪܐ | |
| | | | | | | ܫܝܪ | | | ܚܕܪܐ | |
| | | | | | | | | | ܚܕܪܐ | |
| | | | | | | | ܫܠܐ | | | |
| | | | | | | ܫܝܪ | | | | |
| | | | ܩܪܐ | | | | | | | |

| | | | | | | | | |
|---|---|---|---|---|---|---|---|---|
| 11a | | | | | | | | |
| b | | | | | | | | |
| 12a | | | | | | | | |
| b | | | | | | | | |
| 13a | | | | | | | | |
| b | | | | | | | | |
| c | | | | | | | | |
| 14a | | | | | | | | |
| b/ 15a | | | | | | | | |
| b | | | | | | | | |
| c | | | | | | | | |
| 16a | | | ܪܚܝ | | | | ܚܘܝ | |
| b | | | | | | | | ܡܝ |
| c | | | | | | | | |
| 17a | | | | | ܐܠܗܐ | | | |
| b | | | | | | | | |
| 18a | | | ܪܚܝ 2 | | | | | |
| b | | | | | | | ܪܝܒܐ | |
| 19a | | ܢܒܣ | | | | | | |
| b | | | | ܡܫܝܚܐ | | | | |
| 20a | | | | | | | | |
| b | | | | | | | | |
| 21a | | | | | ܐܠܗܐ | | | |
| b | | | ܡܫܝܒܐܬܐ | | | | | |
| 22a | | | | | | | | |
| b | ܩܝܪ | | | | | | | |
| c | | | | | | | | |

| | | | | | | | | ܐܬܐ | | |
|---|---|---|---|---|---|---|---|---|---|---|
| | | | | | | | | | ܐܬܐ...ܠܝ | |
| | | | | ܬܪܬܝܢ | ܬܪܬܝܢ | | | | | |
| | | | | | | | | ܐܬܐ | | |
| | | | | | | | | | | |
| ܒܬܐܪ | | | | | | | | | | |
| | | | | | | | | | | |
| | | | | | | | | | | |
| ܒܬܐܪ | | | | | | | | | | |
| | | | | | | | | | | ܢܝܐ |
| | | | | | | | | ܐܬܐ | | ܢܝܐ |
| | | | | ܬܪܪܡ | | | | | ܐܬܐ...ܠܝ | |
| | | | | | | | | | | |
| | | | ܡܠܐ | | | | | | | |
| | | | | | | ܒܝܐ | ܐܟܐ | | | |
| | | | | ܬܪܬܝܢ | | | | | | |
| ܒܬܐܪ | | | | | | | | | | |
| | ܬܝܒ | | | | | | | | | |
| | | | | | | | | | | |
| | | ܬܡܐ | | | | | | | | |
| | | | | | | ܐܟܐ | | | | |
| | | | | | | ܒܝܐ | | | | |
| | | | ܬܠܡ | | | | | | | |

ODE 21

| | throughout | | | | | in part |
|---|---|---|---|---|---|---|
| 1a | ܪܘܚܝ, ܡܪܘܬܐ | | | | | |
| b | | | | | | ܚܕܝ |
| 2a | | | | | | |
| b | ܪܘܚܝ | ܡܒܪܟܘ | | | | |
| c | | | | | | ܚܕܝ |
| 3a | | | | | | |
| b | | | ܣܡܗܪ | | | |
| 4a | | | | | | |
| b | | | | | | |
| c | | | | | | |
| 5a | | ܡܒܪܝܬܗ | | | | |
| b | | | | | | |
| c | | | | | | |
| 6a | ܪܘܚܝ | | ܣܡܗܪ | | | |
| b | | | | ܐܠܗܐ | | |
| 7a | | | | | | |
| b | | | | | ܫܒܚ | |
| c | | | | | | |
| 8a | | | | | | |
| b | | | | | | |
| c | | | | | | |
| 9a | | | | ܐܠܗܐ | | |
| b | | | | | ܬܫܒܘܚܬܐ | |

ODE 24

| | throughout | | | | | | in part |
|---|---|---|---|---|---|---|---|
| 1a | ܦܘܝ | ܡܪܐ | | | | | ܐܢܫ |
| b | | | | | | | ܐܢܫ |
| 2a | | | | | | | |
| b | | | | | | | |
| 3a | | | | | | | |
| b | | | | | | | |
| 4a | ܦܘܬܐ | | | | | | |
| b | | | | | | | |
| 5a | | ܬܚܡܘܡ | | | | | |
| b | | ܡܪܝ | | | | | |
| 6a | | | | | | | |
| b | | | | | | | |
| 7a | | ܡܪܝ | ܬܚܡܘܡ | | | | ܠܘܬܐ, ܠܘܬܐ |
| b | | | | ܐܟܒ | ܡܫܒܚܬܐ | | |
| c | | | | | | | |
| 8a | | | | | | | ܚܘܠ |
| b | | | | | | | ܚܘܠܬܐ |
| 9a | | | | ܐܟܒ | | ܚܡܝܢ | |
| b | | | | | | | |
| c | | | | | | | |
| 10a | | ܡܪܝ | | ܐܟܒ | ܡܫܒܚܬܐ | | |
| b | | | | | | | ܟܝܪ |
| 11a | | | | | | ܚܡܝܢ | |
| b | | | | | | | |
| 12a | | | | | | | |
| b | | | | | | | ܟܝܪ |
| 13a | | ܡܪܝ | | | | | |
| b | | | | | | | |
| 14a | | | | | | | ܠܥ |
| b | | | | | | | ܠܥ |

## ODE 25 [Syriac]

| | throughout | | | | in part | |
|---|---|---|---|---|---|---|
| 1a | | | | | | |
| b | | | | | | |
| 2a | ܡܢ | ܦܪܩܘ | | | | |
| b | | | ܕܪܬܝܢ | | | |
| 3a | | | | ܠܩܘܠ | | |
| b | | | | | | |
| 4a | | | | | | |
| b | | ܦܪܩ | | | | |
| 5a | | | | | ܠܢܝ | |
| b | | | | | ܠܢܝ | |
| 6a | | | | | | |
| b | | | ܠܩܝܪܝ | | | |
| 7a | ܡܢ | | | | | |
| b | | | | | | |
| 8a | | | | | ܡܩܘ, ܕܩܘܡܬ | |
| b | | | | | | ܩܘܪܢ |
| 9a | ܡܢ | | | | | ܩܘܪܢ |
| b | | | | | | |
| 10a | | | | | | |
| b | | | | | ܕܩܘܩܬ | |
| 11a | | | | ܠܩܘܠ | | |
| b | | | | | | |
| 12a | | | | | ܩܪܦ | |
| b | | | | | | |

ODE 25 [Coptic]

| | throughout | | | | | | | | | in part |
|---|---|---|---|---|---|---|---|---|---|---|
| 1a | NOYϨM̄ | | | | | | | | | |
| b | | | | | | | | | | |
| 2a | NOYϨM̄ | ϢⲰⲠⲈ | OYⲚAⲘ | | | | | | | |
| b | | | | † | ΤⲰⲠⲈ | | | | | |
| 3a | | | | † | | OYBH | | | | |
| b | | | | | | | | | | |
| 4a | | ϢⲰⲠⲈ | | | | | | | | |
| b | NOYϨM̄ | | | | | | | | | |
| 5a | | | | | | | | | | MTO |
| b | | | | | | | | | | |
| c | | | | | | | EIPE | | | MTO |
| 6a | | ϢⲰⲠⲈ | | | ΤⲰⲠⲈ | | | 6OM | | |
| b | | | | † | ΤⲰⲠⲈ | | | | | |
| 7a | | | | | | | | | ca 2 | |
| b | | ϢⲰⲠⲈ | | | | | | | ca | |
| 8a | | | | | | | | | | |
| b | | | | | | | EIPE | | | |
| 9a | | | OYⲚAⲘ | | | | | | | |
| b | | | | | | | | | (caBOλ) | |
| 10a | | ϢⲰⲠⲈ | | | | | | 6OM | | |
| b | | | | | | | | | | |
| 11 | | | | † | | OYBH | | | | |
| 12a | | | | | | | | | | |
| b | | ϢⲰⲠⲈ | | | | | | | | |

## ODE 26

| | throughout | | | | | | |
|---|---|---|---|---|---|---|---|
| 1a | ܢܒܠ | ܐܬܟܣܝܬܐ | | | | | |
| b | | | | | | | |
| 2a | | | ܡܠܠ | ܘܗܪܝܬܐ | | | |
| b | | | | | | | |
| 3a | | | | | | | |
| b | | | | ܘܗܪܝܬܐ | ܚܝܐ | | |
| 4a | | | | | | | |
| b | | ܒܟܝ | | | | ܪܘܡܪ | |
| 5a | | | | | | | |
| b | | ܐܬܟܣܝܬܐ | | | | | |
| 6a | | | | | | | |
| b | | | | | | | |
| 7a | | | | | | ܪܘܡܒ | |
| b | | | | | | | |
| 8a | | | | ܘܗܪܝܬܐ | | | |
| b | | | | | | | |
| 9a | | | | | | | ܪܗܪ |
| b | | | | | | | |
| 10a | | | | | ܢܚܝ | | |
| b | | | ܡܠܠ | | | | |
| 11a | | | | | | | |
| b | | | | | | | |
| c | | | | | | | |
| 12a | | | | | ܢܚܝ | | |
| b | | | | ܡܕܒܪܘ | ܫܚܬܐ | | |
| 13a | ܡܒܩܘ | | | | | | |
| b | | | | | | | ܪܗܪ |

| in part | | |
|---|---|---|
| | | |
| | | |
| | | |
| ܠܓ | | |
| | | |
| ܠܓ | | |
| | | |
| | | |
| ܓܪܒ...ܓ | | |
| ܡܠܝ... | | |
| ܓܪܒ...ܓ | | |
| ܡܠܝ... | | |
| ܓܪܒ...ܓ | | |
| ܡܠܝ... | | |
| ܡܚ | | |
| ܡܚ (ܐܢ) | | |
| ܡܚ (ܐܢ) | ܦܚܪ | |
| | | ܦܚܪ |
| ܡܚ (ܐܢ) | | |
| | | |
| ܡܚ | | ܬܘܪܟ |
| | | ܬܘܪܟ |
| | | ܬܘܪܟ |
| | | |
| | | |
| | | |
| | | |

ODE 27

| | throughout | |
|---|---|---|
| 1 | ܦܪܝܠ | ܐܝܟ̈ܪ |
| 2 | | ܐܝܟ̈ܪ |
| 3 | ܦܪܝܠ | |

ODE 28

| | throughout | | | | | | |
|---|---|---|---|---|---|---|---|
| 1a | | | | | | | |
| b | | | | | | | |
| c | ܪܘܢܐ | | | | | | |
| 2a | | | | | | | |
| b | | | | | | | |
| 3a | | | | | | | |
| b | | | | | | | |
| c | | | | | | | |
| d | | | | | | | |
| 4a | | | | | | | |
| b | | | | | | | |
| c | | | | | | | |
| d | | | | | | | |
| 5a | | ܩܪܒܡ | ܐܒܬ | | | | |
| b | | | | ܫܠܒܐ | | | |
| 6 | | | | | ܡܒܘܬܐ | | |
| 7a | ܪܘܢܐ | | | | | | |
| b | | | | | ܡܒܘܬ | ܫܒܝܚ | |
| c | | | | | | | |

| in part | | | | |
|---|---|---|---|---|
| ܩܕ݁ | ܩܘܕܢ | | | |
| | ܩܘܕܢ | ܩܘܕܣܐ 2 | | |
| ܩܕ݁ | | | ܠܕܐ | |
| | | | ܠܕܐ | ܕܘܥ |
| | | | | ܕܘܥ |
| ܐܪܓ | | | | |
| ܐܪܓ | | | | |
| ܐܪܓ | | | | |
| ܬܘܪܝ 2 | | | | |
| | | | | |
| | | | | |
| | | | | |
| | | | | |
| | | | | |
| ܣܝܐ | | | | |
| | | | | |
| ܣܝܐ | | | | |

| | | | | | | | |
|---|---|---|---|---|---|---|---|
| 8a | | | | | | | |
| b | | | | | | | |
| 9a | | | | | | | |
| b | | | ܐܒܘ̈ܗܐ | | | | |
| 10a | | | | | | | |
| b | | | | | | | |
| 11a | | | | | | | |
| b | | | | | | | |
| 12a | | | | | | | |
| b | | | | | | | |
| 13a | | | | | | | |
| b | | | | | | | |
| 14a | | | | ܚܒܠ | | | ܬܘܠܕܬܐ |
| b | | | | | | | ܝܠܕܐ |
| 15a | | | | | | | |
| b | | | | | | | |
| 16a | | | ܐܒ | | | | |
| b | | | | | | | |
| c | | | | | | | |
| 17a | | | | | ܡܩܒܠ | ܫܒܚ | |
| b | | | | | | | |
| c | | | | | | | |
| 18a | | | | | | | |
| b | | ܩܡ ܛ | ܐܒ | | | | |
| 19a | | ܩܡ ܛ | | | | | ܬܘܠܕܬܐ |
| b | | | | | | | |

| ܐܝܟ | | | | |
|---|---|---|---|---|
| | | | | |
| | | | | |
| ܐܝܟ | | | | |
| | | | | |
| | | | | |
| | | | | |
| | | | | |
| | | | | |
| | | | | |
| | | | | |
| | | | | |
| | | | | |
| | | | | |
| | | | | |
| | | | | |
| | | | | |
| | | | | |
| | | | | |
| ܠܒ | | | | |
| | | ܩܕܡܘܗܝ | | |
| | | | | |
| | | | | |
| ܠܒ | | ܩܕܡܘܗܝ | | |
| | | | | |
| | | | | |

## ODE 29

| | throughout | | | | | | |
|-----|------|------|------|------|------|------|------|
| 1a | | | | | | | |
| b | | | | | | | |
| 2a | ܟ̈ܬܘܢܣܪܬ | ܠܒܕ | | | | | |
| b | | | ܟܗܢ̈ܐ | ܗܘ | | | |
| 3a | | | | | | | |
| b | | | | | ܟܗܢ̈ܐ | | |
| 4a | | | | | | | |
| b | | | | | | | |
| 5a | | | | | | ܚܪ | ܟܬܠܠܢ |
| b | | | ܟܗܢ̈ܐ | | | | |
| 6a | | | | | | | |
| b | | | | | | | |
| 7a | | | | | | | |
| b | | | | | | | |
| 8a | | | | ܗܘ | | | |
| b | | ܠܒܕ | | | | | |
| c | | | | | | ܚܪ | |
| 9a | | ܠܒܕ | | | | | ܟܬܠ |
| b | | | | | | | |
| 10a | | | | | | ܟܬܠܠܢ | ܟܬܠ |
| b | | | | | | | |
| 11a | ܟ̈ܬܘܢܣܪܬ | | | ܗܘ | | | |
| b | | | | | ܗܪ | | |
| c | | ܟܬܠ | | | | | |

| in part |
|---------|
|         |
|         |
| ܙܘܡܪ |
| ܙܘܡܪ |
|         |
|         |
|         |
|         |
|         |
| ܫܠܘܛܬܐ |
|         |
| ܫܠܐ |
|         |
|         |
|         |
|         |

## ODE 30

|     | throughout | | | | in part |
|-----|-----|-----|-----|-----|-----|
| 1a  | ܟܠܗ |  |  |  | ܒܟܠܗ |
| b   |  |  |  |  |  |
| 2a  |  | ܐܝܟ | ܒܐܝܟ |  |  |
| b   |  |  |  | ܒܘ | ܒܟܠܗ |
| 3   |  |  |  | ܒܘ |  |
| 4a  | ܟܠܗ |  |  |  |  |
| b   |  |  |  |  |  |
| 5a  |  |  |  |  |  |
| b   |  |  |  |  |  |
| 6a  |  | ܐܝܟ |  |  |  |
| b   |  |  |  |  |  |
| 7a  |  |  |  |  |  |
| b   |  |  |  | ܒܘ |  |

## ODE 32

|     | throughout | |
|-----|-----|-----|
| 1a  | ܟܘ |  |
| b   | ܟܘ |  |
| 2a  | ܟܘ |  |
| b   | ܟܘ |  |
| 3a  |  |  |
| b   |  | ܕܠܝܬ, ܕܠܝܬ |

ODE 31

| | throughout | | | | | in part | |
|---|---|---|---|---|---|---|---|
| 1a | | | | | | | |
| b | | | | | | | |
| 2a | | | | | | ܠܝ, ܠܘܬܗ | |
| b | ܣܩܘܒ | | | | | | |
| c | | ܫܪܝܪ | | | | | |
| 3a | | | | | | | |
| b | | | ܠܘܬܗܘܢ | ܠܘܬܗ | | ܒܠܝ | |
| c | | | | | | ܒܠܝ | |
| 4a | | | | | | | |
| b | | | | | | | |
| 5a | | | | | | | |
| b | | | | | | | |
| 6a | | | | | | | |
| b | | | | ܠܘܬܗ | | | |
| 7a | | | ܠܘܬܗܘܢ | | | | |
| b | ܣܩܘܒ | | | | | | |
| 8a | | | | | | ܥܒܕ | |
| b | | | | | ܩܡܕ | | |
| c | | | | | | ܥܒܕ | |
| 9a | | | | | | | |
| b | | | | | | ܥܒܕ | |
| 10a | | | | | | ܣܒܪܐ | |
| b | | | | | | | ܗܘܠ |
| 11a | | ܫܪܝܪܐ | | | ܩܡܕ | | ܗܠܘܬܐ |
| b | | | | | | ܣܒܪܐ | |
| 12a | | | | | | | |
| b | | | | | | | |
| c | | | | | | ܦܘܩ | |
| d | | | | | | | |
| 13a | | | | | | | ܫܘܬܘܪܐ |
| b | | | | | | ܦܘܠܚܐ | ܚܝ |

ODE 32 (cf. page 380)

ODE 33

| | throughout | | | | | | | in part |
|---|---|---|---|---|---|---|---|---|
| 1a | ܬܫܒܘܚܬܐ | | | | | | | |
| b | | ܝܕܥ | ܚܝܠ | | | | | |
| c | | | | | | | | |
| d | | | | | | | | |
| 2a | | | | ܐܡܪ, ܐܡܪܐ | | | | |
| b | | | ܚܝܠ | | | | | |
| 3a | | | | | ܩܕܡ | | | |
| b | | | | | | | | |
| c | | | | | | | | ܡܗܘ |
| d | | | | | | | | ܡܗܘ |
| 4a | | | | | | ܫܡܥ | | |
| b | | | | | | | | |
| 5a | | | | | ܩܕܡ | | | |
| b | | | | | | | | |
| 6a | | | | | | | | |
| b | | | | | | | | |
| 7a | | ܝܕܥ | ܚܝܠ | | | | ܐܘܪܚܬܐ | |
| b | | | | | | | | |
| 8a | | | | | | | | |
| b | | | | ܐܡܪܐ | | | | |
| c | | | | | | | ܐܘܪܚܬܐ | |

| | | | | | | | | | |
|---|---|---|---|---|---|---|---|---|---|
| 9a | | | ܚܝܠ | | | | | | |
| b | | | | ܐܒܐ | | | | | |
| 10a | | | | | | ܫܒܠ | | | |
| b | | | | | | | | | ܦܪܩ |
| c | ܛܝܒܘܬܐ | | | | | | | | |
| 11a | | | | | | | | | ܦܪܩ |
| b | ܛܘܒܐ | | | | | | | | |
| c | | | | | | | | | |
| 12a | | | | | | | | | |
| b | | | ܚܝܠܐ | | | | | | |
| 13a | | | | | | | | | |
| b | | | | | | | ܐܘܪ̈ܚܬܐ | | |
| c | | | | | | | | | |

ODE 34

| | in part | |
|---|---|---|
| 1a | | |
| b | | |
| c | | |
| d | ܦܫܝܛܘܬܐ | |
| 2a | | |
| b | ܦܫܝܛܘܬܐ | |
| 3a | | |
| b | | |
| 4a | ܠܬܚܬ | |
| b | | ܠܥܠ |
| 5a | | ܠܥܠ |
| b | ܠܬܚܬ | |
| c | | |
| 6a | ܦܘܪܩܢܐ | |
| b | ܦܪܩ | |

ODE 35

| | throughout | | | in part | |
|---|---|---|---|---|---|
| 1a | ܢܝܚܘܬܐ | ܛܠ | | | |
| b | | | | | |
| 2a | | | | | |
| b | | | ܦܘܪܩܢܐ | | |
| 3a | | | | | |
| b | | | | | |
| 4a | | | | | |
| b | | ܛܠܠܐ | | ܝܬܝܪ ܡܢ | |
| c | | | | ܝܬܝܪ ܡܢ | |
| 5a | | | | | |
| b | | | | | ܝܗܒ |
| c | | ܛܠܐ | | | |
| 6a | | | | | ܡܘܗܒܬܐ |
| b | ܚܘ | | | | |
| 7a | | | | | |
| b | | | | | |
| c | | | ܦܪܩ | | |

ODE 36

| | throughout | | | in part | |
|---|---|---|---|---|---|
| 1a | ܪܚܡܐ | | | | |
| b | | | | ܡܪܝܐ, ܪܚܡܐ | |
| 2a | | | | | |
| b | | | | ܪܚܡܐ | |
| c | ܫܒܚܬܐ | ܬܫܒܘܚܬܐ | | | |
| d | | | ܫܒܚ | | |
| 3a | | | | | |
| b | | | | ܒܪܝ | |
| c | | | | | |
| d | | | | ܒܪܝ | |
| 4a | | | ܫܒܚ, ܡܫܒܚܘ | | |
| b | | | | ܪܝ, ܪܘܚܐ | |
| 5a | | | ܪܚܡܬܐ | | |
| b | | | | | |
| c | | | | ܚܕܘܬܐ | |
| d | | | | ܚܕܬ | |
| 6a | ܡܫܒܚܘܬܐ | | | | |
| b | | | | ܩܪܒܝ | |
| 7a | | | | | |
| b | | | | | |
| c | | | | | ܥܠܡ |
| d | | | | | ܥܠܡܬܐ |
| 8a | | | | ܩܪܝܒ | |
| b | ܪܚܡܐ | | | | |

ODE 37

| | | throughout | | |
|---|---|---|---|---|
| 1a | ܡܪܝܐ | | | |
| b | | (ܡܥܩ ܢ, ܡܪܝܬܗ) | ܟܠ | |
| 2a | | | | |
| b | | | | |
| c | | | ܟܠ | |
| 3a | | | | |
| b | | | | ܢܗܡܒ |
| 4 | ܡܪܝܐ | | | ܢܗܡܒ |

## ODE 38

| | | | | | | | | |
|---|---|---|---|---|---|---|---|---|
| | throughout | | | | | | | |
| 1a | ܗܠܘ | ܫܪܝܪܐ | | | | | | |
| b | | | | | | | | |
| c | | ܫܪܝܪܐ | | | | | | |
| 2a | | | | | | | | |
| b | | | ܦܘܡ | | | | | |
| 3a | | | ܦܘܡܗ | | | | | |
| b | | | | ܣܡܝ | ܚܝ | ܩܘܬܐ | | |
| 4a | | | | | | | ܐܝܠ | |
| b | | | | | | | | ܫܒܩ |
| c | | ܫܪܝܪܐ | | | | | | |
| 5a | | | | | | | | |
| b | | | | | | | | |
| c | | | | | | | | |
| d | | | | | | | | |
| 6a | | | | | | | | |
| b | | | | | | | | |
| 7a | | ܫܪܝܪܐ | | | | | ܐܝܠ | |
| b | | | | | | | | |
| c | | | | | | | | |
| 8a | | | | | | | | |
| b | | | | | | ܩܘܬܐ | | |
| 9a | | | | | | | | |
| b | | | | | | | | |
| c | | | | | | | | |
| 10a | | ܫܪܝܪܐ | | | | | | |
| b | | | | | | | | |
| c | | | | | | | | |
| d | | | | | | | | |
| 11a | | | | | | | | |
| b | | | | | | | | |
| c | | | | | | | | |

| | | | |
|---|---|---|---|
| | | | |
| | | | |
| | | | |
| | | | |
| | | | |
| | | | |
| | | | |
| | | | |
| | | | |
| ܐܠ | | | |
| | | | |
| | | | |
| | | | |
| ܐܠ | | | |
| | | | |
| ܟܬܐܠ | | | |
| | | | |
| | | | |
| | ܝܠ | | |
| | | | |
| ܟܬܐܠ | | | |
| | | ܟܠܒܚܡ, ܚܠܫ | |
| | | ܚܠܫ | ܒܐܠܒ |
| | | ܝܠܫ 2 | |
| | | | |
| | | | |
| | | | |
| ܟܬܐܠ, ܟܠܬܝܡ | | | |
| | | | ܒܐܠܒ |
| ܐܠ | | | |
| | | | |

| | throughout | | | | | | | |
|---|---|---|---|---|---|---|---|---|
| 12a | | | | | | | | |
| b | | | | | | | | |
| 13a | | | | | | | | |
| b | | | | | | | | |
| 14a | | | | | | | ܚܕܒ | |
| b | | | | | | | | |
| c | | | | | | | | |
| d | | | | | | | | |
| e | | | | | | | | |
| 15a | | | | | | | | |
| b | | | | | | | | ܠܕ |
| c | | | | | | | | |
| d | | ܚܘܪܐ | | | | ܐܪܠ | | |
| 16a | | ܪܚ | ܦܘܒ | | ܫܘ | | | |
| b | | | | ܒܘܪ | | | | |
| c | | | | | | | | |
| 17a | | | | | | | | |
| b | | | | | | | | |
| c | | | | | | | | |
| 18a | ܗܠܒ | | | | | | | |
| b | | | | | | | | |
| 19a | | | | | | | | |
| b | | | | | | | | |
| 20a | | | | | | | | |
| b | | | | | | | | |
| c | | | | | | | | |
| 21a | | | | | | | | |
| b | | | | | | | | |

| | | | | | | | in part |
|---|---|---|---|---|---|---|---|
| | | | | | | | ܡܫܘܚܬܐ |
| | | | | | | | ܫܬܐ |
| ܡܒܥ | | | ܫܘܬܦܬܐ | | | | |
| | | | ܪܐܝܐ | | | | |
| | | | | | | | |
| | | | | | | | |
| | ܫܟܠ | | | | | | |
| | | | | | | | |
| | | | | | | | |
| | | ܫܟܥܩ | | | | | |
| | | | | | | | ܐܘܟ |
| | | | | | | | |
| | | | | | | | |
| | | | | | | | ܐܘܟ |
| | | | | ܝܕܒ | | | |
| | | | | | | | |
| | | | | | ܒܪܝ | | |
| | | | | | | | |
| | | | | | | | |
| | | | | | | | |
| | | | | | ܥܒܬܐ | | |
| | | | | | | | |
| | | | | | | ܒܣܝܘܬܐ | |
| | | | | | ܥܒܬܐ | | |
| | | | | | ܥܒܬܐ | | |
| ܡܒܥ | | | ܬܘܠܬܐ | | | | |

ODE 39

| | throughout | | | | | |
|---|---|---|---|---|---|---|
| 1a | ܐܬܘܪܘܬܐ | | | | | |
| b | | | | | | |
| 2a | | ܐܬܠܡ | | | | |
| b | | | ܐܬܘܪܝܕ | | | |
| 3a | | | | | | |
| b | | | | ܠܒܝ | | |
| 4a | | | | | | |
| b | | | | | | |
| 5a | | | ܒܠ | | ܐܬܘܒܪܘܗ | |
| b | | | | | | |
| 6a | | ܡܠܝ | | | | |
| b | | | | | | |
| 7a | | | | | | |
| b | | | | | | ܐܝܢܐ |
| c | | | ܒܠ | | | ܚܝܐ |
| 8a | | | | | | ܚܝܐ |
| b | | | | | | |
| c | | | ܒܠ | | | |
| d | ܐܬܘܪܘܬܐ | | | | | |
| 9a | | | | | | |
| b | | ܡܠܝ | ܒܠ | | | |
| 10a | | | | | | |
| b | | | | ܠܒܝ | | |
| c | | | | | | |
| 11a | | | | | | |
| b | | | | | | |
| 12 | | | | ܠܒܝ | | |
| 13a | | | ܒܠ | | | ܐܝܢܐ |
| b | | ܐܬܠܡ | | | ܐܬܘܒܪܘܗ | |
| c | | | | | | ܚܝܐ |

## ODE 40

| | in part | |
|---|---|---|
| | | |
| | | |
| | | |
| | | |
| | | |
| | | |
| | | |
| | | |
| | | |
| | | |
| | | |
| | | |
| | | |
| | ܐܬܐ | |
| | ܐܬܐ | |
| | | |
| | | |
| | | |
| | | |
| | | |
| ܡܪܝ | ܚܠܒܬܐ | |
| | | |
| ܡܪܝ | ܚܠܒܬܐ | |
| | | |
| | | |
| | | |

| | | in part | |
|---|---|---|---|
| 1a | | | |
| b | | | |
| c | | | |
| 2a | ܠܗܘ | | |
| b | ܠܗܘ | ܬܫܒܘܚܬܐ | |
| c | | ܬܫܒܘܚܬܐ | |
| 3a | | | |
| b | | | |
| 4a | ܕܝ | | |
| b | ܕܗ | | |
| c | | | |
| 5a | | | |
| b | | | |
| 6a | | | |
| b | | | |

## ODE 41

| | throughout | | | | | | | |
|---|---|---|---|---|---|---|---|---|
| 1a | ܟܒܪ | ܐܠܗܐ | | | | | | |
| b | | | ܫܝܪܐ | | | | | |
| 2a | | | | ܬܠ | ܩܕ | | | |
| b | | | | | | ܩܘܗ | | |
| 3a | | | | | | ܚܝ | | |
| b | | | | | | ܚܝ | | |
| 4a | | | | | | | ܩܘܗ | ܗܘܝ |
| b | ܬܫܒܚܬܐ | | | | | | | . |
| 5a | | | | | | | | |
| b | | | | | | | | |
| 6a | | | | | | | | ܗܘܝܗܝ, ܗܘܝ |
| b | | | | | | ܩܘܗ | ܐܟܬܒܗ | |
| 7 | | | | | | | | |
| 8a | | | | | | | | |
| b | | | | | | | | |
| 9a | | | ܫܝܪܐ | | | | | |
| b | | | | | | | | |
| 10a | | ܠܝ | | | | | | |
| b | | | | | | | | |
| 11a | | | | | | | | |
| b | | | | | | ܚܝ | | |
| c | | | | | | | | |
| 12a | | | | | | | | |
| b | | | | | | | | |
| 13a | | | | | ܩܕ | | | |
| b | | | | | | | | |
| 14a | | | | | | | | ܗܘܝ |
| b | | | | | | | | |
| 15a | | | ܫܝܪܐ | | | | | |
| b | | | | ܬܠ | | | | |
| 16a | | | ܫܝܪܐ | | | ܚܝ | | |
| b | ܬܫܒܬܐ | | | | ܒܠ | | | |

| | | | | | in part |
|---|---|---|---|---|---|
| | | | | | |
| | | | | | |
| | | | | | |
| | | | | | |
| | | | | | |
| | | | | | |
| | | | | | |
| | | | | | |
| ܟܢܫܐ | | | | | |
| | | | | | |
| | | | | | |
| | ܓܠܐ | | | | |
| | | | | | ܟܝܢ̈, ܗܕ̈ |
| | | ܚܠܐ | | | |
| | | | | | |
| | | | ܐܘܪ | | |
| | | | | | |
| | | | | | |
| | ܓܠܐ | | | | |
| | | | | | ܡܠܐܟܐ |
| | | | | | |
| | | | ܩܚܕܐ | | |
| | | | | | |
| | | | | | |
| | | ܚܠܐ | | | |
| | | | ܐܘܪ | | |
| | | | | | ܡܠܐܟܐ |
| | | | | | |
| | | | | | |
| | | | | | |
| ܟܢܫܐ | | | ܩܚܕܐ | | |
| | | | | | |

## ODE 42

| | throughout | | | | | | | | | |
|---|---|---|---|---|---|---|---|---|---|---|
| 1a | ܩܘܒ | | | | | | | | | |
| b | | ܟܘܬܐ | | | | | | | | |
| 2a | | | | | | | | | | |
| b | | | | | | | | | | |
| 3a | | | ܠܢ | | | | | | | |
| b | | | | | | | | | | |
| 4 | | | | ܢܠ | | | | | | |
| 5a | | | | | ܗܘܬ | | | | | |
| b | | | | | | ܪܒܘܗ | | | | |
| c | | | | | | | ܚܐ | | | |
| 6a | | | | | | | | | | |
| b | | | | | | | | | | |
| c | | | | | | | | ܠܟ | | |
| 7a | | | | | | | | | ܡܠܐ | |
| b | | | | ܢܘܚ | | | | | | |
| 8a | | | | | | | | | | |
| b | | | ܠܢ | | | | | | | |
| 9a | | ܗܬܝ | | | | | | | | |
| b | | | | ܢܘܚ | | | | | | ܐܪܬ |
| 10a | | | | | | ܪܒܘܗ | | | ܡܠܐ | |
| b | | | | | | | | | | |
| 11a | | | | | | | | | | |
| b | | | | | ܡܗܬܐ | | | | | |
| 12a | | | | | | | | | | |
| b | | | | | | | | | | |
| 13a | | | | | | | | | | |
| b | | | | | | ܪܒܘܗ | | | | |
| 14a | | | | | ܒܪܬܐ | | ܚܐ | | | |
| b | | | | | | | ܚܬܐ | ܠܟ | | |
| c | | | | | | | | | | |

| | | | in part | |
|---|---|---|---|---|
| | | | ܦܪܚ | ܐܪܙ |
| | | | | ܐܪܙ |
| | | | ܦܪܚ, ܦܪܚܬܐ | |
| | | | | |
| | | | | |
| | | | | |
| | | | | |
| | | | ܦܪܕܘܢ | |
| | | | | |
| | | | | |
| | | | | |
| | | | | |
| | | | | |
| | | | | |
| | | | ܦܪܕ | |
| | | | ܫܪܐ | |
| | | | | ܫܪܬ |
| | | | ܫܪܐ | |
| | | | | ܫܪܬ |
| | | | | |
| | | | | |
| | | | | |
| ܚܪܐ | | | | |
| | | | | |
| | | | | |
| | | | | |
| | ܪܚܡ | | | |
| | | | | |
| | | ܓܒܪ | | |
| | | | | |
| | | | | |

| | | | | | | | | | |
|---|---|---|---|---|---|---|---|---|---|
| 15a | | | | | ܐܝܬ | | | | |
| b | | | | | | | | | |
| c | | | | | | | | | |
| 16a | | | | | | | | | |
| b | | | | | | | | | |
| 17a | | | | | | | | | |
| b | ܗܘ | | | | ܐܝܬܪ | | | | |
| 18a | | | | | | | | | |
| b | | | | | | | | | |
| 19a | | | | | | | | | |
| b | | | | | | | | | ܗܢܘܬܐܪ |
| 20a | | | | | | | | | |
| b | | | | | | | | | |
| c | | | | | | | | | |

| | | | | |
|---|---|---|---|---|
| | | | | |
| | | | | |
| | | | | |
| | | ܠܒܬ | | |
| | | | ܩܘܡ | |
| | | | ܩܘܡ | |
| ܐܡ | | | | |
| | | | | ܩܘܡ |
| | | | | ܩܘܡܬܐ |
| | | | ܩܡܛ | |
| | ܪܝܐ | | ܩܡܛ | |
| | | | | |
| | | | | |

# APPENDIX B: PARALLEL WORD-PAIRS

The word-pairs below occur at least once in a parallel relationship in the Odes.
The list concentrates on nouns, verbs, adjectival/adverbial expressions, with
limited reference to prepositions.

ABBREVIATIONS

*       the word-pair occurs once only in the Odes but is supported by parallels
        either in the Hebrew or Christian scriptures. All references to these
        scriptures are from the Peshitta version. In the compilation of the sam-
        ple parallels Dahood 1972-81 has proved especially helpful.

rev     the word-pair occurs in reversed order.

assoc   the elements of the word-pair are associated but are not parallel. Either
        or both of the associated elements may be in a different form (noun,
        verb) to that of the word-pair given.

syn     another word-pair using synonymous terms.

---

ٳܪܐ cf ܟܝܡܥ
ܟܐ cf ܟܢܝܒܢ
ܟܐܟ (father) - ܟܝܒ /ܟܝܢ (son/s) 19:2; 23:22; rev 31:4,5; rev 41:13; assoc
14:1; assoc 23:18
ܒܐܟ cf ܝܒܘ, ܝܒܠ, ܝܥ, ܟܡ, ܢܩܒ, ܟܝܙ
ܟܘܝܐ cf ܟܡ
ܟܝܐ cf ܟܘܠ
ܝܝܐ cf ܘܒܙ
ܟܝܝܐܟ cf ܝܐ
ܟܝܝܐܟ (way) - ܟܢܒܠ (grace) 24:13 *; Ps 25:10
ܝܐ cf ܒܙ
ܝܐ (go) - ܟܘ (see) 7:18; 23:10

ܐܙܠ (go) - ܠܐ ܛܥܐ (not to err) 17:5; 38:4; syn ܫܒܩ ܐܘܪܚܐ ܕܛܥܝܘܬܐ (abandon the way of error) - ܐܙܠ 15:6

ܐܟܪ cf ܒܥܠ, ܦܠܚ

ܐܟܪܘܬܐ cf ܪܥܝܬܐ

ܐܟܪ cf ܚܩܠ

ܐܝܕܐ (hands) - ܨܒܥܬܐ (fingers) 16:6; 23:7,8

ܐܠܗܐ cf ܒܪܝܐ

ܐܠܗܐ (God) - ܡܪܝܐ (Lord) 17:1-2 *; Pss 16:1-2; 114:7; 135:1-2

ܐܡܢ cf ܒܥܠ

ܐܡܢ (have faith in) - ܬܟܠ (trust in) 15:10 *; Job 39:11,12; Mic 7:5

ܐܡܬܐ cf ܒܪܐ

ܐܢܐ cf ܢܦܫ

ܐܣܪ cf ܫܪܐ

ܐܦܐ cf ܠܒܐ

ܐܦܐ (face) - ܠܒܐ (heart) 21:8,9; 40:4; 41:6

ܐܪܙܐ (mystery) - ܗܝܡܢܘܬܐ (faith) 8:10,11 *; 1Cor 13:2

ܐܪܝ cf ܦܬܐ

ܐܪܥܐ cf ܫܡܝܐ

ܐܪܥܐ (land) - ܝܡܐ (sea) 16:10 *; Ps 46:2; Gen 1:10

ܐܪܥܐ (earth) - ܦܪܕܝܣܐ (paradise) 11:18,21,23; Joel 2:3

ܐܪܥܐ (earth) - ܫܡܫܐ (sun) 11:12-13 *; Amos 8:9

ܐܬܐ cf ܢܦܩ, ܦܩ, ܫܠܚ

ܐܬܐ (sign) - ܩܝܣܐ (wood) 27:2; 42:1

ܒܪܐ cf ܒܪܐ

ܒܓܠܠ cf ܟܣܐ

ܒܗܠ cf ܢܣܒ

ܒܢܝܐ (sons [of men]) - ܒܢܬܐ (daughters) 33:6 *; Ps 143:12; Is 43:6; 49:22

ܒܣܝܡܘܬܐ cf ܪܚܡܐ

ܒܣܝܡܘܬܐ (gentleness) - ܛܝܒܘܬܐ (grace) 20:9 *; Eph 2:7

ܒܣܝܡܘܬܐ (gentleness) - ܪܒܘܬܐ (greatness) 19:11; assoc 7:3

ܒܣܪܐ (flesh) - ܠܒܘܫܐ (garment) 8:9 *; assoc Job 10:11

ܒܪܐ cf ܐܒܐ, ܒܢܝ, ܠܒܐ

ܒܪܐ (son) - ܪܘܚܐ (spirit) 19:2; 23:22

ܒܪܝܬܐ (creatures) - ܚܝܠܘܬܐ (hosts) 4:7-8; 16:13-14

ܒܬܪ (after) - ܩܕܡ (before) 28:18 *; Job 21:33; Is 43:10

ܓܠܐ cf ܩܪܝܒ

ܓܠܐ cf ܚܛܡܐ ܠܐ

ܓܪܡܐ cf ܚܠܐ

ܕܓܠܘܬܐ cf ܛܥܘܬܐ
ܕܚܠ (fear) - ܙܘܥ (shaken) 5:10,11,12; 24:3; syn assoc ܙܘܥ - ܪܗܒ (Ethpe. be disquieted) 35:3
ܕܝܨܐ (exultation) - ܚܘܒܐ (love) 40:4 *; assoc Zeph 3:17
ܕܟܐ cf ܙܕܝܩܘܬܐ
ܕܟܝܘܬܐ cf ܙܕܝܩܘܬܐ
ܕܨ (exult) - ܢܗܪ (shine) 40:4; rev 41:6,7
ܗܕܪ̈ܐ cf ܠܒܐ
ܗܝܡܢܘܬܐ cf ܐܪܙܐ
ܗܝܡܢܘܬܐ (faith) - ܫܡܐ (name) 39:13; 42:19,20
ܗܠܟ cf ܡܣܩ ܐܘܪܚܬܐ...
ܗܠܟ (walk) - ܝܕܥ (know) 23:4; 33:13
ܗܠܟ (walk) - ܥܒܪ (pass over) 39:2,6,9,13
ܗܠܟ (walk) - ܦܪܩ (save) 10:6; 17:4
ܗܦܟ cf ܦܢܐ
ܙܕܝܩܘܬܐ (righteousness) - ܕܟܝܘܬܐ (purity) 20:4 *; Job 17:9 (ܙܕܩ - ܕܟܐ)
ܙܘܥ cf ܕܚܠ, ܙܘܥ ܠܐ
ܙܡܪ cf ܦܬܚ ܦܘܡܐ
ܙܡܪ (sing) - ܩܪܒ (offer) 7:22; syn ܦܬܚ ܦܘܡܐ (open the mouth)/ܡܠܠ ܬܫܒܘܚܬܐ (speak a hymn)/ܪܘܡ ܩܠܐ (lift up the voice) - ܩܪܒ 31:3-4
ܚܒ (love) - ܢܛܪ (keep) 8:22; 19:11
ܚܒܠ cf ܛܒܐ, ܩܘܡ, ܫܚܩ
ܚܒܠ (destroy) - ܐܒܕ (perish) 24:7-9; 31:1-2; 33:2,9; assoc 28:5
ܚܒܠ (destroy) - ܚܠܦ (pervert) 28:14 *; assoc 1Cor 15:52
ܚܒܠ (labour) - ܝܠܕ (bring forth) 19:8 *; Is 23:4;66:8
ܚܒܠ (destroy) - ܬܩܢ (fix) 39:10; assoc 33:2
ܚܒܠܐ cf ܛܒܐ, ܚܒܠܐ ܠܐ
ܚܕܘܬܐ (joy) - ܛܝܒܘܬܐ (grace) 23:1,2; 31:6,7; assoc 31:3
ܚܕܘܬܐ (joy) - ܚܘܒܐ (love) 23:1,3 *; Gal 5:22
ܚܘܒܐ cf ܕܝܨܐ, ܚܕܘܬܐ, ܛܝܒܘܬܐ, ܝܕܥܬܐ
ܚܘܒܐ (love) - ܦܐܪ̈ܐ (fruits) 16:2; assoc 14:6
ܚܙܐ cf ܐܙܠ, ܡܬܚܙܐ ܠܐ
ܚܙܐ (see) - ܓܠܐ (uncover) 16:8; 23:18
ܚܙܐ (see) - ܝܠܦ (learn) 13:1,2 *; Is 26:10; Phil 4:9
ܚܙܐ (see) - ܣܒܪ (consider) 17:6; 18:11,12; 28:8,9
ܚܙܐ (see) - ܫܡܥ (hear) 15:3; 16:9
ܚܝܐ cf ܡܝܬ, ܫܬܐ
ܚܝܐ (live) - ܦܪܩ (save) 8:22c-d; 17:15; 26:9 (ܚܝܢ̈ܐ); 34:6; 38:16; assoc 10:6

ܚܝܐ cf ܛܝܒܘܬܐ, ܡܘܬ, ܦܐܪܐ/ܦܐܪ̈ܐ, ܦܘܪܩܢܐ
ܚܝܠ cf ܚܝܠܬܢܘܬܐ
ܚܝܠܐ cf ܡܠܬܐ
ܚܐܪܘܬܐ cf ܒܪ̈ܬܐ
ܚܝܠܬܢܘܬܐ (power) - ܛܝܒܘܬܐ (grace) 7:25; assoc 9:5
ܚܟܝܡ (wise) - ܝܕܥ (know) 7:8,9; assoc 3:11; assoc 38:13
ܚܟܡܬܐ/ܚܟܝܡܘܬܐ (wisdom) - ܠܒܐ (heart) 24:11; rev 28:19
ܚܠܒܐ cf ܬܕܝܐ
ܚܠܒܐ (milk) - ܕܒܫܐ (honey) 40:1; assoc 4:10
ܚܠܦ cf ܚܒܠ
ܚܠܦ (pervert) - ܪܥܝܐ/ܬܪܥܝܬܐ (determine, mind) 4:1-3; 28:14
ܚܣܝܘܬܐ cf ܛܝܒܘܬܐ
ܚܪܝܦܐ/ܚܪܝܦܘܬܐ (swift/swiftness) - ܩܠܝܠܐ/ܩܠܝܠܘܬܐ (rapid/rapidity) 39:4; assoc rev 12:5.
ܚܫܘܟܐ cf ܢܘܗܪܐ
ܚܬܢܐ cf ܟܠܬܐ
ܛܒܥ (sink) - ܐܒܕ (perish) 24:7; 31:2
ܛܒܥ (seal) - ܬܩܢ (fix) 8:15c-16a *; Prov 8:25 has ܬܩܢ for טבע (MT)
ܛܝܒܘܬܐ cf ܒܣܝܡܘܬܐ, ܚܝ̈ܘܬܐ, ܚܝܠܬܢܘܬܐ, ܡܫܝܚܐ, ܬܫܒܘܚܬܐ
ܛܝܒܘܬܐ (grace) - ܚܘܒܐ (love) 23:2,3 *; 1Cor 16:23,24; 2Cor 8:7; Eph 6:23, 24
ܛܝܒܘܬܐ (grace) - ܚܝ̈ܐ (life) 31:7 *; assoc Rom 5:17; assoc Tit 3:7
ܛܝܒܘܬܐ (grace) - ܚܣܝܘܬܐ (holiness) 20:9; 24:13,14
ܛܝܒܘܬܐ (grace) - ܡܫܝܚܐ (Messiah) 29:5,6; 41:3
ܛܠܐ (dew) - ܪܣܝܣܐ (sprinkling) 35:1,5 *; Deut 32:2; Mic 5:6
ܛܠܡ cf ܠܒܫ
ܛܠܡ/ܛܠܘܡܝܐ (oppress/oppression) - ܦܪܩ/ܦܘܪܩܢܐ (save/salvation) 28:10; rev 33:11-12
ܛܥܝܐ cf ܣܡܝܐ
ܛܥܐ cf ܐܙܠ
ܛܥܐ/ܛܥܝܘܬܐ (to err/error) - ܚܒܠ/ܚܒܠܐ (corrupt/corruption) 38:8-9,11 *; 2Cor 11:3
ܛܥܝܘܬܐ cf ܐܙܠ
ܛܥܝܘܬܐ (error) - ܫܪܪܐ (truth) 18:14,15; 38:6; assoc 17:5; assoc 31:2; syn ܫܪܪܐ - ܕܓܠܘܬܐ (falsehood) 18:6
ܝܐܝܘܬܐ cf ܬܫܒܘܚܬܐ
ܝܕ cf ܝܡܝܢܐ
ܝܕܥ cf ܗܠܟ, ܚܟܝܡ, ܝܕܥܬܐ, ܝܕܥܬܐ ܠܐ

ܝܕܥ (know) - ܐܚܕ (possess) 4:7,8; 42:3
ܝܕܥ (know) - ܐܡܢ (have faith in) 42:8; rev 41:2; assoc 15:10
ܝܕܥ (know) - ܝܗܒ (give) 6:6; 15:10; rev 30:6
ܝܕܥ (know) - ܣܒܪ (suppose) 7:12; assoc 34:5
ܝܕܥܬܐ cf ܠܐ ܝܕܥܬܐ, ܦܬܓܡܐ
ܝܕܥܬܐ (knowledge) - ܚܘܒܐ (love) 8:13; assoc 17:12
ܝܕܥܬܐ (knowledge) - ܫܪܪܐ (truth) 8:12; assoc11:4-5; assoc 12:3; assoc 12:13; assoc rev 8:8
ܝܗܒ cf ܝܕܥ
ܝܗܒ (give) - ܢܣܒ (take) 4:13; 19:5; rev 9:10
ܝܗܒ (give) - ܥܒܕ (make/do) 15:7; rev 29:2
ܝܘܢܐ (dove) - ܪܘܚܐ (spirit) 28:1 *; Matt 3:16 and parallels
ܝܠܕ cf ܚܒܠ, ܒܠܝܢܐ ܢܣܒ
ܝܠܕ (bring forth) - ܩܢܐ (gain) 19:10; 41:9-10
ܝܠܘܕܐ (babe) - ܒܪܐ (son) 41:2 *; Is 9:6 (ܝܠܕܐ); Jer 31:20 (ܝܠܕܐ)
ܝܠܦ cf ܚܙܐ
ܝܡܐ cf ܐܪܥܐ
ܝܡܝܢܐ (right hand) - ܝܕ (hand) 22:7 *; Pss 26:10; 74:10; 89:13,25; 137:7; 138:10
ܝܡܝܢܐ (right hand) - ܡܥܕܪܢܐ (helper) 8:6; 22:6,7; 25:2
ܝܡܝܢܐ (right hand) - ܣܡܠܐ (left hand) 25:7 *; Gen 24:49; 48:13; Is 9:20
ܝܪܬ (take possession) - ܢܣܒ (take) 31:7; assoc 23:19
ܟܘ̈ܟܒܐ cf ܫܡܝܐ
ܟܘܠܝܬܐ cf ܠܒܐ
ܟܘ... cf ܢܦܫܐ
ܟܠܠܐ cf ܦܘܪܩܢܐ
ܟܠܡܕܡ (everything) - ܠܐ/(ܠܝܬ) ܡܕܡ (nothing) 11:23; 17:10; 34:5
ܟܠܬܐ (bride) - ܚܬܢܐ (bridegroom) 38:9; assoc 42:8
ܟܢܫ (gather together) - ܒܕܪ (scatter abroad) 10:5; 22:2,3
ܟܣܐ cf ܦܬܚ, ܫܠܚ
ܟܬܒ (write) - ܩܪܐ (read) 26:8 *; Deut 17:18,19; Josh 8:32,34; Hab 2:2
ܠܐ ܙܘܐ (not be shaken) - ܩܘܡ (stand firm) 5:12,13; 31:10b-11a
ܠܐ ܚܒܠܐ (incorruptible/incorruption) - ܚܒܠܐ (corruptible/corruption) 15:8; 22:11
ܠܐ ܚܒܠܐ (incorruptible) - ܫܘܡܠܠܐ (perfection) 7:11; assoc 9:4
ܠܐ ܝܕܥܬܐ (ignorance) - ܝܕܥܬܐ (knowledge) 7:21 *; Is 48:7,8 (ܝܕܥ - ܠܐ ܝܕܥ); Jer 5:4,5; 8:7 (ܝܕܥ - ܠܐ ܝܕܥ)
ܠܐ ܡܕܡ cf ܟܠܡܕܡ

ܠܐ ܡܘܬܐ cf ܦܘܪܣܢܐ
ܠܐ ܡܝܬܢ cf ܚܝܐ
ܠܐ ܡܬܚܙܝܢܐ (invisible) - ܓܠܐ (be manifest) 16:8 *; 1Tim 3:16 (ܚܙܐ - ܓܠܐ)
ܠܒܐ cf ܐܦܐ, ܡܚܫܒܬܐ, ܪܥܝܢܐ, ܦܘܡܐ
ܠܒܐ (heart) - ܗܕ̈ܡܐ (members) 18:1,2; 26:4; 40:2,3
ܠܒܐ (heart) - ܟܘ̈ܠܝܬܐ (kidneys) 20:4,5 *; Pss 7:9; 26:2; Jer 11:20; 17:10; 20:12
ܠܒܐ (heart) - ܡܚܫܒܬܐ (thought) 34:1; assoc 41:10; syn ܬܪܥܝܬܐ (mind) - ܠܒܐ 28:19
ܠܒܐ (heart) - ܣܦܘ̈ܬܐ (lips) 16:2; 21:8; 40:2; rev 30:5; rev 37:2; assoc 8:1; assoc 20:4
ܠܒܘܫܐ cf ܡܐܢܐ, ܫܠܚ
ܠܒܘܫܐ (garment) - ܢܘܗܪܐ (light) 11:11 *; assoc Ps 104:1,2
ܠܒܘܫܐ (garment) - ܬܟܣܝܬܐ (covering) 25:8 *; Gen 49:11; Job 24:7
ܠܒܫ cf ܡܐܢܐ, ܠܒܘܫܐ, ܫܠܚ
ܠܒܫ (put on) - ܛܠܠܡ (Eth. be rejected) 4:6; 33:12
ܠܫܢܐ cf ܣܦܘ̈ܬܐ
ܡܪܝܡ cf ܒܠܡܪܝܡ
ܡܕܥܐ (mind) - ܠܒܐ (heart) 8:20 *; Phil 4:7; Heb 8:10
ܡܘܥ̈ܠܐ cf ܬܪ̈ܥܐ
ܡܘܬܐ cf ܡܝܬ, ܦܘܪܣܢܐ
ܡܘܬܐ (death) - ܫܝܘܠ (Sheol) 15:9; rev 29:4; rev 42:11
ܡܚܫܒܬܐ cf ܠܒܐ, ܡܠܬܐ, ܥܒܕܐ, ܨܒܝܐ
ܡܝܬ cf ܩܘܡ
ܡܝܬ/ܡܘܬܐ (die/death) - ܚܝܐ/ܚܝ̈ܐ (live/life) 3:8,9; 15:9,10; 28:7; 42:5; rev 11:7
ܡܝܬܢ cf ܚܝܐ
ܡܟܟ cf ܩܘܡ
ܡܟܟ (humble) - ܪܘܡ (lift up) 41:12 *; Is 2:11; 57:15
ܡܠܠ cf ܦܬܚ ܦܘܡܐ, ܫܡܠ
ܡܠܠ ܬܫܒܘܚܬܐ cf ܪܢܡ, ܦܬܚ ܘܠܐ ܕܦܘܡܐ
ܡܠܬܐ (word) - ܚܝܠܐ (power) 29:9 *; 1Cor 1:18; 2Cor 6:7
ܡܠܬܐ (word) - ܡܚܫܒܬܐ (thought) 16:8,19; rev 41:10
ܡܠܬܐ (word) - ܢܘܗܪܐ (light) 10:1; assoc 41:14; cf ܦܬܓܡܐ - ܢܘܗܪܐ
ܡܚܝܢܐ cf ܡܚܝܐ
ܡܪܝܐ cf ܐܠܗܐ, ܡܪܝܡܐ, ܦܘܡܐ, ܫܡܫܐ
ܡܪܝܡܐ (Most High) - ܐܒܐ (father) 41:13; assoc 23:18
ܡܪܝܡܐ (Most High) - ܐܠܗܐ ... ܐܒܐ (God ... Father) 9:5; 10:4

ܡܪܝܡܐ (Most High) - ܡܪܝܐ (Lord) 5:1,2; 23:4 (H only); 37:1; assoc 3:6; assoc 7:22
ܡܫܝܚܐ cf ܛܝܒܘܬܐ
ܡܫܒܐ cf ܪܘܚܐ
ܢܗܪ cf ܕܓ
ܢܘܗܪܐ cf ܠܒܘܫܐ, ܡܠܬܐ, ܦܬܓܡܐ
ܢܘܗܪܐ (light) - ܚܫܘܟܐ (darkness) 16:15,16; 18:6; 21:3; assoc 11:19; assoc 15:2; syn ܥܢܢܐ ܕܡܛܠܠܐ (cloud of gloom)/ܐܐܪ ܕܥܪܦܠܐ (air of thick darkness) - ܢܘܗܪܐ 5:5,6; Job 38:8-9 (ܥܢܢܐ - ܥܪܦܠܐ)
ܢܚ cf ܫܬܐ
ܢܚ (rest/refresh) - ܩܘܡ (stand) 6:14; 26:12; assoc 36:1,2
ܢܚܬ (descend) - ܣܠܩ (ascend) 22:1 *; Pss 104:8; 107:26
ܢܚܬ (descend) - ܪܗܛ (run) 23:16; rev 33:1
ܢܛܪ cf ܚܒ
ܢܛܪ (keep) - ܦܪܩ (save) 8:22; assoc 18:7; assoc 35:2
ܢܝܚܐ/ܢܝܚܘܬܐ (rest) - ܦܐܪ̈ܐ (fruits) 11:12; 14:6; rev 37:3-4
ܢܣܒ cf ܝܗܒ, ܝܪܬ, ܩܒܠ
ܢܣܒ ܒܛܢܐ (receive conception) - ܝܠܕ (bring forth) 19:6; syn ܒܛܢ (conceive) - ܝܠܕ Gen 21:2; 30:5
ܢܦܠ (fall) - ܐܒܕ (perish) 9:6-7 *; 2Sam 1:27
ܢܦܠ (fall) - ܩܘܡ (stand) 6:16; 12:6; 18:2,3
ܢܦܩ cf ܦܢܐ
ܢܦܩ (go out) - ܐܬܐ (come) 6:8; 30:5-6; assoc 7:17
ܢܦܫܐ cf ܦܓܪܐ, ܪܘܚܐ
ܢܦܫܐ (soul) - ܐܢܐ (I) 3:5; 21:4; similarly ܢܦܫܐ - ...ܟܘܢ (you) 31:7
ܢܫܩ cf ܓܦܩ
ܣܒܪ cf ܚܝܐ, ܒܣܪ, ܦܬܚ ܡܠܐ ܕܦܘܡܐ
ܣܘܠܐܝܐ cf ܣܠܐ
ܣܠܐ/ܣܘܠܝܐ (reject/refuse) - ܐܒܕ/ܐܒܝܕܐ (perish/lost) 24:7,9,10,12; 42:10; rev 28:9,11
ܣܠܩ cf ܢܚܬ
ܣܡܟ cf ܫܪ
ܣܡܟ ܥܩܒܬܐ ܕܢܘܗܪܐ ܥܠ... (set footprints of light upon) - ܗܠܟ (go/walk) 7:14; 10:6
ܣܟܠܐ cf ܚܟܝܡܐ
ܣܢܐ/ܣܢܐܬܐ (hate/hatred) - ܛܢܢܐ (jealousy) 7:20; 28:12
ܣܦܘ̈ܬܐ cf ܠܒܐ, ܦܘܡܐ
ܣܦܘ̈ܬܐ (lips) - ܠܫܢܐ (tongue) 40:2-3 *; Pss 118:171-172; 119:2; 139:3

ܥܒܕ cf ܝܗܒ
ܥܒܕ (work) - ܒܛܠ (be idle) 16:13 *; Ex 5:17,18
ܥܒܕܐ (servant) - ܒܪܐ ܕܐܡܬܐ (son of maidservant) 29:11 *; Pss 86:16; 115:16
ܥܒܕܐ/ܥܒ̈ܕܐ (work/works) - ܡܚܫܒܬܐ (thought) 8:18; 12:4,7; 16:9; syn ܬܪܥܝܬܐ (mind) - ܥܒ̈ܕܐ 12:4
ܥܒܕܐ (work) - ܦܘܠܚܢܐ (service) 16:1,2,6
ܥܒܘܕܐ cf ܣܠܐ
ܥܒܪ cf ܗܠܟ, ܪܘܡ
ܥܝܢܐ/ܥܝ̈ܢܐ (eye/s) - ܐܕܢܐ/ܐܕ̈ܢܐ (ear/s) 15:3,4; 16:9
ܥܝ̈ܢܐ (eyes) - ܦܪܨܘܦܐ (face) 11:14; syn ܥܝ̈ܢܐ - ܐܦ̈ܐ (face) 13:1,2
ܥܠ cf ܬܚܬ
ܥܡ cf ܐܝܠ
ܥܡܘܪ̈ܐ (inhabitants) - ܬܘܬܒ̈ܐ (sojourners) 24:3 *; Gen 23:4; Hos 10:5
ܥܡܛܢܐ cf ܢܘܗܪܐ
ܥܦܩ (embrace) - ܢܫܩ (kiss) 28:6 *; Gen 29:13; 33:4
ܥܪ̈ܦܠܐ cf ܢܘܗܪܐ
ܦܐܪܐ cf ܒܛܠ, ܚܘܒܐ, ܚܝܐ/ܚܝܘܬܐ, ܫܪܪܐ
ܦܐܪܐ/ܦܐܪ̈ܐ (fruit /s) - ܚ̈ܝܐ (life) 8:2; rev 10:2
ܦܓܪ̈ܐ (bodies) - ܢܦ̈ܫܬܐ (souls) 39:3 *; Matt 10:28; 1Thess 5:23
ܦܘܠܚܢܐ cf ܥܒܕܐ
ܦܘܡܐ cf ܦܬܚ ܦܘܡܐ, ܦܬܚ ܡܠܐ ܦܘܡܐ
ܦܘܡܐ (mouth) - ܠܒܐ (heart) 10:1; 21:8; 28:1; 36:7
ܦܘܡܐ (mouth) - ܣܦܘ̈ܬܐ (lips) 12:2; 21:8
ܦܘܡܗ ܕܡܪܝܐ (mouth of the Lord) - ܦܬܓܡܐ (word) 12:3; assoc 12:10,11
ܦܘܪܩܢܐ cf ܛܠܡ
ܦܘܪܩܢܐ (salvation) - ܚܝܐ ܕܠܐ ܡܘܬܐ (immortal life) 38:3; 40:5
ܦܘܪܩܢܐ (salvation) - ܟܠܝܠܐ (crown) 5:11,12; rev 17:1,2
ܦܢܐ cf ܫܒܩ
ܦܢܐ (turn back) - ܐܬܐ (come) 33:6; assoc 10:3; syn ܐܬܐ - ܗܦܟ (turn) 5:4,7; syn ܐܬܐ - ܢܦܩ (go out) 7:17
ܦܪܕܝܣܐ cf ܐܪܥܐ
ܦܪܚܬܐ (flying creature) - ܪܚܫܐ (creeping thing) 24:4 *; Gen 1:20,21,26,28, 30
ܦܪܨܘܦܐ cf ܥܝܢܐ
ܦܪܣ cf ܗܠܟ, ܚܝܐ, ܛܠܡ, ܢܛܪ, ܡܒܠ
ܦܫܛ (extend) - ܬܪܨ (stand upright) 34:1; 35:7; 42:2; assoc 27:3
ܦܬܐ (spread out widely) - ܐܪܟ (lengthen) 7:13 *; Is 54:2

ܦܬܓܡܐ cf ܡܠܬܐ, ܦܘܡܗ ܕܡܪܝܐ
ܦܬܓܡܐ (word) - ܝܕܥܬܐ (knowledge) 8:8; 12:3; assoc 7:7
ܦܬܓܡܐ (word) - ܢܘܗܪܐ (light) 12:3; rev 32:1,2; cf ܡܠܬܐ - ܢܘܗܪܐ
ܦܬܚ (open) - ܐܚܕ (shut) 17:10; assoc 17:8; syn ܦܬܚ - ܟܣܐ (Ethpa. be covered) 24:5
ܦܬܚ ܦܘܡܐ cf ܙܡܪ, ܦܬܚ ܩܠܐ ܕܦܘܡܐ
ܦܬܚ ܦܘܡܐ (open the mouth) - ܡܠܠ (speak) rev 8:4; 16:5; 31:3; syn ܙܡܪ (sing) - ܦܬܚ ܦܘܡܐ 16:3,5; syn ܪܘܡ ܩܠܐ (lift up the voice) - ܡܠܠ 37:1-2; syn ܦܬܚ ܦܘܡܐ - ܪܘܡ ܩܠܐ 31:3,4
ܦܬܚ ܩܠܐ ܕܦܘܡܐ (open the voice of the mouth) - ܫܒܚ (praise) 7:24; syn ܦܬܚ ܦܘܡܐ (open the mouth)/ܡܠܠ ܬܫܒܘܚܬܐ (speak a hymn [syn ܣܒܪ ܬܫܒܘܚܬܐ (declare a hymn)13:2]/ܪܘܡ ܩܠܐ (lift up the voice) 16:5; 31:3-4; 37:1-2; assoc ܦܬܚ ܩܝܬܪܐ (open the harp) - ܫܒܚ 14:8
ܨܒܝܐ (desire) - ܡܚܫܒܬܐ (thought) 9:3; rev 23:5
ܨܒ̈ܘܬܐ cf ܐܪ̈ܐ
ܨܘܪ cf ܚܬܡ
ܩܒܠ cf ܫܡܥ
ܩܒܠ (receive) - ܦܪܩ (save) 9:5; 17:14; assoc 15:6; syn ܢܣܒ (receive) - ܦܪܩ 17:4
ܩܕܝܫܐ (holy) - ܓܒܝܐ (chosen) 23:1,2,3 *; Col 3:12; 1Pet 2:9
ܩܘܡ cf ܒܬܪ
ܩܘܐ cf ܫܪܐ
ܩܘܡ cf ܝܗܒ, ܠܐ, ܚܝ, ܢܦܠ, ܫܪܐ, ܬܡ
ܩܘܡ (stand up/be established) - ܐܒܕ (perish, destroy) 5:12; 6:3,5; 22:5; 33:2, 3; syn ܩܘܡ - ܚܒܠ (corrupt) 39:10; syn ܩܘܡ - ܡܟܟ (bring low) 8:3
ܩܘܡ (stand up/be established) - ܡܝܬ (die) 5:13,14; assoc 6:14-16; assoc 42:5-6
ܩܝܣܐ cf ܐܬܐ
ܩܝܬܪܐ cf ܦܬܚ ܩܠܐ ܕܦܘܡܐ
ܩܠܐ cf ܦܬܚ ܦܘܡܐ, ܦܬܚ ܩܠܐ ܕܦܘܡܐ
ܩܠܝܠܐ/ܩܠܝܠܘܬܐ cf ܚܪܝܦܐ/ܚܪܝܦܘܬܐ
ܩܢܐ cf ܝܠ
ܩܪܐ cf ܟܬܒ
ܩܪܐ (read) - ܫܡܥ (hear) 23:10 *; Rev 1:3
ܩܪܒ cf ܙܡܪ, ܫܒܩ
ܩܪܒ (draw nigh) - ܫܬܐ (drink) 11:6,7; 19:1
ܩܪܒܐ cf ܫܠܡܐ
ܪܒܘܬܐ cf ܒܣܝܡܘܬܐ

ܪ̈ܓܠܐ (feet) - ܪܫܐ (head) 42:13 *; Is 7:20
ܪܗܒ cf ܕܚܠ
ܪܗܛ cf ܢܚܬ
ܪܘܙ cf ܫܘܚ
ܪܘܚܐ cf ܒܪܐ, ܚܘܐ
ܪܘܚܐ (spirit) - ܡܫܟܐ (skin) 25:8 *; Job 10:11,12
ܪܘܚܐ (spirit) - ܢܦܫܐ (soul) 40:4 *; Job 7:11;12:10; Is 26:9
ܪܘܡ cf ܡܟܟ, ܦܬܚ ܦܘܡܐ, ܦܬܚ ܡܠܐ ܕܦܘܡܐ, ܫܠܚ
ܪܘܡ (lift up) - ܥܒܪ (pass) 21:6; 25:9
ܪܘܡ/ܪܘܡܐ (lift up/height) - ܫܒܚ/ܬܫܒܘܚܬܐ (glorify/glory) 18:1; 21:6,7; 36:1,2; rev 17:7; rev 26:4
ܪ̈ܚܡܐ (mercy) - ܒܣܝܡܘܬܐ (gentleness) 14:3 *; Col 3:12
ܪܚܫܐ cf ܦܪܚܬܐ
ܪܫܝܬ (beginning) - ܐܚܪܝܬܐ (end) 6:4; 7:14; 11:4; 24:8
ܪܡܫܐ cf ܠܠܝܐ
ܪܥܐ cf ܢܠܦ
ܫܒܚ cf ܦܬܚ ܡܠܐ ܕܦܘܡܐ, ܪܘܡ
ܫܒܚ/ܬܫܒܘܚܬܐ (glorify/glory) - ܐܘܕܝ/ܬܘܕܝܬܐ (praise/confession) 21:7; 26:6
ܫܒܩ (abandon) - ܐܙܠ (go) 15:6; 17:11; syn ܫܒܩ - ܦܢܐ (turn back) 11:8,9; syn ܫܒܩ - ܩܪܒ (draw near) 33:7
ܫܘܐ cf ܫܠܚ
ܫܘܚ (sprout) - ܪܘܙ (laugh) 11:12; θάλλω - γελάω 11:12,16
ܫܘܡܠܝܐ cf ܠܐ ܢܒܠܐ, ܬܫܒܘܚܬܐ
ܫܚܩ (shatter) - ܐܬܐ (come) 6:8; syn ܚܒܠ (destroy) - ܐܬܐ 7:21
ܫܝܘܠ cf ܡܘܬܐ
ܫܠܚ (strip off) - ܠܒܫ (put on) 11:10-11 (ܠܒܘܫܐ); 21:3; rev 15:8; syn ܟܣܐ (cover) - ܪܘܡ (lift up) 25:8; syn ܫܘܐ (wipe) - ܠܒܫ 13:3
ܫܠܡܐ (peace) - ܩܪܒܐ (war) 8:7;9:6
ܫܡܐ cf ܗܝܡܢܘܬܐ, ܬܫܒܘܚܬܐ
ܫܡܐ (name) - ܛܝܒܘܬܐ (grace) 8:6-7; 15:8; assoc 31:3
ܫܡܝܐ (heaven) - ܐܪܥܐ (earth) 16:10-11; Gen 1:30; 9:2; Ps 68:8
ܫܡܝܐ (heaven) - ܟܘ̈ܟܒܐ (stars) 16:11 *; Job 22:12; Ps 148:3-4; Is 14:13; 47:13
ܫܡܥ cf ܚܙܐ, ܩܪܐ
ܫܡܥ (hear) - ܡܠܠ (speak) 33:10; 37:2
ܫܡܥ (hear) - ܩܒܠ (receive) 8:8 *; Ps 6:10; Prov 4:10; 19:20
ܫܡܫܐ cf ܐܪܥܐ

ܫܡܫܐ (sun) - ܡܪܝܐ (Lord) 15:1,2; assoc 11:13
ܫܪ (set fast) - ܬܩܢ (fix) 11:5; syn ܫܪ - ܣܡܟ (set) 38:16
ܫܪܐ (dissolve) - ܐܣܪ (bind) 17:11; assoc rev 22:4
ܫܪܐ (dissolve) - ܩܘܐ (abide) 26:11; syn ܐܒܕ (perish/destroy) - ܩܘܐ 24:9
ܫܪܐ (refresh, release) - ܩܘܡ (stand) 6:14; rev 15:2
ܫܪܪܐ cf ܛܝܒܘܬܐ, ܕܟܬܐ
ܫܪܪܐ (truth) - ܦܐܪ̈ܐ (fruits) 12:2; 14:7
ܫܬܐ cf ܩܪܒ
ܫܬܐ (drink) - ܚܝܐ (live) 8:16; assoc 11:7
ܫܬܐ (drink) - ܢܘܚ (rest) 30:2,7
ܬܕ̈ܝܐ (breasts) - ܚܠܒܐ (milk) 8:16; 19:3; assoc 19:4
ܬܘܕܝܬܐ cf ܫܒܚ
ܬܘܬܒ̈ܐ cf ܠܡܘܪ̈ܐ
ܬܚܬ (below) - ܠܥܠ (above) 34:4-5 *; Job 18:16; 37:3
ܬܒܠ cf ܐܡܢ
ܬܟܣܝܬܐ cf ܠܒܘܫܐ
ܬܩܢ cf ܚܒܠ, ܛܒܠ, ܫܪ
ܬܩܢ (fix) - ܩܘܡ (set up/made to stand) 16:12; rev 39:10
ܬܪ̈ܥܐ (gates) - ܡܘܟ̈ܠܐ (bolts) 17:8-9 *; Ps 107:16; Is 45:2
ܬܪܥܝܬܐ cf ܚܠܦ, ܠܒܐ
ܬܪܨ cf ܦܫܛ
ܬܫܒܘܚܬܐ (glory) - ܛܝܒܘܬܐ (grace) 6:6-7; 20:9; 29:2
ܬܫܒܘܚܬܐ (glory) - ܝܐܘܬܐ (beauty) rev 12:4; 16:5; 29:3; assoc 18:16
ܬܫܒܘܚܬܐ (glory) - ܫܘܡܠܝܐ (perfection) 26:5; rev 36:2
ܬܫܒܘܚܬܐ (glory) - ܫܡܐ (name) 6:7; 14:5; 16:20; 18:16

# APPENDIX C: ASSOCIATED PHRASES, WORDS/ROOTS, NON-PARALLEL WORD-PAIRS

ABBREVIATIONS

| | |
|---|---|
| * | the association of the elements occurs once only in the Odes but can be supported by associations either in the Hebrew or in the Christian scriptures. All references to these scriptures are from the Peshitta version. |
| syn | another association using synonymous terms. |

---

ܐܒܐ (father) ... ܦܝܐ (gain) 41:9; syn ܡܪܝܐ (Lord) ... ܦܝܐ 11:11
ܐܘܪܚܐ cf ܝܗܒ, ܦܬܐ, ܫܒܩ
ܐܘܪܚܐ (way) ... ܚܒܠܐ (corruption) 22:11; 33:7
ܐܘܪܚܐ (way) ... ܝܕܥ (know) 3:10; 12:6; 33:13
ܐܘܪܚܐ (way) ... ܫܪܪܐ (truth) 11:3; 33:8
ܐܘܪܚܐ (way) ... ܬܪܝܨ (upright) 38:7; 42:2
ܐܝܩܪܐ cf ܬܫܒܘܚܬܐ
ܐܡܐ cf ܚܠܒܐ
ܐܡܬܐ cf ܒܪܐ
ܐܢܬܬܐ cf ܚܠܒܐ
ܐܣܘܪܐ (chains) ... ܚܫܘܟܐ (darkness) 21:2,3; 42:16
ܐܦܐ cf ܐܪܥܐ
ܐܦܐ (face) ... ܪܘܙܐ (exultation) 21:9; 40:4
ܐܪܥܐ cf ܢܨܒ
ܐܪܥܐ (earth) ... ܡܢ ܣܘܦܗ...ܘܥܕܡܐ ܠܣܘܦܗ (from one end...to the other) 33:3 *; Deut 13:7; 28:64; Jer 12:12; 25:33
ܐܪܥܐ (earth/land) ... ܥܠ ܐܦܝܗ (upon its face/surface) 11:13; 16:16
ܐܪܥܐ (earth) ... ܦܐܪܐ (fruits) 11:12 *; Ps 104:13; Jer 2:7
ܐܬܪ cf ܒܪܟ
ܐܬܪܐ (place) with the idea of totality (ܟܠ) 18:7; 22:6; 23:17; 34:3
ܐܬܪܐ (place) ... ܦܪܕܝܣܐ (paradise) 11:18,23

ܒܘܣܡܐ cf ܦܪܕܝܣܐ
ܒܛܝܠ (idle) ... ܦܐܪ̈ܐ (fruits) 4:4; 11:23
ܒܢܐ cf ܚܠܒܐ
ܒܪܐ (son) ... ܐܡܬܐ (maidservant) 29:11 *; Gen 21:13; Ex 23:12; Pss 86:16; 115:16
ܒܪܝܫܝܬ cf ܪܝܫܐ
ܠܒܗܐ cf ܠܒܐ
ܕܒܘܪ̈ܬܐ cf ܒܪܬܐ
ܕܒܪ cf ܫܪܪ
ܕܒܫܐ cf ܪܕܐ
ܕܘܝܐ cf ܐܘܐ
ܕܡܐ ܕܢܦܫܐ (blood of the soul) 20:6 *; Jer 2:34; Sir 33:31
ܕܡܘܬܐ cf ܢܣܒ
ܕܡܪ (marvel) ... ܚܙܐ (see) 28:8,9; 41:8; syn ܚܙܐ - ܬܡܗ 17:6
ܕܢܚ/ܕܢܚܐ cf ܢܘܗܪܐ
ܗܕ̈ܡܐ cf ܗܘܘ ܠܝ
ܗܕ̈ܡܐ (members) ... ܢܦܠ (fall) 6:16; 18:2
ܗܘܘ ܠܝ ܗܕ̈ܡܐ (they were to me members) 17:15; 21:4
ܗܘܐ ܠܝ ܦܘܪܩܢܐ (it was to me salvation) 11:3; 28:10; 35:2; 38:3
ܗܠܟ (walk) ... ܛܥܝܘܬܐ (error) 18:14; 38:5
ܗܠܒܬܐ cf ܝܗܒ
ܙܕܝܩܘܬܐ cf ܙܕܩ, ܬܪܘܨ
ܙܕܝܩܘܬܐ (righteousness) ... ܠܒܐ (heart) 20:4; 36:7
ܙܕܩ/ܙܕܝܩܘܬܐ (declare righteous/righteousness) ... ܟܠܠ/ܟܠܝܠܐ (crown) 9:10; 17:2
ܙܡܪ (sing) ... ܚܘܒܐ (love) 16:3; 41:2
ܚܒܠܐ cf ܐܘܪܚܐ, ܚܒܠܐ ܠܐ, ܫܒܠ, ܫܒܩ
ܚܕܘܬܐ (joy) ... ܡܪܝܐ (Lord) 7:2; 15:1; syn ܚܕܘܬܐ - ܪܚܝܡܐ (beloved) 7:1
ܚܕܬ (new) ... ܬܫܒܘܚܬܐ (hymn) 31:3; 41:16
ܚܘܒܐ cf ܙܡܪ, ܦܘܐ
ܚܘܒܐ (love) ... ܠܒܐ (heart) 8:1; 16:2; 18:1
ܚܙܐ cf ܕܡܪ
ܚܙܐ (see) ... ܥܝܢܐ/ܥܝ̈ܢܐ (eye/s) 5:4,5; 13:1; 15:3; 16:9
ܚܝܐ cf ܡܪܝܐ
ܚܝܐ (life) ... ܠܥܠܡ (eternal) 6:18; 9:4; 41:16
ܚܝܐ (life) ... ܠܐ ܡܘܬܐ (immortal) 10:2; 11:7; 15:10; 28:6; 31:7; 38:3; 40:6
ܚܝܠܐ cf ܟܫܪ
ܚܟܡ (be wise) ... ܫܪܪܐ (truth) 33:8; 38:1

ܚܠܒܐ cf ܪܕܐ
ܚܠܒܐ (milk) ... ܐܡܐ (mother)/ܐܢܬܬܐ (woman) ... ܛܠܝܐ (child)/ܒܢ̈ܝܐ (sons) 35:5; 40:1
ܚܠܝܘܬܐ cf ܡܪܝܪܘܬܐ
ܚܣܡ cf ܛܝܒܘܬܐ
ܚܣܪ cf ܝܗܒ
ܚܫܘܟܐ cf ܢܘܗܪܐ
ܛܒܐ cf ܥܒܕ/ܥܒܕܐ
ܛܝܒܘܬܐ cf ܠܒܫ, ܡܠܐ, ܦܪܩ
ܛܝܒܘܬܐ (grace) ... ܚܣܡ ܠܐ (generous) 20:7; 23:4
ܛܠܝܐ cf ܚܠܒܐ
ܛܠܝܘܬܐ cf ܗܠܟ, ܫܒܩ
ܝܐܝܘܬܐ cf ܪܒܘܬܐ
ܝܕ cf ܡܬܚܐ, ܦܫܛ
ܝܕܥ cf ܐܘܪܚܐ
ܝܕܥ (know) ... ܥܒܕ (make) 7:12; 12:10
ܝܕܥܬܐ cf ܣܟܐ
ܝܗܒ (give) ... ܐܘܪܚܐ (way) 17:8; syn ܝܗܒ - ܗܒܠܬܐ (path) 31:2 (ms H)
ܝܗܒ (give) ... ܚܣܪ (be in need) 4:9; 15:10
ܝܗܒ (give) ... ܬܫܒܘܚܬܐ (glory) 6:7; 29:11; 41:4
ܝܘܡܐ cf ܫܡܫܐ
ܝܘܡܐ (day) ... ܢܗܪ/ܢܗܝܪ (shine/light) 16:16; 41:4
ܝܘ̈ܡܬܐ (days) ... ܫܢ̈ܝܐ (years) 4:5 *; Pss 61:6; 77:5; 78:33; 90:14-15
ܝܡܝܢܐ cf ܝܫܐ
ܝܡܝܢܐ (right hand) ... ܣܡ (set) 8:20; 18:7; 25:7
ܝܡܝܢܐ (right hand) ... ܪܘܡ (lift up) 8:5-6; 25:9
ܝܫܛ (hold out) ... ܝܡܝܢܐ (right hand) 14:4 *; Gen 48:14
ܟܘܪ̈ܬܐ ܕܕܒܘܪ̈ܝܬܐ (honeycomb of bees) 30:4; 40:1
ܟܠ cf ܐܬܪܐ, ܚܕܪ
ܟܠܝܠܐ cf ܙܘܩ, ܣܡ
ܟܠܝܠܐ (crown) ... ܫܪܪܐ (truth) 1:2; 9:8
ܟܠܠ cf ܙܘܩ
ܚܕܪ (surround) ... ܟܠ ܐܬܪ (every place) 22:6; 34:3
ܠܐ ܚܒܠܐ (incorruption) ... ܠܥܠܡ̈ܐ (aeons) 7:11; 8:23; ܚܒܠܐ ... ܠܥܠܡܐ 22:11
ܠܒܐ cf ܕܘܝܘܬܐ, ܚܘܒܐ, ܡܠܐ
ܠܒܐ (heart) ... ܓܣܐ (belch up) 36:7; 40:2
ܠܒܐ (heart) ... ܦܐܪ̈ܐ (fruits) 11:1; 17:13
ܠܒܫ (put on) ... ܛܝܒܘܬܐ (grace) 4:6; 20:7

ܠܒܫ (put on) ... ܠܐ ܚܒܠܐ (incorruption) 15:8; 33:12
ܠܥܠܡ cf ܚܝܐ
ܡܒܘܥܐ cf ܡܝܐ, ܥܬܪܐ
ܡܘܬܐ cf ܚܝܐ, ܦܘܡܐ
ܡܚܫܒܬܐ cf ܫܪܪ
ܡܝܐ (water) ... ܚܝܐ (living) 6:18; 11:7
ܡܝܐ (water) ... ܡܒܘܥܐ (spring/fountain) 11:7; 30:1; 40:2
ܡܠܠ (speak) ... ܛܝܒܘܬܐ (grace) 31:3; 33:10
ܡܠܠ (speak) ... ܠܒܐ (heart) 26:2; 37:2
ܡܠܠ (speak) ... ܣܦ̈ܘܬܐ (lips) 37:2; 42:14
ܡܠܠ (speak) ... ܦܐܪ̈ܐ (fruits) 8:2; 10:2
ܡܠܠ (speak) ... ܦܘܡܐ (mouth) 26:10; 42:6
ܡܠܠ (speak) ... ܪܘܚܐ (spirit) 6:2; 16:5
ܡܕܒܪܢܐ cf ܦܘܪܢܣܐ
ܡܪܘܡܐ (height) ... ܢܚܬ (descend) 22:1; 23:5
ܡܪܘܡܐ (height) ... ܪܘܡ (lift up) 21:1; 36:1 (Ms H)
ܡܪܝܐ cf ܐܒܐ, ܚܘܬܐ, ܡܫܝܚܐ
ܡܪܝܪܘܬܐ (bitterness) ... ܚܠܝܘܬܐ (sweetness) 28:15 *; Prov 27:7; Is 5:20
ܡܫܝܚܐ (Messiah) ... ܡܪܝܐ (Lord) 17:16; 24:1; 29:6; 39:11
ܡܫܝܚܐ (Messiah) ... ܪܝܫܐ (head) 17:16; 24:1
ܡܬܝܚܐ (stretching out) ... ܝܕ (hand) 27:2; 42:1
ܢܓܗ cf ܝܘܡܐ
ܢܗܪ cf ܒܢ̈ܐ
ܢܘܗܪܐ cf ܒܢ̈ܐ
ܢܘܗܪܐ (light) ... ܕܢܚ/ܕܢܚܐ (dawn/dawning) 12:7; 41:14
ܢܚ (rest) ... ܡܢ ܥܒ̈ܕܘܗܝ (from his works) 16:12 *; Gen 2:2
ܢܚܬ cf ܡܪܘܡܐ
ܢܣܒ (receive) ... ܕܡܘܬܐ (likeness) 7:4; 17:4
ܢܦܠ cf ܗܕ̈ܡܐ
ܢܦܫܐ cf ܕܡܐ
ܢܨܒ (plant) ... ܐܪܥܐ (earth/land) 11:18,21
ܣܓܐ (increase) ... ܝܕܥܬܐ (knowledge) 6:6; 12:3
ܣܘܓܐܐ/ܣܓܝܐܐ (multitude/great) ... ܪܚܡܐ (mercy) 14:9; 16:7; 19:7
ܣܘܦܐ cf ܐܪܥܐ
ܣܠܩ (ascend) ... ܡܢ ܬܚܬܝ̈ܬܐ (from parts below) 22:1; syn ܣܠܩ ... ܡܢ ܥܘܡ̈ܩܐ (from depths) 29:4
ܣܡ cf ܣܡܐ
ܣܡ (set) ... ܟܠܝܠܐ (crown) 9:8,11; 20:7

ܣܦܘ̈ܬܐ cf ܡܠܠ
ܣܦܘ̈ܬܐ (lips) ... ܦܐܪ̈ܐ (fruit) 12:2; 16:2
ܣܪܝܩܘܬܐ cf ܦܪܩ
ܥܒܕ cf ܐܝܕ, ܪܒܘܬܐ
ܥܒ̈ܕܐ cf ܢܘܚ
ܥܒܕ/ܥܒ̈ܕܐ (make/works) ... ܛܒܐ (good) 11:20; 28:12
ܥܒܕ (make) ... ܦܐܪ̈ܐ (fruits) 11:1; 14:7
ܥܘܡܩ̈ܐ cf ܣܠܩ
ܥܝܢܐ/ܥܝ̈ܢܐ cf ܚܙܐ
ܥܝܢܐ (eye) ... ܢܘܗܪܐ/ܢܗܪ (light/shine) 5:5; 6:17; 11:14
ܥܠܡ cf ܚܝܐ
ܥܠܡܐ/ܥܠܡ̈ܐ cf ܠܐ ܚܒܠܐ
ܥܡܐ cf ܦܪܩ
ܥܫܢ (strengthen) ... ܚܝܠܐ (power) 18:2; 32:3
ܥܬܝܪܐ (abundant) ... ܡܒܘܥܐ (spring/fountain) 4:10; 26:13
ܦܐܪ̈ܐ cf ܐܪܥܐ, ܓܒܠ, ܛܒܐ, ܡܠܠ, ܣܦܘ̈ܬܐ, ܥܒܕ, ܪܘܝ
ܦܘܡܐ cf ܡܠܠ
ܦܘܡܐ (mouth) ... ܡܘܬܐ (death) 18:8; 29:4
ܦܘܪܩܢܐ cf ܠܐ ܗܘܐ
ܦܘܪܩܢܐ (salvation) ... ܡܥܕܪܢܐ (helper) 20:2; 25:2
ܦܪܕܝܣܐ cf ܐܬܪܐ
ܦܪܕܝܣܐ (paradise) ... ܒܘܣܡܐ (luxury) 11:16,24
ܦܪܩ (save) ... ܥܡܐ (people) 10:6; 31:12
ܦܪܩ (save) ... ܛܝܒܘܬܐ (grace) 9:5; 25:4
ܦܫܛ (extend) ... ܐܝܕ (hand) 27:1; 35:7; 37:1; 42:1
ܦܫܪ (melt) ... ܩܕܡ (before) 17:9; 31:1
ܦܬܐ/ܦܬܝܘܬܐ (spread out widely/wide) ... ܐܘܪܚܐ (way) 7:13; 23:15
ܦܬܓܡܐ (word) ... ܫܪܪܐ (truth) 8:8; 12:1,3,12; 24:9,10; 32:2
ܦܬܚ (open) ... ܬܪܥܐ/ܬܪ̈ܥܐ (gate/s) 17:8; 42:17
ܨܒܝܢܐ (desire) ... ܫܘܡܠܝܐ (perfection) 9:4; 18:8
ܩܕܡ cf ܦܫܪ, ܩܘܡ
ܩܘܐ (abide) ... ܪܚܡܬܐ (love) 8:22; syn ܩܘܐ ... ܢܘܚܐ 14:6
ܩܘܡ (stand) ... ܩܕܡ (before) 36:2 *; Gen 23:3; Num 16:2; Josh 7:12,13
ܩܘܡ (stand) ... ܪܡܐ/ܪܘܡܐ (height) 33:3; 36:2
ܩܠܐ cf ܫܡܥ
ܩܢܐ cf ܐܒܐ
ܩܢܐ (gain) ... ܡܢ ܪܫܝܬ (from the beginning) 23:3; 41:9
ܪܒܐ (rear) ... ܫܘܡܠܝܐ (perfection) 17:7; 35:6

ܪܒܘܬܐ (greatness) ... ܝܐܝܘܬܐ (beauty) 7:23; 15:7; 18:16; 29:3
ܪܒܘܬܐ (greatness) ... ܥܒܕ (make) 15:7; 36:5
ܪ̈ܓܠܐ cf ܪܝܫܐ
ܪܕܐ (flow) ... ܚܠܒܐ (milk) 4:10 (... ܕܒܫܐ (honey); 40:1
ܪܘܙ (laugh) ... ܦܐܪ̈ܐ (fruits) 11:12; Gk γελάω ... οἱ καρποὶ 11:12,16
ܪܘܚܐ cf ܡܠܐ
ܪܘܡ cf ܡܪܝܡܐ, ܡܪܘܡܐ
ܪܘܡ (lift up) ... ܙܕܝܩܘܬܐ (righteousness) 8:5; 41:12
ܪܘܡܐ cf ܩܘܡ
ܪܚܡܐ cf ܚܕܘܬܐ
ܪ̈ܚܡܐ cf ܡܣܓܠܐ/ܡܣܓܐܐ
ܪܚܡܬܐ cf ܩܘܐ
ܪܝܫܐ cf ܡܫܝܚܐ
ܪܝܫܐ (head) ... ܪ̈ܓܠܐ (foot) 23:16; rev 42:13
ܪܡܐ cf ܩܘܡ
ܫܒܩ (abandon) with, for the most part, negative elements: ܣܪܝܩܘܬܐ (the vain one) 11:8; ܫܛܝܘܬܐ (folly) 11:10; ܐܘܪܚܐ ܕܛܥܝܘܬܐ (way of error) 15:6; ܚܒܠܐ (corruption) 33:1; ܐܘܪ̈ܚܬܗ ܕܚܒܠܐ (ways of corruption) 33:7
ܫܘܠܛܢܐ/ܫܠܝܛܐ (authority) ... ܫܪܐ (release) 22:4; 23:9
ܫܘܡܠܝܐ cf ܓܡܝܪܐ, ܪܒܐ
ܫܛܝܘܬܐ cf ܫܒܩ
ܫܠܝܛܐ cf ܫܘܠܛܢܐ
ܫܡܥ cf ܬܫܒܘܚܬܐ
ܫܡܥ (hear) ... ܩܠܐ (voice) 24:2; 37:2; 42:19
ܫܡܥ (hear) ... ܫܪܪܐ (truth) 8:8 (word of truth);15:4
ܫܡܫܐ (sun) ... ܝܘܡܐ (day) 15:1; 16:16
ܫܢܐ cf ܝ̈ܘܡܬܐ
ܫܪܐ cf ܫܘܠܛܢܐ
ܫܪܪܐ cf ܐܘܪܚܐ, ܢܒܥ, ܟܠܝܠܐ, ܦܬܓܡܐ, ܫܡܥ
ܫܪܪܐ / ܕܫܪܪܐ ܡܚܫܒܬܐ (truth/thought of truth) ... ܕܒܪ (lead) 17:5; 38:1
ܬܫ̈ܬܝܬܐ cf ܡܠܦ
ܬܡܗ cf ܕܡܪ
ܬܪܥܐ / ܬܪ̈ܥܐ cf ܦܬܚ
ܬܪܓ cf ܐܘܪܚܐ
ܬܫܒܘܚܬܐ cf ܚܕܬ, ܝܗܒ
ܬܫܒܘܚܬܐ (glory) ... ܐܝܩܪܐ (honour) and ܫܡܐ (name) 16:20; 20:10

## APPENDIX D: REPEATED STYLISTIC FEATURES

### a. REPETITION OF ROOTS

Two roots are associated in one line and are subsequently repeated in the same form in reverse order in two subsequent lines (almost always adjacent):

line 1 - element 1 ... element 2
line 2 - element 2
line 3 - element 1

This occurs in 4:1 (x 2: ܚܠܦ...ܐܬܪܐ...ܚܠܦ...ܐܬܪܐ) and 2c, 3a; 7:1b (ܚܕܘܬܐ ...ܪܗܛܐ) and 2a-b; 7:8a (ܒܪܐ...ܚܟܝܡ) and 8b-9a; 17:8b (ܦܬܚ...ܐܚ) and 10a-b; 28:6 (ܚܝܐ...[ܠܐ] ܡܝܬ) and 7b, 7c; 31:3b (ܚܕܘܬܐ...ܛܝܒܘܬܐ) and 6b, 7a.

The order of repetition is not reversed in 6:11a (ܫܬܐ...ܨܗܐ) and 11b-12a; 42:7b (ܚܪܐ...ܚܘܒܐ) and 8b, 9b.

A mirror image of the pattern is provided by 11:16a-b and 24, where the two elements occur separately in 16a and 16b and are subsequently associated in 24 (ܦܪܕܝܣܐ...ܒܘܣܡܐ). The order of repetition of the elements is reversed in the Greek (ΠΑΡΑΔΕΙΣΟΣ...ΤΡΥΦΗΣ); cf. also 41:11b-c and 16 (ܚܝܐ...ܦܘܪܩܢܐ) and the use of the pattern with three elements in 9:8a-b and 11a (...ܟܠܠܐ...ܣܡ ܥܛܪ...).

A root is repeated within one line in adjacent position or with some element/s between, such as a relative particle, *nota dativi*, or preposition. The same form of the root occurs in 4:13a; 6:7b; Copt 6:9b; 7:22a; 8:22b,22d; 17:11b; 20:5b, 5c; 28:1b; 36:4a, 4b; 38:9c. The most frequent pattern of forms is verb + noun - 4:10a; 6:9a; 7:10a; 9:11b; 10:3b; 11:19a (Syr and Gk), 20b; 17:7d; 20:2; 25:8a; 36:1b; 38:9a; 41:6a, 7; or noun + verb - 9:3b; 16:13a, 13b; 18:15b. Other variations of forms occur in 3:7b; 6:18b; 11:5a (Syr and Gk), 15; 42:2a. (Cf. also, e.g., Didascalia Apostolorum XIII, ܘܦܬܓܡܐ ܕܐܠܗܐ ܚܝܐ ܕܚܝܝܢ ܘܡܚܝܝܢ; Vööbus 2: 151, lines 19-20).

This pattern of repetition is found in parallel over two lines in 16:13a-b; 20:5b-c; 36:4.

A root is repeated over two lines in the same form in 1:2b-3a, 5a-b; 3:7c-d, 8a-b, 10b-11a; 4:1a-b, 7a-b, 9b-c; 5:12b-13a; 6:5a-b, 6c-7a, 9a-b (Syr and Copt), 12-13a (Syr and Copt); 7:1a-b, 7a-b, 21a-b, 24a-b; 9:2a-b, 4a-b, 11b-12a; 10:3b-4a; 11:10a-b, 12b-13, 21a-b; 17:9a-b, 15b-16; 20:5c-6a, 9c-10. The pattern of verb + noun occurs in 9:11b-12a; 17:1a-b; 41:3a-b; and noun + verb in 4:11a-b; 6:6a-b, 7a-b; 7:8a-b, 18a-b; 20:1a-b; 34:6a-b; 40:4a-b. Other variations in form are found in 3:7b-c, 9a-b; 6:5a-b, 11a-b; 7:22a-b; 20:3b-c.

A root is repeated in three consecutive lines in Copt 5:7a-8a; 6:1b-2b; 38:9a-c; in six consecutive lines in 3:3a-5b.

There is a triple repetition of ܒ ܬ ܒ (with only the insertion of the preposition ܒ between two of the repetitions) in 9:11b-12a.

### b. OTHER COMMON FEATURES

Series of three verbs with a common subject - e.g. 3:11; 6:8c-d; 7:13b; 8:22a; 10:4a, 6b-c; 31:10a; 34:6; 38:4a-b.

Rhetorical questions - 3:4a-b; 4:6a-b; 8:19a, 19b; 23:1b-c, 2b-c, 3b-c; 26:8a, 8b, 9a-b, 10a-b, 11a-c.

Imperative + ...ܪ ܘܗܢ - e.g. 8:3-5, 10-12; 31:6a.

ܐܝܟ + noun + 3rd masc. sing. suffix (ref. the Lord) + 3rd masc. sing. verb (subj. generally the Lord) + 1st sing. obj. suffix - 15:7; 29:2-3; 36:5 (cf. also 14:9).

# APPENDIX E: THE UNIQUE OCCURRENCE OF A ROOT WITHIN THE SYRIAC ODES

In the following table the figures in the second column represent the number of times a root occurs uniquely within an Ode (cf. the concordance, Lattke 1979-86, vol. 2); the third column indicates the length of each Ode by the number of lines according to my edition; the fourth column gives the proportion of occurences to the number of lines in any Ode.

The data is helpful for the question of whether certain sections of the Odes belong to material borrowed by the Odist from other sources. For those sections considered as possibly from other sources because of their highly structured style (cf. Chapter III.b.3: The small structured sections), it is significant that the data below cannot be used to support such an argument. In fact, most of those sections do not contain any occurences of a unique root. The clusters of lines which do contain a number of unique occurences are 5:5a-7a (x 4); 7:1a (x 2); 16:1a-2b (x 5), 11 (x 2); 17:9a-b (x 4); 19:4a-7b (x 6); 20:6a-c (x 3); 22:5a (x 3); 23:6a-b (x 4), 11-16 (x 5); 28:1-2 (x 3), 4c-6 (x 5), 13a (x 2); 34:1-2a (x 3); 35:3b-5a (x 4); 38:1b-3a (x 5); 39:1b-2b (x 3); 40:3a (x 2); 41:6b (x 2); 42:7b-13a (x 6).

| Ode | Unique root | No. of lines | Proportion |
|-----|-------------|--------------|------------|
| 3 | 2 | 25 | 8 |
| 4 | 5 | 33 | 15.2 |
| 5 | 4 | 30 | 13.3 |
| 6 | 6 | 37 | 16.2 |
| 7 | 9 | 64 | 14 |
| 8 | 4 | 52 | 7.7 |
| 9 | - | 27 | - |
| 10 | 1 | 14 | 7.1 |
| 11 | 10 | 49 | 20.4 |
| 12 | 5 | 36 | 13.9 |
| 13 | 2 | 7 | 28.6 |
| 14 | 3 | 19 | 15.8 |

| 15 | 1 | 23 | 4.3 |
|----|----|----|------|
| 16 | 10 | 36 | 27.8 |
| 17 | 6 | 34 | 17.6 |
| 18 | 3 | 33 | 9.1 |
| 19 | 7 | 25 | 28 |
| 20 | 5 | 24 | 20.8 |
| 21 | 1 | 23 | 4.3 |
| 22 | 6 | 24 | 25 |
| 23 | 10 | 55 | 18.2 |
| 24 | 3 | 30 | 10 |
| 25 | 5 | 24 | 20.8 |
| 26 | 3 | 27 | 11.1 |
| 27 | - | 3 | - |
| 28 | 12 | 45 | 26.7 |
| 29 | 3 | 24 | 12.5 |
| 30 | 2 | 13 | 15.4 |
| 31 | 3 | 29 | 10.3 |
| 32 | - | 6 | - |
| 33 | 3 | 34 | 8.8 |
| 34 | 3 | 15 | 20 |
| 35 | 4 | 17 | 23.5 |
| 36 | - | 24 | - |
| 37 | 1 | 8 | 12.5 |
| 38 | 11 | 59 | 18.6 |
| 39 | 7 | 30 | 23.3 |
| 40 | 4 | 15 | 26.7 |
| 41 | 3 | 32 | 9.4 |
| 42 | 7 | 44 | 15.9 |

# BIBLIOGRAPHY

Abbott, E.A. 1912. Light on the Gospel from an Ancient Poet. Diatessarica 9. Cambridge : UP.

Abbott, E.A. 1914. The Fourfold Gospel: The Beginning. Diatessarica 10,2. Cambridge: UP.

Abramowski, L. 1984. "Sprache und Abfassungszeit der Oden Salomos." OrChr 68: 80-90.

Abramowski, L. 1987. Rev. of Drijvers (1984). JThS NS 38: 218-9.

Abramowski, R. 1936. "Der Christus der Salomooden." ZNW 35: 44-69.

Aland, K., ed. 1975. The Greek New Testament. 3rd ed. United Bible Societies.

Alès, A. d' 1911. "Les Odes de Salomon." Études 129: 753-70.

Allberry, C.R.C., ed. 1938. Manichaean Manuscripts in the Chester Beatty Collection. Vol. 2. A Manichaean Psalm-Book Part II. Stuttgart: Kohlhammer.

Allen, L.C. 1986. "The Value of Rhetorical Criticism in Psalm 69." JBL 105: 577-98.

Altaner, B., and A. Stuiber. 1966. Patrologie. Leben, Schriften und Lehre der Kirchenväter. 7., völlig neubearbeitete Auflage. Freiburg: Herder.

Amstutz, J. 1968. ΑΠΛΟΤΗΣ. Eine begriffsgeschichtliche Studie zum jüdisch-christlichen Griechisch. Theoph. 19. Bonn: Hanstein.

Apuleius cf. Griffiths.

Arnold-Döben, V. 1978. Die Bildersprache des Manichäismus. Als Manuskript veröffentlicht. Arbeitsmaterialen zur Religionsgeschichte 3. Köln: Religionswissenschaftliches Seminar der Universität Bonn in Kommission bei Brill.

Aune, D.E. 1982. "The Odes of Solomon and Early Christian Prophecy." NTS 28: 435-60.

Aune, D.E. 1983. Prophecy in Early Christianity and the Ancient Mediterranean World. Grand Rapids, Michigan: Eerdmans.

Bacon, B.W. 1911. "The Odes of the Lord's Rest." Exp. 8,1: 193-209.

Bardenhewer, O. 1913-32. Geschichte der altkirchlichen Literatur. 2nd ed. 5 vols. Freiburg: Herder.

Bardtke, H., ed. 1963. Qumran-Probleme: Vorträge des Leipziger Symposiums über Qumran-Probleme vom 9. bis 14. Okt. 1961. SSA 42. Berlin: Akademie. 75-108.

Barnes, W. E. 1910a. "An Ancient Christian Hymn Book." Exp. 7,10: 52-63.

Barnes, W.E. 1910b. "The Text of the Odes of Solomon." JThS 11: 573-5.

Barnstone, W. 1984. "The Odes of Solomon." The Other Bible. San Francisco: Harper & Row. 267-85.

Barrett, C.K. 1978. The Gospel according to St John: An Introduction with Commentary and Notes on the Greek Text. 2nd ed. London: SPCK.

Batiffol, P. 1911. "Les Odes de Salomon." RB 8: 21-59, 161-97.

Bauer, W. 1933. Die Oden Salomos. KlT 64. Berlin: de Gruyter.

Bauer, W. 1964. "Die Oden Salomos." Hennecke 1964, 576-625.

Baumeister, Th. 1984. "Gebet V. Alte Kirche." TRE 12: 60-5.

Becker, H. 1956. Die Reden des Johannesevangeliums und der Stil der gnostischen Offenbarungsrede. Ed. R. Bultmann. FRLANT 68 = NF 50. Göttingen: Vandenhoeck & Ruprecht.

Berger, K. 1977. Exegese des Neuen Testaments: Neue Wege vom Text zur Auslegung. UTB 658. Heidelberg: Quelle & Meyer.

Berger, K. 1984a. Formgeschichte des Neuen Testaments. Heidelberg: Quelle & Meyer.

Berger, K. 1984b. "Gnosis/Gnostizismus: I. Vor- und außerchristlich." TRE 13: 519-35.

Berger, P.L., and T. Luckmann. 1971. The Social Construction of Reality: A Treatise in the Sociology of Knowledge. 1967. U.K.: Penguin University Books.

Berlin, A. 1987. "On the Interpretation of Psalm 133." Follis 1987, 141-7.

Bernard, J.H. 1912. The Odes of Solomon: Edited with introduction and notes. TaS 8,3. Cambridge: UP.

Bertram, G. 1928. "Höllenfahrt: II. Höllenfahrt Christi." RGG 2nd ed. 2: 1968-70.

Bertram, G. 1966. "Erhöhung." RAC 6: 22-43.

Bethge, H.-G., and O.S. Wintermute, trans. 1984. "On the Origin of the World (II, 5 and XIII, 2)." Robinson, J.M. 161-79.

Betz, J. 1984. "Die Eucharistie als Gottes Milch in frühchristlicher Sicht." ZKTh 106: 1-26,167-85.

Bianchi, U., ed. 1967. The Origins of Gnosticism. Colloquium of Messina, 13-18 April 1966. SHR 12. Leiden: Brill.

Black, C.C. 1989. "Keeping up with Recent Studies: XVI. Rhetorical Criticism and Biblical Interpretation." ET 100: 252-8.

Blaszczak, G.R. 1985. A Formcritical Study of Selected Odes of Solomon.
HSM 36. Atlanta: Scholars.

Boman, T. 1968. Das hebräische Denken im Vergleich mit dem griechischen.
5th ed. Göttingen: Vandenhoeck & Ruprecht.

Brandt, S., and G. Laubmann, eds. 1890. L. Caeli Firmiani Lactanti Opera
Omnia. 1. Lactantius, Divinae Institutiones et Epitome Divinarum Institutio-
num. CSEL 19. Wien.

Braun, F.-M. 1959. L'Évangile dans l'église ancienne. EtB. Paris: Gabalda.

Brock, S.P. 1974. Rev. of Charlesworth (1973), JBL 93: 623-5.

Brock, S.P. 1975. Rev. of Charlesworth (1973), BSOAS 38: 142-3.

Brock, S.P. 1980. "Bibelübersetzungen. I. Die alten Übersetzungen des Alten
und Neuen Testaments. 1.1 Bibelübersetzungen im Altertum." TRE 6: 161.

Brock, S.P. 1987. "The Odes of Solomon." The History of the Jewish People
in the Age of Jesus Christ (175 B.C.- A.D. 135). Vol. 3/2. E. Schürer. 1885.
Rev. and ed. G. Vermes et al. Edinburgh: T. & T. Clark. 787-9.

Brockelmann, C. 1912. Rev. of Grimme (1911). LZD 63: 313-5.

Brockelmann, C. 1951. Syrische Grammatik mit Paradigmen, Literatur,
Chrestomathie und Glossar. 6th ed. PLO 5. Leipzig: Harrassowitz.

Brockelmann, K. 1966. Lexicon Syriacum. 1928. Hildesheim: Olms.

Brownson, J. 1988. "The Odes of Solomon and the Johannine Tradition." JSP
2: 49-69.

Brueggemann, W. 1975. Rev. of Hayes (1971) [2nd ed. 1974?]. Religious Studies Review 1,1: 8-13.

Bruston, Ch. 1911. "Les plus anciens cantiques chrétiens: Les Odes de Salomon." RThPh 44: 465-97.

Bruston, Ch. 1912a. "La seconde édition du texte des Odes de Salomon." RThQR 21: 74-8, 138-51.

Bruston, Ch. 1912b. Les plus anciens cantiques chrétiens traduits sur la seconde édition du texte syriaque avec une introduction et des notes. Genève: Fischbacher.

Bruston, Ch. 1912c. "Rectifications à la traduction des plus anciens cantiques chrétiens." RThQR 21: 440-2, 536-7.

Bruston, Ch. 1913. "Rectifications à la traduction des plus anciens cantiques chrétiens." RThQR 22: 54-64, 367-75.

Buber, M. 1954. Zu einer neuen Verdeutschung der Schrift: Beilage zu dem Werk "Die fünf Bücher der Weisung" verdeutscht von Martin Buber in Gemeinschaft mit Franz Rosenweig. Olten, Schweiz: Hegner.

Buhl, Fr. 1911. "Salomos Oder." TT 3,2: 97-128.

Bultmann, R. 1941. Das Evangelium des Johannes. KEK 2. Göttingen: Vandenhoeck & Ruprecht.

Burchard, C. 1983. Unterweisung in erzählender Form: Joseph und Aseneth. JSHRZ 2,4. Gütersloh: Mohn.

Burkitt, F.C. 1911/12. "A New MS of the Odes of Solomon." JThS 13: 372-85.

Buss, M.J. "The Study of Forms." Hayes 1974, 1-56.

Carmignac, J. 1961. "Les affinités qumrâniennes de la onzième Ode de Salomon." RdQ 3: 71-102.

Carmignac, J. 1963. "Un qumrânien converti au christianisme: l'auteur des Odes de Salomon." Bardtke 75-108.

Carmignac, J. 1986. Unpublished notes, translation and strophic division of the Odes of Solomon.[1]

Champollion le Jeune, J.F. 1815. "Lettre sur les Odes Gnostiques attribuées à Salomon: adressée à M. Grégoire." Magasin encyclopédique 2: 383-92.

Charles, R.H. 1910. Rev. of Harnack (1910). RTP 6: 220-3.

Charlesworth, J.H. 1967. "A Critical Examination of the Odes of Solomon: Identification, Text, Original Language, Date." Diss. Duke University.

Charlesworth, J.H. 1969. "The Odes of Solomon - Not Gnostic." CBQ 31: 357-69.

Charlesworth, J.H. 1970a. "Les Odes de Salomon et les manuscrits de la mer morte." RB 77: 522-49.

Charlesworth, J.H. 1970b. "Paronomasia and Assonance in the Syriac Text of the Odes of Solomon." Semitics 1: 12-26.

Charlesworth, J.H. 1972. "Qumran, John and the Odes of Solomon." John and Qumran. Ed. J.H. Charlesworth. London: Chapman. 107-36.

Charlesworth, J.H. 1973. The Odes of Solomon: Edited with Translation and Notes. Oxford: Clarendon.

Charlesworth, J.H. 1977. The Odes of Solomon: The Syriac Texts, edited with translation and notes. SBLTT 13. Pseudepigrapha Series 7. Chico, California: Scholars.

Charlesworth, J.H. 1979. "Haplography and Philology: A Study of Ode of Solomon 16:8." NTS 25: 221-7.

---

[1] These were given generously by Jean Carmignac to the author to copy during her short stay in Paris in March 1986. Carmignac intimated that they had been written many years previously and that he did not want them published in their present form.

Charlesworth, J.H., ed. 1981. <u>Papyri and Leather Manuscripts of the Odes of Solomon</u>. Dickerson Series of Facsimiles of Manuscripts Important for Christian Origins 1. Duke University: International Center for the Study of Ancient Near Eastern Civilizations and Christian Origins.

Charlesworth, J.H., and R.A. Culpepper. 1973. "The Odes of Solomon and the Gospel of John." <u>CBQ</u> 35: 298-322.

Charlier, C. 1948. "Odes de Salomon." <u>EeV(M)</u> 1: 239-44.

Clines, D.J.A. 1987. "The Parallelism of Greater Precision: Notes from Isaiah 40 for a Theory of Hebrew Poetry." Follis 1987, 77-100.

Collins, R.F. 1983. <u>Introduction to the New Testament</u>. London: SCM.

Collins, T. 1978. <u>Line-Forms in Hebrew Poetry: A Grammatical Approach to the Stylistic Study of the Hebrew Prophets</u>. StP.SM 7. Rome: Biblical Institute P.

Collins, T. 1987. "Decoding the Psalms: A Structural Approach to the Psalter." <u>JSOT</u> 37: 41-60.

Colpe, C. 1979. "Die gnostische Anthropologie zwischen Intellektualismus und Volksfrömmigkeit." Nagel 1979b, 31-44.

Colpe, C. 1981. "Gnosis II (Gnostizismus)." <u>RAC</u> 11: 537-659.

Colpe, C. 1982. "Heidnische, jüdische und christliche Überlieferung in den Schriften aus Nag Hammadi X." <u>JAC</u> 25: 65-101.

Colson, F.H., and G.H. Whitaker. 1930. <u>Philo</u>. Vol. 3. LCL 247. Cambridge, Massachusetts: Harvard UP.

<u>The Concordance to the Peshitta Version of the Aramaic New Testament</u>. 1985. Ed. The Way International Research Team. New Knoxville, Ohio: American Christian P.

Connolly, R.H. 1911/12. "The Odes of Solomon: Jewish or Christian?" JThS 13: 298-309.

Connolly, R.H. 1912/13a. "Greek the Original Language of the Odes of Solomon." JThS 14: 530-8.

Connolly, R.H. 1912/13b. Rev. of Abbott (1912), JThS 14: 311-3.

Connolly, R.H. 1913/14. Rev. of G. Kittel (1914). JThS 15: 464-8.

Corwin, V. 1960. St. Ignatius and Christianity in Antioch. New Haven: Yale UP.

Crum, W.E. 1939. A Coptic Dictionary. Oxford: Clarendon P.

Cuddon, J.A. 1982. A Dictionary of Literary Terms. London: Penguin.

Dahood, M. 1972-81. "Ugaritic-Hebrew Parallel Pairs." Ras Shamra Parallels: The Texts from Ugarit and the Hebrew Bible. 3 vols. AnOr 49, 50, 51. Roma: Pontificum Institutum Biblicum. 1:71-382, 2:1-39, 3:1-206.

Dalmais, I.-H. "L'apport des églises syriennes à l'hymnographie chrétienne." OrSyr 2: 243-60.

Deichgräber, R. 1967. Gotteshymnus und Christushymnus in der frühen Christenheit. Untersuchungen zu Form, Sprache und Stil der frühchristlichen Hymnen. StUNT 5. Göttingen: Vandenhoeck & Ruprecht.

Deichgräber, R. 1983. "Formeln, Liturgische II. Neues Testament und Alte Kirche." TRE 11: 256-63

Dhorme, P. 1912. Rev. of Grimme (1911) et al. RB 21. N.S. 9: 463-6.

Dibelius, M. 1966. Die Formgeschichte des Evangeliums. 5th ed. Tübingen: Mohr.

Didascalia Apostolorum cf. Vööbus 1979.

Diettrich, G. 1910. "Eine jüdisch-christliche Liedersammlung (aus dem apostolischen Zeitalter)." Refor. 9: 306-10, 370-6, 513-8, 533-6.

Diettrich, G. 1911. Die Oden Salomos unter Berücksichtigung der überlieferten Stichengliederung: Aus dem Syrischen ins Deutsche übersetzt und mit einem Kommentar versehen. NSGTK 9. Berlin: Trowitzsch.

Dölger, F.J. 1925. Sol Salutis. Gebet und Gesang im christlichen Altertum. Mit besonderer Rücksicht auf die Ostung in Gebet und Liturgie. 2nd ed. LF 4/5. Münster i.W.: Aschendorff.

Douglas, M. 1969. "Social Preconditions of Enthusiasm and Heterodoxy." Forms of Symbolic Action: Proceedings of the 1969 Annual Spring Meeting of the American Ethnological Society. Ed. R.F. Spencer. Seattle: American Ethnological Society. 69-80.

Douglas, M. 1970. Purity and Danger. An Analysis of Concepts of Pollution and Taboo. U.K.: Penguin.

Douglas, M. 1982. Natural Symbols. Explorations in Cosmology. With a New Introduction by the Author. 1970. N.Y.: Pantheon.

Drijvers, H.J.W. 1978. "Die Oden Salomos und die Polemik mit den Markioniten im syrischen Christentum." OrChrA 205 (Symposium Syriacum 1976): 39-55.

Drijvers, H.J.W. 1979. "Kerygma und Logos in den Oden Salomos dargestellt am Beispiel der 23. Ode." Kerygma und Logos: Beiträge zu den geisteswissenschaftlichen Beziehungen zwischen Antike und Christentum. Festschrift für C. Andresen zum 70. Geburtstag. Ed. A.M. Ritter. Göttingen: Vandenhoeck & Ruprecht.

Drijvers, H.J.W. 1980. "The 19th Ode of Solomon: Its Interpretation and Place in Syrian Christianity." JThS NS 31: 337-55.

Drijvers, H.J.W. 1981. "Odes of Solomon and Psalms of Mani: Christians and Manichaeans in Third-Century Syria." Studies in Gnosticism and Hellenistic Religions presented to G.Quispel on the occasion of his 65th Birthday. Eds. R. van den Broek and M.J. Vermaseren. EPRO 91. Leiden: Brill. 117-30.

Drijvers, H.J.W. 1984. East of Antioch: Studies in Early Syriac Christianity. Collected Studies series 198. London: Variorum reprints.

Drijvers, H.J.W. 1986. "The Peshitta of Sapientia Salomonis." Scripta Signa Vocis: Studies about Scripts, Scriptures, Scribes and Languages in the Near East, presented to J.H.Hospers by his pupils, colleagues and friends. Eds. H.L.J. Vanstiphout et al. Groningen: Forsten. 15-30.

Drijvers, H.J.W. 1987. "Solomon as Teacher: Early Syriac Didactic Poetry." OrChrA 229 (Symposium Syriacum 1984): 123-34.

Drijvers, H.J.W. 1987/88. "Marcionism in Syria: Principles, Problems, Polemics." The Second Century 6: 153-72.

Drower, E.S. 1962. The Mandaeans of Iraq and Iran: Their Cults, Customs, Magic, Legends, and Folklore. 1937. Leiden: Brill.

Drower, E.S., and R. Macuch. 1963. A Mandaic Dictionary. Oxford: Clarendon.

Dubois, J.D. 1987. "Le quatrième évangile à la lumière des recherches gnostiques actuelles." FV 86:75-87.

Duensing, H. 1911. "Zur vierundzwanzigsten der Oden Salomos." ZNW 12: 86-7.

Eißfeldt, O. 1964. Einleitung in das Alte Testament unter Einschluß der Apokryphen und Pseudepigraphen sowie der apokryphen- und pseudepigraphenartigen Qumrān-Schriften. Entstehungsgeschichte des Alten Testaments. 3rd ed. NTG. Tübingen: Mohr.

Emerton, J.A. 1984. "The Odes of Solomon." The Apocryphal Old Testament. Ed. H.F.D. Sparks. Oxford: Clarendon.

The Facsimile Edition of the Nag Hammadi Codices. 1972-84. 12 vols. Leiden: Brill.

Fanourgakis, B.D. 1979. Αἱ ᾽Ὠδαὶ Σολομῶντος. Συμβολὴ εἰς τὴν ἔρευναν τῆς ὑμνογραφίας τῆς ἀρχαϊκῆς ἐκκλησίας. Analecta Vlatadon 29. Thessaloniki: Patriarchal Institute for Patristic Studies.

Feininger, B. 1981. "A Decade of German Psalm-Criticism." JSOT 20: 91-103.

Ferguson, E. 1988. "Spiritual Circumcision in Early Christianity." SJTh 41: 485-97.

Flemming 1910. cf. Harnack 1910.

Follis, E.R., ed. 1987. Directions in Biblical Hebrew Poetry. JSOT Suppl. Ser. 40. Sheffield: JSOT P.

Frankenberg, W. 1911. Das Verständnis der Oden Salomos. BZAW 21. Gießen: Töpelmann.

Franzmann, M. 1985. "The Odes of Solomon, Man of Rest." OrChrP 51: 408-21.

Franzmann, M. 1986a. "A Study of the Odes of Solomon with Reference to the French Scholarship 1909-1980." Lattke 1979-86, 3: 65, 68, 78, 81, 86-7, 95, 113, 115, 118-21, 133-4, 136-7, 139, 143-4, 147-8, 150, 153, 160, 163, 193-4, 211-4, 226, 228, 230, 234, 238, 240-3, 245, 247-8, 252, 255-7, 263-4, 266-7, 287, 290, 293, 295, 298, 301-2, 305, 311, 317, 320, 327-9, 332, 334, 342, 368-9, 371-425.

Franzmann, M. 1986b. "'Wipe the harlotry from your faces': a brief note on Ode of Solomon 13,3." ZNW 77: 282-3.

Franzmann, M. 1987. "Portrait of a Poet: Reflections on 'the Poet' in the <u>Odes</u> <u>of Solomon</u>." <u>Perspectives on Language and Text. Essays and Poems in Honor of F.I. Andersen's Sixtieth Birthday July 28 1985</u>, Eds. E.W. Conrad and E.G. Newing. Winona Lake, Indiana: Eisenbrauns. 315- 26.

Franzmann, M. 1989. "The Parable of the Vine in <u>Odes of Solomon</u> 38.17-19? A Response to Richard Bauckham." <u>NTS</u> 35: 604-8.

Franzmann, M. 1990. "Strangers from Above: An Investigation of the Motif of Strangeness in the Odes of Solomon and Some Gnostic Texts." <u>Muséon</u> 103: 27-41.

Freedman, D.N. 1987. "Another Look at Biblical Hebrew Poetry." Follis 1987, 11-28.

Freeman, E.E. 1979. "Hymns of the Lord's Rest." <u>The Holy Week Book</u>. San Jose, California: Resource Publications. 174-83.

Gager, J. 1982. "Body-Symbols and Social Reality: Resurrection, Incarnation and Asceticism in Early Christianity." <u>Religion</u> 12: 345-63.

Gamber, K. 1966. "Die Oden Salomos als frühchristliche Gesänge beim heiligen Mahl." <u>OstKSt</u> 15: 182-95.

Girard, M. 1984. <u>Les psaumes: Analyse structurelle et interprétation. 1-50</u>. Recherches, nouvelle série 2. Montréal: Bellarmine.

Gödel, K. 1962. <u>On Formally Undecidable Propositions of Principia Mathematica and Related Systems</u>. Edinburgh: Oliver & Boyd.

Goodman, P. 1954. <u>The Structure of Literature</u>. Chicago: UP.

<u>The Gospel of Philip</u> cf. Isenberg, W.W.

<u>The Gospel of Truth</u> cf. MacRae, G.W.

Greßmann, H. 1911a. "Die Oden Salomos." <u>ChW</u> 25: 633-5, 650-2, 674-7, 703-5.

Greßmann, H. 1911b. "Die Oden Salomos." IWW 5: 1-20.

Greßmann, H. 1913. "Les Odes de Salomon." RThPh NS 1: 195-217.

Greßmann, H. 1924. "Die Oden Salomos." Hennecke 1924, 437-72.

Griffiths, J.G. 1975. The Isis-Book (Metamorphoses, Book XI): Edited with an Introduction, Translation and Commentary. EPRO 39. Leiden: Brill.

Grimme, H. 1893. Der Stophenbau in den Gedichten Ephraems des Syrers mit einem Anhange über den Zusammenhang zwischen syrischer und byzantinischer Hymnenform. Collectanea Friburgensia. Commentationes Academicae Universitatis Friburgensis Helvetiorum 2. Freiburg: Commissionsverlag der Universitaetsbuchhandlung.

Grimme, H. 1911a. "Die 19. Ode Salomos." ThGl 3: 11-18.

Grimme, H. 1911b. Die Oden Salomos syrisch - hebräisch - deutsch: Ein kritischer Versuch. Heidelberg: Winters Universitätsbuchhandlung.

Grimme, H. 1912. "Zur Handschrift N der Oden Salomos." OLZ 15: 492-6.

Grundmann, W. 1963. "Stehen und Fallen im qumrânischen und neutestamentlichen Schrifttum." Bardtke 147-66.

Gunkel, H. 1910. "Die Oden Salomos." ZNW 11: 291-328.

Gunkel, H. 1913a. "Die Oden Salomos." Reden und Aufsätze von H. Gunkel. Göttingen: Vandenhoeck & Ruprecht. 163-92.

Gunkel, H. 1913b. Rev. of Frankenberg (1911). ThLZ 38: 9-13.

Gunkel, H., and J. Begrich. 1975. Einleitung in die Psalmen: Die Gattungen der religiösen Lyrik Israels. Zu Ende geführt von J. Begrich. 3rd ed. Göttingen: Vandenhoeck & Ruprecht.

Haase, F. 1927. "Bardesanes (syr. Bardaisan)." RGG. 2nd ed. 1: 762.

Hamman, A. 1979. Naissance des Lettres chrétiennes: Odes de Salomon -
Lettre de Barnabé - Symbole des Apôtres - Didaché - Pasteur d'Hermas. 3rd
ed. Paris: Desclée de Brouwer.

Harnack, A. 1891. Über das gnostische Buch Pistis-Sophia. TU 7,2. Leipzig:
Hinrichs'sche Buchhandlung.

Harnack, A. 1910. Ein jüdisch-christliches Psalmbuch aus dem ersten Jahrhun-
dert (The Odes ... of Solomon, now first published from the Syriac version
by J.Rendel Harris, 1909): Aus dem Syrischen übersetzt von J.Flemming.
TU 35,4. Leipzig: Hinrichs'sche Buchhandlung.

Harnack, A. 1921. Rev. of Harris and Mingana (1916-20). ThLZ 46: 6-7.

Harris, J.R. 1909. The Odes and Psalms of Solomon, now first published from
the Syriac version. Cambridge: UP.

Harris, J.R. 1911a. The Odes and Psalms of Solomon, published from the Syriac version: 2nd edition revised and enlarged, with a facsimile. Cambridge:
UP.[1]

Harris, J.R. 1911b. "The Thirty-eighth Ode of Solomon." Exp. 8,2: 28-37.

Harris, J.R. 1911c. "Two Flood-Hymns of the Early Church." Exp. 8,2: 405-
17.

Harris, J.R. 1930/31. "The Odes of Solomon and the Apocalypse of Peter." ET
42: 21-3.

Harris, J.R., and A. Mingana. 1916-20. The Odes and Psalms of Solomon re-
edited. 2 vols. Manchester: UP.

Hayes, J.H., ed. 1974. Old Testament Form Criticism. San Antonio: Trinity
UP.

---

[1] Harris' personal copy with marginal notes was presented to the author by Tony Brown,
senior tutor at Woodbrooke College, Birmingham, in February 1987.

Helderman, J. 1984. Die Anapausis im Evangelium Veritatis: Eine vergleichende Untersuchung des valentinianisch-gnostischen Heilsgutes der Ruhe im Evangelium Veritatis und in anderen Schriften der Nag Hammadi-Bibliothek. NHS 18. Leiden: Brill.

Hengel, M. 1969. Judentum und Hellenismus. Studien zu ihrer Begegnung unter besonderer Berücksichtigung Palästinas bis zur Mitte des 2.Jh. v.Chr. WUNT 10. Tübingen: Mohr (Siebeck).

Hengel, M. 1987. "Das Christuslied im frühesten Gottesdienst." Weisheit Gottes, Weisheit der Welt. Festschrift für Joseph Kardinal Ratzinger zum 60. Geburtstag. Ed. W. Baier et al. 2 vols. St. Ottilien: EOS. 1: 357-404.

Hennecke, E., ed. 1924. Neutestamentliche Apokryphen. 2nd ed. Tübingen: Mohr.

Hennecke, E., ed. 1964. Neutestamentliche Apokryphen in deutscher Übersetzung. 3., völlig neubearbeitete Auflage herausgegeben von W. Schneemelcher. II. Apostolisches, Apokalypsen und Verwandtes. Tübingen: Mohr (Siebeck).

Holm-Nielsen, S. 1960. Hodayot: Psalms From Qumran. AThD 2. Aarhus: Universitetsforlaget.

Horst, P.W. van der. 1988. Rev. of Lattke (1979-86, vol. 3). NedThT 42: 343.

Isenberg, S.R. 1975. "Mary Douglas and Hellenistic Religions: The Case of Qumran." SBLSP 1: 179-85.

Isenberg, S.R., and D.E. Owen. 1977. "Bodies, Natural and Contrived: The Work of Mary Douglas." Religious Studies Review 3: 1-17.

Isenberg, W.W. 1984. "The Gospel of Philip (II, 3)." Robinson, J.M. 131-51.

Käsemann, E. 1947. Rev. of Bultmann (1941). VF 3: 182-201.

Kittel, B.P. 1981. The Hymns of Qumran: Translation and Commentary. SBLDS 50. Missoula, Montana: Scholars.

Kittel, G. 1913. "Eine zweite Handschrift der Oden Salomos." ZNW 14: 79-93.

Kittel, G. 1914. Die Oden Salomos - überarbeitet oder einheitlich? BWAT 16. Leipzig: Hinrichs.

Klijn, A.F.J. 1960. Rev. of Testuz. NedThT 14: 447-8.

Knierim, R.P. 1973. "Old Testament Form Criticism Reconsidered." Interp. 27: 435-68.

Knierim, R.P. 1981. "Old Testament Form-critical Project." The Institute for Antiquity and Christianity: Report 1972-80. Ed. M.W. Meyer. Claremont, California: The Institute for Antiquity and Christianity. 9-12.

Knight, D.A. 1974. "The Understanding of 'Sitz im Leben' in Form Criticism." SBL 1974 Seminar Papers. 1: 105-25.

Koch, K. 1967. Was ist Formgeschichte? Neue Wege der Bibelexegese. 2nd ed. Neukirchen-Vluyn: Neukirchener Verlag des Erziehungsvereins.

Köbert, R. 1977. "Ode Salomons 20,6 und Sir 33,31." Bib 58: 529-30.

Köster, H. 1983. "Formgeschichte/Formenkritik. II. Neues Testament." TRE 11: 286-99.

Korpel, M.C.A., and J.C. de Moor. 1988. "Fundamentals of Ugaritic and Hebrew Poetry." Meer and Moor. 1-61.

Koschorke, K. 1978. Die Polemik der Gnostiker gegen das kirchliche Christentum: Unter besonderer Berücksichtigung der Nag-Hammadi-Traktate "Apokalypse des Petrus" (NHC VII,3) und "Testimonium Veritatis" (NHC IX,3). NHS 12. Leiden: Brill.

Kroll, J. 1914. Die Lehren des Hermes Trismegistos. BGPhMA 12, 2-4. Münster i.W.: Aschendorff.

Kroll, J. 1921/22. Die christliche Hymnodik bis zu Klemens von Alexandreia. Libelli 240. Darmstadt: Wissenschaftliche Buchgesellschaft, 1968. [= Photographic reproduction of Verzeichnis der Vorlesungen an der Akademie zu Braunsberg im Sommer 1921 (3-46), im Winter 1921/22 (47-98)].

Kugel, J.L. 1981. The Idea of Biblical Poetry: Parallelism and Its History. New Haven/London: Yale UP.

Labourt, J. 1910. "Les Odes de Salomon." RB 7: 483-500.

Labourt, J. 1911. "Les Odes de Salomon." RB 8: 5-21.

Labourt, J., and P. Batiffol. 1911. Les Odes de Salomon: Une oeuvre chrétienne des environs de l'an 100-120: Traduction française et introduction historique. Paris: Lecoffre.

Lagrand, J. 1980. "How Was the Virgin Mary 'Like a Man' (ܐܢܫ ܐܝܟ)?" NT 22: 97-107.

Lampe, G.W.H., ed. 1961. A Patristic Greek Lexicon. Oxford: Clarendon.

Langbrandtner, W. 1977. Weltferner Gott oder Gott der Liebe: Der Ketzerstreit in der johanneischen Kirche: Eine exegetisch-religionsgeschichtliche Untersuchung mit Berücksichtigung der koptisch-gnostischen Texte aus Nag-Hammadi. BBET 6. Frankfurt: Lang.

Lattke, M. 1975. Einheit im Wort: Die spezifische Bedeutung von ἀγάπη, ἀγαπᾶν, und φιλεῖν im Johannesevangelium. StANT 41. München: Kösel.

Lattke, M. 1979-86. Die Oden Salomos in ihrer Bedeutung für Neues Testament und Gnosis. 4 vols. OBO 25/1, 1a, 2, 3. Freiburg/Göttingen: Universitätsverlag/Vandenhoeck & Ruprecht.

Lattke, M. 1982. "Zur Bildersprache der Oden Salomos." Symb. NF 6: 95-110.

Lattke, M. 1987. Rev. of Blaszczak (1985) ThLZ 112: 183-5.

Lattke, M. 1989. "Salomo-Ode 13 im Spiegel-Bild der Werke von Ephraem Syrus." Muséon 102: 255-66.

Lattke, M. 1991. Hymnus: Materialien zu einer Geschichte der antiken Hymnologie. NTOA. Freiburg/Göttingen: Universitätsverlag/Vandenhoeck & Ruprecht.

Lewis, C.T., and C. Short, comps. 1879. A Latin Dictionary Founded on Andrews' Edition of Freund's Latin Dictionary: Revised, Enlarged, and in Great Part Rewritten. Oxford: Clarendon.

Liddell, H.G., and R. Scott, comps. 1968. A Greek-English Lexicon with a Supplement. Rev. H.S. Jones. Oxford: Clarendon.

Lindblom, J. 1911. Om lifvets idé hos Paulus och Johannes samt i de s.k. Salomos oden. UUA. Uppsala: Almqvist & Wiksell.

Loisy, A. 1911. Rev. of Harnack (1910) RCHL NS 71: 101-5.

Lüdemann, G. 1975. Untersuchungen zur simonianischen Gnosis. GTA 1. Göttingen.

McNeil, B. 1977/78. "The Provenance of the Odes of Solomon: A Study in Jewish and Christian Symbolism." Diss. Cambridge University.

McNeil, B. 1978. "The Odes of Solomon and the Sufferings of Christ." OrChrA 205 (Symposium Syriacum 1976): 31-8.

McNeil, B. 1980. Rev. of Lattke (1979-86, vols. 1, 1a, 2). OstKSt 29: 193-4.

MacRae, G.W. 1984a. "The Gospel of Truth (I, 3 and XII, 2)." Robinson, J.M. 37-49.

MacRae, G.W. 1984b. "The Thunder, Perfect Mind (VI, 2)." Robinson, J.M. 271-7.

Malina, B.J. 1985. "The Gospel of John in Sociolinguistic Perspective." Center for Hermeneutical Studies in Hellenistic and Modern Culture. Protocol of the Forty-eighth Colloquy, 11 March, 1984. Ed. H.C. Waetjen. Berkeley, California. 1-23.

Manichaean Psalm-Book cf. Allberry.

Margoliouth, J.P. cf. Smith, J.P.

MarYosip, M. 1948. The Oldest Christian Hymn-Book. Temple, Texas: privately printed.

Meeks, W.A. 1972. "The Man from Heaven in Johannine Sectarianism." JBL 91: 44-72.

Meeks, W.A. 1973/74. "The Image of the Androgyne: Some Uses of a Symbol in Earliest Christianity." HR 13: 165-208.

Meer, W. van der, and J.C. de Moor, eds. 1988. The Structural Analysis of Biblical and Canaanite Poetry. JSOT Suppl. Ser. 74. Sheffield: JSOT P.

Melugin, R.F. 1979. "Muilenburg, Form Criticism, and Theological Exegesis." Encounter with the Text: Form and History in the Hebrew Bible. Ed. M.J. Buss. SBL Semeia Supp. Philadelphia: Fortress.

Ménard, J.É. 1962. L'Évangile de Vérité. Rétroversion grecque et commentaire. Paris: Letouzey & Ané.

Ménard, J.É. 1972. L'Évangile de Vérité. NHS 2. Leiden: Brill.

Ménard, J.É. 1975. L'Évangile selon Thomas. NHS 5. Leiden: Brill.

Meynet, R. 1989. "Analyse rhétorique du Prologue de Jean." RB 96: 481-510.

Morawe, G. 1963. "Vergleich des Aufbaus der Danklieder und hymnischen Bekenntnislieder (1 QH) von Qumran mit dem Aufbau der Psalmen im Alten Testament und im Spätjudentum." RdQ 4: 323-56.

Morrison, A.T. 1980. "A Literary and Theological Comparison between the Odes of Solomon and the Johannine Literature." Diss. Durham University.

Mosca, P.G. 1985. "Psalm 26: Poetic Structure and the Form-Critical Task." CBQ 47: 212-37.

Müller, H.-P. 1983. "Formgeschichte/Formenkritik. I. Altes Testament." TRE 11: 271-85.

Münter, F. 1812. Odae Gnosticae Salomoni tributae, Thebaice et Latine,praefatione et adnotationibus philologicis illustratae. Copenhagen: Schultz.

Muilenburg, J. 1961. "The Linguistic and Rhetorical Usages of the Particle כי in the Old Testament." HUCA 32. New York: Ktav. 135-60.

Muilenburg, J. 1969. "Form Criticism and Beyond." JBL 88: 1-18.

Musurillo, H. 1964. "The Odes of Solomon." ClF 18: 54-6.

Musurillo, H. 1966. The Fathers of the Primitive Church. New York: Mentor-Omega.

Nag Hammadi cf. The Facsimile Edition of the Nag Hammadi Codices; cf. Robinson, J.M. 1984.

Nagel, P. 1979a. "Anatomie des Menschen in gnostischer und manichäischer Sicht." Nagel 1979b, 67-94.

Nagel, P., ed. 1979b. Studien zum Menschenbild in Gnosis und Manichäismus. Wissenschaftliche Beiträge 1979/39 (K 5). Halle: Martin-Luther-Universität Halle-Wittemberg.

Nestle, E. 1911. Rev. of Harnack (1910) and Diettrich (1911). ThLZ 36: 586-8.

Newbold, W.R. 1911. "Bardaisan and the Odes of Solomon." JBL 30: 161-204.

Nida, E.A. 1961. Bible Translating: An Analysis of Principles and Procedures, with Special Reference to Aboriginal Languages. 2nd ed. London: United Bible Societies.

Nida, E.A. 1964. Towards a Science of Translating with Special Reference to Principles and Procedures Involved in Bible Translating. Leiden: Brill.

Nida, E.A. 1980. "Problems of Biblical Exegesis in the Third World." Text - Wort - Glaube: Studien zur Überlieferung, Interpretation und Autorisierung biblischer Texte. Kurt Aland gewidmet. Ed. M. Brecht. AKG 50. Berlin: de Gruyter. 159-65.

Nida, E.A., and C.R. Taber. 1969. The Theory and Practice of Translation. HeTr 8. Leiden: Brill.

Nöldeke, T. 1904. Compendious Syriac Grammar. Trans. J.A. Crichton. London: Williams & Norgate.

On the Origin of the World cf. Bethge, H.-G. and O.S. Wintermute.

Patrologiae cursus completus. Accurante J.-P.Migne. Series Graeca. 1857. 162 vols. Paris.

Patte, D. 1976. What Is Structural Exegesis? Philadelphia: Fortress.

Paulsen, H. 1978. Studien zur Theologie des Ignatius von Antiochien. FKDG 29. Göttingen: Vandenhoeck & Ruprecht.

Pausanias. 1918-35. Description of Greece. Trans. W.H.S. Jones. 5 vols. LCL. London: Heinemann.

Payne Smith, J. cf. Smith, J.P.

Payne Smith, R. cf. Smith, R.P.

PG cf. Patrologiae cursus completus.

Philonenko, M. 1962. "Conjecture sur un verset de la onzième Ode de Salomon." ZNW 53: 264.

Pistis Sophia cf. Schmidt 1978b.

Potterie, I. de la. 1977. La vérité dans Saint Jean. 2 vols. AnBib 73,74. Rome: Biblical Institute P.

Preisendanz, K. 1956. "Salomo." PRE Suppl. 8. Ed. K. Ziegler. 660-704.

Ragot, A. 1971. "De l'essénisme au christianisme." CCER 19,73: 5-24.

Ras Shamra cf. Dahood.

Reitzenstein, R. 1924. "Weltuntergangsvorstellungen. Eine Studie zur vergleichenden Religionsgeschichte." KHÅ 24: 129-212.

Richard, L. 1984. "Anthropology and Theology: The Emergence of Incarnational Faith According to Mary Douglas." EeT 15: 131-54.

Richter, W. 1971. Exegese als Literaturwissenschaft: Entwurf einer alttestamentlichen Literaturtheorie und Methodologie. Göttingen: Vandenhoeck & Ruprecht.

Robinson, J.M., ed. 1984. The Nag Hammadi Library in English. 2nd ed. Leiden: Brill.

Robinson, T.H. 1947. The Poetry of the Old Testament. London: Duckworth.

Robinson, T.H. 1962. Paradigms and Exercises in Syriac Grammar. 4th ed. Rev. by L.H. Brockington. Oxford: Clarendon.

Rücker, A. 1954. "Die syrische Literatur." HO 1,3 (Semitistik). Ed. B. Spuler. 168-204.

Rudolph, K., ed. 1975. Gnosis und Gnostizismus. WdF 262. Darmstadt: Wissenschaftliche Buchgesellschaft.

Rudolph, K. 1979. "Zur Soziologie, soziologischen 'Verortung' und Rolle der Gnosis in der Spätantike." Nagel 1979b, 19-29.

Rudolph, K. 1980. Die Gnosis: Wesen und Geschichte einer spätantiken Religion. 2nd ed. Leipzig: Koehler & Amelang.

Ryle, H.E., and M.J. James. 1891. ΨΑΛΜΟΙ ΣΟΛΟΜΩΝΤΟΣ. Psalms of the Pharisees, commonly called the Psalms of Solomon: The text newly revised from all the MSS: Edited, with introduction, English translation, notes, appendix, and indices. Cambridge: UP.

Sanders, J.T. 1971. The New Testament Christological Hymns: Their Historical Religious Background. MSSNTS 15. Cambridge: UP.

Schille, G. 1965. Frühchristliche Hymnen. Berlin: Evangelische Verlagsanstalt.

Schmidt, C., ed. 1962. Koptisch-gnostische Schriften. I. Die Pistis Sophia. Die beiden Bücher des Jeû. Unbekanntes altgnostisches Werk. GCS 45 (13). 3rd ed. Rev. by W. Till. Berlin: Akademie.

Schmidt, C., ed. 1978a. The Books of Jeu and the Untitled Text in the Bruce Codex. Trans. V. Macdermot. NHS 13. Leiden: Brill.

Schmidt, C., ed. 1978b. Pistis Sophia. Trans. V. MacDermot. NHS 9. Leiden: Brill.

Schökel, L.A. 1988. A Manual of Hebrew Poetics. SubBi 11. Roma: Pontificio Istituto Biblico.

Schulthess, F. 1910. "Textkritische Bemerkungen zu den syrischen Oden Salomos." ZNW 3: 250-8.

Schwertner, S., comp. 1976. Theologische Realenzyklopädie: Abkurzungsverzeichnis. Berlin/New York: de Gruyter.

The Second Treatise of the Great Seth cf. Wisse, F. 1984a.

Segal, A.F. 1981. "Ruler of This World: Attitudes about Mediator Figures and the Importance of Sociology for Self-Definition." Jewish and Christian Self-Definition. Vol. 2. Aspects of Judaism in the Graeco-Roman Period. Eds. E.P. Sanders et al. London: SCM.

Segal, J.B. 1953. The Diacritical Point and the Accents in Syriac. LOS 2. London: Oxford UP.

Severus, E. 1972. "Gebet I." RAC 8: 1134-258.

Smith, J.P., ed. 1903. A Compendious Syriac Dictionary Founded Upon the Thesaurus Syriacus of R. Payne Smith. Oxford: Clarendon.

Smith, J.P. (J.P. Margoliouth), comp. 1981. Supplement to the Thesaurus Syriacus of R. Payne Smith. 1927. Hildesheim: Olms.

Smith, R.P., ed. 1981. Thesaurus Syriacus. 1879-1901. 2 vols. Hildesheim: Olms.

Southwell, P.J.M. 1987. Rev. of Blaszczak (1985). JThS NS 38: 176-7.

Sprengling, M. 1948. Foreword. MarYosip (1948). v-viii.

Spurgeon, C.F.E. 1958. Shakespeare's Imagery and What It Tells Us. 1935. Boston: Beacon.

Stählin, O., and L. Früchtel, eds. 1985. Clemens Alexandrinus. II. Stromata Buch I-VI. 4. Auflage mit Nachträgen von U. Treu. GCS. Berlin: Akademie.

Steidle, B. 1948. "Die Oden Salomons." BenM 24: 242.

Storfjell, J.B. 1987. "The Chiastic Structure of Psalm 151." Andrews University Seminary Studies 25: 97-106.

Testuz, M., ed. 1959. Papyrus Bodmer X-XII. X. Correspondance apocryphe des Corinthiens et de l'apôtre Paul. XI. Onzième Ode de Salomon. XII. Fragment d'un hymne liturgique: Manuscrit du III<sup>e</sup>siècle. Cologny-Genève: Bibliothèque Bodmer.

The Thunder, Perfect Mind cf. MacRae 1984b.

Till, W.C. 1970. Koptische Grammatik (saïdischer Dialekt). Mit Bibliographie, Lesestücken und Wörterverzeichnissen. 4th ed. (= 2nd ed.) Lehrbücher für das Studium der orientalischen und afrikanischen Sprachen 1. Leipzig: VEB Verlag Enzyklopädie.

Tondelli, L. 1914. Le Odi di Salomone: Cantici cristiani degli inizi del II secolo: Versione dal siriaco, introduzione e note: Prefazione del Angelo Mercati. Roma: Ferrari.

Träger, C., ed. 1986. Wörterbuch der Literaturwissenschaft. Leipzig: VEB Bibliographisches Institut.

Träger, Chr. 1986. "Hymne." Träger, C. 225.

Trimorphic Protennoia cf. Turner, J.D.

Tsakonas, B.G. 1974. Ἀι Ὠδαὶ Σολομῶντος (Εἰσαγωγή - Κείμενον - Ἑρμηνεία). Athens.

Tsumura, D.T. 1983. "Literary Insertion (AXB Pattern) in Biblical Hebrew." VT 33: 468-82.

Tsumura, D.T. 1988. "'Inserted Bicolon', the AXYB Pattern, in Amos I 5 and Psalm IX 7." VT 38: 234-6.

Turner, J.D. 1984. "Trimorphic Protennoia (XIII, 1)." Robinson, J.M. 461-70.

Turner, V. 1969. The Ritual Process: Structure and Antistructure. London: Routledge & Kegan Paul.

Turner, V. 1974. Dramas, Fields, and Metaphors: Symbolic Action in Human Society. Ithaca/London: Cornell UP.

Turner, V. 1985. On the Edge of the Bush: Anthropology as Experience. Ed. E.L.B. Turner. Tucson, Arizona: University of Arizona P.

Ullmann, W. 1979. "Bild- und Menschenbildterminologie in koptisch-gnostischen Texten." Nagel 1979b, 45-54.

Ungnad, A., and W. Staerk. 1910. Die Oden Salomos: Aus dem Syrischen übersetzt, mit Anmerkungen. KlT 64. Bonn: Marcus and Weber.

Vööbus, A. 1979. The Didascalia Apostolorum in Syriac. 2 vols. CSCO 401, 407 = CSCO.S 175, 179. Louvain: Secrétariat du CorpusSCO.

Vogl, A. 1978. "Oden Salomos 17, 22, 24, 42: Übersetzung und Kommentar, herausgegeben von B. McNeil." OrChr 62: 60-76.

Watson, W.G.E. 1986. Classical Hebrew Poetry: A Guide to its Techniques. 2nd ed. JSOT Suppl. Ser. 26. Sheffield: JSOT P.

Watson, W.G.E. 1989. "Internal or Half-Line Parallelism in Classical Hebrew Again." VT 29: 44-66.

Watters, W.R. 1976. Formula Criticism and the Poetry of the Old Testament. BZAW 138. Berlin/New York: de Gruyter.

Wensinck, A.J. 1911. "De Oden van Salomo, een oudchristelijk psalmboek." ThSt(U) 29: 1-60.

Werner, J. 1986. "Ode." Träger, C. 380-1.

Widengren, G., and D. Hellholm. 1977. Proceedings of the International Colloquium on Gnosticism: Stockholm, August 20-25 1973. (Filologisk-filosofiska serien 17), Stockholm/Leiden: Almqvist & Wiksell/Brill.

Willis, J.T. 1987. "Alternating (ABA'B') Parallelism in the Old Testament Psalms and Prophetic Literature." Follis 1987, 49-76.

Wilson, R. McL. 1975. "The Trials of a Translator: Some Translation Problems in the Nag Hammadi Texts." Les Textes de Nag Hammadi. Colloque du Centre d'Histoire des Religions (Strasbourg, 23-25 octobre 1974). Ed. J.-É. Ménard. NHS 7. Leiden: Brill. 32-40.

Wilson, R. McL. 1984. "Gnosis/Gnostizismus. II. Neues Testament, Judentum, Alte Kirche." TRE 13: 535-50.

Wisse, F., ed. 1984a. "The Second Treatise of the Great Seth (VII, 2)." Robinson, J.M. 329-38.

Wisse, F., ed. 1984b. "The Teaching of Silvanus (VII, 4)." Robinson, J.M. 346-61.

Wittgenstein, L. 1961. Tractatus Logico-Philosophicus. London: Routledge & Kegan Paul.

Wootton, R.W.F. 1980. "Bibelübersetzungen. V. Bibelübersetzungen in außereuropäische Sprachen." TRE 6: 299-311.

Worrell, W.H. 1911/12. "The Odes of Solomon and the Pistis Sophia." JThS 13: 29-46.

Zahn, Th. 1910. "Die Oden Salomos." NKZ 21: 667-701, 747-77.

# INDEX

## I. MODERN AUTHORS

## II. ANCIENT WRITERS/WRITINGS

## III. ODES OF SOLOMON

(within Chapters I-IV; bold numbering refers to the analysis section)

*Book description*

This volume provides the first analysis of the collection of the Odes of Solomon in its entirety from the aspect of the structure of its vocabulary and syntax. It offers primarily a detailed study of the patterns of words/roots, cola, strophes, stanzas, and sub-odes, working from the most basic level to the larger relationships within an Ode and beyond to relationships between Odes. From this basis, the study moves to an investigation of how the Odes might be arranged into groups according to the shared patterns of syntax especially, and also of imagery.

For the structural analysis, there are invaluable lists of word-pairs, lists of frequently occurring phrases and associated words/roots, and word-frequency tables. The study also offers a new English translation together with the complete texts of the Syriac, Coptic and Greek Odes.

This book promises to be a useful scholarly tool for those wishing to make a serious study of the Odes of Solomon. It makes a major contribution towards the treatment of the Odes as an historically significant text in its own right. The work was originally completed as a doctoral thesis at the University of Queensland, Australia, under the supervision of Prof. Dr. Michael Lattke.

ISBN 3-7278-0780-6 (Universitätsverlag)
ISBN 3-525-53921-5 (Vandenhoeck & Ruprecht)

Bd. 1    MAX KÜCHLER, *Schweigen, Schmuck und Schleier*. Drei neutestamentliche Vorschriften zur Verdrängung der Frauen auf dem Hintergrund einer frauenfeindlichen Exegese des Alten Testaments im antiken Judentum. XXII + 542 Seiten, 1 Abb. 1986. [vergriffen]

Bd. 2    MOSHE WEINFELD, *The Organizational Pattern and the Penal Code of the Qumran Sect*. A Comparison with Guilds and Religious Associations of the Hellenistic-Roman Period. 104 Seiten. 1986.

Bd. 3    ROBERT WENNING, *Die Nabatäer – Denkmäler und Geschichte*. Eine Bestandesaufnahme des archäologischen Befundes. 360 Seiten, 50 Abb., 19 Karten. 1986.

Bd. 4    RITA EGGER, *Josephus Flavius und die Samaritaner*. Eine terminologische Untersuchung zur Identitätsklärung der Samaritaner. 4 + 416 Seiten. 1986.

Bd. 5    EUGEN RUCKSTUHL, *Die literarische Einheit des Johannesevangeliums*. Der gegenwärtige Stand der einschlägigen Forschungen. Mit einem Vorwort von Martin Hengel. XXX + 334 Seiten. 1987.

Bd. 6    MAX KÜCHLER/CHRISTOPH UEHLINGER (Hrsg.), *Jerusalem. Texte – Bilder – Steine*. Im Namen von Mitgliedern und Freunden des Biblischen Instituts der Universität Freiburg Schweiz herausgegeben ... zum 100. Geburtstag von Hildi + Othmar Keel-Leu. 238 S.; 62 Abb.; 4 Taf.; 2 Farbbilder. 1987.

Bd. 7    DIETER ZELLER (Hrsg.), *Menschwerdung Gottes – Vergöttlichung von Menschen*. 8 + 228 Seiten, 9 Abb., 1988.

Bd. 8    GERD THEISSEN, *Lokalkolorit und Zeitgeschichte in den Evangelien*. Ein Beitrag zur Geschichte der synoptischen Tradition. 10 + 338 Seiten. 1989.

Bd. 9    TAKASHI ONUKI, *Gnosis und Stoa*. Eine Untersuchung zum Apokryphon des Johannes. X + 198 Seiten. 1989.

Bd. 10   DAVID TROBISCH, *Die Entstehung der Paulusbriefsammlung*. Studien zu den Anfängen christlicher Publizistik. 10 + 166 Seiten. 1989.

Bd. 11   HELMUT SCHWIER, *Tempel und Tempelzerstörung*. Untersuchungen zu den theologischen und ideologischen Faktoren im ersten jüdisch-römischen Krieg (66–74 n. Chr.). XII + 432 Seiten. 1989.

Bd. 12   DANIEL KOSCH, *Die eschatologische Tora des Menschensohnes*. Untersuchungen zur Rezeption der Stellung Jesu zur Tora in Q. 514 Seiten. 1989.

Bd. 13   JEROME MURPHY-O'CONNOR, O.P., *The École Biblique and the New Testament: A Century of Scholarship (1890-1990)*. With a Contribution by Justin Taylor, S.M. VIII + 210 Seiten. 1990.

Bd. 14   PIETER W. VAN DER HORST, *Essays on the Jewish World of Early Christianity*. 260 Seiten. 1990.

Bd. 15    CATHERINE HEZSER, *Lohnmetaphorik und Arbeitswelt in Mt 20, 1–16.* Das Gleichnis von den Arbeitern im Weinberg im Rahmen rabbinischer Lohngleichnisse.
346 Seiten. 1990.

Bd. 16    IRENE TAATZ, *Frühjüdische Briefe.* Die paulinischen Briefe im Rahmen der offiziellen religiösen Briefe des Frühjudentums.
132 Seiten. 1991.

Bd. 17    EUGEN RUCKSTUHL/PETER DSCHULNIGG, *Stilkritik und Verfasserfrage im Johannesevangelium.* Die johanneischen Sprachmerkmale auf dem Hintergrund des Neuen Testaments und des zeitgenössischen hellenistischen Schrifttums.
284 Seiten. 1991.

Bd. 18    PETRA VON GEMÜNDEN: Vegetationsmetaphorik im Neuen Testament und in seiner Umwelt. Eine Bildfelduntersuchung. ca. 440 Seiten. 1991. [noch nicht erschienen]

Bd. 19    MICHAEL LATTKE: *Hymnus.* Materialien zu einer Geschichte der antiken Hymnologie. 524 Seiten. 1991.

Bd. 20    MAJELLA FRANZMANN: *The Odes of Solomon:* An Analysis of the Poetical Structure and Form. 500 Seiten. 1991.